W9-BNS-059

Bolivia

Andrew Dean Nystrom
Morgan Konn

Contents

THE CORDILLERAS & YUNGAS pp108–48

AMAZON BASIN pp306–44

LAKE TITICACA pp86–107

LA PAZ pp42–85

CENTRAL HIGHLANDS pp190–247

SANTA CRUZ & EASTERN LOWLANDS pp268–305

THE SOUTHERN ALTIPLANO pp149–89

SOUTH CENTRAL BOLIVIA & THE CHACO pp248–67

Destination: Bolivia

Unparalleled natural beauty. Vibrant indigenous cultures. *Muy tranquilo* cities. Whispers of ancient civilizations. With the notable exception of beaches, Bolivia has attractions to satisfy travelers of many inclinations. A landlocked country lying astride the widest stretch of the Andes, its climate and awesome geography run the gamut, from jagged icy peaks and hallucinogenic salt flats to steamy jungles and vast wildlife-rich savannas. From trekking the Cordilleras and rafting Yungas' whitewater to wildlife watching in the Pantanal and bushwacking through the Amazon, Bolivia is heaven for adventure seekers. Surprisingly, it still falls below many travelers' radar, so unlimited opportunities for off-the-beaten-track exploration await.

Bolivia is called the Tibet of the Americas – it's the highest, most isolated and most rugged of the Latin American republics. With two major indigenous groups and several smaller ones, it's also South America's most traditional country. A majority of the population claims pure Amerindian blood and many people maintain unique cultural values and belief systems.

History abounds in such wonders as the ancient ceremonial site of Tiahuanaco; the legendary mines of Potosí, which date from the 16th century and are still worked under tortuous conditions; the ornate Jesuit missions of the eastern lowlands; and the vestiges of Inca culture set against the dramatic backdrop of the Andean mountain ranges and Lake Titicaca.

Bolivia has certainly had a turbulent and explosive history, but nowadays its image as a haunt of drug barons and revolutionaries is greatly overstated. Although the country still faces some difficult problems, it remains one of South America's most peaceful, secure and welcoming destinations.

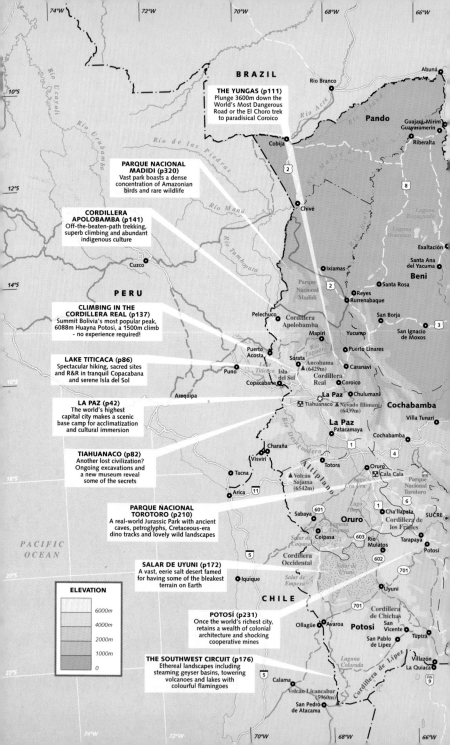

BRAZIL

THE YUNGAS (p111)
Plunge 3600m down the World's Most Dangerous Road or the El Choro trek to paradisical Coroico

PARQUE NACIONAL MADIDI (p320)
Vast park boasts a dense concentration of Amazonian birds and rare wildlife

CORDILLERA APOLOBAMBA (p141)
Off-the-beaten-path trekking, superb climbing and abundant indigenous culture

PERU

CLIMBING IN THE CORDILLERA REAL (p137)
Summit Bolivia's most popular peak, 6088m Huayna Potosi, a 1500m climb - no experience required!

LAKE TITICACA (p86)
Spectacular hiking, sacred sites and R&R in tranquil Copacabana and serene Isla del Sol

LA PAZ (p42)
The world's highest capital city makes a scenic base camp for acclimatization and cultural immersion

TIAHUANACO (p82)
Another lost civilization? Ongoing excavations and a new museum reveal some of the secrets

PARQUE NACIONAL TOROTORO (p210)
A real-world Jurassic Park with ancient caves, petroglyphs, Cretaceous-era dino tracks and lovely wild landscapes

SALAR DE UYUNI (p172)
A vast, eerie salt desert famed for having some of the bleakest terrain on Earth

POTOSÍ (p231)
Once the world's richest city, retains a wealth of colonial architecture and shocking cooperative mines

THE SOUTHWEST CIRCUIT (p176)
Ethereal landscapes including steaming geyser basins, towering volcanoes and lakes with colourful flamingoes

PACIFIC OCEAN

CHILE

ELEVATION
6000m
4000m
2000m
1000m
0

Pando

Beni

Cochabamba

La Paz

Oruro

Potosí

Abuná
Rio Branco
Cobija
Guajará-Mirim
Guayaramerín
Riberalta
Chivé
Exaltación
Santa Ana del Yacuma
Ixiamas
Santa Rosa
Reyes
Rurrenabaque
San Borja
San Ignacio de Moxos
Cuzco
Pelechuco
Mapiri
Yucumo
Puerto Linares
Puerto Acosta
Sorata
Ancohuma (6429m)
Caranavi
Puno
Copacabana
Isla del Sol
Coroico
La Paz
Chulumani
Arequipa
Tiahuanaco
Nevado Illimani (6439m)
Villa Tunari
Patacamaya
Cochabamba
Charaña
Totora
Oruro
Cala Cala
Visviri
Volcán Sajama (6542m)
Tacna
Cha'llapata
Arica
SUCRE
Sabaya
Coipasa
Río Mulatos
Tarapaya
Iquique
Potosí
Uyuni
Ollagüe
Avaroa
San Vicente
Tupiza
San Pablo de Lipez
Villazón
La Quiaca
Calama
Volcán Licancabur (5960m)
San Pedro de Atacama

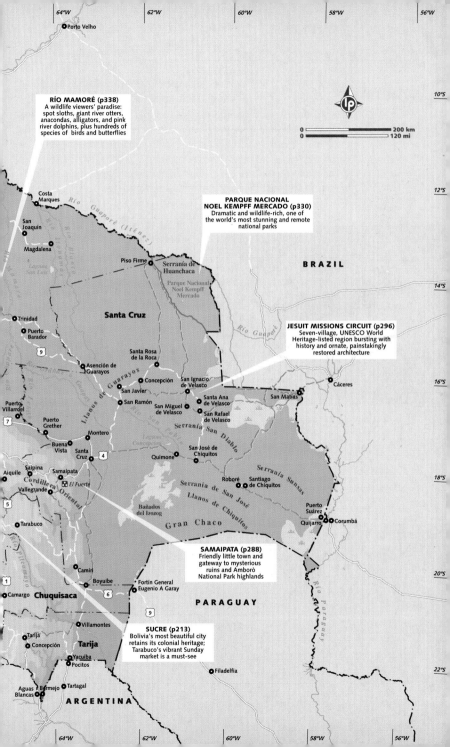

RÍO MAMORÉ (p338)
A wildlife viewers' paradise: spot sloths, giant river otters, anacondas, alligators, and pink river dolphins, plus hundreds of species of birds and butterflies

PARQUE NACIONAL NOEL KEMPFF MERCADO (p330)
Dramatic and wildlife-rich, one of the world's most stunning and remote national parks

JESUIT MISSIONS CIRCUIT (p296)
Seven-village, UNESCO World Heritage-listed region bursting with history and ornate, painstakingly restored architecture

SAMAIPATA (p288)
Friendly little town and gateway to mysterious ruins and Amborò National Park highlands

SUCRE (p213)
Bolivia's most beautiful city retains its colonial heritage; Tarabuco's vibrant Sunday market is a must-see

0   200 km
0   120 mi

BRAZIL

PARAGUAY

ARGENTINA

Porto Velho

Costa Marques
San Joaquin
Magdalena
Piso Firme
Serranía de Huanchaca
Parque Nacional Noel Kempff Mercado

Trinidad
Puerto Barador
Asención de Guarayos
Santa Rosa de la Roca
Concepción
San Ignacio de Velasco
San Matías
Cáceres

Puerto Villarroel
San Javier
San Ramón
Santa Ana de Velasco
San Miguel de Velasco
San Rafael de Velasco

Puerto Grether
Montero
Serranía San Diablo

Buena Vista
Santa Cruz
Quimone
San José de Chiquitos
Serranía Sunsas

Aiquile
Saipina
Samaipata
El Fuerte
Roboré
Santiago de Chiquitos

Vallegrande
Serranía de San José
Puerto Suárez
Quijarro
Corumbá

Tarabuco
Bañados del Izozog
Llanos de Chiquitos

Camiri
Gran Chaco

Boyuibe
Fortín General Eugenio A Garay

Camargo
Chuquisaca

Villamontes

Tarija
Concepción
Tarija
Yacuiba
Pocitos

Aguas Blancas
Bermejo
Tartagal
Filadelfia

Santa Cruz

Río Mamoré
Río Guaporé (Iténez)
Río Guaporé
Río paraguay
Río Pilcomayo

Cordillera Oriental
Llanos de Guarayos
Serranía San Pablo

Bolivia's biggest draws are its colorful traditions, vibrant festivals and other-worldly landscapes. In addition to the highlights illustrated, you can mountain bike the **World's Most Dangerous Road** (p55), fly over the remote **Parque Nacional Noel Kempff Mercado** (p330) or dig deep into the mines at **Potosí** (p231). Hike the diverse **El Choro Trek** (p131) or check out the wildlife of **Río Mamore** (p328). Barter with locals at **Tarabuco's Sunday market** (p227) or Cochabamba's nerve-shattering **La Cancha** (p197) marketplace. Must-see festivals include Oruro's devilish **La Diablada** (p156) and La Paz' unique **Alasitas** (p61).

Check out Isla del Sol's impressive **Chincana ruins** (p99)

GREG CAIRE

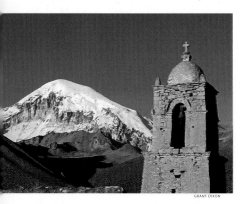

GRANT DIXON

Climb Bolivia's highest peak, **Nevado Sajama** (p161)

Enjoy traditional music at Tarabuco's **Phujllay fiesta** (p227)

ERIC L WHEAT

WOODS WHEATCROFT

Ascend the popular 6088m-high peak of **Huayna Potosí** (p137)

ERIC L WHEATER

Experience everyday islander life on **Isla Suriqui** (p104)

Grab a guide and head out on one of the many treks around **Sorata** (p127)

GREG CAIRE

DEANNA SWAN

Be awed by the surreal landscape of **Salar de Uyuni** (p172)

Wander around La Paz' fascinating
Witches' Market (p50)

KRZYSZTOF DYDYŃ

ANDREW PETERS

Look out for Bolivia's most common fauna,
the **alpaca** (p32)

Getting Started

Foreign visitors have only recently begun to discover this intriguing and underrated country, so it's still surprisingly easy to stray from the worn routes. Every corner of Bolivia will overwhelm curious and motivated travelers with cultural and natural beauty, as well as unforgettable experiences and characters to match the classic expectations of those who dream of South America. There are plenty of opportunities for adventure, with a wide variety of luxury levels and travel choices on offer. The going isn't always easy, but the rewards are worth the effort.

WHEN TO GO

See climate charts (p349) for more information.

Travelers will encounter just about every climatic zone, from stifling humidity and heat to Arctic cold. Summer (November to April) is the rainy season when overland transportation becomes difficult, if not impossible in some areas. The most popular, and arguably most comfortable, time for exploring the whole country is during winter (May to October) with its dry, clear days. This is also the best season for climbing.

Most of Bolivia lies as near to the equator as Tahiti or Hawaii, but its elevation and unprotected expanses result in unpredictable weather. Bolivia's two poles of climatic extremes are Puerto Suárez with its overwhelming heat, and Uyuni for its icy, cold winds. But there are no absolutes; there are times when you can sunbathe in Uyuni and freeze in Puerto Suárez.

Summer in the lowlands can be utterly miserable, with mud, high humidity, biting insects and relentless tropical downpours. However washed-out roads necessitate an increase in river transport, making summer the best time to hop on a cargo boat. Winter in the Altiplano means extreme heat during the day, and freezing winds and subzero temperatures at night. The highland valleys are refuges, having a comfortable climate with little rain year-round.

August is the most popular month of the high tourist season which runs from late June to early September: it has the most reliable weather,

---

DON'T LEAVE HOME WITHOUT...

- Checking the visa situation (p358) – those with Asian passports may be subject to extra hassles here
- Checking travel advisory warnings (p350)
- Proof of vaccination for yellow fever (p369)
- A copy of your travel insurance policy details (p353)
- Your camera, plenty of film and extra camera batteries
- Binoculars for watching wildlife (p32)
- Sunscreen for crystal-clear skies at 4000m
- Tampons for periods spent outside the city
- Photos from home to share with new friends
- Ear plugs for disco nights you want to sleep through
- Self-sealing (zip-lock) bags for all your wet, stinky and messy stuff
- A pack lock or other luggage security for peace of mind
- Your sense of humor – patience and courage will no doubt be tested by long bus rides

is the time of European and North American summer holidays and of most of Bolivia's major festivals, so many Bolivians and South Americans also travel at this time. This can be an advantage if you are looking for people to form a travel group, but prices are generally higher than during the rest of the year.

COSTS & MONEY

Overall, prices are slightly lower here than in neighboring countries. When converted to US dollars, prices for most goods and services are actually lower now than they were a decade ago. The biggest cost in any trip to Bolivia will be transport, both getting to the country and getting around, simply because the distances involved are great.

While ultra-budget travelers can get by on less than US$15 a day, most people will spend between US$25 and US$50. Visitors who want to enjoy the best Bolivia has to offer can travel comfortably for US$150 a day. All prices in this book are quoted in US dollars (US$) unless otherwise noted.

If you encounter 'gringo pricing', a deliberate overcharging of foreigners, an approach somewhere between suspicion and acceptance is advised. Before hailing a taxi or setting off to buy something, ask locals for a ballpark idea of what you can expect to pay. To avoid unpleasant scenes, agree on food, accommodation and transport prices before the goods or services are consumed or rendered.

TRAVEL LITERATURE

At the top of the South American travelogue list is the humorous and well-written *Inca-Kola* by Matthew Parris. It follows the meanderings of several Englishmen on a rollicking circuit through Peru and parts of Bolivia.

Chasing Ché – A Motorcycle Journey in Search of the Guevara Legend by Patrick Symmes chronicles the author's motorcycle trip around South America, in a naïve but well-intentioned attempt to balance the legendary figure with the curious reality of this controversial man.

An intrepid sailor's journeys through landlocked Bolivia are recorded in *The Incredible Voyage*, by Tristan Jones. It includes a narrative about several months' sailing and exploring on Lake Titicaca and a complication-plagued haul across the country to the Paraguay River.

An offbeat historical character is portrayed in *Lizzie – A Victorian Lady's Amazon Adventure*, compiled by Anne Rose from the letters of Lizzie Hessel, who lived in the Bolivian Amazon settlement of Colonia Orton during the early 20th-century rubber boom.

Henry Shukman's *Sons of the Moon – A Journey in the Andes* is a well-written account of a fairly unremarkable journey from northwestern Argentina, across the Bolivian Altiplano and on to Peru. It does, however, include superb observations of typically introverted Altiplano cultures.

INTERNET RESOURCES

Bolivia.com (www.bolivia.com) Current news and cultural information (in Spanish).

Bolivia web (www.boliviaweb.com) A good starting point, good cultural and artistic links (in English).

Bolivian.com (www.bolivian.com) A thorough, searchable Spanish-language index of Bolivian sites.

Enlaces Bolivia (www.enlacesbolivia.net) An extensive collection of well-organized and up-to-date links (in Spanish).

Lanic-Bolivia (http://lanic.utexas.edu/la/sa/bolivia) Outstanding collection of links from the University of Texas (in both Spanish and English).

Lonely Planet (www.lonelyplanet.com) Succinct summaries of travel in Bolivia, and the Thorn Tree bulletin board for gleaning travel tips (in English).

HOW MUCH?

Hotel double US$20

Dorm bed US$2-5

Set lunch US$1-2

Restaurant dinner US$5-10

Day's worth of coca leaves US$0.15

LONELY PLANET INDEX

Liter of gasoline US$0.50

Liter of bottled water US$0.50

Liter of domestic beer US$1

Souvenir T-shirt US$4-5

Street snack (coffee & a salteña) US$0.75

TOP TENS

OUR FAVORITE FESTIVALS & EVENTS

Bolivians are big on celebrating and there's almost always something interesting on around the country, especially during the high travel season. The following list is subjective; also see the comprehensive listing of festivals and events throughout the country (p351).

- Alasitas (La Paz) January (p61)
- La Virgen de Candelaria (Copacabana) February (p93)
- Carnaval (nationwide, best in Tarija) February/March (p255)
- La Diablada (Oruro) February/March (p156)
- Phujllay (Tarabuco) March (p227)
- El Gran Poder (La Paz) May/June (p61)
- Fiesta de la Cruz (Lake Titicaca) May 3 (p94)
- Fiesta del Santo Patrono de Moxos (San Ignacio de Moxos) July 31 (p324)
- Independence Day (nationwide, best in Copacabana) August 6 (p94)
- Chu'tillos (Potosí) August (p241)

EXTREME ADVENTURES

Bolivia's rugged landscape and outgoing tour guides offer innumerable, unforgettable adventures. Whether you're into 3600m mountain-bike descents or want to shoot some Class V rapids, Bolivia's got all the thrills you're seeking.

- Conquer 6088m Huayna Potosí (p137)
- Hike El Choro Trek, a 3250m descent (p117)
- Ski Chacaltaya, the world's highest developed slope (p79)
- Bike the World's Most Dangerous Road – before it's gone (see the boxed text, p55)
- Raft Class II–V whitewater on the Río Coroico (see the boxed text, p114)
- Float the Río Mamoré through pristine Amazon jungle (p328)
- Kayak the Chapare – after some serious jungle bashing (p348)
- Soak in hot springs at the base of Nevado Sajama (p161)
- Walk on the wild side on a jungle or pampas trip from Rurrenabaque (p316)
- Trek the Trans Cordillera Real route from Sorata to Huyana Potosí and Illimani (p128)

NATIONAL PARKS & NATURAL ATTRACTIONS

Bolivia boasts a number of protected areas, and access and visitor infrastructure is improving all the time. For more suggestions on where to get off the bus and launch into the backcountry, see the Environment chapter (p32).

- Parque Nacional Madidi (p30)
- Reserva Nacional de Fauna Andina Eduardo Avaroa (p176)
- Parque Nacional & Área de Uso Múltiple Amboró (p283)
- Parque Nacional Sajama (p161)
- Parque Nacional Torotoro (p210)
- Reserva de la Biosfera Pilón Lajas (p319)
- Parque Nacional Noel Kempff Mercado (p330)
- Reserva Biosférica del Beni (p322)
- Área Protegida Apolobamba (p144)
- Reserva de la Biosfera Sama (p259)

Itineraries

CLASSIC ROUTES

FROM HIGH TO LOW: BOLIVIA 101

Two weeks / Lake Titicaca, La Paz, Cordillera & the Yungas

A popular way to enter Bolivia is to come in overland from Peru. Get to know the festive Bolivian spirit in **Copacabana** (p89), where the scenery is amazing and R&R inevitable. After a day or two, hike to the tiny port of **Yampupata** (p97), where boats ferry passengers across **Lake Titicaca** (p86) to tranquil **Isla del Sol** (p99). After a couple of days exploring Inca ruins and watching the moon rise over **Isla de la Luna** (p103), head back to the mainland.

From Copacabana, catch a bus (it'll be crowded) across the Tiquina Strait to **La Paz** (p42). The Altiplano at sunset with the Cordillera Real as a backdrop is stunning. Spend a few days exploring the hectic markets, museums and streets of Bolivia's de facto capital city before taking a day-trip to **Tiahuanaco** (p81) or climbing to the 5395m summit of **Chacaltaya** (p79), the world's highest developed ski slope.

Once you're acclimated, it's time to pick up the pace by hiking the **Choro Trek** (p117) or mountain biking the **World's Most Dangerous Road** (see the boxed text, p55) down to the serene little town of **Coroico** (p111) in the Yungas. Starting out in thick fog at 4275m, you'll descend a thrilling 3600m past waterfalls and an incredible range of spectacular scenery. In Coroico many people prefer a poolside hammock but thrill seekers will want to hit the **Río Coroico** (p348) for some whitewater rafting or kayaking before returning to La Paz.

The area around La Paz is packed with highlights, from ancient Inca ruins to jagged peaks and sleepy weekend re-treats. Two weeks is just enough time to introduce adventurous travelers to the diverse range of activities on offer in Bolivia.

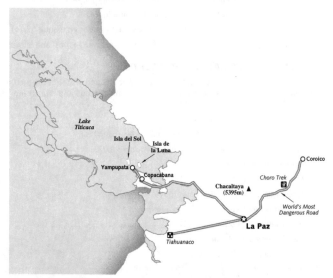

BREATHTAKING CIRCUIT

One month / Southern Altiplano, Central Highlands, Amazon Basin

Many people who come to Bolivia stay for at least a month, which is just about the right amount of time to experience the highlights.

After acclimating around Lake Titicaca and La Paz while doing **Bolivia 101** (p12), head south across the unforgettable emptiness of the **Southern Altiplano** (p149). If it's Carnaval time, don't miss Oruro's wild **La Diablada** festivities (p156). Take the train to **Uyuni** (p165) and get together with a group for a **Southwest Circuit** tour (p176) of the astounding **Salar de Uyuni** (p172) and the extraordinary **Reserva Eduardo Avaroa** (p176). After a hot shower back in Uyuni, catch the bus to **Potosí** (p231).

Even if the altitude didn't get you in La Paz, it might slow you down here. Allow a couple of days to adapt by taking guided tours of the **Casa Real de la Moneda** (p235) and a **cooperative mine** (p240). Then share a taxi to relatively balmy **Sucre** (p213), where you should time your visit to coincide with **Tarabuco's** vibrant Sunday market (p227).

Had enough of the highlands? Catch a flight from Sucre back to La Paz, where you can wing or bus it to tropical **Rurrenabaque** (p314). Chill in a hammock while gearing up for wildlife watching on a **jungle** or **pampas tour** (see the boxed text, p316). Or treat yourself to a few days of hiding in the jungle at a community-run ecolodge such as **Mapajo** (p315) or **Chalalán** (p320).

If Bolivia's range of landscapes doesn't leave you breathless, hanging out and hoofing it around the Altiplano (where the oxygen is limited) will. Add the sights and sounds of the jungle to the mix and, by the end of your stay, you may well be planning your next visit to Bolivia.

ROADS LESS TRAVELED

UP THE RIVER & THROUGH THE JUNGLE   One month / Big adventure loop

Any true offbeat Bolivian adventure will involve many varied modes of transport – and at least one break-down or road blockade.

From **La Paz** (p42) fly or go overland to **San Borja** (p321) to arrange a visit to the wildlife-rich **Reserva Biosférica del Beni** (p322). After exploring the lakes, rainforest and savanna by canoe and horseback, head east through sleepy **San Ignacio de Moxos** (p323) to **Trinidad** (p324), where a night of *moto-taxi* cruising awaits.

Ship out on a cargo boat from nearby **Puerto Barador** (p328) upriver to **Puerto Villarroel** (p313) in the Chapare. Head west to do some hiking or splashing around in the swimming holes around **Villa Tunari** (p311). Continue overland to **Cochabamba** (p194) where you can shop for almost anything at the country's best stocked and most crowded market.

From Cochabamba optional adventurous excursions include flying or driving a four-wheel drive into the remote **Parque Nacional Torotoro** (p210); or climbing to some of the country's highest summits in nearby **Parque Nacional Tunari** (p203).

Parque Nacional Sajama (p161) is just off the major highway linking La Paz to Arica in Chile, but attracts little more than a trickle of mountaineers with their sights set on **Nevado Sajama** (p161) volcano, generally considered Bolivia's highest peak.

Is there any better way to finish a back country escapade than with a dip in a pristine hot spring? Try a soak in the natural pools near the geyser field outside Sajama village.

Off-the-beaten-path travel in Bolivia can be slow going, and traveling by river-boat and charter plane means it is difficult to stick to set schedules. This trip takes in a wide range of little-visited landscapes and easily could be extended another month by surprise layovers and enticing detours.

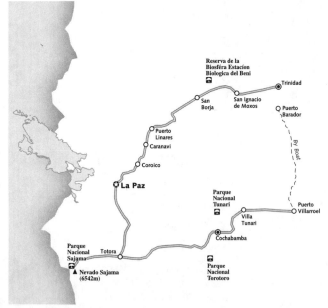

TAILORED TRIPS

NATIONAL PARKS, RESERVES & WATCHING WILDLIFE

Bolivia has protected a third of its territory in 60 national parks and reserves. From **Reserva de la Biosfera Sama's** (p259) slice of the Altiplano and **Kaa-Iya's** (p304) vast chunk of the Gran Chaco, to the inundated savannas of the remote, but spectacular, **Parque Nacional Noel Kempff Mercado** (p330), flora and fauna fans have much to choose from. Although some of these protected areas can be difficult to access, the following places are worth every ounce of the effort they take to reach.

Parque Nacional Sajama (p161) with its *vicuñas*, soaring volcanoes and heavenly hot springs was Bolivia's first preserve. After *National Geographic's* feature in 2000, **Parque Nacional Madidi** (p320) became the best known, encompassing the widest habitat range and most numerous protected species.

Parque Nacional Carrasco (p312) and **Parque Nacional Tunari** (p203) are two of the more accessible, middle altitude cloudforests, while **Parque Nacional Amboró** (p283) is a prime place for bird-watching.

Apolobamba (p144) is one of the least visited national parks while the most popular, **Eduardo Avaroa** (p176), receives more than 40,000 visitors per year.

PLANES, TRAINS & CAMIONES

In Bolivia getting there is often half the fun. The means of transport can either be a pain or the highlight of your adventure.

From the **world's highest funicular** (p58) to the sluggish **Death Train** (p280), you're spoiled for choice when it comes to mobility options.

Foolhardy adventurers shouldn't pass up the chance to conquer the **World's Most Dangerous Road** (p55). Flying in a small plane along the **Cordillera Real** (p137) or into remote **Noel Kempff Mercado National Park** (p330) merits a million rolls of aerial photography. Piling yourself, your pack and your driver on a *moto-taxi* in **Trinidad** (p324) is almost as much fun as renting one and zipping around independently.

Romantic reed boat journeys or hydrofoil cruises on **Lake Titicaca** (p88) provide a refreshing change of pace. Several days of 4WD off-road rambling across the **Salar de Uyuni** (p172) will more than rack your back.

At the end of the day, there's always your feet: Bolivia has more than its share of awe-inspiring trekking, from **Inca trails** (p119) to the **Yunga Cruz Trek** (p122). As for travelling on the buses and *camiones* – there are no words.

The Authors

ANDREW DEAN NYSTROM   Coordinating Author

Andrew has been fascinated by Bolivia ever since his Californian soccer club played Santa Cruz' famous Tahuichi side in a Texas youth tournament. A summer conducting scientific field research in Yellowstone National Park sparked Andrew's interest in all things wild and geothermal. As home to some of the world's highest hot springs, the Bolivian Altiplano fit the bill perfectly, and Andrew's grand tur boliviano was determined. He has contributed to Lonely Planet's Mexico, South America on a Shoestring and Yellowstone & Grand Teton National Parks titles, and his writing for the Webby-award-winning lonelyplanet.com has been translated into a dozen languages.

MORGAN KONN

Bolivia sat in the back of Morgan's mind since age 10, when she wrote a report on the country. Aching with curiosity, she had to see for herself what life at 4000m was like. After a journey north from Antarctica, she found her fingers numb, nose running and was mind boggled by the emptiness of the Bolivian southwest. Four months, three flights, two peaks and one case of ameobic dysentery later, she still finds the country surreal and dreamlike. Morgan started her Lonely Planet affair in the US Marketing Department before trying her hand at writing. She has contributed to Lonely Planet's South America on a Shoestring and Mexico.

Our Favorite Trips

Wildlife, wide open spaces, the world's highest everything. We'll never forget the *charque kan tamales* in **Tupiza** (p179); condors soaring over the **Cordillera de Lípez** (p176); breathtaking *fútbol* at 4000m; Altiplano ghost towns inhabited by only foxes, *vicuñas* and *vischacas*; soaking at sunrise in the **Termas de Polques** (p177) and in the shadow of **Nevada Sajama** (p161); thousands of stately pink flamingos in the **Reserva Eduardo Avaroa** (p176); and gliding across the flooded **Salar de Uyuni** (p172). After four days in a Jeep, the hot showers and pizza in **Uyuni** (p165) were heavenly. Relaxing moments included flying into **La Paz** (p42) at sunset, watching the moon rise over **Isla del Sol** (p99) and the lunar eclipse in **Sorata** (p127), and staying at the **Chalalán** (p320) and **Mapajo** (p315) Lodges.

CONTRIBUTING AUTHOR

David Goldberg MD wrote the Health chapter. Dr Goldberg completed his training in internal medicine and infectious diseases at Columbia-Presbyterian Medical Center in New York City, where he has also served as voluntary faculty. At present, he is an infectious diseases specialist in Scarsdale, New York and the editor-in-chief of the website MDTravelHealth.com.

Snapshot

Hot-button topics since the short-lived re-election of US-educated President Gonzalo 'Goni' Sánchez deLozada in August 2002 have included coca eradication, economic reform and the privatization of natural resources. If you haven't heard much about any of it, it's because Bolivia rarely makes the headlines, or even in the front section for that matter.

Coca production is estimated to generate up to US$500 million annually; the US government has spent more than US$1.3 billion on anti-coca insurgency in the past decade. Ex-president Banzer's plan to eradicate coca by 2000 was met by widespread protests and violent clashes. In 2002 *cocalero* (coca leaf grower) leader Evo Morales of the Movimiento al Socialismo (MAS) tied with Sánchez de Lozada in the first round of the presidential election with a surprise 22% of the popular vote, but Goni won the congressional tie-breaker vote by 84–43.

In reaction to Goni's return to office, teachers went on strike nationwide on the day of his inauguration, and 300,000 bus drivers did the same in January 2003. February 2003 (aka Black February) saw widespread protests against proposed tax increases, pension program tinkering and other 'structural reforms' advocated by International Monetary Fund and World Bank austerity advisors. Bullets riddled government buildings around Plaza Murillo in La Paz, 17 people were killed, hundreds were injured and the central business district came to a complete standstill for several days. Goni subsequently withdrew the proposal and has yet to implement other belt-tightening measures.

Legal wrangling continues in the wake of the Cochabamba water revolt, when protestors won the reversal of a US$2.5 billion privatization scheme headed by the California-based Bechtel Corporation in 2000. Bechtel (which reports annual revenues in excess of US$14 billion) has filed a legal demand with the arbitration arm of the World Bank seeking US$25 million in damages from the government, which has an annual budget of US$2.7 billion.

Then there's the multibillion-dollar Cuiabá natural gas pipeline across the Bolivian Chaco to the Brazilian state of Mato Grosso, constructed with US-taxpayer supported loans by Shell and the bankrupt US energy behemoth Enron (whose overseas assets are now held by the newly incorporated InternationalCo). See www.amazonwatch.org or the horse's official mouth (www.enron.com/corp/pressroom/factsheets/egs/egsi.html - find on 'Bolivia') for extensive documentation of the facts surrounding this case. In 2000 indigenous protesters blocked access to construction camps after Enron failed to deliver land titles promised as part of a compensation package for allowing the pipeline to be built through their homeland. Environmentalists are still waiting for a promised US$30 million for wildlife protection that never materialized. In March 2003 the pipeline's daily capacity was increased from 17 to 30 million cubic meters. Before the increase the pipeline generated annual revenue of US$42 million.

In early 2003 the government expressed interest in exporting natural gas to California and Mexico. In addition to widespread public unease about the prospect of giving away the nation's natural resources, the government will need to ease public concerns about how the gas might be delivered to the north. The only feasible options require building a pipeline to the coast via Peru or Chile. Peru is the current favorite as Bolivians haven't forgiven Chile for usurping their coastal access over a century ago. In October 2003, incoming President Carlos Mesa promised to hold a national referendum on the controversial gas export issue.

FAST FACTS

Population: 8.3 million humans, 2.5 million llamas

Average annual income: US$2500

Birth rate: 5.53 births/1000

Literacy rate: 87.2%

Population below poverty line: 70%

Merchant marines: 53 ships

Airports with unpaved landing strips: 1069

Annual military spending: US$187 million

Tourist arrivals in 2002: 335,000

History

Tangible history lives on in most of Bolivia's best-known destinations. From pre-Hispanic archaeological sites and living indigenous traditions to colonial architecture and the most recent headline-making political upheaval, the country's history reflects influences that have shaped South America as a whole.

THE CENTRAL ANDES

The great Altiplano (High Plateau), the largest expanse of arable land in the Andes, extends from present-day Bolivia into southern Peru, northwestern Argentina and northern Chile. It's been inhabited for thousands of years, but the region's early cultures were shaped by the imperial designs of two major forces: the Tiahuanaco culture of Bolivia and the Inca of Peru.

The Andes Web Ring (www.jqjacobs.net/andes) is loaded with Andean prehistory, cosmology and archaeology links.

Most archaeologists define the prehistory of the Central Andes in terms of 'horizons' – Early, Middle and Late – each of which was characterized by distinct architectural and artistic trends. Cultural interchanges between early Andean peoples occurred mostly through trade, usually between nomadic tribes, or as a result of the diplomatic expansionist activities of powerful and well-organized societies. These interchanges resulted in the Andes' emergence as the cradle of South America's highest cultural achievements.

During the initial settlement of the Andes, from the arrival of nomads probably from Siberia until about 1400 BC, villages and ceremonial centers were established, and trade emerged between coastal fishing communities and farming villages of the highlands.

EARLY & MIDDLE HORIZONS

The so-called Early Horizon (1400 to 400 BC) was an era of architectural innovation and activity, which is most evident in the ruins of Chavín de Huantar, on the eastern slopes of the Andes in Peru. During this period it is postulated that a wave of Aymará Indians, possibly from the mountains of central Peru, swept across the Andes into Alto Perú (Bolivia), driving out most of the Altiplano's original settlers. Chavín influences resounded far and wide, even after the decline of Chavín society, and spilled over into the Early Middle Horizon (400 BC to AD 500).

The Middle Horizon (AD 500 to 900) was marked by the imperial expansion of the Tiahuanaco and Huari (of the Ayacucho valley of present-day Peru) cultures. The ceremonial center of Tiahuanaco, on the shores of Lake Titicaca, grew and developed into the religious and political capital of the Alto Peruvian Altiplano.

The Tiahuanacans produced technically advanced work, most notably the city itself. They created impressive ceramics, gilded ornamentation, engraved pillars and slabs with calendar markings and designs representing their bearded white leader and deity, Viracocha, as well as other undeciphered hieroglyphs.

By 700 BC, Tiahuanaco had developed into a thriving civilization. Considered as advanced as ancient Egypt in many respects, it had an extensive system of roads, irrigation canals and agricultural terraces. Over the following centuries wooden boats were constructed to ferry 55,000kg

1400 BC–AD 400

Initial settlement by first peoples in what is now the Bolivian Altiplano

500–800

The ceremonial center for the Tiahuanaco people grew and prospered on the shores of Lake Titicaca slabs 48km across the lake to the building site, and sandstone blocks weighing 145,000kg were moved from a quarry 10km away.

Tiahuanaco was inhabited from 1500 BC until AD 1200, but its power lasted only from the 6th century BC to the 9th century AD. One theory speculates that Tiahuanaco was uprooted by a drop in Lake Titicaca's water level, which left the lakeside settlement far from shore. Another postulates that it was attacked and its population massacred by the warlike Kollas (sometimes spelt Collas; also known as Aymará) from the west. When the Spanish arrived, they heard an Inca legend about a battle between the Kollas and 'bearded white men' on an island in Lake Titicaca. These men were presumably Tiahuanacans, only a few of whom were able to escape. Some researchers believe that the displaced survivors migrated southward and developed into the Chipaya people of western Oruro department.

Today the remains of the city lie on the plain between La Paz and the southern shore of Lake Titicaca, and collections of Tiahuanaco relics can be seen in several Bolivian museums. For further information, see Tiahuanaco in the La Paz chapter (p81).

LATE HORIZON – THE INCA

The Late Horizon (AD 1476 to 1534) marked the zenith of Inca civilization. The Inca, the last of South America's indigenous conquerors, arrived shortly after the fall of Tiahuanaco. They pushed their empire from its seat of power in Cuzco (Peru) eastward into present-day Bolivia, southward to the northern reaches of modern Argentina and Chile, and northward through present-day Ecuador and southern Colombia. However the Inca political state thrived for less than a century before falling to the invading Spanish.

The Inca inhabited the Cuzco region from the 12th century and believed they were lead by descendents of the Sun God. The 17th-century Spanish chronicler Fernando Montesinos believed the Inca descended from a lineage of Tiahuanaco sages. There were many similarities between Tiahuanaco and Inca architecture, and when the Inca arrived to conquer the shores of Lake Titicaca, the Kollas who inhabited the Tiahuanaco area regarded the city's site as taboo.

Renowned for their great stone cities and skill in working with gold and silver, the Inca also set up a hierarchy of governmental and agricultural overseers, a viable social welfare scheme and a complex road network and communication system that defied the difficult terrain of their far-flung empire. The Inca government could be described as an imperialist socialist dictatorship, with the Sapa Inca, considered a direct descendant of the Sun God, as reigning monarch. The state technically owned all property, taxes were collected in the form of labor and the government organized a system of mutual aid in which relief supplies were collected from prosperous areas and distributed in areas suffering from natural disasters or local misfortune.

Around 1440 the Inca started to expand their political boundaries. The eighth Inca, Viracocha (not to be confused with the Tiahuanaco leader/deity of the same name), believed the mandate from the Sun God was not just to conquer, plunder and enslave, but to organize defeated tribes and absorb them into the realm of the benevolent Sun God. When the Inca arrived in Kollasuyo (present-day Bolivia), they assimilated local tribes as they had done elsewhere: by imposing taxation, religion and

Striking photos by Stephen Ferry illustrate the tales of modern Potosí miners in the book *I am Rich Potosí – The Mountain that Eats Men.*

their own Quechua language (the empire's *lingua franca*) on the region's inhabitants. The Kollas living around the Tiahuanaco site were essentially absorbed by the Inca and their religion was supplanted, but they were permitted to keep their language and social traditions.

By the late 1520s internal rivalries began to take their toll on the empire. In a brief civil war over the division of lands, Atahuallpa, the true Inca emperor's half-brother, imprisoned the emperor and assumed the throne himself.

SPANISH CONQUEST

The arrival of the Spanish in Ecuador in 1531 was the ultimate blow. Within a year Francisco Pizarro, Diego de Almagro and their bands of merry *conquistadores* arrived in Cuzco. Atahuallpa was still the emperor, but was not considered the true heir of the Sun God. The Spanish were aided by the Inca belief that the bearded white men had been sent by the great Viracocha Inca as revenge for Atahuallpa's breach of established protocol. In fear, Atahuallpa ordered the murder of the real king, which not only ended the bloodline of the Inca dynasty, but brought shame on the family and dissolved the psychological power grip of the Inca hierarchy. Within two years the government was conquered, the empire dissolved and the invaders had divided Inca lands and booty between the two leaders of the Spanish forces.

Alto Perú, which would later become Bolivia, fell for a brief time into the possession of Diego de Almagro, who was assassinated in 1538. Three years later Pizarro suffered the same fate at the hands of mutinous subordinates. But the Spanish kept exploring and settling their newly conquered land, and in 1538 La Plata (now known as Sucre) was founded as the Spanish capital of the Charcas region.

The Legacy of Potosí

By the time the wandering Indian Diego Huallpa revealed his earth-shattering discovery of silver at Cerro Rico (Rich Hill) in Potosí in 1544, Spanish conquerors had already firmly implanted their language, religion and customs on the remnants of Atahuallpa's empire.

Spanish Potosí, or the 'Villa Imperial de Carlos V', was officially founded in 1545 and quickly grew to 160,000 residents, making it the largest city in the western hemisphere. The Potosí mine became the world's most prolific, and the silver extracted from it underwrote the Spanish economy, particularly the extravagance of its monarchy, for at least two centuries.

Atrocious conditions in the gold and silver mines of Potosí guaranteed a short life span for the local Indian conscripts and African slaves who were herded into work gangs. Those not actually worked to death or killed in accidents succumbed to pulmonary silicosis within a few years. Africans who survived migrated to the more amenable climes of the Yungas northeast of La Paz, and developed into an Aymará-speaking minority. The indigenous peoples became tenant farmers, subservient to the Spanish lords, and were required to supply their conquerors with food and labor in exchange for subsistence-sized plots of land.

Coca, ace at numbing nerves and once the exclusive privilege of Inca nobles, was introduced among the general populace to keep people working without complaint (see the boxed text, p110).

1531	1544
The Spanish, led by conquistador Francisco Pizarro, arrive in Ecuador and claim Alto Perú, which would later become Bolivia	Diego Huallpa's discovery of silver in Potosí's Cerro Rico leads to the development of the world's most prolific silver mine

INDEPENDENCE

In May 1809 Spanish America's first independence movement had gained momentum and was well underway in Chuquisaca (Sucre), with other cities quick to follow suit. By the early 1820s General Simón Bolívar succeeded in liberating both Venezuela and Colombia from Spanish domination. In 1822 he dispatched Mariscal (Major General) Antonio José de Sucre to Ecuador to defeat the Royalists at the battle of Pichincha. In 1824 after years of guerrilla action against the Spanish and the victories of Bolívar and Sucre in the battles of Junín (August 6) and Ayacucho (December 9), Peru won its independence.

At this point Sucre incited a declaration of independence for Alto Perú, and exactly one year later the new Republic of Bolivia was born (see the boxed text, p214). The republic was loosely modeled on the USA, with legislative, executive and judicial branches of government. Bolívar and Sucre served as Bolivia's first and second presidents, but after a brief attempt by Andrés Santa Cruz, the third president, to form a confederation with Peru, things began to go awry. One military junta after another usurped power from its predecessor, setting a pattern of political strife that haunts the nation to this day.

Few of Bolivia's 192 governments to date have remained in power long enough to have much intentional effect, and some were more than a little eccentric. The bizarre and cruel General Mariano Melgarejo, who ruled from 1865 to 1871, once drunkenly set off with his army on an overland march to aid France at the outset of the Franco-Prussian War. History has it that he was sobered up by a sudden downpour and the project was abandoned (to the immense relief of the Prussians, of course).

DID YOU KNOW?

The first coins in the Americas were minted in Potosí.

DID YOU KNOW?

As of 2003 Bolivia had endured 192 changes of government in its 178 years as a republic.

SHRINKING TERRITORY

At the time of independence Bolivia's boundaries encompassed well over 2 million sq km, but its neighbors soon moved to acquire its territory, removing coastal access and much of its amazonian rubber trees, as well as attempting to control the potentially oil-rich Chaco; only half the original land area remained.

The coastal loss occurred during the War of the Pacific fought against Chile between 1879 and 1884. Many Bolivians believe that Chile stole the Atacama Desert's copper- and nitrate-rich sands and 850km of coastline from Peru and Bolivia by invading during Carnaval. Chile did attempt to compensate for the loss by building a railroad from La Paz to the ocean and allowing Bolivia free port privileges in Antofagasta, but Bolivians have never forgotten this devastating *enclaustromiento* (landlocked status). In fact the government still uses the issue as a rallying cry to unite people behind a common cause.

The next major loss was in 1903 during the rubber boom when Brazil hacked away at Bolivia's inland expanse. Brazil and Bolivia had been

TERRITORY LOSS 1825-1935

ACRE — To Brazil 251,000 km² 1867

To Brazil 188,704 km² 1903 — PURUS

To Peru 250,000 km² 1909

PERU

BRAZIL

To Brazil 50,733 km² 1867

BOLIVIA

MATO GROSSO

PACIFIC OCEAN — CHILE

PUNA DE ATACAMA 4753 km²

To Paraguay 243,500 km² 1935

LITORAL

PARAGUAY

To Chile 120,000 km² 1879-1884

To Argentina 130,095 km² 1862

CHACO BOREAL

To Argentina 35,910 km² 1883

CHACO CENTRAL

ARGENTINA

ransacking the forests of the remote Acre territory, which stretched from Bolivia's present Amazonian borders to halfway up Peru's eastern border. The area was so rich in rubber trees that Brazil engineered a dispute over sovereignty and sent in its army. Brazil convinced the Acre region to secede from the Bolivian republic, and promptly annexed it.

Brazil attempted to compensate Bolivia's loss with a railway, intended to open up the remote northern reaches of the country and provide a coastal outlet for the Amazon Basin. However the tracks never reached Bolivian soil. Construction ended at Guajará-Mirim on the Brazilian bank of the Río Mamoré.

Finally Paraguay went in for the kill. In 1932 a border dispute for control of the potentially huge deposits of oil in the Chaco was revved up by rival foreign oil companies. With Standard Oil backing Bolivia and Shell siding with Paraguay, Bolivia entered into the Chaco War.

Bolivia fell victim to Paraguayan pride and, within three years, lost another 225,000 sq km, 65,000 young men and a dubious outlet to the sea via the Río Paraguai before the dispute was finally settled in 1935 in Paraguay's favor. The anticipated oil reserves were never discovered, but several fields in the area that remained Bolivian territory now keep the country self-sufficient in oil production.

'Brazil convinced the Acre region to secede from the Bolivian republic, and promptly annexed it'

CONTINUING POLITICAL STRIFE

During the 20th century wealthy tin barons and landowners controlled Bolivian farming and mining interests, while the peasantry was relegated to a non-feudal system of peonage known as *pongaje*. The beating Bolivia took in the Chaco War made way for reformist associations, civil unrest among the *cholos* (indigenous people who dress traditionally but live in cities) and a series of coups by reform-minded military leaders.

The most significant development was the emergence of the Movimiento Nacionalista Revolucionario (MNR) political party, which united the masses behind the common cause of popular reform. It sparked friction between peasant miners and absentee tin bosses. The miners' complaints against outrageous working conditions, pitifully low pay and the export of profits to Europe, raised the political consciousness of all Bolivian workers. Under the leadership of Victor Paz Estenssoro, the MNR prevailed in the 1951 elections, but a last-minute military coup prevented it from actually taking power. The coup provoked a popular armed revolt by the miners, which became known as the April Revolution of 1952. After heavy fighting the military was defeated and Victor Paz finally took power. He nationalized mines, evicted the tin barons, put an end to *pongaje* and set up Comibol (Corporación Minera de Bolivia), the state entity in charge of mining interests.

The revolutionaries also pressed ahead with a diverse reform program, which included redistribution of land among sharecropping peasants and the restructuring of the education system to include primary education in villages.

The miners and peasants felt they were being represented, which enabled the MNR to stay in power for a notable 12 years under various leaders. But even with US support the MNR was unable to raise the standard of living or increase food production substantially, and its effectiveness and popularity ground to a halt. Victor Paz was forced to become

1884	1952
Bolivia loses her coastline to Chile	A military coup provokes a popular armed revolt by the miners, the April Revolution, and Victor Paz Estenssoro takes power

increasingly autocratic, and in 1964 his government was overthrown by a military junta headed by General René Barrientos Ortuño.

Five years later Barrientos died in a helicopter accident and a series of coups, military dictators and juntas followed. Right-wing coalition leader General Hugo Banzer Suárez eventually took over in 1971 and served a turbulent term, punctuated by reactionary extremism and human-rights abuses. In 1978 amid demand for a return to democratic process, he scheduled general elections, lost, ignored the results, accused the opposition of ballot-box tampering and was forced to step down in a coup by General Juan Pereda Asbún.

The next three years were filled with failed elections, appointed presidents, military coups and hideous regimes, and a rash of tortures, arrests and disappearances, as well as a substantial increase in production and cocaine trafficking. One military leader, General Luis García Meza Tejada, eventually fled the country and was convicted in absentia of genocide, treason, human-rights abuses and armed insurrection, and sentenced to 30 years' imprisonment. He was extradited from Brazil to Bolivia in 1995 to serve his sentence.

In 1982 Congress elected Hernán Siles Zuazo, the civilian left-wing leader of the Communist-supported Movimiento de la Izquierda Revolucionaria (MIR). His term was beleaguered with labor disputes, ruthless government spending and monetary devaluation, resulting in a staggering inflation rate that at one point reached 35,000% annually.

When Siles Zuazo gave up after three years and called general elections, Victor Paz Estenssoro returned to politics to become president for the third time. He immediately enacted harsh measures to revive the shattered economy: he ousted labor unions, removed government restrictions on internal trade, slashed the government deficit, imposed a wage freeze, eliminated price subsidies, laid off workers at inefficient government-owned companies, allowed the peso to float against the US dollar and deployed armed forces to keep the peace.

Inflation was curtailed within weeks, but spiraling unemployment, especially in the poor Altiplano mining areas, caused enormous suffering and threatened the government's stability. Throughout his term, however, Victor Paz remained committed to programs that would return the government mines to private cooperatives and develop the largely uninhabited lowland regions. To encourage the settlement of the Amazon, he promoted road building (with Japanese aid) in the wilderness and opened up vast indigenous lands and pristine rainforest to logging interests.

DEMOCRACY PREVAILS

Free from the threat of military intervention, the 1989 presidential elections were characterized mostly by apathy. Hugo Banzer Suárez of the Acción Democrática Nacionalista (ADN) resurfaced, the MIR nominated Jaime Paz Zamora and the MNR put forth mining company president and economic reformist Gonzalo Sánchez de Lozada ('Goni'). Although Banzer and Sánchez were placed ahead of Paz Zamora, no candidate received a majority, so it was left to the National Congress to select a winner. Rivals Banzer and Paz Zamora formed a coalition and Congress selected Paz Zamora as the new president.

DID YOU KNOW?

The Bolivian congress appointed a woman, Lidia Gueilar, as interim president in 1982.

For all you ever wanted to know about the Andean wonder drug, see the cult classic *The History of Coca – The Divine Plant of the Incas*, by W Golden Mortimer. It's been in print since 1901 and was reprinted in 2000.

1967	1985
Argentine-born Marxist folk hero Ernesto 'Ché' Guevara, who failed to foment a peasant revolt in Bolivia, is executed	Victor Paz Estenssoro's New Economic Policy promotes spending cuts and privatization, resulting in massive unemployment

In the 1993 election Sánchez returned to defeat Banzer. Sánchez's Aymará running mate, Victor Hugo Cárdenas, appealed to *cholos* and *campesinos*, while European urbanites embraced his free-market economic policies. This administration attacked corruption and began implementing *capitalización* by opening up state-owned companies and

THE DRUG WAR

If outsiders know one thing about Bolivia and its neighboring countries, it's their affiliation with the coca leaf and the refinement and trafficking of cocaine and other illicit coca derivatives. While this factor isn't as prevalent as the Western media would have people believe, at any given time up to one third of the Bolivian work force has been dependent on the coca industry. Far and away the most lucrative of Bolivia's economic mainstays, it has been estimated to generate more than US$1 billion a year, of which less than half is thought to stay in the country.

As early as 1987 US Drug Enforcement Agency (DEA) squadrons were sent into the Beni and Chapare regions, and by the early 1990s US threats to cease foreign aid unless efforts were made to stop cocaine production forced Bolivia to comply with a half-baked coca eradication program.

In response to appeals by Bolivian President Jaime Paz Zamora in 1990, US President George Bush I sent US$78 million in aid and stepped up US anti-coca activities in northern Bolivia. More recently the US government points to the forgiveness of US$450 million of Bolivian debt (of a total debt of more than US$6 billion) when Bolivia seeks financial support for coca eradication, but this has hardly helped those most affected by coca eradication.

Initially the Bolivian government refused to chemically destroy coca fields, and instead urged farmers to accept US$2000 per hectare to replace their crops with alternative commodities. In 1992 the government upped the fee to US$2500 and in 1998 they forcibly destroyed plants in Chapare. That use of force is said to have sparked the militant opposition to eradication which culminated in riots and road blockades in 2001.

The 1990s were spotted with raids and eradication by the DEA and Bolivian police. In 1991 Bolivian police and DEA agents staged a daylight helicopter raid on Santa Ana del Yacuma, north of Trinidad, and seized 15 cocaine labs, nine estates, numerous private aircraft and 110kg of cocaine base; however no traffickers were captured, having been given sufficient warning to escape. Several surrendered later under Bolivia's lenient 'repentance law'. Most US government support of the Bolivian drug war since 1993 has been directed at militarized solutions. As of September 1998 their efforts resulted in 1206 arrests and seizures of 3201kg of cocaine hydro-chloride, 5392kg of cocaine base and US$15.8 million in seized assets.

Unfortunately the effect of most of the coca-eradication measures has been increased violence on both sides – and coca growing continues. At its peak, 100,000 acres were committed to coca plantations. In 1998 production was said to be down to 4000 acres and dwindling, but in 2002 the estimated number was closer to 24,000 acres. In 2001 coca growers leader Evo Morales demanded each family be allowed to plant 1600 square meters (17,000 sq ft) of coca.

In early 2003 the US Congress received US$91 million from tax payers to fund another year of the Bolivian drug war. Bolivia became eligible for 'Excess Defense Articles' and the US government planned to build several new bases in the Yungas, Beni and Pando regions. Despite eradication attempts, the Chapare region alone is said to still cultivate much of the world's illicit coca, yielding up to 100,000kg of cocaine annually. (In contrast, most coca grown in the Yungas region is used domestically to chew or make tea.)

In October 2003, incoming President Carlos Mesa failed to mention the C-word in his acceptance speech but indicated he will continue coca eradication soon after meeting with US ambassador David Greenlee.

1987	1988
USA begins sending Drug Enforcement Administration anti-coca squadrons into the Beni and Chapare regions	In response to growing interest in Andean countries as a toursim destination, Lonely Planet publishes 1st edition of *Bolivia*

mining interests to overseas investment. Officials hoped privatization would stabilize and streamline companies, making them profitable. Overseas investors in formerly state-owned companies received 49% equity, total voting control, license to operate in Bolivia and up to 49% of the profits. The remaining 51% of the shares were distributed to Bolivians as pensions and through Participación Popular, which was meant to channel spending away from cities and into rural schools, clinics and other local infrastructure.

Initially Participación Popular drew widespread disapproval; city dwellers didn't want to lose their advantage, and rural people, who stood to benefit most, feared a hidden agenda or simply didn't understand the program. Most working-class people viewed it as privatization by another name, and believed it would lead to the closure of unprofitable operations that didn't attract investors, resulting in increased unemployment. They had a point: while potential investors clamored for the oil company YPFB and the huge agribusinesses of the Santa Cruz department, the antiquated Comibol mining operations and the hopelessly inefficient ENFE railways drew little more than polite sneers (and many components of these operations have indeed closed down).

In 1995 labor grievances over these new policies resulted in a 90-day state-of-siege declaration and the arrest of 374 labor leaders. By mid-year measures were relaxed, but as the year progressed, reform issues were overshadowed by violence and unrest surrounding US-directed coca eradication in the Chapare. Even the establishment of a Spanish-managed private pension scheme and a subsequent payment of US$248 to each Bolivian pensioner – with the promise of future payments from the less-than-fluid plan – did little to boost the administration's popularity.

In 1997 voters upset by the reforms cast 22.5% of the ballot in favor of comeback king General Hugo Banzer Suárez over MNR's Juan Carlos Duran, former president Jaime Paz Zamora and Santa Cruz millionaire Ivo Kuljis. After cobbling together a disparate coalition – with little in common but a distaste for contender Paz Zamora – Congress deemed Banzer the victor, and he was sworn in on August 6 to a five-year term, up from four by a 1996 constitutional amendment.

In the late 1990s Banzer faced swelling public discontent with his coca eradication measures, widespread corruption, unrest in response to increasing gas prices and a serious water shortage and economic downturn in the Cochabamba department. In 2000 public protests over increasing gas prices versus government-controlled transport fares resulted in the blockade of the Yungas Highway for several weeks, and several issues inspired marches, demonstrations and occasional violence, which sporadically halted all traffic (in some cases even vendor and pedestrian traffic) in La Paz and other cities.

In August 2002 'Goni' Sánchez de Lozada was appointed president after winning only 22.5% of the vote. In February 2003 his International Monetary Fund-endorsed economic policies, including steep tax hikes, were met with widespread protests and several days of police lock-down in La Paz. In October 2003, Lozada resigned amidst massive popular protests and fled to Miami. His vice president and respected historian Carlos Mesa automatically took office. Opposition leaders have given Mesa 90 days to renounce coca eradication or face a new wave of protests.

DID YOU KNOW?

During the past 25 years, the United States has spent more than US$1.2 billion dollars on coca eradication in Bolivia.

The concise, up-to-date and extremely informative *Bolivia in Focus* by Paul van Lindert and Otto Verkoren provides an excellent synopsis of Bolivia's history, economics, politics and culture.

1995

Labor grievances over privatization result in a 90-day state-of-siege declaration and the arrest of hundreds of labor leaders

2002–2003

Gonzalo Sánchez de Lozada ('Goni') wins presidency with 22% of the vote. Widespread protests force his resignation in October 2003

Culture

THE NATIONAL PSYCHE

In Bolivia attitude depends on climate and altitude. *Cambas* (lowlanders) and *kollas* (highlanders) enjoy expounding on what makes them different (ie, better) than the other. Lowlanders are said to be warmer, more casual and more generous to strangers; highlanders are supposedly harder working but less open-minded. In reality nearly every *kolla* has a kindly *kolla camba* living in La Paz and all the jesting is good-natured.

Bolivians are keen on greetings and pleasantries. Every exchange is kicked off with the usual *Buen día* or *Buenos días,* but also with a *Cómo está?* or *Qué tal?* (How are you?). Bolivian Spanish is also liberally sprinkled with endearing diminutives such as *sopita* (a little soup) and *pesitos* (little pesos, as in 'it only costs 10 little pesos').

Bolivia has been described as a beggar sleeping in a golden bed. The nation is among the top five recipients of foreign aid worldwide and always seems to have its hand out for more. Stubborn pride and an overriding desire to protect the country's natural wealth make it nearly politically impossible to export abundant resources like oil or natural gas, even when the potential financial rewards are huge.

A collective, landlocked longing for the ocean is manifest in the military airline's logo, a lost pelican in a thunderstorm over Illimani.

LIFESTYLE

Day-to-day life varies from Bolivian to Bolivian, mostly depending on whether they live in the city or the country. Many *campesinos* live without running water, heat or electricity, and some wear clothing that has hardly changed style since the Spanish arrived. But in cities, especially Santa Cruz (the country's richest city), thousands of people enjoy the comforts of modern conveniences.

The average spending power per person per year is US$2600 in Bolivia (the lowest in South America after Guyana). Not everyone is complacent about the economy. In 2003 disgruntled teachers blocked roads in efforts to drastically increase their US$200 a month salaries, and other public servants and farmers strike regularly as well. A large percentage of the underemployed supplement their income by participating in the informal street-market and coca-production economy.

Most Bolivians' standard of living is alarmingly low, marked by substandard housing, nutrition, education, sanitation and hygiene. Bolivia suffers from a Third World trifecta: a high infant mortality rate (57 deaths per 1000 births), a high birth rate (3.3 per woman) and a low female literacy rate (77%). Overall 87% of primary-school-aged children are enrolled in classes, but attendance isn't necessarily a high priority.

On the higher education front there are 30 universities, 10 of which are public. The growing ranks of well-educated college graduates are frustrated by the lack of domestic opportunity and are increasingly seeking work abroad.

With no social welfare system in place to sustain the elderly, disabled, mentally ill and underemployed, they take to the streets, hoping to arouse sympathy. One ethnic group in Potosí department has even organized a begging syndicate that sends brown-clad older women into larger cities around the country, provides accommodation and supplies them with suitably grubby-looking children.

Yes, machismo is alive and well in Bolivia, but women's rights and education organizations are popping up, most notably in El Alto. The Bolivian congress appointed a woman as interim president in 1982 and many women have been elected as members of the national legislature.

Naturally, homosexuality exists in Bolivia. It's fairly widespread among rural communities and it's perfectly legal (though the constitution does prohibit same-sex marriages).

POPULATION

Bolivia is thinly populated with just 1½ million people. The Altiplano supports nearly 70% of the population – despite its frigid climate and simmering social and political strife – mostly in the La Paz, Lake Titicaca and Oruro regions.

More than half of the population claims pure indigenous heritage; nearly 1% is of African heritage, mostly descendants of slaves conscripted to work in the Potosí mines. The remainder of Bolivia's citizens are largely of European extraction. Not all are descendants of the early Spanish conquerors; there are Mennonites colonies, Jewish refugees from Nazi Europe, Eastern European refugees and hordes of researchers, aid workers and missionaries. Small Middle Eastern and Asian minorities, consisting mainly of Palestinians, Punjabis, Japanese and Chinese, have also immigrated. Most have opened restaurants in urban areas or settled in the rapidly developing lowlands of the Santa Cruz department.

The Fat Man from La Paz: Contemporary Fiction from Bolivia, edited by Rosario Santos, is a less-than-gripping collection of 20 shorts. The stories offer insider perspectives about typical Bolivians and their life experiences.

GIFT GIVING

When traveling around Bolivia, particularly in rural areas, some visitors may be shocked by the often primitive living conditions they encounter. In response some are moved to compare the locals' lot with their own, and experience pangs of conscience and outrage at inequalities. In an attempt to salve the guilt or inspire goodwill, many visitors indiscriminately distribute gifts of sweets, cigarettes, money and other items to local children and adults.

What people from Western societies may not realize is that in Bolivia and many other developing countries is that the lack of money, TV, automobiles, modern conveniences or expensive playthings does not necessarily indicate poverty. Most of the people of rural Bolivia have crops, animals and homes that provide sufficient food, clothing and shelter. They work hard on the land and it, in turn, takes care of them.

While it may be difficult for Westerners to understand this lifestyle, many of the proud and independent Bolivians have known nothing else for thousands of years, and are as comfortable with it as foreigners are in their own environment. When short-term visitors hand out sweets or cigarettes, they cause dental and health problems that cannot be remedied locally; when they give money, they impose a foreign system of values and upset a well-established balance.

It's undoubtedly well meaning, but the long-term consequences of indiscriminate gift giving are undeniable. As more visitors venture into traditional regions, the local people come to associate the outside world with limitless bounty – which appears to be theirs for the asking. Visitors are pestered with endless requests, and locals become confused as once-generous foreigners begin to regard them with contempt. Communication breaks down and the meeting of cultures becomes a strain on everyone.

If you wish to be accepted by local people, you can perhaps share a conversation, teach a game from home or share a photograph of your friends or family. If you wish to make a bigger difference, you can donate money and supplies to organizations working to improve rural conditions. Alternatively bring a supply of bandages, rehydration mixture or other medicines and leave them with the local health-care nurse (larger rural villages have a clinic), or buy a handful of pens and a stack of exercise books and give them to the schoolteacher.

When a personal gift becomes appropriate – if you're invited for a meal, for example, or someone goes out of their way to help you – share something that won't disrupt or undermine the local culture or lifestyle, such as some fruit, bread or a handful of coca leaves.

SPORTS

Like its Latin American neighbors, Bolivia's national sport is *futból* (soccer). Their teams typically fare well in *futsal* or *futból de salon* (five-vs-five mini-soccer) world championships. Professional matches are held every weekend in big cities, and impromptu street games are always happening. Some communities still bar women from the field, but in the Altiplano womens' teams have started popping up, where they play clad in petticoats, skirts and jerseys. A couple of years ago a national women's team was started too. Bolívar and The Strongest (both from La Paz) usually participate (albeit weakly) in the Copa Libertadores, the annual showdown of Latin America's top clubs.

In rural communities volleyball is a sunset affair, with mostly adults playing a couple of times a week. Racquetball, billiards, chess and *cacho* (dice) are also popular. The unofficial national sport, however, has to be feasting and feting – competition between dancers and drinkers knows no bounds.

Surf the Bolivian Educational & Cultural Network's site www.llajta.org to hear samples of a wide range of traditonal and modern Bolivian music.

RELIGION

Roughly 95% of Bolivia's population professes Roman Catholicism and practices it to varying degrees. The absence of Roman Catholic clergy in rural areas has led to a mixing of Inca and Aymará belief systems with Christianity in an interesting amalgamation of doctrines, rites and superstitions, and some *campesinos* still live by a traditional lunar calendar.

Indigenous religions believe in natural gods and spirits, which date back to Inca times and earlier. *Pachamama*, the ubiquitous earth mother, is the most popular recipient of sacrificial offerings, since she shares herself with human beings, helps bring forth crops and distributes riches to those she favors. She has quite an appetite for coca (see the boxed text, p110), alcohol and the blood of animals, particularly llamas. If you're wondering about all the llama fetuses in the markets, they are wrapped up and buried under new constructions, especially homes, as an offering to *Pachamama*.

Among the Aymará, mountain gods, the *apus* and *achachilas*, are important. The *apus*, mountain spirits who provide protection for travelers, are often associated with a particular *nevado* (snow-capped peak). *Achachilas* are spirits of the high mountains, who are believed to be ancestors of the people and look after their *ayllu* (native group of people, loosely translated as 'tribe') and provide bounty from the earth.

Ekeko, which means 'dwarf' in Aymará, is the jolly little household god of abundance. Since he's responsible for matchmaking, finding homes for the homeless and ensuring success for businesspeople, he's well looked after, especially during the Alasitas festival in La Paz (p61).

Talismans are also used in daily life to encourage prosperity or to protect a person from evil. A turtle is thought to bring health, a frog or toad carries good fortune, an owl signifies wisdom and success in school, and a condor talisman will ensure a good journey.

ARTS

Bolivia enjoys a wide range of artistic expression. Traditional music and textiles are more prevalent than contemporary gallery art. The Museo de Arte Contemporaneo (p000) in La Paz, opened in 2001, represents a growing appreciation of contemporary art, but by international standards, it's little more than a private gallery. In the way of performances, theater is limited mostly to the cinematic type or traditional *peñas*. Bolivia does have several artists and writers of note, many museums worth a full afternoon and a wealth of undiscovered musical talent.

Artesanía (Textiles)

Weaving methods have changed little in Bolivia for centuries. In rural areas girls learn to weave before they reach puberty, and women spend nearly all their spare time with a drop spindle or weaving on heddle looms. Prior to colonization llama and alpaca wool were the materials of choice, but sheep's wool has now emerged as the least expensive material, along with synthetic fibers.

Bolivian textiles come in diverse patterns. The majority display a degree of skill that results from millennia of artistry and tradition. The most common piece is a *manta* or *aguayo*, a square shawl made of two hand-woven strips joined edge to edge. Also common are the *chuspa* (coca pouch), the *falda* (skirt) with patterned weaving on one edge, woven belts and touristy items such as camera bags made from remnants.

Regional differences are manifest in weaving style, motif and use. Weavings from Tarabuco often feature intricate zoomorphic patterns, while distinctive red-and-black designs come from Potolo, northwest of Sucre. Zoomorphic patterns are also prominent in the wild Charazani country north of Lake Titicaca and in several Altiplano areas outside La Paz, including Lique and Calamarka.

Some extremely fine weavings originate in Sica Sica, one of the many dusty and nondescript villages between La Paz and Oruro, while in Calcha, southeast of Potosí, expert spinning and an extremely tight weave – more than 150 threads per inch – produce Bolivia's finest textiles.

Music

All Andean musical traditions have evolved from a series of pre-Inca, Inca, Spanish, Amazonian and even African influences, but each region of Bolivia has developed distinctive musical traditions, dances and instruments. The strains of the Andean music from the cold and bleak Altiplano are suitably haunting and mournful, while those of warmer

Arturo von Vacano's *Morder el Silencio* (translated as *The Biting Silence*) is an autobiographical novel of the life, career and ultimate arrest of the journalist narrator, who penned a critique of the military government and is accused of being a communist.

Renato Prada Oropeza's prize-winning *Los Fundadores del Alba* (translated as *The Breach*) revolves around the experiences of two people, a saintlike guerrilla modeled on Ché Guevara and a young soldier who lacks ideals and is fighting only because he has been drafted.

CHOLA DRESS

The characteristic dress worn by many Bolivian Indian women was imposed on them in the 18th century by the Spanish king, and the customary center parting of the hair was the result of a decree by the Viceroy Toledo.

This distinctive ensemble, both colorful and utilitarian, has almost become Bolivia's defining image. The most noticeable characteristic of the traditional Aymará dress is the ubiquitous dark green, black or brown bowler hat that would seem more at home on a London street than in the former Spanish empire. You'd be hard pressed to find a *chola* or *campesina* without one.

The women normally braid their hair into two long plaits that are joined by a tuft of black wool known as a *pocacha*. The short *pollera* skirts they wear are constructed of several horizontal bands tucked under each other. This garment tends to make the women appear overweight (most actually aren't), especially when several skirts are combined with multiple layers of petticoats.

On top, the outfit consists of a factory-made blouse, a woolen *chompa* (sweater/jumper), a short vestlike jacket and a cotton apron, or some combination of these. Usually, women add a woolen shawl known as a *llijlla* (sometimes spelled *llica*) or *phullu*.

Slung across the back and tied around the neck is the *aguayo* (also spelled *ahuayo*), a rectangle of manufactured or handwoven cloth decorated with colorful horizontal bands. It's used as a carryall and is filled with everything from coca or groceries to babies.

The Quechua of the highland valleys wear equally colorful but not so universally recognized attire. The hat, called a *montera*, is a flat-topped affair made of straw or finely woven white wool. It's often taller and broader than the bowlers worn by the Aymará. The felt *monteras* (aka *morriones*), of Tarabuco, patterned after Spanish conquistadores' helmets, are the most striking.

Tarija, with its complement of bizarre musical instruments, take on more vibrant and colorful tones.

Original Andean music was exclusively instrumental, but recent trends toward popularization of the melodies has inspired the addition of appropriately tragic, bittersweet or morose lyrics.

In the lowland regions Jesuit influences on Chiquitano, Moxos and Guaraní musical talent left a unique legacy that is still in evidence, and remains particularly strong. Extremely able artists and musicians, the Indians handcrafted musical instruments – the renowned harps and violins featured in contemporary Chaco music – and mastered Italian baroque forms, including opera. In the remotest of settings they gave concerts, dances and theater performances that could have competed on a European scale. For more information, see the boxed text, p59.

Dance

Traditional Altiplano dances celebrate war, fertility, hunting prowess, marriage and work. After the Spanish arrived, European dances and those of the African slaves were introduced, resulting in the hybrid dances that now characterize most Bolivian celebrations.

Bolivia's de facto national dance is the *cueca*, derived from the Chilean original and danced by handkerchief-waving couples to three-quarter time, primarily during fiestas. The most unusual and colorful dances are performed at Altiplano festivals, particularly during Carnaval. Oruro's La Diablada (Dance of the Devils) celebration draws huge international crowds. The most famous and recognizable Diablada dance is La Morenada, which reenacts the dance of African slaves brought to the courts of Viceroy Felipe III. The costumes consist of hooped skirts, shoulder mantles and devilish dark-faced masks adorned with plumes.

Architecture

Tiahuanaco's ruined structures and a handful of Inca remains are about all that's left of pre-Columbian architecture in Bolivia. The classic Inca polygonal-cut stones that distinguish many Peruvian sites are rare in Bolivia, found only on Isla del Sol and Isla de la Luna in Lake Titicaca.

Some colonial-era houses and street façades survive, notably in Potosí, Sucre and La Paz. Most colonial buildings, however, are religious, and their styles are divided into several major overlapping periods.

Renaissance (1550 to 1650) churches were constructed primarily of adobe, with courtyards and massive buttresses. One of the best surviving examples is in the village of Tiahuanaco (p81). Renaissance churches indicating *mudéjar* (Moorish) influences include San Miguel (p221) in Sucre, and the cathedral (p92) in Copacabana, on the shores of Lake Titicaca.

Baroque (1630 to 1770) churches were constructed in the form of a cross with an elaborate dome. The best examples are the Compañía (p155) in Oruro, San Agustín (p238) in Potosí and Santa Bárbara in Sucre.

Mestizo style (1690 to 1790) is defined by whimsical decorative carvings including tropical flora and fauna, Inca deities and designs, and bizarre masks, sirens and gargoyles. See the amazing results at the San Francisco church (p51) in La Paz, and San Lorenzo, Santa Teresa and the Compañía in Potosí (p238).

In the 18th century the Jesuits in what is now known as the Beni and Santa Cruz lowlands went off on neoclassical tangents, designing churches with Bavarian rococo and Gothic elements. Their most unusual effort was the bizarre mission church at San José de Chiquitos.

DID YOU KNOW?

Bolivian milliners don't want for work: at last count there were more than 100 hat styles worn countrywide.

DID YOU KNOW?

The song which became the worldwide pop hit *Lambada* was based on *Llorando Se Fue* by the late Bolivian composer Ulisses Hermosa and his brother Gonzalo.

Charangos Famosos is a recording of Bolivia's finest *charango* masters, including Ernesto Cavour, Willy Centellas, Alejandro Camara, Eddy Navia, Celestino Campos and Mauro Núñez.

Since the 1950s many modern high-rises have appeared in the major cities. Though most are generic, there are some gems. Look for triangular pediments on the rooflines, new versions of the Spanish balcony and the use of hardwoods of differing hues. In La Paz chalet-type, wooden houses are all the rage, and the new cathedral in Riberalta sings the contemporary gospel of brick and cedar like nobody's business.

Visual Arts

In the early colonial days Bolivian art was largely inspired by religion, the major contribution being represented by the Escuela Potosina Indígena. Hallmarks of this tradition include gilded highlights and triangular representations of the Virgin Mary.

Notable modern artists include Alejandro Mario Yllanes, an Aymará tin miner turned engraver and muralist, and Miguel Alandia Pantoja who, in the late 1940s, painted scenes of popular revolution.

Contemporary Aymará artist Mamani Mamani from Tiahuanaco village strives to portray the true 'color' of the Altiplano – not the landscape but the images that inspire the people – and it's brilliant. The *paceño* artist Gil Imana brings out the stark, cold and isolated nature of life in the Andes, using only tiny splashes of color on drab backgrounds to hint at the underlying vibrancy of the culture. See 'Marina Núñez del Prado' (boxed text, p54) for a biography of Bolivia's foremost sculptor.

Librería Boliviana: www.libreriaboliviana.com stocks an extensive collection of books, videos, traditional instruments and music (plus MP3 samples) and ships worldwide.

Contemporary Ayamará visual artist Mamani Mamani (www.mamani.com), renowned for his brilliant, inspired imagery of every-day Altiplano life, has exhibited internationally.

Environment

The 1990s saw a dramatic surge in international and domestic interest in ecological and environmental issues in the Amazon region. Environmental problems have not yet reached apocalyptic proportions, but change is coming rapidly and it is not being accompanied by the measures required to maintain a sound ecological balance. Bolivia fortunately lacks the population pressures of Brazil, nevertheless it is promoting indiscriminate development of its lowlands. Settlers continue to leave the highlands to clear lowland forest and build homesteads. Though several local and international NGOs have crafted innovative ways to preserve select habitats, in other areas insensitive development continues apace, and many regions risk exhaustion of their forest and wildlife resources.

Manuel Córdova-Ríos' *Wizard of the Upper Amazon* is an autobiographic tale of modern, Peruvian-Amazonia, village life and a non-anthropological introduction to the region's endangered religion, culture and unique ecosystems.

THE LAND

Despite the huge loss of territory in wars and concessions, landlocked Bolivia is South America's fifth-largest country – 1,098,581 sq km or 3½ times the size of the British Isles.

John Kricher's *A Neotropical Companion* is a clearly written, hard-hitting examination of the workings of a rainforest, including regeneration pathways and ecological succession.

Two Andean mountain chains define the west of the country, with many peaks above 6000m. The western Cordillera Occidental stands between Bolivia and the Pacific coast. The eastern Cordillera Real runs southeast then turns south across central Bolivia, joining the other chain to form the southern Cordillera Central.

The haunting Altiplano, which ranges in altitude from 3500m to 4000m, is boxed in by these two great *cordilleras*. It's an immense, nearly treeless plain punctuated by mountains and solitary volcanic peaks. At the Altiplano's northern end, straddling the Peruvian border, Lake Titicaca is one of the world's highest navigable lakes. In the far southwestern corner, the land is drier and less populated. Here are the remnants of two vast ancient lakes, the Salar de Uyuni and the Salar de Coipasa.

East of the Cordillera Central are the Central Highlands, a region of scrubby hills, valleys and fertile basins with a Mediterranean-like climate.

Search through Project Underground's www.moles.org Drillbits & Tailings archive for news about mining, gas and petroleum developments.

North of the Cordillera Real, the Yungas form a transition zone between arid highlands and humid lowlands. More than half of Bolivia's total area is in the Amazon Basin. The northern and eastern lowlands are sparsely populated and flat, with swamps, savannas, scrub and rainforest.

In the country's southeastern corner is the flat, nearly impenetrable scrubland of the Gran Chaco.

WILDLIFE

Thanks to its varied geography, sparse human population and lack of extensive development, Bolivia is one of the best places on the continent to observe wildlife. Even the most seasoned wildlife observers will be impressed by Parque Nacional Madidi (p320) and Parque Nacional Noel Kempff Mercado (p330).

Animals

The distribution of wildlife is largely directed by the country's geography. The Altiplano is home to the camelids, flamingos and condors. The jaguar, tapir and *javeli* (peccary), which occupy the nearly inaccessible, harsh expanses of the Chaco in relatively healthy numbers, are quite elusive. The Amazon Basin contains the richest density of species on earth, featuring an incredible variety of lizards, parrots, monkeys, snakes, butterflies, fish and bugs (by the zillions!). Bolivia is home to many rare and endangered species such as *vicuñas*, *guanacos*, giant anteaters, spectacled bears, maned wolves and many more.

The Southern Altiplano is the exclusive habitat of the James flamingo. The versatile rhea or *ñandú* (the South American ostrich) inhabits the Altiplano to the Beni, the Chaco and the Santa Cruz lowlands. In the highlands lucky observers may see a condor; highly revered by the Inca, these rare vultures are the world's heaviest birds of prey.

River travelers are almost certain to spot capybaras (large amphibious rodents), turtles, alligators, pink dolphins and, occasionally, giant river otters. It's not unusual to see anacondas in the rivers of the Beni department, and overland travelers frequently see armadillos, rheas, sloths and the agile, long-legged *jochis* (agoutis).

You won't have to travel very far to spot the most common Bolivian fauna – the llama and the alpaca – but having been domesticated for centuries, they are hardly wild. A boat journey along a northern river or a rail trip through the far southwest or the Oriente will present at least a glimpse of Bolivia's unique inhabitants.

ENDANGERED & RARE SPECIES

The extremity of the landscape has kept many areas uninhabited by people for a long time, preserving pristine habitats for many exotic species.

Vicuñas, which fetch a bundle on the illicit market for their fuzzy coats, are declining in the wild, but in a couple of Bolivian reserves their numbers have been increasing. Other wild Altiplano species include Andean wolves, foxes and *huemules* (Andean deer). The best place to see all of these, however, is just across the Chilean border in the Parque Nacional Lauca (p164).

Guanacos are seen throughout the remote southwestern part of the country. The *viscacha*, a longtailed rabbitlike creature, spends most of its time huddled under rocks in the highlands.

The tracks of puma, which is native throughout the Americas and was once indigenous to Bolivia, are occasionally seen in remote mountain ranges, but there's little chance of spotting one without mounting a special expedition.

Rarer still, but present in national parks and remote regions, are jaguars, peccaries, maned wolves, tapirs, giant anteaters and spectacled bears. These animals can be seen in the Parque Nacional Noel Kempff Mercado (p330).

Plants

Because of its enormous range of altitudes, Bolivia enjoys a wealth and diversity of flora rivaled only by its Andean neighbors.

In the overgrazed highlands, the only remaining vegetable species are those with some defense against grazing livestock or those that are unsuitable for firewood. Much of what does grow in the highlands, grows slowly and is endangered. While there's remarkably little forest above 3000m elevation, the rare dwarf *queñua* trees live as high as 5300m. The uncommon giant *Puya raimondii* century plant is found only in Bolivia and southern Peru.

The lower elevations of the temperate highland hills and valleys support vegetation similar to that of Spain or California. Most of southeastern

Amateur birdwatchers will find John Stewart Dunning's well-illustrated *South American Birds: A Photographic Aid to Identification* a fascinating introduction. Experts will want to track down Jon Fjeldsa's *Birds of the High Andes*.

DID YOU KNOW?

The elusive Andean condor, the world's heaviest bird of prey, has a 3m wingspan and can effortlessly drag a 20kg carcass.

Margaret Mee's beautifully illustrated *In Search of the Flowers of the Amazon Forest* comes highly recommended for anyone (not only botanists) interested in the Amazon.

Bolivia is covered by a nearly impenetrable thicket of cactus and thorn scrub, which erupts into colorful bloom in the spring.

The moist upper slopes of the Yungas are characterized by dwarf forest. Further down the slopes is the cloudforest, where the trees grow larger and the vegetation thicker.

Northern Bolivia's lowlands are characterized by true rainforest dotted with vast soaking wetlands and open savannas. The Amazon Basin contains the richest botanical diversity on earth with thousands of endemic species.

Scour the Friends of the Earth's Amazonia homepage www.amazonia.org.br for news and views on current environmental developments throughout the Amazon.

NATIONAL PARKS & RESERVES

Bolivia has protected 35% of its total land by declaring 60 national parks, reserves and protected areas. Although many are just lines drawn on a map, they are home to much of Bolivia's most amazing landscapes and wildlife. The Servicio Nacional de Areas Protegidas (Sernap; ☎ 02-243-4420/72; www.sernap.gov.bo; 20 de Octubre 2659, La Paz) manages all protected areas. Their website has a good overview (in Spanish) of each area.

The following areas are accessible to visitors – albeit often with some difficulty:

Amboró (p283) Near Santa Cruz, home to the rare spectacled bear, jaguars and an astonishing variety of bird life.

EL CHAQUEO: THE BIG SMOKE

Each September Bolivia's skies fill with a thick pall of smoke, obscuring the air, canceling flights, aggravating allergies and causing respiratory strife. Illimani is obliterated from La Paz' skyline, visitors to Lake Titicaca are deprived of spectacular views and there are all manner of aviation problems.

This is all the result of *el chaqueo*, the slashing and burning of the rainforest for agricultural and grazing land, which has been going on for hundreds of years. A prevailing notion is that the rising smoke forms rain clouds and ensures good rains for the coming season. In reality the hydrological cycle, which depends on transpiration from the forest canopy, is interrupted by the deforestation, resulting in diminished rainfall. In extreme cases deforested zones may be sunbaked into wastelands. The World Bank estimates that each year Bolivia loses upwards of 200,000 hectares of forest in this manner.

Ranchers in the Beni department have long set fire to the savannas annually to encourage the sprouting of new grass. Now, however, the most dramatic defoliation occurs along the highways of the northern frontier. In the mid-1980s this was largely virgin wilderness accessible only by river or air, but the new roads connecting the region to La Paz have turned it into a free-for-all. Forest is consumed by expanding cattle ranches – only charred tree stumps remain. Although the burned vegetable matter initially provides rich nutrients for crops, those nutrients aren't replenished. After two or three years the land is exhausted and takes 15 years to become productive again. That's too long for most farmers to wait; most just pull up stakes and search for more virgin forest to burn.

Ironically all this burning is prohibited by Bolivian forestry statutes, but such laws are impossible to enforce in an area as vast as the Bolivian lowlands. When relatively few people were farming the lowlands, the *chaqueo's* effects were minimal, but given Bolivia's annual population growth rate of 1.6%, the country must feed an additional 140,000 people each year. Because much of this population growth is rural, more farmers' children are looking for their own lands.

Although the long-term implications aren't yet known (hint: take a look at the devastated Brazilian states of Acre and Rondônia), the Bolivian government has implemented a program aimed at teaching forest-fire control and encouraging lowland farmers to minimize the *chaqueo* in favor of alternatives that don't drain the soil of nutrients. Despite these efforts, it seems that the *chaqueo* will be a fact of life in Bolivia for many years to come.

Apolobamba (p144) Excellent hiking in this remote park abutting the Peruvian border beneath the Cordillera Apolobamba.

Carrasco (p312) Remote extension to Amboró protects remaining stands of cloudforest in the volatile Chapare region.

Cotapata (p112) Most of El Choro trek passes through here, midway between La Paz and Coroico in the Yungas.

Madidi (p320) Protects a wide range of wildlife habitats, home to more than 1100 bird species.

Noel Kempff Mercado (p330) Remote park on the Brazilian border contains a variety of wildlife and some of Bolivia's most inspiring scenery.

Sajama (p161) Adjoining Chile's magnificent Parque Nacional Lauca, contains Volcán Sajama (6542m), Bolivia's highest peak.

Torotoro (p210) Enormous rock formations with dinosaur tracks from the Cretaceous period, plus caves and ancient ruins.

Tunari (p203) Within hiking distance of Cochabamba, features the Lagunas de Huarahuara and lovely mountain scenery.

Reserva Nacional de Fauna Eduardo Avaroa (p176) A highlight of the Southwest Circuit tour, including wildlife-rich lagoons and loads of pink flamingoes.

ENVIRONMENTAL ISSUES

Contact the following non-profit groups for information on countrywide environmental conservation efforts:

Armonía (www.birdbolivia.com) Everything you need to know about Bolivian birding and bird conservation.

Conservación Internacional (CI; www.conservation.org.bo) Promotes community-based ecotourism and biodiversity conservation.

Fundación Amigos de la Naturaleza (FAN; www.fan-bo.org) Works in Parques Nacionales Amboró & Noel Kempff Mercado.

Proteción del Medioambiente del Tarija (Prometa; www.prometabolivia.org) Works in Gran Chaco, Sama, Tariquía and El Corvalán reserves and Parque Nacional Aguaragüe.

DID YOU KNOW?

The World Bank estimates that Bolivia loses upwards of 200,000 hectares of rainforest anually to *chaqueo* slashing and burning for agricultural and grazing land.

Food & Drink

While the Bolivian national cuisine may not win any international awards, it's based on an admirable versatility derived from a few staple foods. Altiplano fare tends to be starchy and loaded with carbohydrates, while in the lowlands, fish and fresh produce feature more prominently.

Meat invariably dominates and is usually accompanied by rice, a starchy tuber (usually potato or *oca*) and shredded lettuce. Often the whole affair is drowned in *llajhua* (fiery tomato-based salsa).

STAPLES & SPECIALITIES

Desayuno (breakfast) consists of little more than coffee and a bread roll, and is often followed by a mid-morning street snack.

The South American Table by Maria Baez Kijac includes 450 home cooking recipes from Tierra del Fuego to Rio de Janiero and is spiced with a generous pinch of history.

Lunch is the main meal of the day. Most restaurants offer a set lunch (*almuerzo*), which consists of soup, a main course and tea or coffee; sometimes salad and dessert too. Depending on the class of the restaurant, *almuerzos* cost anywhere from US$1 to US$4; meals from the à la carte menu costs roughly twice as much. The evening meal, *la cena*, is less elaborate and served à la carte.

Quick Eats

After a light breakfast, Bolivians hit the street and bakeries for *salteñas*, *tucumanas* or *empanadas* These snacks are football-shaped and consist of a pastry shell stuffed with juicy, spiced mixtures of meat and vegetables, but each has a distinct flavor and texture.

Browse www.boliviaweb .com/recipes for recipes and ideas on how to put together a Bolivian meal.

Originating from Salta (Argentina), *salteñas* are crammed with beef or chicken, olives, eggs, potatoes, onions, peas, carrots, raisins and sundry spices. The best ones dribble all over the place. The *tucumana* has a puffier pastry shell which is filled with a piquant mix of egg, potatoes, chicken and onions. *Salteñas* tend to be sweeter and *tucumanas* pack a picante punch. *Empanadas* have a slightly more bready encasement that is sometimes deep-fried rather than baked. Vendors supply spicy condiments, if you are so inclined.

Other popular street snacks include *tamales* and *humintas* (aka *humitas*), both cornmeal dough pockets filled with spiced beef, vegetables, potatoes and/or cheese.

Soup

A large bowl of *sopa* is the start of every great Bolivian meal. Most soups include meat, which varies depending on where you're eating. Mid- to top-end restaurants use chicken or a bit of bone with tough but edible meat attached. In cheap spots a scrap of bone and gristle is typical.

Chupe, chaque and *lawa* are the most common thick stew-like soups. *Quinoa* and *maní* (peanuts) are often used to thicken broth.

Meat & Fish

Beef, chicken or fish are the backbone to nearly all Bolivian dishes; pork (*carne de chancho*) is considered a delicacy. *Campesinos* eat more *cordero* or *carnero* (mutton), *cabrito* or *chivito* (goat) or llama.

Beef is typically barbecued or grilled (*carne asado* or *carne parrillada*) in various cuts (*lomo, brazuelo* and *churrasco*). Jerked beef, llama or other red meat is called *charque* On the Altiplano it's served with mashed hominy; in the lowlands it's served with *yuca* or mashed plantain. In the Beni beef may be served as *pacumutus*, enormous chunks of grilled meat accompanied by *yuca*, onions and other trimmings.

Chicken is either fried (*pollo frito*), cooked on a spit (*pollo al spiedo*) or broiled (*pollo asado or pollo dorado*). Any combination of the above is called *pollo a la broaster* and is commonly served as *pollo a la canasta* (chicken-in-a-basket), with mustard, fries or *yuca*, and *ají* (chile sauce).

On the Altiplano the most popular fish (*pescado*) is *trucha* (trout) from Lake Titicaca. The lowlands have a wide variety of other freshwater fish; *surubí*, a catfish caught throughout the lowlands, is arguably the best of the lot.

Tubers

Tuberous plants are the bulk of the Bolivian diet. There are nearly 250 potato varieties. *Chuños* or *tunta* (freeze-dried potatoes) are rehydrated, cooked and eaten as snacks or with meals. Few foreigners find them appealing, mainly because they have the consistency of polystyrene when dry, and are tough and tasteless when cooked.

Ocas are tough, purple, potato-like tubers, which taste best roasted or fried. In the lowlands the potato and its relatives are replaced by plantain or the root of the *yuca* (*manioc* or cassava). It's good – if rather bland – provided it has been sufficiently cooked.

Cereals

Other common foods include *choclo*, a large-kernel corn (maize) that's ubiquitous on the Altiplano. *Habas*, similar to *fava* beans, grow wild and are eaten roasted or added to stews. They're also used to make a coffee-like beverage.

Quinoa, a unique Andean grain, is high in protein, and is used to make flour and to thicken stews. Recent research has shown that it's the only edible plant that contains all essential amino acids in the same proportions as milk, making it especially appealing to vegans. It's similar in most respects to millet or sorghum, except it grows on a stalk and resembles caviar when it's in the field.

Fruit

Many uniquely South American fruits are cultivated in Bolivia. Most notable are the custard apple (*chirimoya*), prickly pear cactus (*tuna*), and passion fruit (*maracuya*); unripe *maracuya* is known as *tumbo* and makes an excellent juice.

In the lowlands the range of exotic tropical fruits defies middle-latitude expectations. Among the more unusual are the human-hand shaped *ambaiba*; the small, round, green-and-purple *guaypurú*; the spiny yellow *ocoro*; the lemon-like *guapomo*; the bean-like *cupesi*; the *marayau*, which resembles a bunch of giant grapes; the currant-like *nui*; the scaly onion-looking *sinini*; and the stomach-shaped *paquio*. A good place to sample exotic fruits is at the Mercado Los Pozos (p278) in Santa Cruz.

TRAVEL YOUR TASTEBUDS

Want to take your tastebuds off the eaten track while you're in Bolivia? You won't find these at home:

Batidas – fruit juice whipped with milk, sugar and a syrupy nonalcoholic brew known as *bi-cervecina*

Boiled ocas – a cross between potato and skunk spray

Ckocko – spicy chicken cooked in wine or *chicha* and served with *choclo*, olives, raisins, grated orange peel; a Potosí original

Jolque – kidney soup; a Cochabamba specialty

We dare you to try rostro asado (sheep's head) or falso conejo (false rabbit,) a greasy, glutinous substance that appears to be animal-based.

DRINKS
Nonalcoholic Drinks
The most common international drinks like coffee, soda and bottled water are widely available. But don't leave the country without trying any of the local specialty drinks; many are gastronomic highlights.

Api and *mate de coca* are heated morning-time treats. *Refresco* (refreshment), an anonymous fruit-based juice with a floating dried peach, is a bus and train station favorite. Less prevalent are the sweet and nutty *tostada*, the walnut-based *horchata* and *licuados* (fruit-shakes blended with water or milk).

Check out www.bolivia.com/ El_sabor_de_bolivia/ for typical Bolivian recipes, a full culinary glossary and other gastronomic pointers.

Alcoholic Drinks
When Bolivians gather for recreational drinking – beer or harder – they intend to get plastered. Remember altitude increases both froth and effect. Bolivia produces its own wines, lagers and local concoctions of varying qualities.

Enjoyable Bolivian lagers include the fizzy and strange-tasting Huari, the good but rather nondescript Paceña, the pleasant but weak-flavored Sureña, the refreshing Taquiña, the robust Potosina, the slightly rough Ducal and the cold and tasty Tropical Extra.

Wines are fermented around Tarija with varying degrees of success. The best – and most expensive – is Bodega La Concepción's Cepas de Altura, from some of the world's highest vineyards, which sells for around US$10 for a 750ml bottle.

Drunk more for effect than flavor and created by fermenting corn, *chicha cochabambina* is favored by the Bolivian masses. The rumors about additional fermentation-starting ingredients are best ignored if you plan to imbibe. It's produced mostly around Cochabamba, where white plastic flags on long poles indicate *chicherías*, places where the funky stuff is sold.

Campesinos rarely consider taste or personal health when looking for a cheap and direct route to inebriation – thus their willingness to swill the head-pounding *puro* or *aguardiente* (firewater). This burning, gut-wrenching stuff is essentially pure alcohol, so if you're offered a glass, you may wish to make a particularly generous offering to Pachamama (see the boxed text, below).

WHERE TO EAT & DRINK
Larger towns and cities have a range of eateries, from family-run operations to upscale cloth-napkin restaurants. All towns have cheap food stalls in the market *comedores* (dining halls) that serve filling and tasty meals and snacks. When there is a menu, it normally reflects the propietor's wishes more than what's actually cooking. Sometimes it's more efficient to ignore the menu and ask what's on offer.

There are a growing number of western-style fast-food joints in the big cities. Restaurants serving typical European or North American foods

---

SPIRITS FOR THE SPIRITS

The world of the original Andean inhabitants is populated by hosts of well-respected supernatural beings, the *apus* and *achachilas* (mountain spirits believed to be ancestors of the people). They mainly pervade wild areas and are prone to both favorable behavior and fits of temper. The people believe themselves are literally descended from the earth mother, *Pachamama*, who is also respected and venerated.

The spirits are taken into consideration in facets of everyday life, and certain things are done to keep on their better side. Before a person takes the first sip of alcohol from a glass, it's customary to spill a few drops on the ground as an offering, or *t'inka*, to Pachamama. This demonstrates to *Pachamama* that she takes precedence over her human subjects. Alcohol is also splashed or sprinkled over homes and cars as a *cha'lla* (blessing).

are found around larger hotels or in middle-class districts of larger cities. Italian restaurants are becoming increasingly popular, and *chifas* (Chinese restaurants) exist in most major cities. More exotic cuisines such as vegetarian, Mexican, Swiss, Peruvian and Japanese are starting to catch on.

Quick Eats
Markets and street stalls are the places for cheap, on-the-go bites. They're everywhere, but aren't always open all day, everyday. They're often the best place to sample local specialties. Hygiene at some of these places isn't a top prioroty, so your internal plumbing may need time to adjust, but don't give up on market food just because you got the runs the first time you tried it.

Confiterías and pastelerías sell little more than snacks and coffee. Heladerías (ice cream parlors) are becoming increasingly worldly, offering pizza, pasta, doughnuts, salteñas, coffee specialties and even full (if bland) meals.

VEGETARIANS & VEGANS
Vegetarians who speak some Spanish and can be a little flexible (putting up with meat stock in soups, or picking meat out of a dish) will be fine. Vegans will find themselves eating a lot of potatoes in the highlands, and fresh fruits and vegetables elsewhere. Bigger cities and popular tourist areas have at least one vegetarian restaurant.

HABITS & CUSTOMS
Nearly everything stops from noon to at least 3pm when families get together and lull over a multi-hour lunch. It's the main meal of the day and no one rushes through it. *Campesinos* may eat with their fingers among family, but Bolivians in general use western-style utensils. Tipping up to 10% is standard at upscale restaurants when service is up to snuff; locals leave small change, if anything at all, elsewhere.

EAT YOUR WORDS
Want to know a *pacumutu* from a *pique lo macho*? *Chupe* from *chaque* from *charque*? Get behind the *comida* scene by getting to know the lingo. For pronunciation guidelines, see p378.

Useful Phrases

Do you have a menu in English?	*¿Tiene una carta en inglés?*
	tee-en oon-ah kahr-tah en een-gles?
What do you recommend?	*¿Qué me recomienda?*
	keh meh re-ko-mee-en-dah?
Do you have any vegetarian dishes?	*¿Tienen algún plato vegetariano?*
	tee-en-eh al-goon plat-ee-yoh ve-het-ar-ee-ah-noh?
Not too spicy please.	*No muy picoso/picante, por favor.*
	no moo-ee pee-koh-soh/pee-cahn-teh, por fah-vor.
I'll try what he/she is having.	*Voy a pedir lo que el/ella pedío.*
	voy ah pee-deer loh keh ehl/eh-yah pee-dee-oh.
I'd like the set lunch.	*Quisiera el almuerzo, por favor.*
	kee-see-ehr-ah ehl all-moo-erh-soo, por fah-vor.
This food is delicious.	*Esta comida está exquisita.*
	es-tah koh-mee-dah es-tah eks-kee-sit-a.
The bill (check), please.	*La cuenta, por favor.*
	lah kwen-tah, por fah-vor.

DID YOU KNOW?

Ceremonial *confites* (colored balls of sugar around a nut or fruit filling) are intended as religious offerings and are not meant to be eaten.

See www.bolivian.com/cocina to learn how to make your own empanadas and other favorite Bolivian treats .

Menu Decoder

anticuchos – beef-heart shish-kebabs

chancao – chicken with yellow pepper and tomato-and-onion sauce; a Tarija specialty

chajchu – beef with *chuño*, hard-boiled egg, cheese and hot red pepper sauce

charque kan – meat jerky (often llama meat) served with mashed *choclo*

chicharrón de cerdo – fried pork

chupe – thick meat, vegetable and grain soup with a clear broth flavored with garlic, *ají*, tomato, cumin or onion

escabeche – vinegar pickled vegetables, mainly carrots, onion and peppers

fritanga – spicy-hot pork with mint and hominy

kala purkha – soup made from corn that is cooked in a ceramic dish by adding a steaming chunk of heavy pumice; a Potosí and Sucre specialty

llapa – bargaining practice in which a customer agrees to a final price provided that the vendor augments or supplements the item being sold

masaco – *charque* served with mashed plantain, *yuca* and/or corn, a Bolivian Amazonian staple sometimes served with cheese

milanesa – a fairly greasy type of beef or chicken schnitzel (see *silpancho*)

pacumutu – enormous chunks of beef grilled on a skewer, marinated in salt and lime juice, with cassava, onions and other trimmings; a Beni specialty

papas rellenas – mashed potatoes stuffed with veggies or meat, and fried; tasty when piping hot and served with hot sauce

pique lo macho – chunked grilled beef and sausage heaped over french-fried potatoes, lettuce, tomatoes, onions and *locoto* (chile peppers)

silpancho – a schnitzel pounded till very thin and able to absorb even more grease than a *milanesa*. A properly prepared *silpancho* is said to be perfect for viewing a solar eclipse!

Spanish-English Glossary

BASICS

almuerzo – set lunch
cena – dinner
comedor – cheap dining hall
confitería – snack bar
cuchara – spoon
cuchillo – knife
desayuno – breakfast

mercado – market
panadería – bakery
parrillada/churrasquería – steakhouse
restaurante – restaurant
restaurante chifa – Chinese restaurant
tenedor – fork
wiskería – classy bar

SNACKS

buñuelo – sticky type of doughnut dipped in sugar syrup
cuñape – cassava and cheese roll
empanada – meat or cheese pasty
huminta – (aka *humita*) like a *tamale* but filled with cheese only and normally quite dry
licuado – fruit shake made with either milk or water
llaucha paceña – a doughy cheese bread
mani – peanuts
panqueques – pancakes
pastel – a deep-fried *empanada*; may be filled with chicken, beef or cheese
pukacapa – circular *empanada* filled with cheese, olives, onions and hot pepper sauce and baked in an earth oven

salteña – delicious, juicy meat and vegetable pasty, originally created in Salta, Argentina; it's now a popular mid-morning snack
tamale – cornmeal dough filled with spiced beef, vegetables and potatoes then wrapped in a corn husk and fried, grilled or baked
tucumana – *empanada*-like pastry stuffed til bursting with meat, olives, eggs, raisins and other goodies; originated in Tucuman, Argentina

SOUP

chairo – mutton or beef soup with *chuños*, potatoes and *mote*
chaque – like *chupe* but much thicker and contains more grain
chupe – thick meat, vegetable and grain soup with a clear broth flavored with garlic, ají, tomato, cumin or onion
fricasé – pork soup, a La Paz specialty

lawa – meat-stew broth thickened with corn starch or wheat flour
saíce – hot meat and rice stew
thimpu – spicy lamb and vegetable stew
tomatada de cordero – lamb stew with tomato sauce
witu – beef stew with pureed tomatoes

MEAT & FISH

brazuelo – shoulder
cabrito – goat
carne – beef
carne de chancho – pork
charque – jerked meat; the source of the English word 'jerky'
churrasco – steak
cordero – lamb or mutton

lomo – loin (of meat)
parrillada- meat grill or barbecue
pejerrey – the most common fish served in Bolivia; it's tasty, and is found everywhere from the Altiplano to the Amazon
pescado – generic term for fish
pollo – chicken

FRUIT & VEGETABLES

camote – sweet potato
chirimoya – custard apple, a green scaly fruit with creamy white flesh
choclo – large-grain Andean corn (maize)
chuños – freeze-dried potatoes
haba – bean of the *palqui* plant found on the Altiplano, similar to fava beans
maracuya – a sweet and delicious fruit (aka passion fruit), also see *tumbo*

mote – freeze-dried corn
oca – tough edible tuber similar to a potato
pomelo – large, pulpy-skinned grapefruit
quinoa – nutritious grain similar to sorghum
tarhui – legume from Sucre
tumbo – unripe *maracuya*, makes a superb juice
tuna – prickly pear cactus
yuca – cassava (*manioc*) tuber

OTHER DISHES & CONDIMENTS

llajhua – spicy-hot tomato sauce
locoto – small, hot pepper pods

queso – cheese
tallerines – long, thin noodles

DRINKS

api – syrupy form of *chicha* made from sweet purple corn, lemon, cinnamon and staggering amounts of white sugar
chicha – popular beverage that is often alcoholic and made from fermented corn; it may also be made from such ingredients as *yuca*, sweet potato or peanuts
cerveza – beer; Taquiña is the best, Huari the fizziest
chuflay – a blend of *singani*, lemon-lime soda, ice and lemon
despepitado – aka *mocachinchi*, a dried and shriveled peach used to flavor a *refresco*

gaseosa – soft drink
horchata – sweet walnut-based, milky-looking drink
mate de coca – coca leaf tea
mate de manzanilla – chamomile tea
singani – distilled grape spirit
tostada – tasty corn, barley, honey, cinnamon and clove brew (*aloja* in southern Bolivia)
trimate – common chamomile, coca and anise tea mixture
vino – wine; Kohlberg is the cheapest, Concepción is the best

LA PAZ

La Paz

CONTENTS

Although Sucre remains the judicial capital, La Paz, Bolivia's largest city and centre for commerce, finance and industry, is the de facto capital. It is one of the world's most intoxicating cities and, in terms of spectacular setting, is in the same scenic league as Rio de Janeiro, Cape Town, San Francisco and Hong Kong.

A visitor's first glimpse of La Paz will never be forgotten. Standing at the edge of the canyon the earth drops away, obliterating the poverty and ugliness of El Alto and revealing, 400m below, the sprawling city, which fills the bowl and climbs the walls of the gaping canyon. On a clear day the snowcapped triple peak of Illimani (6402m) towers in the background. If you're fortunate enough to arrive on a clear, dark night, the cityscape will appear like a mirrored reflection of the glittering sky.

But you won't realize La Paz' magnificent location if you approach through the poverty-plagued sprawl of El Alto, via muddy streets that appear not to have been swept since Inca times. Once a La Paz suburb, El Alto's ongoing influx of immigrants from the countryside has morphed it into Latin America's fastest growing city. Here unkempt children play in potholes, *cholas* pound laundry in sewage-choked streams and every other garage seems to house an auto repair shop.

Since La Paz is sky-high, warm clothing is desirable most of the year. In summer (November to April) the climate can be harsh: rain falls most afternoons, the canyon may fill with clouds and steep streets often become torrents of runoff. In winter (May to October) days are slightly cooler, but the crisp air is invigorating.

TOP FIVE

- Peruse Artesanía Alley off **Calle Sagárnaga** (p72) for fine woven wares
- Catch a **peña** (p70) for a taste of traditional dancing and folk music
- Stroll through El Alto's sprawling **markets** (p59) to taste and smell indigenous La Paz
- Bike the **World's Most Dangerous Road** (p55) – claim your bragging rights, before it's gone!
- Explore the ancient ruins of **Tiahuanaco** (p82)

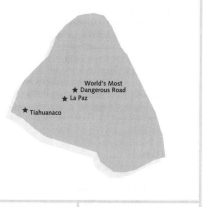

★ World's Most Dangerous Road
★ La Paz
★ Tiahuanaco

■ TELEPHONE CODE: 02   ■ POPULATION: 1.5 MILLION   ■ ELEVATION: 3660M

HISTORY

La Ciudad de Nuestra Señora de La Paz (the City of Our Lady of Peace) was founded and named on October 20, 1548, by a Spaniard, Captain Alonzo de Mendoza, at present-day Laja on the Tiahuanaco road. Soon after, La Paz was shifted to its present location, the valley of the Chuquiago Marka (now called the Río Choqueyapu), which had been occupied by a community of Aymará miners.

The 16th-century Spanish historian Cieza de León remarked of the new city: 'This is a good place to pass one's life. Here the climate is mild and the view of the mountains inspires one to think of God.' In spite of León's lofty assessment (perhaps he mistakenly got off at Cochabamba), the reason behind the city's founding was much more terrestrial. The Spanish always had a weakness for shiny yellow metal, and the now-fetid Río Choqueyapu, which today flows beneath La Paz, seemed to be full of it. The Spaniards didn't waste any time in seizing the gold mines, and Mendoza was installed as the new city's first mayor. The conquerors also imposed their religion and lifestyle on the Indians, and since most colonists were men, unions between Spanish men and Indian women eventually gave rise to a primarily *mestizo* population.

If the founding of La Paz had been based on anything other than gold, its position in the depths of a rugged canyon probably would have dictated an unpromising future. However the protection this setting provided from the fierce Altiplano climate and the city's convenient location on the main trade route between Lima and Potosí – much of the Potosí silver bound for Pacific ports passed through La Paz – offered the city some hope of prosperity once the gold had played out. By the time the railway was built, the city was well enough established to continue commanding attention.

In spite of its name, the City of Our Lady of Peace has seen a good deal of violence. Since Bolivian independence in 1825, the republic has endured 192 changes of leadership. An abnormally high mortality rate once accompanied high office in Bolivia, thus with the job of president came a short life expectancy. In fact the presidential palace on the plaza is now known as the Palacio Quemado (Burned Palace), owing to its repeated gutting by fire. As recently as 1946 then-president Gualberto Villarroel was publicly hanged in Plaza Murillo.

ORIENTATION

It's almost impossible to get lost in La Paz. There's only one major thoroughfare and

---

LA PAZ IN...

Two Days

Start your day with a snack (try *salteñas*) around Plaza Isabel la Católica or breakfast on The Prado – the perfect spots for watching the world's highest city wake up. Stroll the historic cobblestone streets around **Iglesia de San Francisco** (p51), then wander the nearby **Calle Linares** (Artesanía Alley; p72) and **Mercado de Hechicería** (Witches' Market; p50) while shopping for fine alpaca wear. No visit to Bolivia is complete without a stop at the **Museo de la Coca** (Coca Museum; p58).

Treat yourself to fine dining at an international eatery in **Lower Sopacachi** (p65) or in the trendy Zona Sur. Treat yourself to great local cuisine at homely **Casa de los Paceños** (p66). Finish off with a night at historic **Gran Hotel Paris** (p65) overlooking Plaza Murillo or at one of the world's highest five-star hotels (p65).

The highlight of a wander along colonial Calle Jéan is the **Museo de Instrumentos Musicales** (p56), best followed by an evening dinner show accompanied by traditional music at **Peña Marka Tambo** (p70).

Four Days

Follow the two-day itinerary, then on your third day take a day-trip out to **Tiahuanaco** (Tiwanaku; p82) to explore the excavated ruins. Depending on the season, on the fourth day you may want to relax at **Urmiri's rustic hot springs** (p85), ski or climb **Chacaltaya** (p79) or bicycle the **World's Most Dangerous Road** (p55) down to Coroico.

it follows the Río Choqueyapu canyon (fortunately for your olfactory system, the river flows mostly underground). The main street changes names several times from the top to bottom: Avenidas Ismael Montes, Mariscal Santa Cruz, 16 de Julio (the Prado) and Villazón. At the lower end, it splits into 6 de Agosto and Aniceto Arce. Away from the Prado and its extensions, streets climb steeply uphill and many are cobbled or unpaved. Above the downtown skyscrapers, the adobe neighborhoods and the informal commercial areas climb toward El Alto, perched on the canyon's rim. If you become disoriented and want to return to the center just head downhill.

City Center, Zona Sur & El Alto

La Paz' business districts and wealthier neighborhoods occupy the lower altitudes, which is the reverse of many US and European cities. The best-preserved colonial section of town is near the intersection of Calles Jaén and Sucre, where narrow cobbled streets and colonial churches offer a glimpse of early La Paz. The most prestigious suburbs are found far down in the canyon in the Zona Sur (Southern Zone), which includes the suburbs of Calacoto, Cotacota, San Miguel, La Florida, Obrajes and a growing throng of other upmarket *barrios* (districts). Numbered streets run perpendicular to the main road in Zona Sur, making navigation easier; the numbers increase from west to east.

Above the city center and Zona Sur are the cascades of cuboid, mud dwellings and makeshift neighborhoods of El Alto which literally spill over the canyon rim and down the slopes on three sides.

Maps

Most hotels hand out free photocopied city maps. Ómnium's glossy *Info Map La Paz* is the best of the freebie bunch. The best map of the city is the *Mapa Referencial de la Ciudad de La Paz* (US$1.50), available from the municipal tourist office. It also sells a map of a couple of La Paz-area hikes (US$1) and assorted booklets on Bolivia's most popular tourist cities. Another useful map is Polyjake's *Guía Cultural* (US$0.75), available at bookshops and hotels. It includes maps of Plaza Murillo, Sopocachi, Miraflores, Calacoto and San Miguel, and features museums, galleries

and embassies. Inside the central post office, opposite the poste restante counter, gift shops sell a range of maps.

Stock up on maps for the rest of your trip in LaPaz. For information on buying topo sheets and climbing maps, see p347.

Instituto Geográfico Militar (IGM; Map pp52-3; ☎ 237-0118; Oficina 5, Juan XXIII 100) In a blind alley off Rodríguez, offers original 1:50,000 topographic maps (US$8), or photocopies (US$5) if a sheet is unavailable.

Los Amigos del Libro (Map pp52-3; ☎ 220-4321; www.libro sbolivia.com; Mercado 1315; also at El Alto Airport) Also stocks 1:50,000 topographic maps, plus Walter Guzmán Córdova's colorful, mostly accurate 1:50,000 trekking maps.

INFORMATION
Airline Offices

AeroSur (Map pp52-3; ☎ 243-0430, 231-3233; 16 de Julio 1616) 224 4705

Amazonas (☎ 222-0840/48; Saavedra 1649, Miraflores)

American Airlines (Map pp52-3; ☎ 235-5384; www.aa.com; Plaza Venezuela 1440, Edificio Busch)

Grupo Taca (Map pp52-3; ☎ 231-3132; www.taca.com; 16 de Julio 1479, Edificio San Pablo, 4th fl)

LanChile/LanPeru (Map pp52-3; ☎ 235-8377; www.lanchile .com, www.lanperu.com; 16 de Julio 1566, Edificio Ayacucho, Suite 104)

Lloyd Aéreo Boliviano (LAB; Map pp52-3; ☎ toll-free 800-10-3001/4321, 237-1020/24; www.labairlines.com; Camacho 1460)

TAM Mercosur (Map pp52-3; ☎ 244-3442; www.tam.com.py; Plaza del Estudiante 1931)

Transportes Aéreos Militares (TAM; Map pp52-3; ☎ 212-1582/89; TAM airport ☎ 02-284-1884; Montes 738)

Varig (Map pp52-3; ☎ 231-4040; www.varig.com.bo; Santa Cruz 1392, Edificio Cámara de Comercio)

Bookshops & Book Exchanges

For used paperbacks in English, check the stalls in Paseo María Nunez del Prado and the booksellers' section of **Mercado Lanza** (Map pp52-3). To trade books, try **Ángelo Colonial** (Map pp52-3), the side-by-side offices of **America Tours** (Map pp52-3) and **Gravity Assisted Mountain Biking** (Map pp52-3) or **Café Sol y Luna** (Map pp52-3) or any of the hotels near Sagárnaga.

Gisbert & Co (Map pp52-3; Comercio 1270) Spanish-language literature and maps.

Librería Olimpia (Map pp52-3; ☎ 235-3833; Galería Handal, Local 14) Stationery shop with good map selection.

Los Amigos del Libro (☎ 220-4321; www.librosbolivia .com; Mercado 1315; also at El Alto Airport) Widest selection of foreign-language novels and periodicals, plus a good selection of Lonely Planet guides.

Cultural Centers

Centro Boliviano-Americano (CBA; Map pp48-50; ☎ 234-2582; www.cba.com.bo; Parque Zenón Iturralde 121) Language classes and US periodicals library.
Goethe Institut (Map pp52-3; ☎ 244-2453; www.goethe .de; 6 de Agosto 2118) Films, language classes and good German-language library.

Emergency

Numbers for emergency services (police, fire and ambulance) are the same for all Bolivia.
Ambulance (☎ 118)
Fire (Bomberos; ☎ 119)
Police (Radio Patrulla; ☎ 110)
Private ambulance (Auxilio Medico; ☎ 772-68502)
Tourist police (Policía Turistica; Map pp52-3; ☎ toll-free 800-10-8686/7, 222-5016; www.policiaturistica.gov .bo; Sagárnaga & Murillo) English-speaking. Report thefts to obtain an affidavit *(denuncia)* for insurance purposes – they won't recover any stolen goods.

Immigration

Migración (Map pp52-3; ☎ 237-0475; Camacho 1433; ☽ 8:30am-4pm Mon-Fri) Length of stay extensions are granted with little ado.

Internet Access

La Paz has nearly as many cybercafés as shoeshine boys. Charges range from US$0.35 to US$0.50 an hour, and connections are generally fastest in the morning or late evening. See @ icons on maps for other recommended places not mentioned here.
Internet Alley (Map pp52-3; Pasaje Iturralde, just off Prado near Plaza del Estudiante) Fastest, cheapest connections in town and several places are open late.
Tolomeo's (Map pp52-3; Loayza at Comercio, around the corner from Hostal República) Fast, friendly, warm, high-tech and reliably open late.

Internet Resources

Happening (www.happening.tk) Current culture and nightlife listings focusing on Sopocachi and San Miguel; pick up free weekly flyer at clubs and cafés.
La Paz municipal website (www.ci-lapaz.gov.bo) Flash site with good cultural and tourism sections.

Laundry

La Paz' climate makes handwashing impossible – nothing ever dries – so *lavanderías* are the rule. Most hotels offer some sort of laundry service. Calle Illampu, at the top of Sagárnaga, is lined with laundry places. For reliable same-day machine wash-and-dry service (US$1 per kilo), try the following.

Lavandería Maya (Map pp52-3; Sagárnaga 339 at Hostal Maya)
Limpieza Laverap (Map pp52-3; Illampu 704) Delivery to nearby hotels with pre-paid service.
Limpieza Sucre (Map pp52-3; Nicolás Acosta near Plaza San Pedro)

Left Luggage

Most recommended places to stay offer inexpensive or free left-luggage storage, especially if you make a return reservation. The main bus terminal (Map pp48–50) also has a cheap *deposito*. Think twice about leaving valuables as there have been numerous reports of items gone missing.

Media

Keep an eye out for the free, more or less monthly English-language *Llama Express* newspaper, which features funny and informative articles about attractions in the area. It's worth a look to see if the English-language *Bolivian Times* newspaper has been resurrected. *La Razon* (www.la-razon.com), *El Diario* (www.eldiario.net) and *La Prensa* are La Paz' major daily newspapers. National media chains **ATB** (www.bolivia.com) and **Grupo Fides** (www.fidesbolivia.com) host the most up-to-date online news sites.

Medical Services

For medical emergencies, it's best to avoid the hospitals. For serious conditions, ask your embassy for doctor recommendations. The 24-hour **Trauma Klinik** (☎ 277-1819; Aliaga 1271, San Miguel, Zona Sur) has been recommended for emergencies.

There's a well-stocked **24-hour pharmacy** (Map pp52-3; 16 de Julio at Bueno) on the Prado and there's another open until midnight on circular Plaza Egunio, the most convenient to Sagárnaga. Other after-hours pharmacies *(farmacias de turno)* are listed in daily newspapers.

The best optical outlet providing glasses and contact lenses is **Óptica Paris** (Map pp52-3; Camacho btwn Colón & Loayza).

The following are reputable medical and dental contacts.
Centro Epidemiológico Departamental La Paz (Centro Pilote; Map pp52-3; ☎ 245-0166; Vásquez 122 at Peru; ☽ 8:30-11:30am Mon-Fri) Off upper Ismael Montes near the brewery. Anyone heading for the lowlands can pick up antimalarials, and rabies and yellow fever vaccinations for the cost of a sterile needle – bring one from a pharmacy.

Clínica del Sur (☎ 278-4001; Siles 3539 at Calle 7, Obrajes) Frequently recommended by readers and embassies as friendly, knowledgeable and efficient. It's the best 24-hour trauma facility.

Dr Elbert Orellana Jordan (Unidad Medica Preventiva; ☎ 242-2342, ☎ 725-20964; Freyre & Mujia) Gregarious English-speaking doctor makes 24/7 emergency house calls for US$20.

Dr Fernando Patiño (Map pp48-50; ☎ 243-1664/0697, ☎ 772-25625; fpatino@ceibo.entelnet.bo; Arce 2677, Edificio Illimani, 2nd fl, opposite the US embassy) American-educated, English-speaking, high-altitude medical expert.

Dr Jorge Jaime Aguirre (Map pp48-50; ☎ 243-2682; Arce 2677, Edificio Illimani, 1st fl) Frequently recommended dentist for everything from routine cleaning to root canals.

High Altitude Pathology Institute (☎ 224-5394, 222-9504; www.geocities.com/zubietaippa; Saavedra 2302, Miraflores) Bolivian member of the International Association for Medical Assistance to Travelers (IAMAT). Offers computerized high-altitude medical check-ups and maintains a hyper-oxygen acclimatization chamber near the Chacaltaya ski lift.

Money
Casas de cambio in the city center are quicker and more convenient than banks. Most places open from 8:30am to noon and 2pm to 6pm weekdays, and on Saturday mornings. Outside these times, try Hotel Rosario (p63), El Lobo (p66) or Hotel Gloria (p65) which has the most convenient ATM to Sagárnaga.

Be wary of counterfeit US dollars, especially with street moneychangers (cambistas) who loiter around the intersections of Colón, Camacho and Santa Cruz. Outside La Paz you'll get 3% to 10% less for checks than for cash. **Cambios América** (Map pp52-3; Camacho 1223) and **Casa de Cambio Sudamer** (Map pp52-3; Colón 206 at Camacho) change travelers checks for minimal commission. Sudamer also sells currency from neighboring countries.

Cash withdrawals of bolivianos and US dollars are possible at Enlace ATMs at major intersections around the city. For cash advances (bolivianos only) of up to US$1000 a day on major credit cards with no commission and little hassle, try **Banco Mercantil** (Map pp52-3; Mercado & Ayacucho), **Banco Nacional de Bolivia** (Map pp52-3; Colón & Camacho) and **Banco de Santa Cruz** (Map pp52-3; Mercado 1078).

The helpful American Express representative, **Magri Turismo** (Map pp52-3; ☎ 44-2727; Ravelo 2101), does everything (including holding client mail) except change travellers checks. For urgent international money transfers, try **DHL/Western Union** (Map pp52-3; Montes 693), which has other outlets scattered all around town.

Post
Ángelo Colonial (Map pp52-3; Linares 922; ☺ 9am-7pm) Convenient, gringo-friendly branch with Internet, tourist information and outgoing-only service.

Central post office (ECOBOL; Map pp52-3; Santa Cruz & Oruro; ☺ 8am-8pm Mon-Fri, 8am-6pm Sat, 9am-noon Sun) A tranquil oasis off the bustling Prado and a quiet place to make card-phone calls while admiring the architecture. Holds poste restante (lista de correos) mail for three months for free – bring your passport. Mail is sorted into foreign and Bolivian stacks, so those with Latin surnames should check both stacks. A downstairs customs desk facilitates international parcel posting.

Telephone & Fax
Convenient Punto Entels (public phones) are scattered throughout the city. Street kiosks, which are on nearly every corner, also sell phone cards, and offer brief local calls for B$1. Hawkers with mobiles on a leash offer mobile calls for B$1 per minute.

Internet Call Centers (Map pp52-3; Sagárnaga & Murillo/México, Galería Doryan; ☺ 8am-8pm) Cheap worldwide Net2Phone calls.

Main Entel office (Map pp52-3; Ayacucho 267; fax 213-2334; ☺ 7am-10pm) Best place to receive incoming calls and faxes. Internet service.

Tourist Information
Ángelo Colonial (Map pp52-3; Linares 922; ☺ 9am-7pm) Privately run tourist-info office with a book exchange, noticeboard and guidebook reference library.

Information kiosks Outside the main bus terminal (Map pp48-50). Also on the southeast side of Plaza Alonso de Mendoza (Map pp52-3).

Municipal tourist office (Map pp52-3; ☎ 237-1044; north side of Plaza del Estudiante; ☺ 8:30am-noon & 2:30-7pm Mon-Fri) Sells maps and has free brochures (mostly in Spanish, but some in English, French and German). Moved several times during research, so ask around before making a long trek here.

National Tourist Authority (Senatur; Map pp52-3; ☎ 236-7463; Edificio Ballivián, Mercado 1328, 18th fl) Inconvenient and unhelpful.

Travel Agencies
America Tours (Map pp52-3; ☎ 237-4204; jmiranda@ceibo.entelnet.bo; www.america-ecotours.com; 16 de Julio 1490, Ground fl, No 9) Warmly recommended

LA PAZ

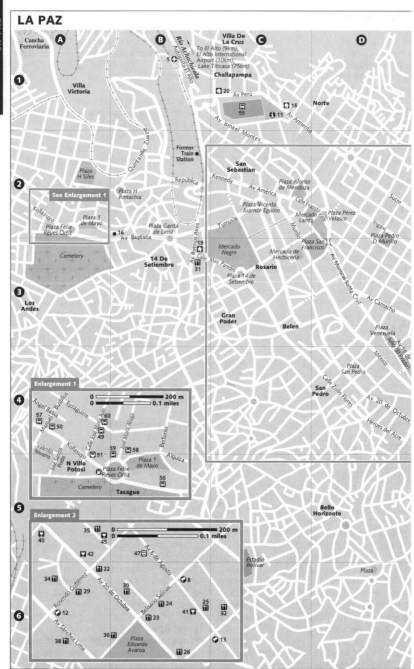

Cancha
Ferroviaria

Villa De
La Cruz

A **B** **C** **D**

Río Achuchalla

Autopista El Alto

To El Alto (9km);
El Alto International
Airport (10km);
Lake Titicaca (75km)

5

1

Villa
Victoria

Challapampa

20
Av Perú

55
18
11 Av Armentia

Norte

Av Ismael Montes

Quintanilla Zuazo

Former
Train
Station

San
Sebastian

Kennedy
Av América

Plaza Alonso
de Mendoza

Sucre

Plaza
H Siles

2

República

Plaza H
Rimachia

Plaza Vicenta
Juariste Eguino

Calle Evaristo

Mercado
Lanza

Plaza Pérez
Velasco

Ingavi

See Enlargement 1

Kollasuyo
Plaza Felix
Reyes Ortiz

Plaza 1
de Mayo

16
Av Baptista

Plaza Garita
de Lima

Tumusla

Murillo

Plaza San
Francisco

Plaza Pedro
D Murillo

19
Av Buenos Aires

Calle Max Paredes

Mercado
Negro

Mercado de
Hechiceria

Av Mariscal Santa Cruz

Cemetery

14 De
Setiembre

31

Rosario

Plaza 14 de
Setiembre

Av Camacho

3

Los
Andes

Gran
Poder

Belen

Plaza
Venezuela

Av 16 de Julio (El Prado)

Mexico

Plaza
San Pedro

Calle Zoilo Flores

San
Pedro

Av 20 de Octubre

Héroes del Acre

Enlargement 1

Angel Baña

Bustillos

Eyzaguirre

0   200 m
0   0.1 miles

57
50

Manuel M

60

Calle José María Asin

49

José María Aliaga

Berfonio

4

Valentin
Navarro

Kollasuyo

José Santos

59
51

58

Alquiza

Plaza 1
de Mayo

N Villo
Potosi

Plaza Félix
Reyes Ortiz

56

Cemetery
Tacagua

5

Bello
Horizonte

Enlargement 2

40
35
45

0   200 m
0   0.1 miles

42
47 Av 6 de Agosto

22

Estadio
Bolivar

Plaza

34
Rosendo Gutiérrez

29

Av 20 de Octubre

30

8

Belisario Salinas

24
23

25
41 32

6

12

Av Sánchez Lima

36

Plaza
Eduardo
Avaroa

13

38

26

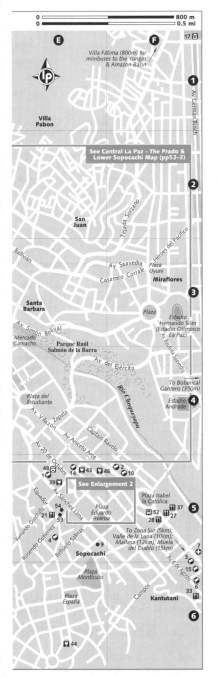

English-speaking agency organizes trips to anywhere in the country. Specializes in new routes and community-based ecotourism projects.

Travel Center (Map pp52-3; ☎ 231-1416, mobile ☎ 715-76883; travelcenter2001@hotmail.com; 16 de Julio 1764) Multilingual owner, Ivan. Best place to book flights.

Valmar Tours (Map pp52-3; ☎ 220-1499/1519; www .valmartour.com; Riva 1406, Edificio Alborada, 1st fl) Specializes in student travel; sells ISIC cards (US$15).

DANGERS & ANNOYANCES

La Paz is a great city to explore on foot, but take local advice '*camina lentito, come poquito...y duerme solito*' ('walk slowly, eat only a little bit... and sleep by your poor little self') to avoid feeling the effects of *soroche* (altitude sickness). More annoying than dangerous, shoeshine boys *(lustrabotes)* hound everyone with footwear. Many affect a menacing and anonymous appearance, wearing black ski masks and baseball caps pulled so low you can just make out two eye sockets. It's said that they often do so to avoid social stigma, as many are working hard to support families or pay their way through school – you can support their cause for B$1.

Scams

La Paz is incredibly safe by South American standards, but there are still a number of ruses aimed at separating gringos from their goods. Authentic police officers will always be uniformed (undercover police have strict orders not to hassle foreigners) and will never insist that you get in a taxi with them or that they search you in public. If confronted by an imposter, refuse to show them your valuables (wallet, passport, money, etc), try to get the attention of a uniformed police officer or insist on going to the nearest police station on foot. See Dangers & Annoyances (p350) in the Directory for a complete rundown of current cons, swindles and rip-offs.

SIGHTS

When the sun shines, La Paz invites leisurely exploration. The steep city is short on breath-taking attractions but long on lively markets and colorful street life. Most of La Paz' major sights are found in the city center or suburban Zona Sur. Keep your eyes peeled for fantastic glimpses of Illimani's triple peak towering between the world's highest high-rises. Many visitors allow another day or two to acclimatize during a day-trip to Tiahuanaco (p82) or Lake Titicaca (p86).

Bolivia's de facto capital has its share of cultural and historical museums. Most are closed over the Christmas holiday (December 25 to January 6). If you want to meet people or just observe the rhythms of local life, spend a couple of hours exploring one of the city's dozen or so lively markets.

Cathedral & Plaza Murillo
Although it's a recent addition to La Paz's collection of religious structures, the 1835 **cathedral** (Map pp52-3; entrance on south side of Plaza Murillo) is an impressive structure – mostly because it is built on a steep hillside. The main entrance is 12m higher than its base on Calle Potosí. The structure's sheer immensity, with its high dome, hulking columns, thick stone walls and high ceilings, is overpowering, but the altar is relatively simple. Inside, the main attraction is the profusion of stained-glass work; the windows behind the altar depict a gathering of Bolivian politicos being blessed from above by a flock of heavenly admirers.

Beside the cathedral is the **Presidential Palace** (Map pp52–3), and in the center of Plaza Murillo, opposite, stands a statue of President Gualberto Villarroel. In 1946 he was dragged from the palace by vigilantes and hanged from a lamppost in the square. Interestingly enough, Don Pedro Domingo Murillo, for whom the plaza was named, met a similar fate here in 1810.

The Cathedral's **Museo de Arte Sacro** (Map pp52-3; enter at Socabaya 432; admission US$1; 🕙 9:30am-12:30pm & 3-7pm Tue-Fri, 10am-1pm Sat) consists mostly of typical religious paraphernalia, but there are two unusual mother-of-pearl coffins and well-executed portraits of the 12 Apostles.

Museo Nacional de Arqueología
Two blocks east of the Prado, the **National Archaeology Museum** (Museo Arqueologico Tiwanaku; Map pp52-3; ☎ 231-1621; Tiwanaku 93; admission US$1.35 with official guide; 🕙 9am-12:30pm, 3-6:30pm Mon-Sat, Sun 10am-1pm) holds a small but well-sorted collection of artifacts that illustrate the most interesting aspects of the Tiahuanaco culture's five stages (p83). Most of Tiahuanaco's treasures were stolen or damaged during the colonial days, so the extent of the collection isn't overwhelming and can be easily digested in an hour. Some of the ancient stonework disappeared into Spanish construction projects, while valuable pieces – gold and other metallic relics and artwork – found their way into European museums or were melted down for royal treasuries. Most of what remains in Bolivia – pottery, figurines, trepanned skulls, mummies, textiles and metal objects – is housed in one room. Mandatory guided tours are usually in Spanish, with infrequent English tours.

Mercado de Hechicería (Witches' Market)
The city's most unusual market (Map pp52–3) lies along Jiménez and Linares between Sagárnaga and Santa Cruz, amid lively

tourist *artesanía* shops. What they're selling isn't exactly witchcraft as depicted in horror films and Halloween tales; the merchandise is mainly herbs and folk remedies, as well as a few more unorthodox ingredients intended to manipulate and supplicate the various malevolent and beneficent spirits that populate the Aymará world.

If you're opening a new business, for example, you can buy a llama fetus to bury beneath the cornerstone as a *cha'lla* (offering) to *Pachamama*, encouraging her to inspire good luck therein. This practice is strictly for poor *campesinos*, however; wealthier Bolivians are expected to sacrifice a fully functioning llama. If someone is feeling ill, or is being pestered by unwelcome or bothersome spooks, they can purchase a plateful of colorful herbs, seeds and assorted critter parts to remedy the problem. As you pass the market stalls, watch for wandering *yatiri* (witch doctors), who wear dark hats and carry coca pouches, and circulate through the area offering fortune-telling services.

Museo Nacional del Arte

The **National Art Museum** (Map pp52-3; ☎ 240-8600; Comercio at Socabaya; admission US$1.35; ☼ 9am-12:30pm & 3-7pm Tue-Sat, 9am-12:30pm Sun) near Plaza Murillo, is housed in the former Palacio de Los Condes de Arana. The building was constructed in 1775 of pink Viacha granite and has been restored to its original grandeur. In the center of a huge courtyard, surrounded by three stories of pillared corridors, is a lovely alabaster fountain. The various levels are dedicated to a range of artists: Marina Núñez del Prado's contemporary sculptures, the late-Renaissance paintings of Melchor Pérez de Holguín and students of his Potosí school, and works of other Latin American artists. Modern visiting exhibitions are shown in the outer salon.

Calle Jaén Museums

These four, small, interesting **museums** (Map pp52-3; ☎ 237-8478; combo admission US$0.50; ☼ 9:30am-12:30pm & 3-7pm Mon-Fri, 9am-1pm Sat & Sun) are clustered together along Calle Jaén, La Paz' finest colonial street, and can easily be bundled into one visit. Buy tickets at the Museo Costumbrista (see this page).

Also known as the Museo del Oro, the **Museo de Metales Preciosos Pre-Colombinos** (Jaén 777) houses three impressively presented salons of pre-Columbian silver, gold and copper works. A fourth salon in the basement has examples of ancient pottery.

Sometimes called the Museo de la Guerra del Pacífico, the diminutive **Museo del Litoral** (Jaén 798) incorporates relics from the 1884 war in which Bolivia became landlocked after losing its Litoral department to Chile. The collection consists mainly of historical maps that defend Bolivia's emotionally charged claims to Antofagasta and Chile's Segunda Región.

Once the home of a leader in the La Paz Revolution of July 16, 1809, the **Casa de Don Pedro Domingo Murillo** (Jaén 790) displays collections of colonial art and furniture, textiles, medicines, musical instruments and household items of glass and silver that once belonged to Bolivian aristocracy. Other odds and ends include a collection of Alasitas miniatures (see Festivals & Events, p61). Murillo was hanged by the Spanish on January 29, 1810, in the plaza now named after him. The most intriguing painting on display is entitled *The Execution of Murillo*.

The **Museo Costumbrista Juan de Vargas** (Jaén & Sucre) contains art and photos, as well as some superb ceramic figurine dioramas, of old La Paz. One of these is a representation of *akulliko*, the hour of coca-chewing; another portrays the festivities surrounding the Día de San Juan Bautista on June 24; another depicts the hanging of Murillo in 1810. Also on display are colonial artifacts and colorful dolls wearing traditional costumes.

Museo Tambo Quirquincho

This intriguing **museum** (Map pp52-3; off Evaristo Valle at Plaza Alonzo de Mendoza; admission US$0.15; ☼ 9:30am-12:30pm & 3-7pm Tue-Fri, 9:30am-12:30pm Sat & Sun), a former *tambo* (wayside market and inn), displays old-fashioned dresses, silverware, photos, artwork and a collection of Carnaval masks.

Iglesia de San Francisco

The hewn stone basilica of San Francisco (Map pp52–3), on the plaza of the same name, reflects an appealing blend of 16th-century Spanish and mestizo trends. The church was founded in 1548 by Fray Francisco de los Ángeles, and construction began the following year. The original structure collapsed under heavy snowfall

CENTRAL LA PAZ – THE PRADO & LOWER SOPOCACHI

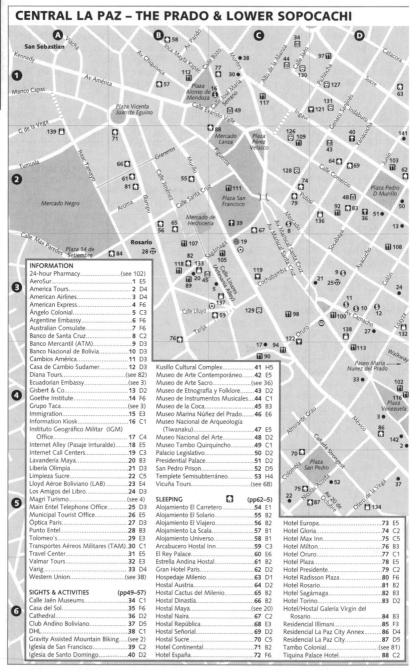

LA PAZ

0 ————————— 300 m
0 ————————— 0.2 mi

EATING 🍴 (pp65–9)
100% Natural..............................**89** B3
Acuario II..................................**90** C4
Alexander Coffee & Pub............**91** E5
Alexander Coffee & Pub............**92** D2
Andrómeda................................**93** F6
Ángelo Colonial......................(see 5)
Bar Tiwanaku............................**94** C4
Cafe La Terraza........................**95** E4
Café Ciudad..............................**96** E5
Café Pierrot............................(see 74)
Café Torino.............................(see 83)
Casa de los Paceños.................**97** D1
Cevichería Portales..................**98** C3
Chifa Luqing.............................**99** F6
Confitería Club de La Paz........**100** D3
Confitería Manantial...............(see 74)
El Lobo....................................(see 56)
Eli's Pizza Express...................**101** E5
Eli's Pizza Express...................**102** D4
Heladería Napoli......................**103** D2
La Bodeguita Cubana...............**104** E4
Laksmi....................................**105** C3

Las Velas...............................**106** G4
Le Pot-Pourri des Gourmets......(see 45)
Limpieza Laverap....................(see 81)
Pepe's Coffee Bar...................**107** B3
Pollo Copacabana....................**108** D3
Pollo Copacabana....................**109** C2
Pollo Copacabana....................**110** E5
Profumo di Caffé....................**111** C2
Restaurant Laza......................**112** B1
Restaurant Verona..................**113** D4
Restaurant Vienna..................**114** F5
Sergio's..................................**115** F6
Snack El Montañés..................(see 20)
Unicornio................................**116** D4
Vigor.......................................**117** C1
Yussef....................................**118** B3

DRINKING 🍷 (p69)
Café Sol y Luna........................**119** C3
Disco Love City........................**120** H3
La Choperia.............................**121** D1
La Luna...................................**122** C3
Malegria..................................**123** F6

ENTERTAINMENT 🎭 (pp69–71)
Camping Caza y Pesca.............(see 21)
Cine 16 de Julio......................**124** E5
Cine Monje Campero................**125** E4
Cinema Nameless....................**126** C2
Cinemateca Boliviana..............**127** D1
El Calicanto............................**128** C2
La Casa del Corregidor............**129** C3
Los Escudos...........................(see 100)
Peña Huari..............................(see 20)

Peña Marka Tambo..................**130** C1
Peña Parnaso..........................(see 19)
Teatro Municipal.....................**131** D1

SHOPPING 🛍 (pp71–2)
Adolfo Andino.........................(see 20)
AGFA Bolivia...........................**132** D3
Artesanía Sorata.....................**133** B3
Asarti.....................................(see 79)
Asarti.....................................(see 80)
Bodega La Concepción............**134** D5
Breick Chocolate Shop.............**135** E4
Casa Kavlin.............................**136** D2
Comart Tukuypaj/Inca Pallay....**137** C3
Condoriri...............................(see 133)
Foto Capri...............................**138** D3
Foto Linares...........................(see 32)
Galería Handal........................(see 21)
Sarañani..................................(see 19)
Sweet Snack Shops.................**139** A2

TRANSPORT (pp72–5)
International Rent-a-Car............**140** G6
Tour Agencies.........................(see 133)

OTHER
Academía de Música Helios......**141** D2
Fremen Tours...........................(see 21)
LanChile.................................**142** D4
LanPeru.................................(see 142)
Pachamama Tours....................(see 19)
SpeakEasy Institute.................**143** F6
TAM Mercosur........................**144** E5
Turisbus.................................(see 81)

in about 1610, but it was reconstructed between 1744 and 1753. The second building was built entirely of stone quarried at nearby Viacha. The façade is decorated with stone carvings of natural themes such as *chirimoyas* (custard apples), pinecones and tropical birds. A new religious antiquities museum adjacent to the church is planned to open in 2004.

After looking at the church, turn toward the bizarre sculpture on the upper portion of Plaza San Francisco. This mass of rock pillars and stone faces in suspended animation is intended to represent and honor Bolivia's three great cultures – Tiahuanaco, Inca and modern.

MARINA NÚÑEZ DEL PRADO

Bolivia's foremost sculptor, Marina Núñez del Prado, was born on October 17, 1910 in La Paz. From 1927 to 1929 she studied at the Escuela Nacional de Bellas Artes (National School of Fine Arts) and from 1930 to 1938 worked there as a professor of sculpture and artistic anatomy.

Her early works were in cedar and walnut, and represented the mysteries of the Andes: indigenous faces, groups and dances. From 1943 to 1945 she lived in New York and turned her attentions to Bolivian social themes, including mining and poverty. She later went through a celebration of Bolivian motherhood with pieces depicting indigenous women, pregnant women and mothers protecting their children. Other works dealt largely with Andean themes, some of which took appealing abstract forms. She once wrote, 'I feel the enormous good fortune to have been born under the tutelage of the Andes, which express the richness and the cosmic miracle. My art expresses the spirit of my Andean homeland and the spirit of my Aymará people.'

During her long career she held more than 160 exhibitions, which garnered her numerous awards and she received international acclaim from the likes of Pablo Neruda, Gabriela Mistral, Alexander Archipenko and Guillermo Niño de Guzmán. In her later years Marina lived in Lima, Peru, with her husband, Peruvian writer Jorge Falcón. She died there in September 1995 at the age of 84.

Iglesia de Santo Domingo

Like Iglesia de San Francisco, the exterior of the **Iglesia de Santo Domingo** (Map pp52-3; Ingavi & Yanacocha), a block northwest of Plaza Murillo, shows evidence of Baroque and mestizo influences. The rest of the structure, which was closed for restoration in 2003, is of limited interest.

Mercado Negro & Upper Market Areas

The entire section of town from Plaza Pérez Velasco uphill (west) to the cemetery – past Mercado Lanza, and Plazas Eguino and Garita de Lima – has a largely indigenous population and is always bustling. The streets are crowded and noisy with traffic honking its way through the narrow cobbled streets, *cholas* rushing about socializing and making purchases, and pedestrians jostling with sidewalk vendors. The market stalls sell all manner of practical items from clothing and fast food to groceries, healthcare products and cooking pots. The focus of activity is near the intersection of Calles Buenos Aires and Max Paredes, especially on Wednesday and Saturday.

The **Mercado Negro** (Black Market; Map pp52-3) along upper Graneros and Eloy Salmón, is the place to pick up undocumented merchandise and just about anything else you may hope for. Most of it isn't stolen, exactly, although some of it is bootlegged. In the case of CDs, vendors make no effort to conceal the fact: the covers are merely photocopied. It's also good for electronics, imitation designer clothing and inexpensive Fuji and Agfa film, including slide film. Be especially careful when wandering around this part of town: it's notorious for rip-offs and light fingers.

Between Plaza Pérez Velasco and Calle Figueroa is **Mercado Lanza** (Map pp52–3), one of La Paz' main food markets (the other major one is **Mercado Camacho**; Map pp52–3). It sells all manner of fruits, vegetables, juices, dairy products, breads and canned foods. There are also numerous stalls where you can pick up a sandwich, soup, *salteña*, *empanada* or full meal.

The **Flower Market** (Av Tumusla), appropriately located opposite the cemetery, is a beautiful splash of color amid one of the city's drabber areas. Unfortunately it also sits alongside a festering open sewer and garbage dump, which makes it rather confusing to the nostrils.

Museo de Etnografía y Folklore

This free **ethnography & folklore museum** (Map pp52-3; ☎ 235-8559; Ingavi at Sanjinés; ☺ 9:30am-12:30pm, 3-7pm Mon-Sat, 9:30am-12:30pm Sun) is one for the anthropology buffs. The building, which is itself a real treasure, was constructed between 1776 and 1790, and was once the home of the Marqués de Villaverde. The highlight is the Tres Milenios de Tejidos exhibition of 167 stunning weavings from around the country – ask a guide for a look inside the drawers beneath the wall hangings. It also has a fine collection of Chipaya artifacts from western Oruro department, a group whose language, rites and customs have led some experts to suggest that they are descendants of the vanished Tiahuanaco culture.

Museo de Arte Contemporaneo

Better modern art may be found in various other collections around town, but this

---

THE WORLD'S MOST DANGEROUS ROAD

It's official: the road between La Paz and Coroico is 'The World's Most Dangerous Road' (WMDR), according to an Inter-American Development Bank (IDB) report. Given the number of fatal accidents that occur on it, the moniker is well deserved. An average of 26 vehicles per year disappear over the edge into the great abyss.

Those up for an adrenaline rush will be in their element, but if you're unnerved by a gravel track just 3.2m wide – just enough for one vehicle – sheer 1000m drops, hulking rock overhangs and waterfalls that spill across and erode the highway, your best bet is to bury your head and not look until it's over. Conventional wisdom asserts that minibuses traveling by day are safer than larger overnight buses or *camiones*.

The trip starts off innocuously enough. On leaving La Paz to cross La Cumbre, you'll notice a most curious phenomenon: dogs stand like sentinels at 100m intervals, presumably awaiting handouts. *Camión* drivers feed them in the hope that the *achachilas* (ancestor spirits who dwell in the high peaks) will look after them on their way down. At the pass, drivers also perform a *cha'lla* for the *apus* (ambient mountain spirits), sprinkling the vehicle's tires with alcohol before beginning the descent.

Crosses (aka 'Bolivian caution signs') lining the way testify to the frequency of vehicular tragedies. The most renowned occurred in 1983 when a *camión* plunged over the precipice, killing the driver and 100 passengers in the worst accident in the sordid history of Bolivian transport.

Accidents along the WMDR stem from several causes. Drunk driving is probably the most prevalent, followed by carelessness and right-of-way disputes. However, these human weaknesses pale in comparison to the undeniable weakness of the earth beneath the precarious turnouts. In 1999 an attempt was made to mitigate the dangers by allowing only downhill traffic in the morning and uphill traffic in the afternoon. However Yungas' residents complained that it limited access to their markets, and the plan was scrapped after a few months.

Owing to general international dissatisfaction with the road's safety hazards, a new paved route, which will cut travel time in half, was constructed on the opposite wall of the valley, thanks to a US$120 million loan from the IDB. Additional costs involved in tunnel building to connect the two completed ends of the road delayed its opening until mid-2003. What will become of the old route is anyone's guess. If left for the *apus* and *achachilas* to maintain, it could become a killer single track or trekking route. For the time being, it looks as though *camiones* will continue to use the old route, while smaller vehicles will be given preference on the new route.

The good news is that the risks of traveling from La Paz to Coroico are balanced by the reward of seeing some of South America's most amazing 'vertical' scenery. Those who remain under their own power all the way down (with only a little help from gravity) might choose to hike the La Cumbre to Coroico Trek (see the boxed text, p138) or navigate it on a mountain bike (p56).

Note: Although Bolivian traffic normally keeps to the right, downhill traffic on the Yungas road passes on the outside, whether that's the right or the left side of the road. Vehicles heading downhill must maneuver onto the sliver-like turnout ledges bordering the big drop and wait while uphill traffic squeezes past, hugging the inside wall. In fact this makes sense, as it ensures that the risk is taken by the driver with the best possible view of the outside tires.

private **museum** (MAC; Map pp52-3; ☎ 233-5905; 16 de Julio 1698; admission US$1.35; ⏰ 9am-9pm) wins the gold star for the most interesting building: a restored 19th-century mansion (only one of four left on the Prado) with a glass roof and stained-glass panels designed by Gustave Eiffel. The museum's eclectic collection is a mix of Bolivian and international work. The 1st floor is given over to university art and architecture students.

Museo de Instrumentos Musicales

The exhaustive, hands-on collection of unique instruments at this **museum** (Museo de Instrumentos Nativos; Map pp52-3; ☎ 233-1075; Jaén 711; admission US$0.65; ⏰ 10am-1pm & 2-6pm) is a must for musicians. The brainchild of *charango* master Ernesto Cavour, it displays all possible incarnations of *charangos* and other indigenous instruments used in Bolivian folk music and beyond. If you don't happen on an impromptu jam session, check out **Peña Marka Tambo** (p70) across the street. You can also arrange *charango* and wind instrument lessons here for around US$5 per hour.

Museo de Textiles Andinos Bolivianos

Fans of Bolivia's lovely traditional weaving consider this small **textile museum** (☎ 224-3601; Plaza Benito Juárez 488, Miraflores; admission US$1.35; ⏰ 9:30am-noon, 3-6:30pm Mon-Sat, 10am-12:30pm Sun) a must-see. Examples of the country's finest traditional textiles (including pieces from the Cordillera Apolobamba, and the Jal'qa and Candelaria regions of the Central Highlands) are grouped by region and described in Spanish. The creative process is explained from fiber to finished product. The gift shop sells originals of museum quality; 90% of the sale price goes to the artists. To get there, walk 20 minutes northeast from the Prado or catch *micro* No 131 or 135, or minibus No 203, 244, 269, 281 or 352.

Templete Semisubterráneo (Museo al Aire Libre)

The open pit **museum** (Map pp52-3; admission free) opposite the stadium contains replicas of statues found in Tiahuanaco's Templete Semisubterráneo (p84). The showpiece Megalito Bennetto Pachamama (Bennett monolith) was moved to Tiahuanaco's new site museum to avoid further smog-induced deterioration. This place is worth a quick look if you aren't able to visit the actual site.

Museo Marina Núñez del Prado

This recently restored **museum** (Map pp52-3; ☎ 232-4906; Ecuador 2034; ⏰ 9:30am-1pm & 3-7pm Tue-Fri, 9:30am-1pm Sat-Mon) is dedicated to the work of the late sculptor (see the boxed text, p54), whose works focus on Quechua and Aymará cultural subjects. Located in her former Sopocachi home, it contains her personal collection of cultural paraphernalia and numerous examples of her work.

ACTIVITIES

You'll get plenty of exercise gumshoeing up and down the Prado but you don't have to head far out of town for a real adrenaline rush.

Mountain Biking

For an unforgettable experience, try a trip with the highly regarded **Gravity Assisted Mountain Biking** (Map pp52-3; ☎ 231-3849; gravity@unete.com; www.gravitybolivia.com; 16 de Julio 1490, Edificio Avenida, No 10). Two of the most popular full-day options (each US$49 per person) are to zoom

---

WORLD'S HIGHEST RECREATION

Golf and tennis buffs looking for some high-altitude practice must join a club since public facilities do not exist. For tennis, racquetball and swimming in a lovely setting, try the Strongest Club at the Achumani Complejo in Zona Sur (take any *micro* or minibus labeled 'Achumani Complejo'). On weekdays they charge US$3.25 per person, and on weekends, US$4.50.

Watch your drives go further than you ever imagined at the **La Paz Golf Club** (☎ 274-5124/5462; www.lapazgolfclub.com; Mallasa, Zona Sur), the world's highest 18-hole course (3318m) – Oruro's course is much higher but lacks grass. Green fees are around US$70 and a caddie and rental clubs are US$10 each.

In town at the swank Hotel Europa (Map pp52-3), nonguests can use the swimming pool and sauna for US$9 from 1pm to 9pm; afterward you can opt for a massage for an additional US$9. The Hotel Plaza (Map pp52-3) also lets you use the pool for a similar fee, but the facilities aren't quite as nice.

LA PAZ

down the World's Most Dangerous Road (see the boxed text, p55) from La Cumbre to Coroico, or down from Chacaltaya to La Paz. Many other outfits on Sagárnaga offer the La Cumbre to Coroico trip for a few bucks less but consider what corners are being cut before you go hurtling downhill. Also think twice before contracting any of the agencies who offer these trips during the rainy season (January and February). Reserve ahead in high season and prepare to be thrilled.

Skiing, Hiking & Climbing

The world's highest downhill skiing (5320m down to 4900m), which is strictly for enthusiasts, is on the slopes of **Chacaltaya** (see the boxed text, p79), a rough 35km drive north of La Paz. The ski season (February to late April) is increasingly uncertain because the piste is on a retreating glacier. There is just one primitive rope tow (constantly undergoing repair), and the high altitude means most people can manage only a couple of runs before they're gasping for oxygen.

Established in 1939, the **Club Andino Boliviano** (Map pp52-3; ☎ 232-4682; www.geocities.com/yosemite/trails/7553/cab1.html; México 1638, La Paz) operates the lift and the basic lodge, where you can buy hot drinks, rent ski gear and stay the night (US$5). It arranges weekend ski trips when conditions are suitable (US$10 to US$20, plus transportation). Make sure you're well acclimatized before setting out, and bring good UV protection. Out of

season, many La Paz tour agencies offer daily hiking tours to Chacaltaya, an easy way to bag a high peak. For rock-climbing and other extreme adventure possibilities, contact the Oruro-based **Club de Montañismo Halcones** (www.geocities.com/msivila), who have pioneered many routes around La Paz.

WALKING TOUR

> **INFORMATION**
>
> Distance: 2.5km
> Duration: approximately 2–3 hours

A good starting point is **Iglesia de San Francisco (1)** where it's easy to find breakfast on the street. Watch for colorful wedding processions on weekend mornings. From **Plaza San Francisco (2)**, huff up **Calle Sagárnaga**, which is lined with shops and stalls selling beautiful weavings, musical instruments, antiques, 'original' Tiahuanaco artifacts and handmade leather bags.

Turn right at **Calle Linares** and poke around the **Mercado de Hechicería** (Witches' Market) **(3)**, which is crammed with herbs, magical potions and dried toucan beaks intended to cure ills and protect supplicants from malevolent spirits. If you're lucky, you might convince a *yatiri* (Aymará healer) to toss the coca leaves and tell your fortune, but they usually refuse gringo customers. Photographing here may be met with

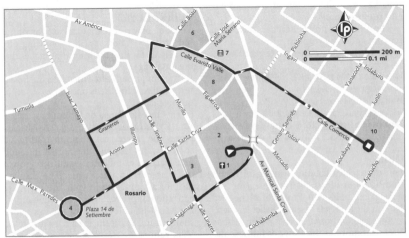

unpleasantness – unless you are a customer and first ask politely.

Higher up Calle Santa Cruz, around **Plaza 14 de Septiembre (4)** and **Calle Max Paredes**, you'll find the **Mercado Negro (5)**, a clogged maze of makeshift stalls that spreads over several blocks. From here, wander downhill, north and east of the markets, through streets choked with people and *micros* to **Plaza Alonso de Mendoza (6)** where you can grab a seat and watch the world go round. Adjacent is the **Museo Tambo Quirquincho (7)** notable for its mask and photography collection. Continue past the bustling **Mercado Lanza (8)** where you can buy a freshly squeezed juice along pedestrian-only **Calle Comercio (9)** past street vendors hawking everything imaginable to end at **Plaza Murillo (10)** where ice cream awaits at Heladería Napoli.

COURSES
Language
Note that not everyone advertising language instruction is accredited or even capable of teaching Spanish, however well they speak it, so seek local and personal recommendations, and examine credentials before signing up. Plan on paying around US$5 per hour. Private and group lessons are offered by the **Centro Boliviano Americano** (CBA; Map pp48-50; ☎ 234-2582; www.cba.com.bo; Parque Zenón Iturralde 121) and the **Instituto de la Lengua Española** (ILE; ☎ 279-6074; www.bolivialanguageinst.com; Aviador 180, Achumani). The **SpeakEasy Institute** (Map pp52-3; ☎ /fax 244-1779; www.speakeasyinstitute.com; Arce 2047) has specialized courses for travelers and professionals.

The following private teachers have been recommended by readers:

Cecilia C de Ferreira (☎ 248-7458; Camacho 1664, San Pedro)

Isabel Daza Vivado (☎ /fax 231-1471; maria_daza@ hotmail.com; Murillo 1046, 3rd fl)

William Ortiz (ABC Spanish; ☎ 772-62657; williamor@hotmail.com; Linares 980, 2nd fl)

Zenaida Gutiérrez (☎ 222-6749; zenaidagutierrez@ hotmail.com; Mercedes Torre Sur, Piso 6B, Cuba, Miraflores)

Music
For musical instruction (in Spanish) on traditional Andean instruments (see the boxed text, p59) visit Professor Heliodoro Niña at the **Academía de Música Helios** (Map pp52-3; ☎ 240-6498/99; www.academiahelios.com; Indaburo 1166) or inquire at the **Museo de Instrumentos**

Musicales (Map pp52-3; ☎ 233-1075; Jaén 711; US$0.65; ☺ 10am-1pm & 2-6pm daily).

Other courses
Yoga, Tai Chi and meditation classes are offered at **Casa del Sol** (Map pp52-3; ☎ 244-0928; Goitia 127), where a single class costs US$2 and monthly membership is US$25; ask about student discounts and massage services.

LA PAZ FOR CHILDREN
On Sunday afternoon, when traffic is restricted and the city empties out, the **Prado** hosts promenading families, and the sidewalks fill with balloon and cotton-candy sellers, and people renting kites, bicycles and toy cars. There's a festive atmosphere that may recall a bit of lost childhood, especially when the sun shines.

Kusillo Cultural Complex & Children's Museum
This complex overlooking La Paz has an awesome **lookout** (mirador; Map pp52-3; admission US$0.15; ☺ 9am-5:30pm) in a tranquil park setting. Alongside is the **Museo Kusillo** (Map pp52-3; ☎ 222-6187; Av del Ejército; admission US$0.65 Mon-Fri, US$1.35/1 Sat & Sun; ☺ 10:30am-6:30pm Tue-Sun), an interactive museum of science and play that hosts artesanía shops, open-air theater and dance programs. For big kids there are great sunset views from the café atop the world's highest funicular. The complex is a 20-minute walk east of the Prado along Pérez Zapata, which turns into Av del Ejército.

QUIRKY LA PAZ
You'll quickly realize that La Paz is anything but ordinary. Check out the following offbeat sights for insights into what makes this breathtaking city tick.

The unique **San Pedro Prison** (see the boxed text, p60) tops the list as one of La Paz' more quirky places.

The terrific **Museo de la Coca** (Map pp52-3; ☎ 231-1998; Linares 906; US$1; ☺ 10am-7pm) explores the sacred leaf's role in traditional societies, its use by the soft-drink and pharmaceutical industries and the growth of cocaine as an illicit drug. The displays (ask for a translation in your language) are educational, provocative and evenhanded. For a first-hand look at how the raw goods change hands, visit the legal coca market in Villa Fatima.

TRADITIONAL ANDEAN MUSICAL INSTRUMENTS

Although the martial honking of tinny and poorly practiced brass bands seems an integral part of most South American celebrations, the Andean musical tradition does employ a variety of pre-colonial instruments. The only instrument with European roots is the popular ukulele-like *charango*, based on the Spanish *vihuela* and *bandurria* – early forms of the guitar and mandolin.

Pre-*charango*, melody lines were carried exclusively by woodwind instruments such as the *quena* and the *zampoña* (pan flute), both of which still feature in traditional musical performances today. *Quenas* are reed flutes played by blowing into a notch at one end. *Zampoñas* are played by forcing air across the open ends of reeds lashed together in order of their size, often in double rows. Both instruments come in a variety of sizes and tonal ranges. The *bajón*, an enormous pan flute, which must be either rested on the ground or carried by two people, accompanies festivities in the Moxos communities of the Beni lowlands.

By the early 17th century Andean Indians had blended and adapted Spanish *charango* designs into one that would better reproduce their pentatonic scale: a 10-stringed instrument with llama-gut strings arranged in five pairs and a *quirquincho* (armadillo carapace) soundbox. Because of the paucity and fragility of *quirquinchos*, together with the desire to improve sound quality, wood is the current choice for *charango* soundboxes. Another stringed instrument, the *violín chapaco*, originated in Tarija in south central Bolivia, and is a variation on the European violin (for information on other instruments unique to Tarija, see the boxed text, p255).

Percussion also figures in most festivals and folk music performances as a backdrop for the typically lilting strains of the woodwind melodies. In highland areas the most popular drum is the largish *huankara*. The *caja*, a tambourine-like drum played with one hand, is used exclusively in Tarija.

El Alto

At first glance it would seem that the entire city of El Alto (Map pp48–50) is one big market. From the canyon rim at the top of the El Alto Autopista (toll road) or the top of the free route at Plaza Ballivián, the streets hum with almost perpetual activity. In the lively La Ceja (Brow) district you'll find a variety of electronic gadgets and mercantile goods. Try the Thursday and Sunday **Mercado La Ceja**, which stretches along the main thoroughfare and across Plaza 16 de Julio. If you keep your wits about you, speak Spanish and bargain politely, you're sure to have an excellent time, meet some friendly, down-to-earth Bolivians and find some great deals. The activity starts at about 6am and peters out after 3pm.

Cemetery District

As in most Latin American cemeteries, bodies are first buried in the traditional way or placed in a crypt, then within 10 years they're disinterred and cremated. After cremation, families purchase or rent glass-fronted spaces in the cemetery walls for the ashes, and affix plaques and mementos of the dead, and place flowers behind the glass door. Each wall has hundreds of these doors, and some of the walls have been expanded upward to such an extent that they resemble three- or four-storied apartment blocks. As a result the **cemetery** (Map pp48–50) is an active place, full of people passing through to visit relatives and leave or water fresh flowers. On November 2, the **Día de los Muertos** (All Saints Day), half the city turns out to honor their ancestors.

There are also huge family mausoleums, as well as sections dedicated to mine workers and their families, and common graves for soldiers killed in battle. You may even see the black-clad professional mourners who provide suitable wails and tears during burials.

Museo de la Revolución Nacional

The first question to ask when approaching this **museum** (Plaza Villarroel at end of Av Busch; US$0.15; ☺ 9:30am-12:30pm & 3-7pm Tue-Fri, 10am-1pm Sat & Sun) is 'Which Revolution?' (Bolivia has had more than 100 of them). The answer is the one of April 1952, the popular revolt of armed miners that resulted in the nationalization of Bolivian mining interests. It displays photos and paintings from the era and describes the creation of the government mining corporation Comibol, which was an economic failure and was recently transferred to private interests.

TOURS

Most of Bolivia's tour agencies are based in La Paz and there are at least 100 of them. Some are clearly better than others

and many specialize in particular interests or areas. Most agencies run day tours (US$10 to US$40 per person) in and around La Paz, to Lake Titicaca, Tiahuanaco and other sites. For details and contact information, as well as information on tours further afield, see Tours, in the Directory, p357.

SAN PEDRO PRISON – AN INSIGHT INTO THE WORLD'S MOST UNIQUE JAIL

Inside San Pedro prison (Map pp52-3) there are no guards. Inmates don't wear uniforms. They hold the keys to their own cells. Their wives, children and pets can stay with them. In fact San Pedro is more like a city within a city than what most would consider a 'normal' jail.

The prison population functions as an independent community, with its own distinctive economy, social norms and political process. As a microcosm of a society characterized by a bizarre mix of injustice and hope, of poverty and dignity, San Pedro encapsulates many of the contradictions that make Bolivia so intriguing and bewildering.

Once through the main gates, the sights are somewhat reminiscent of typical La Paz street scenes – you could almost be forgiven for not believing you are actually in a prison. During the day, the atmosphere is peaceful. Inmates – the majority of whom are in for drug-related offenses – mill about, conversing, while others move freely through the maze of winding corridors that link the open courtyards of the various sections. A quick stroll reveals various churches, restaurants, market stalls, small businesses, handicraft workshops, classrooms, billiard rooms and gymnasiums, as well as a soccer field and childcare center. The prison's inner walls are, ironically, lined with adverts from a certain American cola company.

However, life for inmates isn't as easy as it first appears. For a start, they are obliged to pay for everything, including their cells and utilities. The cash-strapped administration does not provide much beyond the barest necessities – so inmates must fend for themselves. Leaders nominated in annual democratic elections maintain order. Income is generated through working – anything from running errands, cleaning shoes, washing laundry to selling handicrafts.

Women and children are treated with great respect inside. The prison hierarchy is based primarily on wealth instead of violence, which is relatively infrequent. The eight sections that resemble small suburbs more than cellblocks are ranked according to a star system. Wealthy inmates live in spacious, carpeted, fully furnished 'five-star' apartments, complete with private bathrooms, views over the city and cable TV. In the 'one-star' sections, tiny, filthy hovels, known as 'coffins', are crammed with as many as five men.

Near unfettered liberty can also be a mixed blessing. Many spend their time productively – studying university courses or working – for which they receive sentencing reductions. Others become trapped in a cycle of dependence upon drugs, which, as in many prisons around the world, are freely available.

The most colorful days are Thursdays and Sundays, when hundreds of visitors cram into the complex between 9am and 5pm, filling its corridors and courtyards with laughter and the noise of children playing, and the influx of hungry family members stretches the capacity of the prison's restaurants.

On and off over the last decade, enterprising English-speaking inmates have conducted guided prison tours for foreigners, resulting in one of the world's most bizarre tourist attractions. Most recently, multilingual signs outside the main entrance announced that the prison is officially off-limits to 'tourists'. Only relatives with official permission (supposedly) are allowed inside to visit inmates or for interviews.

Rusty Young, Sydney, Australia
(Australian law-graduate Rusty Young is the author of the best-selling Marching Powder *Pan Macmillan, 2003; www.marchingpowder.com Inspired by Lonely Planet's description of San Pedro prison, he spent four months inside interviewing a British inmate.)*

Most day trips provide easy sightseeing in the city's environs, including such popular destinations as Tiahuanaco, Copacabana, Zongo Valley, Chacaltaya and Valle de la Luna. Inexpensive agency transfers to Puno are the most straightforward way of getting to Peru, and they allow a stopover in Copacabana en route. Agencies are also useful for arranging climbing in the Cordilleras; many rent equipment. For information on specialist operators, see Activities in the Directory, p347.

Agencies frequently recommended by readers include the following:

America Tours (Map pp52-3; ☎ 237-4204; www
.america-ecotours.com; 16 de Julio 1490, No 9)

Diana Tours (Map pp52-3; ☎ 235-1158; hotsadt@ceibo
.entelnet.bo; Sagárnaga 326-328)

Pachamama Tours (Map pp52-3; ☎ 211-3179;
Sagárnaga 189, Galería Doryan, 2nd floor)

Vicuña Tours (Map pp52-3; ☎ 239-0915; Comercio
1455, at Hostal República)

City Bus Tours

It's hard to miss the red, double-decker, city-tour bus run by **Viajes Planeta** (☎ 279-1440, ☎ 719-70826; with flyer US$9.35, on board US$14, valid for 2 days), which runs jump-on, jump-off downtown and southern circuits. Short stops include Mirador Killi Killi and the Valle de la Luna (p75). It's not the most independent way to see the city, but the narration is in seven languages and you'll see a lot in four hours.

FESTIVALS & EVENTS

La Paz, like all of Bolivia, is always looking for an excuse to celebrate. Check with the tourist office (p47) for a complete list of what's on.

January
ALASITAS

During Inca times the **Alasitas Fair** ('buy from me' in Aymará, in Spanish it's *comprame*) coincided with the spring equinox (September 21), and was intended to demonstrate the abundance of the fields. The date underwent some shifts during the Spanish colonial period, which the *campesinos* weren't too happy about. In effect they decided to turn the celebration into a kitschy mockery of the original. 'Abundance' was redefined to apply not only to crops, but also to homes, tools,

---

EKEKO

Ekeko is the household god and the keeper and distributor of material possessions. During Alasitas his devotees collect miniatures of those items they'd like to acquire during the following year and heap them onto small plaster images of the god. He's loaded down with household utensils, baskets of coca, wallets full of miniature currency, lottery tickets, liquor, chocolate and other luxury goods. The more optimistic devotees buy minature souped-up *camiones*, first-class airline tickets to Miami and three-story suburban homes! Once purchased, all items must be blessed by a certified *yatiri* (shaman) before they can become real. If this apparent greed seems not to be in keeping with Aymará values – the community and balance in all things – it's worth noting that Ekeko is also charged with displaying that which a family is able to share with the community.

---

cash, clothing and, lately, cars, trucks, airplanes and even 12-story buildings. The little god of abundance, Ekeko ('dwarf' in Aymará), made his appearance and modern Alasitas traditions are now celebrated every January 24.

May/June
EL GRAN PODER

Held in late May or early June, **La Festividad de Nuestro Señor Jesús del Gran Poder** (Festival of Our Lord Jesus) began in 1939 as a candle procession led by an image of Christ through the predominantly *campesino* neighborhoods of upper La Paz.

The following year the local union of embroiderers formed a folkloric group to participate in the event. In subsequent years other festival-inspired folkloric groups joined in, and the celebration grew larger and more lively. It has now developed into a unique La Paz festival and a strictly *paceño* (local) affair, with dancers and folkloric groups from around the city participating. The embroiderers prepare elaborate costumes for the event and upwards of 25,000 performers practice for weeks in advance.

El Gran Poder is a wild and exciting time, and offers a glimpse of Aymará culture at its most festive. A number of dances are featured, such as the *suri sikuris* (in which the dancers are bedecked in ostrich feathers), the lively *kullasada*, *morenada*, *caporal* and the *inkas*, which duplicates Inca ceremonial dances. Several of these dances are from Oruro's La Diablada festivities, brought to La Paz' festival by the Altiplano migrants.

If you'd like to catch the procession, go early to stake out a place along the route, keeping a lookout for stray or unruly water balloons. The tourist office (p47) can provide specific dates and details about a particular year's celebration.

AYAMARÁ NEW YEAR & SAN JUAN (WINTER SOLSTICE)

The Ayamará New Year is celebrated across the Altiplano around June 21, the longest and coldest night of the year. Festivities feature huge bonfires and fireworks in the streets, plus lots of drinking to stay warm. San Juan (June 24) is the Christian version of the solstice celebration. The solstice celebrations are most lively at Tiahuanaco (p84).

July
FIESTAS DE JULIO

This month-long cultural series at the Teatro Municipal features much folk music.

VIRGEN DEL CARMEN

The patron saint of La Paz department gets her own public holiday (July 16), which includes many dances and parades.

August
INDEPENDENCE DAY

This lively public holiday (August 6) sees lots of gunfire in the air, parades galore and mortar blasts around the city center.

November/December
DÍA DE LOS MUERTOS (ALL SAINTS DAY)

Colorful celebrations of ancestors fill cemeteries around the city and country.

NEW YEAR'S EVE

Look out for fireworks – many at eye level – which are best seen from high above the city at a *mirador*.

SLEEPING

Most backpackers beeline for Central La Paz to find a bed. The downtown triangle between Plazas Mendoza, Murillo and 14 de Septiembre is full of popular budget and mid-range places, and many of the services travelers need. If you want to live closer to movie theaters, a wider array of restaurants and a bar or two, consider staying closer to Sopocachi around Plaza San Pedro. The area around the Witches' Market (between Santa Cruz and Sagárnaga) is about as close as Bolivia gets to a travelers' ghetto. For upmarket luxury (at very reasonable rates) look in the historic center around Plaza Murillo or along the Lower Prado and further south in Zona Sur.

Budget

La Paz has dozens of low-cost hotels and *residenciales*, the vast majority of which are in the area between Manco Capac and Ismael Montes. Some bottom-of-the-barrel places impose a midnight curfew. All places listed below claim to have hot water at least part of the day; few have it all the time. Bargaining is fair game during the low season. Bathrooms are shared and prices per person, unless otherwise noted.

Hospedaje Milenio (Map pp52-3; ☎ 228-1263; hospe dajemilenio@hotmail.com; Yanacocha 860; s/d US$3/5.35) Clean and simple, with hot showers all day and kitchen use, and it's close to the bus terminal. The best rooms, including the single room in the tower, are upstairs. The staff are friendly and will organize cheap bus trips; extra blankets are available on request.

Hostal Maya (Map pp52-3; ☎ 231-1970; mayahostal@hotmail.com; Sagárnaga 339; with breakfast US$6; 🖳) A new, central, budget favorite. All rooms are tidy and have good beds. Some have balconies but the ones at the back are quieter. A stumble away from Peña Huari (the popular, folk-music venue).

Alojamiento El Solario (Map pp52-3; ☎ 236-7963; elsolariohotel@yahoo.com; Murillo 776; dm/s/d US$2.65/3.35/6.25; 🖳) A mellow hangout with clean, spare rooms, 24/7 hot showers, laundry service, shared kitchen and luggage storage. Check out the sunny roof terrace.

Hostal Cactus del Milenio (Map pp52-3; ☎ 245-1421; Jiménez 818; US$3) Smack in the middle of the Witches' Market and the home of cranky, but fair, Señora Bicho, the hostal has a communal kitchen, hot showers all day, a nice rooftop terrace and clean rooms with saggy beds.

Hotel Torino (Map pp52-3; ☎ 240-6003; Socabaya 457; s/d/tr US$4/6.65/10, with bath US$6.50/10.50/16; ☐) Central backpacker hangout in a modernized (in the 1950s) colonial building that's seen better days; more popular for its services – restaurant, book exchange and luggage storage – than its creature comforts.

Hostal Señorial (Map pp52-3; ☎ 240-6042; Yanacocha 540; with bath & TV US$7.50) A family-run place with gas showers and kitchen facilities where you'll meet more Bolivians than foreigners.

Hostal Austria (Map pp52-3; ☎ 240-8540; Yanacocha 531; US$3.35-4) This is an old travelers' haunt known for overbooking (give a clear arrival time and don't be late) and treating its clientele like chattel (in English and French!). A bit pricey for what you get (short beds, dicey shared bath with good but too few gas-heated showers); worth it if you are looking for cooking facilities or to hook up with other travelers. *Cuidado*: some of the rooms are windowless cells.

Residencial La Paz City (Map pp52-3; ☎ 249-4565; Acosta 487; US$3.50-4) A friendly, safe, helpful, former Peace Corps favorite near Plaza San Pedro. The affiliated **Residencial La Paz City Annex** (☎ 236-8380; México 1539; US$3.35) has some rooms with balconies, and a good restaurant and cooking school in the courtyard below.

Alojamiento El Carretero (Map pp52-3; ☎ 228-5271; Catacora 1056; US$2) Classic cheapie, with a kitchen, laundry and lots of traveler traffic – mind your gear.

Alojamiento Universo (Map pp52-3; ☎ 246-0731; Kapac 575; dm/r US$1.85/2) Cheap, cleanish, friendly place with hot showers until noon. Go for a ground-floor unit and, as in all dormitory scenarios, keep your gear locked up.

Alojamiento El Viajero (El Lobo; Map pp52-3; ☎ 245-3465; Illampu & Santa Cruz; dm/s US$2/2.65; ☐) Just like your college dorm, only colder and everything is in Hebrew. The few shared baths are grubby, and rates include all the partying your Israeli neighbors can throw. Its suggestion books are good for finding out which places are on their way to becoming travelers' ghettos.

Alojamiento La Scala (Map pp52-3; ☎ 245-6342; Unión 425 btwn Chuquisaca & América; US$2) A safe, clean, friendly option. Even though it's tucked away in a quiet alley, the nearby disco can render it noisy on weekends.

Residencial Illimani (Map pp52-3; ☎ 220-2346; Illimani 1817; s/d US$4.75/7.75) In a quiet (some would say dead) area near the stadium. A friendly family place with a laundry sink, and leafy patio where you can cook.

NEAR THE MAIN BUS TERMINAL

There are a couple of handy, decent places to crash opposite the main bus terminal. **Hostal Tambo del Oro** (Map pp48-50; ☎ 228-1565; fax 228-2181; Armentia 367; s/d US$5.25/8, with bath & cable TV US$9.50/12) is the best of the bunch. It's pleasantly quiet, cozy and colonial-looking with good-value, carpeted rooms and gas showers. Early breakfast available. **Residencial Rosinho II** (Map pp48-50; ☎ 228-1578; Perú 125; US$3) has basic rooms with shared bath.

Mid-Range

Hotel Rosario (Map pp52-3; ☎ 245-1658; www.hotelrosario.com; Illampu 704; s/d/tr US$28/37/49, with bath US$31/41/54; free ☐) Let the professional, English-speaking staff at La Paz' best three-star hotel pamper you with five-star treatment. The ultra-clean rooms in the colonial residence all have private baths, solar-powered hot showers, satellite TV and heaters. The included breakfast buffet at the Tambo Colonial restaurant (p66) is worth a trip, even if you can't get a room here. It's base camp for many expeditions, so book ahead online. Large family and honeymoon suites fetch US$67 to US$74.

Hostal República (Map pp52-3; ☎ 220-2742; www.angelfire.com/wv/hostalrepublica; Comercio 1455; s/d/tr/q US$10/16/21/28, with bath US$16/25/33/44; free ☐) Three blocks from the historic heart of the city, this sparkling hotel occupies a lovely historic bolivida that was once home to one of Bolivia's first presidents. It has two large courtyards, a garden and a warm reception area with a small library of foreign-language books. Request an upstairs room in the front (downstairs tends towards dank) or a newer and quieter room at the back. The friendly English-speaking staff really aim to please. The cozy café does great breakfast and evening snacks, and has cable TV and free Internet for guests. Family rooms and a fully-equipped *casita* (separate apartment) are also available.

Hostal Naira (Map pp52-3; ☎ 235-5645; www.hostalnaira.com; Sagárnaga 161; s/d/tr with bath & breakfast US$25/32/42; ☐) At the bottom of Sagárnaga, near Plaza San Francisco, Naira is repeatedly recommended for its location, cleanliness and heating, which make it quite popular with tour groups.

Arcabucero Hostal Inn (Map pp52-3; ☎ /fax 231-3473; ar_hostal@hotmail.com; Liluyo 307; s/d with bath US$12/18.65) The nine quiet rooms at this restored antique colonial home are arranged around an ornate indoor courtyard. The electric showers are unpredictable, and a few rooms have national TV. Breakfast (US$2) is served in the common TV room. Avoid the downstairs rooms as they are dark.

Hotel España (Map pp52-3; ☎ 244-2643; www.hotel -espana.com; 6 de Agosto 2074; s/d US$15/20, with bath s/d/tr US$20/30/40; ☐) At the lower end of the city center, the comfortable and friendly España has a solarium and a lovely, sunny courtyard that receives direct sun most of the day. The newer rooms at the front are better than the older section out the back around the lawn. It's within an easy stroll of many of the city's best restaurants. Rates include cable TV, half-hour free Internet and a basic breakfast. The attached restaurant also offers inexpensive meals.

Hotel/Hostal Galería Virgen del Rosario (Map pp52-3; ☎ 246-1015; hotelgaleria@hotmail.com; Santa Cruz 583; s/d hostel US$5/9, hotel US$20/35; ☐) This novel and very pleasant option rises above the bustling streets overlooking the Mercado Negro. The interior, which loosely resembles a cathedral shopping mall, features lots of greenery and a good mezzanine restaurant. The gas-heated showers are good, and rooms are cheaper without optional services like cable TV or buffet breakfast. The front rooms overlooking the street are sunny but noisy. Guests staying multiple nights are offered free bus transfers to Copacabana and Peru.

Hotel Milton (Map pp52-3; ☎ 236-8003; www.hotel -milton-bolivia.com; Illampu 1224; high season s/d US$18/24, low season US$11/15) This clean two-star hotel in the heart of the hectic Rodriguez market area is excellent value. It's totally disco 1970s, but in the best kitschy, John Travolta way possible. Views facing the street (and from the roof) are superb, but rooms at the back are more *tranquilo*. Rooms with bath, hot showers, telephone and cable TV include breakfast, with discounts for more than two nights. It also offers cheap (US$0.65 per kilo) laundry services; free, safe luggage storage; book exchange; safe boxes; and a travel agency with transfers to Peru.

Hostal Sucre (Map pp52-3; ☎ 249-2038; Colombia 340; US$6.50, with bath & cable TV s/d US$10/15) A more upmarket choice facing Plaza San Pedro. The management is helpful and the freshly painted rooms are set around a pleasant courtyard.

Hostal Dinastía (Map pp52-3; ☎ 245-1076; hostel dinastia@yahoo.com; Illampu 684; US$4, with bath & cable TV US$6; ☐) Basic, clean carpeted rooms in the middle of the action. The friendly owner speaks English, and breakfast is available.

Hotel Continental (Map pp52-3; ☎ 245-1176; Illampu 626; US$4.50, s/d with bath & cable TV US$10/12) This older two-star HI-affiliate on Plaza Eguino is used by climbers, thrifty tour groups and Bolivian business types. It's clean, well located and has terrific showers, but rooms without bath are cramped.

Tiquina Palace Hotel (Map pp52-3; ☎ 245-7373; hoteltiquina@hotmail.com; Pasaje Tiquina 150; s/d with bath US$20/23) A quiet choice in the heart of La Paz' traditional action. Modern, carpeted rooms all include bath, cable TV, telephone and a buffet breakfast. Airport transfers are free for guests staying three nights, but otherwise they cost US$6.

Hotel La Joya (Map pp48-50; ☎ 245-3841; www .hotelajoya.com; Max Paredes 541; s/d/tr US$13/17/23, with bath US$20/27/34; ☐) A fine, friendly, relatively elegant, three-star near Plaza Garita de Lima amid the bustle of the Mercado Negro. It's very clean and includes breakfast, cable TV, phones and good hot showers. When space is available during the low season, backpackers can stay for around US$5 per person. It's away from the center of town but on numerous *micro* and *trufi* lines.

Hotel Max Inn (Map pp52-3; ☎ 249-2247; southwest side of Plaza San Pedro; s/d US$35/47) In a relatively quiet part of town, this hotel is recommended for its large, bright, carpeted rooms with bath. Kitchen suites also available. Probably the only three-star hotel in the world with views of a five-star prison.

Hotel Sagárnaga (Map pp52-3; ☎ 236-0831; hotsadt@ ceibo.entelnet.bo; Sagárnaga 326; s/d US$5.35/9, with bath s US$18, d US$25-35) Overlooking La Paz' main tourist drag, private bath rates include breakfast and cable TV, but rooms are gloomy. *Peñas* are sometimes held here when the onsite travel agency, Diana Tours (p61), has a group in town.

Hotel Oruro (Map pp52-3; ☎ 245-9992; northeast side Plaza Alonzo de Mendoza; s/d/tr US$5.35/9/15.25, with bath & TV US$10/13/17.50) Opposite the *trufi* terminus, this older, family-run place is decent value, and popular with Bolivians. The elevator actually works – a rarity – and some rooms have bath tubs and views over the plaza.

Also recommended is the modern and friendly **Estrella Andina Hostal** (Map pp52-3; ☎ 245-6421; juapame_2000@hotmail.com; Illampu 716; US$10-15; 🖳), a couple of doors down from Hotel Rosario.

Top End

The number of top-end options is growing all the time. If you're after a bit of luxury, they're bargains in comparison to similar accommodations in most other world capitals. Expect such amenities as health clubs, spas, swimming pools, pubs, coffee shops and discos.

Gran Hotel Paris (Map pp52-3; ☎ 220-3030; north side of Plaza Murillo; s/d/ste US$85/110/130; 🗶 🖳) A relatively elegant and charming hotel. The original 1911 Baroque Imperial structure was restored in 1995 (and again in 2003 after the riot on Plaza Murillo which left several bullet holes), but retains its historic Louis XVI details. Electric stoves are lit in the rooms before guests' arrival in winter and the best of the 41 rooms have balconies with panoramic views overlooking Plaza Murillo. The gourmet Café Paris, which features a piano bar and live tango music nightly, is open all day and has an excellent salad buffet on Sundays.

Hotel Gloria (Map pp52-3; ☎ 240-7070; www.hotel gloriabolivia.com; Potosí 909; s/d with bath & breakfast US$49/58; 🗶 🖳) At the lower range of the top-end towers above the snarling traffic of the Prado, the hotel standards make this place excellent value.

Hotel Plaza (Map pp52-3; ☎ 237-8311; www.plaza bolivia.com.bo; 16 de Julio 1789; s/d US$99/119; 🗶 🔀 🖳 🖵) Amazingly friendly, helpful and convenient, but nothing fancy, and with all the amenities: cable TV, a continental buffet breakfast and use of the swimming pool, gym and jacuzzi. Nonguests may use the pool and fitness facilities for US$10 per day.

El Rey Palace (Map pp52-3; ☎ 241-8541; www .hotel-rey-palace-bolivia.com; 20 de Octubre 1947; s/d US$70/80, ste US$85-105; 🔀 🖳) This business-oriented, four-star boutique hotel has 43 rooms offering European-standard services, including

buffet breakfast, telephones and cable TV. Request a room with a private jacuzzi. The Rey Arturo restaurant serves à la carte dishes and does executive *almuerzos* for US$4, and the bar is open nightly.

Hotel Europa (Map pp52-3; ☎ 231-5656, toll-free 800-10-5656; www.hoteleuropa.com.bo; Tiahuanacu 64; s/d US$160/190; 🗶 🔀 🖳 🖵) The newest, sleekest, most luxurious, biz-focused place in town. All the amenities, like in-room Internet, are executive, and thoughtful touches like radiant bathroom heating, a humidification system and telephones in the bathrooms justify the high rack rates. The Picasso suite on the 12th floor and the El Solar restaurant have amazing city views, and original prints by the namesake artist. Nonguests can use the spa, heated pool and fitness center for US$9 per day.

Hotel Presidente (Map pp52-3; ☎ 240-6666; www .hotelpresidente-bo.com; Potosí 920; s/d/tr/ste US$115/135/155/185; 🗶 🔀 🖳 🖵) The highest five-star hotel in the world (oxygen tanks are available), just a few meters higher than the competition. Rack rates include a buffet breakfast and airport transfers. Weekend specials are common, and the hotel also has a couple of fine restaurants, including the 16th-floor Bella Vista and the simpler La Kantuta.

Hotel Radisson Plaza (Map pp52-3; ☎ 244-1111, toll-free 800-10-9999; www.radisson.com/lapazbo; Arce 2177; s/d/ste US$130/150/170; 🗶 🔀 🖳 🖵) The Radisson has everything you'd expect in a five-star hotel, but the impersonal atmosphere isn't for everyone. There is also a range of more luxurious options, up to the presidential suite for US$550. The top-floor restaurant affords a superb view over the city and surrounding mountains.

EATING

La Paz has a good variety of eateries of generally high quality. All are reasonably priced compared to what you'd pay at home. Mid-range and upmarket restaurants are concentrated at the lower end of town: in **Lower Sopocachi** around Avs 20 de Octubre and 6 de Agosto, on the **Lower Prado** around 16 de Julio and in **Zona Sur**.

At the cheap end, don't expect much variation from local standards. Nearly all places specialize in some sort of beef or chicken. Most offer set meals (mainly *almuerzos*, but sometimes *cenas* too) and a short list of common dishes, with the occasional regional specialty. Go easy on the grease if you're attempting to acclimatize.

Restaurants
BREAKFAST

Few places that serve breakfast are open before 8am or 9am, but early risers desperate for a caffeine jolt before they can face the day will find bread rolls and coffee concentrate at the markets for US$0.35. The *salteñas* and *tucumanas* sold in the markets and on the streets – for a third of what they cost in sit-down cafés – are normally excellent. The street stalls near **Plaza Isabel la Católica** are particularly good, so too are those opposite the cemetery, where you'll pay just US$0.15 for a hearty snack.

Tambo Colonial (Map pp52-3; Illampu 704, Hotel Rosario; 7-10:30am, 7-10:30pm; breakfast buffet US$2.50) Nothing beats its fresh fruit, juices, delicious bread and sundry elements of continental and American breakfasts.

Café Torino (Map pp52-3; Socabaya 457, Hotel Torino; 7:30am; breakfast US$1-2) Serves breakfasts of rolls, *salteñas* and fruit juices. *Almuerzos* and *cenas* are also available.

Café La Terraza Prado (Map pp52-3; 231-0701; 16 de Julio 1615); Sopocachi (Map pp48-50; 242-2009; 20 de Octubre 2331); San Miguel (279-5696; Montenegro Bloque B3; mains US$1-3) This stylish chain offers quality espresso and other coffee treats, as well as incredible chocolate pie and cooked breakfasts that include North American-style pancakes and *huevos rancheros*.

LUNCH

Cheap set meals offered at countless cubbyhole restaurants can be excellent, varied and cheap – look for the chalkboard menus out front. As a general rule, the higher you climb from the Prado, the cheaper the meals will be. Many lunch spots also serve dinner and vice versa.

Ángelo Colonial (Map pp52-3; 236-0199; Linares 922-924; mains US$2-5) A fabulous café (and travelers' nirvana) housed in an old colonial mansion tastefully decorated with antiques. The coffee is excellent, sandwiches are enormous and all the food is well presented.

Andrómeda (Map pp52-3; 244-0726; Arce 2116 at Aspiazu stairs; 9am-midnight Mon-Sat; lunch US$2, mains US$3-7) Gourmet *almuerzos* with meat and vegetarian options (fish on Friday),

and an excellent salad bar. In the evening the intimate country-cosmopolitan atmosphere is candlelit, and there are homemade pastas, French-Mediterranean and Bolivian dishes and a full bar.

Mongo's Rock Bottom Café (Map pp48-50; 244-0714; Manchego 2444; from noon Mon-Fri, from 6pm Sat & Sun; lunch US$2.75, mains US$2-4) Hopping American-style bar popular with expats and NGO workers. Specialties include nachos, enormous burgers and vegetarian dishes. They screen major sporting events and stage free live acoustic music on Tuesday nights.

Casa de los Paceños (Map pp52-3; 228-0955; Sucre 856; lunch Tue-Sun, dinner Tue-Fri; lunch US$1.75, mains US$3-5) Friendly, family-run place for upscale versions of classic *paceño* dishes like *saice*, *sajta*, *fricasé* and *chairo*, and *fritanga*. Also in Zona Sur.

Café Ciudad (Map pp52-3; 244-1827; Plaza del Estudiante 1901; 24/7/365; mains US$1.50-3) Slow service and mediocre food but the full menu of burgers, pasta, steak and pizza is always available, and you're free to linger over its two redeeming features, coffee and apple pie.

El Lobo (Map pp52-3; Illampu & Santa Cruz; mains US$2-3) Favorite for cheap, filling meals. The curry, pasta, chicken and veggie options are slightly better than the surly service. El Lobo is cluttered with whacky photos of naked Israelis, and is often open when everything else on Sagárnaga is shut.

Gringo Limón (Map pp48-50; 241-8097; Plaza Avaroa 2497; lunch only Sun, closed Mon; US$2-3 per kilo, mains US$3-6) Brazilian-style by-the-kilo Bolivian and European grilled meat specialties, with salad bar, plus à la carte dinners. Good for takeout. Also in Zona Sur.

Chifa Luqing (Map pp52-3; 20 de Octubre 2090; 11am-11pm; lunch US$1.75) Serves big Chinese *almuerzos* in a bright atmosphere.

Jalapeños (Map pp48-50; 236-9876; Arce 2549; mains US$3-5) The most central Mexican option. At lunchtime they offer a good three-course *almuerzo*, and a lunch buffet on Friday. Dinner is served from 6:30pm.

There are heaps of acceptable budget restaurants on Evaristo Valle, near Mercado Lanza (Map pp52–3); also cheap are the places along the lower (eastern) end of Calle Rodríguez, which also boasts a handful of excellent, cheap Peruvian-style *ceviche* places in the 200 block. The best is **Acuario II** (Map pp52-3; mains under US$2), which has no sign, but is opposite Acuario I (which does have a sign). A bit more sophisticated is **Cevichería Portales** (Map pp52-3; Santa Cruz s/n), a block uphill from the main post office.

Other recommended, central, set-lunch places include the following:

Bar Tiwanaku (Map pp52-3; Oruro & México; lunch US$0.75) Hosts occasional live music on weekends.

Restaurant Laza (Map pp52-3; Bozo 244; Plaza Alonso de Mendoza; lunch US$0.75)

Restaurant Verona (Map pp52-3; Colón near Santa Cruz; mains US$1-2)

DINNER

Many of the lunch spots listed above also serve dinner. For more dinner options – with live folk programs – see Peñas, p70.

Tambo Colonial (Map pp52-3; ☎ 245-1658; Illampu 704 at Hotel Rosario; ☺ 7-10:30pm; mains US$2.50-5) Known for its salad bar and excellent mains such as trout in white wine sauce and llama medallions with mushroom sauce, as well as good veggie lasagna. Afterward indulge in what may be the best chocolate mousse south of the equator. Don't miss the live acoustic folk music performances on Thursday, Friday and Saturday nights.

Restaurant Vienna (Map pp52-3; ☎ 244-1660; Zuazo 1905; ☺ lunch only Sun, closed Sat; mains US$4-10) Arguably La Paz' best continental restaurant, classy Vienna serves traditional, central European cuisine and unique takes on Bolivian *criolla* classics. Try the hearty Austrian Farmer's plate or the legendary black and white chocolate mousse. Filled with antiques, the restaurant also has live piano music.

Wagamama (Map pp48-50; ☎ 243-4911; Pinilla 2257 behind Jalapeños; ☺ lunch only Sun, closed Mon; meals US$4-10) Bolivia's best Japanese joint does superb teppanyaki and wonders with landlocked trout. The atmosphere is classy and the service is friendly.

Pronto Ristorante (Map pp48-50; ☎ 244-1369; Jáuregui 2248; ☺ 6:30-10:30pm Mon-Sat; mains US$3.50-7) Although fairly posh, Pronto delivers good-value Italian and there's no fuss about appearances. It's repeatedly recommended for its few meaty mains, good house salad and homemade pastas. In an alley off Guachalla near 6 de Agosto.

Chifa New Hong Kong (Map pp48-50; Salinas & 20 de Octubre; mains US$1.50-3) Inexpensive, MSG-laden, Chinese grub. *Sin Agí-no-moto* is the key phrase to avoid the glutamate.

La Québecoise (Map pp48-50; ☎ 212-1682; 20 de Octubre 2387; ☺ closed Sun; mains US$5-10) Fine French-Canadian and American cuisine in a homey, romantic atmosphere. It's not cheap, but the food, service and ambience are top quality.

El Arriero (Map pp48-50; ☎ 244-0880; 6 de Agosto 2535; mains US$4-8) Big beef fans shouldn't miss this Argentine gem, which also boasts fine South American wines.

Pronto Pettirosso (Map pp48-50; ☎ 232-4853; Pasaje Medinacelli 2282; mains US$5-15) Superb food in a chic ambience. The lively orange and blue decor features a wealth of original Botero paintings. Expect to pay around US$20 per person for a fine Italian meal with wine.

La Bodeguita Cubana de Eugenio (Map pp48-50; ☎ 231-0782; Zuazo 1665; ☺ lunch & dinner Mon-Sat, lunch only Sun; mains US$3-5) Sophisticated Cuban cuisine (mainly pork, lamb and chicken dishes) is the specialty at this warm and agreeable hangout. Of course there are strong *mojitos*, but try one of the other rum-based cocktails (sorry, no stogies) for desert.

New Tokyo (Map pp48-50; ☎ 243-3654; 6 de Agosto 2932; ☺ noon-2:30pm & 6-11pm Mon-Sat, noon-3pm Sun; meals US$4-10) The second-best bet for sushi, with a less classy ambience and less attention to detail.

Abracadabra (☎ 279-1880; Ballivián 969; mains US$3-6) Classic American fare – steaks, ribs, pizza and salads – with homemade sausage, pastrami and sauces. Run by an expat upstate New Yorker, it's in Calacoto, between Calles 15 and 16 in Zona Sur, accessible by *micro* or *trufi*.

VEGETARIAN

Armonía (Map pp48-50; Ecuador 2286; ☺ noon-2:30pm Mon-Fri; buffet US$2.75) La Paz' best all-you-can-eat vegetarian lunch is found above Librería Armonia in Sopocachi.

Confitería Manantial (Map pp48-50; Potosí 909 at Hotel Gloria; ☺ noon-2:30pm & 7-10pm Mon-Sat; lunch & dinner buffet US$2.25) Also has a popular veggie buffet. Arrive before 12:30pm or you risk missing the best dishes.

Yussef (Map pp52-3; ☎ 279-3549; Sagárnaga 380; mains US$2-4.50) Bolivia's best Middle Eastern food. Great mixed vegetarian plate of Lebanese specialties like hummus, falafel, tabouli and babaganoush. The extensive menu also has many meaty choices. Skip the baklava – everything else is divine. Also in Zona Sur on Ballivian.

Laksmi (Map pp52-3; Sagárnaga 213, Galería Chuquiago, 1st fl; ☺ all day) Cheap, hearty, wholesome veggie lunches with East Indian leanings.

Le Pot-Pourri des Gourmets (Map pp52-3; ☎ 715-40082; Linares 906 above Coca Museum; set lunch US$2.25, mains US$2-4.50) An ambitious menu; the creative takes on traditional Bolivian dishes don't always meet their mark. Pros include an arty, inviting setting, table games and good music.

Coffee & Cafés

Pepe's Coffee Bar (Map pp52-3; ☎ 245-0788; Jimenez 894; ☺ 8am-9pm Mon-Sat, 9:30am-3pm Sun; breakfast & sandwiches US$1-3.50) This cheery, inviting, little arty café is tucked away on a sunny bend in the Witches' Market. It's a cozy place for coffee or cocktails. Big breakfasts and veggie lunch options go down easy while browsing the library of guidebooks and English-language periodicals.

Alexander Coffee & Pub (Map pp52-3; ☎ 231-2790, 16 de Julio 1832; Map pp52-3, ☎ 240-6482, Potosí 1091; Map pp48-50, ☎ 243-1006, 20 de Octubre 2463; ☎ 277-3410; Montenegro 1336, Zona Sur; ☺ 7am-2am; mains US$1-3) Trendy café serving all manner of java drinks, pastries and sandwiches. Near Plaza del Estudiante is the wonderful original that spawned the successful chain. It's renowned for its excellent espresso and cappuccino, as well as fruit juices and tasty snacks, from pastries to vegetarian quiche.

Café Pierrot (Map pp52-3; ☎ 237-0018; Potosí 909, Hotel Gloria; mains US$1) Fine coffee and fresh *salteñas* are served in the hotel's friendly, ground-floor café.

Profumo di Caffé (Map pp52-3; ☎ 231-3824; Plaza San Francisco 502-504; ☺ 8:30am-8pm; mains US$1-2) A very Italian coffee shop where you'll find excellent coffee specialties plus a rotating selection of tiramisu, cakes, pastries and other snacks. The café may be relocating to inside the church's new antiquities museum in 2004.

Confitería Club de La Paz (Map pp52-3; ☎ 719-26265; Camacho & Santa Cruz; mains US$1-3) For a quick coffee or *salteña*, hit this literary café and haunt of politicians (and, formerly, of Nazi war criminals) known for its strong espresso, and lemon meringue pie.

Quick Eats & Snacks

100% Natural (Map pp52-3; Sagárnaga 345; mains US$1-2.50) A convenient spot for big breakfasts, healthy snacks and salads.

Snack El Montañés (Map pp52-3; Sagárnaga 323; mains US$1-2) A hole-in-the-wall serving excellent sandwiches, fruit juices, light meals and desserts.

Sergio's (Map pp52-3; 6 de Agosto 2040; ☺ from 5pm; under US$1) Arguably the best pizzas in town come from this rockin', evening-only hole-in-the-wall near the Aspiazu steps. Besides pizza, you'll find gyros, chili and lasagna.

Pollo Copacabana (Map pp52-3; Comercio at Sanjinés, Potosí at Colón, 16 de Julio near Plaza del Estudiante; mains US$1-2) The queen of quick chicken offers roasted bird, french fries and fried plantain smothered in ketchup, mustard and *ají* (hot chili sauce) for US$2.

Eli's Pizza Express (Map pp52-3; 16 de Julio 1491 & 1800; mains US$1-3) Prado fast food favorite where you can choose between pizza and pasta, pastries and ice cream. The food is not great – but there's no wait. Other outlets in Sopacachi and San Miguel.

Vigor (Map pp52-3; Ingavi near Alianza; under US$1.50) Great fruit shakes and yogurt drinks.

Kuchen Stube (Map pp48-50; Gutiérrez 461; ☺ noon-8pm Mon, 10am-12:30pm & 2:30-7pm Tue-Fri; sweets US$1-2) A favorite for European coffee, decadent German pastries, fresh juices and quiche Lorraine.

Las Velas (Map pp52-3; Bolívar s/n; under US$1) Near the Kusillo Cultural Complex. Vendors in this warren of smoky cubicles whip up everything from burgers to kebabs, sausages, sandwiches and other fast delights for an utter pittance. It's very good and is open until late.

A good choice for Italian ice cream is **Heladería Napoli** (Map pp52-3; north side of Plaz Murillo). In addition to ice cream concoctions, it serves breakfasts, pastry, cakes and other snacks. There are also several popular ice-cream parlors along the Prado, such as the circus-like **Unicornio** (Map pp52-3).

Markets & Street Food

If you don't mind the hectic settings, your cheapest food scene is the markets. Unfortunately the most central, **Mercado Lanza** (Map pp52-3) has a rather dirty and unpleasant *comedor* (basic eatery) – but don't miss the rank of fruit drink stalls outside the Figueroa entrance. Better is **Mercado Camacho** (Map pp52-3), where takeout stalls sell *empanadas* and chicken sandwiches, and *comedores* dish up filling, set meals. **Mercado Uruguay** (Map pp52-3; off Max Paredes) has one particularly hygienic stall that serves fresh *pejerrey* (a tasty freshwater fish) with vegetables and sauce for around US$1.35. It's the only one serving the fish, so you're sure to find it eventually. Other areas to look for cheap and informal meals include the street markets around Ava Buenos Aires and the cemetery district.

For excellent *empanadas* and *tucumanas*, try the first landing on the steps between the Prado and Calle México. For US$0.25, you'll get an enormous beef or chicken *empanada* served with your choice of sauces – hot, hotter and hottest. In Sopocachi, the northwest border of Plaza Avaroa is lined with *salteña* stands; try Salteña Chic.

Self-Catering
Cheap DIY meals can easily be cobbled together from the abundance of fruit, produce and bread at the markets (p54). If you're after sweet snacks, go to Calle Isaac Tamayo (Map pp52–3), near Manco Capac.

If you're headed off to a picnic, load up on everything from olives to beer at **Ketal Hipermercado** (Map pp48-50; Arce near Pinilla, Sopocachi). **ZATT** (Map pp48-50; Sánchez Lima near Plaza Avaroa) is a smaller US-style supermarket option. Opposite Sopocachi Market, **Arco Iris Market** (Map pp48-50; ☎ 242-1999; Guachalla 554; ☽ 8am-8pm Mon-Sat) has an extensive *pastelería* and deli featuring fine specialty regional meat and dairy treats like smoked llama salami, plus artisanal products like fresh palm hearts and dried Beni fruits. There's also the decent but more basic **Ketal Express** (Map pp48-50; Plaza España).

DRINKING
There are scores of inexpensive, drinking dens where local men go to drink *singani*, play *cacho* (dice) and, eventually, pass out. Unaccompanied women should steer clear of these dens (even accompanied women may have problems) and only devoted sots will appreciate the drunken marathon that typifies Bolivian partying.

You'll also find lots of more elegant bars, which are frequented by foreigners and middle-class Bolivians. Local, gilded youth mingle with upmarket expats at tony clubs along 20 de Octubre in Lower Sopocachi and in Zona Sur, where US-style bars and discos spread along Av Ballivián and Calle 21.

A great, central, gringo-friendly bar with a mixed scene is bohemian **La Luna** (Map pp52-3; ☎ 233-5523; Murillo at Oruro), which hosts occasional live music.

Mongo's (Map pp52-3; ☎ 244-0714; Manchego 2444; ☽ happy hour 5-7pm Fri, 6:30-8:30pm Sat) is the expat local, and gets crazy after the café shuts down around 11pm.

Café Sol y Luna (Map pp52-3; Murillo & Cochabamba) A low-key, Dutch-run hangout offering cocktails, bar snacks and good coffee. It has big booths, a book exchange and an extensive guidebook reference library (many current Lonely Planet titles), a dart alley and couches downstairs for watching TV.

Malegria (Map pp52-3; ☎ 244-0983; Goitia 155; ☽ closed Sun) A good place to mingle with student types. It also offers darts, backgammon, pub meals and a variety of imported beer. Wednesday's Afro-Cuban percussion and Thursday's Saya Afro-Boliviana gets gringos and locals mixing on the dance floor.

Dead Stroke (Map pp48-50; ☎ 243-3472; 6 de Agosto 2460; ☽ from 5pm Mon-Sat) An upbeat – and only marginally sleazy – billiards bar with cable TV. It attracts lots of night owls with pool, snooker, darts, chess and dominoes, and also serves standard bar meals.

Coyote Bar (Map pp48-50; 20 de Octubre 2228; ☽ closed Sun) Brightly lit and desert-themed. Features tequila, Corona beer and other Mexican elements. Offers all-you-can drink beer for US$5 every Wednesday from 7pm to 11pm.

Thelonious Jazz Bar (Map pp48-50; ☎ 242-4405; 20 de Octubre 2172; ☽ 7pm-3am Mon-Sat; weekend cover charge US$3.50) Bebop fans love this charmingly low-key bar for its live performances and great atmosphere.

Reineke Fuchs (Map pp48-50; ☎ 244-2979; Jáuregui 2241; ☽ from 6pm Mon-Sat) Sopocachi *brewhaus* featuring imported German beers, schnapsladen and hearty sausage-based fare.

La Choperia (Map pp52-3; ☎ 231-1034; Pichincha off Ingavi) Opposite the Mormon church, its rustic interior, retro photographs from the 1920s and 1930s, Western pop music and pitchers/jugs of beer make it a favorite with middle-class locals.

ENTERTAINMENT
Pick up a copy of the free weekly *Happening* leaflet (www.happening.tk) for a day-by-day rundown of what's on at Sopocachi's

and San Miguel's most popular bars, pubs, clubs and cafés. Otherwise, watch hotel noticeboards for underground clubbing flyers and live music posters, or check the **Agenda Cultural** (www.utopos.org) for current arts and theater listings. The municipal tourist office (p47) distributes a free monthly cultural and fine arts schedule, and the **Teatro Municipal** (Map pp52-3; Sanjinés & Indaburo) has an ambitious theater and folk-music program.

Cinema

Your best chances of catching a quality art film are at the **Cinemateca Boliviana** (Map pp52-3; ☎ 240-6444; Pichincha & Indaburo; tickets US$1.35), which shows subtitled foreign films daily at 4pm and 7:30pm. German films are screened regularly at the Goethe Institut (p46). The **nameless cinema** (Map pp52-3; Comercio near Sanjinés) does an afternoon double feature for US$1.35. Modern cinemas on the Prado show recent international releases, usually in the original language with Spanish subtitles, for around US$2. The following are recommended movie houses:

Cine 6 de Agosto (Map pp48-50; ☎ 244-2629; 6 de Agosto btwn Gutierrez & Salinas)

Cine 16 de Julio (Map pp52-3; ☎ 244-1099; 16 de Julio at Plaza del Estudiante)

Cine Monje Campero (Map pp52-3; ☎ 212-9033/34; 16 de Julio at Bueno)

Nightclubs

Forum (Map pp48-50; Victor Sanjinés 2908; cover charge US$2-10) The granddaddy of La Paz' discos appeals to the young and restless, and offers a different musical theme each night of the week.

Salsa Club (R&S Club; Map pp48-50; ☎ 234-2787; Gutiérrez & 6 de Agosto) The club formerly known as Loro en su Salsa (Parrot in His Own Sauce) still gets pretty riotous, especially on Friday. Happy hour runs from 8:30pm to 10:30pm, but the dancing doesn't heat up until midnight. The rest of the week sees lots of trance, house and electronica on the turntables.

Other discos include the optimistically named **Disco Love City** (Map pp52-3; ☎ 222-2626), a local teenage favorite near the stadium. Sopocachi's 20 de Octubre strip is the new nightlife hotspot, with several swanky clubs catering to local monied youth.

Bizarro (Map pp48-50; Guachalla 356; Ⓨ from 7pm Wed-Sat) Sopocachi's hip alternaclub throws bumpin' 18-and-up DJ parties every Friday and Saturday night. Thursday is ladies' night and Wednesday features three rooms of electronica.

Diesel Nacional (Map pp48-50; 20 de Octubre 2271; Ⓨ from 7:30pm Mon-Sat) The post-modern place to escape reality for an overpriced drink with the rich kids. It doesn't really get going until late.

Also check out **Dragonfly** (Map pp48-50; ☎ 244-0735; dragonfly@hotmail.com; Guachalla 319).

Peñas

Typical of La Paz (and most of Bolivia) are folk-music venues known as *peñas*. Most present traditional Andean music, rendered on *zampoñas*, *quenas* and *charangos*, but also often include guitar shows and song recitals. Many *peñas* advertise nightly shows, but in reality most only have shows on Friday and Saturday nights. Most start at 9pm or 10pm and last until 1am or 2am. Admission ranges from US$4 to US$7 and usually includes the first drink. Check the daily newspapers for advertisements and details about smaller unscheduled *peñas* and other musical events.

El Calicanto (Map pp52-3; Genaro Sanjinés 467; mains US$3-6, dinner buffet US$4) Housed in an old colonial home two blocks from Plaza Murillo, it consists of the café El Molino, which does coffee and lunches, a bar with a nightly *peña*, and the Restaurant Las Tres Parrillas. The food is reasonably priced and excellent, especially if you like *parrillada*; the broiled steaks are cooked over steaming volcanic rocks.

Peña Marka Tambo (Map pp48-50; ☎ 228-0041; Jaén 710; Ⓨ from 10pm Thu-Sat; cover charge US$3.35) A less expensive – and some claim more traditional – *peña*. The music is much better than the food.

Peña Huari (Map pp52-3; ☎ 231-6827; Sagárnaga 339; Ⓨ from 9pm nightly; cover charge US$5.35) The city's best known *peña* is aimed at tourists and Bolivian business people. The attached restaurant specializes in Bolivian cuisine, including llama steak, Lake Titicaca trout, *charque kan* and salads. It's run by the same folks as Parnaso.

Peña Parnaso (Map pp52-3; ☎ 231-6827; Sagárnaga 189; Ⓨ from 8:30pm Mon-Sat; cover charge US$5) You can sample all sorts of local specialties, including various llama dishes – *charque kan*, shish kebab and even llama fondue. It bills itself as 'a space for art', and features Andean music and dancing. Watch for flyers offering a free welcome drink.

La Casa del Corregidor (Map pp52-3; ☎ 236-3633; Murillo 1040; ⏰ 7pm-midnight Mon-Sat; mains US$4-6; cover charge US$3.35) Housed in a beautiful colonial building, this upmarket *peña* is called El Bodegón de Cinti, and the Sucre theme dictates southern specialties and drinks based on *singani* from Cinti province in Chuquisaca department. Go before the show to enjoy a meal of trout, chicken or vegetarian dishes at its recommended lunch and dinner restaurant, El Horno.

Los Escudos (Map pp52-3; ☎ 231-2133; Santa Cruz 1201; ⏰ Mon-Sat from 9pm; set meal US$7.50; cover US$4) Another large touristy peña, in the same building as Confitería Club de La Paz.

Sport
The popularity of *fútbol* (professional soccer) in Bolivia is comparable to that in other Latin American countries. Matches are played at Estadio Hernando Siles (Map pp52-3) on Sunday year-round, as well as on Thursday evening during the winter. You can imagine what sort of advantage the local teams have over mere lowlanders; players from elsewhere consider La Paz games a suicide attempt! Check newspapers for times and prices.

Theater
The **Teatro Municipal Alberto Saavedra Pérez** (Map pp52-3; Sanjinés & Indaburo; tickets US$3-5) has an ambitious program of folklore shows, folk-music concerts and foreign theatrical presentations. It's a great old restored building with a round auditorium, elaborate balconies and a vast ceiling mural. The newspapers and tourist office (p47) have information about what's on here.

SHOPPING
Musical Instruments
Many La Paz artisans specialize in *quenas*, *zampoñas*, *tarkas* and *pinquillos*, among other traditional woodwinds. There's a lot of low-quality or merely decorative tourist rubbish around. Visit a reputable workshop where you'll pay a fraction of gift-shop prices, and contribute directly to the artisan

rather than to an intermediary. Clusters of artisans work along Juan Granier near Plaza Garita de Lima. Other recommended shops in La Paz include those on Isaac Tamayo near the top of Sagárnaga, and those at Linares 855 and 859.

Outdoor Gear
A good selection of new and secondhand climbing, trekking and camping equipment can be found at **Condoriri** (Map pp52-3; ☎ /fax 231-9369; Sagárnaga 343). It sells everything from ropes and backpacks to boots, compasses and headlamp batteries, plus a selection of high-quality climbing hardware, books and maps. It also rents out equipment and has a repair service. **Adolfo Andino** (Map pp52-3; ☎ 231-7151; adolfo1andino@hotmail.com; Sagárnaga 380) sells good-quality, locally made, breathable waterproof gear. You'll find one of Bolivia's widest, if expensive, ranges of basic camping equipment at **Camping Caza y Pesca** (Map pp52-3; ☎ 240-8095; Galería Handal, Mariscal, Local 9), a good place to pick up gas-stove canisters.

If you prefer to rent equipment, try **Sarañani** (Map pp52-3; ☎ 237-9806; saranani@ceibo .entelnet.bo; Galería Doryan, Local 25, Sagárnaga 189), which has decent Vietnamese-made Doite equipment. For all kinds of backpack protection – wire mesh, plastic sacks, chains, padlocks, and so on – check the street stalls along Calle Isaac Tamayo.

Photography & Film
Official Kodak one-hour developing outlets are springing up all around touristy parts of town; alternatively try **AGFA Bolivia** (Map pp52-3; Loayza 250). For camera problems, track down master repairman Rolando Calla at **Foto Capri** (Map pp52-3; ☎ 237-0134; Santa Cruz at Colón; ⏰ 10:30am-noon Mon Fri). Otherwise, try him at **home** (☎ 222-3701; rccrcc@entelnet.bo; tecnologiafotografica.8m.com; Victor Eduardo 2173, Parque Triangular; ⏰ 2:30-7:30pm).

Slide film is widely available for around US$5 per roll; be cautious about buying film at street markets where it is exposed to strong sun all day. Print film costs about US$2.50 per roll of 36 exposures. Lots of photo shops cluster around the intersection of Comercio and Santa Cruz, and in the street stalls along Buenos Aires. It's difficult to find anything over 400 ASA, and, even if you do, it will probably be expired. For relatively inexpensive cameras and electronics, try the small shops at Eloy Salmón 849 and 929, off the west end of Santa Cruz.

The following are recommended film-processing places:

Casa Kavlin (Map pp52-3; ☎ 240-6046; Potosí 1130) Good for one-hour slide or print processing.

Foto Linares (Map pp52-3; ☎ 232-7703; Loayza & Juan de la Riva, Edificio Alborda) Best choice for specialist processing.

Souvenirs, Clothing & Artesanía

La Paz is a shopper's paradise; not only are prices very reasonable, but the quality of what's offered can be very high. The main tourist shopping area, which features both *artesanía* and tourist kitsch, lies along the very steep and literally breathtaking **Calle Sagárnaga** (Map pp52-3) between Santa Cruz and Tamayo, and spreads out along adjoining streets. Here expensive shops compete with street vendors, and as a general rule, the lower their elevation, the higher their prices. Shopkeepers are usually less willing to haggle over prices than street vendors, who charge less as a matter of course.

Some shops specialize in Oriente wood-carvings and ceramics, and Potosí silver. Others deal in rugs, wall-hangings, woven belts and pouches. In the **Mercado de Hechicería** (p50) you'll find all sorts of figurines, including such Aymará good-luck charms as toads and turtles. Music recordings are available in small shops along **Evaristo Valle** and more established places on **Calle Linares**. Quite a few shops also sell tourist kitsch, an art form in itself, and amid the lovely weavings and other items displaying real craftsmanship, you'll find ceramic ashtrays with Inca designs, fake Tiahuanaco figurines, costume jewelry and all manner of mass-produced woolens.

For less expensive llama or alpaca sweaters, bowler hats and other clothing items that weren't produced specifically for tourists, stroll **Calles Graneros** and **Max Paredes**.

Comart Tukuypaj (Map pp52-3; ☎ /fax 231-2686; www.terranova.nu/comart; Linares 958) has export-quality, fair-trade llama, alpaca and *artesanías* from around the country. Upstairs the Inca Pallay women's weaving cooperative has a gallery with justly famous Jalq'a and Candelaria weavings. **Asarti** (Map pp52-3; ☎ 244-2726; www.asarti.com.bo; Arce 2177) has a boutique at the Hotel Radisson Plaza featuring fine textile art and alpaca and

pima cotton knitwear. **Artesanía Sorata** (Map pp52-3; ☎ 239-3041; www.peoplink.org/partners/bo/so; Sagárnaga 363 & Linares 862) specializes in export-quality handmade dolls and original alpaca and sheep's wool designs for children.

Wine & Food

Bodega La Concepción (Map pp52-3; ☎ 248-4812; Cañada Strongest 1620 at Otero de la Vega, San Pedro) Award-winning high-altitude vintages at wholesale prices from this Tarija-based winery.

Breick Chocolate Shop (Map pp52-3; Zuazo at Bueno) Bolivia's best chocolate at rock-bottom prices.

Campos de Solana (☎ 222-8364; Estados Unidos 1427) A Tarija winery best known for its Malbec and Riesling.

GETTING THERE & AWAY

Air

El Alto International Airport (LPB; ☎ 281-0240) is 10km via the toll-road from the city center on the Altiplano. At 4050m, it's the world's highest international airport; larger planes need 5km of runway to lift off and must land at twice their sea-level velocity to compensate for the lower atmospheric density. Stopping distance is much greater too, and planes are equipped with special tires to withstand the extreme forces involved.

Airport services include a newsstand, ATMs, Internet, souvenir shops, a bookstore with Lonely Planet guides, a coffee shop, fast food, a bistro and a duty-free shop in the international terminal. The currency exchange desk outside the international arrivals area gives poor rates on travelers checks – if possible, wait until you're in town. The domestic departure tax is US$2; the international departure tax is US$25.

Bus

The **main bus terminal** (Terminal de Buses; Map pp48-50; ☎ 228-0551; Plaza Antofagasta; terminal fee US$0.15) is a 15-minute uphill walk north of the city center. Fares are relatively uniform between companies, but competition on most routes is such that discounts are available for the asking. This full-service terminal serves all destinations south and east of La Paz, as well as international destinations. Other destinations are served mainly by *micros* and minibuses departing from the cemetery district (Map pp48–50) and Villa Fátima.

MAIN TERMINAL
Southern & Eastern Bolivia

Buses to Oruro run about every half-hour (US$2, three hours) 5am to 9:30pm. To Uyuni (US$6 to US$10, 13 hours), Panasur buses depart Tuesday and Friday at 5:30pm. Several companies serve Cochabamba (US$2 to US$3, seven hours) daily, with most departures between 7am and 10am or 7pm and 10:30pm. Many Cochabamba buses continue to Santa Cruz (US$8 to US$15, 18 hours) but it can be cheaper to buy separate tickets. El Dorado runs the best direct service.

Most overnight buses to Sucre (US$8 to US$10, 14 hours) pass through Potosí (US$5 to US$7, 11 hours) and some require a layover there. Have warm clothes handy for this typically chilly trip. Some Potosí buses continue on to Tarija (US$10 to US$15, 24 hours), Tupiza (US$10 to US$12, 20 hours) or Villazón (US$7 to US$12, 23 hours).

International Services

Several companies offer daily departures to Arica (US$10 to US$13, eight hours) and Iquique (US$12 to US$17, 11 to 13 hours); to Cusco (US$15 to US$20, 12 to 17 hours) via either Desaguadero or Copacabana, with connections to Puno (US$6 to US$8, eight hours), Lima and Arequipa; and even to Buenos Aires (normal/bus cama US$65/75, 50 hours), via either Villazón or Yacuiba.

CEMETERY DISTRICT BUS STOPS

Several companies run frequent services to Copacabana (US$2, three hours) between 5am and 8pm from Calle José María Aliaga (Map pp52–3) near Plaza Felix Reyes Ortíz (Plaza Tupac Katari). In Copacabana, you'll find *camiones* and *colectivos* to Puno and beyond. Alternatively there are more comfortable tourist minibuses (US$4 to US$5, 2½ hours) that do hotel pick-ups; you can book them at any La Paz travel agency (p47).

Most companies offer daily services to Puno (with a change in Copacabana) for about US$10, including hotel pick-up. The trip takes nine to 10 hours, including lunch in Copacabana and the border crossing. If a company doesn't fill its bus, passengers may be shunted to another company so no one runs half-empty

buses. All companies allow stopovers in Copacabana.

Between 5am and 6pm, **Autolíneas Ingavi** (Map pp48-50; Calle José María Asín) has departures every 30 minutes to Desaguadero (US$1, two hours) via Tiahuanaco (US$1, half-hour) and Guaqui. Across the street, **Unión Ingavi** (Map pp48–50) services the same route. Nearby is **Trans-Unificado Sorata** (Map pp48-50; Babia & Bustillos), which operates 10 daily buses to Sorata (US$1.50, 4½ hours). Seats are in short supply, so book your ticket early; sit on the left for views. Buses to Huarina and Huatajata (US$0.80, two hours) leave nearby from the corner of Calles Bustillos and Kollasuyo.

Be sure to watch your bags in this area, especially while boarding or leaving buses.

VILLA FÁTIMA BUS STOPS

Several *flotas* offer daily bus and minibus services to the Yungas and beyond. **Flota Yungueña** (☎ 221-3513) has two offices; the one at Yanacachi 1434, behind the gasoline station, serves Coroico, and the one on Av Las Américas, just north of the gas station, serves Amazon Basin routes. Nearby **Trans Totaí** (☎ 221-6774/6592), on San Borja, and **Trans San Bartolomé** (☎ 221-1674), on Ocobaya, serve Chulumani. Other companies serving the region are clustered along Virgen del Carmen, just west of Av Las Américas. Except for Rurrenabaque, most Amazon Basin routes only operate during the dry season. For all services, it's wise to reserve seats in advance. *Camiones* depart from behind the gasoline station.

Sample fares include Coroico (US$2, four hours), Chulumani (US$2, four hours), Guanay (US$8, eight hours), Rurrenabaque (US$7 to US$10, 18 to 20 hours), Guayaramerín (US$21.50, 35 to 60 hours), Riberalta (US$18.50, 35 to 60 hours) and Cobija (US$26.50, 50 to 80 hours).

Train

La Paz' old train station is now defunct (although rumors of restarting a La Paz to Arica or La Paz to Tiahuanaco *ferrobus* linger). Trains for Chile and the Argentine border, via Uyuni and/or Tupiza, all leave from Oruro (p159). For information and bookings, contact the **Empresa Ferroviaria Andina** (FCA; ☎ 241-6545/46; www.fca.com.bo; Guachalla 494; ticket office ☺ 8am-noon Mon-Sat).

For information about rail services within Peru, contact **Peru Rail** (www.perurail.com).

GETTING AROUND
To/From the Airport

There are two access routes to El Alto International Airport: the autopista (US$0.20) toll-road and the sinuous free route, which leads into Plaza Ballivián in El Alto, La Paz.

The cheapest but least convenient way to El Alto airport is on a La Ceja *micro* (US$0.20), which will drop you at the brow of the canyon; from there it's a level 2km walk to the airport. Much easier is *trufi* 212 (US$0.50) which runs frequently between Plaza Isabel la Católica (Map pp48–50) and the airport. Heading into town from the airport, this service will drop you anywhere along the Prado.

Radio taxis (US$5 to US$6 for up to four passengers) will pick you up at your door; confirm the price with the dispatcher when booking, or ask the driver to verify it when you climb in. For a fifth person, there is an additional US$1 charge. Transportes Aéreos Militares (TAM) flights leave from the **military airport** (☎ 237-9286) in El Alto, accessible via TAM's gondola (US$0.65) which departs from the TAM office (Map pp52–3) daily at 6:45am and drops arrivees at San Francisco Church. Alternatively catch a Río Seco *micro* from the upper Prado. Taxi fares should be about the same as for the main El Alto airport.

To/From the Bus Terminals

The main bus terminal is 1km uphill from the center. *Micros* marked 'Prado' and 'Av Arce' pass the main tourist areas but are usually too crowded to accommodate swollen rucksacks. If walking, snake your way down to the main drag, Av Ismael Montes, and keep descending for 15 minutes to the center.

Micros and minibuses run to the cemetery district constantly from the center. Catch them on Av Santa Cruz or grab *micro* No 2 along Av Yanacocha. Heading into the city from the cemetery by day you can catch *micros* along Av Baptista. At night it's best to take a taxi.

You can reach Villa Fátima by *micro* or minibus from the Prado or Av Camacho. It's about 1km uphill from Plaza Gualberto Villarroel.

Around Town

La Paz is well served by public transport. Basically you can choose between *micros* (buses), which charge US$0.15 (B$1.50); *trufis* – either cars or minibuses – which charge US$0.20 (B$1.80) around town, US$0.80 (B$5) to the airport and US$0.40 (B$1.70) to Zona Sur; taxis, which charge US$0.40 (B$3) per person around the center (a bit more for long uphill routes); and radio taxis, charging US$0.80 (B$6) around the center, US$1 (B$8) to the cemetery district and US$1.60 (B$12) to Zona Sur. Radio taxi charges are for up to four passengers and include pickup, if necessary, while other taxis charge a per-person rate. Any of these vehicles can be waved down anywhere, except near intersections or in areas cordoned off by the police.

MICRO

La Paz's sputtering and smoke-spewing *micros* mock the law of gravity and defy the principles of brake and transmission mechanics as they grind up and down the city's steep hills. In addition to a route number or letter, *micros* plainly display their destination and route on a signboard posted in the front window. You'll see *micro* stops, but they're superfluous; *micros* will stop wherever you wave them down.

TRUFI & COLECTIVO

Trufis and *colectivos* are small cars or minibuses that ply set routes, and provide reliable and comfortable transport that falls somewhere between the taxis and *micros*. Destinations are identified on placards on the roof or windscreen.

TAXI

Although most things worth seeing in La Paz lie within manageable walking distance of the center, the bus terminals are all rather steep climbs from the main hotel areas. Especially considering the altitude, struggling up the hills through traffic with bulky luggage isn't fun.

Fortunately taxis aren't expensive, but if the journey involves lots of uphill travel, drivers may expect a bit more. Most regular taxis – as opposed to radio taxis, which carry roof bubbles advertising their telephone numbers – are actually collective taxis. Don't be concerned if the driver picks up additional passengers, and don't hesitate to flag down a taxi already carrying passengers. If you're traveling beyond the city center, or your journey involves a long uphill climb, arrange a fare with the driver before climbing in and, if possible, pay the fare in exact change.

Taxi drivers may not always be well versed in the geography of the city. It's a good idea to have a map handy so you can explain roughly where you want to go.

Long-distance taxis gather at the Centro de Taxis (Map pp48–50) on Aniceto Arce near Plaza Isabel la Católica. Prices are negotiable; as a general rule, plan on around US$40 per day.

CAR & MOTORCYCLE

Driving the steep, winding, one-way streets of La Paz may be intimidating for the un-initiated, but for longer day trips into the immediate hinterlands, renting a car isn't a bad idea. For rental rates and policy details, see Getting Around in the Transport chapter (p365).

International Rent-a-Car (Map pp52-3; ☎ 244-1906; Zuazo 1942)

Kolla Motors (Map pp48-50; ☎ 241-9141; www.kolla motors.com; Gutiérrez 502)

Localiza Rent-a-Car (Map pp52-3; ☎ 228-3132; Arce 2177 at Radisson Hotel)

Petita Rent-a-Car (☎ 242-0329; www.rentacarpetita .com; Valentin Abecia 2031, Sopocachi Alto) Swiss-owned and specializing in 4WDs.

AROUND LA PAZ

VALLE DE LA LUNA

The Valley of the Moon is a pleasant and quiet half-day break from urban La Paz, and may be visited easily in a morning or combined with another outing such as a hike to **Muela del Diablo** (p76) to fill an entire day. It isn't a valley at all, but a bizarre, eroded, hillside maze of canyons and pinnacles technically known as badlands. It lies 10km down the canyon of the **Río Choqueyapu** from the city center. The desert-like landscape and its vegetation inspire the imagination and invite exploration. Several species of cactus grow here, including the hallucinogenic *choma*, or San Pedro cactus.

The route is badly eroded, and un-consolidated silt makes it slippery and dangerous; the pinnacles collapse easily, and some of the canyons are more than 10m deep. Be cautious, carry drinking water and wear a good pair of hiking shoes.

Getting There & Away

If you visit Valle de la Luna as part of an or-ganized tour, you'll have only a five-minute photo stop. On your own, however, you'll have time to explore the intriguing forma-tions on foot.

From Av México, which parallels the Prado, catch any form of transport marked 'Mallasa' or 'Zoológico'. Continue past

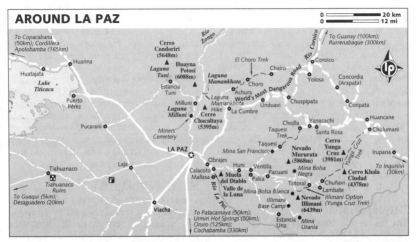

AROUND LA PAZ

0 _____ 20 km
0 _____ 12 mi

RÍO CHOKE

If statistics are anything to go by, the name of the Río Choqueyapu, which flows through La Paz, might as well be shortened to the Río Choke (or 'Omo River'. after the quantity of laundry soap flowing in it). This fetid stream, which provided the gold that gave La Paz its present location, is now utterly dead and beyond help. According to one source, 'the Río Choqueyapu receives annually 500,000 liters of urine, 200,000 tons of human excrement and millions of tons of garbage, animal carcasses and industrial toxins.' The industrial toxins include cyanide from tanneries and a cocktail of chemicals and dyes from textile and paper industries, which cause the river to flow bright orange in places, or red topped with a layer of white foam.

The Choqueyapu fortunately flows underground through the city, but as it emerges in the Zona Sur, it's used by *campesinos*, who have to make their way around heaped trash and animal carcasses to take water for washing, cooking and drinking. Most people heat the water before drinking it, but few boil it, and even boiling wouldn't eliminate some of the chemical pollutants from industrial wastes. The potential for health problems is staggering.

Currently no one can be fined or cited for dumping waste into the river because, incredibly, the city has no laws against it. In 2000 the Mayor's Environmental Quality office proposed a raft of projects aimed at controlling water pollution, vehicle emissions, rubbish dumping and noise. As always the problem with implementation has been funding, and still the foul stream continues to flow.

Calacoto and Barrio Aranjuez, and up the hill to the fork in the road; the right fork goes to the La Paz Golf Club at Malasilla. Get off after the *cactario* (cactus garden); it's not marked as such but is identifiable by its stand of cacti. Walk for a few minutes uphill toward Mallasa village and, when you see a green house on your right, you're at the top of the Valle.

For a taxi from the center, you'll pay around US$10 for up to three people, and the driver will wait for an hour or so while you look around.

MALLASA

After a traipse around Valle de la Luna, you can also visit the blossoming resort village of Mallasa. Just east of Mallasa is La Paz' spacious, but sorely underfunded, **Vesty Pakos Zoo** (☎ 274-5992; admission US$0.40; ☺ 10am-5pm), where there are photo opportunities a plenty and feeding time (10am) is raucous.

From the overlook immediately behind the zoo, you can take the clearly marked walking track that passes the rubbish dump, then descends to and crosses the fetid Río Choqueyapu, before beginning a lung-bursting 600m climb to the **Muela del Diablo** (see Muela del Diablo walk, this page).

Sleeping & Eating

The Swiss-run **Hotel Oberland** (☎ 274-5040; www.h-oberland.com; Calle 2-3, Mallasa; s/d/ste US$30/

40/50, walk-ins US$15; ☐ ☺) is a well-designed country-style hotel 30 minutes by *trufi* from the center of La Paz. It sits at an altitude of just 3200m, so it's a good 5°C warmer than central La Paz. Cacti grow in the garden, which is frequented by butterflies and dragonflies. The hotel has an indoor pool and sauna, squash and beach volleyball courts, and table tennis. It also offers guests Internet access (US$3 an hour) and cable TV. Transfers from La Paz cost US$10. All rates include a full American buffet breakfast. The lovely à la carte restaurant has tables in the garden, a fine place to sip a German beer, and is popular on weekends for BBQs.

Several shops in Mallasa sell snacks, beer and soft drinks; the snack stands outside the zoo only function on weekends.

Getting There & Away

From La Paz take minibus No 11 or No 380, or any form of transport marked 'Mallasa' or 'Zoológico'. From the top of Valle de la Luna, catch a *micro* headed downvalley or continue a couple of kilometers on foot to Mallasa. To return to La Paz, catch anything that moves back up the valley.

MUELA DEL DIABLO WALK

The prominent rock outcrop known as the **Devil's Molar** is actually an extinct volcanic plug which rises between the **Río Choqueyapu** and the recently established outer suburb of

Pedregal. A hike to its base makes a pleasant, half-day, walking trip from La Paz, and can be easily combined with a visit to Valle de la Luna. **Warning**: Several robberies have been reported; inquire locally about safety before heading out.

From the **cemetery** in Pedregal, the trail climbs steeply (several times crossing the new road that provides access to the hamlet near the base of the Muela) and affords increasingly fine views over the city and the surrounding tortured landscape. After a breathless hour or so, you'll reach a pleasant grassy swale where the tooth comes into view, as well as some precarious pinnacles further east.

At this point the walking track joins the road and descends through the hamlet. About 300m further along, a side route branches off to the left and climbs toward the Muela's base. From the end of this route you can pick your way with extreme caution up to the cleft between the **double summit**, where there's a large cross. Without technical equipment and expertise, however, it's inadvisable to climb further.

After descending to the main track, you can decide whether to return the way you came, or follow the steep track that circles the Muela in a counterclockwise direction and descends to the Río Choqueyapu before climbing the other side of the valley to the zoo in Mallasa. The latter option will turn this hike into a full-day trip, as it takes about six hours for the hike between Pedregal and Mallasa.

The marginally useful map *Trekking en La Paz* (US$ 0.75), which shows both routes, is sometimes on sale at La Paz' municipal tourist office (p47).

Getting There & Away

From La Paz the best access to the start of the hike is on minibus No 288, marked 'Pedregal', from the lower Prado. The end of the line is the parking area a couple hundred meters downhill from Pedregal's cemetery. Coming from Valle de la Luna, you can board these minibuses at Zona Sur's Plaza Humboldt or follow the difficult walking track from near the zoo in Mallasa, which involves a descent to the Río Choqueyapu and then a stiff 600m ascent to the eastern side of the Muela. To return

to La Paz from Pedregal, catch a 'Prado' minibus from the parking area.

VALLE DE LAS ÁNIMAS WALKS

The name Valley of Spirits is used to describe the eerily eroded canyons and fantastic organ-pipe spires to the north and northeast of the *barrios* of Chasquipampa, Ovejuyo and Apaña (which are rapidly being absorbed into the Zona Sur neighborhoods of La Paz). The scenery resembles that of Valle de la Luna, but on a grander scale.

There are two walking routes through the valley; for either, you need an early start from La Paz.

Río Ovejuyo Route

This route begins at Calle 50, near the Instituto de Biología Animal in Chasquipampa. This point is accessible from La Paz on *micro* Ñ or minibus No 288 or No 203, marked 'Chasquipampa' or 'Ovejuyo'. From the northern side of the road the route descends slightly through new developments. When you reach the diminutive **Río Ovejuyo**, turn right and follow its southern bank northeast past the spectacularly eroded formations.

After about 6km, the river valley turns to the north. If you don't want to return the way you came, you'll need a compass, the 1:50,000 topo sheet *5944-II* and, for a very short section along the upper Río Ovejuyo, topo sheet *5944-I*. Traverse up the slope to your right and head south over **Cerro Pararani**, until you arrive at the head of Quebrada Negra. From here you can follow the Quebrada Negra route (described below) either back to Ovejuyo or down to the village of Huni. This option can be challenging, especially because of the altitude, and you have to carry enough water for the entire day, as there's no drinkable surface water along the way.

Quebrada Negra Route

The 7km route up Quebrada Negra, over Cerro Pararani and down to Huni is a demanding day hike that requires six to seven hours. It begins at the Quebrada Negra ravine, which crosses the road at the upper (eastern) end of Ovejuyo village. *Micros* and *trufis* marked 'Ovejuyo' stop about half a kilometer short of this ravine, but *micro* Ñ and minibus No 385, marked 'Ovejuyo', or minibus No 42, marked 'Apaña', all travel right past the ravine mouth.

The easy-to-follow 4km route up Quebrada Negra will take you through the most dramatic of the eroded Valle de las Ánimas pinnacles. Near the head of the ravine, you need to traverse southeast around the northern shoulder of Cerro Pararani, until you find the obvious route that descends steeply to Huni village (not Huni chapel, which is also marked on the topo sheet). In fine weather, you'll have good views of Illimani along this section.

To return to La Paz, follow the road for 2km up over Paso Huni and then for another 1.5km downhill to Apaña, where you'll catch up with regular *micros* and *trufis* returning to the city.

For this route you'll need a compass and either the tourist office's *Trekking en La Paz* map, or the 1:50,000 topo sheets *5944-I* and *6044-III*.

CAÑÓN DE PALCA (QUEBRADA CHUA KHERI)

The magnificent Palca Canyon (marked on the topo sheet as Quebrada Chua Kheri) brings a slice of grand canyon country to the dramatic badland peaks and eroded amphitheaters east of La Paz. Although it's now a motorable track, a walk through this wonderful gorge makes an ideal day hike from La Paz.

The Route

Heading in an easterly direction from Paso Huni, about 2km above Ovejuyo, you'll pass a small lake just near the point where the road begins to descend the other side. Several hundred meters past the summit, on your left you'll see some magnificent 'church-choir' formations – rows of standing pinnacles that resemble an ensemble in song.

About 2km beyond the pass, take the right (south) fork of the road into the village of **Huni** (aka Uni). After less than 1km, the road begins to descend in earnest. Much of this route originally followed an ancient Inca road, with good examples of pre-Hispanic paving, but it was ripped up to make it passable to vehicles.

The route drops slowly toward the gravelly canyon floor, and offers sensational views along the way. The approach to the canyon is dominated by a 100m-high natural obelisk, and in the opposite wall is the rock formation **Ermitaño del Cañón**, which resembles a reclusive human figure hiding in an enormous rock niche. The route then winds alongside the usually diminutive Río Palca for about 2km between spectacular vertical walls. On exiting the canyon you'll have a gentle 3km climb through green farmland to the former gold-mining village of Palca.

Sleeping & Eating

If you don't find transport back to La Paz on the same day, you can stay at the alojamiento in Palca or camp around Palca or nearby Ventilla. Beware of the badly polluted surface water, and ask permission before you set your tent up in a field or pasture.

Huni is a small town above the entrance to Cañón de Palca. It has a shop selling basic supplies, including bottled water and snack foods, and also provides Bolivian set-menu meals.

Palca is a pleasant but basic town located relatively close to the exit of the canyon. It has a simple **hostal** (US$2-4), which offers set meals and is popular with Bolivian tourists on weekends.

Getting There & Away

For the start of this hike, you need to reach Huni, which is served only by *micros* and *trufis* headed for Ventilla and Palca. These leave at least once daily from near the corner of Boquerón and Lara, two blocks north of Plaza Líbano in the San Pedro district of La Paz. There's no set schedule, but most leave in the morning. You'll have the best luck on Saturday and Sunday, when families make excursions into the countryside. Alternatively take *micro* Ñ, or minibus No 385, marked 'Ovejuyo/Apaña', get off at the end of the line, and slog the 1.5km up the road to Paso Huni.

From Palca back to La Paz, you'll find occasional *camiones*, *micros* and minibuses, particularly on Sunday afternoon, but don't count on anything after 3pm or 4pm. Alternatively you can hike to Ventilla, an hour uphill through a pleasant eucalyptus plantation, and try hitching from there.

SKIING IN BOLIVIA – THIN AIR & THIN ICE

The improvement of the Chacaltaya ski lift, the highest in the world, has been on the Club Andino Boliviano agenda for almost as long as the club has been in existence (since 1939). Built in 1940, it was South America's first ski lift, and it hasn't changed much since. An automobile engine in an aluminum hut turns a steel cable loop. You clip on to the cable at the bottom of the slope using a length of steel fashioned into a hook (*gancho*), which is attached to a short length of rope and bit of wood. This fits between your legs and acts as a seat that theoretically drags you to the top of the hill, where you disengage from the cable. As you can imagine, there's lots of scope for complications.

In 1994 a retired – but still relatively modern (25 years old) – ski lift was shipped to Chacaltaya from Sestriere ski resort in northern Italy. It languished in an El Alto warehouse as a rather large and formidable jigsaw puzzle, until two engineers were flown over from Sestriere to install it nearly a year later, The engineers determined that, yes, the jigsaw puzzle could be reassembled but, because the piste was on a glacier (that is, slowly moving ice), the lift would have to be re-erected every year to make adjustments for glacial motion. It was decided that this would make it uneconomical, and in 1995 the old steel cable was replaced and bits of the Sestriere lift were cannibalized to improve the existing lift.

More bad news for Chacaltaya lies in global warming, which is causing the glacier to recede at a rate of 6m to 10m per year. Glacial shrinkage is not new at Chacaltaya – Club Andino Boliviano helped pay to construct the road to the piste by selling chunks of the glacier – but this time it's probably terminal. According to current estimates, unless there's a change in the present climatic trends, the Chacaltaya glacier will completely disappear within 30 years. In fact the bottom of the ski lift is now below the snow line, and will require some further engineering work if skiing is going to continue.

As a result the search is on for another piste, however all of Bolivia's glaciers are shrinking (as they are all over the world – only the Patagonian ice cap is expanding), and there's very little permanent ice left on any Bolivian peak under 5000m. Higher glaciers still have a long way to go before the big meltdown, but they're so high that day-trippers from La Paz would risk cerebral or pulmonary edema. The future of skiing in Bolivia looks bleak – it probably won't continue past 2005 – so enjoy it while you can.

Yossi Brain

If you arrive in Palca geared up for more hiking, you can always set off from Ventilla along the Taquesi Trek (p119).

CHACALTAYA

The world's highest developed ski area (the term 'developed' is used loosely) is at an altitude of more than 5000m, atop a dying glacier on the slopes of 5395m-high Cerro Chacaltaya. It's a steep 90-minute ride from central La Paz, and the accessible summit is an easy 200m ascent from there.

Those who fly into La Paz from the lowlands will want to wait a few days before visiting Chacaltaya or other high-altitude places. For guidelines on avoiding or coping with altitude-related ailments, see the Health chapter (p374).

Snacks and hot drinks are available at the lodge; if you want anything more substantial, bring it from town. Also bring warm (and windproof) clothing, sunglasses (100% UV proof) and sunscreen.

Most La Paz tour agencies take groups to Chacaltaya for around US$10 per person. For prospective skiers, Club Andino Boliviano (p80) is the best bet.

Skiing

The steep, 700m ski piste runs from 5320m (75m below the summit of the mountain) down to about 4900m. The ski season is from February to April, but it's often possible to ski on snow rather than ice even later in the year. There is no 'bunny hill', but beginners who can cope with bumps can have a good time. The major problem is the lift; real beginners often spend the entire day at the bottom of the hill because they can't come to grips with the utterly confounding cable tow. The club has long intended to replace it, but the project has been less than successful. Wear expendable clothing; it will suffer if you do manage to hook up to the cable.

The **Club Andino Boliviano** (Map pp52-3; ☎ 231-2875; México 1638, La Paz; ✆ 9:30am-noon & 3-7pm Mon-Fri) organizes transport to Chacaltaya on weekends throughout the year when there is sufficient interest, but the ski lift operates only when snow conditions are favorable. Ski trips leave from the club office at 8:30am and arrive at Chacaltaya around 11am. You ski until 4pm and are back in La Paz by 6:30pm.

Transport alone costs US$10 to US$20 per person; equipment rental is an additional US$10, including a *gancho* (hook) for the ski tow. Admission for nonskiers is US$1.35. The equipment rental shop is in the warm-up hut. When you're choosing equipment, make sure your *gancho* has a complete U-shaped curl, otherwise it won't clip onto the cable tow.

Hiking

For nonskiers or out-of-season visitors, a trip to Chacaltaya can still be rewarding. The views of La Paz, Illimani, Mururata and 6088m Huayna Potosí are spectacular, and it's a relatively easy (but steep) 1km, high-altitude climb from the lodge to the summit of Chacaltaya. Remember to carry warm clothing and water, and take plenty of rests, say a 30-second stop every 10 steps or so, and longer stops if needed, even if you don't feel tired. If you start to feel lightheaded, sit down and rest until the feeling passes. If it doesn't, you may be suffering from mild altitude sickness; the only remedy is to descend.

From Chacaltaya it's possible to walk to Refugio Huayna Potosí, at the base of Huayna Potosí, in half a day. Climb to the second false summit above the ski slope, and then wind your way down past a turquoise lake until you meet up with the road just above the nearly abandoned mining settlement of Milluni. Turn right on the road and follow it past Laguna Zongo to the dam, where you'll see the refuge on your left and the trailhead for Laguna Mamankhota (p81) on your right.

Mountain Biking

It's a long way down from the summit to the base of Cerro Chacaltaya, and Gravity

Assisted Mountain Biking (p56) in La Paz takes advantage of this descent by running riveting full-day rides downhill along the sinuous route. For US$49, it offers a variety of itineraries, depending on the weather and skill level of the participants. You reach Chacaltaya by 4WD, which provides the opportunity to savor the view before you're assaulted by a serious adrenaline rush on the downhill route to the Prado in La Paz.

Sleeping & Eating

For overnight stays at Chacaltaya, you can crash in Club Andino's well-ventilated **mountain hut** (r/dm US$4/5). Meals are available during the ski season. Alternatively you might try the La Paz UMSA research lab, which is heated and just downhill from the warm-up hut. The friendly scientific personnel may welcome visitors.

A warm sleeping bag, food and some sort of headache/*soroche* relief are essential for an overnight stay in either location.

Getting There & Away

There's no public transport to Chacaltaya. You'll have to go with either Club Andino Boliviano (p57) or a La Paz tour operator (p60). The Chacaltaya road, especially from March to May, may become impassable to 2WD vehicles, so check the situation before choosing a tour that can't arrive at its destination, or you'll have a long, uphill slog at high altitude.

If you go with Club Andino Boliviano on Saturday, you should be able to catch a lift back to La Paz with its Sunday trip, if the bus isn't full. On other days tour groups may have space for extra people; they'll charge about half the tour price for the one-way trip.

MILLUNI & THE ZONGO VALLEY

The dramatic Zongo Valley plunges sharply down from the starkly anonymous mining village of Milluni – from 4624m to 1480m within 33km. At its head, between Chacaltaya and the spectacular peak of Huayna Potosí, is the glacial blue Laguna Zongo, which was created to run the Zongo hydroelectric power station.

Not strictly a town, Milluni is a collection of hydroelectricity-company buildings and huts at the head of the Paso Zongo (along the road below Huayna Potosí, which skirts the east side of Laguna Zongo).

Laguna Mamankhota (Laguna Cañada) Hike

Once upon a time a lovely set of ice caves high above the valley floor provided a good excuse for day hikes and tours, but in 1992 they melted away, leaving not even an ice cube. Today the best excuse to climb to the former site is the impressive views of Huayna Potosí across Laguna Mamankhota.

To reach the trailhead, take the route northeast of Milluni and continue for about 5km. Along the way Milluni will be visible downhill on your left; stop to have a look at the unusual roadside miners' cemetery overlooking Milluni. If you're traveling by vehicle, you'll reach **Laguna Zongo**, an artificial lake with milky blue-green water, and the Compañía Minera del Sur gate a few minutes later. On your right you'll see a trail climbing up the hillside. From there the road winds steeply downward into Zongo Valley.

The hike begins at 4600m. From the parking area, strike off uphill to the right. After about 100m, you'll reach an aqueduct, which you should follow for about 50 minutes along a rather treacherous precipice. Watch on your left for the plaque commemorating an Israeli's final motorbike ride along this narrow and vertigo-inspiring route.

About 20m further along you cross a large bridge, then turn right along a vague track leading uphill, following the cairns that mark the way. After a short climb you'll reach Laguna Mamankhota, and stunning views of Huayna Potosí, Tiquimani, Telata and Charquini – if the peaks aren't shrouded in clouds. A further 25 minutes up the vague trail will bring you to the site of the former ice caves.

Sleeping & Eating

There are two accommodations options.

Refugio Huayna Potosí (☎ 232-3538; dm low/high season with breakfast US$6/9) At Paso Zongo, above the dam at the head of Zongo Valley, this mountain hut provides basic accommodations for climbers and trekkers. Additional meals cost US$4 to US$5, and there is hot water.

Casa Blanca (☎ 715-37 737; near Observatorío San Calixto) is a new hostel under construction on the road to Paso Zongo, on the left a few kilometers before Refugio Huayna Potosí is reached. It should be complete by 2004 and is located beside a water and weather station for the region's hydroelectric scheme, on the road to Milluni.

Camping is possible at the seismic station on the western end of Laguna Zongo.

Getting There & Away

Camiones leave for Zongo Valley, via Paso Zongo, from Kollasuyo in the La Paz cemetery district and from Plaza Ballivián in El Alto around midday on Monday, Wednesday and Thursday, and usually return the following day. *Micros* (US$0.75 per hour) leave daily when full from the same places, normally between 5am and 7am.

The half-day trip by hired taxi costs about US$35 for up to five people. Make sure the driver understands that you want the Zongo Valley via Milluni, as drivers may expect you to ask for Chacaltaya and try to take you there anyway. At the trailhead, the driver will wait while you walk up the mountain to the lake; allow a minimum of three hours for the walk.

To hire a 4WD and driver from La Paz to Paso Zongo costs about US$50 for up to nine people.

LAJA

This tiny village (formerly known as Llaxa or Laxa) is 38km west of La Paz, or about halfway to Tiahuanaco, and a brief stop here is included on many Tiahuanaco tours.

In 1548 the Spanish captain Alonzo de Mendoza was charged with founding a city and rest stop along the route from Potosí to the coast at Callao, Peru. On October 20, 1548 he arrived in Laxa and declared it his chosen location. He changed his mind, however, and the site was shifted to the gold-bearing canyon where La Paz now stands.

Over Laja's plaza towers a grand **church** built in commemoration of Spanish victories over the Incas. The interior is ornamented with colonial artwork, including lovely wooden carvings adorned with gold and silver. The mestizo-style façade bears the indigenized visages of King Ferdinand and Queen Isabella. Due to looting that has occurred in the past, the church is

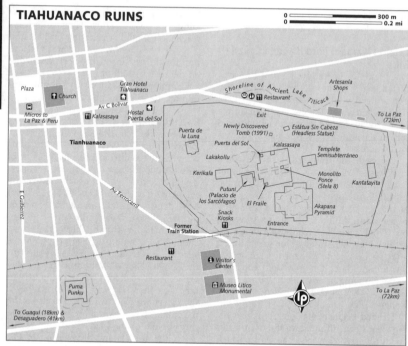

TIAHUANACO RUINS

0 ————— 300 m
0 ————— 0.2 mi

Plaza
Church
Gran Hotel Tiahuanacu
Shoreline of Ancient Lake Titicaca
Restaurant
Artesanía Shops
Micros to La Paz & Peru
Av C Bolivar
Kalasasaya
Hostal Puerta del Sol
Exit
To La Paz (72km)
Tianhuanaco
Puerta de la Luna
Newly Discovered Tomb (1991)
Estátua Sin Cabeza (Headless Statue)
Puerta del Sol
Kalasasaya
Templete Semisubterráneo
Lakakollu
Av Ferrocarril
Kerikala
Monolito Ponce (Stela 8)
Kantatayita
Putuni (Palacio de los Sarcófagos)
El Fraile
Akapana Pyramid
E Guiterrez
Snack Kiosks
Entrance
Former Train Station
Restaurant
Visitor's Center
Puma Punku
Museo Lítico Monumental
To La Paz (72km)
To Guaqui (18km) & Desaguadero (41km)

only open to the public on Sunday mornings and during festivities every October 20.

TIAHUANACO (TIWANAKU)

Little is actually known about the people who constructed the great Tiahuanaco ceremonial center on the southern shore of Lake Titicaca more than 1000 years ago. Archaeologists generally agree that the civilization which spawned Tiahuanaco rose around 600 BC. Construction on the ceremonial site was under way by about AD 700, but around AD 1200 the group had melted into obscurity, becoming another 'lost' civilization. Evidence of its influence, particularly its religion, has been found throughout the vast area that later became the Inca empire.

The treasures of Tiahuanaco have literally been scattered to the four corners of the earth. Its gold was looted by the Spanish, and early stone and pottery finds were sometimes destroyed by religious zealots who considered them pagan idols. Some of the work found its way to European museums; farmers destroyed pieces of it

as they turned the surrounding area into pasture and cropland; the church kept some of the statues or sold them as curios; and the larger stonework went into Spanish construction projects, and even into the bed of the La Paz–Guaqui railway line that passes just south of the site.

Fortunately a portion of the treasure has been preserved, and some of it remains in Bolivia. A few of the larger anthropomorphic stone statues have been left on the site. Others are on display at the Museo National de Arqueología (p50) in La Paz. New finds from the earliest Tiahuanaco periods are being added to the collection of the new onsite **Museo Lítico Monumental** (9am-5pm; admission US$2.35). The star of the show is the massive **Megalito Bennetto Pachamama**, rescued from its former smoggy home at the outdoor Templete Semisubterráneo (p560) in La Paz.

Pieces from the three more recent Tiahuanaco periods may be found scattered around Bolivia, but the majority are housed in archaeological museums in La Paz and Cochabamba. The ruins themselves have been so badly looted, however, that much of the information they could have revealed about their builders is now lost forever.

Labeling at the onsite museums is sparse and almost exclusively in Spanish. The single admission ticket includes the site, the **Puma Punku** excavation site (not included on most tours), the new museum and the visitor center. People selling cheap clay trinkets (fortunately all fake; don't pay more than US$0.25 for a small one) are no longer permitted inside the ruins – neither are clientless guides; guides (US$2 to US$10) can be hired only outside the fence.

A major research and excavation project is ongoing, which means that some of the main features may be cordoned off during your visit.

History

Although no one is certain whether it was the capital of a nation, Tiahuanaco undoubtedly served as a great ceremonial center. At its height the city had a population of 20,000 inhabitants and encompassed approximately 2.6 sq km. While only a very small percentage of the original site has been excavated – and what remains is less than overwhelming – Tiahuanaco represents the greatest megalithic architectural achievement of pre-Inca South America.

The development of the Tiahuanaco civilization has been divided by researchers into five distinct periods, numbered Tiahuanaco I through V, each of which has its own outstanding attributes.

The Tiahuanaco I period falls between the advent of the Tiahuanaco civilization and the middle of the 5th century BC. Significant finds from this period include multicolored pottery and human or animal effigies in painted clay. Tiahuanaco II, which ended around the beginning of the Christian Era, is hallmarked by ceramic vessels with horizontal handles. Tiahuanaco III dominated the next 300 years, and was characterized by tricolor pottery of geometric design, often decorated with images of stylized animals.

Tiahuanaco IV, also known as the Classic Period, developed between AD 300 and 700. The large stone structures that dominate the site today were constructed during this period. The use of bronze and gold is considered evidence of contact with groups further east in the Cochabamba valley and further west on the Peruvian coast. Tiahuanaco IV pottery is largely anthropomorphic. Pieces uncovered by archaeologists include some in the shape of human heads and faces with bulging cheeks, indicating that the coca leaf was already in use at this time.

Tiahuanaco V, or the Expansive Period, is marked by a decline that lasted until Tiahuanaco's population completely disappeared around AD 1200. Pottery grew less elaborate, construction projects slowed and stopped, and no large-scale monuments were added after the early phases of this period.

When the Spanish arrived in South America, local Indian legends recounted that Tiahuanaco had been the capital of the bearded white god called Viracocha, and that from his city Viracocha had reigned over the civilization.

Visiting the Ruins

Scattered around the Tiahuanaco site, you'll find heaps of jumbled basalt and sandstone slabs weighing as much as 25 tons each. Oddly enough the nearest quarries that could have produced the basalt megaliths are on the Copacabana peninsula, 40km away beyond the lake. Even the sandstone blocks had to be transported from a site more than 5km away. It's no wonder, then, that when the Spanish asked local Aymará how the buildings were constructed, they replied that it was done with the aid of the leader/deity Viracocha. They could conceive of no other plausible explanation.

Tiahuanaco's most outstanding structure is the **Akapana pyramid**, which was built on an existing geological formation. At its base this roughly square 16m hill covers a surface area of about 200 sq m. In the center of its flat summit is an oval-shaped sunken area, which some sources attribute to early, haphazard, Spanish excavation. The presence of a stone drain in the center, however, has led some archaeologists to believe it was used for water storage. Because much of the original Akapana went into the construction of nearby homes and churches, the pyramid is now in a rather sorry state.

North of the pyramid is **Kalasasaya**, a partially reconstructed 130m by 120m ritual platform compound with walls constructed of huge blocks of red sandstone and andesite. The blocks are precisely fitted to form a platform base 3m high. Monolithic uprights flank the massive entrance steps up to the restored portico of the enclosure, beyond which is an interior courtyard and the ruins of priests' quarters.

Other stairways lead to secondary platforms, where there are other monoliths including the famous **El Fraile** (Priest). At the far northwest corner of Kalasasaya is Tiahuanaco's best-known structure, the **Puerta del Sol** (Gateway of the Sun). This megalithic gateway was carved from a single block of andesite, and archaeologists assume that it was associated in some way with the sun deity. The surface of this fine-grained, gray volcanic rock is ornamented with low-relief designs on one side and a row of four deep niches on the other. Some believe these may have been used for offerings to the sun, while others maintain that the stone served as some kind of calendar. The structure is estimated to weigh at least 44 tonnes.

There's a smaller, similar gateway carved with zoomorphic designs near the western end of the site that is informally known as the **Puerta de la Luna** (Gateway of the Moon).

East of the main entrance to Kalasasaya, a stairway leads down into the **Templete Semisubterráneo**, an acoustic, red sandstone pit structure measuring 26m by 28m, with a rectangular sunken courtyard and walls adorned with 175 crudely carved stone faces.

West of Kalasasaya is a 55m by 60m rectangular area known as **Putuni** or Palacio de los Sarcófagos, which is still being excavated. It is surrounded by double walls and you can see the foundations of several houses.

The heap of rubble at the eastern end of the site is known as **Kantatayita**. Archaeologists are still trying to deduce some sort of meaningful plan from these well-carved slabs; one elaborately decorated lintel and some larger stone blocks bearing intriguing geometric designs are the only available clues. It has been postulated – and dubiously 'proven' – that they were derived from universal mathematical constants, such as pi; but some archaeologists simply see the plans for a large and well-designed building.

Across the railway line south of the Tiahuanaco site, you'll see the excavation site of **Puma Punku** (Gateway of the Puma). In this temple area megaliths weighing more than 440 tonnes have been discovered. Like Kalasasaya and Akapana, there is evidence that Puma Punku was begun with one type of material and finished with another; part was constructed of enormous sandstone blocks and, during a later phase of construction, notched and jointed basalt blocks were added.

Festivals & Events

On June 21 (the southern hemisphere's winter solstice), when the rays of the rising sun shine through the temple entrance on the eastern side of the complex, the **Aymará New Year** (Machaj Mara) is celebrated at Tiahuanaco. As many as 5000 people – including a large contingent of New Agers – arrive from all over the world. Locals don colorful ceremonial dress and visitors are invited to join the party, drink *singani*, chew coca, sacrifice llamas and dance until dawn. Artisans hold a crafts fair to coincide with this annual celebration.

Special buses leave La Paz around 4am to arrive in time for sunrise. Dress warmly because the pre-dawn hours are bitterly cold at this time of year. Die-hard participants turn up a few days early and camp outside the ruins.

Smaller, traditional, less touristed celebrations are held here for the other solstices and equinoxes.

Tours

Many La Paz agencies offer reasonably priced, guided, full- and half-day Tiahuanaco tours (US$10 to US$20 per person), including transport and a bilingual guide. These tours are worth it if you prefer to avoid the crowded local buses.

Sleeping & Eating

You'll find several basic eateries around the entrance to the ruins. Tiahuanaco village, 1km west of the ruins, has several marginal restaurants and an incredibly colorful Sunday market. As a tour participant you may want to carry your own lunch; otherwise you'll likely be herded into an overpriced restaurant.

The nicest place to stay is **Gran Hotel Tiahuanacu** (☎ 289-8548; La Paz ☎ 241-4154; Bolívar 903; US$4, with bath US$4.65). The rooms are clean, breezy and comfortable. There's an Entel phone there and the restaurant is open on weekends. Across the street the restaurant **Kalasasaya** (Bolívar 937; r per person US$1.35) also offers informal sleeping possibilities. The reasonable **Hostal Puerta del Sol** (US$2.50), at the La Paz end of the village, is the closest to the ruins. It offers simple meals and some bizarre stories about Tiahuanaco, including tales of UFOs seen near the site.

Getting There & Away

Most travelers visit Tiahuanaco on a guided day tour from La Paz. For those who prefer to go it alone, Autolíneas Ingavi (p73) leaves for Tiahuanaco (US$1, 1½ hours) about eight times daily from José María Asín in La Paz. Most buses continue to Guaqui and Desaguadero. The buses are crowded beyond comfortable capacity – even when passengers are hanging out the windows and doors, drivers are still calling for more.

Thanks to the new road, buses now pass the museum near the entrance to the complex. To return to La Paz, flag down a *micro* along the road south of the ruins. However they'll likely be overflowing, so it may be worth catching one in Tiahuanaco village. *Micros* to Guaqui and the Peruvian border leave from the plaza in Tiahuanaco village, or may be flagged down just west of the village – again, expect crowds.

Taxis to Tiahuanaco from La Paz cost around US$30 round-trip.

URMIRI

Urmiri lies at an elevation of 3800m in the Valle de Sapahaqui, 30km east of the La Paz–Oruro highway and 2½ hours southeast of La Paz. It features the mineral- and ion-rich **Termas de Urmiri** (Urmiri Hot Springs) which emerge from the source at 72°C, and to which the Hotel Gloria Urmiri owes its existence. This resort-style hotel boasts two outdoor pools, which are allowed to cool to a comfortable temperature.

Sleeping & Eating

The Hotel Gloria in La Paz runs the rustic but charming **Hotel Gloria Urmiri** (☎ 237-0010; La Paz ☎ 240-7070; www.hotelgloria bolivia.com; standard/luxury with bath US$15/20, camping US$1.35). Rates include breakfast and use of the hot springs and eucalyptus saunas. Aromatic herbal baths and several styles of massage are available. Luxury rooms have their own private Roman bath fed by the hot springs. Off-season, two-night, room-and-board package deals include transport and start at US$17 per person during the week and US$19 on weekends. Lunch and dinner cost US$5 each, and campers and nonguests may use the pools for US$2.50. Make accommodation and transport reservations at least two days in advance through the Hotel Gloria in La Paz (p65), and note that the pools are closed on Monday for cleaning.

Getting There & Away

The easiest way to reach Urmiri from La Paz is with Hotel Gloria's shuttle (US$6 per person round-trip), which leaves the hotel at least a couple of times a week in the morning.

To attempt to reach Urmiri independently, take a bus or *camión* from La Paz toward Oruro and get off near the bridge in Villa Loza, 70km south of La Paz and 15km north of Patacamaya. From here turn east along the unpaved road and pray for a lift, because if nothing is forthcoming, you're in for a very long walk.

Lake Titicaca

CONTENTS

LAKE TITICACA

Surprisingly reminiscent of the Aegean Sea, Lake Titicaca is an incongruous splash of sapphire amid the parched landscape of the Altiplano. Set in the rolling, scrub-covered hills in the heart of the high plains northwest of La Paz, South America's second-largest body of freshwater (after Venezuela's Lake Maracaibo) straddles the Peru–Bolivia border like a bridge between the two countries. Bolivians crudely but proudly proclaim that they got the 'titty' and Peru has the *caca*!

The lake is a remnant of the ancient inland sea known as Lago Ballivián, which covered much of the Altiplano before geological faults and evaporation brought about a drop in the water level. Its average dimensions are 230km long and 97km wide, but during recent flooding the water level rose several meters and inundated an additional 1000 sq km. Long rumored to be unfathomable, the depth of the lake has now been measured at up to 457m.

It's one of the world's highest major lakes, but ignore 'the world's highest navigable lake' claims, as both Peru and Chile have higher bodies of water that can be navigated by small craft.

LAKE TITICACA

TOP FIVE

- Join the revelry at one of several riotous annual fiestas in **Copacabana** (p93)
- Watch the sun set or moon rise over Lake Titicaca from tranquil **Yumani** (p100) on Isla del Sol
- Check out a baptism or *cha'lla* (vehicle blessing) at **Copacabana's cathedral** (p92)
- Walk the lakeshore from **Copacabana to Yampupata** (p97) and take a spin in a reed boat
- Trek **Isla del Sol** (p99) and enjoy spectacular lakeshore views, ancient ruins and lovely Mediterranean-like landscapes

★ Isla del Sol
★ Yampupata
★ Copacabana

| ■ TELEPHONE CODE: 02 | ■ AREA: 9000 SQ KM | ■ ELEVATION: 3820M |

HISTORY

When you first glimpse Lake Titicaca's crystalline, gemlike waters, beneath the looming backdrop of the Cordillera Real in the clear Altiplano light, you'll understand why pre-Inca people connected it with mystical events. These early inhabitants of the Altiplano believed that both the sun itself and their bearded, white leader/deity, Viracocha, had risen out of its mysterious depths, while the Incas believed that it was the birthplace of their civilization.

When the Spanish arrived in the mid-16th century, legends of treasure began to surface, including the tale that certain Incas, in desperation, had flung their gold into the lake to prevent the Spanish carting it off. Because of the obvious fluctuation in the water level, other rumors alleged that entire ruined cities existed beneath the surface.

Although evidence of submerged cities is inconclusive, archaeologists have discovered interesting finds around Isla Koa, north of Isla del Sol. These include 22 large stone boxes containing a variety of artifacts: a silver llama, some shell figurines and several types of incense burners.

Water-level changes from year to year are not uncommon, and previous fluctuations may have inundated other ruins and artifacts. In the floods of 1985 to 1986 highways, docks, fields and streets disappeared beneath the rising waters, adobe homes turned to mud and collapsed, and 200,000 people were displaced. It took several years for the Río Desaguadero, the lake's only outlet, to drain the flood waters.

CLIMATE

From February to November the climate around the lake is mostly pleasant and sunny, but there's often a cool wind off the lake and nights can be bitterly cold. Most of the rainfall occurs in midsummer (December and January).

GETTING THERE & AWAY

Lake Titicaca is a focal point for visitors from both Peru and Bolivia. Whether you arrive independently or with a tour, the journey between La Paz and Copacabana is

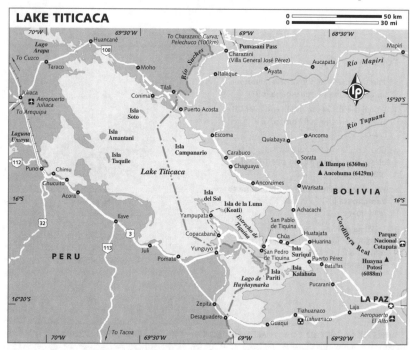

impressive. It follows a scenic route across the Altiplano and along the shoreline to the Tiquina Straits. Vehicles are ferried by barge across these straits, between San Pablo and San Pedro, while passengers ride in launches.

You can choose from several guided lake excursions that begin in La Paz and include a stop in Copacabana, usually around lunchtime, and there's a choice of hydrofoils, catamarans, launches and several types of land transportation (including tourist coaches and minibuses). If you have limited time, this is a quick way to 'do' Titicaca.

The most popular companies are Balsa Tours (p105) which offers motor excursions around the lake; Crillon Tours (p105), an upmarket agency with a hydrofoil service (the posh Posada del Inca complex on Isla del Sol is part of their business); and Transturin (p106), which runs day and overnight cruises in covered catamarans.

COPACABANA

pop 54,300 / elevation 3800m

The bright town of Copacabana on the southern shore of Lake Titicaca was established around a splendid bay between two hills. As a stopover along the Tiquina route between La Paz and Cuzco, it served as a site of religious pilgrimage for centuries, beginning with the Incas.

Copacabana is still well known for its fiestas, which bring this ordinarily sleepy place to life with pilgrims and visitors from all over Bolivia. At other times, it's visited mainly as a pleasant stopover between La Paz and Puno in Peru, and also serves as a convenient base for visits to Isla del Sol and Isla de la Luna.

History

After the fall and disappearance of the Tiahuanaco culture, the Kollas (Aymará) rose to power in the Titicaca region. Their most prominent deities included the sun and moon (who were considered husband and wife), the earth mother Pachamama and the ambient spirits known as *achachilas* and *apus*. Among the idols erected on the shores of the Manco Capac peninsula was Kota Kahuaña or Copacahuana ('lake view' in Aymará), an image with the head of a human and the body of a fish.

Once the Aymará had been subsumed into the Inca empire, Emperor Tupac Yupanqui founded the settlement of Copacabana as a wayside rest for pilgrims visiting the *huaca* (shrine). This site of human sacrifice (gulp!) was at the rock known as Titicaca (Rock of the Puma), at the northern end of Isla del Sol.

Before the arrival of Spanish priests in the mid-16th century, the Incas had divided local inhabitants into two distinct groups. Those faithful to the empire were known as Haransaya and were assigned positions of power. Those who resisted, the Hurinsaya, were relegated to manual labor. It was a separation which went entirely against the grain of the community-oriented Aymará culture, and the floods and crop failures that befell them in the 1570s were attributed to this social aberration.

This resulted in the rejection of the Inca religion, and the partial adoption of Christianity and establishment of the Santuario de Copacabana, which developed into a syncretic mishmash of both traditional and Christian premises. The populace elected La Santísima Virgen de Candelaria as its patron saint, and established a congregation in her honor. Noting the lack of an image for the altar, Francisco Tito Yupanqui, a direct descendant of the Inca emperor, fashioned an image of clay and placed it in the church. However his rude effort was deemed unsuitable to represent the honored patron of the village and was removed.

The sculptor, who was humiliated but not defeated, journeyed to Potosí to study arts. In 1582 he began carving a wooden image that took eight months to complete. In 1583 La Virgen Morena del Lago (The Dark Virgin of the Lake) was installed on the adobe altar at Copacabana, and shortly thereafter the miracles began. There were reportedly 'innumerable' early healings and Copacabana quickly became a pilgrimage site.

In 1605 the Augustinian priesthood advised the community to construct a cathedral commensurate with the power of the image. The altar was completed in 1614, but work on the building continued for 200 years. In 1805 the *mudéjar* (Moorish-style) cathedral was finally consecrated, although construction wasn't completed until 1820.

LAKE TITICACA

In 1925 Francisco Tito Yupanqui's image was canonized by the Vatican.

Orientation

Copacabana is set between two hills that offer views over both the town and the lake. All the action in 'Copa' centers around two main plazas and everything of interest is within walking distance. The main drag, 6 de Agosto, runs east to west. At its western end is the lake and a walkway (aka Costañera) which traces the lakeshore, past the two main plazas.

MAPS

The best map of Copacabana and Lake Titicaca is *Lago Titikaka* (US$2.50) by Freddy Ortiz. It is available for sale at better hotels and sometimes at the tourist office.

Information

BOOK EXCHANGE

La Cúpula hotel (☎ 862-2029; www.hotelcupula.com; Michel Peréz 1-3) and **Café Sol y Luna** (at Hotel Gloria; 16 de Julio & Manuel Mejía) have the best book exchanges and lending libraries (with many Lonely Planet guides).

INTERNET ACCESS

The best connections are available at the friendly **alf@net** (6 de Agosto & 16 de Julio; ⏱ 8am-10pm; US$2 per hr), which also has a café-bar, cheap video rentals and a couple of nice pool tables. Other similarly priced options include **Sol de Los Andes** (6 de Agosto) above Café Europa and **Ciber Copacabana** (6 de Agosto), half a block up from the lake.

LAUNDRY

Lavanderías are noticeably scarce. **Coyote** (east side of Plaza 2 de Febrero) charges around US$1.50 per kilo, but figure a few days for dry time. Otherwise try your hotel or keep an eye out for signs advertising handwashing services along 6 de Agosto.

LEFT LUGGAGE

Most hotels will hold luggage for free for customers for a few days while they visit Isla del Sol.

MEDICAL SERVICES

There is a basic hospital on the southern outskirts of town with medical and dental facilities, but for serious situations you're better off going to La Paz.

MONEY

There's no ATM in town. Casa de Cambio Copacabana, adjacent to Hotel Playa Azul, is open weekdays during business hours and on weekends until 1:30pm; it changes both cash (near official rates) and most brands of travelers checks (5% commission). Banco Unión with Western Union facilities changes travelers checks for a US$5 fee and does cash advances for a 3% fee. It's open daily except Monday (weekends until 1pm). Numerous *artesanía* shops also change US cash and travelers checks, but watch out for excessive commissions. You can buy *soles* at most *artesanía* shops, but you'll normally find better rates in Yunguyo, just beyond the Peruvian border. Street moneychangers sometimes operate near the cathedral.

PHOTOGRAPHY

With its constant stream of pilgrims and tourists, Copacabana is a good place to buy film. The vendors in front of the cathedral sell 36-exposure print film for US$2 and 36-exposure slide film for US$6. Reasonably priced, one-hour developing is available at the color lab on Calle Pando.

POST & TELEPHONE

Post office (north side of Plaza 2 de Febrero; ⏱ Tue-Sat 9am-noon & 2:30-6pm, Sun 9am-3pm) You may have to hunt for the attendant.
Entel (Plazuela Tito Yupanqui; ⏱ 7am-11pm) In a modern building behind the cathedral.

TOURIST INFORMATION

Tourist office (northeast cnr of Plaza 2 de Febrero) Has some informative brochures, but doesn't maintain reliable hours.

Dangers & Annoyances

Transit officials at Copacabana's highway police post *(tranca)* reportedly attempt to extract a petty 'entry tax' from tourists and pilgrims when they arrive, ostensibly a donation for the upkeep of the sanctuary and the Virgin. The church claims that they receive none of it.

Travelers entering from Peru continue to report spontaneous 'fines' for a variety of bogus infractions, including taking photos without a permit and carrying 'illegal' US dollars.

Be wary of light-fingered revelers, especially during festivals. Stand well back

LAKE TITICACA

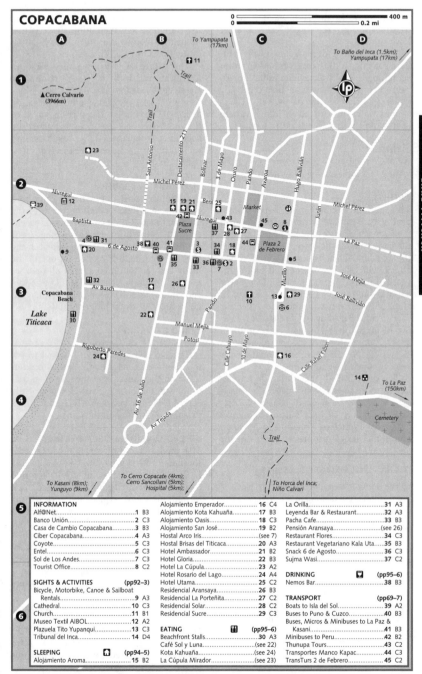

COPACABANA

during fireworks displays; when it comes to explosive fun, crowd safety takes a rather low priority.

The thin air and characteristically brilliant sunshine in this area combine to admit scorching levels of ultraviolet radiation. To minimize the risk, wear a hat, especially when you're out on the water. Hikers should watch out for an insidious variety of thorn bush that shreds skin on contact.

Sights

All of Copacabana's main attractions can be visited in a long but relaxing day.

CATHEDRAL

The sparkling white Moorish-style cathedral, with its *mudéjar* domes and colorful *azulejos* (blue Portuguese-style ceramic tiles), dominates the town. During festivals the cathedral's beautiful courtyard is often ablaze with the blooms of wild and cultivated flowers. Baptisms take place every Saturday at 4pm; check the noticeboard in front of the entrance for the mass schedule. The colorful **Benedicion de Movilidades** (blessing of automobiles) occurs daily at 10am and 2:30pm in front of the cathedral. For a requested US$1.35 per vehicle donation, it's a cheap alternative to insurance!

The cathedral's black Virgen de Candelaria statue **Camarín de la Virgen de Candelaria** (11am-noon & 2-6pm Mon-Fri, 8am-noon & 2-6pm Sat & Sun), carved by Inca Tupac Yupanqui's grandson, Francisco Yupanqui, is encased above the altar upstairs in the niche or *camarín*. The statue is never moved from the cathedral, as superstition suggests that its disturbance would precipitate a devastating flood of Lake Titicaca.

The cathedral is a repository for both European and local religious art and the **Museo de la Catedral** (admission US$0.30; 8am-noon & 2:30-6pm) contains some interesting articles. Don't miss the ostrich vases or the hundreds of paper cranes donated by a Japanese woman hedging her bets with the Virgin in the hope of bearing an intelligent child.

COPACABANA BEACH

OK, Bolivia's only public beach can't hold a candle to the better-known beach of the same name in Rio de Janeiro, but on weekends the festive atmosphere is a magnet for families. Along the shore you can sit in the sun, eat trout and drink beer in one of the many little restaurants, or rent all manner of sailing craft, bicycles (US$1.25 per hour) and motorbikes (US$5 per hour); bargain for reduced rates on longer rentals.

CERRO CALVARIO

The summit of Cerro Calvario can be reached in half an hour and is well worth the climb, especially in the late afternoon to watch the sunset over the lake. The trail to the summit begins near the **church** at the end of Calle Destacamento 211 and climbs past the 14 Stations of the Cross.

NIÑO CALVARIO & HORCA DEL INCA

The small but prominent hill **Niño Calvario**, southeast of town, is known variously as Little Calvary, Seroka and by its original name, Kesanani. Its weirdly rugged rock formations merit exploration. From near the end of Calle Murillo, a signposted trail leads uphill to the **Horca del Inca** (Inca Gallows; admission US$1.35), an odd trilithic gate perched on the hillside. This pre-Inca observatory is surrounded by pierced rocks that permit the sun's rays to pass through onto the lintel during the solstices. Foreigners approaching the site may also find themselves besieged by aspiring young guides.

CERRO SANCOLLANI & CERRO COPACATE

The higher hill behind Niño Calvario, **Cerro Sancollani**, is flanked by Inca-era *asientos* (seats), agricultural terraces and numerous

---

CHA'LLA – A RITUAL BLESSING

The word *cha'lla* is used for any ritual blessing, toasting or offering to the powers that be, whether Inca, Aymará or Christian. On weekend mornings in front of Copacabana's cathedral, cars, trucks and buses are decked out in garlands of real or plastic flowers, colored ribbons, flags and even stuffed ducks. Petitions for protection are made to the Virgin, and a ritual offering of alcohol is poured over the vehicle, thereby consecrating it for the journey home. The vehicle *cha'lla* is especially popular with pilgrims and long-distance bus companies with new fleets between Good Friday and Easter Sunday.

unrestored and little-known ruins. To get here, follow Calle Murillo to its end, where it becomes a cobbled road. After 50m a crumbling stone route (which might once have served as an irrigation aqueduct) leads off to the left about 1m above the road level. The easiest access to the summit is from the saddle between it and Niño Calvario.

A further 4km down this road toward Kasani lies **Cerro Copacate**, which features pre-Inca ruins and pictographs. The best known is the **Escudo de la Cultura Chiripa**, a unique icon attributed to the pre-Inca Chiripa culture.

TRIBUNAL DEL INCA (INTIKALA)

North of the cemetery on the southeastern outskirts of town is a field of artificially sculpted boulders known as the **Inca Tribunal** (admission free; ☺ 9am-noon & 1-5pm). Its original purpose is unknown, but there are several carved stones with *asientos*, basins and *hornecinos* (niches), which probably once contained idols. During the rainy season, the place hops with thousands of tiny frogs.

KUSILLATA & BAÑO DEL INCA

A 2km walk along the shoreline from the end of Calles Junín or Hugo Ballivián leads to a colonial manor building known as **Kusillata** (admission US$0.50), where there's a small archaeological display. Hours vary but weekends are the best time to find someone to let you in. The pre-Columbian tunnel beside the manor was originally used to access the subterranean water supply. The carved-stone water tank and tap are known as the **Baño del Inca** (Inca Bath).

MUSEO TEXTIL AIBOL

The new museum of **Arte Indigena Bolivia** (AIBOL; ☎ 719-59611; Jáuregui 5; admission by donation) features colorful, well-preserved examples of pre-Columbian weavings, textiles and other antiquities from the 16th century to the present.

Tours

A number of tour agencies, most clustered on the corner of 6 de Agosto and 16 de Julio, organize tours around Copacabana's environs. They change names frequently and they all offer roughly the same things, so there's little use in running down a long list. The most popular tour is the half- or full-day trip to Isla del Sol with departures at 8am and 1:30pm daily. You can also buy Peruvian train tickets at these agencies.

Festivals & Events

Copacabana hosts several major annual fiestas. The town also celebrates the **La Paz departmental anniversary** on July 15. Wednesday and Sunday are market days.

JANUARY

One local tradition is the blessing of miniature objects, like miniature cars or houses, at the **Alasitas festival** (January 24) as a prayer that the real thing will be obtained in the coming year. These miniatures are sold in stalls around the Plaza Sucre and at the top of Cerro Calvario.

FEBRUARY

From February 2 to 5, the **Fiesta de la Virgen de Candelaria** honors the patron saint of Copacabana and all Bolivia. Although the feast day is celebrated to varying degrees around Bolivia, Copacabana stages an especially big bash, and pilgrims and dancers come from Peru and around Bolivia. Traditional Aymará dances are performed, and there's much music, drinking and feasting. On the third day celebrations culminate with the gathering of 100 bulls in a stone corral along the Yampupata road, and the town's braver (and drunker) citizens jump into the arena and try to avoid being attacked.

MARCH/APRIL

On **Good Friday** the town fills with pilgrims – a few of whom make the 158km journey from La Paz on foot – to do penance at the Stations of the Cross on Cerro Calvario. Beginning at the cathedral at dusk pilgrims join a solemn candlelit procession through town, led by a statue of Christ in a glass coffin and a replica of the Virgen de Candelaria. Once on the summit they light incense and purchase miniatures representing material possessions in the hope that they will be granted the actual by the Virgin during the year. A local priest relates the significance of the holiday through a microphone, a military band plays dirges and the city hall's audio system broadcasts 'Ave Maria' for all to hear.

MAY
Fiesta de la Cruz (Feast of the Cross) is celebrated over the first weekend in May all around the lake, but the biggest festivities are in Copacabana.

AUGUST
Copacabana stages its biggest event, **Bolivian Independence Day**, during the first week in August. It's characterized by pilgrimages, round-the-clock music, parades, brass bands, fireworks and amazing alcohol consumption.

Sleeping

During fiestas accommodations are full and prices increase up to threefold; at other times Copacabana is Bolivia's least expensive town for accommodations. Despite its proximity to the lake Copacabana's water (and electric) supply is unpredictable. Better hotels go to extreme efforts to fill water tanks in the morning (the supply is normally switched off at 11am).

BUDGET
Hostal Emperador (☎ 862-2083, La Paz ☎ 228-1251; Murillo 235; US$1.35, with bath US$2) This budget travelers' choice is an upbeat and colorfully speckled place, which has hot showers all day and a raft of extras, including laundry service, a small shared kitchen, luggage storage and a sunny mezzanine that's ideal for lounging. You can even order breakfast in bed. It's often full but they are building a new annex across the street with private bathrooms.

Residencial Sucre (☎ 862-2080; Murillo 228; US$3.35, with bath US$4.65) Ever expanding, this option feels more like a mid-range hotel (with color national TV, room service, carpeted rooms, reliable hot water, etc) than a budget place. It's often recommended for its friendliness and machine laundry service.

Hotel Utama (☎ 862-2013; Michel Peréz s/n; r per person with bath & breakfast US$5) A comfortable and good-value hotel, applauded for its breakfasts; it often absorbs the overflow from the nearby La Cúpula.

Residencial Aransaya (☎ 862-2229; 6 de Agosto 121; US$2) Quite comfortable rooms, an inviting sunny patio and a restaurant which is popular with the locals.

Residencial La Porteñita (☎ 862-2006; Jáuregui at Pando; US$2, with bath US$2.65) A friendly choice with clean rooms, a sundrenched court-

yard and a well-traveled, English-speaking owner.

Alojamiento Kota Kahuaña (Busch 15; US$1.35, with bath US$2) A mellow, family-run option near the lake. It's basic but friendly, and there's (usually) hot water all day. There are shared kitchen facilities and some upstairs rooms enjoy lake views.

Residencial Solar (☎ 862-2009; Jáuregui 140; US$2, with bath US$3.35) If you don't mind tiny rooms (ask for No 1), the friendly Solar is a good choice. The spacious rooftop patio has panoramic lake views and full exposure to the sun. There are only a few shared showers, but the water is hot 24/7.

Hostal Arco Iris (☎ 862-2247; 6 de Agosto at Oruro; US$2) Increasingly popular with comfortable rooms and an attached dining room.

Alojamiento Aroma (☎ 862-2004; Jáuregui at 16 de Julio; US$1.35) This oddly designed but friendly pad has cozy top-floor doubles that open onto a sunlit patio with tables and a superb lake view.

Alojamiento Oasis (☎ 862-2037; Pando at 6 de Agosto; US$1.35, with bath US$2) Yes, it's dominated by a multicolored pastel paint job and can get noisy, especially when family members switch on the TV, but the rooms (some with carpet) are decent and hot water pours from the communal showers at all hours. Request room No 14.

Alojamiento San José (☎ 862-2066; Jáuregui 146; US$1.35) A no-frills choice that supposedly has hot water all day. Unfortunately, the sunny terrace overlooks a chronically hectic bus-parking area.

Hotel Ambassador (☎ 862-2216, La Paz ☎ 224-3382; Jáuregui at Bolívar; r per person with bath & TV US$5.35-6) It's not that friendly, but the rooms are comfortable and the facilities are a step up from the cheaper places that dominate in town. A limited number of space heaters are available upon request. Note that it's no longer an HI-affiliate.

Hostal Brisas del Titicaca (☎ 862-2178, La Paz ☎ 245-3022; hbrisastiticaca@hotmail.com; 6 de Agosto at Costañera; US$3.35, with bath US$4.65; 🖵) Right on the beach this new HI-affiliate is good value, with very amenable (albeit retro 1970s) rooms. A few rooms with shared baths don't have windows, but several others with private baths have their own lake-view terraces with good views.

Although the slopes around Copacabana are generally steep and rocky, there are several excellent free wild camping sites. The summits of both Niño Calvario and Cerro Sancollani have smooth, grassy saddle areas with magnificent views. There's also a pleasant campsite at the high point along the Inca road toward Kasani (the Peruvian border), 1km from the end of Calle Murillo.

MID-RANGE & TOP END

La Cúpula (☎ 862-2029; www.hotelcupula.com; Michel Pérez 1-3; s US$6-12, d US$8-17, tr US$20, with bath US$14-20, US$20-24, US$28) Gleaming white domes mark this much-lauded oasis on the slopes of Cerro Calvario, overlooking the lake. None of the 17 rooms are alike; all are inviting. Guests enjoy access to the TV/video room, library and shared kitchen and laundry facilities, and the attached Mirador restaurant (below) is a favorite. The grounds include shady spots with hammocks for reading and relaxing. The helpful staff speak several languages and are full of travel tips. There's a sweet honeymoon suite (US$32). No matter what room you end up in, you'll be glad you booked ahead via the website.

Hotel Gloria (☎ 862-2094, La Paz ☎ 237-0010; 16 de Julio & Manuel Mejía; www.hotelgloriabolivia.com; without/with views US$14/20) This large yet inviting ex-prefectural hotel has been tastefully upgraded and offers a lovely view of the lake and surrounding mountains. It's dead quiet during the week but springs to life on weekends. Clean, spacious rooms with private baths and lake views (some even have sundecks) include breakfast, and good-value all-inclusive packages are available. There's billiards and table tennis upstairs and the Café Sol y Luna (p96) downstairs.

Hotel Rosario del Lago (☎ 862-2141, La Paz ☎ 245-1341; www.travelperubolivia.com; Paredes at Costañera; s/d/tr/ste US$36/47/63/87; 🖥) The neocolonial, three-star sister of Hotel Rosario in La Paz is the nicest place in town. The small but charming rooms all have solar-heated showers and lake views, and a breakfast buffet in the classy Kota Kahuaña restaurant (below). Rates rise 10% to 20% in high season.

Eating & Drinking

The local specialty is *trucha criolla* (salmon trout) from Lake Titicaca. The fish were introduced in 1939 by foreign pisciculturists in order to increase protein content in the local diet. For years the trout were also canned and exported, but that ended when fish stocks became severely depleted. Although dozens of tourist-oriented places serve trout, the best seem to be Kala Uta, La Cúpula, Kota Kahuaña and Sujma Wasi which are listed below.

Nearly every place in town now serves breakfast in its many incarnations.

RESTAURANTS

Restaurant Vegetariano Kala Uta (☎ 862-2332; 6 de Agosto at 16 de Julio; set meals under US$2, mains US$2-4) An artsy, appealing Andean atmosphere pervades Copa's most original, family-run vegetarian option. Imaginative breakfasts include the *poder Andino* (Andean power), which features *quinoa* pancakes topped with jam, bananas, yogurt, brazil nuts, raisins and coconut, accompanied by an Andean grain drink, fruit juice or coffee. Set vegetarian lunches and dinners, and the huge creative salads are highlights. The Andean salad is most unusual: potatoes, oca, *quinoa*, toasted fava beans, tomatoes and peanut sauce. They also do trout, pasta and pizza.

Sujma Wasi (☎ 862-2091; Jáuregui 127; set meals US$1.50-3, mains US$3-5) With delightful courtyard tables and a rustic interior, 'your friend's home' offers a varied menu including many Bolivian, vegetarian and international specialties for breakfast, lunch and dinner. Allow enough time to savor the meal and appreciate the lovely wooden tables, simple ceramic dishes and tasteful Andean décor. For desert, try the unique homemade *licor de coca* (coca leaf liquor) or something from the full bar.

La Cúpula Mirador restaurant (☎ 862-2029; www.hotelcupula.com; Michel Peréz 1-3; 🕑 closed Tue morning; mains US$2.50-4) The glassy surroundings admit lots of Altiplano light and maximize the fabulous view of the lake. There's an excellent vegetarian range with something for meat eaters too. Plan on spending around US$5 for a memorable meal.

La Orilla (The Water's Edge; 6 de Agosto s/n; mains US$2-4) This is another creative winner, especially at dinnertime. There's heating, a full bar and huge portions of pasta pesto, stuffed trout and coconut curry.

Kota Kahuaña (☎ 862-2141, La Paz ☎ 245-1341; at Hotel Rosario del Lago, Paredes at Costañera; mains US$4-7) Hotel Rosario del Lago's restaurant, the most expensive one in town, has a good salad bar and a select range of imaginatively prepared main courses that justifies its prices. It's a romantic place for a fine meal with wine and a lake view. Be aware that when tour groups take over the dining room, the service suffers.

Pensión Aransaya (☎ 862-2229; at Residencial Aransaya, 6 de Agosto 121; set meals US$1-2, fish US$3) Super-friendly local favorite for a tall, cold beer and trout heaped with all the trimmings.

Leyenda Bar & Restaurant (☎ 862-2288; Costañera at Busch; ⏰ 10am-11pm; mains US$2-4) Lakefront place open all day, with good music and a wide variety of local (trout) and international (pizza) dishes, plus juice and cocktails. Upstairs they have a few rooms with private bath (US$4 per person) and a suite with a balcony and lake views (US$8 per person).

QUICK EATS
Snack 6 de Agosto (☎ 862-2114; 6 de Agosto near Oruro) The service may be crusty but the food is well prepared, and the patio seating can be heavenly on a sunny day. The *pejerrey* is especially recommended, as are the breakfasts and the specialty, suckling pig.

Restaurant Flores (6 de Agosto at Oruro) Frequently recommended by readers, Flores is a great place to spend a mellow afternoon lingering over a *Paceña* while letter writing. And, of course, they serve trout.

Pacha Café (6 de Agosto at Bolívar; set meals US$1.35, mains US$1-4) A cozy, popular spot for light meals and good pizza. It also has a bar and occasional live entertainment.

On the waterfront, a row of informal beachfront stalls sells snacks and drinks. The stalls are especially pleasant on weekends, when you can sip a drink and observe the quintessential Bolivian beach life.

As usual, the bargain basement is the market comedor, where numerous eateries compete fiercely for your business. You can eat a generous meal of trout or beef for a pittance, while a contingent of the town's canine population patiently awaits handouts. If you're up to an insulin shock in the morning, treat yourself to a breakfast of hot *api morado* and syrupy *buñuelos*.

CAFES & PUBS
New nightspots come and go as frequently as tour boats. Wander along 6 de Agosto towards the water to see what's new. The following are established traveler favorites.

The atmospheric, kickback **Café Sol y Luna** (at Hotel Gloria; 16 de Julio & Manuel Mejía; ⏰ 6pm-late, happy hour 7-9pm) has java drinks, bar munchies and good cocktails, plus satellite TV, board games and a groovin' by-request CD library.

Nemos Bar (6 de Agosto 684) is a warm, dimly lit, late-night hangout run by British Bolivians and is a popular place for a tipple.

Shopping
Local specialties include handmade miniatures of *totora* reed boats, unusual varieties of Andean potatoes, and *pasankalla* (puffed choclo corn with caramel). This last item is a South American version of popcorn that, if crispy, can be fairly palatable. You'll also find dozens of shops selling llama- and alpaca-wool sweaters for fair prices; a nice alpaca piece will cost around US$10. Vehicle adornments used in the *cha'lla*, miniatures and religious paraphernalia are sold in stalls in front of the cathedral.

Getting There & Away
TO/FROM LA PAZ
Trans Manco Kapac (☎ 862-2234, La Paz ☎ 245-9045) and **TransTurs 2 de Febrero** (☎ 862-2233, La Paz ☎ 245-3035) both have several daily connections from La Paz' cemetery district via Tiquina to Copacabana (US$2, 3½ hours), with extra weekend departures. Both booking offices are near Plaza 2 de Febrero, but buses sometimes arrive at and depart near Plaza Sucre. More comfortable (but often more crowded) nonstop tour buses from La Paz to Copacabana cost as little as US$2 to US$5 in high season.

TO/FROM PERU
Many tour buses go all the way to Puno (Peru), and you can arrange to break the journey in Copacabana and then continue with the same agency. You can do just the Copa–Puno leg (US$3 to US$4, three to four hours) or go all the way to Cuzco (US$9.50, 15 hours) – book ahead. These buses depart and arrive in Copacabana from Av 6 de Agosto.

To reach Peru, either book a direct minibus through a tour agency (US$2.50, 2½ hours) or catch a public minibus from Plaza Sucre to the border at Kasani (US$0.35, 15 minutes). After crossing the border, you'll find frequent onward transport to

Yunguyo (US$0.25, five minutes) and Puno (US$2, 2½ hours), but be warned that the buses get quite crowded and you may not have a seat. If you're headed straight to Cuzco, check out any of the Copacabana agencies offering tickets on the daily buses (they also offer efficient bus journeys to Arequipa, Lima and other Peruvian destinations). The least expensive seems to be **Thunupa Tours** (La Paz ☎ 278-4130; at Residencial Copacabana, Oruro 555), which charges around US$9 for the 12-hour trip (most others charge a negotiable US$10 to US$15). All require layover (two to three hours) in Puno, which will give you time to change money.

Note that Peruvian time is one hour behind Bolivian time. For further information on travel to and around the Peruvian portion of Lake Titicaca and beyond, see Lonely Planet's *Peru*.

TO/FROM ISLA DEL SOL

The days of haggling over transport to Isla del Sol are effectively over. Now you just go down to the beach in the morning and buy a ticket (around US$3) from one of the cooperative offices. For details, see p103.

COPACABANA TO YAMPUPATA TREK

A particularly enjoyable way of reaching Isla del Sol is to trek from Copacabana along the lakeshore to the village of **Yampupata**, which lies just a short boat ride from the ruins of Pilko Kaina on Isla del Sol. If you're arriving from La Paz, this three- to four-hour walk will help accustom your lungs to the altitude, and the glorious scenery along the way presents a suitable prologue to a couple of days' trekking around Isla del Sol.

For a longer trek you can opt to walk the pre-Hispanic route from **Cruce Paquipujio**, near the Tiquina Straits. This route passes through the village of Chisi, where there's a *templete semisubterráneo* (sunken temple) that dates back to the pre-Tiahuanaco Chavín culture. The route then continues through San Francisco, Chachacoyas, Kollasuyos, Santa Ana and the lovely cobblestoned village of Sampaya, on the hilltop about 5km from Yampupata. This route joins up with the Copacabana to Yampupata trek at Titicachi.

The Route

From **Copacabana**, strike out northeast along the road running across the flat plain. After about 40 minutes, the road turns sharp left and climbs gently onto a ledge overlooking the lake. About one to 1½ hours from Copacabana, you'll pass the isolated **Hinchaca fish hatchery** in the forest on your left. Beyond the hatchery cross the stream on your left and follow the Inca road up the steep hill. Just above the stream you'll pass the **Gruta de Lourdes** (aka Gruta de Fátima), a cave that for locals evokes images of its French or Portuguese namesake, respectively. This stretch includes some fine stone paving and provides a considerable shortcut, rejoining the main road at the crest of the hill.

From here the road passes through more populated areas. At the fork just below the crest of the hill bear left and descend to the shore and into the village of **Titicachi**, where there's a shop selling soft drinks and staple items.

In and around Titicachi are several sites of interest, among them the **Tiahuanacota Inca cemetery**, some pre-Inca walls and, on the offshore islet of Jiskha Huata, the **Museo de Aves Acuáticos** (Museum of Aquatic Birds). This small display of Lake Titicaca birdlife is reached only by boat. While you're in the area, look in the reeds for the live versions.

At the next village, **Sicuani**, the amenable Mamani family run the Hostal Yampu. Basic accommodations with bucket showers cost US$1 per person, and meals are US$1 each. Hikers can pop in for a beer or soft drink, and you can take a spin around the bay in a *totora* reed boat for US$1.50 per person.

Three to four hours from Copacabana, you'll reach **Yampupata**, a collection of lakefront adobe houses where you can camp on the beach or hire a motorboat for a minimum of US$8, or a rowboat for around US$3 for two people, to take you across the **Estrecho de Yampupata** to the **Pilko Kaina** ruins (p99) or the **Escalera del Inca** (p100). If you opt for the Escalera del Inca, make sure that's where you're dropped off; some boat owners may well try to drop you at Pilko Kaina anyway. Also, resist attempts to add extra charges, such as invented 'landing fees'.

Getting There & Away

For those who don't want to walk, the easiest ways to travel between Yampupata and

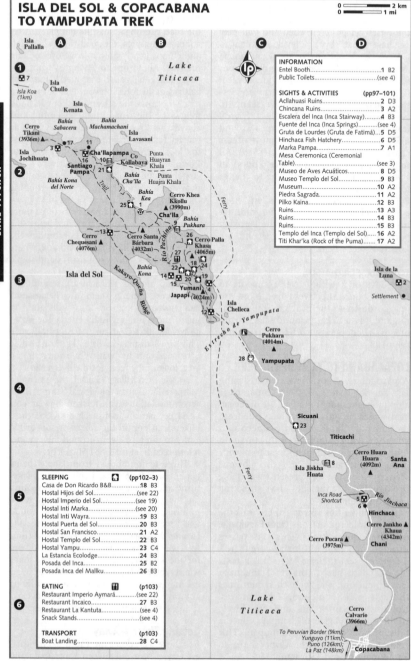

ISLA DEL SOL & COPACABANA TO YAMPUPATA TREK

0 —————— 2 km
0 —————— 1 mi

INFORMATION
Entel Booth.....................................1 B2
Public Toilets..............................(see 4)

SIGHTS & ACTIVITIES   (pp97–101)
Acllahuasi Ruins.............................2 D3
Chincana Ruins.............................3 A2
Escalera del Inca (Inca Stairway)....4 B3
Fuente del Inca (Inca Springs)........(see 4)
Gruta de Lourdes (Gruta de Fatimá)...5 D5
Hinchaca Fish Hatchery..................6 D5
Marka Pampa..................................7 A1
Mesa Ceremonica (Ceremonial
Table)..(see 3)
Museo de Aves Acuáticos...............8 D5
Museo Templo del Sol....................9 B3
Museum......................................10 A2
Piedra Sagrada.............................11 A2
Pilko Kaina.................................12 B3
Ruins..13 A3
Ruins..14 B3
Ruins..15 B3
Templo del Inca (Templo del Sol)...16 A2
Titi Khar'ka (Rock of the Puma).....17 A2

SLEEPING   (pp102–3)
Casa de Don Ricardo B&B.............18 B3
Hostal Hijos del Sol.....................(see 22)
Hostal Imperio del Sol...............(see 19)
Hostal Inti Marka.......................(see 20)
Hostal Inti Wayra.........................19 B3
Hostal Puerta del Sol....................20 B3
Hostal San Francisco.....................21 A2
Hostal Templo del Sol...................22 B3
Hostal Yampu.............................23 C4
La Estancia Ecolodge....................24 B3
Posada del Inca.........................25 B3
Posada Inca del Mallku................26 B3

EATING   (p103)
Restaurant Imperio Aymará...........(see 22)
Restaurant Incaico.......................27 B3
Restaurant La Kantuta.................(see 4)
Snack Stands..............................(see 4)

TRANSPORT   (p103)
Boat Landing...............................28 C4

Copacabana are by infrequent camión or by minibus (US$0.50, 30 minutes) which run most frequently on market days (Sunday and Thursday). On most days there's a bus from the corner of Junín and Michel Pérez in Copacabana at around 11am and from Yampupata in the afternoon.

ISLA DEL SOL

The Island of the Sun was known to early inhabitants as Titi Khar'ka (Rock of the Puma) from which Lake Titicaca takes its name. This island has been identified as the birthplace of several revered entities, including the sun itself. There the bearded white leader/deity Viracocha and the first Incas, Manco Capac and his sister/wife Mama Ocllo, mystically appeared under direct orders from the sun. In fact, most modern-day Aymará and Quechua peoples of Peru and Bolivia accept these legends as their creation story.

Isla del Sol's 2500 permanent residents are distributed between the main settlements of **Cha'llapampa**, near the island's northern end; **Cha'lla**, which backs up to a lovely sandy beach on the central east coast; and **Yumani**, which straddles the ridge above the Escalera del Inca.

With a host of ancient ruins, tiny traditional villages, beautiful walking routes and a distinctly Aegean look, Isla del Sol merits a couple of days. Visitors can wander through the ruins at the island's northern and southern ends; explore the island's dry slopes, covered with sweet-smelling *koa* (incense) brush; and hike over the ancient *pampas* (terraces), which are still cultivated.

There are no vehicles on Isla del Sol, so visitors are limited to hiking or traveling by boat. The main ports are at **Pilko Kaina**, the **Escalera del Inca** in Yumani and near the **Templo del Inca** and **Chincana** ruins at Cha'llapampa. There's also a small port at **Japapi** on the southwest coast.

Extensive networks of walking tracks make exploration easy, except the 4000m altitude may take its toll. You can do a walking circuit of the main sights in a long day, but if you have the time, devote a day each to the northern and southern ends. Hikers should carry lunch and ample water. The sun was born here and is still going strong; a good sunscreen is essential, particularly by the water.

A BOLIVIAN ATLANTIS?

At low tide an innocuous-looking column of rock peeps just a few centimeters above Lake Titicaca's surface, north of Isla del Sol. Most locals dismiss it as a natural, stone column, similar to many others along the shoreline. In 1992 stone boxes containing artifacts (including several made of pure gold) were discovered at the underwater site known as **Marka Pampa** (aka La Ciudad Submergida). In August 2000 further excavations near the site revealed a massive stone temple, winding pathways and a surrounding wall, all about 8m underwater. Although it remains unclear who was responsible for the structures, it has been postulated that they are of Inca origin. Investigations are ongoing.

Visitors who arrive on whirlwind tours almost invariably depart wishing they had more time to come to grips with this magical place. While a full-day tour provides a decent introduction to the island (the half-day tour is strictly for the been-there-done-that crowd), most travelers will want to allow at least a night or two on the island.

Southern Half
PILKO KAINA

This prominent ruins complex (admission US$0.65) near the southern tip of the island sits well camouflaged against a steep terraced slope. The best-known site is the two-level **Palacio del Inca** which is thought to have been constructed by the Incan Emperor Tupac Yupanqui. The rectangular windows and doors taper upward from their sill and thresholds to narrower lintels that cover them on top. The arched roof vault was once covered with flagstone shingles and then reinforced with a layer of mud and straw.

Ask the ticket-taker at the ruins about the possibility of basic lodging next door to the ruins if you don't feel up to walking the rest of the way to Yumani. Your admission ticket may also be valid for entry to the museum between Cha'lla and Yumani, depending on whether the two communities are fighting or cooperating with each other when you arrive.

FUENTE DEL INCA

Early Spaniards believed Yumani's spring was a fountain of youth, and for the Incas the three streams represented their national motto: *Ama sua, ama llulla, ama khella*, meaning 'Don't steal, don't lie, don't be lazy'. Today, the fountain is a crucial source of water for locals, who come daily with their donkeys to fetch water and carry it up the steep trail.

FUENTE DEL INCA & ESCALERA DEL INCA

About 30 minutes' walk north of Pilko Kaina, incongruous streams of fresh water gush from the natural spring **Fuente del Inca** and pour down three artificial stone channels alongside a beautifully constructed Inca-era staircase **Escalera del Inca**; the springs feed a lovely terraced and cultivated water garden.

YUMANI

Yumani's small church, **Iglesia de San Antonio**, serves the southern half of the island. Nearby you'll find a growing cluster of guesthouses and fabulous views over the water to Isla de la Luna. You can also climb to the ridge for a view down to the deep sapphire-colored **Bahía Kona** on the western shore. From the crest you'll find routes leading downhill to the village of **Japapi** and north along the ridge to Cha'llapampa and the Chincana ruins.

About midway up the hill between the Fuente del Inca and the ridge, a short side track leads north to the **Inti Wata Cultural Complex**, which is only open to clients of the Transturin catamaran tours and includes the Ekako underground archaeological and anthropological museum, an Andean botanical garden, captive llamas and a typical Aymará house.

With extra time you can make your way over the isthmus and up onto the prominent **Kakayo–Queña Ridge**, the island's southwestern extremity. The serene walk along the ridge to the **lighthouse** on the southern tip and back takes at least half a day from Yumani.

CHA'LLA

This agreeable little village, the site of the island's secondary school, stretches along a magnificent sandy beach that appears to be taken straight out of a holiday brochure for the Greek islands. It's a great place to soak up the sun and watch people playing soccer and families strolling. Literally 1m off the sand is the popular snack bar and **Posada del Inca** guesthouse (p102).

In the pastoral valley over the low pass between Cha'lla and Yumani is a **Museo Templo de Sol** (admission US$1.35), with exhibits that reveal the history and lifestyle of the hardy Aymará people who inhabit the Altiplano region. Depending on the political climate this ticket may or may not be good for the southern tip of the island.

Northern Half

There are two major routes between the northern and southern ends of Isla del Sol. The lower route winds scenically through fields, hamlets and villages, and around the bays and headlands above the eastern coast. The more dramatic ridge route begins on the crest in Yumani and heads north, roughly following the uninhabited ridge to the Chincana ruins. The views down to both coasts of the island are nothing short of spectacular. About half an hour from Yumani, you'll reach a four-way trail junction: the track to the left leads to the shore at Bahía Kona, the one to the right descends to Bahía Kea, and straight ahead it continues along the ridge to the ruins.

CHA'LLAPAMPA

Most boat tours visiting the northern ruins land at Cha'llapampa, which straddles a slender isthmus. The wall dividing the village from the Co Kollabaya peninsula was designed to keep people out of the planted area on the peninsula; in the growing season, children aren't allowed there lest they trample the precious crops.

The main attraction is the well-presented **museum** (admission US$1.35) of artifacts excavated in 1992 from **Marka Pampa** (see the boxed text, p99), an archaeological site under 8m of water, at the center of a triangle formed by the islands of Chullo, Koa and Pallalla. It's fancifully referred to by locals as *la ciudad submergida* (the sunken city), in reference to a legend that a city and temple existed between the islands of Koa and Pallalla in an age when the lake level was lower than it is today.

This small museum displays a boggling variety of interesting stuff: anthropomorphic figurines, animal bones, Tiahuanaco-era artifacts, skull parts, puma-shaped ceramic *koa* censers and cups resembling Monty Python's Holy Grail. Most interesting, however, are the Marka Pampa stone boxes and their contents, all made of gold: a medallion, a cup, a puma and a woman. The boxes were so expertly carved and capped that their contents remained dry until their relatively recent discovery.

It's normally open only in the mornings when there are tour groups about; in the afternoon, try asking around for Señor Hiriberto Ticoma, who has the key and may or may not be willing to open it for you (and once you're in, don't let anyone charge you extra to use the toilet). Keep your ticket, because it's also good for entry to the Chincana ruins (and visa versa).

PIEDRA SAGRADA & TEMPLO DEL INCA
From Cha'llapampa, the Chincana route continues parallel to the beach, climbing gently along an ancient route to the isthmus at **Santiago Pampa** (Kasapata).

Immediately east of the trail an odd, artificially carved boulder stands upright in a small field. This is known as the **Piedra Sagrada** (Sacred Stone). There are theories that it was used as an execution block for those convicted of wrongdoing or as a *huaca* (a rainmaking stone), but no one is entirely certain of its purpose. Today its main function seems to be as a picnic table. Flagging tourists can rest here, put their feet up and enjoy cold beers and sandwiches, which are served up by an enterprising local.

Over the track, just southwest of the Piedra Sagrada, are the ancient walls of the complex known as the **Templo del Inca**, also called the Templo del Sol. Although little remains of this temple built for an unknown purpose, it contains the only Bolivian examples of expert Inca stonework comparable to the renowned walls found in Cuzco.

CHINCANA RUINS & TITI KHAR'KA
The island's most spectacular ruins complex, the **Chincana ruins**, (admission US$1.35) lies near the island's northern tip. Its main feature is the **Palacio del Inca**, also known as El Laberinto (Labyrinth) or by its Aymará name, Incanotapa. This maze of stone walls and tiny doorways overlooks a lovely white beach lapped by deep blue waters.

About 150m southeast of the ruins is the **Mesa Ceremónica** (Ceremonial Table), which also happens to be a convenient picnic spot. It's thought to have been the site of human and animal sacrifice. East of the table stretches the large rock known as Titicaca – or more accurately, **Titi Khar'ka**, the Rock of the Puma – which is featured in the Inca creation legend. The name is likely to derive from its shape which, when viewed from the southeast, resembles a crouching puma.

Three natural features on the rock's western face also figure in legend. Near the northern end is one dubbed the **Cara de Viracocha** (Face of Viracocha), which takes some imagination to distinguish – it could be the face of a puma. At the southern end are four distinctive elongated niches. The two on the right are locally called the **Refugio del Sol** (Refuge of the Sun) and those on the left, the **Refugio de la Luna** (Refuge of the Moon). According to tradition it was here during the Chamaj Pacha (Times of Flood and Darkness), that the sun made its first appearance, and later Manco Capac and Mama Ocllo appeared and founded the Inca empire.

In the surface stone immediately south of the rock you'll pass the **Huellas del Sol** (Footprints of the Sun). These natural markings resemble footprints and have inspired the notion that they were made by the sun after its birth on Titicaca Rock.

A ticket from the museum in Cha'llapampa also covers entry to the Chincana ruins and vice versa. Most north-end tours begin at the boat landing in Cha'llapampa and follow the prominent Inca route past the Piedra Sagrada and Templo del Inca to the Chincana ruins. Another access route is along the ridge from Yumani. When you reach a point directly above Cha'llapampa, leave the main trail and continue straight ahead along a jumble of light tracks for 2km, picking your route through the maze of goat tracks over shrub-covered slopes (mostly below the ridge) and around bizarre rock outcrops.

Tours
Numerous Copacabana tour agencies offer informal Isla del Sol tours (half day/full day US$2/3.35). Launches embark from the beach around 8am and stop at the Escalera

LAKE TITICACA

del Inca to drop off passengers before continuing north to Cha'llapampa. They allow just enough time to hike up to the Chincana ruins, then return to the Escalera del Inca and Pilko Kaina. Some full-day tours also buzz over to Isla de la Luna (for an extra US$2 or US$3) for a quick look around before returning to Copacabana.

Those who wish to hike can get off at Cha'llapampa in the morning and walk south to the Escalera del Inca, rejoining the tour in the afternoon. Alternatively you can opt to stay overnight or longer on the island, which is highly recommended, then find your own way back to Copacabana.

Turisbus (www.travelperubolivia.com), at the Hotel Rosario del Lago (p95), offers guided half-day trips (US$19) to the southern end of the island, including a ride on a reed boat at Sicuani and admission to the ruins and museum. As well they do a full-day tour (US$35) that also takes in the northern end of Isla del Sol.

Sleeping

The most scenic place to stay is Yumani – as it is high on the ridge – where there are a growing number of guesthouses. On arrival you'll likely be met by kids who, for a small tip, will help you find a place to rest your head. You can wild camp just about anywhere on the island. It's best to set up away from villages, avoiding cultivated land. There are plenty of deserted beaches and the island's western slopes are especially appealing and secluded.

YUMANI

Just below the ridge in Yumani village, above the Fuente del Inca, there are a growing number of hostal options.

Hostal Inti Wayra (☎ 719-42015, La Paz ☎ 246-1765; US$2) The beautiful and amicable Inti Wayra affords great views from every room; those upstairs are larger and more open. There's a fabulous rooftop vista over the lake to Isla de la Luna and, coincidentally, the full moon rises behind the island. American breakfasts are US$1, and other meals (including vegetarian options) are US$2. The new rooms being built with hot water and private bath on the top floor will have fantastic views.

Hostal Templo del Sol (US$2) A real favorite and with good reason. It's upbeat but rundown, and sits right on the ridge with unsurpassed views down both sides of the island, including a rather haunting vista of the Kakayo–Queña ridge from the typically sunny patio area. The ambience here creates a real backpackers' scene, and many people who arrive for two days wind up staying a week. Meals, staples and cooking facilities are available.

Hostal Imperio del Sol (US$2.50) Friendly Gualberto Mamani's simple hostal has seven clean rooms plus new rooms with private bath.

Other budget options include the **Hostal Hijos del Sol** (US$2) and the **Hostal Inti Marka** (US$2). About 20 minutes north of Yumani on the coastal trail is **Posada Inca del Mallku** (US$2.50), which has rooms perched over the lake.

Hostal Puerta del Sol (☎ 719-55181; US$3, with bath US$10) Cheery and scenic but the rooms with private bath are overpriced.

Casa de Don Ricardo B&B (☎ 719-34427; birdyze hnder@hotmail.com; s/d with bath & breakfast US$12/20) Argentine community activist Ricardo and his Aymará neighbors run this delightful four-room retreat. Meals and guided boat trips are available upon request.

La Estancia Ecolodge (☎ 715-67287, La Paz ☎ 244-2727; walk-in s/d with bath US$28/36) Magri Turismo's spacious new solar-powered adobe cottages sport traditional Aymará thatch roofs and are set above pre-Incan terraces with great views of the lake. The lodge is most often used as an overnight stop for lake tours en route to La Paz or Puno, but rooms are available on a drop-in basis.

Posada del Inca (☎ 715-28062, La Paz 233-7533; www.titicaca.com; s/d with bath US$49/57) The island's most luxurious choice is only open to clients of Crillon Tours (p105). It occupies a historic colonial compound next to the San Antonio church. The rooms are comfortable but rustic with solar-powered electric blankets. Packages include breakfast and dinner.

CHA'LLA

Right on the beach at Cha'lla is the simple, family-run **Posada del Inca** (Alojamiento Juan Mamani; US$1.35). The owners are an excellent source of information and the outdoor tables tempt nonguests to stop for snacks and conversation. Meals are available and you get a bed, blankets and use of a stove.

Inquire here about the new hostal the family is building on the ridge along the trail to the Chincana ruins.

CHA'LLAPAMPA

The best option here is the flowery **Hostal San Francisco** (US$1.35), run by friendly Señor Francisco Ramos. Choose between two basic four-bed sleeping huts. Note that you'll need a flashlight to climb to the outhouse at night. Meals are available and the facilities are supposedly being improved with a real bathroom promised. To get here from the landing site, follow the beach road to your left and look for the violet-colored house. Along the main ridge route to Chicana, look for a new hostal being built in a saddle, a 30-minute walk north from the four-way junction.

Eating

Yumani has the best, albeit limited, eating options, including a small bakery and the friendly, recommended Restaurant Incaico, which serves excellent breakfasts, soup, *pejerrey* and trout. Hostal Templo del Sol and Inti Wayra are good bets for breakfasts and dinners (US$1 to US$2). On the hilltop, Restaurant Imperio Aymará and, at the top of the Escalera del Inca, Restaurant La Kantuta are the best bets for simple meals.

Burgers, sandwiches and US$1 *almuerzos* are available from snack stands at the foot of the Escalera del Inca. You'll also find snacks and light meals beside the Piedra Sagrada. The Mamani family runs a snack shack along the ridge walk to the Chincana ruins, and cooks up the catch of the day for as little as US$2 at the Posada del Inca in Cha'lla.

The lake water is generally clean, especially along the western shore, but it's still wise to boil or purify it before drinking.

Getting There & Around

BOAT

From the beach in Copacabana, several private *lanchas* and tour companies offer transport to Isla del Sol. The return fare between Copacabana and Isla del Sol is around US$3 per person. In theory the return portion is valid for two or three days, but in practice it's difficult to link up with your original boat for the return trip. For a one-way ticket, you'll pay US$1.35 to reach the island and US$2 for the return to Copacabana. In addition to the private tour boats, cooperative Mallku community boats leave several times daily from Cha'llapampa and the Escalera del Inca.

Tickets may be purchased at the ticket kiosks on the beach or from Copacabana agencies. Boats to the northern end of the island land at Cha'llapampa, while those going to the southern end land at either Pilko Kaina or the Escalera del Inca; many also make a circuit of all three landing sites.

WALKING

Although there have been many miracles reported at Lake Titicaca, you can't really walk to Isla del Sol. It is possible, however, to walk from Copacabana to the village of Yampupata on the mainland, a short distance from the island's southern tip. From there, it's a short boat ride across the Estrecho de Yampupata to the island. See the Copacabana to Yampupata Trek, p97.

ISLA DE LA LUNA (KOATI)

Legend has it that the small Island of the Moon was where Viracocha commanded the moon to rise into the sky. This peaceful little island is surrounded by clear aquamarine water. A walk up to the eucalyptus grove at the summit, where shepherds graze their flocks, is rewarded by a spectacular vista of Cerro Illampu and the entire snow-covered Cordillera Real.

The ruins of an **Inca nunnery** (admission US$0.75) for the Vírgenes del Sol (Virgins of the Sun), also known as Acllahuasi or Iñak Uyu, occupy an amphitheater-like valley on the northeast shore. It's constructed of well-worked stone set in adobe mortar.

It's possible to camp anywhere away from the settlement, but expect a bit of attention. The only source of drinking water is the lake, which locals drink without problems, but you may want to boil or purify first.

Some tours, after dropping tourists at Cha'llapampa on Isla del Sol, continue on to Isla de la Luna. Alternatively you can charter a launch from Yampupata or the Escalera del Inca for around US$8 round-trip (for up to 12 people).

ISLAS DE HUYÑAYMARKA

Lago de Huyñaymarka's most frequented islands – **Suriqui**, **Kalahuta** and **Pariti** are easily visited in a half-day. Tourism has become an island mainstay, but unfortunately the once-proud Kalahuta and Suriqui – and to a lesser extent, Pariti – have been corrupted by outside influences. Please behave sensitively; ask permission before taking photos and refuse requests for money or gifts.

It's also possible to camp overnight, particularly on sparsely populated Pariti. Those who dare to camp on Kalahuta will have the island to themselves since residents are reluctant to venture out at night for fear of encountering spirits. However, as campers will probably draw some measure of criticism from the locals, camping there is not recommended.

Isla Suriqui

The best known of the Huyñaymarka islands is world renowned for the *totora* reed boats that were, until just a few years ago, used by many islanders in everyday life. Their construction was relatively simple. Green reeds were gathered from the lake shallows and left to dry in the sun. Once free of moisture, they were gathered into fat bundles and lashed together with strong grass. Often a sail of reeds was added. These bloated little canoes didn't last long as far as watercraft go; after six months of use they became waterlogged and began to rot and sink. In order to increase their life span, the canoes were often stored some distance away from the water.

In the early 1970s Dr Thor Heyerdahl, the unconventional Norwegian explorer, solicited the help of Suriqui's shipbuilders, the Limachi brothers and Paulino Esteban, to design and construct his vessel *Ra II*. Dr Heyerdahl wanted to test his theory that migration and early contact occurred between the ancient peoples of North Africa and the Americas. He planned to demonstrate the feasibility of traveling great distances using the boats of the period. Four Aymará shipbuilders accompanied him on the expedition from Morocco to Barbados.

Isla Kalahuta

When lake levels are low, Kalahuta ('stone houses' in Aymará) becomes a peninsula. Its shallow shores are lined with beds of *totora* reed, the versatile building material for which Titicaca is famous. By day

fisherfolk ply the island's main bay in their wooden boats; just a few years ago you'd also have seen the *totora* reed boats, and men paddling around to gather the reeds to build them. Wood, however, has won out, and the typical *totora* reed boats are no longer used.

During Inca times, the island served as a cemetery, and it is still dotted with stone *chullpas* (funerary towers). Legends abound about the horrible fate that will befall anyone who desecrates the cemetery, and locals have long refused to live in the area surrounding the island's only village, Queguaya, which is now almost abandoned.

Isla Pariti

Like Kalahuta much of Pariti is surrounded by *totora* reed marshes. A visit to this small island provides a glimpse of the tranquil lifestyle of its friendly inhabitants. Locals trade cheese, fish and woolen goods in Huatajata for items from the Yungas and La Paz. Their sailing boats, which are used for fishing, are beautiful to watch as they slice through the Titicaca waters in search of a bountiful catch.

Getting There & Around

The most experienced guides are the Catari brothers (p105). Thor Heyerdahl's *balsa* builder, Paulino Esteban, also conducts island tours, which may be booked in La Paz through **Calacoto Tours** (☎ 279-2524; www.hotel-calacoto-bolivia.com).

On any of these trips you'll get informative commentary (in Spanish) on the legends, customs, people, history and natural features of the lake. You're allowed as much time as you'd like on each island, and if you'd like to camp on one of the islands, you can arrange to be picked up the following day.

Those who aren't pressed for time may want to speak with the Aymará fisherfolk

---

ISLA INCAS

It doesn't show up on many maps, but legend has it that this tiny, uninhabited island near Suriqui was part of an Inca network of underground passageways, apocryphally reputed to link many parts of the Inca empire with the capital at Cuzco.

GREG CAIRE

Laguna Glacial (p128), the Yungas

Textiles, La Paz

KRZYSZTOF DYDYNSKI

KRZYSZTOF DYDYNSKI

Colonial architecture, La Paz

Outskirts of La Paz

WOODS WHEATCROFT

WOODS WHEATCR

Japapi (p99), Isla del Sol

SARAH JH HUBBARD

Spinning alpaca wool into yarn,
Isla del Sol

Courtyard of the **cathedral** (p92) in Copacabana

RICHARD I'ANS

Chincana ruins (p101), Isla del Sol

DEANNA SWANEY

in Huatajata, who may agree to take a day off to informally shuttle visitors around the islands for a pre-negotiated price.

AROUND LAKE TITICACA

PUERTO PÉREZ

Established in the 1800s by English entrepreneurs as a home for the Lake Titicaca steamship service, Puerto Pérez is 67km northwest of La Paz. Today it's the home port of **Balsa Tours** (☎ 244-0817; www.turismobalsa.com) and its five-star lake resort, **Complejo Náutico Las Balsas** (☎ /fax 244-0620, La Paz ☎ 235-6164; US$25-40). Amenities include a health and fitness center, racquetball, massage, sauna and restaurants. Using the hotel at the resort as a base, Balsa operates tours to the islands of Kalahuta, Suriqui and Pariti for around US$25 per person.

Most people arrive at the Complejo Náutico Las Balsas on a transfer arranged by Balsa Tours. If you are independent and require public transport, board anything headed for Copacabana or Sorata and get off at Batallas. From here you may have to walk the last 7km if you can't hitch or connect with infrequent public transport.

HUARINA

This nondescript little village, midway between Copacabana and La Paz, serves as a road junction, particularly for the town of Sorata, a popular visitor destination. If you're traveling between Sorata and Copacabana, you'll have to get off at the intersection here and wait for the next bus going in your direction.

HUATAJATA

This tiny community is mostly just a jumping-off point for trips to the Islas Huyñaymarkas (p103) and tourist cruises on Lake Titicaca. Life around this part of the lake remains much as it was when the Incas were capturing the imaginations – and the lands – of the Aymará inhabitants with dazzling tales of their origins. The tourist scene aside, daily life in Huatajata is dominated by age-old routines. In the morning men take out their fishing boats, and each afternoon they return with the day's haul. Women mostly spend their days

repairing nets, caring for children, weaving, cooking, cleaning and selling the previous day's catch.

The Hotel Inca Utama's **Andean Roots Museum** (Museos de Raíces Andinos; admission free for hotel guests, US$5 for nonguests) focuses on the anthropology and archaeology of the Altiplano cultures, as well as the natural history of the Lake Titicaca region. It features the traditions, agriculture, medicine and building techniques of the Tiahuanaco, Inca and Spanish empires, as well as the Chipayas and Uros cultures and the Kallawayas medicinal tradition. There's even a traditional healer on staff, but his services are available to hotel guests only. Visitors may also get to chat with the Limachi brothers, who helped construct Thor Heyerdahl's reed boats (p104). The Aymará observatory at the complex, known as *Alajpacha*, was equipped by NASA and presents nighttime stargazing programs.

Paulino Esteban's free **Museo Paulino Esteban** contains paraphernalia about *Ra II* and other Heyerdahl expeditions that employed watercraft of ancient design, such as the *Ra I*, *Tigris* and the *Kon Tiki*, as well as the Nazca project balloon gondola. Museum displays also include the various types of *totora* reed boats used on the lake, and outside the owner's home sits a large example that was in use only a few years ago.

Tours

The **Catari brothers** (☎ 213-6616) at the Inti Karka restaurant (p106) run informative day visits to Suriqui, Kalahuta and Pariti (p104) from US$25 for groups of up to five people. Sailing trips are also available for as little as US$20 per day. See Islas Huyñaymarka (p103) for details.

Crillon Tours (☎ 233-7533; www.titicaca.com; around US$150 per person) bases its hydrofoil services in Huatajata at its Inca Utama Hotel. The standard tour entails a bus trip from La Paz to Huatajata and a museum visit before hitting the water. The cruise stops at the Tiquina Straits then continues to Copacabana (p89) before calling in at Isla de la Luna (p103). From here it proceeds to Isla del Sol (p99) for a quick stop at Pilko Kaina and lunch at Yumani before cruising back to Huatajata. At Huatajata, passengers are bused back to La Paz. The company also offers two-day lake tours and one-day transfers by bus and hydrofoil between Peru and Bolivia.

Alternatively you can do a catamaran tour with **Transturin** (☎ 242-2222; www.transturin.com; US$50 half-day, US$100 full day), which is based nearby in Chúa. The largest Transturin catamaran accommodates 150 passengers and offers a half-day cruise to Isla del Sol (p99) or an overnight cruise, stopping at Copacabana (p89), Isla del Sol (p99) and the Inti Wata cultural complex.

Sleeping

The Catari brothers' well-situated **Hostal Puerto Inti Karka** (☎ 213-5058; US$4, with bath US$6) offers very basic rooms where the advertised hot water rarely makes an appearance. It sits right on the shore and enjoys magnificent views of the lake, especially at sunset. There's a small museum about reed boats and Thor Heyerdahl's expeditions (p104). This is also the place to ask about excursions to Islas de Huyñaymarka (p103).

A decent alternative is the lakefront **Kantuta Hostal** (s/d US$4.50/5), next to the gas station.

Crillon Tours' five-star **Inca Utama Hotel & Spa** (☎ 213-6614; titicaca@caoba.entelnet.bo; s/d US$45/ 55) is the destination for the agency's Lake Titicaca hydrofoil cruise programs. Amenities include conference rooms, a natural health spa and the floating La Choza Nautica bar.

Midway between Huatajata and Huarina is the upmarket Hotel Titicaca; book through Transturin (above). Amenities include an indoor heated pool, a sauna and racquetball courts.

Eating

Many restaurants here are open only during the high season or on weekends. On the main road the best bet is Inti Karka, which specializes in trout and also prepares frog legs and typical Bolivian dishes. The slew of tourist-oriented eateries along the shore all serve trout and other standard fare, and there's not much to distinguish one from another: try La Playa, La Kantuta, Inti Raymi, Kala-Uta or Panamericano. On weekends the Bolivian Yacht Club is open to nonmembers for lunch.

Getting There & Away

Lakeside communities between La Paz and Copacabana are served by *micros* (US$1, 1½ hours), which leave roughly every half hour between 4am and 5pm from the corner of Calles Manuel Bustillos and Kollasuyo in La Paz' cemetery district.

To return to La Paz, flag down a bus heading east along the main highway. The last *micro* passes through Huatajata no later than 6pm.

ESTRECHO DE TIQUINA

The narrow Tiquina Straits separate the main body of Lake Titicaca from the smaller Lago de Huyñaymarka. Flanking the western and eastern shores respectively are the twin villages of **San Pedro** and **San Pablo**. A bridge across the strait has been in the planning stages for many years, but vehicles are still shuttled across the straits on *balsas* (rafts), while passengers travel across in small launches (US$0.20; 10 minutes). Bus travelers should carry all valuables onto the launch with them.

There are a number of small restaurants and food stalls on both sides to serve people caught up in the bottleneck of traffic. Note that foreigners traveling in either direction may have to present their passports for inspection at San Pedro, which is home to Bolivia's largest naval base.

NORTHWEST OF HUATAJATA

There are a couple of sites of minor interest northwest of Huatajata along the seldom-used route to the Peru–Bolivia border beyond **Puerto Acosta**. About 90km north of La Paz, along the road before the turnoff to Sorata, is the large market town of **Achacachi**, a crucial transportation junction and favorite roadblock staging point of local political boss Felipe Quispe (aka El Mallku). **Ancoraimes**, 20km beyond Achacachi, has a church with a lovely ornamental screen above the altar, and *cholitas* play soccer on Sundays. In the colonial township of **Escoma**, where a road strikes off the Cordillera Apolobamba (p141), there is another vibrant Sunday market.

Getting There & Away

Inexpensive *micros* run occasionally from La Paz' cemetery district to Puerto Acosta, near the Peruvian border. Beyond there you'll probably have to rely on the (almost) daily *camiones* that run from Puerto Acosta to Moho on the Peruvian side, which has an *alojamiento* and several onward daily buses. Sunday is market day in Puerto Acosta, so Saturday is probably the best day to look for *camiones* coming from La Paz. There's also an infrequent *micro* (perhaps three times weekly) between Tilali, near the Peruvian border (a four-hour walk from Puerto Acosta), and the larger town of Huancané, Peru.

Note that to enter Peru by this obscure route, you'll have to check out of Bolivia at immigration in Puerto Acosta. In a hamlet on the Peruvian side of the border, the irritable police will check your documents and order you to beeline for Puno (on the opposite side of the lake), where *migración* will stamp you into Peru.

GUAQUI & DESAGUADERO

Soporific little Guaqui sits beside, and partially beneath, Lago Huyñaymarka, the southern extension of Lake Titicaca. It's 25km beyond Tiahuanaco (p81), and about 30km from the Peruvian frontier at Desaguadero. There's a truly beautiful church with a silver altar and some colonial artwork inside. Guaqui sees most of its excitement during the riotous **Fiesta de Santiago** in the final week of July. Desaguadero's Tuesday and Friday markets have been compared by readers to the exotic Sunday market in Kashgar, China.

Residencial Guaqui (US$1.50), near the port, provides Guaqui's only accommodations. Rooms aren't terribly secure, but there's a pleasant courtyard and an attached restaurant. There's also a basic eatery on the plaza.

The Peruvian side of Desaguadero has plenty of small and inexpensive places to stay. If you're stuck on the Bolivian side after the border closes, try the **Hotel Bolivia** (s/d US$6/9), recommended for its clean rooms; it has a restaurant.

Getting There & Away

Most Tiahuanaco-bound buses from La Paz continue to Guaqui. The first *micros* from Guaqui back to Tiahuanaco and La Paz leave at 5:30am, and there's something at least every hour until about 4pm or 5pm. They depart from the main avenue in the lower part of town.

Direct buses from La Paz to Desaguadero (US$2, three hours) leave from Transportes Ingavi's office in La Paz' cemetery district.

From Guaqui, minibuses also run to Desaguadero (US$0.40, 30 minutes), where you can cross the border on foot, complete the normally quirky immigration formalities, and then catch a connecting bus on to Yunguyo (where you can cut back into Bolivia at Copacabana) or Puno. The border closes at 7pm.

The Cordilleras & Yungas

THE CORDILLERAS
& YUNGAS

The 200km-long Cordillera Real, Bolivia's most prominent range, is also one of the loftiest and most imposing in the Andes. The Yungas, the misty, jungle-filled valleys and gorges to the north and east of the Cordilleras, descend dramatically toward the Amazon Basin, forming a distinct natural division between the cold, barren Altiplano and northern Bolivia's rainforested lowlands. Not only is the Cordillera Real Bolivia's best mountaineering venue, it's also popular as a trekking destination. The bulk of the country's popular walking routes follow ancient roads connecting the high Altiplano with the steamy Yungas.

North of Lake Titicaca lies the remote Cordillera Apolobamba, with scores of little-known valleys and traditional Aymará villages. Here live the renowned Kallawaya healers who employ a blend of herbs and magic to cure ailments. This area also includes the Área Protegida Apolobamba, a vicuña reserve abutting the Peruvian border. Access to this region is difficult – and often uncomfortable – but the isolated landscapes, looming peaks and wonderful trekking possibilities make it worthwhile for an increasing number of visitors.

The wild and even-less-visited Cordillera Quimsa Cruz is a beautifully glaciated southern outlier of the Cordillera Real and holds promise as a trekking and mountaineering destination. It has long been a major tin-mining area, but has only recently been discovered as a visitor destination.

TOP FIVE

- Lounge poolside, hike and eat your fill in cloud-wreathed **Coroico** (p111)
- Follow the pre-Inca paving on the **Choro** (p117), **Takesi** (p119) or **Yunga Cruz** (p122) treks
- Explore medieval-looking **Sorata** (p127) and enjoy its fabulous hiking opportunities
- Climb the glaciated 6088m peak of **Huayna Potosí** (p137) – for fit mountaineers only
- Hike over five high passes between Curva and Pelechuco in the wild **Cordillera Apolobamba** (p141)

★ Cordillera Apolobamba

★ Sorata

Huayna Potosí ★

★ Coroico

Choro, Takesi & Yunga Cruz treks ★

- TELEPHONE CODE: 02
- ELEVATION: 600M TO 6429M

HISTORY

The first settlers of the Yungas were inspired by economic opportunity. In the days of the Inca empire, gold was discovered in the Río Tipuani and Río Mapiri valleys, and the gold-crazed Spanish immediately got in on the act. To enrich the royal treasury, they forced locals to labor for them, and the region became one of the continent's most prolific sources of gold. Today the rivers of the lower Yungas are being ravaged by hordes of wildcat prospectors as well as a growing number of multinational mining outfits. A distressing side effect is water pollution from the mercury used to recover fine particles from gold-bearing sediment.

Agriculture has also played a part in the development of the Yungas. Today most farmland occupies the intermediate altitudes, roughly between 600m and 1800m. Sugar, citrus, bananas and coffee are grown in sufficient quantities for export to the highlands. The area centered on the village of Coripata and extending south toward Chulumani is also prime coca-producing country. The sweet Yungas' coca is mostly consumed locally, while leaves from the Chapare region (p310) generally serve more infamous purposes.

Yungas' coca is also under fire and is slated to be the target of an upcoming eradication scheme, jointly financed by the Bolivian government and foreign-sponsored

---

THINGS GO BETTER WITH COCA

Cocaine, marijuana, hashish and other drugs are illegal in Bolivia, but the coca leaf, which is the source of cocaine and related drugs, is chewed daily by many Bolivians and is even venerated by indigenous peoples. Mama Coca is revered as the daughter of Pachamama, the earth mother, and coca is considered a gift to the people to be used to drive evil forces from their homes and fields.

Both the Quechua and Aymará people make sacrifices of coca leaves when planting or mining to ensure a good harvest or lucky strike. The *yatiri* (traditional Aymará healers) use them in their healing and exorcising rituals, and in some remote rural areas leaves are often used in place of money. People embarking on a journey also place several leaves beneath a rock at the start, as an offering to Pachamama in the hope that she'll smooth their way. Visitors walking or hiking in the mountains may want to hedge their bets and do the same, or at least carry some leaves as a gift for helpful locals (coca is always gratefully received).

The conquering Spanish found that laborers who chewed the leaf became more dedicated to their tasks, so they promoted its use among the peasants. Today nearly all *campesinos* and *cholos*, men and women alike, take advantage of its benefits. It's also becoming popular among younger middle-class people, particularly those who sympathize with peasant causes. Most Bolivians of European origin however still regard chewing coca as a disgusting 'Indian' habit and generally avoid its use.

Used therapeutically coca serves as an appetite suppressant and a central nervous system stimulant. Workers use it to lessen the effects of altitude and eliminate the need for a lunch break. They also chew it recreationally and socially in much the same way people smoke cigarettes or drink coffee. Among Bolivian miners the 'coca break' is an institution.

The leaf itself grows on bushes that are cultivated in the Yungas and Upper Chapare regions at altitudes of between 1000m and 2000m. Leaves are sold by the kilogram in nearly every market in Bolivia along with *legía*, an alkaloid usually made of mineral lime, potato and *quinoa* ash, which is used to draw the drug from the leaves when chewed. There are two kinds of *legía*: *achura*, which is sweet, and *cuta*, which is salty.

The effects of coca chewing are not startling. It will leave the person feeling a little detached, reflective, melancholy and contented. Locals normally chew around 30 to 35 leaves at a time. A beginner places a few leaves, say five to 10, between gum and cheek until they soften. Then the process is repeated with a little *legía* between the leaves. Chewing doesn't start until the desired amount has been stuffed in. Once it has been chewed into a pulpy mess, the bitter-tasting juice is swallowed, which numbs the mouth and throat. (In fact novocaine and related anesthetics are coca derivatives.)

(mainly US) agencies. It's hoped that this lovely region will be able to avoid the unrest and violence suffered by the Chapare region, since anti-coca programs first came into being during the late 1980s.

CLIMATE

The Yungas' physical beauty is astonishing, and although the hot, humid and rainy climate may induce lethargy, it's nevertheless more agreeable to most people than the chilly Altiplano. Winter rains are gentle, and the heavy rains occur mainly between November and March. The average year-round temperature hovers in the vicinity of 18°C, but summer daytime temperatures in the 30s aren't uncommon. As a result, the region provides a balmy lowland retreat for chilled highlanders, and is a favorite R&R hangout for foreign travelers.

GETTING AROUND

Transport, commerce and administration focus on Coroico and Chulumani, while such outlying towns as Yanakachi, Sorata, Caranavi and Guanay function as regional commercial centers. Access is entirely overland and the region's unpaved roads can get mucky and washed out in the rainy season. Scheduled public transport is infrequent to many trekking and mountaineering base-camps, so chartered private transport from La Paz is used more often here than in other regions of the country.

Road blockades have increased in the Yungas in recent years. They are most common between harvest and planting seasons, which happens to coincide with the high tourist season (June to September). The protesters don't have a beef with you, but they might leave you stranded in paradise for a couple weeks. Keep your ears open for warnings before heading off.

THE YUNGAS

The Yungas – the transition zone between dry highlands and humid lowlands – is where the Andes fall away into the Amazon Basin. Above the steaming, forested depths rise the near-vertical slopes of the Cordillera Real and the Cordillera Quimsa Cruz, which halt Altiplano-bound clouds, causing them to deposit bounteous rainfall. Vegetation is abundant and tropical fruit, coffee, coca, cacao and tobacco grow with minimal tending. The Yungas is composed of two provinces in La Paz department, Nor and Sud Yungas (oddly, most of Sud Yungas lies well to the north of Nor Yungas), as well as bits of other provinces.

COROICO

pop 4500 / elevation 1750m

Serene, tropical Coroico is the Nor Yungas provincial capital. Perched aerie-like on the shoulder of Cerro Uchumachi, it commands a far-ranging view across forested canyons, cloud-wreathed mountain peaks, patchwork agricultural lands,

THE CORDILLERAS & YUNGAS

0 — 30 km
0 — 20 mi

PERU

Moho
Ulla •
Pelechuco
Parque Nacional Madidi
Área Protegida Apolobamba
Apolobamba
Conima
Tilali
Curva
Termas de Charazani
Apolo
Isla Soto
Italaque
Charazani (Villa General José Pérez)
Puerto Acosta
Isla Campanario
Lake Titicaca
Escoma
Aucapata
Iskanwaya
Sorata Limitada
Isla del Sol
Puerto Carabuco
Consata
Río Mapiri
Quiabaya
Ancoma
Mapiri
Isla de la Luna (Koati)
Ancoraimes
Sorata
Río Tupuani
Ancohuma (6427m)
Illampu (6362m)
Achacachi
Tipuani
Guanay
Huatajata
BOLIVIA
Lago de Huiñaymarka
Huarina
La Paz
Puerto Pérez
Cordillera Real
Tiahuanaco
Pucarani
Batallas
To Rurrenabaque
Huayana Potosí (6088m)
Tiahuanaco
Milluni
Parque Nacional Cotapata
Caranavi
Laja
LA PAZ
Chairo
Yungas
Viacha
La Cumbre
Coroico
Yolosa
El Alto Airport
Unduavi
Chuspipata
Ventilla
Yanakachi
Illimani (6439m)
Chulumani
Río La Paz
Irupana
Cordillera Quimsa Cruz
Viloco
Mina Caracoles
Quime

TREKS
1 Curva to Pelechuco Trek
2 Mapiri Trail
3 Illampu Circuit
4 El Camino del Oro
5 El Choro Trek
6 Takesi Trek
7 Yunga Cruz Trek

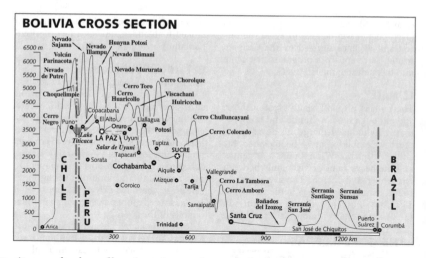

BOLIVIA CROSS SECTION

citrus orchards, coffee plantations and dozens of small settlements. When the weather clears, the view stretches to the snow-covered summits of Mururata, Huayna Potosí and Tiquimani, high in the Cordillera Real. The name is derived from *coryguayco*, which is Quechua for 'golden hill'.

The town's biggest attraction is its slow pace, which allows plenty of time for relaxing, swimming, sunbathing and wandering the surrounding hills. Coroico stays relatively warm year-round, but summer storms bring some mighty downpours. Because of its ridgetop position, fog is common, especially in the afternoon when it rises from the deep valleys and swirls through the streets and over the rooftops. The town festival is October 20th, and Saturday and Sunday are market days. On Mondays the town utterly closes down and most shops and restaurants don't reopen until Tuesday morning

Information

EMERGENCY
There's a basic **regional hospital** near Hostal El Cafetal, but for serious medical treatment you'll be most happy in La Paz.

INTERNET ACCESS
MCM, near the bus offices, and **Internet La Casa**, one block southeast of the plaza, offer sloth-like access for US$2 an hour.

LAUNDRY
Handwashing services are available at **Lavandería Benedita**, near Hotel Gloria (look for the small sign), and at most hotels for US$0.15 per piece.

MONEY
Banco Unión does cash advances and may change cash. **Hotel Esmeralda** (p115) changes travelers checks without commission.

TOURIST INFORMATION
There's no tourist office, but the friendly **Cámara Hotelera** on the plaza has free town maps. Sernap's **Parque Nacional Cotapata office** is upstairs on the plaza's south side; check here for permission to camp at the park's biological research station off the El Choro trek (p117).

Dangers & Annoyances
Women especially should avoid hiking alone, as there have been incidents.

Although Coroico is perfectly tranquil, be aware that it is inhabited by some especially vicious biting insects. While they don't carry malaria, the bites itch for days (or weeks!), so don't forget the repellent.

Activities

HIKING
It can get extremely hot while hiking, so carry plenty of water.

For pretty views head uphill toward **Hotel Esmeralda** and on up to **El Calvario**, an easy 20-minute hike. At El Calvario the Stations of the Cross lead to a grassy knoll and chapel. There are two good trailheads from El Calvario. The one to the left leads to the **cascadas**, a trio of waterfalls 5km and two hours beyond the chapel. The trail to the right leads to **Cerro Uchumachi** (five hours round-trip), which affords terrific valley views.

A good day's walk will take you to **El Vagante**, an area of natural stone swimming holes in the Río Santa Bárbara. Follow the road toward Coripata to Cruce Miraflores, 750m beyond the Hotel Don Quijote. Here you should turn left at a fork in the road and head steeply downhill past Hacienda Miraflores; at the

second fork, bear right (the left fork goes to Santa Ana). After two hours along this route, which features a stretch with some pre-Columbian terraces, you'll reach a cement bridge. Turn right before the bridge and follow the river downstream for 20 minutes to a series of swimming holes and waterfalls. The water isn't drinkable, so carry water or purification tablets – and bear in mind that the return route is uphill all the way.

HORSEBACK RIDING

You can rent horses from Reynaldo at **El Relincho** (☎ 719-23814), 100m past Hotel Esmeralda, for US$5 an hour or US$30 per day, including a guide.

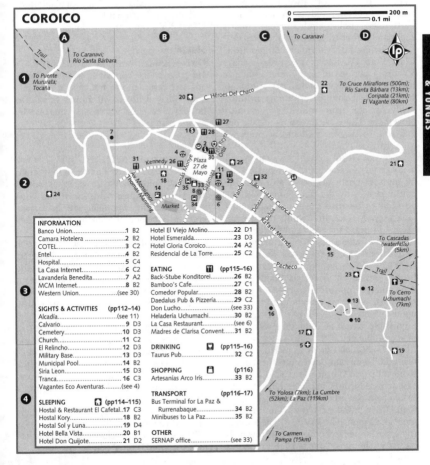

COROICO

SWIMMING

Feeling lazy? Instead of walking down to the river, dip into the **municipal pool** (admission US$0.65) below the market. Several hotels also allow nonguests to use their pool for a small charge.

WHITEWATER RAFTING

About three hours from town is the **Río Coroico**, which flows through the Nor Yungas. This pool-drop river is the country's most popular commercially rafted river, and is the most convenient to La Paz. The river features well over 30 rapids, great surfing holes, dramatic drops and challenging technical maneuvers (most of these can be scouted from the river and from several bridges). It alternates between calm pools and 50m to 900m rapids, with sharp bends, boils, mean holes, undercurrents, sharp rocks and rather treacherous undercuts.

The whitewater normally ranges from Class II to IV, but may approach Class V during periods of high water (when it becomes too dangerous to raft). Although trips run year-round, conditions are normally optimal from mid-March to mid-November. There are few spots to take out and rest, so stay focused and be prepared for surprises.

Access is from the highway between Yolosa and Caranavi; the best put-ins are 20 minutes north of Yolosa and near the confluence with the Río Santa Bárbara, 50 minutes by road north of Yolosa. Just look for any track that winds down from the road toward the river and find one that provides suitable access. Trips average three to five hours. For the take-out, look on the right side of the river for a devastated steel bridge (destroyed in a 1998 flood) across a normally diminutive creek. Don't miss it because after this the climb to the road up the steep jungled slopes is practically impossible, and it's a long, long way to the next possible exit.

The **Río Huarinilla** flows from Huayna Potosí and Tiquimani down into the Yungas to meet the Río Coroico near Yolosa, and is best accessed from Chairo, at the end of the El Choro trek. Although it's normally Class II and III, high water can swell it into a much more challenging Class IV to V. The full-day trip is best suited to kayaks and narrow paddle rafts. The new Yungas Highway passes right by the take-out at the confluence of the Ríos Huarinilla and Coroico.

Several experienced La Paz tour agencies organize daytrips on the Río Coroico and Río Huarinilla (p357).

Courses & Tours

Siria Leon (☎ 719-55431; siria_leon@yahoo.com; JZ Cuenca 062) is recommended for Spanish lessons (US$4 an hour).

The whitewater is great, but unfortunately the high tourist season coincides with the dry season. Several agencies around the plaza offer day-long rafting trips for US$35 to US$50 per person.

On the plaza, **Vagantes Eco Aventuras** (☎ 719-12981; vagantesguias@yahoo.es) runs 4WD tours to local waterfalls, Tocaña, coca plantations and Parque Nacional Cotapata starting at US$20 for groups of up to four.

Sleeping

On weekends from June to August hotels are often booked out. It's possible to make advance reservations, but there's no guarantee that all hotels will honor them. On holiday weekends prices may increase by as much as 100%.

BUDGET

Hostal Kory (La Paz ☎ 243-1311; s/d US$4/7, r with bath US$6; 🏊) Like its budget competition, the deck enjoys fantastic views of valleys and Cordillera peaks. It's clean and convenient, making it popular with backpackers. The large pool is available to nonguests for US$0.75.

Hostal El Cafetal (Rancho Beni; ☎ 715-10670; Miranda s/n, follow signs from plaza; US$3.35, weekends r per person US$4.50; 🏊) In addition to the superb eatery here, there are several clean, secure rooms with splendid views. The lush grounds encourage lazing in a hammock or chilling in the pool.

Residencial de la Torre (half a block northeast of plaza; r per person US$2) Sunny and clean, this is the cheapest acceptable accommodation.

La Senda Verde (☎ 715-32701; vossiop@acelerate .com) Off the main road just below Yolosa. Riverside camping and good food are available here under a thatched *palapa*. If the current structures are any indication, their planned *cabañas* will be delightful.

There are other secluded wild campsites near the church on the hill above town.

MID-RANGE

Hostal Sol y Luna (☎ 715-61626, La Paz ☎ 236-2099; www.solyluna-bolivia.com; camping US$2, s US$4-6, d US$7, cabañas with bath s US$10-15, d US$14-20; ⚉) This splendid German-run retreat is well worth the 20-minute uphill walk east of town. It has scenic campsites, lovely self-contained cabins sleeping up to seven people (nicer ones have views and a patio) and comfortable shared bathrooms down near the pool. Bonuses include a gringo-friendly restaurant with veggie options (recruit a group for the Indonesian buffet), a big multilingual lending library and book exchange, massage (US$10 to US$12 an hour) and a sublime, slate, hot tub (US$6.50 for up to three people). Free taxi pickup is available from the plaza for guests with reservations.

Hotel Bella Vista (☎ /fax 213-6059, 715-69237; US$5, with bath US$10) It's sparkling new and has a racquetball court and video salon but no swimming pool. Rooms are modern and clean, and some have stunning views from the verandas.

Hotel Don Quijote (☎ 213-6007, La Paz ☎ 278-4640; s/d with breakfast US$10/15; ⚉) A flat 10-minute (1km) walk east of the plaza, this friendly pad is popular with Bolivian families. It looks more expensive than it is and makes a good alternative to staying in town. It's clean and has all the amenities of a solid mid-range option – including an inviting pool.

Hotel Esmeralda (☎ 213-6017; www.hotelesmeralda.com; US$7-9, with bath & TV US$12-15; 🖳 ⚉) Everyone (including most tour groups) seems to end up here, 400m uphill east of the plaza. Peripheral amenities include a pool, hammocks, a tropical garden, a video lounge, Internet access (US$3 an hour) and a sunny patio overlooking the universe. Unfortunately, dank downstairs rooms without a view or bath are overpriced; the best rooms with bath are upstairs. If you'd rather not climb the hill with luggage, look around the plaza for their free Jeep; if they aren't there, phone from the Entel office and they'll pick you up. Note that they only hold reservations until 3pm.

Hotel Gloria Coroico (☎ /fax 213-6020, La Paz ☎ 270-4040; www.hotelgloriabolivia.com; s/d US$8/18, with bath US$11/22; ⚉) Downhill from town, just below the soccer fields, is this distinctive red-roofed ex-prefectural resort. In addition to some of Coroico's finest views, it boasts a number of pleasant lounges, a video room and a games room with billiards and ping-pong tables. While the high ceilings and grandiose halls lend a colonial ambience, it's popular with families, and is animated only on weekends. All rates include a continental breakfast; other meals are available from the attached restaurant. Ask about mid-week package deals.

TOP END

Hotel El Viejo Molino (☎ /fax 220-1529/1499; www.valmartour.com; s/d/tw, US$25/35/45, ste US$48-55; ⚉) Coroico's top-end option is a 15-minute downhill walk northeast of town on the road toward the Río Santa Bárbara. All rooms have private bath and TV, and include breakfast and access to the temperamental sauna and jacuzzi, as well as the pool.

Eating & Drinking

For its size, Coroico has an impressive variety of tasty cafés and eateries. Most hotels also have restaurants.

The plaza is ringed by a number of inexpensive local places including Heladería Uchumachi and Don Lucho; all have ordinary menus, acceptable fare and a typically tropical sense of urgency and service. If you're in a rush or on a strict budget, there are many food stalls around the mercado municipal and in the Comedor Popular to placate your growling stomach, but you'll need a bit of gastric stamina.

El Cafétal (Rancho Beni; ☎ 715-10670; Miranda s/n, follow signs from plaza; mains US$1-5) The indisputable travelers' favorite at Hostal El Cafétal is where (with a bit of patience) you can enjoy an incredible, heaped meal in a verdant setting, accompanied by mellow music and an inspiring view. This rustic, relaxing place, expertly run by French expats Dany and Patricio, is consistently rated by travelers as one the best in all of Bolivia. The menu includes sweet and savory crêpes, soufflés, soups, pasta, burgers, sandwiches, curry, vegetarian lasagna, superb Yungas' coffee, chocolate mousse, cakes, cocktails and other goodies. It's near the hospital, a 15-minute walk uphill from the plaza.

Bamboo's Café (one block north of plaza; mains US$2-3; ☾ happy hour 6-7pm) The place for picante

Mexican (tacos, burritos and veggie refried beans) food. There is usually reggae on the radio when live music isn't in the house on Friday and Saturday nights.

Hotel Esmeralda (☎ 213-6017; www.hotel esmeralda.com; buffet breakfast US$2, lunch or dinner US$2.35) A good range of meals, including decent wood-fired pizza and various vegetarian options.

Back-Stube Konditorei (☎ 719-54991; mains US$1.50-3.50) Start your day here with an excellent full breakfast and Yungas' coffee. Later on try the unbeatable pasta, steaks, vegetarian plates and divine German cakes and pastries. The large terrace overlooking the region is the nicest spot in town to take the sun or sip a cocktail.

Restaurant La Casa (☎ 213-6024; half a block southeast of plaza; mains US$2-4) European cuisine is available at this homely German-Bolivian-run restaurant. They do a great range of breakfasts, fondues, coffee, hot chocolate, pancakes, and local or continental dishes. The wonderful *raclette* or *fondue bourguignon* (US$3.75 per person) includes a range of salads and appetizers. If you're planning on a fondue, you'll need a minimum of two people and an advance booking.

Hostal Sol y Luna (☎ 715-61626; www.solyluna -bolivia.com; mains US$1.50-3) The menu is a mix of Bolivian and European dishes including vegetarian options. An extraordinary treat if you have a group – or can muster one – is the Luna Llena Indonesian buffet (US$3.25 per person) for eight to 20 people, which must be booked a day in advance.

Daedalus Pub & Pizzeria is the best spot for beer and wood-fired pizza. The funky French-Bolivian-run **Taurus Pub** also has clay-oven pizza and good music. It's worth checking to see what's shakin' in the kitchen at **Hostal Kory**, which in the past has served everything from pasta and pizza to Argentine *parrillada*.

The **Madres de Clarisa Convent** (down the steps off southwest cnr of plaza; ☺ 8am-8pm) sells homemade brownies, orange cakes, creatively flavored biscuits, and wines. Ring the bell to get into the shop area.

Shopping

For quality handmade jewelry visit **Artesanías Arco Irís**, on the south side of the plaza. It isn't cheap, but most items are unique. During the high season the plaza is frequented by itinerant craftspeople selling a dazzling array of novel jewelry.

Getting There & Away

Flanked by epic scenery, and punctuated with waterfalls in the rainy season, the La Paz–Coroico road plunges more than 3000m in 80km. It's called The World's Most Dangerous Road (p55) because it sees the most fatalities annually, although the road itself is really not that treacherous. True, it's extremely narrow and can be muddy, slippery and deeply rutted, but Andean veterans will recall much worse routes in Peru and Ecuador. What makes the road so dangerous is the drivers – a combination of weekend warriors, macho bus drivers on sleep-deprived benders and tenderfooted tourists. To minimize the danger, travel on a weekday in a minibus (especially if they are using the new road) rather than a big bus. Alternatively you can bicycle or trek (see the boxed text, p138). Traveling at night is a death wish.

BICYCLE

An exhilarating yet (arguably) safe option is to mountain bike from La Paz to Coroico. Gravity Assisted Mountain Biking (p56) guides safe but thrilling one-day downhill mountain-bike tours to Coroico daily during the high season (see the boxed text, p55). It's also possible to rent a bike in La Paz and do the downhill trip independently; then throw your bike in a *camión* for the long haul back to La Paz.

BUS

From the Villa Fátima in La Paz, buses and minibuses leave for Coroico (US$2, 3½ hours). Most weekday departures are in the morning from the plaza, starting around 7am, with extra runs on weekends and holidays. **Flota Yungueña** (☎ 289-5513, La Paz ☎ 221-3513) is experienced and reliable. Minibuses stop in Yolosa where you can catch buses and *camiones* north to Rurrenabaque (US$13, 15 to 18 hours) and farther into Bolivian Amazonia.

CAMIÓN

Camiones from La Paz to Coroico leave mornings and until mid-afternoon from behind the gas station in Villa Fátima. Given the road's terrifying reputation, the few Bolivian dollars saved may not be worth the additional risk.

To reach the Amazon Basin, you must first get to Yolosa, where drivers always stop for a snack. All downhill vehicles must pass through the *tranca* there, so it's a good place to wait for a lift. When the roads are open, there should be no problem finding transport to Caranavi, Rurrenabaque or La Paz.

For Chulumani, head back toward La Paz and get off at Unduavi to wait for onward transport. Alternatively, you can make a trip through Bolivia's main coca-growing region: Take a *camión* from Coroico to Arapata, another from Arapata to Coripata and yet another to Chulumani. It's a pleasant adventure, but don't be in too much of a hurry and don't try it during the rainy season, as this road features some of the deepest mud ever.

EL CHORO TREK

The La Cumbre to Coroico (Choro) trek is one of Bolivia's premier hikes. It begins at La Cumbre (4725m), the highest point on the La Paz–Coroico highway, and climbs to 4859m before descending 3250m into the humid Yungas and the village of Chairo. Along the 70km route (which is in the best condition during the April to September dry season), you'll note distinct differences in the people and their dress, herds, crops and dwellings.

Energetic hikers can finish the trek in two days, but it's more comfortably done in three days. Many people allow even more time to appreciate the incredible variety of landforms and vegetation across the various altitude zones.

Prepare for a range of climates. On the first day you'll need winter gear, but on the second and third days the warm clothing will be peeled off layer by layer. For the lower trail, light cotton trousers or something similar will protect your legs from sharp vegetation and biting insects.

Dangers & Annoyances

In recent years there have been reports of robberies in the lower regions of this trek. The most thefts are reported below Choro village. These appear to be isolated incidents however, and the trail is not generally deemed unsafe. It's still wise to camp out of sight if possible and do not leave anything outside your tent. Don't attempt the route solo.

Tours

A growing number of La Paz outfits offer organized El Choro treks from US$80 to US$120 per person. Most include meals, guides and camping equipment; some include the services of pack animals or porters. For suggestions, see Tours in the Directory chapter, p357.

Access

Once you find the trailhead, the trail is easy to access and follow. From Villa Fátima in

THE CORDILLERAS & YUNGAS

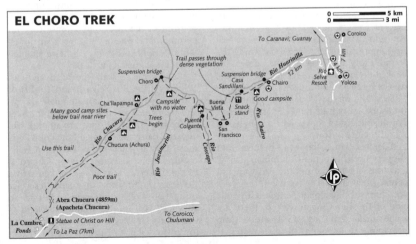

EL CHORO TREK

La Paz, catch any Yungas-bound transport. If there's space (Yungas-bound passengers take priority), you'll pay around US$1 in a bus or minibus, or US$0.75 in a *camión* to be dropped at La Cumbre, marked by a statue of Christ, where the trek begins.

The road climbs steeply out of Villa Fátima, and less than an hour out of La Paz at the 4725m crest of the La Paz–Yungas road is La Cumbre. For the best chance of good clear views of the stunning scenery, start as early as possible, before the mist rises out of the Yungas.

The Route

From the **statue of Christ**, follow the well-defined track to your left for 1km. There you should turn off onto the smaller track that turns right and passes between two small ponds (one often dry). Follow it up the hill until it curves to the left and begins to descend.

At this point follow the light track leading up the gravely hill to your right and toward an obvious notch in the barren hill before you. This is **Abra Chucura** (4859m), and from here the trail tends downhill all the way to its end at Chairo. At the high point is a pile of stones called Apacheta Chucura. For centuries travelers have marked their passing by tossing a stone atop it (preferably one that has been carried from a lower elevation) as an offering to the mountain *apus*. An hour below Abra Chucura lie the remains of a *tambo* (wayside inn) dating from Inca times.

Basic supplies are available at the village of **Chucura** (also known as Achura). An hour's walk from here leads to the best first-night campsites (US$1.35) which are found along the river. Further down the beautifully paved Inca road, the village of **Cha'llapampa** administers a campsite (US$1.35) and basic guest accommodations in a sooty little hut (US$1.75). Water is available from a convenient stream below a bridge close to town.

After two hours following beautiful but slippery stretches of pre-Columbian paving, a **suspension bridge** across the Río Chucura is reached at **Choro**. The track continues descending steadily along the true left (west) side of the Río Chucura where there are some small campsites (US$1) and a shop providing drinks and snacks. Water is

scarce for the next five to six hours. At the time of writing, the Puento Choro suspension bridge was sturdy and safe, but it often gets washed away when the river floods, requiring trekkers to rely on a rudimentary flying fox to cross the river.

From the ridge above Choro, the trail alternately plunges and climbs from sunny hillsides to vegetation-choked valleys, crossing streams and waterfalls. You'll have to ford the **Río Jucumarini**, which can be rather intimidating in the wet season. Further along, the trail crosses the deep gorge of the **Río Coscapa** via the relatively sturdy Puente Colgante suspension bridge.

The trail continues through some tiny hamlets, including **San Francisco** and **Buena Vista**. Some five hours from Choro is the remarkable **Casa Sandillani** (2000m), a Japanese-style home surrounded by beautifully manicured gardens. The friendly owner is full of trail news and enjoys having visitors stop by and sign his guestbook. He's happy to let you camp in his garden; you may want to bring some stamps or postcards from home to augment his extensive collections. There are several snack and soft-drink stalls and a clear water supply is provided by a pipe located diagonally opposite the house (to the right, 20m along the main trail).

From Casa Sandillani it's an easy 7km (2½ hours) downhill to **Chairo**, where camping is possible in a small, flat, grassed area with no facilities, near the bridge above town. Camping is technically free, but you may be asked for a small contribution. It may also be possible to sleep on the porch in front of the local schoolhouse (ask for permission at one of the town's small restaurants, both of which sell basic supplies and serve cheap, set meals).

It's possible to walk the relatively level 12km past the Río Selva Resort (p119) or take transport from Chairo to **Yolosa** (16km) and then catch an onward service the 8km to **Coroico** (p111). A few private vehicles depart Chairo for Coroico (via Yolosa) on most days; if you'd rather ride than walk, inquire about transport leaving Chairo at one of the restaurants as soon as you arrive. Beware: two brothers run a shuttle service using two 4WD *camionetas*, both in an advanced state of decay, and they tend to overcharge unwary trekkers. Minibuses for the entire 23km to Coroico shouldn't cost

---

EL CAMINO DE LAS CASCADAS

An adventurous reader sent the following report on an alternative walking route past the worst of the Yungas road:

'I did the Camino de las Cascadas from the Chuspipata truck stop to Yolosa. It's an easy trek, following an old 4WD route built by Paraguayan POWs during Bolivia's war with that country. You can't get lost, but you should probably bring a machete, as it was pretty overgrown. In any case you'll have a good 'Look-at-me-I'm-in-the-jungle-with-a-machete' sort of experience. There are countless waterfalls along this route, including the 100m monster that the trail curls above.

Begin by getting off the La Paz to Coroico transport at Chuspipata and follow the old 4WD track downhill. Past the power station the road begins to be overgrown. For the next two to three days the track, cut into the hillside (in one 30m stretch, it's quite exposed but still passable), gradually loses altitude, then crosses a ridge into the valley above Yolosa. When the town is clearly visible below, you can cut down through the fields and save several hours.

You can't get lost, there was no trash along the trail, and it was the only place in the Yungas where I heard monkeys in the trees.'

---

more than US$20 for groups of up to 10. From Yolosa there's lots of traffic heading either uphill to La Paz or down to the Amazon lowlands.

YOLOSA

Traveling between La Paz and the Beni – or from anywhere to Coroico – you'll pass through Yolosa, which guards the Coroico road junction. The Yolosa's *tranca* closes between 1 and 5am, impeding overnight traffic between the Yungas and La Paz. Pickup trucks awaiting passengers to Coroico (US$0.35, 20 minutes) line up at the corner by the police checkpoint.

Sleeping & Eating

If you're stuck overnight here, you can crash at **Restaurant El Conquistador** (US$1.35). Streetside stalls sell inexpensive snacks and set meals to passing truckers.

About 5km from the end of the Choro trek in Pacollo is the **Río Selva Resort** (☎ 241-2281/1561; www.rioselva.com.bo; s/d/tw/q US$37/65/65/70; 🏊), a posh five-star riverside retreat that can be a welcome deal for larger groups. Peripheral amenities include racquetball courts, a sauna and swimming pool.

TAKESI (TAQUESI) TREK

Also known as the Inca Trail, the Takesi trek is one of the most popular and impressive walks in the Andes. The route was used as a highway by the early Aymará, the Inca and the Spanish, and it still serves as a major route to the humid Yungas over a relatively low pass in the Cordillera Real.

Nearly half the trail's 40km consists of expertly engineered pre-Inca paving, more like a highway than a walking track.

The walk itself takes only 10 to 15 hours, but plan on two or three days because of transport uncertainties to and from the trailheads. It's hiked by more than 4000 people annually, more than half of whom are Bolivians, and suffers from a litter problem due to its growing popularity.

The May to October dry season is best for this trip. In the rainy season the wet and cold, combined with ankle-deep mud, may contribute to a less-than-optimal experience. Since the trail's end is in the Yungas, however, plan on some rain year-round.

The entire route appears on a single 1:50,000 IGM topo sheet: *Chojlla – 6044-IV*. A good source of information is **Fundación Pueblo** (☎ 241-5832; pueblo@entelnet.bo; Aspiazu 600, Edificio Hertzog, La Paz), an NGO that supports rural development projects that encourage local self-sufficiency. Currently the group is working with villagers along the trail to develop bridges and potable water sources. In Takesi and Kacapi they've built basic solar-powered lodges (minimum four days advance booking required), campsites and places to buy meals and drinks.

Access

If travelling by public transportation, your first destination will be **Ventilla**. A daily *micro* leaves La Paz (US$2, three hours) from the market area above Calle Sagárnaga, at the corner of Calles Rodríguez and Luis Lara. Another option for groups is to charter a

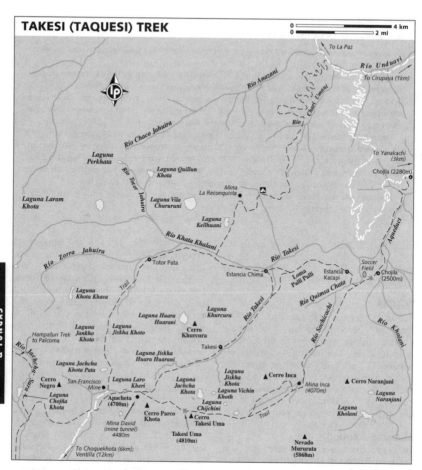

TAKESI (TAQUESI) TREK

minibus to the Choquekhota trailhead. Most La Paz tour agencies can organize this for you or contact Fundación Pueblo.

You can also take an urban *micro* or minibus *trufi* from La Paz to Chasquipampa or Ovejuyo, then either hitch along the road or trek through the beautiful Palca Canyon (and the Valle de las Ánimas if you like; see Around La Paz, p77) to Palca and then to Ventilla. This will add at least one extra day to the trip, but will be a fitting prelude to the longer trek.

There are also minibus *trufis* going from La Paz' Calles Rodríguez and Luis Lara to Ventilla and Palca at least once daily on weekdays and several times daily on weekends. Transport between Ventilla and the

San Francisco mine trailhead is sparse. If you're lucky, you may be able to hitch, but otherwise you should probably resign yourself to paying a negotiable US$10 to US$15 for a taxi, or slogging three hours uphill to the trailhead. Or, with the help of Fundación Pueblo, you can hire mules and a guide to haul your gear for around US$100 per day. A new full-service lodge two-thirds of the way along the route makes it possible to do the hike with only a daypack.

Long-distance taxis departing from near the Plaza Isabél la Católica in La Paz charge around US$40 for up to four people to the San Francisco trailhead. A 4WD and driver will cost around US$100 for up to nine people.

The Route

About 150m beyond Ventilla, turn left and follow the rough road uphill. After climbing for 1½ hours, you'll reach the village of **Choquekhota**, where the landscape is reminiscent of the remotest parts of North Wales. On foot, it's another two to 2½ hours of uphill hiking along the access road to the **San Francisco mine**; after crossing a stream, you'll see the signpost indicating the trailhead. The mine route veers left here, but hikers should continue along the signposted track.

After an hour of climbing you'll begin switchbacking for half an hour for the final ascent, partly on superb pre-Inca paving, to the 4700m **Apacheta**. There, you'll find the *apacheta* (shrine of stones) and a spectacular view of Nevado Mururata (5868m) to the right and the plunging valleys of the Yungas far below. Just beyond the pass you'll see a **mine tunnel**; it's best not to enter, as there's always a danger of collapse, but it can be explored with a flashlight from outside.

From the pass the trail begins to descend into the valley, passing a series of abandoned mining camps and high alpine lakes. If daylight is on your side, look for another lake, **Laguna Jiskha Huara Huarani**, to the left of the trail midway between the pass and Takesi. The trail from here contains some of Bolivia's finest examples of Inca paving. At the ancient-looking village of **Takesi** there's a hut and campsite (US$0.65 per person); you'll also find meals of potatoes and local trout. When exploring the village, watch out for vicious dogs.

Beyond Takesi the trail winds downhill until it crosses a bridge over the **Río Takesi**, then follows the beautifully churning river before it moves upslope from the river and makes a long traverse around the **Loma Palli Palli**, where you're protected from steep drop-offs by a pre-Columbian wall. As you descend, the country becomes increasingly vegetated. Shortly after passing a particularly impressive *mirador* (lookout), you'll enter the village of **Estancia Kacapi**, the heart of the former colonial *estancia* (ranch) that once controlled the entire Takesi valley. Most of the overseers' dwellings have been reclaimed by vegetation, but you can still see the ruins of the Capilla de las Nieves. Kacapi's 10-bed **Albergue Turistico** (per person US$4) and campsite are equipped with solar-powered showers.

Basic meals are available as well. (Note that there are no wild camping sites between Takesi and the trail's end at Chojlla.)

After Kacapi the track drops sharply to a bridge over the **Río Quimsa Chata** (which suffers varying degrees of damage each rainy season), then climbs past a soccer field on the left to a pass at the hamlet of **Chojila**. From there the route descends to the final crossing of the Río Takesi via a concrete bridge. From there it's a 3km, 1½-hour trudge along an **aqueduct** to the ramshackle mining settlement of **Chojlla** (2280m), where there is a cheap *alojamiento*. At dawn, the village bakery turns out fresh bread.

From Chojlla, crowded buses leave for Yanakachi (US$0.15) and La Paz (US$1.50) at 5:30am and around noon daily – buy your ticket on arrival. If you can't endure a night in Chojlla (and few people can), keep hiking 5km (about an hour) down the road past the headquarters of the new hydroelectric power project to the more pleasant village of Yanakachi.

YANAKACHI
elevation 2000m

Yanakachi, 87km southeast of La Paz, is near the fringe of the Yungas. One of the oldest towns in the region, it was an early trading center along the Takesi trail, which was constructed more than 800 years ago as a coca and tropical-produce trade route. During the colonial period, the town's role as a commercial center expanded as *hacienda* owners settled there. By 1522 they'd already constructed the **Iglesia de Santa Bárbara**, the Yungas' oldest existing church. The bells in the tower date from 1735 and 1755, and in the lower part of town you can still see traces of the colonial heritage in the colonial balconies and thick stone walls.

Modern amenities include Entel and Cotel telephone offices on Plaza Libertad, as well as a health clinic. For trekking information, contact Fundación Pueblo which has an office on the plaza and can help arrange transportation, as well as guides and mule hire.

Sleeping & Eating

The nicest place to stay is **Hostal Metropoly** (La Paz ☎ 245-6643; per person US$3), which has a good pool table and newly refurbished rooms.

Alojamiento Tomny (r per person US$2; 🏊) has a pool and pleasant gardens – it's across from the large trail map; ask for Nelly or Tomas at the nearby shop with the Fanta sign if nobody is home. The larger **Hostal San Carlos** (La Paz ☎ 223-0088; US$4) has great views from rooms 5, 6 and 7.

Don Edgar and English-speaking Doña Frida, owner of Hostal Metropoly, run recommended restaurants; these are located on the plaza.

Getting There & Away

Veloz del Norte buses depart Mina Chojlla for La Paz (US$1.50) daily at 5:30am and 1pm, and pass through Yanakachi, stopping in front of Hostal San Carlos at 6am and 1:30pm. It's best to buy tickets in Chojlla, but there's usually little problem getting a seat on the morning bus. Minibuses to La Paz (US$1.50) leave the plaza in Yanakachi less frequently; inquire locally about the departure times. Alternatively, you can walk for an hour down the track out to the main road, where you'll readily find passing transportation to either La Paz or Chulumani.

Veloz del Norte buses leave from their La Paz office (☎ 421-7206; Ocabaya 489-495, Villa Fátima) for Yanakachi daily at 8am and 2pm.

YUNGA CRUZ TREK

This is a relatively little-trodden trek with good stretches of pre-Hispanic paving that connects the village of Chuñavi with the Sud Yungas' provincial capital of Chulumani. There are a couple of variations to the standard trek, including a pass over the northern shoulder of Illimani to get you started, as well as an alternative – and considerably more spectacular – route over Cerro Khala Ciudad, which begins beyond Lambate. It's the hardest of the Inca trails and usually takes five days. Expect to see lots of condors, eagles, hawks, vultures and hummingbirds along the route.

The map in this book is intended only as a rough guide; you'll need to carry the 1:50,000 topo sheets *Palca – 6044-I*, *Lambate – 6044-II* and *Chulumani – 6044-III*.

Access

There's a good case for hiring a 4WD to take you to the trailhead at Tres Ríos, Chuñavi or Lambate. Otherwise you'll first have to get to Ventilla (p119). Beyond Ventilla, the road is poor and vehicles are scarce.

A Bolsa Negra *micro* from Plaza Belzu in La Paz will get you all the way to Tres Ríos, 40km from Ventilla, where the vehicle turns north toward the Bolsa Negra mine. From Tres Ríos, you can either continue walking along the road toward Chuñavi or walk over the northern shoulder of Illimani to Estancia Totoral (not to be confused with Totoral Pampa, 3km west of Tres Ríos). See the Illimani option, below.

Alternatively, you can go straight to Chuñavi by *micro*, which is an all-day trip from La Paz. Buses leave Calle Venancio Burgoa, near Plaza Líbano, at least twice weekly (Friday and Monday are the best bets) at 9am. Advance information is hard to come by and no reservations are taken; you'll just have to turn up early (around 7am) and see if a *micro* is leaving. Failing those options, go to Ventilla and wait for an eastbound *camión*, or begin walking along the road over the Abra Pacuani (4524m).

Taxi access from La Paz (US$70) isn't good owing to the distance and condition of the road; it's at least five hours to the Chuñavi trailhead and six or more to Lambate. It would be preferable to hire a 4WD and driver from La Paz (see the Transport chapter, p365).

The return to La Paz is straightforward; catch one of the many daily buses or *camiónes* from the *tranca* in Chulumani.

The Route
ILLIMANI OPTION

Once you've made it to **Tres Ríos**, cross the bridge over the **Río Khañuma** and follow the **Río Pasto Grande** uphill toward **Bolsa Blanca mine**, on the skirts of Illimani. After 2km a track leads downhill and across the river (it traverses around the northernmost spur of Illimani), but it's better to continue along the western bank of the river to the **Pasto Grande campsite**, at some abandoned buildings at the head of the valley. Here begins a steep and direct huff-and-puff walk up the valley headwall to the 4900m pass below Bolsa Blanca mine, which is overlooked by the triple-peak of Illimani. It takes the best part of two hours to get from the valley floor to the pass.

From the pass, the route becomes more obvious as it descends steeply into the

YUNGA CRUZ TREK

of the altitude as well as the several exhausting climbs and treacherous descents. The best campsite is at the Pasto Grande valley headwall below Bolsa Blanca.

CHUÑAVI TRAILHEAD
Approximately 5km east of Estancia Totoral, turn northeast (left) along the track that descends through the village of **Chuñavi**. Beyond the village the track traverses a long steady slope, high above the **Río Susisa**, and keeps to about 4200m for the next 30km. It passes the westernmost flank of **Cerro Khala Ciudad**, but unfortunately the spectacular views of the mountain's cirques and turrets are hidden from view.

About 2km beyond Cerro Khala Ciudad the track joins the Lambate trailhead route, and 4km later it skirts the peak of **Cerro Yunga Cruz**, before trending downhill along a ridgeline through dense cloud forest. Just below the tree line is a prominent campsite – the last before the trail's end – but unfortunately it's dry, so fill your water bottles at every opportunity. Despite the dampness and the amount of vegetation the trail stays above the watershed areas, and running water is scarce unless it has been raining.

After the track narrows and starts to descend steeply, the vegetation thickens and often obscures the way. Three hours below the tree line the trail forks in a grassy saddle between two hills. The right fork climbs the shoulder of **Cerro Duraznuni** before descending anew. After approximately two hours you'll pass through a steep plantation to the hillside village of **Estancia Sikilini**, a citrus estate across the Huajtata Gorge from Chulumani. When you hit the road, turn left and continue for about two hours into **Chulumani**.

LAMBATE TRAILHEAD
This route is more difficult but also more beautiful than the Chuñavi route. Lambate is about 2½ hours on foot east of Estancia Totoral, and 2km beyond the Chuñavi cutoff. Lambate, which enjoys a commanding view, has a *tienda* – the last place to buy a soft drink or pick up snacks.

Follow the continuation of the road from La Paz toward the village of **San Antonio** until you reach a small house on the left, set on a precipice. Descend to the house on any of the small paths, and just beyond it turn

Quebrada Mal Paso. Once you've entered the valley, cross to the southern bank of the **Río Mal Paso** as soon as possible and follow it down – it's a steep descent – to the village of **Estancia Totoral** back on the Lambate road, where there's a small shop.

Even strong hikers will need two days from Tres Ríos to Estancia Totoral because right to follow a path between some bean fields to an opening in a stone wall. If you take the left fork beyond the wall, you'll descend to a footbridge over the dramatic **Río Chunga Mayu**. Here, you should turn downstream onto a path beside a small house with a cross on top. After crossing the **Río Colani** (collect water here!), head uphill into the village of **Quircoma** (Ranchería).

Follow the main track up through Quircoma; above the village, you'll reach the last possible campsite, but it's waterless. Ascend the only path out of the village; when you reach a gate, cross the pasture – the track continues on the other side. From here the route is fairly straightforward but a real struggle – it's a 10km, 2000m climb past **Laguna Kasiri** to the **pass**.

After the first couple of hours the heat will ease a bit, and two hours later you'll reach a well-watered meadow with good campsites beside the Río Kasiri, which you've been following. At this point, the track makes a steep ascent to the prominent mountain spur to the west, then levels off before the final short climb to **Laguna Kasiri**, which is said to be haunted by an evil spirit. This lovely and mysterious spot lies in a cirque surrounded by the snowy peaks of **Cerro Khala Ciudad**.

Skirt around the right side of the lake; here the path crosses the stream, then switchbacks upward for about 2½ hours to the 4300m pass on Cerro Khala Ciudad, where there's an *apacheta* and an incredible view from the Cordillera Real right down into the Yungas. Immediately after the pass, bear left and pass a narrow section of trail with a vertical drop to the right. After this section, 20 to 30 minutes beyond the pass, you should take the left fork between two large rocks over the ridge or you'll descend into the wrong valley.

After this fork the trail descends and deteriorates. About 2km beyond the pass, you'll meet up with the Chuñavi route, where you should turn right. There's a good campsite just after a small stream crossing; fill up with water here, because it will probably be the last water available.

From this point the increasingly forested route, now marked by green arrows, trends downhill most of the way to Chulumani. When you reach a small meadow before **Cerro Duraznuni**, continue directly across it, then take the right fork, which climbs the hill but skirts the right side of the peak.

At this point you begin a long and occasionally steep descent through increasingly populated countryside to the citrus farm at **Estancia Sikilini**. You can either follow the shortcut across **Huajtata Gorge** – which will seem an excruciating prospect at this stage – or just lumber along the longer but mercifully level road into Chulumani.

CHULUMANI
elevation 1700m
The Sud Yungas' capital used to be the end of the road and it retains that feel. At a subtropically warm and often wet altitude, it's a great trekking base camp and a relaxing weekend retreat with a great view. It's also a center for growing coffee, bananas, citrus and sweet coca. The only time Chulumani breaks its pervasive tranquility is during the week following August 24, when it stages the riotous **Fiesta de San Bartolomé**. Lots of winter-weary highlanders turn up to join in the festivities.

Rebels during the 1781 La Paz revolt escaped to the Yungas and hid out in the valleys around Chulumani. Today the area is home to a large population of African-Bolivians, descendants of slaves brought to work in the Potosí mines. Locals claim the town's name is derived from *cholumanya* (tiger's dew), to commemorate a jaguar's visit to the town; well, it's a good story anyway.

Increasing political pressure on coca growers has recently heated up in this area – never mind that the local crop is used almost exclusively for domestic consumption.

Information
Although Chulumani does have a nominal tourist office, it's inactive. The **Cámara Hotelera** (☎ 213-6109) takes hotel reservations and is planning to open an office near the plaza. In the meantime hotel owners like Xavier Sarabia at the Country Guesthouse are your best source of information. Banco Union changes travelers checks for 5% commission. There are several Entel and Cotel offices near Plaza Libertad. Tune into Radio Yungas (93.1 FM or 730 AM) for a taste of local politics.

Sights & Activities
Chulumani sees few visitors, yet it is a good base for several worthwhile excursions.

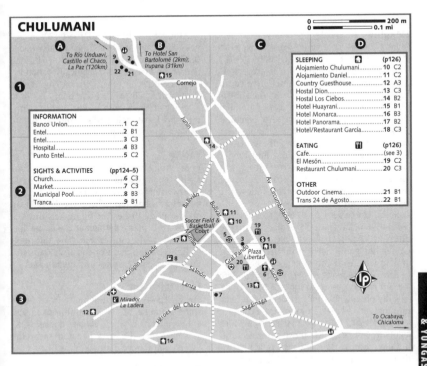

CHULUMANI

INFORMATION
Banco Union	1 C2
Entel	2 B1
Entel	3 C3
Hospital	4 B3
Punto Entel	5 C2

SIGHTS & ACTIVITIES (pp124–5)
Church	6 C3
Market	7 C3
Municipal Pool	8 B3
Tranca	9 B1

SLEEPING (p126)
Alojamiento Chulumani	10 C2
Alojamiento Daniel	11 C2
Country Guesthouse	12 A3
Hostal Dion	13 C3
Hostal Los Ciebos	14 B2
Hotel Huayrani	15 B1
Hotel Monarca	16 B3
Hotel Panorama	17 B2
Hotel/Restaurant García	18 C3

EATING (p126)
Cafe	(see 3)
El Mesón	19 C2
Restaurant Chulumani	20 C3

OTHER
Outdoor Cinema	21 B1
Trans 24 de Agosto	22 B1

Map labels: To Río Unduavi, Castillo el Chaco, La Paz (120km); To Hotel San Bartolomé (2km); Irupana (31km); Cornejo; Junín; Bolívar; Ballivián; Av. Circumbalación; Av. Crispín Andrade; Junín; Salmón; Gral Pando; Plaza Libertad; Sucre; Lanza; Heroes del Chaco; Mirador La Ladera; Sagárnaga; To Ocabaya; Chicaloma; Soccer Field & Basketball Court

When it gets too hot, you might check whether the dry **municipal pool** (US$0.15) is back in action. Several hotels allow nonguests to take a dip for US$1.35.

The most interesting day trip is probably to the **Apa Apa Ecological Forest** (locally pronounced 'Apapa'), 8km from Chulumani. The private 800-hectare forest is one of the last remnants of primary humid montane forest in the Yungas, and is rich in tree, orchid and bird species. It's a beautiful place for day hikes and overnight camping. For information and to arrange transportation, contact **Señor Ramiro Portugal** (☎ 213-6106) in Chulumani or the **forest administration** (La Paz ☎ 279-0381; apaapayungas@hotmail.com; Miraflores) in La Paz. Admission, guide and transportation from Chulumani cost US$25 for groups of up to five people. From La Paz, you can book through **Apa Apa Trek Rainforest Expeditions** (☎ /fax 272-3662; aptrekad@ceibo.entelnet .bo; Zona Sur, La Paz).

HIKING
A lovely five-hour one-way walk will take you to the clean and swimmable **Río Sol-acama**; perhaps catch a *micro* down and walk back. In three to four hours you can also walk to the quaint village of **Ocabaya**, which claims to have Bolivia's second-oldest church. The nearby Afro-Bolivian community of **Chicaloma** is best known for its annual **town festival** on May 27, which feaures lots of traditional *saya* dancing.

WHITEWATER RAFTING
The road to Chulumani follows part of another good whitewater river, the **Río Unduavi**. The upper section ranges from essentially unnavigable Class V to VI, with steep chutes, powerful currents, large boulder gardens, blind corners and waterfalls. Beyond this section it mellows out into some challenging Class IV whitewater followed by Class II and III rapids. Access is limited, but the Chulumani road does offer several put-ins and take-outs. The best access points have been left by construction crews who've mined the riverbanks for sand and gravel. A good take-out point is Puente Villa, which is three to four hours below the best put-ins.

Sleeping

Country Guesthouse (campsite & hot shower per person US$2.65; s/d with bath & breakfast US$8/13.50; 🔊) The friendliest place in town is gregarious Xavier Sarabia Sardon's homely five-room hideaway. To give you an idea of the atmosphere, he once lived in New York, attended Woodstock and hiked the Appalachian trail. Amenities include a pool table, and an extensive video and music library. Good meals are provided on request and Xavier is full of sightseeing and adventurous trip ideas. It's a 10-minute walk from the plaza; head for Mirador Ladera then follow the signs for 100m.

Hostal Los Ceibos (🕿 289-6014; Junin s/n; r per person US$4, with bath US$4.65) Adjacent to the odorous coca-leaf warehouses, this newcomer has good views, a motherly owner, and an ice cream and sweets café below.

Hotel Panorama (🕿 213-6109, La Paz 🕿 278-3899; Murillo at Andrade; r per person with bath US$6; 🔊) A friendly place with a nice garden and restaurant that serves breakfast for an extra charge.

Hotel Monarca (🕿 213-6121, La Paz 🕿 235-1019; with TV US$6.50; 🔊) Like most ex-prefectural holiday camps, the Monarca is a bit run down and lacks character, but the enormous pool is open to nonguests for US$1.50.

Hotel San Bartolomé (🕿 213-6114, La Paz 🕿 244-0208; d from US$30; 🔊) Owned by the upscale Plaza Hotel in La Paz, this relatively posh pad is notable for its odd Z-shaped swimming pool. Deals include four-person *cabañas* for US$60 and all-inclusive weekend packages from US$60 per person. For weekend guests the hotel organizes minibus transportation from La Paz. It's 2km out of town on the road to Urupana.

Hotel García (🕿 715-08058; US$2, with bath US$3.35) A good bet except on Friday or Saturday nights when you'll either have to wear earplugs or join the noisy fun at the attached disco.

Hotel Huayrani (🕿 213-6351; US$6, weekends US$10; 🔊) A complex of kitchen-equipped apartments with a large manicured garden, cable TV and telephones.

Alojamiento Daniel (US$2, with bath US$3.25) Has clean rooms with shared hot showers and serves decent *almuerzos*.

A number of cheap options cluster around the main plaza. In a pinch you might try the good-value **Hostal Dion** (🕿 213-6070; US$3.75-4) or **Alojamiento Chulumani** (US$2).

Along the Chulumani road (20km beyond Unduavi) at 1934m, the idyllic two-star **Castillo el Chaco** (La Paz 🕿 241-0579) is a unique riverfront castle that sporadically functions as a hotel. At last check it was closed, but it's worth a call to see if it's open. It's only a couple of hours from La Paz, and its swimming pool, waterfalls and subtropical climate make it an appealing weekend getaway.

Eating

Food choices are limited. Try the restaurant at the **Country Guesthouse** or one of the basic *comedores* at the *tranca*. The spic-'n'-span **market** also has good cheap meals. **El Mesón** on the plaza dishes up filling set lunches. Across the plaza **Restaurant Chulumani** has an upstairs dining terrace. The **café** next to Entel on the plaza opens at 7:30am and does good coffee, cakes and *empanadas*.

Entertainment

On Friday and Saturday nights **Hotel Garcia** spins karaoke at its cacophonous disco. On weekends a small **outdoor cinema** (OK, a large-screen TV in a pension) near the *tranca* plays second-string films.

Getting There & Away

The beautiful route from La Paz to Chulumani, which extends on to Irupana, is wider, less unnerving and statistically safer than the road to Coroico. Yunga Cruz trekkers finish in Chulumani, and the town is readily accessed from Yanakachi at the end of the Takesi trek. From Yanakachi walk down to the main road and wait for transport headed downhill; it's about 1½ hours to Chulumani.

From Villa Fátima in La Paz, Turbus Totai buses depart when full for Chulumani (US$2, four hours) from 8am to 4pm. *Camiones* (US$1.25, nine hours) leave between 5am and 2pm. From Chulumani, Trans San Bartolomé has daily departures for La Paz at 5:30am, noon and 2pm. Trans Chulumani and 24 de Agosto minibuses leave hourly for La Paz from the *tranca*.

If you're coming from Coroico or Guanay, get off at Unduavi and wait for another vehicle. Carry a range of clothing in order to accommodate the climate range along this route.

It's also possible to go to Coroico via Coripata; take a La Paz-bound bus and get off at the crossroads just after Puente Villa at Km 93. Here, wait for a bus or *camión* to Coripata and then change again for a lift to Coroico. It's a lo-o-o-ng and dusty but worthwhile trip.

SORATA

pop 2500 / elevation 2670m

Sorata is a crumbling colonial gem. Perched on a hillside in a valley beneath the towering snowcapped peaks of Illampu (6362m) and Ancohuma (6427m, but rumored to be taller), it enjoys one of the finest settings of any Bolivian village. It's a popular weekend getaway and a relaxing base camp for a growing number of hikers and mountaineers.

In colonial days Sorata provided a link to the Alto Beni's goldfields and rubber plantations, and a gateway to the Amazon Basin. In 1791 it was the site of a distinctly unorthodox siege by indigenous leader Andrés Tupac Amaru and his 16,000 soldiers. They constructed dikes above the town, and when these had filled with runoff from the slopes of Illampu, they opened the floodgates and the town was washed away.

Now that commercial traffic moves into the Yungas from La Paz, Sorata has slipped into comfortable obscurity. Today it's best known to paradise-seekers who've re-routed the Gringo trail to include this formerly off-the-beaten-track destination. You'd be hard-pressed to find someone who doesn't like the place. The main **town fiesta**, which can be a riotous affair, is held on September 14.

Information

Sunday is market day, and Tuesday, when many businesses are closed, is considered Domingo Sorateño (Sorata's Sunday).

While some shops and tourist businesses may change cash, the place to change travelers checks is **Pete's Place** (p130), which charges customers a 3% commission and has a good guidebook library and book exchange. **Prodem** (east side of Plaza) does cash advances for a hefty fee. For Internet access, try **Buho's** (south side of plaza) or **Residencial Sorata** (p130), which both have temperamental dial-up connections for US$2.65 an hour.

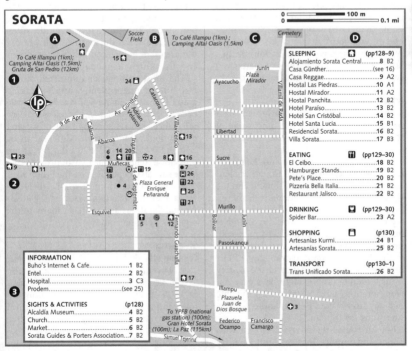

SORATA

0 — 100 m
0 — 0.1 mi

SLEEPING		(pp128–9)
Alojamiento Sorata Central	8	B2
Casa Günther	(see 16)	
Casa Reggae	9	A2
Hostal Las Piedras	10	A1
Hostal Mirador	11	A2
Hostal Panchita	12	B2
Hotel Paraíso	13	B2
Hotel San Cristóbal	14	B2
Hotel Santa Lucia	15	B1
Residencial Sorata	16	B2
Villa Sorata	17	B3

EATING		(pp129–30)
El Ceibo	18	B2
Hamburger Stands	19	B2
Pete's Place	20	B2
Pizzería Bella Italia	21	B2
Restaurant Jalisco	22	B2

DRINKING		(pp129–30)
Spider Bar	23	A2

SHOPPING		(p130)
Artesanías Kurmi	24	B1
Artesanías Sorata	25	B2

TRANSPORT		(pp130–1)
Trans Unificado Sorata	26	B2

INFORMATION		
Buho's Internet & Cafe	1	B2
Entel	2	B2
Hospital	3	C3
Prodem	(see 25)	

SIGHTS & ACTIVITIES	(p128)	
Alcaldía Museum	4	B2
Church	5	B2
Market	6	B2
Sorata Guides & Porters Association	7	B2

Soccer Field

To Café Illampu (1km);
Camping Altaí Oasis (1.5km)

Cemetery

To Café Illampu (1km);
Camping Altaí Oasis (1.5km);
Gruta de San Pedro (12km)

Junín
Plaza
Mirador

Ayacucho

Villami de Rada

9 de April

Av. Günther
Adrián Velasco

Calina
Iturri

Villavicencio

Abaroa

Libertad

Esquivel

Muñecas

14 de Septiembre

Plaza General
Enrique
Peñaranda

Sucre

Murillo

Bolivar

Junín

Pasoskanqui

Fernando Guachalla

To YPFB (national
gas station) (100m);
Gran Hotel Sorata
(100m); La Paz (115km)

Illampu
Plazuela
Juan de
Dios Bosque

Federico
Ocampo

Francisco
Camargo

Samuel Tejerina

THE CORDILLERAS & YUNGAS

Sights

There isn't much of specific interest in Sorata itself – its main attractions are its medieval ambience, which is accentuated when the mists roll in, and its maze of steep stairways and narrow cobbled lanes. It's worth taking a look at **Casa Günther**, a historic mansion that now houses the Residencial Sorata (p129). It was built in 1895 as the home of the Richters, a quinine-trading family. It was later taken over by the Günthers, who were involved in rubber extraction until 1955.

The main square **Plaza General Enrique Peñaranda** is Sorata's showcase. With the town's best view of the *nevados*, it's graced by towering date palms and immaculate gardens. Unfortunately it's fenced off in the evening. Upstairs in the town hall on the plaza there's the free **Alcaldía museum** (☺ 8am-noon & 2-5pm Wed-Mon) containing a number of artifacts from the Inca Marka site near Laguna Chillata and an exhibit of old festival clothing.

Although it's nothing to shout about, many visitors do the scenic 12km hike to the **Gruta de San Pedro** (San Pedro Cave; admission US$1; ☺ 8am-5pm), a six-hour round-trip from Sorata (a taxi one-way costs US$2). An attendant will crank up the lights inside the cave, where there is a tepid lagoon. Bring a flashlight, water and snacks – or, better yet, stop by Café Illampu (p130) en route.

Activities

Sorata is best known as a convenient base for hikers and climbers pursuing some of Bolivia's finest landscapes. The peak hiking season is May to September.

Ambitious adventurers can do the seven-day **El Camino del Oro trek** (p131), an ancient trading route between the Altiplano and the Río Tipuani gold fields. Alternatively there's the steep climb to Laguna Challata (a long day hike), Comunidad Lakathiya (another long day hike), Laguna Glacial (three days), the challenging **Mapiri trail** (five days; p133) or the Illampu circuit (seven days). The ultimate hardcore challenge is the 20-day Trans Cordillera route: eight days gets you from Sorata to Lago Sistaña, with possible four-day (to Huayna Potosi) and eight-day extensions (to Illimani).

For all routes it's advisable to go with guides and inquire locally about security before attempting any treks, as many serious incidents continue to be reported. Hikers should carry the *Alpenvereinskarte Cordillera Real Nord* (Illampu) 1:50,000. Most popular hikes pass through traditional areas, especially the Illampu circuit, so stay tuned to local sensitivities. Unless you're invited, don't set up camp anywhere near a village, and if you feel unwelcome, move on as quickly as possible.

Basic information on climbing Illampu and Ancohuma is included under Cordillera Real (p137). For detailed trekking information, pick up Lonely Planet's *Trekking in the Central Andes*.

Tours

While it's possible to hike independently, some hikes, such as the Illampu circuit and the Mapiri trail, are best done with a guide, mainly because of the need to be aware of local sensibilities and the difficultly finding the routes. Several unlicensed upstart agencies have sprung up and tout heavily on the plaza, but think about where they might cut corners before you opt for the cheapest service in lieu of a licensed agency. Ask around among recent returnees to find the best guides. Top-notch foreign guides often descend on town during the high season, but are often booked out, charge top dollar and are in high demand.

The most economical authorized option is to hire an independent, Spanish-speaking guide from the **Sorata Guides & Porters Association** (☎ /fax 213-6698; guiasorata@hotmail.com; Sucre 302), which also rents equipment of varying quality and arranges many different treks. Budget for US$12 to US$20 a day per group plus food (clients must also provide the guide's meals), depending on the group size.

If you can track him down, Louis Demers, a French Canadian based at the Residencial Sorata, is an expert on many of the region's trekking routes.

Sleeping

Camping Altai Oasis (☎ 715-19856; resaltai@hotmail .com; 20 min walk from town off road to caves; camping US$1.35, s/d US$2.65/6.65, with bath US$10.65, cabins for 3-5 people US$20-40) Welcoming Bolivian hosts Johny and Roxana run this beautiful riverside retreat. In the high season a coffee shop operates in a bizarrely painted structure, courtesy of a South African artist who couldn't tear himself away. There's also a lounge, book exchange, laundry service, table games, hot showers and a communal kitchen with fire pits. The new *cabañas* are yurt-like and simple but very comfortable and romantic. Coming from town, descend the Calle Catacora steps, then follow the downhill track past the soccer field to the Río Challa Suyu. After the bridge, follow the path to the left and climb back up to the road and turn left. After 150m you'll see their sign; the camp sites are on the riverbank 1km down this winding road, a 20-minute walk from the plaza.

Hostal Las Piedras (☎ 719-1634; Ascarrunz s/n; US$2.65) This new, *simpatico* German-run (English spoken) place has six artistically decorated rooms, some with fantastic valley views, and two shared hot showers. The optional breakfast includes homemade wholemeal bread and yogurt courtesy of Café Illampu. It's near the town soccer oval, a 10-minute walk from the plaza down Calle Ascarrunz (a rough track) off the shortcut to the cave.

Villa Sorata (☎ 213-6688; Guachalla 238; s/d with bath & TV US$8/11.50) This newly remodeled four-room earthy colonial house is Swedish- and American-run as a B&B; the price includes breakfast. It has a wonderful courtyard and a sunlit terrace with great Illampu views.

Hotel Paraíso (☎ 213-6671; Villavicencio s/n; r per person with bath US$4-5) This family-run spot has a bright patio, comfortable rooms, lots of flowers and a good restaurant.

Hostal Panchita (☎ 213-5038; south side of plaza; s/d US$2.50/4) The pleasant peach-colored Panchita has ample rooms with shared bath and a nice clean courtyard where travelers gather to chat, flirt and play card games.

Hotel Mirador (☎ 289-5008; Muñecas 400; with breakfast US$2.65) Sorata's pleasant Hostelling International affiliate has a sunny terrace, a restaurant, a bar, basic rooms with shared bath and lovely views down the valley.

Residencial Sorata (☎ 279-3459; northeast cnr of plaza; US$2-5.50; 🖳) The antique rooms in this colonial-style mansion, known as Casa Günther, are nice to look at, but you'll be happier sleeping in one of the newer refurbished rooms with private bath. Amenities include a restaurant, a spacious lounge, ping-pong, Internet access, resident hummingbirds and a good book exchange. The manager, Louis Demers, speaks French,

English and Spanish, and videos are shown nightly.

Casa Reggae (Villa Rosa s/n; US$1.35) Calling all dread-heads to this Rastafarian favorite, with its friendly café, bar, hot showers, kitchen and trekking info. Visiting artisans cram the place in high season and musicians occasionally jam in the outdoor pub on weekends.

Hotel Landhaus Copacabana (☎/fax 213-6670; www.boliviatrek.com; low/high season US$2/4, d with bath US$15/20; 🖳) A German-run hangout including a sunny garden with hammocks, a good restaurant and a huge video collection. It's 10 minutes from the plaza toward San Pedro.

Hotel Santa Lucia (☎ 213-6686; across from soccer field off shortcut to caves; US$2.65, with bath US$4) This new, brightly colored place with carpeted rooms, and laundry sinks also has a *chifa* restaurant. The friendly owner, Serafin, is eager to please – he's pure Al Pacino from *Casino*, white loafers and all.

Gran Hotel Sorata (ex-Prefectural; ☎ 289-5003, La Paz ☎ 272-2846; opposite gas station at entrance to town; low/high season US$6.65/12, all-inclusive US$16.75) This castle-like 1940s republican-style building may have fine stained glass but its slouching beds and sketchy electric showers make it only mildly appealing. It's deserted midweek, but often booked out by groups in high season. Nonguests can plunge in the murky pool for US$0.40.

The cheapest place is the basic but friendly **Alojamiento Sorata Central** (north side of plaza; US$1.35) with plaza views and shared cold showers. Nearby, the spartan **Hotel San Cristóbal** (US$2) also has only cold water.

Camping (US$1) is also available at the friendly Café Illampu (p130) and Hotel Mirador (above). Ask at Café Illampu about a couple of basic, cheap rooms for rent with a local family 15-minutes walk beyond the café in the *tranquilo* countryside.

Eating & Drinking

Small, inexpensive restaurants around the market and the plaza sell cheap and filling *almuerzos*. For a quick B$1 burger piled high with weenies and fries, hit the hamburger stands on the northwest corner of the plaza, where *chollitas* do fry-ups until the wee hours. For a decent budget lunch, there are a couple of small and inexpensive places near the plaza.

Pete's Place (☎ 289-5005; 🕙 8:30am-10pm; mains US$1.50-5, set meals US$1.65-2) In the morning you'll get big breakfasts with real brewed coffee and healthy muesli, pancakes or crêpes. The highlight, however, is the artistically presented vegetarian fare that's served at lunch and dinner. Carnivores can also be accommodated with big burgers or a T-bone steak. Neil Young is often on the stereo and the current *Guardian Weekly* is always in the periodical stack, next to the best reference library in town (including many current LP guides). Trekking maps and info are also available. Credit cards accepted.

Café Illampu (🕙 closed Tue) Out in the *campo*, you can also visit this lovely Alpine-like café which, not surprisingly, is Swiss-run. The owner Stephan is a master baker who crafts sandwiches on homemade bread, as well as preparing magical cakes, pies, yogurt and coffee. Other features include good music, a book exchange and assorted four-footed farmyard types. Passing visitors have left their own marks in the form of artwork, carvings and mosaics. It's an obligatory stop en route back from the San Pedro Cave hike.

Altai Oasis (☎ 715-19856; 20min walk from town off road to caves; mains US$2-5) serves coffee, drinks and its trademark steaks, veggie treats, goulash, borscht and other Eastern European specialties. In case you're wondering, the name is indeed derived from the remote Mongolian range. There's a book exchange, and happy hour is from 4pm to 6pm.

Restaurant Jalisco (east side of plaza; mains US$2-3, set meals US$2-3) delivers an ambitious menu, with Mexican choices being the best bet. There's also standard pizza, pasta, tacos and an admirable attempt at a burrito (wrapped in a sort of crêpe).

Pizzería Bella Italia (☎ 289-5009; east side of plaza; mains US$2-5) Once upon a time Sorata was home to a real Italian pizzeria. When the owner split for La Paz after one too many road blockades, his staff scrambled to set up their own shops, with the same menus, etc. The cooking isn't quite what it used to be, but many travelers end up at one of the several nearly identical places on the plaza nonetheless. You may begin to believe the rumors that several of the pizza places share a kitchen when your order takes a long time to arrive.

Residencial Sorata (☎ 279-3459; northeast cnr of plaza; set meals US$1.65-1.85) The hotel's restaurant serves decent breakfast as well as set lunches and dinners.

Landhaus Copacabana (☎ /fax 213-6670; dinner US$2.50) The evening set menu includes salad, soup, main course, dessert and a hot drink.

Pizzería Kon-Tiki (☎ 719-38889; kontikisorata@ yahoo.com) Keep an eye out near the plaza for pizzas from Italian chef Ermanno – or muesli, milkshakes and gourmet international dinners 3km out of town on the road to the cave, if he hasn't made his planned move back to town yet.

El Ceibo (Muñecas 339; 🕙 7am-11pm) Serves breakfasts, vegetarian dishes, sandwiches, grilled food and typical Bolivian dishes, plus *salteñas* and *tucumanas* on Sunday.

Entertainment

Cocktails (and occasional live music) can be found at the cozy pub formerly known as the Spider Bar, which is 250m west of the plaza and due to re-open under new management, or across the way at the smokin' Casa Reggae.

Shopping

On the east side of the plaza, **Artesanías Sorata** (☎ 213-5061) sells a range of locally produced crafts and textiles, including unique hand-knitted woolens with natural dyes for adults and children, as well as dolls, wall-hangings and carved wooden articles.

For local handiwork look for the friendly **Artesanías Kurmi** (Gunther 107), in a rustic two-story white house. Here Wilma Velasco sells wonderful homemade and hand-dyed clothing, hats, dolls, bags and wall-hangings for excellent prices; also ask to try the homemade orange wine! There's no sign, but if you ring the bell, she'll open up.

Getting There & Away

Sorata is a long way from the other Yungas towns, and there's no road connecting it directly with Coroico, so you must go through La Paz. The rough route to La Paz has been approved for paving, but don't count on it happening anytime soon.

From La Paz, **Trans Unificado Sorata** (☎ 238-1693) departs the cemetery district 10 times daily (US$1.50, 4½ hours). From Sorata, La Paz-bound buses depart from the plaza hourly from 4am to 5pm. For Copacabana you must get off at the junction town of

Huarina and wait for another, probably packed, bus.

The only road route between Sorata and the lowlands is a rough 4WD track that leads to the gold-mining settlement of Mapiri. It strikes out from Sorata and passes through Quiabaya, Tacacoma, Itulaya and Consata, roughly following the courses of the Ríos Llica, Consata and Mapiri all the way. The biggest drawbacks are the horrendous mud, the road construction and some river crossings that are passable only with 4WD. *Camiónetas* leave Sorata daily for the grueling journey to Consata (US$3.50, four hours) and on to the Sorata Limitada mine (US$5, seven hours). From Sorata Limitada, you'll find *camiónetas* on to Mapiri, which is another three hours away.

EL CAMINO DEL ORO (GOLD DIGGER'S TRAIL)

This was once a classic, demanding trek along a paved Inca transport route, but over recent years it has been degraded by road building and indiscriminate gold-mining activity. If the current road-building trend continues, this popular hike between Sorata and the Río Tipuani goldfields may soon disappear.

For nearly 1000 years this Inca road has been used as a commerce and trade link between the Altiplano and the lowland goldfields. Indeed, the Tipuani and Mapiri valleys were major sources of the gold that once adorned the Inca capital, Cuzco.

Today, however, the fields are worked primarily by bulldozers and dredges owned by mining cooperatives. They scour and scrape the landscape for the shiny stuff and dump the detritus, which is picked over by out-of-work Aymará refugees from the highlands. Squalid settlements of plastic, banana leaves and sheet aluminium have sprung up along the rivers, the banks of which are staked out for panning by wildcat miners. It's projected that gold will soon replace tin as Bolivia's greatest source of mineral export income.

Fortunately the upper part of the route remains magnificent, and almost everything between Ancoma and Chusi has been left alone, including some wonderfully exhausting Inca staircases and dilapidated ancient highway engineering.

This trek is more challenging than the Takesi, El Choro or Yunga Cruz routes; if

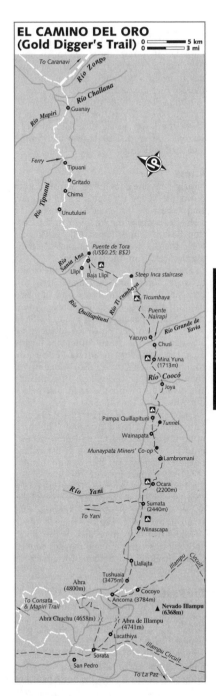

EL CAMINO DEL ORO (Gold Digger's Trail) 0 — 5 km / 0 — 3 mi

To Caranavi
Río Zongo
Río Challana
Río Mapiri
Guanay
Ferry
Río Tipuani
Tipuani
Gritado
Chima
Unutuluni
Puente de Tora (US$0.25; B$2)
Río Santa Ana
Llipi
Baja Llipi
Steep Inca staircase
Río Ti cumbaya
Río Quillapituni
Ticumbaya
Puente Nairapi
Río Grande de Yavia
Yacuyo
Chusi
Mina Yuna (1713m)
Río Coocó
Joya
Pampa Quillapituni
Tunnel
Wainapata
Munaypata Miners' Co-op
Lambromani
Río Yani
Ocara (2200m)
Sumata (2440m)
To Yani
Minascapa
Llallajta
Illampu Circuit
Tushuaia (3475m)
Abra (4800m)
Cocoyo
Ancoma (3784m)
To Consata & Mapiri Trail
Nevado Illampu (6368m)
Abra Chuchu (4658m)
Abra de Illampu (4741m)
Lacathiya
Sorata
Illampu Circuit
San Pedro
To La Paz

THE CORDILLERAS & YUNGAS

you want to get the most from it, plan on six or seven days to walk between Sorata and Llipi, less if you opt for a jeep to Ancoma. At Llipi, find transport to Tipuani or Guanay to avoid a walking-pace tour through the worst of the destruction.

Although it's unlikely the road will reach as far up the valley as Ancoma, the aesthetics of the lower valley have already been scarred and eroded by large-scale mining and road building.

Access

Nearly everyone does the route from Sorata down the valley to Tipuani and Guanay, simply because it's generally downhill. It's a shame, because the final bits of this section pass through devastated landscapes. Nevertheless, tradition demands describing the walk from the top down.

There are three options for the route between Sorata and Ancoma. First, you can rent a 4WD in Sorata and cut two days off the trek. After bargaining, you'll pay US$3.50 per person or around US$40 to rent the entire vehicle. A challenging alternative is the steep route that begins near the cemetery in Sorata. The route roughly follows the Río Challasuyo, passing through the village of Chillkani and winding up on the road just below the Abra Chuchu (4658m) – this is also the access to the Mapiri trail (p133), is a four-hour walk from Ancoma. The third option, which is shorter and more scenic, is to follow the route through the village of Lakathiya and over the Abra de Illampu (4741m) to meet up with the road about 1½ hours above Ancoma. Foreigners are charged US$1.35 per person to camp anywhere in the vicinity of Ancoma, and US$0.40 to cross the bridge there.

Allow two days for either of the *abras*, and before setting out see the Residencial Sorata or Hotel Copacabana for advice on routes and conditions.

The Route

Once you're in **Ancoma**, the route is fairly straightforward. Leave the 4WD track and follow the southern bank of the **Río Quillapituni** (which eventually becomes the Río Tipuani). At a wide spot called **Llallajta**, 4½ hours from Ancoma, the route crosses a bridge and briefly follows the north bank be-

fore recrossing the river and heading toward Sumata. Another Inca-engineered diversion to the north bank has been destroyed by bridge washouts, forcing hikers to follow a spontaneously constructed but thankfully brief detour above the southern bank.

Just past the detour is the village of **Sumata**; just beyond, a trail turns off to the north across the river and heads for **Yani** (which is the start of the Mapiri trail). A short distance further along the trail junction is **Ocara**. From here, the path goes up the slope – don't follow the river. After 1½ hours you'll reach **Lambromani**, where a local may ask foreigners to pay US$0.40 per person to pass. Here you can camp in the schoolyard.

An hour past Lambromani you'll reach **Wainapata**, where the vegetation grows thicker and more lush. Here, the route splits (to rejoin at Pampa Quillapituni); the upper route is very steep and dangerous, so the lower one is preferable. A short distance along, the lower route passes through an interesting tunnel drilled through the rock. There's a popular myth that it dates from Inca times, but it was actually made with dynamite and probably blasted out by the Aramayo mining company early in the 20th century to improve the access to the Tipuani goldfields. At **Pampa Quillapituni**, half an hour beyond, is a favorable campsite. Just east of this spot, a trail branches off to the right toward Calzada Pass, several days away on the Illampu circuit.

Four hours after crossing the swinging bridge at the **Río Coocó**, you'll reach the little settlement of **Mina Yuna**, where you can pick up basic supplies, and it's possible to **camp** on the soccer field.

An hour further down is **Chusi**, which is four hours before your first encounter with the road. There's no place to camp here, but you can stay in the school. **Puente Nairapi**, over the Río Grande de Yavia, is a good place for a swim to take the edge off the increasing heat.

Once you reach the road, the scene grows increasingly depressing. For a final look at relatively unaffected landscape, follow the shortcut trail, which begins with a steep **Inca staircase** and winds up at **Baja Llipi** and the **Puente de Tora** toll bridge (US$0.25; B$2) over the **Río Santa Ana**.

After crossing the bridge climb up the hill and hope for a *camióneta* or 4WD to take you to **Tipuani** and **Guanay**. *Camiónetas* between the Río Santa Ana bridge and **Unutuluni** cost US$0.75 per person; to continue on to Tipuani or Guanay costs an additional US$2.

You can pick up basic supplies at Ancoma, Wainapata, Mina Yuna, Chusi and Llipi, as well as all the lower settlements along the road. Spartan accommodations may be found in Unutuluni, Chima (rough-and-ready and not recommended), Tipuani and Guanay, all of which are along the road.

MAPIRI TRAIL

A longer and more adventurous alternative to the Camino del Oro trek is the six- to seven-day pre-Hispanic Mapiri trail, which was upgraded 100 years ago by the Richter family in Sorata to connect their headquarters with the *cinchona* (quinine) plantations of the upper Amazon Basin.

While the trailhead is technically at the village of Ingenio, you can also begin this unspoiled route by climbing from Sorata over the 4658m Abra Chuchu, then ascending and descending through the open grassy flanks of the Illampu massif to Ingenio. For the next three days it descends along one long ridge through grassland, dense cloud forest and pampa to the village of Mapiri. With the Sorata approach, the entire route takes anywhere from six to eight days, depending on the weather, your

fitness and whether you reach the trailhead at Ingenio on foot or by motor vehicle.

An excellent side trip before you get started will take you from Ingenio up to the lovely and medieval, cloud-wrapped village of **Yani**, where there's a basic *alojamiento*. Bolivia doesn't get much more enigmatic than this (see the boxed text, p134) and adventurers won't regret a visit.

Unfortunately, owing to mining sensitivity in the area, no government mapping is available for this trek. The sketch map in this book (which is derived from several sources) will head you in the right direction, but independent trekkers should ask at the Residencial Sorata (p129) or the Sorata Guides & Porters Association (p128) for the most up-to-date details. Guides for this trek charge around US$100 per group, and porters, US$70 each.

Access

The Mapiri trail begins at the village of **Ingenio**, which has basic *alojamientos*. It can be reached either by 4WD from Sorata (US$35 to US$50 for five people, three to four hours) or on foot over Abra Chuchu (4658m). For the latter, start at the cemetery in Sorata and follow the track up past the tiny settlements of Manzanani and Huaca Milluni to the larger village of Chillkani, about three hours beyond Sorata. From there you have five hours of fairly relentless climbing of the semiforested slopes to the Abra Chuchu. You'll

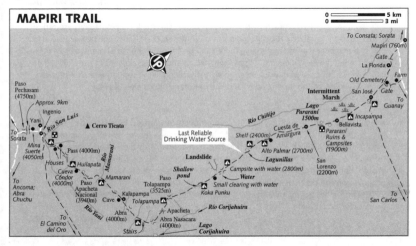

MAPIRI TRAIL

meet up with the road twisting 4km below the pass.

Shortly after the crest, take the left turn (the route straight on leads to Ancoma and the Camino del Oro trek) down toward a small lake. This route will take you over Paso Pechasani Pass (4750m) and down past Mina Suerte to Ingenio and the start of the Mapiri trail at 3550m.

The Route

Past Ingenio you'll cross the **Río Yani**. Here the trail starts downstream, but half an hour later it cuts uphill along a side stream; there's a good campsite where it crosses the stream. The path then twists uphill for 1½ hours over a 4000m **pass**. In the next two hours you'll cross three more ridges, then descend past **Cueva Cóndor**, a cave that is

---

THE MAPIRI EXPERIENCE

Travelers had the following to say about the Mapiri trail, which is often considered Bolivia's most challenging popular route:

This must be one of the world's most staggering walks – in every sense. It is wildly beautiful and unremittingly tough. It follows a 1000-year-old pre-Inca track, remarkable not so much for its stonework (Takesi is better) as for the feat of engineering that accommodated this 3000m drop into the jungle and for its millennium of human uphill and downhill traffic. In 1903 the entire Bolivian army went down it to lose a war with Brazil. It has been overgrown since the 1950s, but in 1990 the Club Sorata Travel Agency in Sorata hacked back the worst obstructions.

You'll almost certainly need a guide and a porter, which can be arranged in Sorata. Believe me, every kilogram of your load soon becomes a very personal matter. Travel light – never more than a 10kg pack, including food and water. Water is available in places en route, but is a constant problem. Take bottles and purification for at least three liters per person (unless you have porters, there goes your 10kg limit!). Camps must be waterproof and insect-excluding: flies, wasps, bees and ants make themselves very much a part of the experience. And don't suppose that because the route drops overall, there aren't many arduous climbs!

The way is rough and you'll spend much of the week cursing yourself, your guide and God. Much of the time is spent crawling over rocks, along branches and under logs, but you'll be rewarded with parrots, butterflies, flowers, tree-ferns, millions of tons of moss and unbelievable views over vast vertical cloud forest, unpenetrated by humans but for this single trail.

Matthew Parris, UK

This is an excellent way down to the Amazon Basin. The track is completely deserted as it isn't used by locals any more. It travels through dense cloud forest for two days, and in places a machete may be necessary. There can also be problems obtaining water as most of the route follows a ridgeline. It's physically tough and it can rain a lot (it certainly did on us). However, there are fantastic views and great walking, and there's the chance of seeing a lot of wildlife, including *huemules* (Andean deer) and spectacled bears.

James A Lind, UK

About the turn of the century, two Bolivian army officers arrived here late one night...and seeing a handsome girl in the doorway of a house adjoining the *tambo*, tossed up to decide who should try his luck at courting her. The loser stayed with the village headman – the Corregidor – and next morning to his horror discovered his brother officer dead on the broken stone floor of a ruined house, which he could have sworn was not only whole but occupied on the previous night.

'The house has been a ruin for years, declared the Corregidor. 'There was no maiden and no doorway, *mi capitán*. It was a...ghost you saw.'

Colonel Percy Harrison Fawcett, Yani, 1906

also a good campsite, to a small lake. From the lake the route ascends to **Paso Apacheta Nacional** (3940m), then twists down **El Tornillo**, a corkscrew-like track that drops 150m. In under an hour you'll cross the **Río Mamarani**, where a good campsite is protected by large rocks.

The next campsite lies three hours further along, beside a stream-crossing at the foot of the next big ascent. At the next stream, half an hour later (collect water here!), is another campsite. Here the trail climbs a long staircase, then descends into another valley before climbing to the next pass, **Abra Nasacara** (4000m). At this stage you're on the ridge that dominates most of the Mapiri trail route, with great views of the Illampu massif. For the next three days, you'll follow this ridge up and down, slowly losing altitude and passing through mostly lush jungle vegetation; fill your water bottles at every opportunity here. The first water along this stretch is at **Tolapampa**, which would also make a good campsite.

The next stretch passes through thick forest and may require a bit of bush bashing with a machete; plan on getting good and wet from all the soaked vegetation. Six hours beyond Abra Nasacara is a very pleasant ridgetop campsite, **Koka Punku**, with water in a shallow pond 50m away. About three hours later, just before a prominent landslide, watch for the water 3m off the track to the right. Four hours and three crests later is the last permanent water source and campsite at **Lagunillas**. An hour later you'll find good (but dry) campsites on the hill **Alto Palmar**.

From Alto Palmar, the trail tunnels through dense vegetation along the **Cuesta de Amargura** (Bitterness Ridge). After three hours the jungle gives way to merely thick bush. Six hours later you'll reach **Pararaní** (1900m), where there's water (which needs to be purified) in a small pond near the ruins of an old house. An hour later there's a semi-permanent lake, and just beyond it the trail leaves the dense vegetation and issues onto a grassy ridge flanked by thick forest. It's then 4½ hours to **Incapampa**, with a semi-permanent marsh and a campsite. Along this stretch, wildlife is rife – mainly in the form of bees, ants, ticks, flies and mosquitoes, as well as plenty of butterflies.

About three hours beyond Incapampa you'll reach the hamlet of **San José** (1400m), where there's a campsite and a view over the village of Santiago. Water can sometimes be found 300m down to the right of the route. After an open area that's actually an old cemetery, the left fork provides the faster track to Mapiri.

Four to five hours of walking from San José brings you to **Mapiri**, which is visible 1½ hours before you arrive. Here you'll find several decent *alojamientos* (avoid the Alojamiento Sorata) and motorized canoes downstream to **Guanay** (US$4, three hours), which is on the bus routes. Boats leave around 9am, but arrive an hour earlier to get a place. Alternatively, catch a *camióneta* along the 4WD track first to Santa Rosa (don't attempt to walk, because there are two large river crossings), which has two small *alojamientos*, and then 175km uphill back to Sorata (US$6, 12 hours).

CONSATA

The semi-abandoned gold-mining town of Consata, which looks like a holdover from the Old West, is accessible every couple of days by vehicle from Sorata (US$7.50, seven hours). This lovely village, characterized by rambling tropical gardens, hasn't yet been discovered by tourists. The place to stay here is the cheap and rather charming Hotel de Don Beto.

AUCAPATA & ISKANWAYA

elevation 2850m

The tiny and remote village of Aucapata is truly an undiscovered gem. Perched on a ledge, on the shoulder of a dramatic peak, it's a great place to hole up for a couple of days' reading, hiking and relaxing. While most of Aucapata's very few visitors want to see Iskanwaya – somewhat optimistically dubbed 'Bolivia's Machu Picchu' – they may well take one look at the 1500m descent to the ruins (and the corresponding climb back up) and seek out the small Iskanwaya museum, which contains artifacts from the site. Admission is free but donations are expected.

Iskanwaya

The major but near-forgotten ruins of Iskanwaya, on the western slopes of the Cordillera Real, sit in a cactus-filled canyon, perched 250m above the Río Llica. Thought to date from between 1145 and 1425, the site is attributed to the Mollu culture.

While Iskanwaya isn't exactly another Machu Picchu, the 13-hectare site is outwardly more impressive than Tiahuanaco. This large city-citadel was built on two platforms and flanked by agricultural terraces and networks of irrigation canals. It contains more than 100 buildings, plus delicate walls, narrow streets, small plazas, storerooms, burial sites and niches.

Note that it's a 1500m descent from Aucapata to Iskanwaya, and there's no accurate map of the area. In the rainy season hiking is dangerous on this exposed route and not recommended.

For more information ask around for Señor Jorge Albaracin, or look for the book *Iskanwaya: La Ciudadela que Solo Vivía de Noche*, by Hugo Boero Roja (Los Amigos del Libro, 1992), which contains photos, maps and diagrams of the site, plus background information on nearby villages.

Sleeping & Eating
Aucapata has one smart-looking little hotel (US$3.50) with clean rooms and hot showers. There's also a small *alojamiento* (US$1.35) behind the church. For meals there's only a small eatery on the corner of the plaza where you'll get whatever happens to be available. They'll probably also be happy to cook up your own supplies. Be sure to bring small change or you're likely to clean out the town!

Getting There & Away
Aucapata lies about 20km northeast of Quiabaya and 50km northwest of Sorata. A weekly *camión* leaves from Calle Reyes Cardona in the cemetery district of La Pazon Friday and returns on Sunday. You'll probably pay around US$4 for this spectacular (and grueling) trip, which may well take more than 24 hours.

There's also a rather difficult access from Sorata, which involves a four-day hike via Payayunga. Guides are available from Sorata Guides & Porters (p128). One other access route, which is quite challenging and very interesting, is a little-known trek from the village of Amarete, in the Cordillera Apolobamba. A guide is essential; you may be able to hire one by asking around Amarete, Curva or Charazani.

GUANAY
Isolated Guanay makes a good base for visits to the gold-mining operations along the Río Mapiri and Río Tipuani. If you can excuse the utter rape of the landscape for the sake of gold, chatting with the down-to-earth miners and panners *(barranquilleros)* can make a visit a particularly interesting experience. This area and points upriver are frontier territory that may be reminiscent of the USA's legendary Old West. Gold is legal tender in shops and saloons, and the foundations of the local culture appear to be gambling, prostitutes and large hunks of beef.

Information
There's no place to change travelers checks, but everyone displaying 'Compro Oro' signs (just about everyone in town) changes US$ cash. The Entel office is in the entrance to the Hotel Minero.

River Trips
Access to the mining areas is by jeep along the Llipi road, or by motorized dugout canoes up the Río Mapiri. The Mapiri trip is easier to organize because boats leave more or less daily. The trip to Mapiri takes five hours upstream and costs around US$5 per person. The exhilarating three-hour downstream run back to Guanay costs US$3.50. The forest has been largely decimated, and bugs are a nuisance, so bring repellent. If you want to spend the night, Mapiri has several *alojamientos* that will put you up for around US$1.35 per person.

Sleeping & Eating
The **Hotel Pahuichi** (US$2.50pp), a block downhill from the plaza, is by far the best value in town, and also has Guanay's best and most popular restaurant. A good alternative is the **Hotel Minero** next door. Friendly **Hospedaje Los Pinos** (d with private bath & fan US$4.50) is near the dock.Other possibilities are the **Panamericana** (US$2pp) and several other basic but friendly places within a block of the plaza. **Alojamiento Plaza** (US$1.35) and **Alojamiento Santos** (US$1.35), both on the plaza, have also been recommended.

For large steaks and fresh juices try **Las Parrilladas** on the road leading to the port. The **Fuente de Soda Mariel** on the plaza offers *empanadas*, cakes, ice cream, *licuados* and other snacks.

Soccer match, Altiplano

JAMES LYON

GREG CAIRE

Inca paving and stone walls, **El Choro Trek** (p117), the Yungas

Huayna Potosí (p137), Cordillera Real

GREG CAIRE

Rock formations around **Tupiza** (p179)

KRZYSZTOF DYDYŃ

Las Payachatas (p164), Parque Nacional Lauca

GRANT DIXON

DEANNA SWANEY

Mounds of salt mined from the **Salar de Uyuni** (p172)

DEANNA SWANEY

San Vicente (p186) where Butch Cassidy and the Sundance Kid died

Getting There & Away

For information on walking routes from Sorata, see El Camino del Oro (p131) and Mapiri trek descriptions (p133). A rough and seasonally unreliable 4WD track connects Mapiri with Sorata, via Consata.

BOAT

Ask around at the dock if you're gung ho for a thrilling motorized canoe ride down the Río Beni to Rurre (US$10 to US$20), which departs only on demand. It's also sometimes possible to find rides through mining country to Mapiri in the early morning.

BUS & CAMIÓN

The bus offices are all around the plaza, but buses actually depart from a block away toward the river. Four companies offer daily runs both to and from La Paz via Caranavi and Yolosa (US$8, eight to 10 hours). For Coroico, get off at Yolosa and catch a lift up the hill. In the dry season there's an overnight bus to Rurrenabaque (US$7.50, 14 hours). Or head to Caranavi and connect with a northbound bus. At around 7am *micros* heading for Caranavi cruise through town honking wildly in search of passengers.

Camiones to Caranavi, Yolosa and La Paz are also plentiful and cheaper, but the trip takes longer.

CARANAVI

All buses between La Paz and the lowlands pass through uninspiring little Caranavi, midway between Coroico and Guanay. Travelers love to knock this place – and the reason is pretty obvious – but those who find themselves stuck here can take a look at the Untucala suspension bridge, which spans a crossing used since Inca times.

Caranavi has several inexpensive hotels, all near the highway. **Hotel Landivar** (US$6) is one of the better ones and has a pleasant pool. More sophisticated is the recommended **Hostal Caturra Inn** (☎ 823-2209; www.hostalcaturra.cjb.net; s/d/tw with bath & breakfast US$13/20/27; ☒), which has hot showers, fans, lovely gardens, a good restaurant and a clean pool. **Hotel Avenida** (US$3), **Residencial México** (☎ 823-2198; US$3.50pp) and the basic but economical **Residencial Caranavi** (US$2.50) are all decent choices. **El Tigre** does basic meals for less than US$1.

CORDILLERA REAL

Bolivia's Royal Range has more than 600 peaks over 5000m, all of which are relatively accessible. They're also still free of the growing bureaucracy attached to climbing and trekking in the Himalayas. The following section is a run-down of the more popular climbs in the Cordillera Real, but it is by no means an exhaustive list. There are many other peaks to entice the experienced climber, and whether you choose one of those described here or one of the lesser known, climbing in the Bolivian Andes is always an adventure.

Note that the climbs described here are technical and require climbing experience, a reputable climbing guide and proper technical equipment. For information on Bolivian mountaineering, see Activities in the Directory chapter, p347.

HUAYNA POTOSÍ

This is Bolivia's most popular major peak because of its imposing beauty and ease of access, as well as the fact that it's 88m over the magic 6000m figure (but 26ft under the magic 20,000ft figure). It's also appealing because it can be climbed by beginners with a competent guide and technical equipment.

Some people attempt to climb Huayna Potosí in one day; this cannot be recommended. It's a 1500m vertical climb from Paso Zongo and a 2500m vertical altitude gain from La Paz to the summit, and to ascend in one day would pose a great risk of potentially fatal cerebral edema.

Dr Hugo Berrios runs the **refugio** (dm low/high season with breakfast US$6/9) in Paso Zongo and also guides climbs on the mountain. As well, he can organize transportation to the hut, mountain guides and rations, as well as porters to carry your kit up to the first camp.

Access

A 4WD from La Paz to the trailhead at Paso Zongo costs around US$40 for up to five people. A taxi should be a bit less with haggling – make sure your driver knows the way. There's also a *camión* from Plaza Ballivián in El Alto at around midday on Monday, Wednesday and Friday. It may be difficult to squeeze on board, and the ride is dusty and uncomfortable, but it's less than US$1 as far as Paso Zongo.

As Huayna Potosí is so popular, lots of climbers are headed out that way during the climbing season. If you only want a lift, check with specialist climbing agencies. Someone will probably have a 4WD going on the day you want, and you can share costs for the trip.

The Route

From the *refugio*, cross the dam and follow the aqueduct until you reach the third path taking off to your left. Follow this to a glacial stream where a signpost points the way. Take this path through and across the rocks to reach the ridge of a moraine. Near the end of the moraine descend slightly to your right and then ascend the steep scree gullies. At

---

DOWNHILL THRILLS

The vertical scenery in the spectacular Cordillera Real will prove a sort of nirvana for mountain bikers who prefer sitting back and letting gravity do the work! The following descriptions of the most prominent rides should start your wheels spinning. For further information on mountain biking in Bolivia, as well as choosing an operator, see Tours in the Directory chapter, p357.

La Cumbre to Coroico

Quite deservedly this ride is Bolivia's most popular, made so by travelers wishing to combine a long and thrilling downhill run with a very appealing destination. It features an incredible range of scenery and a spectacular 3600m descent from the Altiplano, down between snowcapped peaks into the steaming Yungas. Part of the route follows the dramatic and scenic Yungas Highway, which in 1995 was labelled by the Inter-American Development Bank as the 'World's Most Dangerous Road' (see the boxed text, p55). After this thrilling day trip, riders can relax poolside in the quiet Yungas town of Coroico. From here, it's possible to continue to Rurrenabaque, in the Amazon Lowlands, or return to La Paz on public transport.

To reach La Cumbre from La Paz, catch any Yungas-bound transport from Villa Fátima.

Sorata

Sorata is not only Bolivia's trekking capital but it's also saturated with mountain-biking opportunities, and the fun begins with a descent into the town from the mountains astride Lake Titicaca. From La Paz, take a Sorata-bound bus to the pass north of Achacachi and then choose either the main road or any of the downhill routes along unpaved roads. Most routes eventually lead to Sorata – or at least in view of it (but some don't, so it's wise to have a map). Throughout the ride you're presented with superb views of towering snowcapped peaks, plunging valleys and tiny rural villages.

Zongo Valley

This ride includes a descent from the base of spectacular Huayna Potosí (6088m) past Zongo Dam, and then along a dramatic 40km, 3600m descent into the lush and humid Yungas. This is a dead-end road that lacks a great destination at its finish, but there's little vehicular traffic, making it more suitable for nervous beginners or intrepid speed demons than the Coroico ride.

For further information, including access to the start of this route, see Milluni & the Zongo Valley, p80.

Chacaltaya to La Paz

This trip begins with a drive up to the world's highest developed ski slope at 5345m. After taking in the incredible view across the Cordillera Real, riders descend along abandoned mine roads. Along the way you'll have marvelous vistas across the mountain ranges, the Altiplano and the city of La Paz nestling in the bottom of the Choqueyapu canyon. This route is nearly all downhill, descending more than 2000m from Chacaltaya back to central La Paz. For more on Chacaltaya, including access from La Paz, see p79.

the top you should bear left and follow the cairns to reach the glacier. If you got a late start, it may be wise to stop at **Campamento Rocas**, on dry land at the base of the glacier. The glacier is crevassed, especially after July, so rope up while crossing it. Ascend the initial slopes then follow a long, gradually ascending traverse to the right, before turning left and climbing steeply to a flat area between 5500m and 5700m known as **Campo Argentino**. It will take you about four hours to reach this point. Camp on the right of the path, but note that the area further to the right is heavily crevassed, especially later in the season.

The following morning you should leave between 4am and 6am. Follow the path/ trench out of Campo Argentino, and head uphill to your right until you join a ridge. Turn left here and cross a flat stretch to reach the steep and exposed **Polish Ridge** (named in honor of the Pole who fell off it and died while soloing in 1994). Here you cross a series of rolling glacial hills and crevasses to arrive below the summit face. Either climb straight up the face to the summit or cross along the base of it to join the ridge that rises to the left. This ridge provides thrilling views down the 1000m-high west face. Either route will bring you to the summit in five to seven hours from Campo Argentino.

Descent to Campo Argentino from the summit takes a couple of hours; from there, it's another three hours or so back to the *refugio* at Paso Zongo.

ILLIMANI

Illimani, the 6439m giant overlooking La Paz, was first climbed by a party led by WM Conway, a pioneer 19th-century alpinist. Although it's not a difficult climb technically, the combination of altitude and ice conditions warrants serious consideration and caution. Technical equipment is essential above the snow line; caution is especially needed on the section immediately above Nido de Cóndores where six Chileans died on the descent in 1989. The Bolivian media has reported 18 climbing-related deaths here in the last 25 years.

Access

The easiest way to reach the Illimani first camp, **Puente Roto**, is via Estancia Una,

a three-hour trip by 4WD from La Paz (about US$125). From there, it's three to four hours' walk to Puente Roto. At **Estancia Una** you can hire mules to carry your gear to Puente Roto for around US$5. You can hire porters in Estancia Una or Pinaya for US$10 to carry rucksacks from Puente Roto to the high camp at Nido de Cóndores.

A daily 5am bus (US$1.35) goes from near La Paz's Mercado Rodríguez to the village of **Quilihuaya**, from which you'll have a two-hour slog to Estancia Una – complete with a 400m elevation gain. In theory buses return from Quilihuaya to La Paz several days a week at around 8:30am, but if you're relying on public transportation you should still carry extra food to tide you over for at least a couple of days.

An alternative route to the base camp is via Cohoni. Buses and *camiones* leave La Paz for Cohoni (US$1.50, four hours) in the early afternoon Monday to Saturday from the corner of General Luis Lara and Calle Boquerón. They leave Cohoni to return to La Paz around 8:30am and may take anywhere from four hours to all day depending on which route is followed.

The Route

The normal route to Pico Sur, the highest of Illimani's five summits, is straightforward but heavily crevassed. If you don't have technical glacier experience, hire a competent professional guide.

The route to **Nido de Cóndores**, a rock platform beside the glacier, is a four- to six-hour slog up a rock ridge from Puente Roto. There's no water at Nido de Cóndores, so you'll have to melt snow – bring sufficient stove fuel.

From Nido de Cóndores you need to set off at about 2am. Follow the path in the snow leading uphill from the camp; this grows narrower and steeper, then flattens out a bit before becoming steeper again. It then crosses a series of crevasses before ascending to the right to reach a level section. From here aim for the large break in the skyline to the left of the summit, taking care to avoid the two major crevasses, and cross one steep section that is iced over from July onwards. After you pass through the skyline break, turn right and continue up onto the summit ridge. The final three vertical meters involve walking

400m along the ridge at over 6400m elevation.

Plan on six to 10 hours for the climb from Nido de Cóndores to the summit and three to four hours to descend back to camp.

If possible continue down from Nido de Cóndores to Puente Roto on the same day. The 1000m descent is not appreciated after a long day, but your body will thank you the following day and will recover more quickly at the lower altitude. You'll also avoid having to melt snow for a second night.

On the fourth day you can walk from Puente Roto back out to Estancia Una in about two to three hours.

CONDORIRI MASSIF

The massif known as Condoriri is actually a cluster of 13 peaks ranging in height from 5100m to 5648m. The highest of these is Cabeza del Cóndor (Head of the Condor) which has twin winglike ridges flowing from either side of the summit pyramid. Known as Las Alas (The Wings), these ridges cause the peak to resemble a condor lifting its wings on takeoff.

Cabeza del Cóndor is a challenging climb following an exposed ridge, and should be attempted only by experienced climbers. However a number of other peaks in the Condoriri Massif, including the beautiful Pequeño Alpamayo, can be attempted by beginners with a competent guide.

Access

There is no public transportation from La Paz to Condoriri. A 4WD to the start of the walk-in at the dam at **Laguna Tuni** costs around US$55. If you don't want to use a 4WD transfer, you can trek the 24km from Milluni to Laguna Tuni dam on the road to Paso Zongo (see Huayna Potosí, p137).

From Laguna Tuni follow the rough road that circles south around the lake and continues up a drainage trending north. Once you're in this valley, you'll have a view of the Cabeza del Condor and Las Alas.

It isn't possible to drive beyond the dam because there's a locked gate across the road. Some drivers know a way around it, but if you need to hire pack animals you'll have to do so before the dam anyway. Locals charge US$7 per day for mules, and a bit less for llamas, which can carry less.

The Route

From the end of the road, follow the obvious paths up along the right side of the valley until you reach a large lake. Follow the right shore of the lake to arrive at the **base camp**, which is three hours from Laguna Tuni.

Leave base camp at about 8am and follow the path up the north-trending valley through boulders and up the slope of a moraine. Bear to the left here and descend slightly to reach the flat part of the glacier above the seriously crevassed section. You should reach this point in about 1½ hours from base camp.

Here you should rope up and put on crampons. Head left across the glacier before rising to the col (lowest point of the ridge), taking care to avoid the crevasses. Climb to the right up the rock-topped summit called **Tarija** – which affords impressive views of Pequeño Alpamayo – before dropping down a scree and rock slope to rejoin a glacier on the other side. From there either climb directly up the ridge to the summit or follow a climbing traverse to the left before cutting back to the right and up to the summit. The summit ridge is very exposed.

ANCOHUMA

Ancohuma is the highest peak in the Sorata massif, towering on the remote northern edge of the Cordillera Real. It was not climbed until 1919 and remains very challenging.

No one seems to know how high Ancohuma is. At present the generally accepted height is 6427m, but the Times *World Atlas* has it at 7012m, the maps in early 1900s editions of the *South American Handbook* says it's 7014m high and various tourist-board publications put it at 7002m. In 1994 a satellite picture suggested it was in fact nearly 7000m high and recent GPS mapping expeditions claim to have confirmed this. If that's correct, Ancohuma would not only be higher than the 6542m volcano Sajama (which is currently believed to be Bolivia's highest peak) but it would also be the highest peak in the world outside the Himalayas. It would also mean that all those climbers who've slogged up Argentina's Aconcagua believing it to be South America's highest summit would have to come to Bolivia and try again.

THE KALLAWAYA

The origins and age of the Kallawaya tradition are unknown, although some Kallawaya claim to be descended from the vanished people of Tiahuanaco. The Kallawaya language, however, which is used exclusively for healing, is derived from Quechua, the language of the Inca. Knowledge and skills are passed down through generations, although it's sometimes possible for aspiring healers to study under acknowledged masters.

The early Kallawaya were known for their wanderings and traveled all over the continent in search of medicinal herbs. The most capable of today's practitioners will have memorized the properties and uses of 600 to 1000 different healing herbs, but their practices also involve magic and charms. They believe that sickness and disease are the result of a displaced or imbalanced *ajallu* (life force). The incantations and amulets are intended to encourage it back into a state of equilibrium within the body.

Hallmarks of the Kallawaya include the *huincha*, a woven headband worn by women, and the *alforja* (medicine pouch) carried by the men. The Kallawaya of the Charazani region are known for their colorful weavings, which typically bear natural designs, both zoomorphic and anthropomorphic, and for their *llijllas*, striped women's shawls with bands of color representing the landscape of the village of origin.

The Kallawaya's legacy has been recorded by several anthropologists and medical professionals; German university psychiatrist Ina Rössing has produced an immense four-volume work called *El Mundo de los Kallahuaya* about her ongoing research, and Frenchman Louis Girault has compiled an encyclopedia of herbal remedies employed by the Kallawaya, entitled *Kallahuaya, Curanderos Itinerantes de los Andes*.

Access

The peak is accessed via Sorata (p127). From this lovely little town you can hire a 4WD for the long traverse to **Cocoyo**, where the fun begins. (It's also possible to hire a 4WD all the way from La Paz to Cocoyo, which is convenient but expensive.) If you have a serious amount of gear, you can hire a mule train to carry it from Sorata to base camp, which is in the lake basin east of the peaks at about 4500m. Plan on at least two days for these various transport arrangements to get you to the lakes. Alternatively Ancohuma can be climbed from the west, using **Laguna Glacial** as a base camp (p128). Further advice and information is available in Sorata.

The Routes

From the lakes head west up to the glacier following the drainage up through loose moraine. Make camp below the north ridge, the normal route. After a circuitous path through a crevasse field, a steep pitch or two of ice will gain the north ridge. An exposed but fairly easy ridge walk will take you to the summit.

If you've opted for the more easily accessed western route, hike from Sorata to base camp at Laguna Glacial. From there the route climbs the obvious moraine and then ascends the glacier, over fields of extremely dangerous crevasses to a bivouac at 5800m. It then climbs to the bergschrund and across a relatively level ice plateau to the summit pyramid. This is most easily climbed via the north ridge; the first part is quite steep and icy, but it gets easier toward the summit.

CORDILLERA APOLOBAMBA

The remote Cordillera Apolobamba, flush against the Peruvian border north of Lake Titicaca, is becoming a popular hiking, trekking and climbing venue. Mountaineers, in particular, will find a wonderland of tempting peaks, first ascents and new routes to discover.

It must be stressed that, although things are changing rapidly, this remote region is far from set up for tourism. There are few services, transport isn't reliable and the people maintain a fragile traditional lifestyle. Despite the number of foreign researchers passing through, only a few locals – mostly men – speak Spanish. Sensitivity to

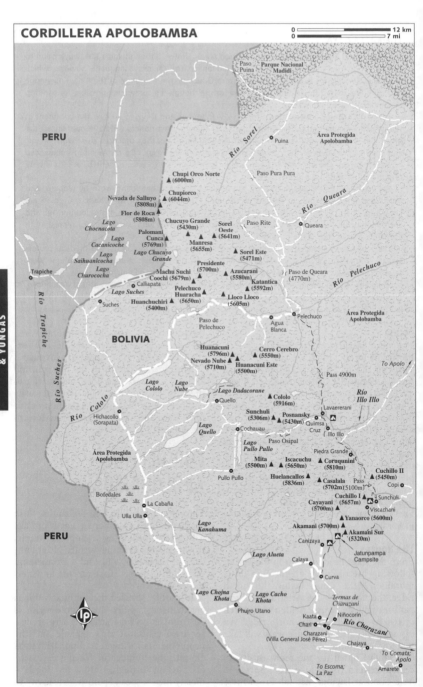

CORDILLERA APOLOBAMBA

0 — 12 km
0 — 7 mi

PERU

Paso Puina
Parque Nacional Madidi

Río Sorel

Puina

Área Protegida Apolobamba

Paso Pura Pura

Chupi Orco Norte
▲ (6000m)

Chupiorco
▲ (6044m)

Nevada de Salluyo
(5808m) ▲

Flor de Roca ▲
(5808m)

Chucuyo Grande
(5430m)

Río Queara

Paso Rite

Queara

Lago Chocnacota

Lago Cacanicoche

Palomani
Cunca ▲
(5769m)

Manresa
(5655m)

Sorel Oeste
▲ (5641m)

Lago Saihuanlcocha

Lago Chucuyo Grande

▲ Sorel Este
(5471m)

Lago Churococha

Presidente
(5700m) ▲

▲ Azucarani
(5580m)

Paso de Queara
(4770m)

Río Pelechuco

Trapiche

Machu Suchi
Coochi (5679m) ▲

▲ Katantica
(5592m)

Calliapata

Lago Suches

Pelechuco
Huaracha ▲
(5650m)

▲ Lloco Lloco
(5605m)

Área Protegida Apolobamba

Río Trapiche

Suches

Huanchuchiri ▲
(5400m)

Paso de Pelechuco

Agua Blanca

Pelechuco

BOLIVIA

Huanacuni
(5796m) ▲

Cerro Cerebro
▲ (5550m)

Pass 4900m

To Apolo

Nevado Nube ▲
(5710m)

▲ Huanacuni Este
(5500m)

Río Suches

Río Cololo

Lago Cololo

Lago Nube

Lago Dadacorane

▲ Cololo
(5916m)

Río Illo Illo

Hichacollo
(Sorapata)

Quello

Sunchuli
(5306m) ▲ ▲ Posnansky
(5430m)

Lavaererani

Lago Quello

Cochauau

Paso Osipal

Quimsa
Cruz

Illo Illo

Área Protegida Apolobamba

Lago Pullo Pullo

Mita
(5500m) ▲ ▲ Iscacuchu
(5650m)

Piedra Grande

▲ Coruqunini
(5810m)

Cuchillo II
▲ (5450m)

Bofedales

Pullo Pullo

Huelancallos
(5836m)

▲ Casalala Pass
(5702m) (5100m)

Copi

Sunchuli

La Cabaña

Cuchillo I
▲ (5657m)

Ulla Ulla

Cayayani
(5700m) ▲

▲ Yanaorco (5600m)

Viscachani

PERU

Lago Kanahuma

Akamani (5700m) ▲ ▲ Akamani Sur
(5320m)

Canizaya

Jatunpampa Campsite

Lago Alueta

Calaya

Curva

Termas de Charazani

Lago Chojna Khota

Lago Cacho Khota

Kaata

Niñocorin

Phujro Utano

Chari

Río Charazani

Charazani
(Villa General José Pérez)

Chajaya

To Comata; Apolo

To Escoma;
La Paz

Amarete

the local sentiments of this highly traditional Aymará- and Quechua-speaking area will help keep its distinctive character intact.

Every town and village in the region holds an annual festival, most of which fall between June and September. The **Fiesta de La Virgen de las Nieves**, one of the best, takes place in Italaque, northeast of Escoma, around August 5. It features a potpourri of traditional Andean dances, including Quena Quenas, Morenos, Llameros, Choquelas, Kapñis, Jacha Sikuris and Chunchos.

CHARAZANI

Charazani is the administrative and commercial center and transport axis of Bautista Saavedra province. The surrounding area of the upper Charazani valley is the home of the Kallawaya (also spelled Kallahuaya or Callawaya). Services in Charazani have increased exponentially in recent years, and several NGOs are working in the area on sustainable development projects, including solar power, textile production and the promotion of sensible tourism.

Information

Two **fiestas** are held, the biggest around July 16 and a smaller one on August 6. There's also a wonderful **children's dance festival** (around November 16).

There are now two telephones at the **Transportes Altiplano** (☎ 213-7439) office on the plaza and in the *alcaldía* (town hall; ☎ 213-7282), a block below the plaza. The **gas station** (a *tienda* opposite the church selling fuel out of plastic jugs) exchanges cash dollars at good rates. If you happen to find it open, the public **Nawiriywasi Library** has books on medicinal plants and the Kallawaya culture, and maps and information for hikers, trekkers and climbers. Market day is Sunday.

Sights & Activities

Along the river about 10 minutes' walk upstream from town, you'll pass the **Termas de Charazani Phutina** (US$0.50; ☯ 7am-9pm, closed Mon until 2pm for cleaning) a hot springs complex where you can bathe and enjoy a hot shower. Other **natural thermal baths**, complete with a steaming hot waterfall, are found a two-hour hike away down the valley from Charazani along the Apolo road alongside the Río Kamata.

The traditional Kallawaya village of **Chari**, 1½ hours' walk from Charazani, is a lovely blend of terraces, flowers and vegetable gardens. A German anthropologist started the Tuwans textile project, which is designed to market the local hand-dyed weavings. The town is also home to a **Kallawaya cultural museum**, a stone and thatch structure with exhibits pertaining to medicinal plants and textile arts. About an hours' walk outside the village are some **pre-Incan ruins**, reached by walking through town and turning left at the enormous boulder that creates a small cave. Follow this path to the cemetery, keep left until you gain the ridge, then continue 200m up to the ruins. Because of local suspicion it's best to advise locals where you're headed before setting off.

Sleeping & Eating

Of the five lodging possibilities, three are relatively comfortable. A block below the plaza, **Hotel Akhamani** (US$1.35-5.50) has the highest standards and the widest variety of options, including a four-bed mini-apartment with a private bath and small kitchen. There are plans for a full-scale restaurant. Just off the plaza on the Curva road is **Residencial Inti Wasi** (US$2.65) on your left, and the two-room **Hotel Charazani** (US$1.35) on your right. The former is arranged around a traditional cobbled courtyard, which provides a pleasant atmosphere. The latter is more basic but offers a fabulous view over the valley, along with immediate access to *duena* Doña Sofia's fine Bolivian cooking.

There are several *pensiones* around the plaza that dish out soup, a main course and coffee (often tasting like *chuño* water) for under US$1. The aforementioned efficient but quick-tempered Doña Sofia serves *almuerzos* at 12:30pm sharp and *cenas* at 6pm or 7pm; reserve early, don't arrive late, stay humble and clean your plate. After dark follow your nose just off the plaza to **Tu Esnack Kiosko**, which lives up to its name with greazy, esnackalicious *pollo al broaster*. If all else fails, cheap burgers are available on the plaza whenever the teens are in town or folks are getting drunk.

Essentials (wheat, oats, canned fish, pasta, rice, bread and a few bruised fruits and vegetables) can be purchased at *tiendas* surrounding the plaza. Trekkers, however, are advised to bring their supplies from La Paz.

Getting There & Away
From La Paz (US$3.25, six or eight hours), **Trans Norte** (☎ 238-2239) and the more reliable **Trans Altiplano** (☎ 238-0859) depart Tuesday, Friday and Saturday at 6:30am from along Calle Reyes Cardona, four blocks up Avenida Kollasuyo from the cemetery near Cancha Tejar. Book tickets in advance and turn up early. Monday through Thursday. Trans Norte buses continue to Curva (US$0.65, two hours) and Lagunillas, and arrive at around 6pm (occasionally, a bus even dares to attempt the road down to Apolo). From Curva, it leaves for La Paz (via Charazani) on Wednesday, Saturday and Sunday at around 4pm. Trans Norte continues to Chari on Friday and Sunday. From Charazani, buses from both companies depart daily for La Paz at around 6pm.

From Charazani, a 4WD route winds down to the Yungas village of Apolo at the edge of the Amazon Basin, where you can stay overnight at the monastery. The route is frequently negotiated by *camiones* during the dry season, but several serious stream crossings and landslide risks mean it's best suited to mountain bikes or foot traffic in the wet.

ÁREA PROTEGIDA APOLOBAMBA
In the late 1990s the Reserva Nacional de Fauna Ulla Ulla was renamed the Área Natural de Manejo Integrado Nacional (ANMIN) Apolobamba and was expanded by nearly 300,000 hectares to 484,000 hectares. It now includes the entire Cordillera Apolobamba and most of the renowned **Curva to Pelechuco trek** (p145) along the range's eastern slopes. At its northern end it abuts Parque Nacional Madidi to form one of the western hemisphere's most extensive protected areas.

The original park – a loosely defined *vicuña* reserve along the Peruvian border - was established in 1972, and was upgraded by Unesco in 1977 into a Man and the Biosphere Reserve. Later that same year the Instituto Nacional de Fomento Lanero (Infol) was created to represent wool

producers and charged with researching, monitoring and preventing habitat degradation of the reserve's camelids. Infol morphed into the Instituto Boliviano de Tecnología Agropecuaria (IBTA), which focuses more on agricultural development and social services.

The modern park is home to several thousand alpacas and *vicuñas*, and also to Bolivia's densest condor population. In addition to the popular hiking routes you'll find excellent wild trekking around Lagos Cololo, Nube, Quello, Kanahuma and Pullo Pullo, all of which enjoy snow-covered backdrops and rich waterbird populations, including black ibis, flamingo and several species of geese.

Information
Twenty-nine park rangers roam between several far-flung **Casas de Guardaparques,** which are all linked via radio communication but infrequently staffed during the daytime. For predeparture information contact **Sernap** (☎ 244-2870; 20 de Octubre 2782, La Paz). In an emergency contact them by radio on frequency 8335 USB.

The traditional village of **Curva** (3780m) has a few basic *tiendas*, but no hotels or restaurants. With a bit of Spanish you may be able to ask around at the bus office and rent a bed in someone's home. Curva's main festival is a colorful affair that takes place on June 29.

Sleeping & Eating
Noncampers can normally find accommodations in local homes for US$2 per person *mas o menos* – just ask around. The biggest *tienda* is in Ulla Ulla. At **La Cabaña**, 5km from Ulla Ulla village, IBTA has a small hostel where you may be able to stay, but it's suggested that you reserve via Sernap in La Paz.

Two new highly publicized *albergues* (US$2) at Lagunillas and Agua Blanca offer dorm beds, kitchen facilities and (sometimes) hot showers, but there's no good way to reserve ahead and you may have to hunt around to find the keeper of the keys. New **ranger stations** have been built at Antaquilla, Charazani, Curva, Kotapampa, Pelechuco, Pullo Pullo, Suches and Hichacollo; the last three were designed by a La Paz architect and blend adobe construction, domed thatched roofs and passive solar walls to reflect both modern and traditional styles.

Hikers can camp at any of these sites – or can even stay inside, space and Spanish skills permitting.

CURVA TO PELECHUCO TREK

This fantastic four- to five-day hike (115km) passes through splendid and largely uninhabited wilderness. The track stays mostly above 4000m and includes five high passes. There's arguably no better scenery in the Andes, and along the way you're sure to see llamas and alpacas, as well as more elusive Andean wildlife, such as viscachas, *vicuñas*, condors and perhaps even a spectacled bear. (The Wildlife Conservation Society runs a bear research center five hours on foot from Pelechuco, where a couple of bears have been tagged and are occasionally observed.)

The trek may be done in either direction, as both Charazani and Pelechuco have relatively reliable – albeit limited – public transportation. Most people do the route from south to north, but starting in Pelechuco would mean an additional day of downhill walking and a grand finale at Charazani's hot springs.

Pack animals are intermittently available in both Curva and Pelechuco for the following prices: llamas (US$3 to US$4 per day), mules (US$5 to US$7 per day) and guides/muleteers (US$5 to US$7 per day). Clients must often carry their own food and stove, and are often expected to provide meals for their guides, porters and muleteers. If possible bring all your trekking food from La Paz, as Curva and Pelechuco have only basics at inflated prices.

Access

Because of the sensitive nature of this frontier territory, no good maps exist. For information on public transportation, see Getting There & Away under Charazani (p144) or Pelechuco (p147).

A more expensive but considerably easier and more comfortable way to go is by 4WD. A vehicle and driver from La Paz to Curva (US$250, seven hours) or Pelechuco (US$250 to US$300, 10 hours) may be worthwhile because it allows daylight travel through the incomparable scenery. Alternatively you can pay to leave the logistics to someone else and

do the trek with an agency (see Tours in the Transport chapter, p357).

The Route

Because most people do the trek from south to north, from Curva to Pelechuco, that's how it's described here. If you're coming from **Charazani**, you can either follow the long and winding road for four to five hours or take the 3½- to four-hour shortcut. Cross the river at the thermal baths, then climb the other bank and back to the road. After about an hour you should follow a path that climbs to a white and yellow church on your left. Beyond the church, descend the other side of the hill, to just above the community of **Niñocorín**. After a short distance you'll strike an obvious path; turn left onto it and follow it as it contours through the fields and then descends to cross a river, where it then starts the steep climb into **Curva**.

From Curva, head toward the cross on the hill north of the village and skirt around the right side of the hill. About an hour out of Curva, you'll go across a stream. Continue uphill along the right bank of the stream. At a cultivated patch about 200m before the valley descending from the right flank of the snow peak, cross the stream to join a well-defined path entering from your left. If you continue along this path, you'll reach an excellent flat streamside campsite. Alternatively, keep following this trail for another 1½ hours to an ideal campsite at **Jatunpampa** (4200m).

From Jatunpampa, head up the valley and across a small flat to the col with a cairn, about two hours along. From this **4700m pass**, you'll have fabulous views of Akamani off to the northwest. One to two hours further along you'll arrive at a good campsite (4100m) near the **Incacancha** (aka Incachani) waterfall.

The following morning's ascent appears a bit daunting, but it isn't that bad. Cross the bridge below the waterfall and follow the switchbacks up the scree gully. As you ascend, enjoy distant views of Ancohuma and Illampu. After two hours or so you'll reach a **4800m pass**.

From the pass, traverse gently uphill to the left until you gain the ridge, which affords great views of the Cordillera Real to the south and Cuchillo II to the north. At this point the obvious trail descends past a small lake before arriving at a larger lake with a good view of Akamani.

Climb up to the next ridge before descending an hour to the small mining settlement of **Viscachani**, where you'll strike the 4WD track toward Illo Illo (aka Hilo Hilo). In another hour this road ascends to a **4900m pass**, which also provides superb views of the Cordillera Real to the south and the Sunchuli Valley to the north and west.

At the pass the road drops into the valley; at the point where it bears right, look for a path turning off to the left. This will take you to a point above the **Sunchuli gold mine**. From Sunchuli, follow a contour line above the aqueduct for about an hour, until you see an idyllic campsite (4600m) below Cuchillo I.

The fourth day of the hike is probably the finest, as it includes sections that have been used for centuries by miners and *campesinos*. From the campsite, the road ascends for about two hours via a series of switchbacks to a **5100m pass**. From the pass, you can scramble up to a cairn above the road for excellent views dominated by **Cololo** (5916m), the southern Cordillera Apolobamba's highest peak.

Descend along the road for a few minutes, then jog right down a steep but obvious path that crosses a stream opposite the glacier lake below Cuchillo II before descending to the valley floor. If you follow the valley floor, you'll rejoin the road a couple of minutes above the picturesque stone-and-thatch village of **Piedra Grande**, three hours from the pass.

Follow the road for about an hour, then join the pre-Hispanic road turning off downhill to your right. After you cross a bridge, you should follow the obvious path to the right, leading you up into the village of **Illo Illo** in about an hour. Here you'll find small shops selling the basics – perhaps even beer and batteries.

When leaving Illo Illo don't be tempted onto the path to the left, which leads west to Ulla Ulla (although this is also a viable trek). The correct route leaves the village above the new school, between the public facilities and the cemetery. From there, cross the llama pastures until the path becomes clear again. After crossing a bridge (about an hour out of Illo Illo)

and beginning up a valley with a sharp rock peak at its head (if it's too overcast to see the rock, look for several small houses on your left and turn there), you'll stumble onto an ideal campsite set in a bend in the valley, where there are a number of large fallen rocks.

From the campsite, head up the valley for about 1½ hours until you reach a bridge over the stream. At this point the route begins to ascend to the **final pass** (4900m), which you should reach in another 1½ hours. From the pass, descend past a lake, crossing camelid pastures and follow some pre-Columbian paving. In less than two hours you'll arrive in **Pelechuco**.

PELECHUCO

pop 800 / elevation 3400m

Founded by Jesuits in 1560 this quaint colonial village nestles beneath the snowy peaks of the Cordillera Apolobamba. It's most often visited as a Curva–Pelechuco trek trailhead or, less frequently, as a staging point for the much longer and more challenging trek from Pelechuco down to Apolo in the northernmost reaches of the Yungas.

Information

Entel (☎ 213-7283) sometimes works and takes messages for folks in town. You might also try ringing **Antiquilla's Entel** (☎ 213-7425), for laughs if nothing else.

Sleeping & Eating

No one will accuse **Alojamiento Rumy Llajta** and **Hotel Llajtaymanta** of trying to outdo each other. Both places are on the plaza, neither has electricity or running water and both charge around US$1 per person. Hot meals are available from *pensiones* on the plaza and staple supplies are sold at a couple of small *tiendas* – but don't bet on finding fresh food here. The good news is that there's normally enough rainwater to keep the village hydrated.

Hotel Llajtaymanta's owner Reynaldo Vasquez is rumored to have stubborn-yet-willing mules for hire for reasonable rates, as are Remy and Justina Roca – look for the house across from the billards place behind the church, the one with the horseshoe faintly painted on the door. Cheap meals and basic beds are available here above the barnyard courtyard where the donkeys dwell.

Getting There & Away

Rickety **Trans Norte** (☎ 238-2239) buses leave La Paz (US$4.25 – ask for the special 'gringo price', 10 or 15 to 24 hours) on Wednesday and Thursday around 6am or 7am from the ex-*tranca* Río Seco in El Alto; they may stop en route – depending on the driver's mood – at the market in Huancasaya on the Peruvian border, before continuing to Ulla Ulla, Agua Blanca and Pelechuco.

From Pelechuco, buses return to La Paz at 2am or 3am and 7pm on Friday, 9am and noon on Saturday and noon on Sunday – double check all these departure times before making any big plans. The earlybird Friday bus normally halts at the international market in Chejepampa, near Suches. At both of the markets you can change US$ cash, *bolivianos* and *soles*, and purchase good-value alpaca wool products.

If you're hiking into Pelechuco and aren't being met by a 4WD, it's worth hoofing it west along the road for four hours or so. About 4km beyond the military post in Antaquilla, a 2km *desvio* (detour) into the Hichacollo *pampa*, you'll find luscious open-air bathing in clean natural *pozos* and an enclosed adobe *piscina*, both fed by hot spring runoff. It's worth camping here because there's no place to stay or eat before Escoma, five hours away by bus. From Escoma it's at least another five hours by bus back to La Paz.

A 4WD and driver cost around US$300 one way to or from La Paz, and must be arranged in La Paz. Try to approach or leave Pelechuco as early as possible so you can enjoy the incredible mountain views across the Altiplano and the scenic drive along Lago Cololo.

CORDILLERA QUIMSA CRUZ

The Cordillera Quimsa Cruz, an as-yet-undiscovered gem for mountaineers, was once described by the Spanish climbing magazine *Pyrenaica* as a 'South American Karakoram'. In 1999, near the summit of Santa Veracruz, the Spaniard Javier Sánchez

discovered the remains of an 800-year-old ceremonial burial site with ancient artifacts and weavings.

The Quimsa Cruz is not a large range – it's only some 50km from end to end – and the peaks are lower than in other Bolivian ranges. The highest peak, Jacha Cuno Collo, rises to 5800m, and the other glaciated peaks range from 4500m to 5300m. Granite peaks, glaciers and lakeside camping make the Quimsa Cruz arguably the most scenically spectacular of Bolivia's four main cordilleras. It lies to the southeast of Illimani, separated from the Cordillera Real by the Río La Paz, and geologically speaking it's actually a southern outlier of that range.

The Quimsa Cruz lies at the northern end of Bolivia's tin belt, and tin reserves have been exploited here since the late 1800s. However, with the replacement of tin by plastics and aluminum, the current tin prices mean that it isn't viable to extract it from such remote sites. The few miners who've stayed on and continue to work some of the mines here, either take their chances with cooperatives or are employed as caretakers for mining companies who don't want to abandon their holdings, and are presumably hoping for better days. In any case all the major mining areas in the region – which includes every valley along the western face of the Quimsa Cruz – are still populated, and most of the remaining mining activity is divided between the villages of Mina Caracoles and Viloco.

ACTIVITIES

The Quimsa Cruz offers some of the finest adventure climbing in all of Bolivia, and in every valley mining roads provide access to the impressively glaciated peaks. Although all of the *nevados* of the Quimsa Cruz have now been climbed, there are still plenty of unclimbed routes, and expeditions are unlikely to encounter other climbing groups.

Trekking is also possible throughout the range, which is covered by IGM mapping. The main route is the two- to three-day from **Viloco to Mina Caracoles trek**. Of interest along this route is the renowned site of a 1971 airplane crash, which had already been stripped by local miners before rescue teams arrived at the scene two days later!

Staples are available in both Viloco and Quimé, but it's still best to carry everything you'll need (food, fuel and other supplies) from La Paz.

GETTING THERE & AWAY

Road access is relatively easy because of the number of mines in the area, and it's possible to drive within 30 minutes' walk of some glaciers. Others, however, are up to a four-hour hike from the nearest road. The easiest access is provided by **Flota Trans-Inquisivi**, which leaves daily from La Paz's main bus terminal for the eastern side of the range (to Quimé, Inquisivi, Cajuata, Circuato, Suri, Mina Caracoles, and, less often, Yacopampa and Frutillani). Alternatively take any bus toward Oruro and get off at the *tranca* at Khonani, 70km short of Oruro. This is the turnoff for the main road into the Quimsa Cruz, and here you can wait for a truck or bus heading into the Cordillera.

A bus service is also available to the communities and mines on the western side of the range. To Viloco, Araca or Cairoma, buses leave most days of the week, but the biggest challenge can be finding its office in El Alto, as it seems to shift around with some frequency; you'll just have to ask locally.

Those with a bit more ready cash can hire a 4WD and driver for the five- to seven-hour journey; any of the services used by mountaineers and trekkers can organize the trip.

THE CORDILLERAS & YUNGAS

Southern Altiplano

CONTENTS

Stretching southward from La Paz to the Chilean and Argentine frontiers is a harsh, sparsely populated wilderness of scrubby windswept basins, lonely peaks and almost lifeless salt deserts. The Altiplano, a Tibet-like land of lonely mirages, is a place of indeterminable distances and an overwhelming sense of solitude. Stark mountains seem to hover somewhere beyond reality, and the nights are just as haunting, with black skies and shining stars. The moment the sun sets – or even passes behind a cloud – you'll realize this air has teeth. Further south towards Argentina the land turns into spectacular red rock country scattered with canyons and peaks; a land of hiding places.

Those who live on the Altiplano are among the world's hardiest souls, existing on the edge of human endurance. Cold, biting winds and drought threaten even the most simple daily needs. However, given the opportunity to potentially prosper in the developing lowlands, few Aymará people have chosen to leave their ancestral homes. These are the same people whose ancestors managed to escape Inca efforts to conquer, long ago. On the surface they may seem as cold as their environment, but many are actually quite friendly and they deserve a great deal of respect for their accomplishments.

TOP FIVE

- Experience the eerie otherworldliness of the **Salar de Uyuni** (p172)
- Join in Oruro's wild annual **La Diablada** (p156) Carnaval celebration
- Feel small at the foot of Parque Nacional Sajama's hulking **Volcán Sajama** (p161)
- Behold the natural wonders of the **Reserva Eduardo Avaroa** (p176) with its steaming volcanoes, flamingo-filled lakes and soothing hot springs
- Follow the ghosts of Butch Cassidy and the Sundance Kid on horseback through the spectacular Wild West landscapes around **Tupiza** (p179)

★ Oruro

★ Nevado Sajama volcano

★ Salar de Uyuni

★ Tupiza

Reserva Nacional de Fauna Andina Eduardo Avaroa

- TELEPHONE CODE: 02
- ELEVATION: 3500M to 6542M

HISTORY

The prehistoric lakes Minchín and Tauca, which once covered most of this highland plateau, evaporated around 10,000 years ago, leaving behind a parched landscape of brackish puddles and salt deserts. Humans haven't left much of a mark on the region; some time in the mid-15th century, the reigning Inca Pachacuti sent his son Tupac Inca Yupanqui southward to conquer all the lands he encountered. He apparently had good public relations skills because the southwestern extremes of Bolivia and deserts of northern Chile were taken bloodlessly. Yupanqui and his gang marched on across the wastelands to the northern bank of Chile's Río Maule, where a fierce band of Araucanian Indians inspired them to stake out the southern boundary of the Inca empire and turn back toward Cuzco.

Owing to the harsh conditions the Inca never effectively colonized this desert area, and today there are still relatively few inhabitants. Beyond the towns of Uyuni, Tupiza and Villazón, most of the people cluster around mining camps, health and military outposts and developing geothermal energy projects.

CLIMATE

Climatically, the best months to visit are August, September and October, after the worst of the winter chills and before the summer rains. From May to early July, night-time temperatures combined with stiff winds can lower the windchill temperature to -40°C. Summer is warmer but, for an arid area, there's quite a lot of rainfall between November and March. At any time of year you'll need protection against sun, wind and cold.

NATIONAL PARKS

Parque Nacional Sajama (p161), Bolivia's first national park, adjoins Chile's Parque Nacional Lauca (p164), preserving a stretch of magnificent peaks, plains and wildlife habitat. Sajama itself is home to the world's highest forest and some of South America's loftiest hot springs. Even if you're not into superlatives or hardcore mountaineering, an evening dip in the crystal clear springs at the base of Volcán Sajama in the company of a few camelids is worth the trek.

The Reserva Nacional de Fauna Andina Eduardo Avaroa (p176) is a highlight of Southwest Circuit tours and the gateway to Chile for those headed for the desert oasis of San Pedro Atacama.

GETTING THERE & AWAY

From La Paz, the Southern Altiplano is easily accessed by bus, although off the paved main roads it can be a long and bumpy ride. The route from the central highland cities of Potosí and Sucre is rough on the back, bum and bladder. The overland route from Chile is a scenic mountain traverse and routes to Argentina are nonstop tours of otherworldly landscapes.

The train between Oruro and Villazon, which stops in Uyuni and Tupiza, provides a fine alternative to grueling overland travel. Rumors of flights starting up to Uyuni, via Sucre and La Paz, linger but tricky Altiplano wind conditions have so far kept regularly scheduled flights grounded.

ORURO

pop 200,000 / elevation 3702m

The Southern Altiplano's only true city lies north of the salty lakes Uru Uru and Poopó and 3½ hours by bus south of La Paz. It sits at the northern end of the passenger railway that serves Chile and Argentina, against a range of mineral-rich low hills. The city's inhabitants, 90% of whom are of pure Indian heritage, refer to themselves as *quirquinchos* (armadillos), after the carapaces (protective shell) used in their *charangos*.

Visitors are rarely indifferent to Oruro; they either love it or hate it. Although it's one of Bolivia's most culturally colorful cities – indeed, it calls itself the 'Folkloric Capital of Bolivia' – there are few tourist attractions, and you'll need time to let the place grow on you. The crusty exterior of some *orureños* is balanced by the warm hospitality of others. If you manage to attend the uncharacteristically riotous **La Diablada**, the wild annual Carnaval celebration, you won't regret a visit.

History

Settled in 1601 and founded in 1606, Oruro owes its existence to the mineral-rich 10-sq-km range of hills rising 350m behind the city. Chock-full of copper, silver and

THE SOUTHERN ALTIPLANO

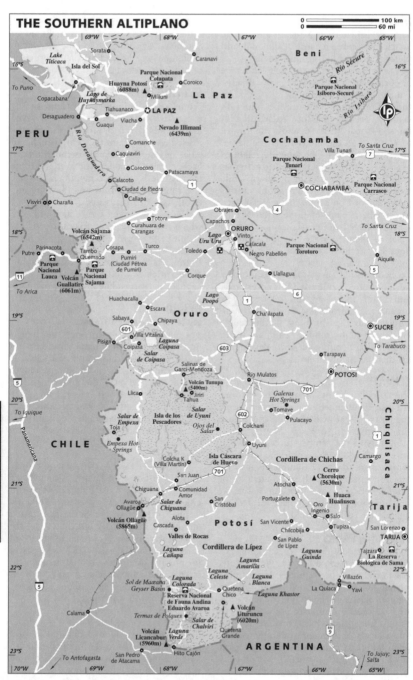

tin, these hills form the city's economic backbone. Early mining activities focused almost exclusively on silver extraction, but in the early 1800s indigenous workers moved on in search of more lucrative prospects, and the community was more or less abandoned. Oruro rebounded as a mining town during the late 19th century, with the increasing world market for tin and copper.

By the 1920s Bolivia's thriving tin-mining industry rested in the hands of three powerful capitalists. The most renowned was Simon I Patiño, an Indian from the Cochabamba valley who arguably became the world's wealthiest man. In 1897 Patiño purchased La Salvadora mine near the village of Uncia, east of Oruro, which eventually became the world's most productive tin source. Patiño's success snow-balled and by 1924 he had gained control of about 50% of the nation's tin output.

Once secure in his wealth, Patiño migrated to Britain, where he started buying up European and North American smelters and tin interests. As a consequence Bolivia found itself exporting both its precious metal and its profits. Public outcry launched a series of labor uprisings, and set the stage for nationalization of the mines in 1952 and the subsequent creation of the government-run Corporación Minera de Bolivia (Comibol).

Decades of government inefficiency, corruption and low world tin prices proceeded the push for *capitalización* (a variation on privatization), which eventually brought about the dissolution of Comibol in the mid-1980s.

Information
EMERGENCY
Tourist police (☎ 525-1923; Plaza 10 de Febrero) They only seem to be out in force during Carnaval.

IMMIGRATION
Immigration (☎ 527-0239; Ayacucho 322, 2nd fl; ⏱ 8:30am-4pm Mon-Fri) Extend your stay here.

INTERNET ACCESS
Compumundo (6 de Octubre near Cochabamba) Opposite the university. The best of several cheap Internet places (US$0.50 an hour) along 6 de Octubre.
Mundial Internet (Bolívar 573; ⏱ 9am-midnight) Charges US$0.65 an hour for the best connection in town.

ICP Internet (Bolívar near 6 de Octubre) Cheap Internet-based international phone calls.

LAUNDRY
Andes Dry Cleaner (Sucre 240) Charges US$0.75 per piece.
Hotel Sucre (cnr Sucre & 6 de Octubre) Charges US$1.25 per dozen for hand wash and dry service.
Lavandería Alemania (Aldana &Pagador)
Lavandería Los Andes (Sucre & Montes)

MAPS
The best city map is the *Plano Turístico* (US$0.65), sold around town before and after Carnaval (until supplies run out). The rest of the year, the tourist information office (cnr Bolívar & Galvarro) hands out an adequate free map.

MEDICAL SERVICES
Policlínica Oruro (☎ 524-2871; 500 block of Rodríguez) Oruro's best hospital is across from the National Tennis Club.

MONEY
You can change cash at any shop displaying *compro dólares* signs. Street moneychangers mill around the corner of 6 de Octubre and Aldana, near Plaza Ingavi. Banks listed below change cash and travelers checks (for 4% to 6% commission).
Banco Boliviano Americano (Bolívar & Galvarro)
Banco de Santa Cruz (Bolívar 460)
Banco Bisa (south side of plaza) Cashes Amex travelers checks into B$ without commission (or 6% commission for US$).
Banco de Crédito (southwest cnr of plaza) Has an ATM.

POST & TELEPHONE
The **main post office** is just north of Plaza 10 de Febrero. Parcels must first be inspected by the **Aduana Nacional** (Velasco Galvarro at Junín). The modern **Entel** office is west of the corner of Galvarro and Bolívar. There's also a **Punto Entel** and last-minute postal kiosk downstairs at the bus station.

TOURIST INFORMATION
The great little booklet *Oruro – Destino Turístico*, by Juan Carlos Vargas, is sometimes sold at the tourist office. *Carnaval de Oruro* provides detailed information (in Spanish) on La Diablada's dances and musical styles and a rundown of visitor attractions around Oruro department.

ORURO

0 — 700 m
0 — 0.4 mi

A **B** **C** **D**

To Rumi Campana (2km);
Mina San José (2km)

To Capachos (10km);
Obrajes Hot Springs (25km)

INFORMATION
Aduana Nacional (Customs)........ 1 C4
Andes Dry Cleaner........................2 C5
Banco Bisa.....................................3 B4
Banco Boliviano Americano...........4 B4
Banco de Crédito (ATM)................5 A4
Banco de Santa Cruz (ATM)..........6 B4
Café Internet.................................7 B4
Compumundo.................................8 B4
Entel..9 B4
ICP Internet.................................10 B4
Immigration.................................11 C4
Internet..12 B4
Lavandería Alemana....................13 B5
Lavandería Los Andes.................14 A4
Mundial Internet.........................15 B4
Municipal Tourist Office..............16 A4
Policlínica Oruro Hospital...........17 B2
Tourist Information Office...........18 B4
Tourist Police..............................19 A4

SIGHTS & ACTIVITIES (pp155–7)
Capilla de Serrato.......................20 A3
Cathedral.....................................21 B4
Faro de Conchupata.....................22 B3

Faro de Conchupata.................22 B3
Museo Etnográfico Minero........23 A3
Museo Patiño..............................24 B4
Museo Sacro Folklorico
  Arqueológico..........................(see 23)
Santuario de la Virgen del
  Socavón...................................(see 23)
Teatro al Aire Libre...................25 B3

SLEEPING (pp157–8)
Alojamiento Copacabana............26 B5
Alojamiento Ferrocarril..............27 C5
Alojamiento San Juan de Dios....28 C5

Gran Hotel Sucre.......................29 B4
Hostal Hidalgo............................30 B4
Hotel Bernal...............................31 D2
Hotel International Park..............32 D2
Hotel Lipton...............................33 D2
Hotel Monarca............................34 C4
Hotel Repostero.........................35 B4
Hotel Samay Wasí......................36 D2
Pub the Alpaca............................37 B2
Residencial Ideal........................38 B4
Residencial San Miguel..............39 B5
Residencial San Salvador...........40 C5
Su Majestad Palace.....................41 B4

Plaza
La Unión

Aroma

Rodríguez

León

Plaza
Rancheria

1 de Noviembre

Herrera

Montecinos

Caro

Mercado
Fermín López

Plaza del
Folklore

To Emisa
Mining
Office (100m)

Cochabamba

Ayacucho

Av del Ejército

Plaza
10 de
Febrero

Calle Junín

Calle Adolfo Mier

To Complejo Metalúrgico
Vinto; Potosí (310km);
Sucre (472km)

Mercado
Campero

Calle Bolívar

EATING (p158)
Confitería Dumbo.......................42 B4
Confitería M & M........................43 B4
El Huerto Vegetariano...............44 B4
Govinda......................................45 B4
La Cabaña...................................46 B4
Las Delicias.................................47 C4
Le' Grill.................................(see 13)
Oggy..48 B4
Restaurant Nayjama...................49 B5
Restaurant Pagador....................50 C4
Salteñería La Casona.................51 B4

Calle Sucre

Murguía

Aldana

Plaza
Ingavi

Balliviián

DRINKING (p158)
Crissol Restaurant & Bar...........52 B4
Discoteque VIP's........................53 B4
Karaoke 1-2-3.............................54 B4

ENTERTAINMENT (p158)
Cinema.......................................55 A4

SHOPPING (pp158–9)
ARAO Artesenía Oruro..............56 B4
Cafe Extrapuro El Chapaco........57 B4

Train
Station

San Felipe

Arce

Santa Barbara

To Museo Mineralógico;
University; Museo
Antropológico
Eduardo López
Rivas (0.5km)

To Uyuni (320km);
Tupiza; Villazón

Jean

TRANSPORT (pp159–60)
Bus Terminal..............................58 D2
Buses to Capachos & Obrajes
  Hot Springs..............................59 C4

Tourist information office (Caseta de Información Turistica; ☎ 525-7881; Bolívar & Galvarro) Friendly kiosk next to Entel, open regular business hours weekdays and weekends for the two weeks before Carnaval.

Municipal tourist office (Unidad de Turismo y Cultura; ☎ 525-0144; west side of plaza, inside the Galería Prefectural)

Dangers & Annoyances

Watch your cash stash – several readers have encountered quite competent pickpockets, bag-slashers and con artists here, notably at the Mercado Campero, around the train station and especially during Carnaval and other rowdy festivals.

Sights

MUSEUMS

Museo Patiño (Casa de Cultura; ☎ 525-4015; Galvarro 5755; admission US$0.80; ☒ 9am-noon & 2:30-6pm Mon-Fri, Sat & Sun by request) This university-administered cultural complex is a former residence of tin baron Simon I Patiño. Exhibits include his furniture, personal effects, fine toys and an ornate stairway. Visiting exhibitions are featured in the downstairs lobby. If it's closed, ask for the key at the office on the ground floor.

Museo Etnográfico Minero (☎ 525-6954; admission for one/both museums US$0.40/60, camera use US$0.40; ☒ 9am-noon & 3-6pm) Adjacent to the Santuario de la Virgen del Socavón, this unique museum is housed in an old mine tunnel. It reveals various methods of Bolivian mining: tunnels, 'mailboxes', tailing dumps and chimneys and discusses El Tío (the devilish character who owns the minerals). Also here is the new **Museo Sacro Folklorico Arqueologico**, which keeps the same hours.

Museo Antropológico Eduardo López Rivas (admission US$0.65; ☒ 8am-noon & 2-6pm) At the south end of town adjacent to the zoo, the anthropology museum has been remodeled and upgraded with the help of the German government. Named after the mid-20th-century scholar who wrote extensively about Andean cultures, it focuses on the early Chipaya and Uros tribes. Take an orange *micro* C (marked 'Sud') of the northwest corner of Plaza 10 de Febrero or opposite the train station, and get off just beyond the old tin-foundry compound.

Museo Mineralógico (☎ 526-1250; admission US$1; ☒ 8am-noon & 2-7pm Mon-Fri, 8am-noon Sat) On the university campus south of town,

the mining museum houses a remarkable collection of more than 5000 minerals, precious stones, fossils and crystals from around the world. If the door is locked, visit the Departamento de Minas and someone will likely let you in. From the patio outside there's a nice view of Lago Uru Uru. Hop on a green *micro* A, blue *micro* F or red minibus 102 (all marked 'Sud' or 'Ciudad Universitaria') from the YPFB gas station opposite the train station.

THE CATHEDRAL

Just east of the main plaza, the cathedral has fine stained glass above the altar. The adjacent tower was constructed by the Jesuits as part of **Iglesia de la Compañía de Jesús** before Oruro was founded. When the Jesuits were expelled, it was designated as the **Cathedral of the Oruro Bishopric**. In 1994, the original baroque entrance was moved and reconstructed at the **Santuario de la Virgen del Socavón** (Virgin of the Grotto), on **Cerro Pie de Gallo** (Cock's Foot Hill), which presents a grand city view. It was here that 16th-century miners began worshiping the Virgen de Candelaria, the patron saint of miners. The present church, which is a 19th-century reconstruction of the 1781 original, figures prominently in La Diablada as the site where good ultimately defeats evil (see the boxed text, p156). **Capilla de Serrato**, a steep climb from the end of Calle Washington, also offers impressive city views.

FARO DE CONCHUPATA

On November 17, 1851 Bolivia's red, gold and green flag was first raised at Faro de Conchupata: red for the courage of the Bolivian army, gold for the country's mineral wealth and green for its agricultural wealth. The spot is now marked by a balcony and column topped by an enormous glass globe. It's illuminated at night and provides a fine vista over the town. Adjacent is the **Teatro al Aire Libre** amphitheater.

HOT SPRINGS

The **Obrajes hot springs** (admission US$0.35), 25km northeast of town, are the best of several nearby soaking spots. From the corner of Caro and Av 6 de Agosto, catch an Obrajes *micro* (US$0.35, half an hour) daily from 7:30am to 5pm, which also passes the funkier **Capachos hot springs**, 10km east of town.

A DEVIL OF A GOOD TIME

La Diablada (Dance of the Devils) has become Bolivia's most renowned and largest annual celebration. In the broad sense, these festivities can be described as reenactments of the triumph of good over evil, but the festival is so interlaced with threads of both Christian and indigenous myths, fables, deities and traditions that it would be inaccurate to oversimplify it in this way.

The origins of a similar festival may be traced back to 12th-century Cataluña, now in Spain, although *orureños* maintain that it commemorates an event that occurred during the early days of their own fair city. Legend has it that one night a thief called Chiruchiru was seriously wounded by a traveler he'd attempted to rob. Taking pity on the wrongdoer, the Virgin of Candelaria gently helped him reach his home near the mine at the base of Cerro Pie del Gallo and succored him until he died. When the miners found him there, an image of the Virgin hung over his head. Today, the mine is known as the Socavón de la Virgen (Grotto of the Virgin). This legend has been combined with the ancient Uros tale of *Huari* and the struggle of Michael the Archangel against the seven deadly sins into the spectacle that is presented during the Oruro Carnaval.

The design and creation of Diablada costumes has become an art form in Oruro, and several Diablada clubs – consisting of members from all levels of Oruro society – are sponsored by local businesses. There are anywhere from 40 to 300 dancing participants. Costumes, which may cost several hundred dollars each, are owned by individual dancers, and rehearsals of their diabolical dances begin on the first Sunday in November, several months in advance of Carnaval.

Festivities begin the first Saturday before Ash Wednesday with a glorious *entrada* (opening parade) led by the brightly costumed Michael the Archangel character. Behind him, dancing and marching, come the famous devils and a host of bears and condors. The chief devil Lucifer wears the most extravagant costume, complete with a velvet cape and an ornate mask. Faithfully at his side are two other devils, including Supay, the Andean god of evil that inhabits the hills and mineshafts.

The procession is followed by vehicles adorned with jewels, coins and silverware (in commemoration of the *achura* rites in which the Inca offered their treasures to Inti – the sun – in the festival of Inti Raymi), and the miners offer the year's highest-quality mineral to *El Tío*, the devilish character who is owner of all underground minerals and precious metals.

Behind them follow the Inca and a host of *conquistadores*, including Francisco Pizarro and Diego de Almagro. When the Archangel and the fierce-looking devilish dancers arrive at the soccer stadium, they complete a series of dances which relates the ultimate battle between good and evil. After it becomes apparent that good has triumphed, the dancers retire to the Santuario de la Virgen del Socavón, and a Mass is held in honor of the Virgen del Socavón, who pronounces that good has prevailed.

For three days following the *entrada*, other dance groups perform at locations throughout the city. Each group has its specific costume and performs its own dance. For a brief rundown of the dances see p30.

MINES

Most of the abandoned mines in the hills behind Oruro are dangerous to enter. Among them is **Mina San José**, which claims to have operated for over 450 years. If you wish to hike around the colorful tailing heaps, take a yellow *micro* D (marked 'San José') from the northwest corner of Plaza 10 de Febrero.

Oruro's main mining operation is now the **Inti Raymi** gold mine. Prospective visitors will need to muster a group, arrange for a guide and obtain permission from **Emisa** (☎ 524-6886/3349; Bolívar 1221).

The US$12 million **Complejo Metalúrgico Vinto** (☎ 527-8078/ 8091; 🕑 9am-noon Mon-Fri) tin smelter was constructed in the early 1970s during the presidency of General Hugo Banzer Suárez. By the time it was put into operation, the Bolivian tin industry was already experiencing a steady decline, but it still processes up to 20,000 tons of ore annually. Vinto is 8km east of Oruro. It's wise to phone in advance for permission to tour the operation. To get here, take *micro* D (marked 'Vinto ENAF') from the northwest corner of Plaza 10 de Febrero.

Activities

Rumi Campana (Bell Rock), named after an unusual acoustic phenomenon, is a climber's playground just 2km northwest of town. On weekends you can practice your skills with the friendly local climbing club, **Club de Montañismo Halcones** (contact Juan Pablo ☎ 524-4082). There's some excellent rock and a range of routes with protection already in place. Try your hand at the challenging overhanging route Mujer Amante, or the wonderful 7-rated route known as Sueño.

Tours

To travel into the wildest reaches of western Oruro department, where there's a wealth of cultural and natural interest – wildlife, volcanoes, hot springs, colorful lakes and lagoons and isolated communities – contact private guide **Juan Carlos Vargas** (☎ 525-4993; sanfelipe@coteor.net.bo) at Hotel Villa Real San Felipe, who can arrange adventurous custom trips.

Sleeping

Accommodations are often booked solid during La Diablada, so make your reservation (usually three days minimum) early or ask the tourist office about rooms in local homes. Note that prices climb considerably during the festivities. The rate for a basic room in a budget *alojamiento* can quintiple and, although it hasn't been the case in recent years, rates for nicer rooms can increase by up to sixfold, depending on demand.

BUDGET

Note that in the cheapest places the cost of a shower may not be included in the price.

Pub the Alpaca (☎ 527-5715; wcamargo_gallegos@hotmail.com; La Paz 690 – no sign; US$3.35) With three sunlit, spacious but simple rooms and a shared kitchen this is by far the coziest budget option in town. During Carnaval the number of beds doubles to 10 and the price almost quintuples to US$15 per night for a minimum of three nights.

Hotel Bernal (☎ 527-9468; Brasil 701; US$2.65, with bath US$5.35) Opposite the bus terminal, this squeaky-clean place with back-friendly beds and gas-heated showers is great value. It's popular with Brazilians on their way to the Chilean coast and the friendly manager

speaks English and Portuguese. Upper level rooms have more modern conveniences like cable TV and new tiles in the bathroom.

Hotel Lipton (☎ 527-6583; 6 de Agosto 625; US$3.35, with bath US$5.35) Convenient to the bus terminal, this semi-modern place has TVs and big double beds.

Residencial Ideal (☎ 527-7863; Bolívar 386; s/d US$3/4) Not quite ideal, but in the center of the evening action and spitting distance from the market.

Residencial San Miguel (☎ 527-2132; Sucre 331; d US$6.65, with bath US$8) The rooms are crowded and scattered, but it's pretty quiet and the staff are friendly.

Hostal Hidalgo (☎ 525-7516; 6 de Octubre 1616; US$4.75, with bath US$8) Spacious, carpeted modern rooms, some of which are very dark.

Near the train station on Velasco Galvarro are several handy, if not classy, *alojamientos*:

Alojamiento Copacabana (☎ 525-4184; No 6352; US$2, with bath US$4.65) Bright, clean and friendly – the best on this strip.

Residencial San Salvador (☎ 527-6771; No 6325; US$2, with bath US$4.65) Recently improved, with firm beds and morning showers.

Alojamiento San Juan de Dios (☎ 527-7083; No 6346; US$2) A short step up from the bottom of the barrel.

Alojamiento Ferrocarril (☎ 527-4079; No 6278; US$2) Like a prison, but without the showers. Was adding new cells at last look that may be a bit nicer.

MID-RANGE

Gran Hotel Sucre (☎ 527-6320/6800, fax 525-4110; Sucre 510; s/d US$8/10, with bath US$16/30) Past grandeur abounds in this reliable standby, which is popular with locals for business conferences. Rooms in the creaky-floored old section without bath are cheaper than the nearly identical rooms with bath in the newer section. The ballroom restaurant, Pukara, is decorated with stained-glass and Carnaval paintings, and serves an abundant buffet breakfast (US$1.35), which is well worth a look even if you're not staying here.

Hotel Samay Wasí (☎ 527-6737; Brasil 392; samay wasioruro@hotmail.com; s/d/tr/ste with breakfast & cable TV US$13/20/28/40; 🖳) If firm beds, 24-hour hot water and telephones are a priority, this modern high-rise HI-affiliate near the bus terminal is your place. The helpful, professional staff make up for what the building lacks in comfort.

Hotel Repostero (☎ 525-8001; Sucre 370; s/d with bath & TV US$11/16) This place is somewhat worn around the edges, but still offers gas-heated showers, and phones. Some rooms have funky carpet and most of the beds have a bowl-like quality about them.

Hotel International Park (☎ 527-6227; lparkhot@ cotelnet.bo; Bakovic s/n; s/d/ste with breakfast US$25/36/ 60) Literally on top of the bus terminal, this lounge-chic modern hotel offers red carpet, magnificent views and a tropical fish tank. It's comfortable, heated and the best choice for travelers with no interest in seeing more of Oruro than necessary.

The modernish **Su Majestad Palace** (☎ 525-5132; Mier 392; s/d with TV, bath & breakfast US$22/25) and the once-stylish **Hotel Monarca** (☎ 525-4300; 6 de Agosto 1145; s/d with bath US$10.50/18.50) are also acceptable.

Eating

Most restaurants don't open until at least 11am. Mercado Campero is the most reliable option for an early breakfast; Mercado Fermín López is good for lunch. Food stalls in both markets feature noodles, mutton soup, beef and *thimpu de cordero* (boiled potatoes, oca, rice and carrots over mutton, smothered with *llajhua*, a hot tomato-based sauce).

Small eateries around the train station offer the best bargain set-lunch specials. Recommended is **Le' Grill** (Aldana near Pagador) which only serves drinks at night. Nearer the center, **Oggy** (Bolívar & Galvarro) and **Restaurant Pagador** (Pagador 1440; mains US$1-2) attract loyal lunch crowds.

Restaurant Nayjama (☎ 527-7699; Aldana at Pagador; mains US$2.50-5) Jet-setting chef Roberto, with Oruro roots and a cordon bleu pedigree, took over his mom's renowned restaurant and has added a gourmet flare to traditional Bolivian dishes. Invite him to sit down for a drink to find out who he has cooked for. It's simple but classy, there's no smoking allowed and vegetarian options are available on request.

Las Delicias (☎ 527-7256; 6 de Agosto 1278; mains US$2-4, set meals US$1) This family-run, smoky hole-in-the-wall is the local and Peace Corps favorite for sizzling tableside *parrillada*. Set *almuerzos* are served outside on the covered patio. The attentive service is a breath of fresh air, with a few of the staff in the running for the Latin American Waiter of the Year title.

Salteñería & Pizzería La Casona (Montes 5969; mains US$1-2, pizzas from US$3) Hot-out-of-the-oven *salteñas* by day, quick sandwiches for lunch and pizza by night keep this place busy.

El Huerto Vegetariano (Bolívar near Pagador; ☉ closed Sat; mains US$1-2.50) Gotta get here early. It's tiny, lunch is cooked to order and it's only available for a couple hours.

Govinda (6 de Octubre 6089; mains US$1-2) Forget you're in Bolivia for a meal or two at this Hare Krishna devotee restaurant where vegetarian meals are fresh, cheap and creative.

La Cabaña (Junín 609; mains US$2-4) The specialty is grilled meat at this cozy cabin that offers both typical Bolivian and international dishes in a pleasant, modern setting.

Confitería M&M (6 de Octubre s/n; mains US$1-2) Cheap burgers, snacks and lemonade – fast food but sloth-like service.

Confitería Dumbo (Junín near Potosí) A decent quick stop for cakes, *empanadas*, *salteñas*, hot drinks and *helados*.

Drinking

If you're after something totally unexpected, check out the Finnish- and Bolivian-run **Pub the Alpaca** (p157), which is like an English pub. The owners Sinikka and Willy speak a range of European languages and there's a multilingual book exchange. It opens at 8:30pm or 9pm for drinks and may offer meals during Carnaval. If the door is locked, just ring the bell. It's off Plaza Ranchería, where snack stands grill up mean sausage sandwiches all day long.

Entertainment

For karaoke **Discoteque VIP's** (Junín at 6 de Octubre) and **Karaoke 1-2-3** (Potosí at Junín) are tough to beat. The *automovilisimo*-themed **Crissol** (☎ 525-3449, Mier at La Plata) is the classiest place in town to play pool, *cacho* and catch a big game on cable TV. There's a full restaurant, full bar, live music and dancing after hours on weekends.

Housed in an opulent baroque-style colonial-era concert hall, the no-name **cinema** (south side of plaza) screens first-run films nightly for US$1.

Shopping

The design, creation and production of artistic Diablada masks and costumes is Oruro's main cottage industry. Av La Paz, between León and Villarroel, is lined with small workshops offering embroidered wall hangings, devil masks, headdresses, costumes and other devilish things from US$2 to more than US$200.

ARAO Artesanías Oruro (☎ 525-0331; Galvarro 5999; arao@coteor.net.bo) offers the best selection of high-quality, cooperatively produced handicrafts from Oruro department and beyond. The naturally dyed wool rugs and wall hangings and Challa'pata shoulder bags are especially notable. **Café Extrapuro El Chapaco** (Potosí s/n) sells Yungas beans – to taste them brewed, visit Confitería Mateos, opposite Confiteria M&M (p158).

Llama and alpaca wool bags and clothing are sold at *artesanía* shops in the center and at the bus terminal, while the cheapest articles are found around the northeast corner of **Mercado Campero**. Hawkers sell cheap *zampoñas*, *charangos* and some other indigenous musical instruments near the train station.

Tucked away in the middle row of the **Mercado Fermín López** is the impressive **Mercado Traditional** (Mercado de Hechicería), which has more dried llama fetuses than a voodoo master has pins – estranged couples should also beware of the love potions. The affable vendors are more than happy to explain the usage of their wares. Natural healers peddle their goods along Junín between Galvarro and 6 de Agosto.

Getting There & Away
BUS
All long-distance buses use the **bus terminal** (Terminal de Omnibuses Hernando Siles; ☎ 527-9535; terminal fee US$0.25), a 15-minute walk or short cab ride northeast of the center.

Numerous companies run buses to La Paz (US$1.35 to US$2, three hours) every half-hour or so. Midway into the trip, watch for a shallow lake about 100m west of the highway that teems with flamingos.

There are also several daily buses to Cochabamba (US$1.75, 4½ hours) with connections to Santa Cruz, Potosí (normal/*cama* US$4/9, eight hours) and Sucre (US$4.50/ 13.50, 10 hours). Several night-time services depart daily for Uyuni (US$3 to US$4, eight hours) along a rough route that is often impassable after rains. To Llallagua (US$1.35, 2½ hours) three companies make the run several times daily. Alternatively, there's a direct Trans Copacabana

bus *cama* (US$13.50, 10 hours) at 10:30pm nightly. For Santa Cruz (US$10, 18 to 20 hours) you must make a connection in Cochabamba.

There are at least five daily sleeper services to Arica, Chile (US$10.75, 8 to 10 hours), via Patacamaya, Tambo Quemado and Chungará (Parque Nacional Lauca). Daily except Saturday, several sleeper services (4am, 1pm and 10pm) make the considerably rougher journey to Iquique, Chile (US$12 to US$14, 20 to 24 hours,) via the Pisiga or Tambo Quemado border crossings.

TRAIN
Thanks to its mines, Oruro is a rail hub and has one of Bolivia's most organized train stations. Back in the lazy days when the government was running the show, timetables were little more than some office slug's fantasy, but since the Chilean-run **Empresa Ferroviaria Andina** (FCA; ☎ 527-4605/ 5676; www.fca.com.bo) took over in 1996 they're now followed surprisingly closely.

From Oruro, you can travel to Uyuni, where the railroad splits: one line goes to Tupiza and Villazón (on the Argentine border); and the other to Ollagüe and Calama, in Chile. It's also worth inquiring about possible high-season Uyuni–Potosí Ferrobus service. Rumors linger about re-opening the eastbound lines to Cochabamba and eventually Sucre.

The *Expreso del Sur* offers reclining seats, heaters, videos, a dining car and a choice of *salón* and *ejecutivo* classes. To Villazón (salon/executive US$10.65/21.50; 15 hours), via Uyuni (US$4.75/10.25, 6½ hours) and Tupiza (US$9.65/19.35, 11¾ hours) it leaves Monday and Friday at 3:30pm and returns Tuesday and Saturday from Villazón at 3:30pm. The *Wara Wara del Sur* runs Wednesday and Sunday at 7pm to Uyuni (salon/ executive US$4/8; seven hours), Tupiza (US$6.75/13.75, 13 hours) and Villazón (US$8.25/16.75, 16¾ hours).

From Uyuni, a s-l-o-w train trundles southwest to the Chilean frontier at Avaroa (US$4.25), leaving Monday at 3:30am. Unfortunately none of the Oruro trains connect with this service.

Getting Around
Micros (US$0.15) and minibuses (US$0.20) connect the city center with outlying areas.

Their routes are designated by their letters, colors and signs (and in the case of minibuses, numbers). It's a fairly confusing system, because two *micros* with the same letter and different colors will follow different routes – unless the signs are clear, you'll probably have to ask locals for advice. Note that *micros* and minibuses are small and crowded, so if possible, avoid carrying luggage aboard.

Taxis around the center, including to and from the terminals, cost a non-negotiable US$0.30 (B$2.50) per person. A **radio taxi** (☎ 527-6222/3399) costs US$0.75.

AROUND ORURO
Few travelers explore the intriguing areas outside of Oruro.

Calacala (Cala Cala)
The archaeological site at Calacala is 15km southeast of Oruro, along the road to Negro Pabellón. It consists of rock paintings and engravings in a rock shelter at the base of a hulking monolith. The llama theme is most prominent, but there is also a puma and some roughly human figures painted in white and earth tones. As yet, no definitive theory of their origin has been formulated, but some investigators suggest an Inca-era camelid cult (see the boxed text, p163).

On weekends, *micros* run from Oruro to Calacala; at other times, you'll have to take a taxi (US$9 round-trip). Once in the village, track down the park guard, who will unlock the gate to the site and act as a guide. The paintings are a 40-minute walk from the village, toward the old brewery.

On September 14, Calacala hosts a pilgrimage and *fiesta* in honor of Señor de las Lagunas (Lord of the Lakes).

Lago Uru Uru (Lago del Milagro)
The Lake of Miracles, a large lake just south of town, offers good fishing for *pejerrey*, and you'll also see flamingos in the shallow water when the lake isn't completely dried up in the winter. There's a small restaurant and a *cabaña* at the shore where you may rent rowboats for fishing or exploring the lake. To reach the shore, take *micro* A (marked 'Sud') to its terminus at the university. From there, it's a 3km walk along the highway.

Three kilometers around the western shore of the lake from Puente Español,

7km southwest of Oruro, are the Chullpas de Chusa K'eri, an ancient necropolis that dates back at least 2000 years. Transport runs occasionally from Plaza Walter Khon to Puente Español; you'll have to walk the last 3km.

Lago de Poopó & Cha'llapata
About 75km south of Oruro is the large but shallow Lago de Poopó, which covers 2530 sq km but has an average depth of only 6m. This oversized puddle attracts flamingos and a host of other waders, making it an appealing spot for bird-watchers.

To visit some lesser-known *chullpas* (funerary towers), seek out the local indigenous leader Juvenal Pérez in Cha'llapata, 110km south of Oruro and 12km east of the lakeshore. Overcrowded buses leave from near Mercado Campero in Oruro (US$1, three hours) a couple of times daily; southbound trains also make a brief stop.

Curahuara de Carangas
Curahuara de Carangas, at the foot of the Jank'l Khollo (Beautiful Little Heaven) mountains, was the site of the final battle between indigenous Paka Jakhes (Eagle Men) and conquering forces of Tupac Inca Yupanqui. After a diligent fight, the defenders were eventually defeated at the terraced hill fortress of Pukara Monterani (where several warriors are buried), and the Inca leader declared his victory by thrusting a golden rod into the summit of the hill. The Quechua for 'golden rod' is *kori wara*, hence the Hispanicized name, Curahuara.

The village's lovely adobe-and-thatch church has rather hopefully been dubbed 'the Sistine chapel of the Altiplano'. While that's rather overblown, the charming little structure does contain a wealth of lovely naive 16th-century frescoes depicting typical *mestizo*-style themes and Biblical scenes. Along the route eastward toward Totora lies the Yaraque archaeological site, with several stone ruins, numerous rock paintings and an Inca-era *chullpa* constructed in fine stonework comparable to that of Cuzco.

The signposted turnoff is 100km west of Patacamaya, accessible on any bus between Oruro and Arica, Chile. Get off at the turnoff and walk 5km south to the village, which has a small *alojamiento*. The area also offers some fabulous rock-climbing.

Ciudad Pétrea de Pumiri

This bizarre complex of stone caves and eroded rock formations 185km southwest of Oruro was named the 'Stone City of Pumiri' because it resembles a prehistoric village. It's 20km west of the village of Turco (where there's an *alojamiento* and restaurant), near the Thica Utha Cameloid Research Station. Getting here is quite an adventure. A weekly bus connects Oruro with Turco, while *camiones* and buses going all the way to Pumiri leave from the Plaza Walter Khon in Oruro.

The new **Hotel Pumiri** (☎ 525-1115; hotelpumiri@ usa.net; Petot 1744) is 15km southeast of Turco, south of the turnoff at Curahuara de Carangas. It's also accessible from Oruro via La Joya, or Ancaravi from the road to Pisiga. It's in an old mining settlement surrounded by *queñua* forests and is a fine if rustic base camp for exploring the surrounding region.

PARQUE NACIONAL SAJAMA

Bolivia's first national park occupies 80,000 hectares abutting the Chilean border. It was created on November 5, 1945, for the protection of the rare wildlife that inhabits this northern extension of the Atacama Desert. Unfortunately, depredation has already eliminated pumas, *huemules* (Andean deer), viscachas and guanacos; and only limited numbers of vicuñas, condors, flamingos, rheas and armadillos survive.

The world's highest forest covers the foothills flanking the hulking **Volcán Sajama** (Nevado Sajama volcano), which at 6542m is generally considered Bolivia's highest peak. The forest consists of dwarf *queñua* trees, an endemic Altiplano species, but unless you're into checking off superlatives, it's nothing to get steamed up about. The 'trees' have the size and appearance of creosote bushes.

Orientation & Information

The best map of the park is the glossy 1:50,000 *Nevado Sajama* published by Walter Guzmán Córdova; it can be found in better La Paz bookstores.

Admission (US$1.35) is payable at the Sernap headquarters in Sajama village. The fee applies to all foreigners, including those just visiting the village. The office will help climbing expeditions organize mules and porters. Señor Telmo Nina, in Sajama village, keeps a log of routes up the mountain. If you are planning to climb it, definitely read Yossi Brain's *Bolivia – A Climbing Guide* (Mountaineers, 1999), which describes several routes up the mountain.

Volcán Sajama

This volcano is unquestionably the centerpiece of all it surveys. It's attracting increasing numbers of mountaineers who'd like to try their abilities (and luck) on its glaciers and wildly eroded slopes. There are no trails per se, so park hiking is strictly of the backcountry variety.

Although it's a relatively straightforward climb, Sajama's altitude and ice conditions make the peak more challenging than it initially appears. Most of the glaciers are receding, turning much of the route into a sloppy and crevasse-ridden mess. Quite a few La Paz agencies (see Tours, p357) offer organized climbs of Sajama.

The easiest access to the mountain is from the village of Sajama, 18km north of the Arica–La Paz highway. Experienced climbers may prefer to start from the north, south (from Lagunas) or west (from Sajama); allow two or three days to reach the summit and prepare for extremely cold and windy conditions. Carry lots of water, though once on the snow cap, there will be plenty in the form of ice and snow.

Hot Springs & Geysers

For a relaxing warm soak, there are some lovely 35°C hot springs 7km northwest of Sajama village. The springs are relatively easy to find, and locals can point you in the right direction. About 1½ hours on foot due west of Sajama is an interesting spouting geyser field.

Sleeping & Eating

Camping is fine just about anywhere in this sparsely populated region, so a tent and a good cold-weather sleeping bag are recommended. Otherwise, contact the **Junta de Vecinos** (via the Entel office ☎ 513-5525) about homestays (US$1 per person) with local families, which are organized on a rotation basis. Most homes are very

PARQUES NACIONALES SAJAMA & LAUCA (CHILE)

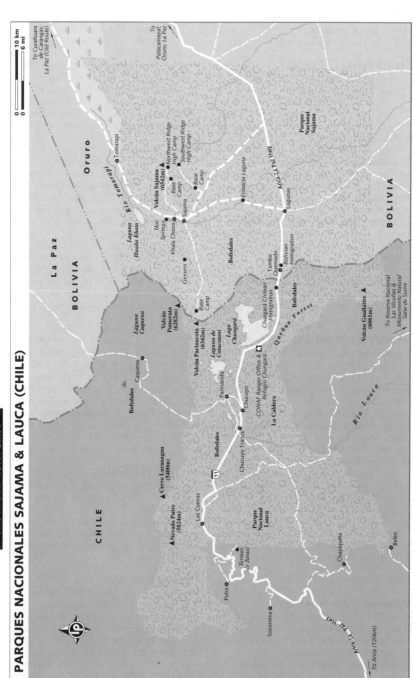

modest, so you'll still need a sleeping bag and many layers of clothing for the typically cold, windy nights. Alternatively, ask at the Sernap office in Sajama village or contact America Tours in La Paz (p47) about the new community-run **Albergue Eco-Turístico** (Tomarapi) on the northern border of the park, which planned to charge around US$25 per person including three meals. Only basic staples are sold in the village, so bring your trail food from elsewhere.

Getting There & Away

All La Paz–Arica buses pass through Sajama National Park, but you'll most likely be expected to pay the entire fare.

ANDEAN CAMELIDS

Unlike the Old World, the western hemisphere had few grazing mammals after the Pleistocene era, when mammoths, horses and other large herbivores disappeared from North and South America. For millennia, the Andean people relied on the New World camelids – the wild guanaco and vicuña and the domesticated llama and alpaca – for food and fiber.

Guanaco *(Lama guanicoe)* and vicuña *(Vicugna vicugna)* are relatively rare today but are the likely ancestors of the domesticated llama *(L. glama)* and alpaca *(L. pacos)*. In fact they were among few potential New World domestic animals – contrast them with the Old World cattle, horses, sheep, goats, donkeys and pigs that have filled so many vacant niches in the Americas. Of the major domesticated animals from across the Atlantic, only the humped camel has failed to achieve an important role here. While the New World camels have lost ground to sheep and cattle in some areas, they are not likely to disappear.

The guanaco ranges from the central Andes to Tierra del Fuego from sea level up to 4000m or higher. In these regions, early native hunters ate its meat and dressed in its skin. In the central Andes, where the human population is small but widely dispersed and domestic livestock numerous, guanaco numbers are small. However, on the plains of Argentine Patagonia and in reserves such as southern Chile's Parque Nacional Torres del Paine, herds of rust-colored guanaco are still a common sight. Bolivia's only guanaco population shelters in the highland plains of the Reserva Nacional de Fauna Andina Eduardo Avaroa (p176).

By contrast, the vicuña occupies a much smaller area, well above 4000m on the puna and Altiplano from southern Peru to northwestern Argentina. Although not as numerous as the guanaco, it played a critical role in the cultural life of pre-Columbian Peru. Its very fine golden wool was the exclusive property of the Inca emperors.

Strict Inca authority protected the vicuña, but the Spanish invasion destroyed that authority. By the middle of this century, poaching reduced vicuña numbers from two million to perhaps 10,000 and caused its inclusion in Appendix I of the Endangered Species List. Conservation efforts in Chile's Parque Nacional Lauca and Bolivia's Parque Nacional Apolobamba have been so successful that economic exploitation of the species is now being allowed in some puna communities. In Lauca and surrounding areas, vicuña numbers grew from barely 1000 in the early 1970s to more than 27,000 two decades later.

The Altiplano's indigenous communities still depend on llamas and alpacas for their livelihood. The two species appear very similar but they differ in several important respects. The taller, rangier and hardier llama has relatively coarse wool that is used for blankets, ropes and other household goods. It also works as a pack animal, but thanks to the introduction of the *camión*, llama trains are increasingly rare in Bolivia.

Llamas can survive and even flourish on relatively poor, dry pastures, whereas the smaller, more delicate alpacas require well-watered grasslands to produce their much finer wool, which has a higher commercial value than that of llamas. Both llama and alpaca meat are consumed by Andean households and are sold in urban markets all over Bolivia.

In recent years, the meager earnings from the sale of wool and meat haven't been sufficient to stem the flow of population from the countryside into urban areas. However, the commercialization of vicuña wool might help achieve this, if there is international agreement. According to a study by Conaf (the Chilean national-park commission), the commercialization of vicuña cloth could bring a price of US$290 per square meter.

Once you've come this far, a visit to Chile's spectacular **Parque Nacional Lauca** (see below) is highly recommended. For onward travel to La Paz or into Chile, go to the paved road (Arica–La Paz highway) and flag down a bus or *camión*; most of the traffic passes after midday, but buses are normally full and passengers aren't permitted to sit in the aisle. The border crossing between **Tambo Quemado** (Bolivia) and **Chungará** (Chile) is straightforward.

PARQUE NACIONAL LAUCA (CHILE)

Across the frontier from Sajama is Chile's poodle-shaped Parque Nacional Lauca – 138,000 hectares of marvelously intact Andean ecosystems. It was declared a national park in 1970 to protect its profusion of wildlife: flamingos, coots, Andean gulls, Andean geese, condors, vicuñas, guanacos, llamas, alpacas, rheas, viscachas, Andean foxes, armadillos, Andean deer and even pumas, as well as unusual vegetation such as the bizarre shaggy-barked *queñua* trees and the rock-hard moss known as *llareta*. Adjacent to the park, but more difficult to access, are Reserva Nacional Las Vicuñas and Monumento Natural Salar de Surire. See www.chilesat.net/conaf-tarapaca/conaf .htm for details (in Spanish) and Lonely Planet's *Chile & Easter Island* book also has more information.

Lago Chungará & Las Payachatas

Near the Bolivian border beneath the volcanoes Pomerata and Parinacota, known collectively as Las Payachatas (both higher than 6000m), is the lovely alpine Lago Chungará. At 4517m, it's one of the world's highest bodies of water and was formed when a lava flow from Volcán Parinacota dammed a snowmelt stream. Visitors may walk at will, but will have to reckon with the high altitude and swampy ground, as well as frequently fierce climatic conditions. Snow is possible at any time of year.

Because of Arica's insatiable appetite for hydroelectricity and the Azapa valley's thirst, the Chilean electric company has built an intricate system of pumps and canals that may compromise Lago Chungará's ecological integrity. Because the lake is so shallow, any lowering of its level would drastically reduce its surface

area and affect the habitat of wading birds, including flamingos and giant coots.

Parinacota

This lovely pre-Columbian stone village (4400m) sits along the Arica–Potosí silver route. In the background stretches the Laguna de Cotacotani and its surrounding *bofedales* (shallow marshes dotted with tussocks of vegetation). Conaf operates a visitor's center, museum and high-altitude genetic research station here.

The imposing whitewashed stone church was originally built in the 1600s but was reconstructed in 1789. Inside, surreal 17th-century frescoes, the work of artists from the Cuzco school, recall Hieronymus Bosch's *The Last Judgment*. Note also the depiction of soldiers bearing Christ to the cross as Spaniards. To gain entrance ask the caretaker for the key, and leave a small donation to the church.

Tours

Numerous Arica tour operators run guided day-trips to Lauca from US$55, but owing to the rapid elevation gain, participants are highly subject to altitude sickness. Based just outside the park, the American-run **Birding Alto Andino** (www.birdingaltoandino.com) offers personalized day-trips for around US$150 for two people.

Sleeping & Eating

Putre is at a much lower elevation, so those with transport will probably find it more comfortable than places inside the park. **Restaurant Oasis** serves good plain meals and offers cheap beds. **Residencial La Paloma** (US$6) has hot showers and good beds. There's also Conaf's **Refugio Putre** (US$6). **Hostería Las Vicuñas** (☎ 58-224-997; s/d with meals US$53/75) caters mainly to mining personnel, but also sees a few tourists.

Inside the park, Conaf runs the following: **Refugio Chungará** (beds US$6, campsites US$8) on Lago Chungará, which has six beds and a warm stove; **Camping Chungará** (sites US$8) with picnic tables and a wind shelter; and the basic **Refugio Parinacota** (beds US$6, campsites US$8) at Parinacota village. Pack food and a warm sleeping bag. Families in Parinacota also rent out basic rooms and welcome campers.

At **Chucuyo** (the Parinacota turnoff), Restaurant Matilde serves alpaca steaks and other simple meals and rents out cheap rooms. A couple of other places here serve inexpensive set meals and sell locally produced alpaca textiles.

Getting There & Away
The entire route from Arica to La Paz (via Tambo Quemado) is paved. Outside Arica it follows the lovely oasis-like Lluta Valley and climbs into the Atacama hills, past ancient petroglyphs and the interesting adobe church at Poconchile. Between 1300m and 1800m you'll see the appropriately named candelabra cactus, which grows just 5mm annually and flowers for only 24 hours. It virtually never rains in the Atacama, so the cactus must take its moisture from the fog.

Independent access to Lauca isn't inordinately difficult. From Arica, several companies leave the main bus terminal in the morning and pass Chungará (US$8 to US$9, three hours), in Lauca National Park, en route to La Paz (US$10 to US$17, eight hours). There are less frequent direct services to Putre and Parinacota. See Oruro's Getting There & Away section (p159) for Oruro–Arica bus details.

SOUTHWESTERN BOLIVIA

Bolivia's bottom-left corner is the country's most remote highland. With few roads, unpredictable weather, few scattered settlements and unreliable transport, travel here is an exercise in patience and creativity. The region's boundaries are demarcated by the railway lines between Uyuni and the Chilean and Argentine frontiers, and by the minor Cordillera de Lípez and Cordillera de Chichas ranges.

Transport is scarce and amenities few, but the reward for adventurous travelers is first-hand experience of other worldly landscapes. The featureless salt deserts (*salares*) are some of the world's flattest terrain, and bleached brine deposits around these *salares* provide an occasional white splash amid the prevailing earth tones. In the far southwest the surreal landscape is punctuated by towering active volcanoes, dozens of hyperactive geothermal features

---

INDEPENDENT TRAVEL

The difficulties of independent travel in the Far Southwest cannot be overstressed. The weather is extremely cold, windy and unpredictable and the area is remote and sparsely populated. The best time to travel here is from July to early October, when the days are dry and cool but not as cold as in winter. From October to March, rainfall causes the *salares* to fill with water and 4WD tracks to deteriorate quickly. Snow may fall at almost any time during the summer months (January to May, which is ironically known locally as *invierno boliviano*, the Bolivian winter).

Puestos sanitarios (health posts) are dotted around but their medical supplies and expertise are basic and shouldn't be counted on. Friendly miners, military personnel and *campesinos* will normally do what they can to provide a place to crash and even share their limited food, but it's unfair to rely on them. Coffee, fruit, magazines, coca, etc – anything that isn't locally available – make good gifts for helpful workers and officials.

The easiest way to explore the region is with an organized tour, which are most easily arranged in Uyuni (p168) or Tupiza (p181).

---

and flamingo-filled lakes stained by algae and minerals into a vast array of colors.

UYUNI
pop 14,000 / elevation 3669m
Mention Uyuni to a Bolivian and the first response is likely to be *harto frío* – extreme cold. One tourist brochure simply describes it as *frígido*. To compound things, buildings are generally drafty, indoor heating is virtually unknown and the icy winds can bite through any number of clothing layers. Although the warmer summer brings some relief – and warm, sunny days are common – this uninspiring desert community does receive more than its share of miserable weather.

Nevertheless Uyuni's isolated position and outlook elicit an affectionate respect from both Bolivians and foreign travelers. It was generously nicknamed La Hija Predilecta de Bolivia (Bolivia's Favorite Daughter), not for looks but because of its pampering of Bolivian troops returning from the Guerra del Pacífico, the war in which Bolivia lost its seacoast to Chile.

Uyuni was founded in 1889 by Bolivian president Aniceto Arce. Most residents are employed in three major enterprises: government (military and police personnel, and city officials), mining (mostly salt extraction from the Salar de Uyuni) and increasingly, tourism.

Information

IMMIGRATION

If you're traveling to Chile, you're best off picking up a Bolivian exit stamp (officially US$2) at the Las Vegas-esque **immigration office** (Sucre & Potosí; ☉ 8:30am-noon & 2-7:30pm Mon-Fri) since the hours of the Bolivian border post at Hito Cajón (just beyond Laguna Verde) are about as reliable as Altiplano transport. Although it's rarely enforced, you're expected to leave Bolivia within three days of getting the stamp, so don't bother until you know you're going.

INTERNET ACCESS

Servinet@Uyuni, the glass box in the middle of Bolívar, offers satellite Internet access for US$1 an hour. There are a couple of other less hectic Internet places opposite the plaza on Potosí and near the bus terminal.

LAUNDRY

Most hotels offer some sort of laundry service. Hotel Avenida (p168) charges US$0.65 per kilo and Toñito Hotel (p169) charges US$0.15 a piece.

MONEY

You can break big Boliviano notes and change cash at decent rates at **Banco de Crédito** (Potosí near Bolívar). Otherwise, try the street-changers near the bank. Bigger tour companies, popular hotels and restaurants will sometimes change travelers checks (3% to 5% commission). Several places on Potosí buy Chilean and Argentine pesos.

TOURIST INFORMATION

Office of Reserva Nacional de Fauna Andina Eduardo Avaroa (REA; ☎ 293-2225; Avaroa at Ferroviaria; ☉ 9am-12:30pm & 2-7pm Mon-Fri) Sernap's helpful office is more user-friendly than the park's name.

Tourist office (☉ 9am-12:30pm & 2-7:30pm) Adjacent to the plaza in the base of the wannabe Big Ben clock tower.

Unidad Regional de Turismo (Potosí at Arce) Has useful area maps and is the place to file formal complaints against tour agencies.

Sights

In town the trippy **Museo Arqueología y Antropológico de los Andes Meridionales** (Arce at Colón; admission adults/students US$0.65/35; ☉ 8:30am-noon & 2-6pm) features mummies and loads of skulls. There are also Spanish descriptions of the practices of mummification and deformation.

Uyuni's only other real tourist attraction is the Cementerio de Trenes (Train Cemetery), a large collection of historic steam locomotives and rail cars, which are decaying in the yards about 3km southwest of the station along Av Ferroviaria (the trashed-out route might well be called the *cementerio de basura* – the garbage cemetery. There have long been plans to turn the collection into a railway museum, but that seems a pipe dream and they'll most likely just keep on rusting.

Tours

The main streets of Uyuni are lined with budget tour agencies, so there's plenty of choice (see the boxed text, p168). The amount of time you wait until there's a full complement of tour participants depends on the season. From July to September, you'll rarely wait more than a day or two. At other times the wait may be longer, but there's still sufficient off-season tourism to ensure that you'll eventually find something.

In the high season (July to early September), the popular four-day circuit around the Salar de Uyuni, Laguna Colorada, Sol de Mañana, Laguna Verde and points in between costs up to US$125 per person and US$20 for each additional day; during slower periods – say, from October to March – you'll pay as little as US$75 (plus US$15 for each additional day). With more time, you can add Laguna Celeste, a lake which is as blue as a swimming pool, one day's drive northeast of Laguna Verde. For one/two days, this option will add US$15/20 to US$20/40 to your total tour price.

Colque Tours (p169) is the main operator offering three-day crossings between Uyuni and San Pedro de Atacama, Chile, via Salar de Uyuni, San Juan, Laguna Colorada, Laguna Verde and intermediate sites of interest. The price is around US$75/100

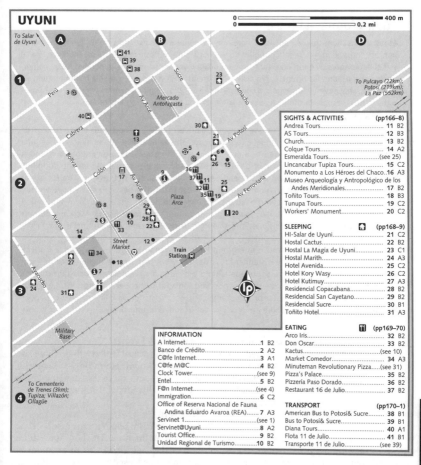

UYUNI

SIGHTS & ACTIVITIES	(pp166–8)
Andrea Tours	**11** B2
AS Tours	**12** B3
Church	**13** B2
Colque Tours	**14** A2
Esmeralda Tours	(see 25)
Lincancabur Tupiza Tours	**15** C2
Monumento a Los Héroes del Chaco	**16** A3
Museo Arqueología y Antropológico de los Andes Meridionales	**17** B2
Toñito Tours	**18** B3
Tunupa Tours	**19** C2
Workers' Monument	**20** C2

SLEEPING	(pp168–9)
HI-Salar de Uyuni	**21** C2
Hostal Cactus	**22** B2
Hostal La Magia de Uyuni	**23** C1
Hostal Marith	**24** A3
Hotel Avenida	**25** C2
Hotel Kory Wasy	**26** C2
Hotel Kutimuy	**27** A3
Residencial Copacabana	**28** B2
Residencial San Cayetano	**29** B2
Residencial Sucre	**30** B1
Toñito Hotel	**31** A3

EATING	(pp169–70)
Arco Iris	**32** B2
Don Oscar	**33** B2
Kactus	(see 10)
Market Comedor	**34** A3
Minuteman Revolutionary Pizza	(see 31)
Pizza's Palace	**35** B2
Pizzería Paso Dorado	**36** B2
Restaurant 16 de Julio	**37** B2

TRANSPORT	(pp170–1)
American Bus to Potosí& Sucre	**38** B1
Bus to Potosí& Sucre	**39** B1
Diana Tours	**40** A1
Flota 11 de Julio	**41** B1
Transporte 11 de Julio	(see 39)

INFORMATION	
A Internet	1 B2
Banco de Crédito	2 A2
C@fe Internet	3 A1
C@fe M@C	4 B2
Clock Tower	(see 9)
Entel	5 B2
F@n Internet	(see 4)
Immigration	6 C2
Office of Reserva Nacional de Fauna Andina Eduardo Avaroa (REA)	7 A3
Servinet 1	(see 1)
Servinet@Uyuni	8 A2
Tourist Office	9 B2
Unidad Regional de Turismo	10 B2

per person in low/high season with food, plus allow a modest amount for accommodations at San Juan and Laguna Colorada. Other companies offer the option to continue to San Pedro de Atacama with a Chilean operator for their regular tour price plus US$10. Travelers clear Bolivian immigration in Uyuni and are stamped into Chile near San Pedro de Atacama. (Note that there have been reports of drivers earning extra cash by transporting illicit substances across the border; before you leave Uyuni, make absolutely sure that this isn't the case on your tour.)

Day-trips to the Salar de Uyuni, stopping at Colchani, the Salt Hotels and Isla de los Pescadores, start at US$20/30 in low/high season. Alternatively, you can opt for a four-day Salar tour that includes Llica, Jiriri, surrounding archaeological sites and a climb up the 5432m Volcán Tunupa (across Salar de Uyuni); this costs around US$60/90 per person. For further information about these destinations, see the Salar de Uyuni (p172) and Southwest Circuit (p176) sections. Note that only larger Uyuni agencies accept credit cards. Since there's no ATM in town, it's best to bring enough cash to cover your tour.

You can either make up your own tour group or let the agency make up your group. For the invariably basic accommodations in private homes, *alojamientos* and *campamentos*, you'll need a warm sleeping bag.

SALAR & SOUTHWEST TOURS

At last count more than 40 agencies were offering to arrange *salar* tours from Uyuni. The explosion of competition has been a double-edged sword. On the positive side it's meant more choice and cheaper tours. The flip side is it's lowered quality, and in many cases generated much corner-cutting and touting for business. Typically, tours are in 4WD vehicles of variable health holding six (or, inadvisably, seven), passengers, a cook and a driver/guide. Bigger agencies may pack tour buses with up to 30 people in the high season. Whoever you go with, bring lots of film.

How to choose an agency

Most local Uyuni agency tours include transport, a driver/guide and food, and some also provide bare-bones lodging (on the standard four-day tour, this is normally at San Juan and Laguna Colorada). While the food in question may be decent, there may not be enough of it, and it can consist of little more than four-day-old bread and boiled potatoes. As for the 'lodging', it may well amount to a space on the earthen floor of an adobe hut; ask in advance about the standards and whether accommodations will cost extra. The best operators have written itineraries outlining meals, accommodations and other trip details – take your own snacks and ask what's available for vegetarians (eggs, eggs and more eggs most likely). Accommodations are typically in super-basic *pensiones* and scientific or military camps. If the trip is not as described notify the Uyuni tourist office.

Trips are much cheaper if you're in a group (easy to arrange in Uyuni) – six people is ideal. Budget US$75 to US$125 for the standard four-day tour, but plan on the higher price or more during the peak season (July to September). More professional operators and bookings outside Uyuni cost extra but are worth it – pay the most you can afford. Cheaper operators inevitably cut corners on basics like food, water or vehicle maintenance. Costs for park and reserve entrances fees and bathroom stops en route are typically not included in tour prices.

If you have any sort of appetite, it's best to supplement the food provided with items purchased in Uyuni. If you don't have a warm sleeping bag, make absolutely certain that the agency will provide one for you; you may have to bug them repeatedly, but no one should make these trips without one.

Previous editions of this book advised travelers to withhold 50% of the payment until they returned from their tour satisfied. Quite a few people were unsatisfied as unfortunately standards on some of these tours are below what even hard-bitten travelers expect (see the boxed text, above). Rather than improve operations, most agencies simply began requiring full payment in advance. Now you'll only get away with paying half in advance if an agency is desperate to fill a group. Therefore the importance of choosing a reputable operator cannot be overemphasized; things still may not run according to plan, but there's less chance of a desert disaster.

For an excellent alternative – which involves doing the circuit in reverse from Tupiza and winding up in Uyuni – see Tours under Tupiza (p181).

Festivals & Events

Uyuni's big **annual festival** falls on July 11 and marks the town's founding. Celebrations entail parades, speeches, dancing, music and naturally, lots of drinking.

Sleeping

Uyuni's tourism boom means new hotels are opening all the time. The best hotels fill up fast in the high season so reservations are recommended, especially if you're chugging in on the train at 2am! In a pinch, you can crash out in the railway station's waiting room; it's toasty with all the bodies in there.

BUDGET

Hotel Avenida (☎ 693-2078; Ferroviaria 11; US$2-3, with bath US$5-6) Near the train station, it's popular for its clean, renovated rooms, laundry sinks and hot showers (available 7am to 1pm). The office locks up at midnight unless there's still space available.

HI Salar de Uyuni (☎ /fax 693-2228; pucara_tours@ yahoo.com; www.hostellingbolivia.org; Potosí & Sucre; dm/d US$2.65/3.35; ▯) A new HI affiliate with good beds and all the typical hostel amenities plus free pick-up from the bus station, which is only 300m away.

The condition of the vehicle is another major consideration. Unfortunately, most vehicles used on these tours are ill-maintained, and the companies run them until they grind to a halt. If this happens in the middle of the Salar de Uyuni or halfway to Laguna Verde, you have a problem. Ascertain that the vehicle can withstand the harsh conditions and that there's sufficient oil and gas for the journey (beyond Uyuni, there's no reliable supply). Also carry enough food and water for several days beyond the projected length of your trip.

All that said, sometimes it's irrelevant which company you choose. If one agency's tour isn't filled, they transfer their clients to another agency to make up a full complement of passengers. It's common to book with one company but end up on a trip with another.

It's very difficult to recommend one agency over another since so much depends on the driver – and his astrological sign. The best bet is to chat to returning travelers and get the latest scoop. The following agencies have been around a few years and consistently receive more yeas than nays from readers:

AS Tours (☎ 693-2772; Ferroviaria s/n) Opposite the train station.
Andrea Tours (☎ 693-2638; Arce 26) Receives high marks for food and accommodation.
Colque Tours (☎ 693-2199; www.colquetours.com; Potosí 56) Often recommended for travel to/from Chile but has received many serious complaints.
Esmeralda Tours (☎ 693-2130; Ferroviaria 11, at Hotel Avenida) Some of best reports at the cheaper end of the scale.
Lincancabur/Tupiza Tours (☎ 693-2996/2988; licancatours@entelnet.bo; Sucre 86) Best choice for reverse circuit trips ending up in Tupiza.
Toñito Tours (☎ 693-2094; www.bolivianexpeditions.com; Ferroviaria 152) Guarantees a price, even without a full group.
Tunupa Tours (☎ 693-2099; Plaza Arce & Ferroviara)

Hotel Kutimuy (☎ /fax 693-2391/2199; kutimuy@ yahoo.com; Potosí & Avaroa; US$2.75, with bath & breakfast US$6.75) Affiliated with Colque Tours, the comfortable, revamped rooms are usually tidy and have good beds. Laundry service is available.

Hostal Marith (☎ 693-2174; Potosí 61; US$2, with bath US$4) Quiet, no-nonsense back-packers' favorite off the main drag. While some of the rooms may be dark, it's clean and cheap. The showers are good and there is hot water all day. Breakfast is available.

Cheap places near the station come in handy as most trains arrive and depart at ungodly hours. If you're not shipping out, however, all the comings and goings can be sleep-depriving:

Hostal Cactus (southwest side of Plaza Arce; US$2.50) Friendly, refurbished, clean, cheap shelter. Plenty of blankets. Expanding in 2004.
Residencial Sucre (☎ 693-2047; Sucre 132; US$2) Marginal with basic but sanitary rooms.
Residencial San Cayetano (southwest side of Plaza Arce; US$2) Servicable. Rise early to use the one decent shower (US$0.50 extra).
Residencial Copacabana (southwest side of Plaza Arce; US$2) Standoffish, with a face that only a parent could love. Showers US$0.50 extra.

MID-RANGE
Toñito Hotel (☎ 693-3186; www.bolivianexpeditions .com/hotel.htm; Ferroviaria 60; US$5, s/d/ste with bath & breakfast US$20/30/40) The cheaper rooms at the new Toñito are deservedly popular with tour groups, so book ahead in the high season. If you have the dough, though, kick it in style in a suite. Just try to resist the waft of pizza aroma from the all-you-can-eat buffet downstairs at Minuteman Pizza – see Eating below.

Hostal La Magia de Uyuni (☎ 693-2541; magia_ uyuni@yahoo.es; Colón 432; s/d with bath & breakfast US$15/20) The charming Magia has spotless, homely rooms arranged around a tidy indoor courtyard. It's one of the nicest places in town, and thus popular with upmarket tour groups.

Hotel Kory Wasy (☎ 693-2670; www.korywasy.com; Potosí 304; r per person with bath & breakfast US$10) The comfort afforded by this sunny, stylish place is worth every penny after four days in a Jeep. It also has a restaurant.

Eating

Thanks to Uyuni's tourism boom visitors now have lots of choices – but thanks to the prevailing copy-cat mentality, most of these options still involve pizza.

RESTAURANTS

Minuteman Revolutionary Pizza (at Toñito Hotel; ☎ 693-2094; Ferroviaria 50; ☽ from 8am; breakfast US$3, dinner buffet US$4.65) Uyuni's best all-around eating choice, owned by a true blue Yankee from Amherst, Mass offers homemade bagels, biscotti and Budweiser. The brick-oven pizza is as out-of-this-world as the nearby landscape. And the all-you-can-eat dinner buffet hits the spot after four days of bland *Si, el chofer es* the cook *tambien* (Yes, the driver is the cook, too) rations.

Arco Iris (northeast side Plaza Arce; mains US$2-4) Habitually recommended for its pizza and as a prime night-time hangout. It's warm inside and there's a decent bar serving up cold beer and occasional live music. It's also the best spot to cobble together a tour group – you'll have plenty of time, as service is at armadillo pace.

Kactus (Potosí near Arce; mains US$1.50-3) This low-lit den offers tasty pastas, simple soups, international dishes and a few typical Bolivian choices. It's a comfortable place to read, chat or write. The music is good and the cocktails are plenty strong.

Restaurant 16 de Julio (☎ 693-2171; Arce 35; mains US$2-4; ☽ from 7am; mains US$1.50-3.50) Offers a mean choice of breakfasts: the Continental, Americano, Ejecutivo (steak and fries), Tor-tuguita (pancakes) or Vegetariano (muesli, yogurt and fruit salad). Later in the day, you'll get (you guessed it) pizza, Bolivian specialties and international cuisine featuring warming, high-carbohydrate fare. It also changes money.

Pizzería Paso Dorado (Arce 49; mains US$3, pizzas US$4-10) Pizza is what they do most, but non-round options are available too. There's a notable variety of *milanesa* incarnations but service is slow.

Don Oscar (Potosí near Bolívar; mains US$1-3) This friendly local favorite opens early for breakfast and also serves filling dinners.

Pizza's Palace (Av Arce) The pizza is decent as are the Bolivian dishes, burgers and snacks, but breakfast is their strong suit.

QUICK EATS

If you've got an iron-clad stomach, cheap meals are on offer at the market comedor and nearby street food stalls. For a piquant dose of Altiplano culture, look for *charque kan* (mashed hominy peppered with strips of dried llama meat), an Uyuni specialty often tucked inside *tamales*. Good snack stands serving burgers, potato cakes, juice and ice cream are lined up like ducks in a row on Av Arce.

Getting There & Away

Getting out of isolated Uyuni can be problematic. Buy your bus ticket the day before or ask your tour agency how much they charge to purchase your train ticket; lines are long and WWF-inspired *quien es mas macho* (who is the most macho) shoving matches can break out for the limited seats. Proposed transport infrastructure upgrades include a high-season Ferrobus rail service to Potosí and TAM flights from La Paz via Sucre, though the latter is a sketchy prospect due to treacherous Altiplano wind conditions.

BUS & JEEP

There's supposedly a new bus terminal in the works (funded by the US$0.20 terminal fee), but at last look all buses were still leaving from the west end of Av Arce, a couple minutes' walk from the plaza. There's a choice of services to most destinations, so ask around to get the best price or the best service.

American and **Transporte 11 de Julio** buses blast off at 10am daily for Potosí (US$2 to US$3, seven hours) and Sucre (US$4 to US$5, 9 to 11 hours). **Diana Tours** runs the same service at 7pm daily. **Flota 11 de Julio** goes to Tupiza (US$4 to US$5, 10 to 12 hours) Wednesday and Sunday at 9am and Calama, Chile (via Avaroa; US$10, 12 to 15 hours) at 4am Monday and Thursday. There are daily 7pm buses to Oruro (US$2 to US$3, 8 to 10 hours). Roads and weather permitting, there are 10am Wednesday departures for Tarija (US$8, up to 24 hours) and Wednesday and Sunday services to La Paz (US$6, 11 to 14 hours).

There's also an international service to Calama, Chile (US$11, 12-15 hours), via the Avaroa border crossing. An alternative route to Chile is with organized tour, which will leave you in San Pedro de Atacama (p168).

4WD Jeep services shuttle between Uyuni and Tupiza (US$6.50, 7 to 8 hours) when there's enough demand. Several companies depart around 7:30am from near the bus terminal – after they've stuffed in as many as 10 passengers.

TRAIN

Uyuni has a modern, well-organized **train station** (☎ 693-2153). When you get to the station, confirm window hours on the blackboard inside, then queue as early as possible.

Comfortable but crowded *Expreso del Sur* trains ramble to Oruro (US$5/9 in salon/executive, 6½ hours) on Tuesday and Friday at midnight and south to Tupiza (US$4/9, five hours) and Villazón (US$6/ 13.75, 9½ hours) on Monday and Friday at 10:20pm. If tickets sell out, you can try to sneak on the train (Bolivian-style) or take a bus 111km south to Atocha, where there are bus connections and the train stops at 12:40am.

Chronically late *Wara Wara del Sur* trains are supposed to chug out of the station at 1:40am on Monday and Thursday for Oruro (US$4/7.75 in salon/executive, seven hours) and on Wednesday and Sunday at 2: 40am for Tupiza (US$3.25/5.75, 5½ hours) and Villazón (US$4.50/9, 9 hours); these engines always seem to be chanting 'I think I can… think I can…'

On Mondays at 3:30am a recently upgraded train trundles west for Avaroa (US$4.25) on the Chilean border, where you cross to Ollagüe and have to wait several hours to clear Chilean customs. Another train continues the journey to Calama (US$12). The whole trip takes 20 to 40 hours and is strictly for rail buffs (see the boxed text, below).

BY RAIL TO CHILE

The rail route between Bolivia and Chile passes through some spectacular landscapes, and if you're prepared for the uncomfortable conditions, the journey is highly worthwhile. Temperatures in the coaches may well fall below zero at night, so a sleeping bag or woolen blanket and plenty of warm clothing are essential. There's a dining car, but it's best to bring food as well. Any sort of fruit, meat or cheese will be confiscated at the border (you'll get a receipt), so eat it up before reaching customs at Ollagüe.

Between Uyuni and the border, the line crosses vast saltpans, deserts and rugged mountains and volcanoes. Flamingos, guanacos, vicuñas and wild burros are common and, thanks to a startling mirage effect, a host of other things. *Remolinos* (dust devils or willy-willys) whirl across the stark landscape beneath towering snowcapped volcanoes. One type of vegetation that flourishes is *llareta* (also spelled – *yareta*), a combustible salt-tolerant moss that oozes a turpentine-like jelly and is used by the locals as stove fuel. It appears soft and spongy from a distance but is actually rock hard. Llareta grows very slowly; a large clump may be several hundred years old. The plant is now an officially protected species in Chile and in the Reserva Nacional de Fauna Andina Eduardo Avaroa (REA).

Before the trip, you'll need to pass by the *migración* office in Uyuni and pick up your Bolivian exit stamp. The Chilean immigration procedures at Avaroa/Ollagüe, a windy, dusty and unprotected outpost in a broad pass through the Andes, can be trying. You must line up for your entrance stamp, and then they may want to do a luggage search. All this takes place outside at nearly 5000m altitude, and it can be a miserable exercise in endurance.

The border crossing will probably also involve a wait for the arrival of the Bolivian or Chilean engine (which may arrive up to 12 hours late) to pull you to either Uyuni or Calama. The excruciatingly slow Chilean engine, especially when it's headed uphill from Calama to the border (max 40km/hr), appears to be the incarnation of *The Little Engine That Could*, but even if 'it thinks it can,' it does so with little conviction. Note also that the Chilean coaches are in surprisingly worse repair than their Bolivian counterparts. The Chilean service is run by British-owned Ferrocarril Antofagasta-Bolivia, which loses money on the line but is required by an 1888 mineral transport treaty to keep the passenger service running indefinitely. Perhaps that explains why the windows are broken and the coaches lack light and heating, why they have wooden benches instead of seats, why the loose boards allow cold winds to whistle through and why the toilets are located outside, exposed to the elements!

From Calama to the coast, there's still a railway, but no rail service, so you'll have a two- to three-hour bus trip to Antofagasta. It's sometimes possible to buy Chilean pesos in Uyuni or Ollagüe, but you'd probably have better luck at a *casa de cambio* in La Paz.

AROUND UYUNI

Pulacayo

At this semi-ghost town 22km northeast of Uyuni brilliantly colored rocks rise beside the road and a mineral-rich stream reveals streaks of blue, yellow, red and green. The Pulacayo mines north of the village, which yielded mainly silver, were first opened in the late 17th century (the grave of the company founder A Mariano Ramírez can still be seen), but they closed in 1832 on account of the Independence war. In 1873, however, the mining Compañía Huanchaca de Bolivia (CHB) took over operations and resumed silver extraction. At the time of its final closure in 1959, it employed 20,000 miners, but today, only a few hundred hardy souls remain.

The little-known **Museo de Minas** (admission US$1.50) mining museum is a worthwhile attempt at reviving Pulacayo from the dead. Here you can explore nearly 2km of mine tunnels (the mine's entire extent is just under 6km) with local guides. Also worthwhile is the **mill** that spins llama wool into cloth, and **Huanchaca**, 15km from Pulacayo, where you'll see the colonial cemetery and the ruins of silver smelters from the same period.

Pulacayo is also home to several decaying steam locomotives that were originally imported to transport ore. They include Bolivia's first steam engine, El Chiripa, which dates from 1890, and others with such names as El Burro, El Torito and Mauricio Hothschild. There's also the ore train that was robbed by legendary bandits Butch Cassidy and the Sundance Kid, including a wooden railcar that bears the bullet holes from the attack.

Another interesting site is the 1878 **Aniceto Arce's home** (admission US$4). This historic house features lovely marble fireplaces, pianos, old telephones and period furniture imported from Britain.

Befitting its more active past, Pulacayo has two basic but surprisingly pleasant hotels, **Hotel El Rancho** (US$1.75) and **El Rancho II** (US$1.50) where simple meals are also available.

Getting There & Away

All transport between Uyuni and Potosí passes through Pulacayo. **Proyecto Turístico Pulacayo** (☎ 694-3459) organizes guided tours from Uyuni. If you can get in touch with them, they charge US$4.50 for round-trip transport to Pulacayo, a sandwich lunch and a folder describing village history.

SALAR DE UYUNI

The world's largest salt flat (12,106 sq km) sits at 3653m and covers nearly all of Daniel Campos province. The Salar de Uyuni is now a center of salt extraction and processing, particularly around the settlement of Colchani, 20km northwest from Uyuni. The estimated annual output of the Colchani operation is nearly 20,000 tons, 18,000 tons of which is for human consumption while the rest is for livestock.

When the surface is dry, the *salar* becomes a blinding white expanse of the greatest nothing imaginable, but when there's a little water, the surface perfectly reflects the clouds and the blue Altiplano sky and the horizon disappears. If you're driving across the surface at such times, the effect is positively eerie, and it's hard to believe that you're not actually flying through the clouds.

History

In recent geologic history, this part of the Altiplano was covered entirely by water. Around the ancient lakeshore, two distinctive terraces are visible, indicating the succession of two lakes; below the lower one are fossils of coral in limestone.

From 40,000 to 25,000 years ago, Lago Minchín, whose highest level reached 3760m, occupied much of southwestern Bolivia. When it evaporated, the area lay dry for 14,000 years before the appearance of short-lived Lago Tauca, which lasted for only about 1000 years and rose to 3720m. When it dried up, it left two large puddles, Lagos Poopó and Uru Uru, and two major salt concentrations, the Salares de Uyuni and Coipasa.

This part of the Altiplano is drained internally, with no outlet to the sea; the salt deposits are the result of the minerals leeched from the mountains and deposited at the lowest available point.

Colchani

There remain at least 10 billion tons of salt in the Salar de Uyuni, and around Colchani, *campesinos* hack it out with picks and

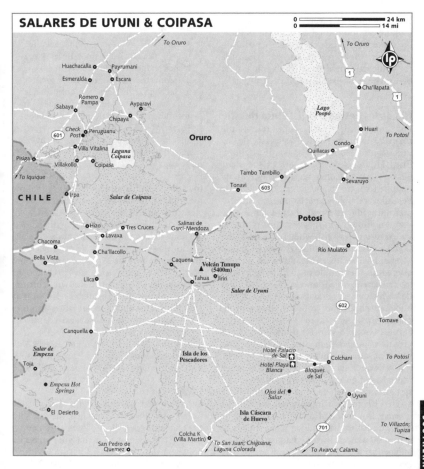

SALARES DE UYUNI & COIPASA

0 ———————— 24 km
0 ———————— 14 mi

shovels and pile it into small conical mounds that characterize the *salar* landscape in this area. In Colchani itself several salt treatment plants iodize the salt according to WHO recommendations and bag it up for distribution to other parts of Bolivia.

Most of the salt is sold to refiners and hauled off by rail, but some is exchanged with local villages for wool, meat and grease. In the winter months, a rapidly decreasing number of people load the salt blocks onto llama caravans and transport them along the salt trail to Tarija, nearly 300km away, where it's traded for honey, chilies, maize, wood, coca leaves and other products that are otherwise unavailable on the Altiplano. This trade has been going on

at least since 1612, when it was described in the Aymará orthography.

A few kilometers southwest of Colchani is the extraordinary **Cooperative Rosario workshop**, also called the Bloques de Sal (Salt Blocks). Here, blocks of salt are cut from the *salar* and made into furniture and lively works of art. You may see anything from souvenir carvings of vicuñas, condors and frogs to lawn chairs and decorative model houses and churches. The operation employs 60 workers and has become a solid attraction on Salar de Uyuni tourist circuits.

Ojos del Salar

In some areas of the *salar*, cold underground water rises to the surface and bubbles up through the salt layer, creating unusual-looking eruptions on the salt. Some of these are quite large, and when there's water on the *salar*, they create dangerous hazards for vehicles. One distinctive example west of Colchani is visited on most dry-season tours.

Isla de los Pescadores (Isla Inca Huasi)

For most Salar de Uyuni tours, the main destination is the lovely Isla de los Pescadores (also known as Isla Inca Huasi, 'Inca Houses'), in the heart of the *salar* 80km west of Colchani. Although many people refer to it incorrectly as Isla de Pescado, reliable experts on the subject maintain that the real 'Fish Island' (the name is thought to derive from its shape, which resembles a fish when reflected in the *salar*) is actually 25km northwest of here.

The Isla de los Pescadores is a hilly outpost in the middle of the *salar*, covered in *Trichoreus* cactus and surrounded by a flat, white sea of hexagonal salt tiles. It was once a remarkably lonely, otherworldly place. However, there's now a tourist complex and around midday, lunching groups trip over each other while chasing photo ops and following a network of well-marked walking tracks to reach the summit. Mongo's (of La Paz fame) opened a bar and restaurant on the island in June 2003.

The island is administered by Daniel Campos Province and at last check overnight accommodation was only available in emergency situations. If you manage to arrive independently, free camping on nearby Isla Pescado, is included in the admission fee (US$1).

Isla Cáscara de Huevo

The small Eggshell Island was named for the broken shells of birds' eggs that litter it. It lies near the southern end of the Salar de Uyuni and is visited mainly to see the strange patterns of salt crystallization in the area, some of which resemble roses.

Volcán Tunupa & Jiriri

Diagonally opposite Colchani, a rounded promontory juts into the Salar de Uyuni and on it rises Volcán Tunupa (5400m). One legend states that Atahualpa slashed the breast of a woman called Tunupa on its slopes, and the milk that spilled out formed

---

SALT HOTELS

At the time of research, the Salar de Uyuni's famous salt hotels, **Hotel Playa Blanca** and the **Palacio de Sal**, were being deconstructed and relocated block by block to the edge of the *salar* near Colchani due to environmental concerns. Inquire at agencies in La Paz or Uyuni, or at **Hidalgo Tours** (☎ 02-622-5186; www.salardeuyuni.net) in Potosí, to find out when they might be up and running again.

---

the *salar*. Altitude aside, this hulking yellow mountain is a relatively easy climb.

At the foot of the volcano is the village of Jiriri, in an area specked with ruined ancient villages and burial grounds. Articles of clothing and artifacts in ceramic, gold and copper have been discovered at some of the sites, indicating the presence of an advanced but little-known culture. Unfortunately, its remoteness has left it vulnerable to amateur treasure hunters who have plundered several items of archaeological value.

Families in Jiriri offer basic accommodations, with a choice of a mattress or a spot on the floor, for a couple of dollars.

Llica

On the opposite side of the *salar* from Colchani is the village of Llica, the unlikely site of a teachers' college. There are a couple basic places to stay each charging a couple dollars a day; ask in the *alcadía's* office. For meals, the *pensiones* Inca Wasi, Bolívar and El Viajero serve soup for US$0.20 and full meals for US$1. *Micros* (US$2.50, four hours) leave Uyuni for Llica more or less daily at noon.

Getting There & Away

From the railway line between Uyuni and Oruro, you'll glimpse the *salar* during the stop at Colchani, but to fully appreciate the place, you need to get out onto the salt. The easiest access is with an organized tour departing from Uyuni (p166), but for those who prefer an independent approach, *camiones* leave for Colchani and Llica from Av Ferroviaria in Uyuni. You'll have the most luck between 7am and 9am. Some salt workers living in Uyuni commute

CHIPAYA

Immediately north of the Salar de Coipasa, on the Río Sabaya delta, live the Chipaya people, who occupy two desert villages (Chipaya and Ayparavi) of unique circular mud huts known as *khuyas* or *putucus*. Chipayas are best recognized by their earth-colored clothing and the women's unique hairstyle, which is plaited African-style into 60 small braids. These are in turn joined into two large braids and decorated with a *laurake* (barrette) at each temple.

Some researchers believe the Chipaya were the Altiplano's first inhabitants, and that they may in fact be a remnant of the lost Tiahuanaco civilization. Much of this speculation is based on the fact that their language, which is vastly different from both Quechua and Aymará, closely resembles Urus. Other researchers note similarities to Mayan, Arawak, Arabic and North African tribal languages.

Chipaya tradition maintains that the people descend from the builders of the *chullpas* scattered around Lake Titicaca. Their religion, which is nature-based, deifies phallic images, stones, rivers, mountains, animal carcasses and Chipaya ancestors. The rather phallic village church tower is worshipped as a demon – one of 40 named demons, who represent hate, ire, vengeance, gluttony, and other deadly sins. These are believed to inhabit the whitewashed sod cones that exist within a 15km radius of the village, where they're appeased with magic amulets, llama fetuses and mummified animals to prevent their evil from invading the village. The people also revere the Volcán Sajama and the Río Lauca, which provide fertile soil and fresh water.

The reverent commemoration of dead ancestors culminates on November 2, **All Saints' Day**, when bodies are disinterred from the *chullpas*. They're feted with a feast, copious drink and coca leaves, and informed about recent village events and the needs of the living. Those who were chiefs, healers and other luminaries are carried to the church where they're honored with animal sacrifices (oddly, a similar practice is salient in the indigenous religion of Madagascar).

Visiting Chipaya

In general, tourists aren't especially welcome. Visitor 'hospitality' in Chipaya has been reported to cost up to US$50 per person, and attempts at bargaining normally only aggravate matters and create ill will. Traditionally, the Chipayas have been rather superstitious about cameras but some will ignore their beliefs for a fee. Accommodations are occasionally available at the school, with permission from the village administration, for a few dollars per person. For food, you're limited to the small village shop, and toilets facilities are four open holes just outside the village, corresponding to the four compass directions.

Chipaya can be reached from Llica, across the Salar de Coipasa, or from Oruro via Toledo, Corque and Huachacalla. On most days, *micros* from Uyuni to Llica (US$2.50, four hours) leave daily around noon. From Llica, you can wait for a *camión* or hire a motorcycle taxi to Pisiga (around US$15); there you'll find Iquique–Oruro buses headed for Sabaya (where you'll find an *alojamiento* and basic meals), Huachacalla and Oruro.

From Oruro, *camiones* leave from the Plaza Walter Khon once or twice a week (most often on Wednesday), while buses, which go only as far as Huachacalla (175km from Oruro and 21km from Chipaya) leave several times weekly, also from Plaza Walter Khon. Alternatively, you can reach Sabaya or Huachacalla on any bus between Oruro and Iquique. In addition, a few tour companies organize visits to the village. *Camiones* (US$2, 20 hours) that fetch the salt from Coipasa village also travel frequently to and from Oruro.

daily to Colchani in private vehicles or on motorcycles, and for a small fee you may be able to hitch along.

Camiones from Uyuni make the trip to Llica in a couple of hours and sometimes continue farther into the southwest region, carrying supplies to sulfur mines and other camps. This is an adventurous way to go,

but come well prepared with food, water and camping gear.

SALAR DE COIPASA

This great 2218 sq km remote salt desert northwest of the Salar de Uyuni at an elevation of 3786m was part of the same system of prehistoric lakes as the Salar de

Uyuni – a system that covered the area over 10,000 years ago. The 4WD-only road to the Salar de Coipasa is extremely poor. The salt-mining village of Coipasa, which (not surprisingly) is constructed mainly of salt, occupies an island in the middle of the *salar*.

THE SOUTHWEST CIRCUIT

Bolivia's southwestern tip is comprised of the provinces of Nor López, Sud López and Baldiviezo, which collectively make up the region known as Los Lípez. Much of it is nominally protected in the **Reserva Nacional de Fauna Andina Eduardo Avaroa** (REA; admission US$4 – rising in 2004), which was created in 1973 and received 44,000 visitors in 2002. Its emphasis is on preserving the vicuña and the llareta plant, both of which are threatened in Bolivia, as well as other unique ecosystems and endemic species.

This high, wide and lonesome desert country represents one of the world's harshest wilderness regions and a final refuge for some of South America's hardiest wildlife. As a hotbed of volcanic and geothermal activity, the landscape literally boils with minerals. When you see the resulting spectrum of wild unearthly colors in the mountains and lakes, you may suspect that Pachamama occasionally takes a walk on the wild side.

TOURS

Most visitors begin their tour in Uyuni, but with more people entering from Argentina, heading out from Tupiza is an increasingly popular option.

Salar de Uyuni to Laguna Colorada

The normal tour route from Uyuni is via **Colchani**, 20km to the northwest, then 80km west across the *salar* to **Isla de los Pescadores**. After a stop to explore the island, the route turns south and 45km later, reaches the edge of the *salar*, where there may be a small snack shack.

After another 22km, you'll pass through a military checkpoint at the village of Colcha K (pronounced col-cha-kah). In the village, there's a pleasant adobe church

and rudimentary accommodations in a private home and shop 100m up the cobbled street.

About 15km further along is the quinoa-growing village of **San Juan** at an elevation of 3660m. It has a lovely adobe church, a population of 1000, and several volcanic-rock tombs and burial *chullpas* in the vicinity. Budget accommodations are provided in private homes, basic *alojamientos* and the clean and well-appointed Posada Don Victor. All charge around US$3 per person. Upmarket tours stay at **Magia de San Juan** (barronhumberto@hotmail.com; s/d with bath & breakfast US$15/20), where the cozy pub has a fireplace and is open to nonguests. With a phone-card, you can call virtually anywhere in the world from the nearby Entel cabin. The new community-run **Museo Kausay Wasi** (admission US$1.35) displays regional archaeological finds and has plans for a salt-block *albergue* on the *salar*.

At this point the route turns west and starts across the borax-producing **Salar de Chiguana**, where the landscape opens up and snowcapped **Ollagüe** (5865m), an active volcano straddling the Chilean border, appears in the distance. There's a rough road leading to a field of steaming fumaroles and sulfur mines at the 5000m level.

At Chiguana, across the Uyuni–Calama railroad, your passport will be scrutinized by lonesome soldiers. The route then turns south and climbs into high and increasingly wild terrain, past the several mineral-rich lakes filled with Andean, Chilean and James flamingos. Several of the lakes are backed by hills resembling spilled chocolate sundaes. After approximately 170km of rough bumping through marvelous landscapes, the road winds down the much-photographed **Árbol de Piedra** (Stone Tree) in the Desierto Siloli, 18km north of Laguna Colorada.

Laguna Colorada

This fiery red lake (4278m) covers approximately 60 sq km and reaches a depth of just 80cm. The rich red coloration is derived from algae and plankton that thrive in the mineral-rich water, and the shoreline is fringed with brilliant white deposits of sodium, magnesium, borax and gypsum. The lake sediments are also rich in diatoms, tiny microfossils used in the production of fertilizer, paint, toothpaste and plastics, and as a filtering agent for oil, pharmaceuticals, aviation fuel, beer and wine. More apparent are the flamingos that breed here, and all three South American species are present (see the boxed text, right)

The sprawling **Huayllajara Hostal Altiplano** (US$5, with bath US$10), 6km from the lake, provides beer, snacks and basic insulation from the cold in six-bed dorms or newer rooms with private bath. At the bottom end is **Señor Eustaquio Bernal's refugio** (US$3).

Upmarket tours stay at Hidalgo Tours' Hospedaría Hidalgo Laguna Colorada, which has rustic rooms with heating, hot water and private bathrooms.

Alternatively, the REA runs the best budget option, the **Albergue de los Guardaparques** (US$4), which has comfortable cots with mattresses in a six-bed dormitory. It was closed for repairs at last look, and may or may not reopen due to environmental impact concerns. It's worth noting that requesting particular accommodations may be futile, since most agencies and drivers have 'special arrangements' with their favorite hotels.

The clear air is bitterly cold and winter night-time temperatures can drop below –20°C. Just as well; if it ever raised much above freezing, the stench would probably make the place unbearable. Instead, the air is perfumed with llareta smoke, which seems ironic given the proximity to potentially limitless solar, geothermal and wind power.

Sol de Mañana Geyser Basin

Apart from tour groups, most vehicles along the tracks around Laguna Colorada will be supplying or servicing mining and military camps or the geothermal project 50km south at Sol de Mañana (which was on hold at last visit). The main interest here is the 4850m-high geyser basin with bubbling mud pots, hellish fumaroles and the thick and nauseating aroma of sulfur fumes. Approach the site cautiously; any damp or cracked earth is potentially dangerous and cave-ins do occur, sometimes causing serious burns.

Termas de Polques & Salar de Chalviri

At the foot of Cerro Polques lie the Termas de Polques, a small 28°C to 30°C hot spring

---

FROZEN FLAMINGOS

Three species of flamingo breed in the bleak high country of southwestern Bolivia, and once you've seen these posers strutting through icy mineral lagoons at 5000m elevation, you'll abandon time-worn associations between flamingos, coconut palms and the steamy tropics.

Flamingos have a complicated and sophisticated system for filtering the foodstuffs from highly alkaline brackish lakes. They filter algae and diatoms from the water by sucking in and vigorously expelling water from the bill several times per second. The minute particles are caught on fine hairlike protrusions that line the inside of the mandibles. The suction is created by the thick fleshy tongue, which rests in a groove in the lower mandible and pumps back and forth like a piston.

The Chilean flamingo reaches heights of just over one meter and has a black-tipped white bill, dirty blue legs, red knees and salmon-colored plumage. The James flamingo is the smallest of the three species and has dark-red legs and a yellow-and-black bill. It's locally known as *jututu*. The Andean flamingo is the largest of the three and has pink plumage, yellow legs and a yellow-and-black bill.

---

pool. Although they're not boiling by any means, they're suitable for bathing and the mineral-rich waters are thought to relieve the symptoms of arthritis and rheumatism. To the east, the adjacent Salar de Chalviri supports populations of flamingos and ducks. A mining operation extracts borax in the middle of the *salar*.

Laguna Verde

This stunning blue-green lake (4400m) is tucked into the southwestern corner of Bolivian territory, 52km south of Sol de Mañana. The incredible green color comes from high concentrations of lead, sulfur, arsenic and calcium carbonates. In this exposed position, an icy wind blows almost incessantly, whipping the water into a brilliant green-and-white froth. This surface agitation combined with the high mineral content means that it can remain liquid at temperatures as low as –20°C.

Behind the lake rises the cone of **Volcán Licancabur** (5960m), whose summit is said to have once sheltered an ancient Inca crypt. Some tours include an ascent of Licancabur, and although it presents no technical difficulties, the wind, temperature, altitude and ball-bearing volcanic pumice underfoot may prove too much for most people.

Where the route splits about 20km south of Sol de Mañana, the more scenic left fork climbs up and over a 5000m pass, then up a stark hillside resembling a freshly raked Zen garden dotted with the enormous **Rocas de Dalí**, which appear to have been meticulously placed by the surrealist master Salvador himself.

Down the far slope are two sulfur mines, a military camp and a **refugio** (US$2) where overnight guests are treated to a mattress on the floor. Behind the complex there's a hot spring in a creek where you can have a welcome bath.

GETTING THERE & AWAY
Most agencies now offer cross-border connections to San Pedro de Atacama by arrangement with Chilean operators. It's wise to check out of Bolivia at immigration in Uyuni; the exit stamp (officially US$2) allows three days to leave the country; the Hito Cajón border post near Laguna Verde is staffed only sporadically.

Laguna Celeste
This 'blue lake' or – more romantically – 'heaven lake,' is still very much a peripheral trip for most Uyuni agencies, but it's gaining popularity with adventurous travelers as a one-day detour. A local legend suggests the presence of a submerged ruin, possibly a *chullpa*, in the lake. Behind the lake, a road winds its way up Volcán Uturuncu (6020m) to the Uturuncu sulfur mine, in a 5900m pass between the mountain's twin cones. That means it's more than 200m higher than the road over the Khardung La in Ladakh, India, making it quite possibly the highest motorable pass in the world.

Other Lakes
In the vast eastern reaches of **Sud Lípez** are numerous other fascinating mineral-rich lakes that are informally named for their odd coloration and have so far escaped

much attention. Various milky-looking lakes are known as **Laguna Blanca**, sulfur-colored lakes are **Laguna Amarilla** and wine-colored ones are known as **Laguna Guinda**. Some of these may eventually find their way onto the circuit.

Quetena Chico
About 120km northeast of Laguna Verde and 30km southwest of Laguna Celeste is the squalid mining settlement of Quetena Chico, which has a few basic services and supplies, a military post and is slated to become another park entrance and registration control point. Otherwise, it's a sleepy spot.

Valles de Rocas & San Cristóbal
The route back to Uyuni turns northeast a few kilometers north of Laguna Colorada and winds through more high, lonesome country and several valleys of bizarre eroded rock formations known as Valles de Rocas. From the village of Alota it's a trying, six-hour jostle back to Uyuni.

If you can still cope with sightseeing at this stage, a short side trip leads to the village of San Cristóbal, in a little valley northeast of Alota. Here you'll find a lovely 350-year-old church constructed on an age-old Pachamama ritual site. The walls bear a series of paintings from the life of Christ, and the altar is made of pure silver and backed up by a beautifully preserved 17th-century organ.

New in 2003, **Hotel Mongo's** (☎ 213-8471; www.llama-mama.com; s/d US$6/8, r with shared bath US$4) offers electricity and hot solar-powered showers, plus the Mad Max bar and restaurant, a unique construction that's worth a look even if you aren't staying the night. The complex, built with mitigation funds from the new massive mining project nearby, also includes a medical and communications center.

Uyuni to Tupiza
The rough track south of Uyuni initially heads out across the high desert. Immediately north of the market village of Cerdas are several impressive fields of sand dunes. After it drops dramatically off the Altiplano, it descends into a riverbed filled with bizarrely colorful, unusual and mineral-rich geology.

Just north of the active mining town of **Atocha**, which retains an Old West feel, you'll pass a picturesque miners' cemetery. In the center of Atocha, don't miss the Cessna that is impaled on a post along the main street. Beyond Atocha, the road enters increasingly scenic country, with excellent views of the stunning cone of **Cerro Chorolque** (5630m). For the next four hours, the road twists through seriously mountainous country, past **Huaca Huañusca** (p185), Butch and Sundance country, then plummets into the fertile **Río Tupiza Valley**, flanked by cactus and brilliant red rock.

TUPIZA

pop 20,000 / elevation 2950

> In the background looms the Tupizan range, very red, or better, a ruddy sepia; and very distinct, resembling a landscape painted by an artist with the animated brilliance of Delacroix or by an Impressionist like Renoir… In the tranquil translucent air, flows the breath of smiling grace…
>
> *Carlos Medinaceli, Bolivian writer*

Tupiza, embedded in some of Bolivia's most spectacular countryside, is a real gem. The capital of Sud Chichas, a province of Potosí department, it is among Bolivia's most literate and educated cities. It's also a comparatively young city – half of its inhabitants are under the age of 20 and its growth rate is one of the country's highest. It's the type of place where you come for a day and end up staying for a week.

The city lies in the valley of the Río Tupiza, surrounded by the rugged Cordillera de Chichas. The climate is mild year-round, with most of the rain falling between November and March. From June to August, days are hot, dry and clear, but night-time temperatures can drop to below freezing.

Economically, the town depends on agriculture and mining. A Yacimientos Petrolíferos Fiscales Bolivianos (YPFB) refinery 5km south of town provides employment, and the country's only antimony (a flame-retardant metallic element) smelter operates sporadically along a dry tributary of the Río Tupiza. Although tourists headed for Argentina have discovered Tupiza, the Chichas area is still well off the rutted track.

Tupiza's charm awaits in the surrounding countryside – an amazing landscape of rainbow-colored rocks, hills, mountains and canyons. If it conjures up visions of the Old West, that's only appropriate, because Tupiza lies in the heart of Butch-Cassidy-and-the-Sundance-Kid country. After robbing an Aramayo payroll at Huaca Huañusca, about 50km north of town, the pair reputedly met their untimely demise in the mining village of San Vicente (see the boxed text, p183).

History

The tribe that originally inhabited the region called themselves Chichas and left archaeological evidence of their existence. Despite this, little is known of their culture or language, and it's assumed they were ethnically separate from the tribes in neighboring areas of southern Bolivia and northern Argentina. Unfortunately, anything unique about them was destroyed between 1471 and 1488 when Tupac Inca Yupanqui made the region an annex to the Inca empire.

Once the Inca empire had fallen to the Spanish, the entire southern half of the Viceroyalty of Alto Peru was awarded to Diego de Almagro by decree of Spain's King Carlos V. When Almagro arrived on a familiarization expedition in 1535, the Chichas culture had been entirely subsumed.

Officially, Tupiza was founded on June 4, 1574, by Captain Luis de Fuentes (who also founded Tarija), but this date is pure conjecture. The origin of the name is similarly hazy. The current spelling was derived from the Chichas word Tope'sa or Tucpicsa, but no one is sure what it meant. It has been suggested that it probably referred to 'red rock,' since that seems to be the area's predominant feature.

During the tumultuous 1781 Campesino Rebellion, the peasants' champion, Luis de la Vega, mobilized the local militia, proclaimed himself governor and encouraged resistance against Spanish authorities. The rebellion was squashed early on, but the mob was successful in executing the Spanish *corregidor* (chief magistrate) of Tupiza. At the same time, 4000 Indian troops led by Pedro de la Cruz Condori, who had been charged with organizing

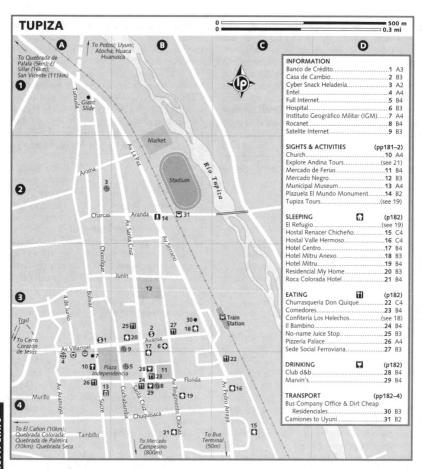

TUPIZA

0 _____ 500 m
0 _____ 0.3 mi

INFORMATION	
Banco de Crédito	1 A3
Casa de Cambio	2 B3
Cyber Snack Heladería	3 A2
Entel	4 A4
Full Internet	5 B4
Hospital	6 B3
Instituto Geográfico Militar (IGM)	7 A4
Rocanet	8 B4
Satelite Internet	9 B3

SIGHTS & ACTIVITIES	(pp181–2)
Church	10 A4
Explore Andina Tours	(see 21)
Mercado de Ferias	11 B4
Mercado Negro	12 B3
Municipal Museum	13 A4
Plazuela El Mundo Monument	14 B2
Tupiza Tours	(see 19)

SLEEPING	(p182)
El Refugio	(see 19)
Hostal Renacer Chicheño	15 C4
Hostal Valle Hermoso	16 C4
Hotel Centro	17 B4
Hotel Mitru Anexo	18 B3
Hotel Mitru	19 B4
Residencial My Home	20 B3
Roca Colorada Hotel	21 B4

EATING	(p182)
Churrasquería Don Quique	22 C4
Comedores	23 B4
Confitería Los Helechos	(see 18)
Il Bambino	24 B4
No-name Juice Stop	25 B3
Pizzería Palace	26 A4
Sede Social Ferroviaria	27 B3

DRINKING	(p182)
Club d&b	28 B4
Marvin's	29 B4

TRANSPORT	(pp182–4)
Bus Company Office & Dirt Cheap	
Residenciales	30 B3
Camiones to Uyuni	31 B2

SOUTHERN ALTIPLANO

and carrying out terrorist acts against the government, were intercepted by Spanish forces before reaching their destination.

On November 7, 1810 the first victory in Alto Peru's struggle for independence was won east of Tupiza at the Battle of Suipacha. At the end of the war, on December 9, 1824, the deciding battle took place at Tumusla in the northern Chichas.

From Tupiza's founding through the War of Independence, its Spanish population grew steadily, lured by the favorable climate and suitable agricultural lands. Later, the discovery of minerals attracted even more settlers, and with them came indigenous people to do the manual labor. In 1840, Argentine revolutionaries fleeing

the dictator Juan Manuel Rosas escaped to Tupiza and were incorporated into the community. More recently, *campesinos* have drifted in from the countryside and many unemployed miners have settled.

Information
INTERNET ACCESS

Several Internet places on the plaza are open late and have decent connections (US$0.65 an hour). Around the corner from Hotel Mitru (and possibly moving into the hotel in 2004), Rocanet is the best, quiet and nonsmoking. Also recommended is the friendly **Cyber Snack Heladería** (Cholorque 131; ⏰ 8am-10pm), which also serves up tea and sandwiches.

LAUNDRY

Hotel Mitru and Hostal Valle Hermoso both offer laundry services for their guests for around US$1 per kilogram, a bit more for nonguests.

MAPS

For maps, try the Instituto Geográfico Militar (IGM), upstairs inside the Municipalidad on the plaza.

MONEY

Shops displaying *compro dólares* signs are happy to exchange US dollars. Hotel Mitru and Hostal Valle Hermoso charge a 3 to 5% commission (depending on how much business you're doing with them) to change travelers checks. Mitru also does cash advances. The casa de cambio in the *libería* on Avaroa often appears closed but a knock on the door often elicits a response. On the plaza's north side, Banco de Crédito changes cash at close to official rates.

TOURIST INFORMATION

There's no tourist office, but the friendly folks at the Hotel Mitru and Hostal Valle Hermoso can answer most of your questions.

Sights & Activities

Tupiza's main attraction is the surrounding countryside, best seen on foot or horseback. The short hike up Cerro Corazón de Jesús, flanked by the Stations of the Cross, is a pleasant morning or evening outing when the low sun brings out the fiery reds of the surrounding countryside.

The permanent Mercado Negro, where you'll encounter a mishmash of consumer goods, occupies an entire block between Santa Cruz and Chicas. Lively street markets convene Thursday and Saturday morning near the train station. A kilometer south of town, the Mercado Campesino features more of the same on Thursday and Saturday. The central Mercado de Ferias has lots of produce stalls and *comedores* upstairs.

Tupiza's free **municipal museum** (⊙ noon-6pm Mon-Fri) houses a dusty mix of historical and cultural artifacts, including an antique cart, old photographs, archaeological relics, old weapons and historic farming implements. If it's closed, ask for a key from the office upstairs.

A favorite activity in Tupiza is horseback riding around the stunning Wild West landscapes, perhaps entertaining illusions of galloping through a shoot-'em-up Western. **Tupiza Tours** offers three-, five- and seven-hour circuits through the red-rock *quebradas* (washes and ravines) south of town for US$2.50 per hour, including lunch. For those who really want to sample the cowboy life, they also offer long-distance trips of two to four days, including tents and campfire cooking, for US$20 per day. The two-day circuit covers Salo and Palala or the *quebradas* south of town, including a lead-mining ghost town. On the three- and four-day circuits, you can visit a rural weaving community, soak in hot springs and camp at the idyllic Huaca Huañusca site where Butch and Sundance committed their last crime.

You can steam in a sauna (admission US$0.65) at Los Alamos Club or play a set of tennis (US$1.35) on Club Deportivo Ferroviaría's clay courts. Nonguests can enjoy Hotel Mitru's sparkling, solar-heated swimming pool all day for US$1. Tupiza Tours and Valle Hermoso both rent bicycles for around US$8 per day.

See Around Tupiza (p184) for hiking options.

Tours

Tupiza Tours (☎ /fax 694-3001, La Paz ☎ 02-224-1738; www.tupizatours.com; at Hotel Mitru;) offers good-value, full-day trips (around US$20 per person) exploring Tupiza's wild *quebradas*. Their innovative Triathalon tour visits Tupiza's best places in a full-day circuit on bicycles, horses and in a 4WD (US$18.50 per person for group of six; minimum two for US$40). They also run two-day tours along the Butch and Sundance trail to Huaca Huañusca and the lonely mining village of San Vicente where the outlaws' careers abruptly ended. Alternatively you can embark on a recommended four-day, three-night Southwest Circuit tours, which pass through the little-seen wild lands of Sud Lípez to connect with the main tourist route at Laguna Verde and continue to Uyuni (around US$100 per person with six people).

Explore Andina Tours (☎ /fax 694-3016; Chichas 220 at Roca Colorada Hotel) offers the standard Jeep and horse tours and rents 4WD vehicles from US$40 a day or US$250 per week with 1000 free kilometers. **Hostal Valle Hermoso** also offers similar excursions at similar prices.

Sleeping

Hotel Mitru (☎ /fax 694-3001/3003; Chichas 187; US$3, with bath US$5.50, El Cactu suite US$20-25; ▢ ▨) The mothership and the affiliated **Hotel Mitru Anexo** (☎ 694-3002; Avaroa s/n) are both bright and friendly and are the best values in town. The simpler, adjacent **El Refugio** (US$2.85) extends laundry and kitchen privileges amid a sunny garden setting. All hotels in the family enjoy use of the swimming pool, rooftop terrace and flowery garden. Bonuses include a book exchange, good breakfasts, money exchange and laundry service. A rooftop Jacuzzi with great views and new suites should be completed in 2004.

Hostal Renacer Chicheño (☎ 719-53801; renacer_ch@hotmail.com; Barrio Ferro Caja No 18; US$2) The newest kid on the block is also the closest to the bus terminal, with bright rooms with good beds, including kitchen use, laundry service and a sunny common TV room.

Hostal Valle Hermoso (☎ 694-2370; www.bolivia.freehosting.net; Arraya 478; US$2.50) The family-run Valle Hermoso is popular more for its services than its cramped rooms. They also have a book exchange, money exchange, optional breakfast and laundry service.

Roca Colorada Hotel (☎ 694-2633; d US$5.50, with bath US$7) Clean rooms with good beds, TV and telephone and some with nice private baths.

Hotel Centro (☎ 694-2705; Santa Cruz 287; US$2.35, with bath US$4) Clean, comfortable and the showers are always hot.

Residencial My Home (☎ 694-2947; Avaroa 288; US$2.50, with bath US$3.50) Another good-value option.

The cheapest options are several basic *residenciales* opposite the train station.

Eating

You can't help but notice the *pollo a la broaster* (ready-to-eat fried chicken and fries) under heat lamps in many storefronts. *Heladerías* crowd around the plaza.

RESTAURANTS

Hotel Mitru Anexo's **Confitería Los Helechos** (Avaroa s/n) is the only restaurant that reliably serves three meals a day. Breakfasts with real coffee (also served at Hotel Mitru) are especially nice. Later in the day, there's good

chicken, burgers, *licuados* and cocktails. The salad bar also wins rave reviews. Try the southern Altiplano's best *salteñas* at friendly **Il Bambino** (Florida & Santa Cruz), which also has good *almuerzos* for US$1.25.

Heartier *parrillada* dinners can be had at **Churrasquería Don Quique** (Arraya 21) or the more staid **Sede Social Ferroviaria** (Avaroa & Chichas), the railway workers' club. For pizza, you can make an attempt to eat at **Pizzería Palace** (Sucre at Florida), which opens sporadically and closes early.

QUICK EATS

The inexpensive market foods are especially good for breakfast. For a real morning treat, head for Mercado Negro after 8am, when the renowned Doña Wala starts serving up her fabulous *charque*-filled *tamales* (US$0.15) – go early because she always sells out. Her stall is outside just to the right of the entrance. A **no-name juice stop** (Av Santa Cruz near Avaroa) in a former beauty parlor blends refreshing alfalfa, papaya and carrot drinks. In the afternoon stalls outside the train station serve filling meals of rice, salad, potatoes and a main dish for under US$1.

For snacks and ice cream, visit **Cyber Snack Heladería** (Chorolque 131; ⏱ 8am-11pm) – try its specialty drink *ratapía*, which is homemade singani with white wine. Residencial My Home also serves a filling *almuerzo*.

Drinking & Entertainment

Karaoke is all the rage in Tupiza. For a novelty evening check out Marvin's or Club d&b, which both have cocktails and a slew of Spanish- and English-language pop hits. Both Hotel Mitru and Hostal Valle Hermoso screen the video *Butch Cassidy & the Sundance Kid* on request.

Getting There & Away

BUS, CAMIÓN & JEEP

Several *flotas* leave the bus terminal morning and evening for Potosí (US$3.35, at least eight hours) and Villazón (US$1.35, 2½ hours) and at night for Tarija (US$4, eight hours), with connections for Villamontes and Santa Cruz. There are daily departures to La Paz (US$12, 16 hours) via Potosí at 10am and 3:30pm. O'Globo leaves for Cochabamba at 10:30am and 8:30pm daily. Flota Boquerón leaves on Monday and Thursday for Uyuni (US$5, 10 to 12 hours) around noon, but the

THE LAST DAYS OF BUTCH CASSIDY & THE SUNDANCE KID

Butch and Sundance came to southern Bolivia in August 1908 and took up residence with the Briton AG Francis, who was transporting a gold dredge on the Río San Juan del Oro. While casing banks to finance their retirement, the outlaws learned of an even sweeter target: a poorly guarded US$480,000 mine-company payroll to be hauled by mule from Tupiza to Quechisla.

On November 3, 1908, manager Carlos Peró picked up a packet of cash from Aramayo, Francke & Compañía in Tupiza and headed north with his 10-year-old son and a servant, but they were discreetly tailed by Butch and Sundance. Peró's party overnighted in Salo, then set off again at dawn. As the trio ascended the hill called Huaca Huañusca, the bandits watched from above with binoculars. In a rugged spot on the far side of the hill, they relieved Peró of a handsome mule and the remittance, which turned out to be a mere US$90,000 – the prized payroll had been slated for shipment the following week.

Dispirited, Butch and Sundance returned to Francis' headquarters at Tomahuaico. The following day, Francis guided them to Estarca, where the three of them spent the night. On the morning of November 6, the bandits bade farewell to Francis and headed west to San Vicente.

Meanwhile, Peró had sounded the alarm, and posses were scouring southern Bolivia. A four-man contingent from Uyuni reached San Vicente that afternoon. Butch and Sundance arrived at dusk, rented a room from Bonifacio Casasola and sent him to fetch supper. The posse came to investigate and had scarcely entered the courtyard when Butch shot and killed a soldier. During the brief gunfight that ensued, Sundance was badly wounded. Realizing that escape was impossible, Butch ended Sundance's misery with a shot between the eyes, then fired a bullet into his own temple.

At the inquest, Carlos Peró identified the corpses as those of the men who had robbed him. Although buried as *desconocidos* (unknowns) in the cemetery, the outlaws fit descriptions of Butch and Sundance, and a mountain of circumstantial evidence points to their having met their doom in San Vicente. For example, Santiago Lowe, Butch's well-known alias, was recently found among the hotel guest list published in the Tupiza newspaper just a few days before the Aramayo holdup, which confirms eyewitness accounts that he was there. Nonetheless, rumors of their return to the USA have made their fate one of the great mysteries of the American West.

In 1991, a team led by forensic anthropologist Clyde Snow attempted to settle the question by excavating the bandits' grave. No one in the village had any knowledge of its location, except one elderly – and as it turned out, imaginative – gentleman, who led them to a specific tombstone. The grave's sole occupant turned out to be a German miner named Gustav Zimmer.

See http://ourworld.compuserve.com/homepages/danne for an exhaustive Butch and Sundance bibliography.

Anne Meadows & Daniel Buck
(Anne Meadows is the author of Digging Up Butch and Sundance, *University of Nebraska Press, 2003)*

SOUTHERN ALTIPLANO

train is much less nerve wracking. Faster, if less comfortable, 4WD

Jeep services to Uyuni (US$6.75, 7 to 8 hours) depart around 7:30am when there is enough demand.

Camiones to Uyuni leave after 7am from just east of Plazuela El Mundo, a traffic circle around an enormous globe. Note that fares for northbound (Oruro, etc) routes double a month before Carnaval.

TRAIN

The scenery is brilliant, so travel by day if possible. The **ticket window** (☎ 694-2529) at the

train station has no set opening hours. Ask for local advice regarding when to queue up or have an agency buy your tickets for a small surcharge.

The *Expreso del Sur* trundles north to Uyuni (US$4/9 in *salón/ejecutivo*; five hours) and Oruro (US$9.65/19.35, 11¾ hours) at 6:20pm on Tuesday and Saturday. At 3:25am on Monday and Friday the *Expreso* speeds south to Villazón (US$1.25/2.50, three hours).

The cheaper *Wara Wara del Sur*, which is always late and crowded, leaves at 7pm on Monday and Thursday for Uyuni (US$2.75/

5.75, six hours) and Oruro (US$8.25/16.75, 13¾ hours), and at 8:35am on Wednesday and Sunday for Villazón (US$1/2, three hours).

AROUND TUPIZA

Much of Tupiza's appeal lies in the surrounding landscape. Hiking opportunities abound: Within 5km of town, the mazes of ridges, *quebradas* and canyons provide a good sampling of what the country has to offer. The IGM office on the plaza sells black-and-white photocopies of topo sheets. Otherwise, you can pick them up in La Paz, but even without a map it would be difficult to get lost.

Hikers should carry at least 3L of water per day in this dry desert climate. It's wise to wear shoes that can withstand assault by prickly desert vegetation, and to carry a compass or GPS if you're venturing away from the tracks. Flash flooding is also a danger, especially in the summer months; avoid camping in the *quebradas*, especially if it looks like rain.

Quebrada de Palala

Just northwest of Tupiza, this broad wash is lined with some very impressive red formations known as fins. During the rainy season it becomes a tributary of the Río Tupiza, but in the winter months it serves as a highway into the backcountry and part of the salt route from the Salar de Uyuni to Tarija. Beyond the dramatic red rocks, the wash rises very gently into hills colored greenish blue and violet by lead and other mineral deposits.

To get a feel for the surrounding country, head north on Av La Paz from Plazuela El Mundo past the giant slide; 2km ahead, along the railroad line, you'll see the mouth of the *quebrada*. About 5km farther along, the route passes some obvious fin formations and continues up the broad *quebrada* into increasingly lonely country, past scrub brush and cacti stands.

El Cañón

A lovely walk leads west of Tupiza through a narrow twisting canyon past dramatic fin formations and makes a great half-day stroll from town. It gently ascends for 2.5km along a sandy riverbed, to end at a waterfall. There are several good campsites

along the route, but any rainfall will raise the risk of flash flooding in this constricted watercourse.

From town, the route begins along Calle Chuquisaca, heading west past the military barracks and cemetery (the route is obvious from the summit of Cerro Corazón de Jesús). The road then narrows to a sandy track running parallel to the mountains. From here you'll have good views of some spectacular fin formations and steep cactus-filled ravines, backed by red hills. Then bear left and follow the narrowing *quebrada* into the hills.

El Sillar (The Saddle)

About 2.5km past the first large fin formations in the Quebrada de Palala, the road turns sharply left and begins to climb up the steeper and narrower **Quebrada Chiriyoj Waykho**. After another 10km of winding and ascending, you'll reach El Sillar, where the road straddles a narrow ridge between two peaks and two valleys. Throughout this area, rugged amphitheaters have been gouged out of the mountainsides and eroded into spires that resemble China's Shilin Stone Forest.

El Sillar is 15km from Tupiza; if you follow this road for another 3½ hours (95km), you'll reach **San Vicente**, of Butch and Sundance fame. This entire route is part of a centuries-old trade route. From May to early July you may see a trickle of llama, alpaca and donkey trains (nowadays more likely *camiones*) humping salt blocks 300km from the Salar de Uyuni to trade in Tarija.

In Tupiza, you can arrange a taxi for up to five people to El Sillar or other sites in the area for US$4 per hour, which isn't bad, especially with a group – and because you're paying by the hour, the drivers will accommodate as many photo stops as you like. Tupiza Tours can arrange cheaper day tours in 4WD Jeeps for larger groups.

Quebrada de Palmira

Between Tupiza and Quebrada Seca lies a wonderful, normally dry wash flanked by tall and precarious fin formations. The right fork of the wash is rather comically known as Valle de los Machos (Valley of Males) or the less genteel Valle de los Penes (Valley of Penises). The names stem from the clusters of exceptionally phallic pedestal formations.

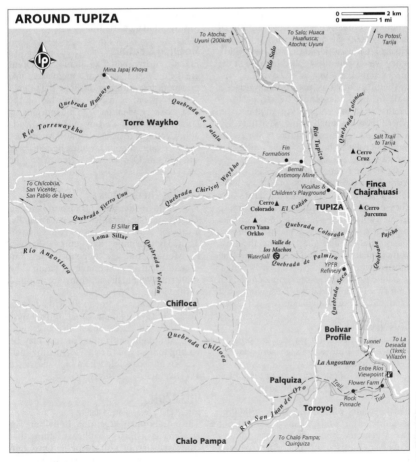

AROUND TUPIZA

To Atocha;
Uyuni (200km)

To Salo; Huaca
Huañusca;
Atocha; Uyuni

To Potosí;
Tarija

Mina Japaj Khoya

Río Salo

Quebrada Huatuyo

Quebrada de Palala

Río Torrewaykho

Torre Waykho

Quebrada Todanias

Río Tupiza

Salt Trail
to Tarija

▲ Cerro
Cruz

Fin
Formations

Bernal
Antimony Mine

To Chilcobija;
San Vicente;
San Pablo de Lípez

Quebrada Fierro Unu

Quebrada Chiriyoj Waykho

Vicuñas &
Children's Playground

**Finca
Chajrahuasi**

Cerro ▲
Colorado   *El Cañón*   **TUPIZA**

▲ Cerro
Jurcuma

El Sillar

Loma Sillar

Quebrada Volcén

Cerro Yana
Orkho

Quebrada Colorada

Pajcha

Río Angostura

Valle de
los Machos
Waterfall ◎

Quebrada de Palmira

YPFB
Refinery

Quebrada Seca

Quebrada

Chifloca

Quebrada Chifloca

**Bolívar
Profile**

Tunnel

To La
Deseada (1km);
Villazón

La Angostura

Entre Ríos
Viewpoint

Palquiza

Trail

Flower Farm

Río San Juan del Oro

Toroyoj

Rock
Pinnacle

Trail

Chalo Pampa

To Chalo Pampa;
Quirquiza

0 ▭▭ 2 km
0 ▬▬ 1 mi

At the head of the main fork of the *quebrada*, you can ascend along a trickle of calcium-rich fresh water, up over boulders and through rock grottoes, into a hidden world beneath steep canyon walls. About 300m up the canyon you'll find several excellent campsites with some water available most of the year.

Quebrada Seca (Dry Wash)

Near the YPFB refinery 9km south of town, a road turns southwest into a dry wash. Unfortunately, Quebrada Seca's lower reaches serve as a garbage dump, but if you continue up the wash, the trash thins out and the route passes into some spectacular red-rock country. At the intersection, the right fork climbs the hill toward the village of Palquiza and the left fork crosses the Río San Juan del Oro, eventually losing itself in the side canyons opening into the main channel. This particularly beautiful route is a good place to see condors.

During the dry season, hikers can turn left just before the Río San Rafael bridge (10km south of Tupiza) and follow the river's northern bank to Entre Ríos. If you wade the Río Tupiza at this point, you can return to town via the road coming from Villazón.

Huaca Huañusca

On November 4, 1908, Butch Cassidy and the Sundance Kid pulled off the last robbery of their careers when they politely and peacefully relieved Carlos Peró of the Aramayo company payroll, which amounted to US$90,000, at the foot of a hill called Huaca Huañusca (Dead Cow). The pueblo's name was apparently applied because of the hill's resemblance to a fallen bovine.

From an obvious pass on the ridge, a walking track descends the steep slopes to the west for about 2km to the river, where there's a small meadow, a tiny cave and some rugged rock outcrops where the bandits probably holed up while waiting for the payroll to pass.

Of special interest along the 25km route from Tupiza is the village of **Salo**, where a local woman produces the Altiplano's best cheese and onion empanadas – coming from Tupiza, it's the first house on the right; also delicious is the local *asado de chivo* (char-broiled goat). Along the way, you can marvel at red spires, pinnacles (the most prominent is known as La Poronga, a crude Argentine expression denoting a feature of male anatomy), canyons, tall cacti and tiny adobe villages.

SAN VICENTE

Kid, the next time I say let's go someplace like Bolivia, let's go someplace like Bolivia.
Paul Newman, in the film
Butch Cassidy & the Sundance Kid

This remote one-mule village (4800m) wouldn't even rate a mention were it not the legendary spot where the outlaws Robert LeRoy Parker and Harry Alonzo Longabaugh – better known as Butch Cassidy and the Sundance Kid – met their untimely demise. The mine in San Vicente is now closed and the place has declined to little more than a ghost town. Most of those remaining are military people, mine security guards and their families.

San Vicente has become a bit of a pilgrimage site for Butch and Sundance fans, as well as for travelers taken with the lure of the Old West. That still amounts to only a trickle of visitors, however, and San Vicente continues to lack any semblance of tourist infrastructure. Bring your imagination: You can still see the adobe house where the bandits holed up and eventually died, the cemetery where they were buried and the sign welcoming visitors to the town: 'Here death's Butch Kasidy Sundance the Kid'.

Sleeping & Eating
El Rancho Hotel and the adjoining restaurant are the only game in town. Otherwise, come prepared for camping at this high, cold altitude. Bread is usually available at the village bakery, identifiable in the morning by lines of people, and a tiny unmarked tienda uphill from the main street may have grocery staples – canned milk, sardines, biscuits, beer and *refrescos*. Occasionally, a comedor on the plaza offers plates of llama *fricassee*.

Getting There & Away
There's no regular public transport between Tupiza and San Vicente. Very occasionally, a *camión* departs for San Vicente early on Thursday morning from Tupiza's Plazuela El Mundo, but it's dependent on San Vicente's current economic situation. The route runs via El Sillar, turning northbound at the village of Nazarenito.

The easiest way to go is with Tupiza Tours (p181), which takes four hours each way but makes for a nice overnight trip. Although Tupiza taxi drivers may be willing to take you to San Vicente, the road is often only passable with a high-clearance 4WD vehicle.

VILLAZÓN
pop 28,000 / elevation 3440m
The most popular Argentina–Bolivia border crossing is a dusty, haphazard burg that contrasts sharply with sleepy La Quiaca in Argentina, just across the river. In addition to being a point of entry, Villazón is a contraband warehousing center for goods being smuggled into Bolivia on the backs of peasants, who form a human cargo train across the frontier. Much of Argentina's Jujuy province is populated by Bolivian expats, lending Villazón the nickname 'Tijuana of Bolivia'.

Despite rampant smuggling the frontier manages to avoid having a sinister feel. That said, you should still be on your guard: petty theft, scams and counterfeit US banknotes are not unheard of. From October to April Bolivian time lags one hour behind Argentine time. The rest of the year, Argentina operates on Bolivian time (only a bit more efficiently).

Information

The **Argentine consulate** (Saavedra 311; ☽ 9am-1pm Mon-Fri) is one block west of the main drag on the street facing the railway line. Numerous *casas de cambio* along Av República Argentina offer reasonable rates for dollars and Argentine pesos, less for Bolivianos. Casa de Cambio Beto changes travelers checks at similar rates, minus 5% commission. **Banco de Crédito** (Oruro 111) changes cash but lacks an ATM. There's a decent Internet node (US$1 per hour) opposite the bus station and several others north of the plaza along Av Independencia.

Sleeping

Accommodations on the Argentine side (p189) are better value, if a tad more expensive. Several passable *residenciales* cater to locals along Villazón's main drag between the bus and train stations – if you must, choose carefully.

Hostal Plaza (☎ 596-3535; Plaza 6 de Agosto 138; s/d US$4.65/6.65, with bath US$6.65/10.50) Villazón's nicest and most modern option, with clean rooms and cable TV.

Residencial Martínez (☎ 596-3562/3353; 25 de Mayo 13; US$2.75) The gas-fired showers make this friendly place opposite the bus terminal the best deal this side of the Río Villazón, especially if you can score one of the rooms with private bath.

Residencial El Cortijo (☎ 596-2093; 20 de Mayo 338; d US$6.65, US$10.50 with bath & cable TV) A clean and cozy travelers' favorite two blocks north of the bus terminal. Hot showers cost an extra US$0.65 for rooms without bath.

Grand Palace Hotel (☎ 596-5333; 25 de Mayo 52; US$2.65, with bath US$4.50-5) Really the bland palace, but the rooms (some windowless) are clean and the café does good breakfast. It's not bad but service is indifferent and the atmosphere less than friendly.

Residencial Bolivia (Belgrano 51-63; US$2, with bath US$3.35) Funky beds occupy most of the room and padlocks barely secure doors, but it's a clean, cheap sleep.

Eating

Villazón's culinary choices are limited; hop over to La Quiaca (p189) for a better selection of cheap 'meateries'. If you're determined to stay in Bolivia, try Charke Kan Restaurant, opposite the bus terminal, which is grimy but good. Next door Snack Pizzeria Don Vicco is a decent choice for burgers, beer and pizza. The stalls upstairs in the main market near the plaza make up in price what they lack in variety. Don't miss the delicious *licuados* and fruit juices – incongruous treats in this climate. Snack stands and ambulatory street food peddlers are plentiful.

Getting There & Away

BUS

All northbound buses depart from the Villazón bus terminal (US$0.25 fee). Daily buses head for Tupiza (US$1.35, two to three hours) at 7am, 3pm and 5pm; it's a beautiful trip, so try to go in the daylight and grab a window seat. Some continue or make connections to Potosí (US$4.75, 10 to 12 hours) with onward connections to Sucre, Oruro, Cochabamba and La Paz. Daily services along the rough but amazing route to Tarija (US$4.75, 8 to 10 hours) continue to Bermejo and Yacuiba at 11am and 8pm. Argentine bus companies have ticket offices opposite Villazón's terminal, but all Argentine buses leave from the La Quiaca bus terminal.

TRAIN

The Villazón train station is 750m north of the border crossing – a taxi costs US$2. The *Expreso del Sur* departs Tuesday and Saturday at 3:30pm for Tupiza (*salón/ejecutivo* US$2.15/4.50, 2¾ hours), Uyuni (US$7/13.60, eight hours) and Oruro (US$11.25/22.50, 15 hours). This is an enjoyable trip with superb scenery for the first few hours. The more crowded and basic *Wara Wara del Sur* departs Monday and Thursday at 3:30pm for Tupiza (US$1.25/2.50, three hours), Uyuni (US$4.25/8.75, 9½ hours) and Oruro (US$7/17, 17 hours). It's a good option as far as Tupiza, but after dark it turns tedious.

TO/FROM ARGENTINA

For quick trips over the border just walk straight across the bridge; there's no need to visit immigration unless you're staying more than a couple of hours. Crossing the border is usually no problem, but avoid the *contrabandistas*' procession; otherwise it may take you hours to clear customs.

On the north side of the international bridge **Bolivian customs and immigration** (☽ 5am-8pm) issues exit stamps and tourist cards

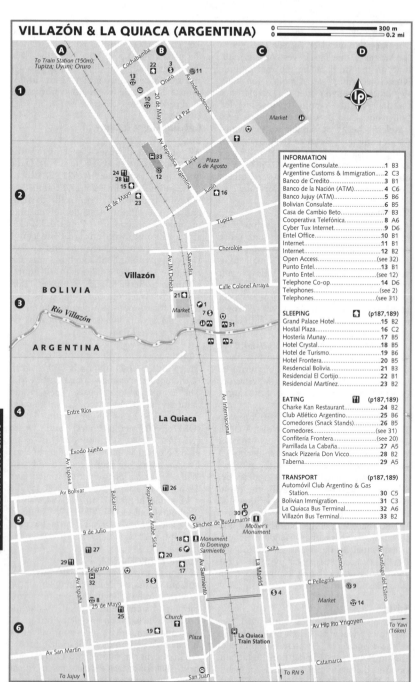

VILLAZÓN & LA QUIACA (ARGENTINA)

0 — 300 m
0 — 0.2 mi

INFORMATION
Argentine Consulate..........................**1** B3
Argentine Customs & Immigration....**2** C3
Banco de Credito.............................**3** B1
Banco de la Nación (ATM)...............**4** C6
Banco Jujuy (ATM)...........................**5** B6
Bolivian Consulate............................**6** B5
Casa de Cambio Beto.......................**7** B3
Cooperativa Telefónica.....................**8** A6
Cyber Tux Internet...........................**9** D6
Entel Office....................................**10** B1
Internet...**11** B1
Internet...**12** B2
Open Access...........................(see 32)
Punto Entel...................................**13** B1
Punto Entel.............................(see 12)
Telephone Co-op............................**14** D6
Telephones.............................(see 2)
Telephones...........................(see 31)

SLEEPING 🏠 (p187,189)
Grand Palace Hotel........................**15** B2
Hostal Plaza.................................**16** C2
Hostería Munay..............................**17** B5
Hotel Crystal.................................**18** B5
Hotel de Turismo............................**19** B6
Hotel Frontera...............................**20** B5
Resdencial Bolivia..........................**21** B3
Residencial El Cortijo......................**22** B1
Residencial Martínez.......................**23** B2

EATING 🍴 (p187,189)
Charke Kan Restaurant....................**24** B2
Club Atlético Argentino...................**25** B6
Comedores (Snack Stands)...............**26** B5
Comedores.............................(see 31)
Confitería Frontera...................(see 20)
Parrillada La Cabaña.......................**27** A5
Snack Pizzeria Don Vicco.................**28** B2
Taberna..**29** A5

TRANSPORT (p187,189)
Automóvil Club Argentino & Gas
    Station.....................................**30** C5
Bolivian Immigration.......................**31** C3
La Quiaca Bus Terminal....................**32** A6
Villazón Bus Terminal......................**33** B2

SOUTHERN ALTIPLANO

(normally only for 30 days) – there is no official charge for these services. Argentine immigration is open 24/7, but Argentine customs is only open 7am to midnight. Formalities are minimal, but those entering Argentina may be held up at several control points further south of the border by exhaustive custom searches.

LA QUIACA (ARGENTINA)

☎ (54) 03885

Villazón's twin town of La Quiaca (3442m) is just across the Río Villazón and *only* 5121km north of Usuhaia, Tierra del Fuego. Since the Argentine economic crisis, the contrast between the two sides has become less striking, but La Quiaca remains a neatly groomed place with tree-lined avenues, surfaced streets, pleasant restaurants and well-stocked shops.

Information

There's no tourist office, but you can sometimes find Argentine maps at the Automóvil Club Argentino (ACA), at Av Internacional (RN9) and Sánchez de Bustamante. The **Bolivian consulate** (Sarmiento 527, 2nd fl; ☺ 8:30-11am Mon-Fri) also opens irregularly on weekday afternoons and Saturday morning and issues visas for US$15. There is also Lonely Planet's *Argentina* guide for information.

Banco Jujuy has a 24/7 ATM. Banco de la Nación exchanges dollars for decent rates and also has an all-hours ATM. It's easy to buy pesos with dollars at good rates. Please note that the province of Jujuy issues its own peso banknotes, which are worthless outside the province.

Services at **Correo Argentino** (San Juan at Sarmiento; ☺ 8am-1pm & 5-8pm Mon-Fri, 9am-1pm Sat) and the **Cooperativa Telefónica** (España at 25 de Mayo) are generally more reliable (and currently cheaper) in Argentina than in Bolivia. At the bus terminal, **Open Access** (US$0.35 per hr) provides Internet connections and is open late. **Cyber Tux Internet** (near the market) offers similar service.

Sleeping

La Quiaca's best bet is the new **Hosteria Munay** (☎ 42-3924; www.munayhotel.jujuy.com; Belgrano 51-61; US$3pp, with bath US$6.50), where spacious modern rooms include breakfast. The slightly run-down **Hotel Crystal** (☎ 45-2255; Sarmiento 543;

s/d/t with bath US$6/10/13) has a loungy feel with decorative mirrors and a wrap-around bar in the lobby. More spartan rooms out back without bath fetch US$2.75 per person. The comfortable **Hotel de Turismo** (☎ /fax 42-2243/ 3390; Árabe Siria at San Martín; s/d with bath, breakfast & TV US$10/17; 🛋) is the fanciest place in town. The basic **Hotel Frontera** (Belgrano at Árabe Siria; US$3) has shared bathrooms with electric showers and a notable lack of heating.

Eating

The food is generally better here than in Villazón, so it's worth tripping across the border for a meal. As you'd expect in Argentina, menus are heavily weighted in favor of carnivores.

The Hotel de Turismo (Árabe Siria at San Martin) has a warm dining room with a stone fireplace; an immense steak with fries goes for US$2. Hotel Frontera's diner-style **Confitería La Frontera** (Belgrano & Árabe Siria; everything under US$2) has savory *tortillas españolas* and decent *tallarines al pesto* (is that really basil?), plus a four-course set *menu economico* for US$1.25. Service is a bit surly at times, but the food compensates. **Parrillada La Cabaña** (España & Belgrano) does decent *parrillada* but the kitchen can be painfully slow. The nicer **Taberna** (España at Belgrano) is also a *parrillada*. The **Club Atlético Argentino** (Balcarce & 25 de Mayo) is worth a try for pizza, *parrillada*, *panchos* (hot dogs) and ice cream. The bus terminal's fast-food counter is the best bet if you have a tight connection. Marginal *comedores* along the route to the *frontera* keep the human cargo train well fed.

Getting There & Away

Buses depart from **La Quiaca bus terminal** (Terminal de Omnibuses, left luggage US$0.35) at the corner of España and Bel-grano. Most long-distance services offer heat, air-conditioning, video *and* bladder-friendly facilities. Several south-bound services depart almost hourly for Huma-huaca and San Salvador de Jujuy (US$5, 5 to 6 hours). The route passes through some stunningly colorful, cactus-studded landscapes. From Jujuy, there are frequent connections to Salta, Cafayate, Rosario and Córdoba and Buenos Aires. Andesmar goes daily to Santiago de Chile and destinations all over Argentina. The short taxi ride to the *frontera* should cost no more than US$0.50.

Central Highlands

Dominating the Bolivian interior, the Central Highlands remain home to an array of wonders and terrors sure to amaze, startle or shock travelers. Visitors to the region have the opportunity to reach back through the eons and touch traces of long-disappeared beasts, to marvel at the faded splendor of unimaginable riches, to recoil from still-horrifying labor conditions, and to experience local traditions that remain steadfastly free from commercialization and its accompanying dilution. These features, in addition to a proud colonial heritage and some of Bolivia's most beautiful and starkly surreal landscapes, render the region ideal for independent exploration.

Perhaps nowhere is the versatile character of the Central Highlands as evident as in the attitude of its people. Aware of their cities' history and stories, and secure in their belief that theirs is one of the most beautiful and enchanting places on earth, the inhabitants of the region live with a quiet dignity that reflects both their pride in a glorious past and their anticipation of a bright future.

TOP FIVE

- Tour historical treasures in Potosí's **Casa Real de la Moneda** (p235) and explore the fascinating **mines** (p240)
- Soak up the charms of **Sucre** (p213) with its culture, cafés and colonial churches
- Browse and carouse at Cochabamba's nerve-shattering **La Cancha market** (p197)
- Discover waterfalls, idyllic swimming holes and fossilized dinosaur footprints in **Parque Nacional Torotoro** (p210)
- Shop for colorful Jalq'a and Candelaria textiles in **Tarabuco** (p227)

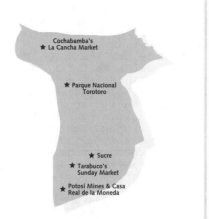

★ Cochabamba's La Cancha Market

★ Parque Nacional Torotoro

★ Sucre
★ Tarabuco's Sunday Market
★ Potosí Mines & Casa Real de la Moneda

| ▦ TELEPHONE CODE: 04 | ▦ POPULATION: 4.7 MILLION | ▦ AREA: 227,420 SQ KM |

CENTRAL HIGHLANDS

HISTORY

Throughout its history Sucre served as the administrative, legal, religious, cultural and educational center of the easternmost Spanish territories. In the 17th century it was known as the Athens of America and today it's the political center of the Central Highlands.

Prior to Spanish domination, the town of Charcas, where Sucre now stands, was the indigenous capital of the valley of Choque-Chaca. It served as the residence of local religious, military and political leaders, and its jurisdiction extended to several thousand inhabitants. When the Spanish arrived, the entire area from Southern Peru to the Río de la Plata in present-day Argentina came to be known as Charcas.

In the early 1530s Francisco Pizarro, the *conquistador* who felled the Inca empire, sent his brother Gonzalo to the Charcas region to oversee Indian mining activities and interests that might prove to be valuable to the Spanish realm. He was not interested in the Altiplano, and concentrated on the highlands east of the main Andean Cordilleras. As a direct result, in 1538 the city of La Plata was founded by Pedro de Anzures, Marques de Campo Redondo, as the Spanish capital of the Charcas. As his Indian predecessors had done, he chose the warm, fertile valley of Choque-Chaca for its site.

During the early 16th century the Viceroyalty of Lima governed all Spanish territories in central and eastern South America. In 1559 King Phillip II created the Audiencia (Royal Court) of Charcas, with its headquarters in the city of La Plata, to administer the eastern territories. The Audiencia was unique in the New World in that it held both judicial authority and executive powers. The judge of the Audiencia also served as the chief executive officer. Governmental subdivisions within the district came under the jurisdiction of royal officers known as *corregidores*.

Until 1776 the Audiencia presided over Paraguay, southeastern Peru, northern Chile and Argentina, and most of Bolivia. When Portuguese interests in Brazil threatened the easternmost Spanish-dominated regions, a new Viceroyalty, also named La Plata, was established in order to govern and ensure tight control. The city of La Plata thereby lost jurisdiction

over all but the former Choque-Chaca, one of the four provinces of Alto Peru, which comprised leftover territories between the Viceroyalties of Lima and La Plata. The city's name was changed to Chuquisaca (the Spanish corruption of Choque-Chaca), presumably to avoid confusion between the city and the new Viceroyalty.

The city had received an archbishopric in 1609, according it theological autonomy. That, along with the establishment of the University of San Xavier in 1622 and the 1681 opening of the Academía Carolina law school, fostered continued development of liberal and revolutionary ideas and set the stage for 'the first cry of Independence in the Americas' on May 25, 1809. The mini-revolution set off the alarm throughout Spanish America and, like ninepins, the north-western South American republics were liberated by the armies of the military genius Simón Bolívar (see the boxed text, p214).

After the definitive liberation of Peru at the battles of Junín and Ayacucho on August 6 and December 9, 1824, Alto Peru, historically tied to the Lima government, was technically free of Spanish rule. In practice, however, it had carried on close relations with the La Plata government in Buenos Aires and disputes arose about what to do with the territory.

On February 9, 1825 Bolívar's second-in-command, General Antonio José de Sucre, drafted and delivered a declaration that stated in part:

The…Viceroyalty of Buenos Aires to which these provinces pertained at the time of the revolution of America lacks a general government which represents completely, legally, and legitimately the authority of all the provinces… Their political future must therefore result from the deliberation of the provinces themselves and from an agreement between the congress of Perú and that… in the Río de la Plata.

Bolívar, unhappy with this unauthorized act of sovereignty, rejected the idea, but de Sucre stood his ground, convinced that there was sufficient separatist sentiment in Alto Peru to back him up. As he expected, the people of the region refused to wait for a decision from the new congress to be installed in Lima the following year and

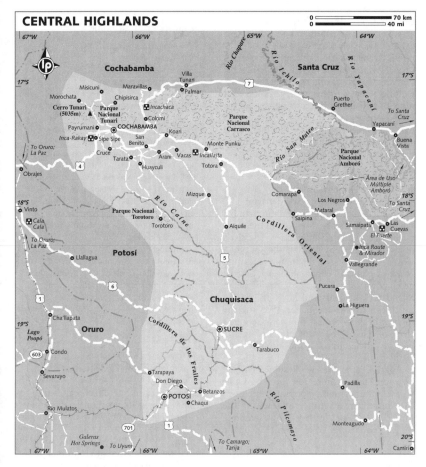

CENTRAL HIGHLANDS

rejected subsequent invitations to join the Buenos Aires government.

On August 6, the first anniversary of the Battle of Junín, independence was declared in the Casa de la Libertad at Chuquisaca and the new republic was christened Bolivia after its liberator. On August 11 the city's name was changed for the final time to Sucre, in honor of the general who promoted the independence movement.

Difficult years followed in the Republic of Bolivia, and at one stage the 'Great Liberator' became disenchanted with his namesake republic. After a particularly tumultuous period of political shuffling, he made this observation: 'Hapless Bolivia has had four different leaders in less than two weeks!

Only the kingdom of Hell could offer so appalling a picture discrediting humanity!'

For more on the region's fascinating past, see the History sections under Cochabamba (p194) and Potosí (p232).

CLIMATE

The saying *Las golondrinas nunca migran de Cochabamba* (The swallows never migrate from Cochabamba) aptly describes what *cochabambinos* believe is the world's most comfortable climate, with warm, dry, sunny days and cool nights. Sucre residents rightfully maintain that their climate is just as salubrious. Winter is a time of clear skies and optimum temperatures, while Potosí is one of Bolivia's few big cities to see snow.

GETTING THERE & AWAY

The Central Highlands' major population centers are well served by all modes of public transportation, except for a train service, which may resume to Cochabamba, Potosí and Sucre at some point in the future. Getting between towns in the region is a bit more of a challenge if venturing beyond the Potosí–Sucre paved highway. Cochabamba has the busiest airport, while for Potosí you must fly into Sucre, where the airport is plagued by weather-related delays.

COCHABAMBA

pop 600,000 / elevation 2558m

This progressive and active departmental capital has a growing population and a vitality that is visibly absent from the more traditional higher-altitude cities. The city's name is derived by joining the Quechua words *khocha* and *pampa*, meaning 'swampy plain.' Cochabamba lies in a fertile green bowl, 25km long by 10km wide, set in a landscape of fields and low hills. To the northwest rises Cerro Tunari (5035m), the highest peak in central Bolivia. The area's rich soil yields abundant crops of maize, barley, wheat, alfalfa, and orchard and citrus fruits.

Apart from the wholesome climate however, there's little for tourists. Once you've done some shopping and seen the museums, it's time to head for the hinterlands. Don't leave without sampling *chicha cochabambina*, a regional alcoholic maize brew.

History

Cochabamba was founded in January 1574 by Sebastián Barba de Padilla. It was originally named Villa de Oropeza in honor of the Count and Countess of Oropeza, parents of Viceroy Francisco de Toledo, who chartered and promoted its settlement.

During the height of Potosí's silver boom, the Cochabamba Valley developed into the primary source of food for the miners in agriculturally unproductive Potosí. Thanks to its maize and wheat production, Cochabamba came to be the 'breadbasket of Bolivia.' As Potosí's importance declined during the early 18th century, so did Cochabamba's, and grain production in the Chuquisaca (Sucre) area,

---

CHICHA COCHABAMBINA

Chicha quiero, chicha busco,
Por chicha mis paseos.
Señora, deme un vasito
Para cumplir mis deseos.

This old Bolivian verse cries, 'I want *chicha*, I search for *chicha*, for *chicha* are my wanderings. Lady, give me a glass to satisfy my longing.'

To most Bolivians, Cochabamba is known for one of two things: Romantics will dreamily remark on its luscious climate, whereas hardcore imbibers, such as the author of the above poem, will identify the city with its luscious, highly intoxicating local beverage *chicha cochabambina*. Both images are well founded.

Throughout the valley and around much of southern Cochabamba department, you'll see white cloth or plastic flags flying on long poles, indicating that *chicha* is available. Traveling outside the town, you'll realize just how popular it is – and, at 2560m elevation, it packs a good punch!

---

much closer to Potosí, was sufficient to supply the decreasing demand.

By the mid-19th century, however, the economic crisis stabilized, and the city again assumed its position as the nation's granary. Elite landowners in the valley grew wealthy and began investing in highland mining ventures. Before long, the Altiplano mines were attracting international capital, and the focus of Bolivian mining shifted from Potosí to southwestern Bolivia. As a result, Cochabamba thrived and its European-*mestizo* population gained a reputation for affluence and prosperity.

Orientation

Cochabamba's central business district lies roughly between the Río Rocha in the north and Colina San Sebastián and Laguna Alalay in the southwest and southeast, respectively.

The largest market areas are on or south of Avenida Aroma, sandwiched between Colina San Sebastián and Laguna Alalay. The long-distance bus terminal and most of the intravalley bus terminals are also in this vicinity.

Cochabamba addresses are measured from Plaza 14 de Septiembre and are preceded by 'N' (*norte*/north), 'S' (*sud*/ south), 'E' (*este*/east) or 'O'(*oeste*/west – although to avoid alphanumeric confusion, a 'W' is sometimes used instead). Addresses north of Av de las Heroínas take an N, those below take an S. Addresses east of Av Ayacucho take an E and those west an O. The number immediately following the letter tells you how many blocks away from these division streets the address falls.

MAPS
The tourist office and news kiosks on the west side of the plaza sell good city maps (US$1.35). See the **Instituto Geográfico Militar** (IGM; ☎ 425-5563; 16 de Julio S-237) for topo sheets from around the Cochabamba department.

Information
BOOKSHOPS
Vendors among the *artesanía* stalls behind the post office sell Spanish-language literature and other books for reasonable and negotiable prices.
Los Amigos del Libro (☎ 425-4114; Ayacucho at Bolívar; Galería Torres Sofer, ☎ 425-6471; Oquendo E-654; also at airport) Stock the best range of English-, French- and German-language paperbacks, plus reference books and Lonely Planet guides.

CULTURAL CENTERS
The following centers sponsor cultural activities and language classes, and have foreign-language reading rooms with current periodicals:
Alliance Française (☎ 425-2997; Santivañez 0-187).
Centro Boliviano-Americano (CBA; ☎ 422-1288/2518; www.cbacoch.org; 25 de Mayo N-365) Can recommend private language teachers.
Instituto Cultural Boliviano-Alemán (ICBA; ☎ 422-8431; icbacbba@supernet.com.bo; Sucre E-693) Offers group Spanish lessons.
Volunteer Bolivia (☎ 452-6028 ; www.volunteerbolivia .org; Ecuador 342) Runs the Café La Republika cultural center and arranges short- and long-term volunteer work, study and homestay programs throughout Bolivia. Also offers language courses.

EMERGENCY
Public ambulance (☎ 165)
Private ambulance (Medicar; ☎ 181 or 453-3222)
Tourist police (☎ 120 or 222-1793; Achá 0-142)

IMMIGRATION
Migración (☎ 422-5553; Arce at Jordán; ☺ 8:30am-4pm Mon-Fri) The place to visit for visa and length-of-stay extensions.

INTERNET ACCESS
Internet places charging US$0.25 to US$0.50 an hour are popping up so fast that nobody has time to come up with unique names:
Black Cat (Bolívar near Aguirre)
CyberNet Café (Colombia & Baptista)
Internet Bolivia (España at Ecuador)

LAUNDRY
Most hotels offer laundry services.
Lavaya (Salamanca & Antezana)
Lavandería Tu-Tu (Ecuador at Oquendo) One-hour service – 5kg for US$2.

MEDICAL SERVICES
Hospital Viedma (☎ 422-0223) Full-service public hospital.
Centro Medico Boliviano Belga (☎ 422-9407; Antezana N-455) Private clinic.

MONEY
Moneychangers powwow around the Entel office and along Av de las Heroínas. Their rates are competitive but they only accept US cash. Cash advances are available at major banks and at widespread Enlace ATMs. The best places to change cash or travelers checks (2% to 3% commission) are:
American (☎ 422-2307; Baptista S-159)
Exprint-Bol (☎ 425-4413; Plaza 14 de Septiembre 0-252)

POST & TELEPHONE
The main **post** and **Entel** (☺ 6:30am-10pm) offices are together in a large complex (Ayacucho btwn Bolívar & Av de las Heroínas). The postal service from Cochabamba is reliable and the facilities are among the country's finest. Downstairs from the main lobby is an express post office. For cheap Internet phone calls try the unnamed place at the corner of Calama and Hamiraya.

TOURIST INFORMATION
Main tourist office (☎ 422-3364; Bolívar near Aguirre; ☺ 8:30am-6:30pm Mon-Fri, 8:30am-noon Sat) In a glass kiosk in front of Entel.
Sernap office (☎ 448-6452/53; Luján N-2882) Has information about Parques Nacionales Torotoro, Carrasco and Isiboro Sécure.

COCHABAMBA

0 |▬▬▬▬▬▬▬▬| 500 m
0 |▬▬▬▬▬▬▬▬| 0.3 mi

A   **B**   **C**   **D**

1

Av America

🏨 82

Av Buenos Aires

🏨🏨 67 71

Av Portales

32 47🛏 🏨 86
🏛 Garden 🍴 95

Av Santa Cruz

Villarroel

P Blanco

Postdam

🏨 87

Beni

68

25 🍴
🏨

Sejas

94

Av Aniceto Padilla

70 🏨

2

57

🏛 Libertador Bolívar

Villazón

100

Av Oblitas

Park

Park

Stadium

Park

Av del Ejército

Park

Av Ramón Rivero

🏨 88

Plaza Quintanilla

Río Rocha

Av Humboldt

Av Villazón

Oruro

Antezana

La Paz

Av Oquendo

Vásquez

79 🏨

93

Av Ballivián

80

🏨🏨 63

Chuquisaca

Salamanca

15

3

La Paz

José de la Reza

México

Major Rocha

Tarapacá

Tumusla

43

23

Junín
Hamayra

106

40🛏

See Enlargement

Paccieri

Plaza
Colón

Venezuela

España

Av San Martín

Ecuador

Colombia

Lanza

16 de Julio

Antezana

🕂
10

To Apart Hotel
Concordia

To Apart Hotel
Concordia

14

Av Aniceto Arce

Av Rubén Darío

4

Achá

39🛏

Santiváñez

Av de las Heroínas

Plaza 14 de
Septiembre

Av Ayacucho

Market

Bolívar

11 🏨 12

Sucre

Jordán

Calama

Ladislao Cabrera

Uruguay

Pasteur

A Melean

Universidad Mayor de San Símon

Julián M López

Mariano R Terrazas

Av Guillermo Urquidi

J A Mendez

Méndez Arcos

6

To Quillacollo (15km);
Sipe Sipe (27km)

Plaza San
Sebastián

Waynakapak

99

33 78
🏨

62

49 18

58 34
102 🏨

44 41 35
45 74

🏨

104

López

Calle Arce

Aguirre

25 de Mayo

Av Ayacucho

42

Montes

Honduras

Punata

Tarata

30

Av Aroma

Brasil

Av República

28

Av 9 de Abril

103

5

Tahuantinsuyo

Av Aroma

cliff

*Heroínes de
la Coronilla
Monument*

Colina San
Sebastián

cliff

cliff

Av de la Independencia

Totora

Former
Train
Station

29

Pulacayo

Barzola

Av Barrientos

Quillacollo

Tapacarí

Lliza

Argostura

Chipirí

Riberalta

República

Moxos

Guayaramerín

Manupiri

107

*Laguna
Alalay*

6

To Airport
(3km)

Arani

Enlargement

C   **D**

José de la Reza

Chuquisaca

84 90

73

Sulamarca

Antezana

Paccieri

🕂 5

96

Plaza
Colón

Venezuela

Av San Martín

Lanza

Baptista

69 89 75

97

38 72

22

4 65

25 de Mayo

España

27

Ecuador

20

🏨 50

@ 13

66

Colombia

7 @

46

55 92

85

81

Av de las Heroínas

105

76 101 59

8 19

16

@ 2

3 @ 9

83

1 26

31

52 21

60 61

56

24 Bolívar

36 53
91

Sucre

51

77

Plaza 14 de
Septiembre

Market

37

17

54 0 |▬▬▬| 500 m
48 0 |▬▬▬| 0.3 mi

Av Ayacucho

Jordán

Bolívar

Dangers & Annoyances

In Cochabamba's rural hinterlands, be especially wary of *vinchuca* beetles, which live in thatched roofing and carry Chagas'-disease (see the Health chapter, p373). The Universidad San Simón's Chagas Institute does testing and distributes pamphlets about the disease.

Readers have reported rip-offs, impromptu passport checks and hassles from bogus police at the main bus terminal; if you're stopped, ask to see some ID. If they continue to hassle you, insist that the matter be settled at the police station. Violent robberies of tourists walking around Colina San Sebastián continue to be reported and it is unfortunately now inadvisable to walk around there at any hour.

Sights

MARKETS

Cochabamba is Bolivia's biggest market town. South of the center, several formerly separate markets around San Antonio have combined into one enormous market, known simply as **La Cancha**, which is one of the most crowded and nerve-shattering places in the country – don't miss the potato section. Around the markets you'll find just about everything imaginable. To experience the chaos is both worthwhile and totally exhausting.

The largest and most accessible area is **Mercado Cancha Calatayud**, which sprawls across a wide area along Av Aroma and south toward the former railway station. Here is your best opportunity to see local dress, which differs strikingly from that of the Altiplano. The **Mercado Incallacta** and **Mercado de Ferias** spill out around the old railway station. *Artesanías* are concentrated near the junction of Tarata and Calle Arce, near the southern end of the market area, where alleys are stuffed with friendly, reasonably priced stalls.

MUSEUMS

The **Museo Arqueológico** (Jordán & Aguirre; admission US$1.35; ☑ 8am-6pm Mon-Fri, 9am-noon Sat) is one of

CENTRAL HIGHLANDS

Bolivia's finest museums. Exhibits include thousands of artifacts, dating from as early as 12,000 BC and as late as the colonial period. The excellent 1½-hour guided tour is in English, French or Spanish.

The **Simón Patiño Cultural Center** (Palacio de Portales; ☎ 424-3137; Potosí 1450; admission US$1.35 with guide; gardens ⏰ 2:30-6:30pm Mon-Fri, 10:30am-12:30pm Sat & Sun; tours in Spanish & English ⏰ 5/5:30pm Mon-Fri, 11/11:30am Sat) in the barrio of Queru Queru, provides evidence of the extravagance of tin baron Simón Patiño. Construction of this opulent French-style mansion began in 1915 and was finalized in 1927. Except perhaps for the brick, everything was imported from Europe. The fireplaces were constructed of flawless Carrara marble, the furniture and woodwork were carved in French wood and the walls were covered with silk brocade – one intricate 'painting' is actually a woven silk tapestry. The gardens and exterior, which were inspired by the palace at Versailles, also reflect inconceivable affluence. In spite of all this extravagance, the house was never occupied, and today it is used as an arts and cultural complex and as a teaching center.

Don't miss the new **Natural History Museum** next door. Take *micro* E north from east of Av San Martín.

CHURCHES
Cochabamba's churches are rarely open during the hours posted at the tourist office; you'll have the most luck in the early morning or late afternoon, particularly Saturday afternoon and on Sunday.

On the arcaded Plaza 14 de Septiembre, the neoclassical 1571 **cathedral** is the valley's oldest religious structure. Because of a myriad of architecturally diverse additions, the composition doesn't hang together well at all, but the frescoes and paintings inside are worth a look.

Constructed in 1581, the **Iglesia & Convento de San Francisco** (25 de Mayo & Bolívar; ⏰ guided tour 9am) is Cochabamba's second-oldest church. Major revisions and renovation occurred in 1782 and 1925, however, and little of the original structure remains. The attached convent and cloister were added in the 1600s. In appreciation of the pleasant Cochabamba climate, the cloister was constructed of wood rather than the stone

that was customary at the time. The pulpit displays fine examples of *mestizo* design.

If you can look past the kitsch halo of lights over the altar, the interior of the **Convento de Santa Teresa** (Baptista & Ecuador; ⏰ 7:30-8am, mass 7:30pm Mon, Wed & Thu, 7pm Sun) is quite impressive. It's actually a combination of two churches, one built on top of the other. Work on the first church was begun by Jesuits in 1753.

The 1875 **Iglesia del Hospicio** (south side of Plaza Colón) is the valley's most recent major church and combines Baroque, Byzantine and neoclassical architectural styles.

The Rococo **Iglesia de Santo Domingo** (Santivañez & Ayacucho) was founded in 1612 but construction didn't begin until 1778. The intriguing main doorway is flanked by two anthropomorphic columns.

North of the river, the Baroque **Iglesia de la Recoleta** was started in 1654. The attraction is a wooden carving entitled Cristo de la Recoleta that was hewn from a single piece of wood.

CHRISTO DE LA CONCORDIA
This immense statue stands atop Cerro de San Pedro behind Cochabamba. It's a few centimeters higher than the famous Cristo Redentor on Rio de Janeiro's Corcovado, which stands 33m high, or one meter for each year of Christ's life. *Cochabambinos* justify the one-upmanship by claiming that Christ actually lived *33 años y un poquito* (33 years and a bit...).

The return walk takes about two hours from the center plus half an hour (and 1250 uphill steps) on the new footpath from the base of the mountain, but beware of vicious dogs. Most people, however, opt for the *teleférico* (cable car), which costs US$0.80 for the round-trip. On Sunday, for another US$0.20, you can climb right to the top of the statue and get an even better overview of the city.

The closest public transport access is on *micro* LL, which leaves from the corner of Heroínas and 25 de Mayo. Taxis charge US$4.50 for the round-trip, including a half-hour wait while you look around.

Courses
Cochabamba is a popular place to hole up for a few weeks of Spanish or Quechua lessons. Several cultural centers offer

courses for around US$5 per hour. One option is the **Instituto Cultural Boliviano Alemán** (p195).

The **Escuela Runawasi** (☎ /fax 424-8923; www .runawasi.org; Blanco s/n, Barrio Juan XXIII) offers a recommended program that involves linguistic and cultural immersion. It also includes a trip to directors Joaquin and Janine Hinojosa's Chapare rainforest hideout when everything is *tranquilo*.

There are plenty of private teachers who offer instruction (most around US$5 per hour), but not all are experienced. You may have to try several before finding one that brings out the best of your abilities. The **Centro Boliviano-Americano** (p195) has a list of recommended teachers.

Readers have recommended:

Reginaldo Rojo (☎ 424-2322; frojo@supernet.com.bo)
Maricruz Almanza Bedoya (☎ 422-7923; maricruz _almanza@ hotmail.com)
Claudia Villagra (☎ 424-8685)
Gloria Ramírez (☎ 424-8697)
Gladys Espinoza (☎ 428-9927)
Daniel Cotani (☎ 424-6820)
Elizabeth Siles (☎ 423-2279)
Katya Claros Vidal (☎ 424-1241; katya_lcv@hotmail.com)

Tours

To visit nearby national parks and reserves contact **Fremen Tours** (☎ 425-9392; www.andes -amazonia.com; Tumusla N-245). This group organizes comfortable yet adventurous excursions around Cochabamba and the Amazon Basin. They're not budget trips, but if you have a group, the costs per person drop to a reasonable level. Intriguing options include the Chapare, Torotoro, Amazon riverboat tours, the indigenous market at Pongo, Incallajta, Parque Nacional Tunari and several Cochabamba Valley villages.

Festivals & Events

A major annual event is the **Heroínas de la Coronilla** (May 27), a solemn commemoration in honor of the women and children who defended the city in the battle of 1812. At the fiesta of **Santa Veracruz Tatala** (May 2) is when farmers gather at a chapel 7km down the Sucre road to pray for fertility of the soil during the coming season. Their petitions are accompanied by folk music, dancing and lots of merrymaking. The **Fiesta de la Virgen de Urcupiña** (August 15 to 18) is the valley's biggest, with pilgrims converging

on the village of Quillacollo, 13km west of Cochabamba.

The village of Vinto (not to be confused with the tin smelter of the same name near Oruro), is best known for two annual celebrations. On March 19 it celebrates the **Fiesta de San José** (St Joseph, the patron saint of carpenters). The **Fiesta de la Virgen del Carmen** is celebrated on July 16 with floric groups, Masses, parades and military bands.

The easiest access is by *trufi* 211Z from the corner of Ayacucho and Aroma in Cochabamba. *Micros* run on Wednesday and Saturday from the same corner, but on other days you have to change in Quillacollo.

Sleeping

BUDGET

Hostal Versalles (☎ 422-1096; Ayacucho S-714; US$3.25, with bath US$4.50, with cable TV US$6) The best budget choice near the bus terminal is this clean, friendly HI-affiliate where breakfast is included.

Residencial Familiar (☎ 422-7988; Sucre E-554; US$3.25, d with bath US$10) and the marginally nicer **Residencial Familiar Anexo** (☎ 422-7986; 25 de Mayo N-234; US$3.25, d with bath US$10) are both popular with Bolivians and foreign travelers alike. The rooms, arranged around a central courtyard, are worn but spacious. Note that the door locks aren't always secure.

Hostal Colonial (☎ 422-1791; Junín N-134; US$3, with bath & breakfast US$4-5) Friendly, clean and secure, this is a traveler's favorite. Spacious family rooms are US$20; ask for a room upstairs overlooking the leafy courtyard gardens.

Hostal Central (☎ 422-3622; Achá 0-235; with bath, breakfast & TV US$6) The quiet rooms are set well back from the street.

Hostal Oruro (☎ 424-1047; López S-864; US$3.25) A secure family-run alternative if the Elisa next door is full. The rooms are a bit bigger than Elisa's and the shared bathrooms have solar-heated showers.

There are several basic – and mostly shabby – rock-bottom *alojamientos* strung out along nerve-wracking Av Aroma. For a bed, shower and little else, you'll pay around US$2 per person. Just off Av Aroma are the following acceptable cheapies:
Alojamiento San Juan de Dios (López S-871) Clean but surly.
Alojamiento Cochabamba (☎ 422-5067; Aguirre S-591) Basic place to flop that's popular with budget travelers. Hot water in the morning only.

Alojamiento Roma (☎ 425-8592; Aguirre S-585) Has a triple room for US$5.

Residencial Escobar (☎ 422-9275; Uruguay E-213)

Alojamiento Escobar (☎ 422-5812; Aguirre S-749)

MID-RANGE

City Hotel (☎ 422-2993; cityhotel42@hotmail.com; Jordán E-341; s/d/tr with breakfast & cable TV US$12/17.25/21.25) Clean and recently renovated, this is the best mid-range choice with spacious terraces, telephones and a restaurant. The superior upper floor rooms are US$22/32.

Hostal Elisa (☎ /fax 423-5102; helisa@supernet .com.bo; López S-834; US$6, with private bath US$10) Despite the sketchy location off odoriferous Av Aroma, it's another world inside. With a grassy courtyard, helpful management and clean garden tables, this place is deservedly recommended throughout Bolivia. Cable TV is available in the lounge and continental breakfasts are US$2 (American ones are US$3).

Hostal Florida (☎ /fax 425-7911; floridah@elsitio .com; 25 de Mayo S-583; US$3.25, with bath, phone & cable TV US$6; 🖳) A favorite old haunt with a quiet patio and lawn furniture downstairs plus a sun deck upstairs. It's well-situated between the center and the bus terminal and is therefore a good place to meet other travelers. There's hot water until 1pm and the friendly owner cooks a mean breakfast (US$1 to US$2) for her guests.

Hostal Jardín (☎ 424-7844; Hamiraya N-248; US$4.65, s/d/tr with bath & breakfast US$6.50/12/17.25) This European favorite has a funky overgrown garden with an enormous star fruit tree. Cable TV is an extra US$2.

Hotel Boston (☎ 422-4421; hboston@supernet.com .bo; 25 de Mayo N-167; s/d with bath & breakfast US$15/25) A reliable central choice with national TV and double beds.

Mary Hotel (☎ 425-2487; camarahotelera@mixmail .com; Aguirre S-601; s/d with breakfast & cable TV US$15/20) A modern family-run highrise within easy reach of the bus terminal. Rooms are carpeted and have phones.

Apart Hotel Concordia (☎ 422-1518; hotelconcordia@ hotmail.com; Arce 690; US$10; 🖳) Family-run and oriented, with grandma and grandpa living on the property. Three- and four-person apartments include a bath, kitchenette (dishes available on request) and phone. Guests have access to the pool and laundry service. It's north of town near the university and accessible on *micro* B.

TOP END

Hotel Portales (☎ 428-5444; www.portaleshotel.com; Pando 1271; s/d/ste US$77/95/155; 🞮 🖳 🖳) Cochabamba's only five-star choice is this comfortable resort-like complex with a full business center, a tropical pool, a steaming jacuzzi, manicured grounds and a classy restaurant. It's across the street from the Palacio de Portales. Ask about discount package deals (s/d from US$60/75 with breakfast).

Hotel Americana (☎ 425-0552; www.hotelamericana .com; Arce S-788; s/d/tr/ste with bath & breakfast US$20/30/40/50) This friendly three-star option is highly recommended. The rooms are all bright and clean and have cable TV.

Cesar's Plaza (☎ 425-0045; www.cesarsplaza.com; 25 de Mayo S-210; s/d/tr/ste US$40/48/58/64; 🞮 🖳) This four-star highrise caters to businessmen and has carpeted rooms with heating, air-con, TV, phone and *frigobar*. Prices include a buffet breakfast and access to a sauna and massage parlor.

Gran Hotel Ambassador (☎ 425-9001, toll-free ☎ 800-10-8282; ambassrv@supernet.com.bo; España N-349; s/d/ste with breakfast US$30/50/60) This four-star, 104-room business and convention hotel has rooms with TV, phone and frigobar. Buffet breakfast is included and some rooms have magnificent views.

Eating

You'll find economical *almuerzos* at dozens of mom-and-pop restaurants, where a cold beer is cheap and US$1.50 will get you at least three courses. Moving up in price, there's a string of sidewalk cafés along Av Ballivián, which will carry you straight to southern California. Most serve European, Bolivian and North American fare and offer hearty *almuerzos* for around US$2.

CAFÉS

Café Express (Aguirre S-443) has Cochabamba's best espresso drinks. The popular **Café Frances** (España N-140; 🕑 8am-8:30pm Mon-Sat) serves excellent coffee, tea, cakes, quiche and both sweet and savory crêpes in a Paris-like setting.

For something more old-fashioned, take tea, strudels and éclairs at **Tea Room Zürich** (☎ 448-5820; Pando 1182; 🕑 closed Tue). **Café Express Bolívar** (Bolívar E-485; 🕑 closed for lunch) steams superb espresso and cappuccino. Along Calle

España, near Ecuador and Venezuela/Major Rocha, you'll find an ever-changing assortment of trendy cafés and *confiterías*.

QUICK EATS

The popular *heladerías* – jumbo-size **Dumbo** (Heroínas E-345) and **Cristal** (Heroínas E-352) – open early in the morning and serve juice, eggs, toast, pancakes, chocolate, coffee, *salteñas* and other breakfast options. Near the corner of Achá and Villazón, street vendors sell delicious *papas rellenas* (potatoes filled with meat or cheese).

Av Heroínas is fast-food heaven and is good for pizza, chicken, burgers and *salteñas*. Near the corner of Achá and Ayacucho, ambulatory street vendors sell piping-hot *papas rellenas* (potatoes stuffed with meat or cheese).

Patio de Comidas El Pasa Tiempo (southwest cnr Plaza Colón; ☺ open until sunrise Thu-Sun; mains US$1-3) Mexican. Chinese. Italian. Churrasco. Bolivian. You name it. Knock yourself out on the cafeteria-style lunch buffet (US$3 per kilo). It's greasy but great and a real student hangout – the spot for post-party snacks. There's also cocktails, billiards and Internet upstairs.

Las Banderas/Charo Tacos (América at Pando; all under US$2) Serving everything from juicy mixed soft tacos with real *pico de gallo* salsa to fresh pasta to typical Bolivian dishes. Check out the organic produce from the owner's sister's farm. Across the street from the IC Norte supermarket.

Eli's Pizza Express (☎ 425-9249; 25 de Mayo N-254; mains US$1-3) Pumps out Manhattan-size (but soggy) pizza slices in a New York minute in NYC-diner surrounds. Call for delivery.

Danielíssimo (Bolívar at Aguirre) Friendly choice across from the tourist office for coffee and sweet treats.

Snack Terminal (Main Bus Terminal) Handy option for overnight travelers arriving by bus in the wee hours of the morning.

El Prado (Ballivián at Mexico) Upmarket ice-creamery with sidewalk seating.

California Burgers & Donuts (25 de Mayo near Heroínas) Delivers on its promise and has decent coffee too.

Porkie's (Heroínas & Ayacucho; burgers US$0.75) Chain of tasty, late-night hamburger stands posted at major intersections around the center.

RESTAURANTS

Metrópolis (España & Ecuador; mains US$2-4) Popular, movie-themed sustenance and socializing spot for expats, travelers and arty locals. The food may seem pricey but the enormous servings of soup, salad and pasta (plus other more imaginative fare) are worth it. The cocktail crowd spills onto the sidewalk at night.

La Estancia (☎ 424-9262; Uyuni E-718, near Plaza Recoleta; salad fare US$1.35, mains US$2.50-5) Well worth the trek across town, this pleasant, upscale restaurant sizzles up thick, juicy steaks, chicken and fish, and the salad bar is often applauded by non-meat eaters.

Kabbab (☎ 424-9149; Potosí N-1392; ☺ 6pm-midnight; mains US$1.50-3) A thousand and one variations on Persian kebabs served in an intimate space adjacent to the Palacio de Portales. Highlights include clay-oven flat bread, Turkish coffee and Bolivia's best baklavah.

Sole Mio (☎ 428-3379; America E-826; ☺ dinner only Mon-Fri, lunch & dinner Sat & Sun; pizzas US$3-6) The Italian owners (from Naples) import their ingredients for their robust wood-fired pizzas – thin crust, light on the sauce. Soft opera music, rich Italian wines and excellent service make this a comfortable place to linger over a meal. They also serve a range of meat and pasta entrees.

Rodizio Grill Americano (beside Hotel Americana; lunch US$2, mains US$2-4) Steak-oriented Rodizio is a carnivore's delight, but also serves great soups and has a full salad bar for vegetarians. It serves three meals daily, including good-value *almuerzos*.

La Cantonata (☎ 425-9222; España & Rocha; ☺ closed Mon; mains US$5-10) You can't beat this place for a decadent dinner. Sip fine Chilean wine before a roaring fire while the executive chef prepares your plate of homemade pasta. The service is superb and it's one of the country's top Italian choices.

Churrasquería Tunari (Bolívar s/n, opposite stadium; kebabs US$2) Mobbed on weekend afternoons when soccer games are on, it's a local favorite for enormous Beni-style grilled beef skewers.

Orale! (Salamanca E-555; ☺ 8:30am-midnight Tue-Sun; mains US$1.50-4) A million varieties of freshly squeezed juices, colorful tequila margaritas and a popular Sunday brunch keep upbeat Orale! hopping. The DF-style *comida* – tacos, tortas, burritos, *quesadillas*, nachos, etc – is presented in a stylish setting and there's breezy patio seating.

Rodizio Búfalo (☎ 425-1597; Torres Sofer, Oquendo N-654, lunch only Sun, dinner only Mon; salad bar US$3.75, dinner buffet US$6.50) Further afield, this all-you-can-eat Brazilian-style grill has an extensive salad bar and much more than just excellent grilled steaks.

Restaurant Jose (Plaza 14 de Septiembre 0-209) A convenient, central spot for an inexpensive lunch or dinner, Chose from Bolivian and pseudo-Chinese meals. It's good value, but don't be in too much of a hurry.

To share a dose of inexpensive *comida criolla* (traditional Bolivian cooking) with locals, try:

Savarín (☎ 425-7051; Ballivián N-626; lunch US$1.65) One of the most frequently recommended *almuerzos*.

Palmar Restaurante Familiar (Aroma near Arce; set meals US$1.50) Hearty four-course set menus. If you're into meat, try a *pacumutu* (think large quantities of beef).

El Caminante (Arce S-628; lunch US$1.25) Weekday-only lunches, including some international options, served in a pleasant open courtyard.

Sucre Manta (Ballivián N-560; mains from US$1) Good for both traditional *almuerzos* and à la carte dishes.

The following locals are also recommended:

Restaurant Marvi (Cabrera at 25 de Mayo; lunch US$1.35) Family-run.

Burger Plaza (south side of Plaza 14 de Septiembre; burgers US$1) Bolivian-style burgers and milkshakes.

El Paseo (☎ 425-9295; Ballivián N-540; mains US$1.50-3) Serves both Bolivian and international cuisine.

Churrasquería Hawaii (Aroma E-141; mains US$1.50-3) Specializes in steak.

SELF-CATERING

Markets (p197) are cheap for simple but varied and tasty meals – don't miss the huge, mouth-watering fruit salads. They're also the cheapest places to find coffee – albeit rather insipid – and a roll for breakfast. If you're up for something more traditional, try the local breakfast specialty, *arroz con leche*.

Super Natural (Pando 1270) Great eco-*mercado*, full of local natural and organic products.

Super Haas (Heroínas E-585) Convenient, if expensive, mini-market with a deli and snack counter.

IC Norte (America at Pando) Well-stocked American-style supermarket with imported and unique export-quality Bolivian products.

VEGETARIAN

Snack Uno's (Heroínas & San Martín; lunch US$1.65) Cochabamba's best vegetarian food: A simple four-course lunch includes a super-fresh salad bar. At night they serve pizza and pasta dishes.

Gopal (España N-250; mains under US$2) Vegetarian lunch or dinner with an Indian flare.

Comida Vegetariana (Heroínas E-262; everything under US$2) Homemade yogurt and freshly squeezed juices, plus dried fruits and granola.

Drinking

Note that by law all nightspots must close by 2:30am. Along El Prado (Av Ballivián) there's more drinking than eating at the Bolivian beer barns **Top Chopp** and **Viking Pub**, which feature loud music. The hard-rock scene jams most nights at **Pancho's** (España N-460; cover US$2) when live bands cover Kiss, Metallica and Deep Purple.

Entertainment

For information about what's on, see the newspaper entertainment listings. Big, bright **Cine Heroínas** (Heroínas s/n) and **Cine Astor** (Sucre & 25 de Mayo) both screen first-run movies nightly.

Popular dancing spots include **Nostalgias** (☎ 425-5955; Plaza Quintanilla beside Los Tiempos) and **Lujos Discoteca y Karaoke** (Beni E-330), both of which operate Wednesday to Sunday night. Expats also like **La Pimienta Verde** (Ballivián s/n) a subterranean dance den.

Local teens hang out at the fully automated, 10-lane **Strike X bowling center** (Pando at Portales) and the go-kart track and arcade complex next door.

Shopping

Locally produced woolens are available at a couple of outlets: the long-standing co-op **Fotrama** (☎ 422-2980; Bolívar 439), their bargain **Fotrama factory outlet** (☎ 424-0567; Circunvalación 1412), and the more expensive **Asarti** (☎ 425-0455; Paccieri at 25 de Mayo, Edificio Colón No 5), which produces export-quality alpaca. Cheaper alpaca and llama wool *chompas* (sweaters) are found in the markets. For inexpensive souvenirs, scour the *artesanía* stalls behind the main post office. For export-quality, high-altitude vintages, visit the retail shop of **La Concepción** (☎ 412-1967; Aguirre 577), Bolivia's foremost winery.

There are several Korean-owned camera shops around the plaza but for repairs you are better off going to La Paz. **Foto Estudio Relieve** (☎ 425-5052; 25 de Mayo N-345) Offers one-hour processing and sells a wide variety of film.

Getting There & Away
AIR
Cochabamba's Jorge Wilstermann Airport (CBB; US$2 domestic departure tax) is served daily by **AeroSur** (☎ 440-0909/0910; Villarroel 105) and **LAB** (☎ 425-0750; office at airport) from La Paz, Santa Cruz and Sucre. The flight between La Paz and Cochabamba must be one of the world's most incredible; coming from La Paz, sit on the left side of the plane for an incredible – and disconcertingly close-up – view of the peak of Illimani, and a few minutes later a bird's-eye overview of the dramatic Cordillera Quimsa Cruz. LAB also flies several times a week to Tarija and Trinidad.

TAM (☎ 458-1552; Hamiraya N-122) lifts off from the military airport to Santa Cruz (US$40) on Tuesday mornings and La Paz (US$27) on Tuesday afternoons. **TAM Mercosur** (☎ 458-2166; Heroínas O-130) connects Cochabamba with Asunción, Buenos Aires and São Paulo daily except Sunday.

BUS & CAMIÓN
Cochabamba's full-service **main bus terminal** (☎ 155; Ayacucho near Aroma) collects a US$0.35 terminal fee. Resist the temptation to buy tickets from hawkers (buy them from bus company ticket windows) to avoid bogus tickets. *Bus cama* (sleeper) service is available on most long-distance routes for about twice the price of those listed below.

Most buses to La Paz (US$2 to US$3, seven hours) – there are at least 20 daily – leave between 7am and 9pm. A baker's dozen of *flotas* have daily services to Oruro (US$2, four hours) between 7am and 10pm. **Jumbo Bus Ballivián** has a Friday-morning service to Vallegrande (US$4, 11 hours). Most Santa Cruz (US$3 to US$6, 10 to 13 hours) buses depart before 9am or after 5pm via the Chapare route. *Flotas* go to Trinidad (US$8, 24 to 30 hours) via Santa Cruz, at 6:30am and 7:30pm.

Frequent buses leave for Sucre (US$4, 10 hours) between 4:30pm and 6:30pm daily. Some then continue on to Potosí (around US$7, 15 hours). *Micros* and buses to Villa Tunari (US$1.75, 3 to 4 hours) and less frequently to Puerto Villarroel (US$2, seven hours) in the Chapare region leave every hour or so from the corner of 9 de Abril and Oquendo.

Flechabus and Almirante Brown offer a marathon international service to Buenos Aires (US$45, 72 hours) leaving at 5:30am and 6:30pm daily.

Trufis and *micros* to eastern Cochabamba Valley villages leave from the corner of República and 6 de Agosto. To the western part of the valley they leave from the corner of Ayacucho and Aroma. Torotoro *micros* leave on Thursday and Sunday at around 6am to 6:30am from República and 6 de Agosto.

Camiones to Sucre and Santa Cruz leave from Av de la Independencia, 1.5km south of the former railway station. In the dry season several weekly *camiones* leave for Torotoro at around 5am from near the Mercado de Ferias which is south of the city centre on Av Barrientos.

Getting Around
TO/FROM THE AIRPORT
Micro B (US$0.20) shuttles between the airport and the main plaza. Taxis to or from the center cost US$2 to US$3.

BUS
Convenient lettered *micros* and *trufis* (both US$0.20) display their destinations and run to all corners of the city.

CAR
Barron's Rent-a-Car (☎ 422-2774; Sucre E-727) **International Rent-a-Car** (☎ 422-6635; Ayacucho 219) **Localiza Rent-a-Car** (☎ 428-3132; Pando 1187) Next to Hotel Portales. Not the cheapest, but the best. Also at Jorge Wilstermann Airport.

TAXI
The taxi fare to anywhere south or east of the river, or north or west of Laguna Alalay, is US$0.35 (B$2.50) per person. Beyond those limits, it doubles. For a radio taxi, ring **CBA** (☎ 422-8856) or **Ciudad Jardín** (☎ 424-1111).

AROUND COCHABAMBA
Parque Nacional Tunari
This easily accessible, 300,000 hectare park was created in 1962 to protect the forested slopes above Cochabamba, as well as the

wild summit of Cerro Tunari. However, in the section directly north of town, the park's fringes have been encroached upon by urban development.

COCHABAMBA AREA

A good dirt road zigzags its way from the park gate (open until 4pm) up the steep mountain face. On foot, you'll find it more interesting to turn left 100m up the track and walk up a stony avenue of eucalyptus toward some farm buildings. About 1km later, several shortcut routes lead up the hill, but all eventually rejoin the road. After 3km from the gate, you'll reach a **picnic site** with BBQs and a playground with slides, firefighters' poles, swings, mini-golf and other amusements.

Immediately beyond the picnic site you'll see the sign for a *sendero ecológico* (nature trail). Don't expect too much in the way of *ecología*, but it's a well-made path that gains altitude rapidly, winding into thickening mature woodland. The views are tremendous, with Cochabamba spread out below, and in the opposite direction, Cerro Tunari and other hills in the Cordillera. At the middle elevations, there's temperate forest with small waterfalls, wildflowers, ferns and mosses, and a variety of colorful butterflies. With an early start and plenty of water, you should be able to make it up to some of the nearer peaks on a long day hike.

At 4000m, 25km from Cochabamba, are the two small trout lakes known as the **Lagunas de Huarahuara**. In a day, you can hike from here to the summit of **La Pirámide**, northwest of the lakes, for views down the other side of the Cordillera. The area offers several wild camping sites.

Coming from town, take *micro* F2 or *trufi* No 35 from Av San Martín, which will drop you three minutes from the park entrance, a big wooden archway with a fire-risk indicator. You may have to show ID and sign into the park. From the gate, turn right, then turn left after 100m; the road zigzags up past the playground to the lakes.

CERRO TUNARI AREA

Snow-dusted Cerro Tunari (5035m) is the highest peak in central Bolivia – it's the second peak from the left on the Taquiña beer label. Its flanks are 25km west of Cochabamba along the road to Independencia. This spectacular area offers excellent hiking and camping, but access is less than straightforward. For climbs, pick up the 1:50,000 map *Cordillera de Tunari* (sheet 6342III) from the IGM.

The first step is to catch a *micro* to **Quillacollo** (below), then walk or take *trufi* No 35 from Plaza Bolívar to **Cruce Liriuni**, 5km north of Quillacollo. From there it's a complicated four- to five-hour ascent to the summit, including some sections requiring technical equipment. Experienced climbers can manage the round-trip in a long day, but the high-altitude ascent will be more pleasant if you allow two days and camp overnight. A guide will be very useful to find the best route.

An easier route ascends from **Estancia Chaqueri** or **Tawa Cruz**, 12km beyond Cruce Liriuni (which has accommodations at the village school) at 4200m. *Micros* and *camiones* toward Morochata leave on Monday, Thursday and Saturday at 7am from three blocks off the main plaza in Quillacollo; they return to Cochabamba in the afternoon on Tuesday, Friday and Sunday. The relatively easy path, which takes around five hours, ascends the north face of the peak.

A two- to four-day route also exists that ascends 2500 vertical meters from the village of **Payrumani** (p207). There's plenty of running water in all but the driest times (late winter), but it needs to be purified, as there's a village at 4200m.

Another option is Fremen Tours (p199). It leads all-inclusive two-day excursions using the northern route.

Cochabamba Valley

QUILLACOLLO

Besides Cochabamba itself, Quillacollo (13km west of Cochabamba) is the Cochabamba Valley's most commercially important community. Apart from the **Sunday market** and the **pre-Inca burial mound** discovered beneath Plaza Bolívar, the main attraction is the **church**, which houses the **Virgen de Urkupiña shrine**. The niche lies to the right of the altar in a little side chapel, which is full of candles and commemorative plaques thanking the Virgin for blessings received. Note the interesting religious statues around this well-kept church.

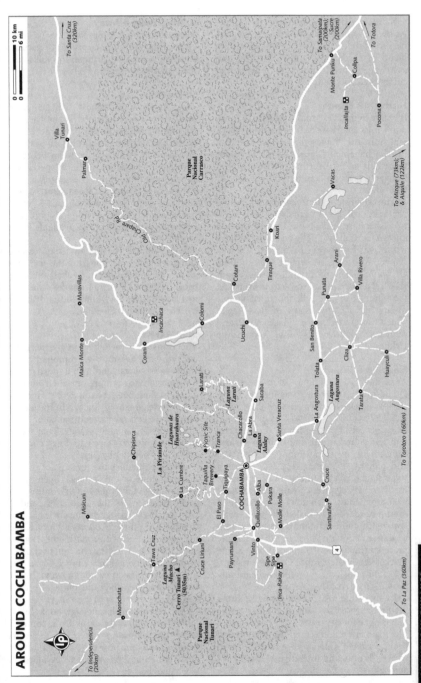

AROUND COCHABAMBA

Sunday visitors may want to sample *garapiña*, Quillacollo's answer to the dessert drink. It's a deceptively strong blend of *chicha*, cinnamon, coconut and *ayrampo*, a local mystery ingredient that colors the drink red.

Festivals & Events
If you're in the area around August 14 to 18, don't miss the **Fiesta de la Virgen de Urkupiña**, which is the biggest annual celebration in Cochabamba department. Folkloric musicians and dancers come from around Bolivia to perform, and the *chicha* flows for three days.

The celebration commemorates repeated visitations of the Virgin Mary and child to a shepherd girl at the foot of the hill known as Calvario. The visits were later witnessed by the girl's parents and a crowd of villagers when she shouted *Orkopiña* (There on the hill) as the Virgin was seen ascending toward heaven. At the summit of the hill, the townspeople discovered a stone image of the Virgin, which was carried to the village church and thereafter known as the Virgen de Urkupiña.

Sleeping & Eating
At Estancia Marquina, 4km north of Quillacollo, is **Eco-Hostal Planeta de Luz** (☎ 426-1234; www.planetadeluz.com; admission US$10, meals US$5; 4 person cabañas US$65; 🔊), an experiment in ecotourism 7km from the natural hotsprings at Liriuni. It's more a bizarre experiment in Gaudi-esque architecture and New Age dogma: vegetarian food, a solar sauna, solar lighting, music therapy, meditation, chanting, tai chi, natural health remedies, a 'clinic of happiness' and even a resident guru called Chamalu, who apparently cuddles trees to encourage them to dance. It might be fun, but you'll get more spirituality watching daily life at the market in Cochabamba! On the practical side, the pool and showers are 'naturally heated' (read: cold).

In the same area, **La Posada de los Cisnes** (cabañas per person US$10; 🔊) is another resort that is open for day use for US$2 per person. The main attraction is their weekend grilled beef *parrillada*. *Cabañas* are rented out on weekends only and include use of the pool and sauna.

Getting There & Away
Micros and *trufis* to Quillacollo (US$0.20, half an hour) leave from the corner of Ayacucho and Aroma in Cochabamba. In Quillacollo, the *trufi* stop is on Plaza Bolívar.

SIPE SIPE
This quiet and friendly village 27km southwest of Cochabamba is the base for visiting **Inca-Rakay**, the most easily accessible of the Cochabamba area ruins. If you're in Sipe Sipe on a Sunday between February and May try to sample the local specialty, a sweet grape liquor known as *guarapo*.

Near Sipe Sipe is **La Cabaña Resort** (☎ 422-2108; r per person with full board US$20), which has good food and a mineral pool and hot spring. Transfers are available from Cochabamba.

On Wednesday and Saturday, *micros* run directly to Sipe Sipe from the corner of Ayacucho and Aroma in Cochabamba. On other days, take a *micro* from the same spot to Plaza Bolívar in Quillacollo and then a *trufi* or a *micro* to Sipe Sipe.

INCA-RAKAY
The ruins of Inca-Rakay, in the Serranía de Tarhuani, are mostly crumbling stone walls these days, and you'll need some imagination to conjure up their former glory. It has been postulated that Inca-Rakay served as an Inca administrative outpost, to oversee agricultural colonies in the fertile Cochabamba Valley. That seems unlikely, however, given its lofty position and the difficulty of access.

The site includes the remains of several hefty buildings and a large open plaza overlooking the valley. One odd rock outcrop resembles the head of a condor, with a natural passageway inside leading to the top. Just off the plaza area is a cave that may be explored with a flashlight. Legend has it that this cave is the remnant of another of those apocryphal Inca tunnels – this one linking Inca-Rakay with faraway Cuzco. On a smog-free day, the plaza affords a spectacular overview of the valley.

The rare Spanish-language book *Inkallajta & Inkaraqay,* by Jesús Lara, contains good site maps and theories about its origins and purposes; it's occasionally available from Los Amigos del Libro in Cochabamba.

Warning

Unfortunately spending the night in the unattended ruins cannot be recommended. A foreign couple was reportedly killed here recently while sleeping in their vehicle, and several other readers have reported serious violent incidents while camping here.

Getting There & Away

Inca-Rakay is accessed on foot from Sipe Sipe. Since staying overnight is not a safe option, you must get an early start out of Cochabamba; the trip takes the better part of a day and you'll need time to explore the ruins.

About once weekly, *camiones* travel to Li'pichi from Sipe Sipe and pass within several hundred meters of Inca-Rakay. If you stay on the road, it's a relatively easy 12km uphill climb that will take about four hours. You'll eventually come across a roadside sign pointing toward the ruins, which are hidden from view amid rocky outcrops and a clump of molle trees (which resemble willows); from the road, it's five minutes downhill to the ruins.

Otherwise, it's a 5km, two-hour cross-country (but well-signed) walk up a steep hill. From the southwest corner of Sipe Sipe's main plaza, follow the road past the secondary school. From there the road narrows into a path and crosses a small ditch. Across the ditch, turn left onto the wider road. Starting several hundred meters up the road from town, follow a water pipeline uphill to the first major ridge; there'll be a large ravine on your left. From there, bear to the right, following the ridge until you see a smaller ravine on the right. At this point you're actually able to see Inca-Rakay atop a reddish hill in the distance, but from so far away it's hard to distinguish.

Cross the small ravine and follow it until you can see a couple of adobe houses on the other side. In front you'll see a little hill with some minor ruins at the top. Climb the hill, cross the large flat area, and then climb up two more false ridges until you see Inca-Rakay.

TIQUIPAYA

The village of Tiquipaya (population 30,000), 11km northwest of Cochabamba, is known for its **Sunday market** and its array of unusual festivals. In late April or early May there's an annual **Chicha Festival**; the second week in September sees the **Trout Festival**; around September 24 is the **Flower Festival**; and in the first week of November there's the **Festival de la Wallunk'a**, which attracts colorfully dressed traditional women from around Cochabamba department.

The classy **Cabañas Tolavi** (☎ 428-8599/8370; www.cabanas-tolavi.com; s/d/tw with breakfast buffet US$30/38/48, cabañas US$55-85; ☒) has chalet-style *cabañas* constructed of perfumed wood, which occupy a gardenlike setting among the trees. Nonguests can enjoy German-style meals, including a buffet breakfast. It's 500m downhill from the *trufi* stop in Tiquipaya.

Micros leave half-hourly from the corner of Avs Ladislao Cabrera and Oquendo in Cochabamba.

PAYRUMANI (VILLA ALBINA)

If you haven't already had your fill of Simón Patiño's legacy in Oruro and Cochabamba, you can visit **Payrumani** (☎ 424-3137; admission free by guided tour; ☽ 3-3:45pm Mon-Fri, 9am-1pm Sat) and tour the home the tin baron actually occupied. This enormous white mansion, which could have inspired the TV home of the Beverly Hillbillies, was named for his wife. Albina was presumably as fussy as her husband when it came to the finer things in life, and the elegant French décor of the main house and the Carrara-marble mausoleum seem typical of royalty anywhere in the world. In 1964 the estate was donated to the nonprofit Salesian Congregation by the Simón I Patiño University Memorial fund, which still represents the tin baron's heirs.

To reach Payrumani, take *trufi* 211Z or *micro* No 7 or 38 from Av Aroma in Cochabamba or from Plaza Bolívar in Quillacollo and get off at Villa Albina. It's only 22km from Cochabamba, but the trip may take a couple of hours.

LA ANGOSTURA

This eponymous village near the large reservoir of the same name lies on the route to Tarata and is known mainly as a place to fill up on fish. Of the several informal restaurants, the best is away from the highway, over the bridge near the railway. Here you'll pay US$3 for excellent meals with enough *pejerrey*, rice, salad and potato to stuff two people. From near the corner of Barrientos and 6 de Agosto in Cochabamba, take any *micro* (US$0.15) toward Tarata or Cliza and get off at the Angostura bridge.

En route, 18km east of the city, is **Lago del Edén Angostura**, a small park and restaurant that is popular with families on weekends, and the waterfront **Cabañas del Edén** (US$12). A 3km walk west of the park is the open-air **Las Carmelitas** restaurant, where on weekends Señora Carmen López bakes delicious cheese, egg, olive and onion *pukacapas* in a large beehive oven.

PUNATA

This small market town 50km east of Cochabamba is said to produce Bolivia's finest *chicha*. Tuesday is market day and May 18 is the riotous **town festival**. Access from Cochabamba is via *micros* (US$0.45) that depart frequently when full from the corner of República (the southern extension of Antezana) and Pulacayo, at Plaza Villa Bella.

If you have been hunting for the perfect alpaca sweater, contact the *alcaldía's* office about visiting **Alpaca Works** (☎ 457-7922; Bolivia 180; www.geocities.com/alpacaworks/home.html), a women's cooperative where you can browse their existing stock or order a customized Western-style sweater.

TARATA & HUAYCULI

Tarata, 35km southeast of Cochabamba, lives in infamy as the birthplace of the mad president General Mariano Melgarejo, who held office from 1866 to 1871. Its name is derived from the abundant *tara* trees, whose fruit is used in curing leather.

Tarata's enormous neoclassical **Iglesia de San Pedro** was constructed in 1788 and restored between 1983 and 1985; several of the interior panels include *mestizo*-style details carved in cedar. The 1792 **Franciscan Convent of San José**, which contains lovely colonial furniture and an 8000-volume library, was founded as a missionary training school. It now contains the ashes of San Severino, Tarata's patron saint, whose feast day is celebrated in grand style on November 30.

The village also has several other **historic buildings**: the government palace of President Melgarejo (built in 1872) and the homes of President Melgarejo, General Don Esteban Arce and General René Barrientos.

Huayculi, 7km from Tarata, is a village of potters and glaziers. The air is thick with the scent of eucalyptus being burned in cylindrical firing kilns. The local style and technique are passed down from generation to generation and remain unique in Bolivia.

Micros leave Cochabamba hourly from Av República and 6 de Agosto. There are no *micros* to Huayculi, but taxis from Cochabamba cost around US$3.

CLIZA

Cliza's **Sunday market** is a good alternative to the total Sunday shutdown in Cochabamba, and it's a good place to sample *squab*, a local specialty. *Micros* make the 30-minute trip to Cliza from Av República and 6 de Agosto in Cochabamba. Other notable times to visit include the **bread festival** (the second week of April) and the festival of the **Virgin de Carmen** on July 16.

ARANI & VILLA RIVERO

Arani, 53km east of Cochabamba, stages a **Thursday market**. The tranquil village is also known for *pan de Arani*, a big round bread concocted from a blend of grains to yield a distinctive flavor. Also look at the intricately carved wooden altars in the restored **church**, which once served as the seat of the Santa Cruz Bishopric. Around August 26 the town celebrates the **Festividad de la Virgen de la Bella**, which dates from colonial times.

At Villa Rivero, 6km south of Arani, men and women weave magnificent carpets in zoomorphic patterns and high relief. A 2m by 2m carpet, which requires 15kg of wool and at least 15 days of handiwork, will start at around US$35. For lunch, stop by the friendly *pensión* **Doña Alicia**, at the corner of the plaza.

Micros to Arani leave from the corner of República and 6 de Agosto in Cochabamba. Taxis from Arani to Villa Rivero cost US$2.50, and from Punata, *micros* are US$0.10.

Incallajta (Inkallajta)

The nearest thing Bolivia has to Peru's Machu Picchu is the remote and rarely visited site of Incallajta (meaning 'land of the

Inca'), 132km east of Cochabamba on a flat mountain spur above the Río Machajmarka. This was the easternmost outpost of the Inca empire and after Tiahuanaco it's the country's most significant archaeological site. The most prominent feature is the immense stone fortification that sprawls across alluvial terraces above the river, but at least 50 other structures are also scattered around the site.

Incallajta was probably founded by Inca Emperor Tupac Yupanqui, the commander who had previously marched into present-day Chile to demarcate the southern limits of the Inca empire. It's estimated that Incallajta was constructed in the 1460s as a measure of protection against attack by the Chiriguanos to the southeast. In 1525, the last year of Emperor Huayna Capac's rule, the outpost was abandoned. This may have been due to a Chiriguano attack, but was more likely the result of increasing Spanish pressure and the unraveling of the empire, which fell seven years later.

The ruins were made known to the world in 1914 by Swedish zoologist and ethnologist Ernest Nordenskiold, who spent a week at the ruins, measuring and mapping them. However, they were largely ignored – except by ruthless treasure hunters – for the next 50 years, until the University of San Simón in Cochabamba launched its investigations. The access road was built in 1977, and the site became a national monument in 1988. The archaeological museum in Cochabamba is now working to restore the ruins and translate Nordenskiold's writings on Bolivia into Spanish.

TOURS
Cochabamba agencies run day-long tours to Incallajta when they have a group large enough to make it worthwhile. Fremen Tours (p199) is recommended. Fridays are the best for joining a pre-organized tour.

SLEEPING & EATING
Without your own transportation, visiting Incallajta will prove inconvenient at best. Additionally, if you can't arrange lodging in private homes, you'll probably have to camp for two or three nights, so be sure to take plenty of water, food, warm clothing and camping gear. Camping and

basic shelters are available at the Centro de Investigaciones (US$1).

GETTING THERE & AWAY
From Cochabamba, take the daily *micro* toward Totora, which leaves from the corner of República and 6 de Agosto, and get off at Inca Cruce. From there, it's a 14km walk (or an unlikely hitch) to Collpa. At the Koari turnoff, opposite a church on the left side of the road, turn west and follow the largely uphill route for 10km. After crossing the Río Machajmarka, you'll enter the Incallajta archaeological park.

Totora
Totora, 142km east of Cochabamba, huddles in a valley at the foot of Cerro Sutuchira, and was once the loveliest colonial village in the department. Unfortunately on May 22, 1998 it was destroyed by an earthquake that measured 6.7 on the Richter scale. Many of the funds that were designated to rebuild Totora and similarly devastated Aiquile were diverted into the black hole of unethical officialdom, but ongoing restorations are finally bringing some of the damaged buildings back to life. The annual **town festival** on February 2 features bullfights.

The colonial-style Gran Hotel Totora collapsed in the earthquake, but there's a small *alojamiento* (US$2.50) and the *alcaldía* is said to be planning a hotel next to the Casa de Cultura.

Micros (US$1, 3½ hours) leave daily for Totora between 1pm and 4pm from the corner of República and 6 de Agosto in Cochabamba. Totora is on the main route between Cochabamba and Sucre, but few travelers ever see it because most buses pass through at night.

Mizque
This pretty colonial village enjoys a lovely pastoral setting on the Río Mizque. Founded as the Villa de Salinas del Río Pisuerga in 1549, it soon came to be known as the Ciudad de las 500 Quitasoles (City of 500 Parasols), after the sunshields used by the locals. It makes a great escape from the cities and main tourist sights, and the few visitors who pass through on trips between Sucre and Cochabamba are impressed by the beauty of the Mizque and Tucuna

Valleys, where you may spot the flocks of endangered scarlet macaws, which squawk and frolic in the early morning.

SIGHTS & ACTIVITIES

The lovely restored **Iglesia Matríz**, which was slightly damaged in the 1998 earthquake, once served as the seat of the Santa Cruz bishopric (until the seat was shifted to Arani in 1767). There's also a small archaeological and historical **museum**. Monday is **market day**.

With the help of Peace Corps volunteers, the *alcaldía* (north side of the plaza) is organizing **self-guided hiking circuits** and **guided trips** to several local sites of natural and historic interest. Ask Moises Cardozo at the Entel office or Restaurant Plaza who will arrange an interesting visit to his beekeeping operation just outside of town.

Besides its cheese and honey, Mizque is best known for its **Fería de la Fruta** (April 19), which coincides with the *chirimoya* harvest and **Semana Santa**. From September 8 to 14, Mizque holds the lively **Fiesta del Señor de Burgos**, which features much revelry and bull- and cock- fighting.

SLEEPING & EATING

Next to the *campesino* market on the road to the river, the brand new **Hotel Bolivia** (US$2, with bath US$2.65) has firm beds and is probably the nicest place in town. There's no phone, but they can be reached through the **Entel** (☎ 413-4512/14) office. Another good option is the rooms with decks at **Hospedaje Graciela** (☎ 413-5616; with bath US$3), which is affiliated with the recommended Restaurant Plaza. Set amid gardens, the clean **Residencial Mizque** (☎ 413-5617; US$1.50) is the easiest place to find if you arrive at night – look for the Prodem sign.

Mizque has several cheap Taquiña-sponsored *pensiones* that serve typical Bolivian meals. They're all within a block of the plaza. Alternatively, you can eat at the street stalls beside the church.

GETTING THERE & AWAY

A daily *micro* (US$2, four hours) leaves Cochabamba from the corner of Avs 6 de Agosto and República at noon; from Mizque they depart for Cochabamba at 8am on Tuesday and Friday and for Aquile at 3pm daily. Overnight Cochabamba-bound buses arriving from Sucre (US$3, five to six hours) pass by around midnight when they are not using the alternative route through Totora.

Aiquile

Dusty little Aiquile, which was decimated by the same 1998 earthquake that damaged Totora, is known for some of Bolivia's finest *charangos*. In late November it holds the **Feria del Charango**. Services include post and Entel offices and a medical clinic. **Market day** is Sunday.

Accommodations are available at the basic Hotel Los Escudos and the pleasant Hostal Campero, which both charge around US$2 per person and serve simple meals. The Campero is in an old colonial building surrounding a pleasant courtyard, and the personable owner likes to chat with guests.

Aiquile lies on the main route between Cochabamba and Sucre, but most buses pass in the wee hours of the night when this already soporific settlement is sound asleep. Buses to Aiquile depart daily at around 3pm from the corner of Avs República and 6 de Agosto in Cochabamba.

It's about a 1½-hour drive between Aiquile and Mizque. There are a couple of *micros* a day, or you can readily thumb a ride on passing *camiones*, but be prepared for a real dust bath.

PARQUE NACIONAL TOROTORO

The diminutive colonial village of **Torotoro** sits on a small plain between the sharp Serranías de Huayllas and Cóndor Khaka. The surrounding 16,570-hectare park was created in 1989. Most of the treasures of this absolute jewel – caves, ruins, rock paintings, waterfalls and fossilized dinosaur tracks – are difficult or uncomfortable to reach without private transport, but that only adds to the appeal. Further information is available from the Servicio Nacional de Áreas Protegidas (Sernap) in Cochabamba (p195) or from the administration office in the village.

Dinosaur Tracks

Most visitors to Torotoro come for the paleontology. The village, which sits in a wide section of a 20km-long valley at a 2600m elevation, is flanked by enormous inclined mudstone rock formations, bearing biped and quadruped Cretaceous-period dinosaur tracks. As the road flattens out beside the stream northwest of Torotoro, it actually crosses the path of a group of three-toed tracks, each measuring about 25cm long.

A short distance from the village, just beyond the Río Torotoro crossing, the area's largest tracks march up from just above the waterline. They were made by an enormous quadruped dinosaur, and they measure 35cm wide, 50cm long and 20cm deep – at a stride of nearly 2m!

Several hundred meters further upstream from the crossing, a group of small three-toed tracks climbs out of the water and under a layer of rocks. More tracks can be found 5km upstream, and dinosaur bone fragments have been found in layers of red earth.

All the tracks in the Torotoro area were made in soft mud which then solidified into mudstone. They were later lifted and tilted by tectonic forces. For that reason, nearly all the tracks appear to lead uphill. The exception is the set known as the **Carreras Pampa site**, along the route to Umajalanta Cave. These tracks, which were made by three-toed biped dinosaurs, run in several different directions, suggesting a dance-like frolic.

Sea Fossils

In a small side gully, an hour's walk southwest of Torotoro, on the Cerro de las Siete Vueltas (Mountain of Seven Turns – so called because the trail twists seven times before reaching the peak), is a major sea-fossil deposit. At the base of the ravine you may see petrified shark teeth, while higher up, the limestone and sedimentary layers are set with fossils of ancient trilobites, echinoderms, gastropods, arthropods, cephalopods and brachiopods. The site is thought to date back about 350 million years. There's another major sea-fossil site in the **Quebrada Thajo Khasa**, southeast of Torotoro.

Batea Cocha Rock Paintings

Above the third bend of the Río Torotoro, 1.5km downstream from the village, are several panels of ancient rock paintings collectively called **Batea Cocha** because the pools below them resemble troughs for pounding laundry. The paintings were executed in red pigments and depict anthropomorphic and geometric designs as well as fanciful representations of serpents, turtles and other creatures.

Llama Chaqui Ruins

A challenging 19km hike around the Cerro Huayllas Orkho from Torotoro will take you to the ruins known as the Llama Chaqui (Foot of the Llama). The multilevel complex, which dates from Inca times, rambles over distinctive terraces and includes a maze of rectangular and semicircular walls, plus a fairly well-preserved watchtower. Given its

strategic vantage point, it probably served as a military fortification, and may have been somehow related to Incallajta, further north. A guide is essential, as the ruins are very difficult to find on your own.

El Vergel

Thanks to the perennial water, the lovely 100m-deep canyon known as El Vergel (or Huacasenq'a – 'cow's nostrils' in Quechua) is filled with incongruous moss, vines and other tropical vegetation. At the bottom a crystal-clear river tumbles down through cascades and waterfalls, forming idyllic swimming pools. To get here, follow the main road out of town to the first big bend, where a 4WD track takes off straight ahead. This track will eventually turn into a footpath and lead to a set of steps down into the canyon. Despite what some locals may tell you, it's not necessary to hire a guide.

Cavernas de Chillijusk'o

These undeveloped caverns ('little eye of the needle' in Quechua) are just 500m from the village. Unlike the more amenable Gruta de Umajalanta, they're comprised of a maze of galleries and labyrinths, and to visit you'll need an experienced guide, several backup light sources and a cord to show you the way back out.

Gruta de Umajalanta

The Río Umajalanta, which disappears beneath a layer of limestone approximately 22m thick, has formed the impressive Umajalanta Cavern, of which 4.5km of passages have been explored. Inside are fanciful stalagmite and stalactite formations; rooms dubbed the Sala de Conciertos, Sala de Inspiraciones, and Sala de La Virgen y El Niño; underground lakes and rivers with blind catfish; and several cascades and waterfalls. Two of the subterranean waterways flowing into the Río Umajalanta have been whimsically dubbed the Río Singani and the Río 7-Up; together, they exit the cavern as the Río Chuflay!

The 8km one-way walk takes two hours from the village. Although the cave remains undeveloped, there are plans to install pathways, stairs and artificial lighting. To see it in a natural state, find a torch, then go to the village administration to pick up the entrance key to the cave (admission US$2pp).

Although most local guides know little about the cave itself, they can show you the safest route through.

Tours

Sernap provides free guides which are obligatory; tips are optional. Independent Spanish-speaking guides can be found near the **tourist office** (☎ 422-1793) in Torotoro. Contact **n2b Adventures** (☎ 429-6959, mobile ☎ 717-95000; www.net2bolivia.com) or Fremen Tours (p199) about organized trips from Cochabamba that take in most of the major sites.

Festivals & Events

From July 24 to 27, the village stages the **Fiesta del Tata Santiago**, which features sheep sacrifices and perhaps some *tinku* fighting (see the boxed text, p233). This may be an interesting time to visit – and a good time to look for a lift – but it's not the best for experiencing the natural attractions.

Sleeping & Eating

Torotoro isn't prepared for mass tourism, but facilities are improving. The new midrange **Hostal Asteria** (☎ 425-9392 in Cochabamba; Anchu s/n; s/d/tr/q with bath & breakfast US$12/20-22/28/35) has comfortable rooms, an ample supply of hot water and a bar and restaurant. Visitors may also lodge with private families near the Entel office. A couple of other families are building new cabins.

If you want to camp, locals will expect you to pay; it's important to set a mutually agreeable price (perhaps US$1 per group per night) and pay only the family in control of the land. Be sure to keep your tent closed to avoid contact with vinchuca beetles.

For meals, you're limited to the Thursday and Sunday markets or a couple of basic *pensiones*. There are also several small shops selling staples but supplies are restricted.

Electricity has eluded the village thus far and the only generator in town peters out soon after sundown, so bring some candles or a flashlight.

Getting There & Away

Parque Nacional Torotoro is 110km (by awful road) southeast of Cochabamba in Potosí department, but much closer as the condor flies. Flying is often the only way to arrive during the rainy season.

AIR

The **Free Swedish Mission of Cochabamba** (☎ 422-7042) occasionaly flies into Torotoro and usually has space for passengers. If you charter their Cessna, the flight costs US$140 for up to five passengers one-way and takes 25 minutes. The local Air Force **Grupo Aéreo 34** (☎ 423-5244) may offer taxi service from the Cochabamba air base. They charge around US$100 for up to five passengers.

BUS

Minibuses (US$3, seven hours) depart on Monday, Thursday and Sunday around 6am from the corner of Avs República and 6 de Agosto in Cochabamba. They return early Monday and Friday morning from near the plaza in Torotoro. During school holidays transport is often completely booked by student groups.

CAMIÓN

During the dry season, there are a couple of weekly *camiones* between Cochabamba and Torotoro (US$2, nine hours), departing at 5am from the Mercado de Ferias in Cochabamba. Alternatively, you can avoid the bone-chilling early-morning departure by taking a *micro* to Cliza and, if there's room to get in, picking up the *camión* as it passes between 6:30am and 9am.

CAR & MOTORCYCLE

You'll be happiest with a good motorbike or a 4WD to do this trip on your own. You can rent 4WDs in Cochabamba (p203) for around US$40 per day plus US$0.40 per kilometer. Follow the highway toward Sucre for 31km, turn right and continue 7km to the village of Cliza. There's no gas available beyond Cliza, so make sure you have enough for the return trip – about 400km. Follow the Oruro road 10km beyond Cliza and turn left onto the very rough Torotoro road. Take the best map you can find and be prepared to ask for directions a lot and to field many requests for rides.

INCACHACA & THE CHAPARE ROAD

In the highlands, 93km northeast along the Santa Cruz road from Cochabamba, you'll pass the 1500-hectare **Corani reservoir**, which was created in 1966 to provide water for the city. On its shores is a popular weekend resort complex. Also look for the bizarre **Casa de los Brujos** (Witches' House), an exceptional but now-dilapidated dwelling constructed by a local eccentric.

Further down the valley, half an hour on foot from Km 84, is the semi-abandoned settlement of **Incachaca** (Inca bridge), which enjoys a Yungas-like microclimate that covers the slopes with lush tropical forest. Here, the Río Alisu Mayu crashes down through convoluted rock formations, and a hanging bridge – the **Puente del Inca** – crosses a 60m deep gorge. An unusual sight is the **Ventana del Diablo** (Devil's Window), where a waterfall issues from the rock. Early in the morning you may see the hooded mountain toucan, the Andean guan and other birds.

For details on the Chapare region of northern Cochabamba department, see the Amazon Basin chapter (p310).

Getting There & Away

From Cochabamba, Incachaca is accessible by *micros* going to Villa Tunari or buses to Santa Cruz. The former leave every half hour from the corner of Oquendo and 9 de Abril. From Km 84, walk 100m down the road, where you'll find an unpaved road leading up the mountain. Follow it for about 30 minutes (or take a shortcut along the power lines) until you reach the site. Allow several hours to look around the small lake, bridge, old hydroelectric plant and the Ventana del Diablo. For the last two sites, visitors must register at the caretaker's office.

SUCRE

pop 225, 000 / elevation 2790m

Most Bolivians who know Sucre will tell you it's their nation's most beautiful city. As a result its inhabitants have reverently bestowed endearing nicknames upon it: 'The Athens of America,' 'The City of Four Names,' 'The Cradle of Liberty' and 'The White City of the Americas'. Set in a valley surrounded by low mountains, it enjoys a mild and comfortable climate nearly as appealing as that of Cochabamba.

The city of Sucre was declared a Unesco cultural heritage site in 1991 and it won't take long to see why. Beautiful colonial architecture abounds, with many original buildings still intact. All buildings within

BOLÍVAR – EL LIBERTADOR

'There have been three great fools in history: Jesus, Don Quixote and I.' So Simón Bolívar, the man who brought independence from Spanish rule to modern-day Venezuela, Colombia, Panama, Ecuador, Peru and Bolivia summed up his life shortly before he died abandoned, poor and rejected.

Simón Bolívar was born on July 24, 1783. His father died five years later, and his mother when he was nine years old. The boy was brought up by his uncle and was taught by tutor Simón Rodríguez, an open-minded mentor who had a strong formative influence on his pupil.

In 1799 the young Bolívar was sent to Spain and France to continue his education. After mastering French, he turned his attention to that country's literature. Voltaire and Rousseau became his favorite authors. Their works introduced him to the progressive ideas of liberalism and, as it turned out, would determine the course of his life.

In 1802 Bolívar married his Spanish bride, María Teresa Rodríguez del Toro, and a short time later the young couple sailed for Caracas, but eight months later María Teresa died of yellow fever. Although Bolívar never remarried, he had many lovers. The most devoted of these was Manuela Sáenz, whom he met in Quito in 1822 and who stayed with him almost until his final days.

The death of María Teresa marked a drastic shift in Bolívar's destiny. He returned to France, where he met with the leaders of the French Revolution and then traveled to the USA to take a close look at the new order after the American Revolution. By the time he returned to Caracas in 1807, he was full of revolutionary theories and experiences taken from these two successful examples. It didn't take him long to join the clandestine pro-independence circles.

At the time, disillusionment with Spanish rule was close to breaking into open revolt. On April 19, 1810 the Junta Suprema was installed in Caracas, and on July 5, 1811 the Congress declared independence. This turned out to be the beginning of a long and bitter war, most of which was to be orchestrated by Bolívar.

Simón Bolívar's military career began under Francisco de Miranda, the first Venezuelan leader of the independence movement. After Miranda was captured by the Spanish in 1812, Bolívar took over command. Battle followed battle with astonishing frequency until 1824. Of those battles personally directed by Bolívar, the independence forces won 35, including a few key ones: the Battle of Boyacá (August 7, 1819), which secured the independence of Colombia; the Battle of Carabobo (June 24, 1821), which brought freedom to Venezuela; and the Battle of Pichincha (May 24, 1822), which led to the liberation of Ecuador.

In September 1822 the Argentine liberator General José de San Martín, who had occupied Lima, abandoned the city to the Spanish, and Bolívar took over the task of winning in Peru. On August 6, 1824 his army was victorious at the Battle of Junín, and on December 9, 1824 General Antonio José de Sucre inflicted a final defeat at the Battle of Ayacucho. Peru, which included Alto Perú, had been liberated and the war was over. On August 6, 1825, the first anniversary of the Battle of Junín, Bolivia declared independence from Peru at Chuquisaca (Sucre), and the new republic was christened 'Bolivia', after the liberator.

the central core of the city are either whitewashed or painted white.

Like the Netherlands, Libya and South Africa, Bolivia divides its bureaucracy between multiple capitals. La Paz has usurped most of the governmental power, but the Supreme Court still convenes in Sucre; *sureños* maintain that their city remains the real heart of Bolivian government. It's still a center of learning, and both Sucre and its university enjoy reputations as focal points of progressive thought within the country.

Orientation

Sucre is compact and laid out in an easily negotiated grid pattern. Tourist offices sell a good town map (US$0.40) and better hotels and tour agencies include maps on the back of their brochures.

Purchase topo sheets of Chuquisaca department from the **Instituto Geográfico Militar** (☎ 645-5514; Arce 172).

Information
CULTURAL CENTERS
Check the noticeboards along Av Argentina

Bolívar could now get down to his long-awaited dream: Gran Colombia, the unified state comprising Venezuela, Colombia (which then included Panama) and Ecuador, became a reality. However, the task of setting the newborn state on its feet proved even more difficult than winning battles. 'I fear peace more than war', Bolívar wrote in a letter, aware of the difficulties ahead.

The main problem was the great regional and racial differences in Gran Colombia, which Bolívar, as president, was unable to hold together, even with strong central rule. The new state began to collapse from the moment of its birth. However, the president insisted upon holding the union together, although it was rapidly slipping from his hands. The impassioned speeches for which he was widely known could no longer sway the growing opposition, and his glory and charisma faded.

In August 1828 he took drastic action: he ousted his vice president Santander and set up a dictatorship, maintaining that 'Our America can only be ruled through a well-managed, shrewd despotism'. His popularity waned further, as did his circle of friends and supporters, and a short time later, he miraculously escaped an assassination attempt in Bogotá. Disillusioned and in poor health, he resigned from the presidency in early 1830 and planned to leave for Europe, just in time for the formal disintegration of Gran Colombia.

Venezuela broke away in 1830, approved a new congress and banned Bolívar from his homeland. A month later, Antonio José de Sucre, Bolívar's closest friend, was assassinated in southern Colombia. These two news items reached Bolívar just as he was about to board a ship for France. Depressed and ill, he accepted the invitation of a Spaniard, Joaquín de Mier, to stay in his home in Santa Marta, Colombia.

Bolívar died on December 17, 1830 of pulmonary tuberculosis. A priest, a doctor and a few officers were by his bed, but none of these were his close friends. Joaquín de Mier donated one of his shirts to dress the body, as there had been none among Bolívar's humble belongings. Perhaps the most important figure in the history of the South American continent had died.

It took the Venezuelan nation 12 years to acknowledge its debt to the man to whom it owed its freedom. In 1842 Bolívar's remains were brought from Santa Marta to Venezuela and deposited in the cathedral in Caracas. In 1876 they were solemnly transferred to the Pantheon in Caracas, where they now rest. Today, Bolívar is once again a hero, his reputation polished and inflated to almost superhuman dimensions. His cult is particularly strong in Venezuela, but he's also widely venerated in the other nations he freed. His statue graces nearly every central city plaza and at least one street in every town bears his name.

El Libertador – as he was called at the beginning of his liberation campaigns and is also called today – was undoubtedly a man of extraordinary gifts. An idealist with a poetic mind and visionary ideas, his goal was not only to topple Spanish rule but also to create a unified America. This, of course, proved an impossible ideal, yet the military conquest of some five million square kilometers remains a phenomenal accomplishment. This inspired amateur with no formal training in war strategy won battles in a manner that still confounds the experts.

One of the final remarks in Bolívar's diary reads, 'My name now belongs to history. It will do me justice.' And history has duly done so.

off the northwest corner of the plaza for announcements of cultural events.

Alliance Française (☎ 645-3599; Arce 35) French-language library, foreign films and La Taverna restaurant (p225).

Casa de la Cultura (☎ 645-1083; Argentina 65) Hosts art exhibitions and music recitals and runs a café and public library.

Centro Boliviano-Americano (CBA; ☎ 645-1982; www.cba.com.bo; Calvo 301) Rainbow Room Café has an English-language library. Referrals for private Spanish-language teachers.

Instituto Cultural Boliviano Alemán (ICBA; ☎ 645-2091; www.icba-sucre.edu.bo; Avaroa 326) German-

language library, listings of rooms for rent, Kultur Café Berlin (p224). Also offers Spanish lessons (see Courses, p222).

IMMIGRATION
Immigration (Sainz 117; ☼ 8:30am-4:30 Mon-Fri) A no-fuss place to extend visas and lengths of stay.

INTERNET ACCESS
Internet 2000 (San Alberto near España; US$0.35 per hr; ☼ until 10:45pm) Smoky but convenient to budget hotels.
Cybercafé Samael (Estudiantes 33 & 79 US$0.35 per hr; ☼ until 11pm) The best alternative.

LAUNDRY

Lavandería LG (☎ 642-1243; Loa 407) Charges US$1 per kilo and delivers to hotels.

Lavandería Laverap (☎ 644-2598; Bolívar 617; ☺ am only Sun) Full-service laundry in 90 minutes (up to 4.5kg for US$2.75).

Hostal Charcas (☎ 645-3972; hostalcharcas@ yahoo.com; Ravelo 62) Does laundry for nonguests for US$0.80 per kilo and can handle washing, drying and ironing in three hours.

MEDICAL SERVICES

Dr Gaston Delgadillo (☎ 645-1692; Colón 33) Reader-recommended. Speaks Spanish, English, French and German.

MONEY

Enlace ATMs are numerous in the city center. **Casa de Cambio Ambar** (San Alberto 7) and **Casa de Cambio El Arca** (España 134) both change travelers checks – the latter normally at better rates. **Banco Nacional de Bolivia** (España & San Alberto) changes travelers checks to dollars for 3% commission but lines can be long. Many businesses display 'Compro Dólares' signs, but they only change cash. Street moneychangers, who operate outside the market along Av Hernando Siles, are handy on weekends when banks are closed. Cash advances are available for a fee at the **Banco de Santa Cruz** (San Alberto & España), the Banco Nacional de Bolivia and some *casas de cambio*.

POST & TELEPHONE

The tranquil **main post office** (Estudiantes & Junín) has an *aduana* (customs) office downstairs for *encomiendas* (parcels), doesn't close for lunch and is open late. The high-rise **Entel office** (España & Urcullo) opens at 8am.

TOURIST INFORMATION

In addition to the following, there are municipal tourist offices at the airport and bus terminal.

Municipal tourist office (Plazuela Zudáñez; Bustillos & Olañeta)

Unidad Departamental de Turismo (☎ 645-5983; Argentina 65) Not terribly helpful, but staff can usually answer specific questions.

Oficina Universitario de Turismo (☎ 645-2831; SE cnr Plaza 25 de Mayo 25) Dispenses good info and provides student guides for city tours (US$10 for groups of up to four) when classes are in session.

Dangers & Annoyances

Sucre long enjoyed a reputation as one of Bolivia's safest towns, but occasionally visitors are harassed by bogus police. If you have a problem, report it to the **tourist police** (☎ 648-0467; Junín pedestrian mall) or the **radio patrulla** (☎ 110; 645-2332). Whistle-blowing private security forces are a common sight (and sound).

Sucre's colonial streets and sidewalks are noticeably narrow and they get packed at night and the bus smog can be annoying if you're walking around a lot. Like in much of Bolivia, nearly everything essential (banks, etc) shuts down after midday on weekends when locals head for the countryside.

Sights & Activities

Sucre boasts several impressive museums and colonial churches but opening hours are unpredictable. For the best view in town, inquire with the National Police or at the Comunicacion Social office inside the Prefectura de Chuquisaca (ex-presidential palace) building next to the cathedral. If they're not otherwise engaged, someone may take you up inside the Mansard roof to the cupola of the building for free. Note the murals depicting the struggle for Bolivian independence as you come upstairs.

CASA DE LA LIBERTAD

For a dose of Bolivian history, it's hard to beat this **house** (☎ 645-4200; Plaza 25 de Mayo 11; admission US$1.35, free Sun; ☺ 9am-noon & 2:30-6:30pm Mon-Sat, 9am-noon Sun) on the main plaza where the Bolivian declaration of independence was signed on August 6, 1825. It's been designated a national memorial, and a replica of the actual document (the original is in Banco Nacional's Sucre branch) and numerous other mementos of the era are on display.

The first score of Bolivian congresses were held in the Salon, originally a Jesuit chapel. Doctoral candidates were also examined here. Behind the pulpit hang portraits of Simón Bolívar, Hugo Ballivián and Antonio José de Sucre. General Bolívar claimed that this portrait, by Peruvian artist José Gil de Castro, was the most lifelike representation ever done of him.

The museum also includes portraits of presidents, military decorations, war- and independence-related art and relics, and old governmental documents. The most memorable is a huge wooden bust of Bolívar carved by artist and musician

Mauro Núñez. Don't miss the magnificent gilded loft in the Aula de Independencia. Guided tours are available in English, French, German or Spanish.

MUSEO TEXTIL-ETNOGRÁFICO (MUSEO DE ARTE INDÍGENA)

Inside the 17th-century Casa Capellánica, the Fundación Antropólogos del Surandino's **museum of indigenous arts** (ASUR; ☎ 645-3841; www.bolivianet.com/asur; San Alberto 413; admission US$1.60; ☟ 8:30am-noon & 2:30-6pm Mon-Fri, 9:30am-noon Sat) is highly recommended. The museum conducts art workshops and displays permanent and itinerant art exhibitions. These feature lovely local ceramics and beautiful and practical weavings, known as *aqsus*, from both the Candelaria (Tarabuco) and Jalq'a (Potolo) traditions, among others, all tastefully displayed.

The contiguous shop (ASUR Proyecto Textil) markets locally produced ceramics and weavings and ensures that a decent share of the profits goes to the artisans. However it's more interesting (and cheaper) to visit the weaving villages and buy directly from the artisans (see Shopping, p226).

IGLESIA DE LA MERCED

Contrary to its ordinary exterior, the **Iglesia de la Merced** (☎ 645-1483; Pérez 512; admission US$0.80; ☟ 10am-noon & 3-5pm Mon-Fri) is blessed with the most beautiful interior of any church in Sucre and possibly in Bolivia. Because the order of La Merced left Sucre for Cuzco in 1826, taking its records with it, the church's founding date is uncertain, but it's believed to be sometime in the early 1550s. The building was completed no later than the early 1580s.

The Baroque-style altar and carved *mestizo* pulpit are decorated with filigree and gold inlay. Several paintings by the esteemed artist Melchor Pérez de Holguín – notably El Nacimiento de Jesús, El Nacimiento de María and a self-portrait of the artist rising from the depths of Purgatory – are on display, as are sculptures by other artists. The views from the bell tower are splendid.

CAL ORCKO (FANCESA DINOSAUR TRACKS)

It seems that 60 million years ago the site of Sucre's Fancesa cement quarry served as a sort of Grumman's Chinese Theater for large and scaly types. When the grounds were being cleared in 1994, plant employees uncovered a nearly vertical mudstone face bearing hundreds of tracks – some of which measure up to 80cm in diameter – from tyrannosauri rex, iguanadons and other dinosaurs. There are also petrified remains of prehistoric algae and fish.

The new **Dino Truck** (☎ 645-1863; US$3.35 for transport, admission & English-speaking guide) departs daily from in front of the cathedral at 9:30am, noon and 2:30pm. Alternatively, you can take a tour with an agency or taxi driver (US$8), get within a dusty 2km walk of the complex via *micro* A or walk the pleasant 6km north of town – but you'll still have to join a guided tour.

CATEDRAL & CAPILLA DE LA VIRGEN DE GUADALUPE

The **cathedral** (☎ 645-2257; southwest side of Plaza 25 de Mayo; ☟ mornings) was begun in 1551 and completed 15 years later, but major sections were added between 1580 and 1650. Of interest is the bell tower, a Sucre landmark, and the statues of the 12 Apostles and four patron saints of Sucre. The tower clock was ordered from London in 1650 and installed in 1772. Unfortunately, the cathedral's interior is rather overburdened with kitsch.

Around the corner is the **Capilla de la Virgen de Guadalupe**, which was completed in 1625. Encased in the altar is the Virgen de Guadalupe de la Extremadura, named after a similar image in Spain. She was originally painted by Fray Diego de Ocaña in 1601. The work was subsequently coated with highlights of gold and silver and adorned in robes encrusted with diamonds, amethysts, pearls, rubies and emeralds donated by wealthy colonial parishioners. The jewels alone are said to be worth millions of dollars, and one can only wonder why the priceless Virgin's head is ringed with cheap incandescent Christmas bulbs!

MUSEO DE LA RECOLETA

Overlooking the city of Sucre from the top of Calle Polanco, **La Recoleta** (☎ 645-1987; Plaza Pedro Anzures; admission US$1.35; ☟ 9:30-11:30am & 2:30-4:30pm Mon-Fri) was established by the Franciscan Order in 1601. It has served not

CENTRAL HIGHLANDS

SUCRE

To Airport
(5.5km)

Parque
Bolívar

Rosenda Villa

Urriolagoitia

Pastor Sáinz

Ayacucho

Moreno

Olta 111

Olañeta

Loa

Colón

Junín

Pilinco

44

12

13

73

Plaza

Tarapaca

Arenales

Estudiantes

Ravelo

58

91

61

48

5

47

53

37

94 83
36

62
9 25

31

Av Hernando Siles

17

81

34

57

56
52
6

2

69

71

74

Plaza 25
de Mayo

33

Plazuela
Zudáñez

50

84

18

60

46

88

10

23

26

95

40

77

79

67

68

78

86
45
85
49
19

80

La Paz

Plaza

28

1

Azurduy

54

32

89
43
92

Bolívar

Ayarda

Pérez

27

To La Glorieta (7km);
Potosí (162km)

To Teatro al Aire
Libre (350 m)

Nicolás Ortiz

Bustillos

INFORMATION
Academia Latinoamericano de
  Español...1 D4
Alliance Française............................2 D3
Banco de Santa Cruz (ATM).............3 E3
Banco Nacional de Bolivia (ATM)......4 E3
Brazilian Consulate..........................5 C2
Casa de Cambio Ambar....................6 D3
Casa de Cambio El Arca...................7 E3
Centro Boliviano-Americano.............8 F5
Cybercafé Samael............................9 D3
Dr Gaston Delgadillo......................10 C4
Entel Office...................................11 E2
German Consulate..........................12 B1
Immigration...................................13 A2
Instituto Cultural Boliviano Alemán
  (ICBA)..14 E4
Instituto Geográfico Militar............15 E2
Internet 2000.............................(see 6)
Lavandería Laverap........................16 E4
Lavandería LG...............................17 D1
Municipal Tourist Office.................18 C4
Officina Universitario de Turismo...19 D4
Peruvian Consulate........................20 E5
SurAndes...................................(see 77)
Unidad Departamental de Turismo.21 C4

CENTRAL HIGHLANDS

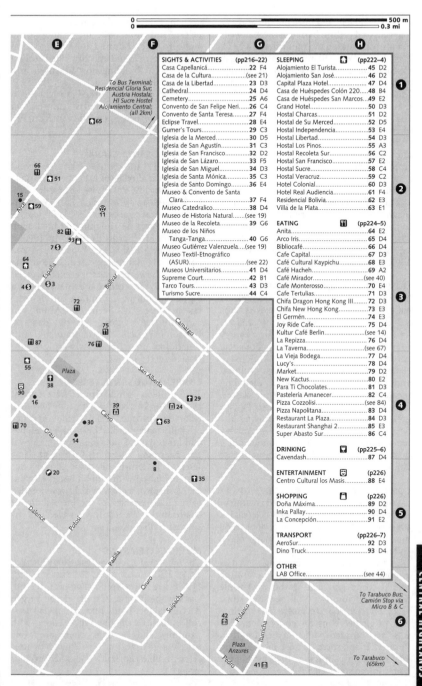

0 ⌷⌷⌷⌷⌷⌷⌷⌷⌷⌷⌷⌷⌷⌷⌷ **500 m**
0 ⌷⌷⌷⌷⌷⌷⌷⌷⌷⌷⌷⌷⌷⌷⌷ **0.3 mi**

SIGHTS & ACTIVITIES	(pp216–22)
Casa Capellanicá	22 F4
Casa de la Cultura	(see 21)
Casa de la Libertad	23 D3
Cathedral	24 D4
Cemetery	25 A6
Convento de San Felipe Neri	26 C4
Convento de Santa Teresa	27 F4
Eclipse Travel	28 E4
Gumer's Tours	29 C3
Iglesia de la Merced	30 D5
Iglesia de San Agustín	31 C3
Iglesia de San Francisco	32 D2
Iglesia de San Lázaro	33 F5
Iglesia de San Miguel	34 D3
Iglesia de Santa Mónica	35 C3
Iglesia de Santo Domingo	36 E4
Museo & Convento de Santa Clara	37 F4
Museo Catedralico	38 D4
Museo de Historia Natural	(see 19)
Museo de la Recoleta	39 G6
Museo de los Niños Tanga-Tanga	40 G6
Museo Gutiérrez Valenzuela	(see 19)
Museo Textil-Etnográfico (ASUR)	(see 22)
Museos Universitarios	41 D4
Supreme Court	42 B1
Tarco Tours	43 D3
Turismo Sucre	44 C4

SLEEPING	(pp222–4)
Alojamiento El Turista	45 D2
Alojamiento San José	46 D2
Capital Plaza Hotel	47 D4
Casa de Huéspedes Colón 220	48 B4
Casa de Huéspedes San Marcos	49 E2
Grand Hotel	50 D3
Hostal Charcas	51 D2
Hostal de Su Merced	52 D5
Hostal Independencia	53 E4
Hostal Libertad	54 D3
Hostal Los Pinos	55 A3
Hostal Recoleta Sur	56 C2
Hostal San Francisco	57 E2
Hostal Sucre	58 C4
Hostal Veracruz	59 C2
Hotel Colonial	60 D3
Hotel Real Audiencia	61 F4
Residencial Bolivia	62 E3
Villa de la Plata	63 E1

EATING	(pp224–5)
Anita	64 E2
Arco Iris	65 D4
Bibliocafé	66 D4
Cafe Capital	67 D4
Café Cultural Kaypichu	68 E3
Café Hachem	69 A2
Café Mirador	(see 40)
Cafe Monterosso	70 E4
Cafe Tertulias	71 D3
Chifa Dragon Hong Kong III	72 D3
Chifa New Hong Kong	73 E3
El Germén	74 E3
Joy Ride Cafe	75 D4
Kultur Café Berlin	(see 14)
La Repizza	76 D4
La Taverna	(see 67)
La Vieja Bodega	77 D4
Lucy's	78 D4
Market	79 D2
New Kactus	80 E2
Para Ti Chocolates	81 D3
Pastelería Amanecer	82 C4
Pizza Cozzolisi	(see 84)
Pizza Napolitana	83 D4
Restaurant La Plaza	84 D3
Restaurant Shanghai 2	85 E3
Super Abasto Sur	86 C4

DRINKING	(pp225–6)
Cavendash	87 D4

ENTERTAINMENT	(p226)
Centro Cultural los Masis	88 E4

SHOPPING	(p226)
Doña Máxima	89 D2
Inka Pallay	90 D4
La Concepción	91 E2

TRANSPORT	(pp226–7)
AeroSur	92 D3
Dino Truck	93 D4

OTHER	
LAB Office	(see 44)

To Bus Terminal;
Residencial Gloria Sur;
Austria Hostala;
HI Sucre Hostel
Alojamiento Central;
(all 2km)

To Tarabuco Bus;
Camión Stop via
Micro B & C

To Tarabuco
(65km)

CENTRAL HIGHLANDS

only as a convent and museum but also as a barracks and prison. In one of the stairwells is a plaque marking the spot where, in 1828, President D Pedro Blanco was assassinated. Outside are courtyard gardens brimming with color and the renowned Cedro Milenario – the ancient cedar – a huge tree that was once even larger than its current size. It is the only remnant of the cedars that were once abundant around Sucre.

The museum is worthwhile for its anonymous sculptures and paintings from the 16th to 20th centuries, including numerous interpretations of St Francis of Assisi.

The highlight is the church choir and its magnificent wooden carvings dating back to the 1870s, each one intricate and unique. They represent the Franciscan, Jesuit and Japanese martyrs who were crucified in 1595 in Nagasaki, Japan.

MUSEO DE LOS NIÑOS TANGA-TANGA

Near La Recoleta, the interactive children's **museum** (☎ 644-0299; Plaza La Recoleta; admission adult/child US$1/0.65; ☼ 9am-noon & 2:30-6pm Tue-Sun) focuses on renewable energy sources. Highlights include the botanical gardens and explanations of Bolivian ecology. The museum also hosts cultural and environmental programs, including theater performances and ceramic classes. The attached Café Mirador (p224) is a great place to relax while enjoying the best view in town. The adjacent Ananay handicrafts shop (p226) sells unique high-quality *artesanías*, including especially cute children's clothing.

CONVENTO DE SAN FELIPE NERI

A visit to the bell tower and tiled rooftop of the **San Felipe Neri convent** (☎ 645-4333; Ortiz 165; admission US$1.35; ☼ 4-6pm Mon-Fri, Sat in high season) more than explains Sucre's nickname of the 'White City of the Americas'.

In the days when the building served as a monastery, asceticism didn't prevent the monks from appreciating the view while meditating; you can still see the stone seats on the roof terraces. The church was originally constructed of stone but was later covered with a layer of stucco. Poinsettias and roses fill the courtyard, and an interesting painting of the Last Supper hangs in the stairwell.

In the catacombs there are tunnels where priests and nuns once met clandestinely and also where, during times of political unrest, guerrillas hid and circulated around the city. The building now functions as a parochial school.

Visitors may be asked to check in with the university tourist information office and procure a guide (free but tip suggested).

MUSEO DE SANTA CLARA

Located in the Santa Clara Convent the **museum of religious art** (☎ 645-2295; Calvo 212; admission US$0.65; ☼ 9am-noon & 2-6pm Mon-Fri, 9:30am-noon Sat), founded in 1639, contains several works by Bolivian master Melchor Pérez de Holguín and his Italian instructor, Bernardo de Bitti. In 1985 it was robbed and several paintings and gold ornaments disappeared. One of the canvases, however, was apparently deemed too large to carry off, so the thieves sliced a big chunk out of the middle and left the rest hanging – it's been restored but you can still see evidence of the damage. Guides may also demonstrate the still-functional pipe organ, which was fabricated in 1664.

CONVENTO DE SANTA TERESA

The brilliant white **Santa Teresa convent** (☎ 645-1986; San Alberto near Potosí; ☼ 10am-noon) belongs to an order of cloistered nuns. They sell homemade candied oranges, apples, figs and limes daily. Don't miss strolling down the charming adjacent **Callejón de Santa Teresa**, a lantern-lit alleyway. It was once partially paved with human bones laid out in the shape of a cross, which was intended to remind passersby of the inevitability of death. In the 1960s it was repaved with its current cobbles.

MUSEO ECLESIASTICO

The renovated eclesiastical **museum** (Caterdralico; ☎ 645-2257; entrance at Ortiz 61; admission US$1.25; 10am-noon & 3-5pm Mon-Fri, 10am-noon Sat, mass 8am Sun), beside the Capilla de la Virgen de Guadalupe, holds one of Bolivia's best collections of religious relics. Along with paintings and carvings, there are some priceless gold and silver religious articles set with rubies, emeralds and other precious stones.

IGLESIA DE SAN FRANCISCO

The **San Francisco church** (☎ 645-1853; Ravelo 1 at Arce; ☼ 7-9am & 4-7pm, for Mass Sat & Sun) was established in 1538 by Francisco de Aroca soon after the founding of La Plata. It began as a makeshift structure; the current church wasn't completed until 1581. In 1809, when the struggle for Bolivian independence got under way, a law passed by Mariscal Sucre transferred San Francisco's religious com-munity to La Paz and turned the building over to the army, to be used as a military garrison, market and customs hall. In 1838 the top floor collapsed, but it was rebuilt and later used as a military bunkhouse. It wasn't re-consecrated until 1925.

Architecturally, San Francisco's most interesting feature is its *mudéjar* ceiling. In the belfry is the Campana de la Libertad, Bolivia's Liberty Bell, which called patriots to revolution in 1825.

IGLESIA DE SANTA MÓNICA

The mestizo-style **Santa Mónica church** (Junín 601 at Arenales) was begun in 1574 and was originally intended to serve as a monastery for the Ermitañas de San Agustín. However the order ran into financial difficulties in the early 1590s, eventually resulting in its closure and conversion into a Jesuit school. The interior is adorned with *mestizo*-tradition carvings of seashells, animals and human figures; the ceiling features impressive woodwork; and the courtyard is one of the city's finest, with lawns and a variety of semitropical plants. The church now serves as a civic auditorium and is only open to the public only during special events.

IGLESIA DE SAN MIGUEL

Built between 1612 and 1621, the **San Miguel church** (☎ 645-1026; Arenales 10; ☼ 11:30am-noon Mon-Fri) reflects *mudéjar* influences, mainly in the arched galleries around the courtyard and the Doric columns supporting the choir. Originally a Jesuit church, it was rededicated when the order was expelled from Bolivia. Highlights include the painted ceiling, the silver altar and several period sculptures and paintings. The interior is open for Mass on weekends; the dress code excludes short sleeves, short skirts and shorts.

IGLESIA DE SANTO DOMINGO

The Baroque-style **Santo Domingo church** (☎ 645-1483; Bolívar 13) was constructed in the mid-16th century by the Dominican order. During the fight for Bolivian independence, the Spanish crown forced the church to liquidate its gold and silver in order to pay for the war effort. After independence, it was transformed into the official residence of the governor, and was also used as a post office. The building is now part of the University's Junín College. It contains a superb wooden carving of Christ.

IGLESIA DE SAN LÁZARO

The 1544 **San Lázaro church** (☎ 645-1448; Calvo 404; ☼ Mass 7am) was the first church in the historic Audiencia de Charcas. The original building was constructed of simple adobe brick and covered with a thatched roof, but it has been thoroughly reworked. Items of note include the original silverwork on the altar and several paintings attributed to Zurbarán, of the Polanco school.

MUSEOS UNIVERSITARIOS

The university's trio of **museums** (☎ 645-3285; Bolívar 698; admission US$1.35; ☼ 8:30am-noon & 2-6pm Mon-Fri; 9am-noon & 3-6pm Sat) are also worth a look:

Museo de Arte Virreinal Charcas occupies a home with 21 large rooms. It houses Bolivia's best-known works of art, including some by Holguín, Padilla, Gamarra and Villavicencio. There's also a collection of ornate furniture that was handcrafted by the Indians of the Jesuit missions.

Museo Antropológico contains separate exhibits dealing with folklore, archaeology and ethnography. Highlights include mummies, skulls and artifacts from Bolivia's eastern jungles. There's also an array of pottery, tools and textiles.

Museo de Arte Moderna features excellent examples of modern Bolivian painting and sculpture, as well as pieces from around Latin America. Don't miss the handcrafted *charangos* by Bolivian artist and musician Mauro Núñez, and the section devoted to indigenous art.

CEMETERY

The enthusiasm surrounding Sucre's **cemetery** (admission free; ☼ 8:30am-noon & 2-5:30pm) seems disproportionate to what's there. There are some arches carved from poplar trees, as well as unkempt gardens and the mausoleums of wealthy colonial families, but it's a mystery why it should inspire such local fervor. To enliven the experience, visit on a weekend when it's jam-packed with families, or hire one of the enthusiastic child guides for a few B$s or a professional for US$1.35. You can walk the eight blocks from the plaza south along Junín, or take a taxi or *micro* A.

Courses

Cochabamba has long been the preferred city in Bolivia for Spanish and Quechua classes, but students have discovered that Sucre also has a healthy climate and vibrant atmosphere. The **Instituto Cultural Boliviano Alemán** (ICBA; ☎ /fax 645-2091; www.icba-sucre.edu.bo; Avaroa 326) offers recommended Spanish and salsa lessons. The **Academiá Latinoamericano de Español** (☎ 646-0537; www.latinoschools.com/bolivia; Dalence 109) has a comprehensive program featuring language, dance and cooking lessons, homestay options and volunteer opportunities.

There are plenty of private teachers who provide more personal and equally professional service (US$5 per hour for one-to-one sessions). The **Centro Boliviano-Americano** (p215) gives referrals for private teachers. Recommended teachers include **Sofía Sauma** (☎ 645-1687; fsauma@hotmail.com; Loa 779) and **Margot Macías Machicado** (☎ 642-3567; m_macias_machiado@hotmail.com; Olañeta 345). Both teachers include plenty of practice while visiting sites of interest around the city. The former is currently setting up the Instituto Charcas, in affiliation with the Hostal de Su Merced.

Tours

Most Sucre tour companies run Sunday excursions to Tarabuco and offer jaunts into the Cordillera de los Frailes. Groups of two or more pay roughly US$20 to US$30 for day-trips and US$50 to US$70 for two-day trips. For unforgettable independent treks, contact the local trekking enthusiasts, Lucho and Dely Loredo (p228).

A unique option is offered by **Joy Ride Bolivia** (☎ 642-5544; www.joyridebol.com; Ortíz 14), which runs motorcycle and ATV tours around Sucre and to Potosí, Uyuni and the Southwest Circuit. For trips on a Honda XR400 motorcycle, you'll pay US$70 per person per day; for a Honda Foreman ES ATV, the price is US$85. Costs include gas, insurance, a guide, protective gear, a T-shirt and a drink if you make it back to the bar.

Mountain-bike tours cost US$12 to US$40 per day or you can rent a bicycle and explore on your own for US$2.50 an hour.

Other agencies offering tours of Sucre and its surroundings include:
Altamira Tours (☎ /fax 645-3525; altamirasucre@hotmail.com; Av del Maestro 50)
Eclipse Travel (☎ /fax 644-3960; eclipse@mara.scr.entelnet.bo; Avaroa 310)
Gumer's Tours (☎ 644-1876; Junín 442)
Sur Andes (☎ /fax 645-2632; surandes@bolivia.com; Ortíz 6)
Tarco Tours (☎ 646-1688; tarco@mara.scr.entelnet.bo; Plaza 25 de Mayo, Multicentro Céspedes)
Turismo Sucre (☎ 645-2936; Bustillos 117) Runs Jatun Yampara artesanía shopping tours.

Festivals & Events

On the evening of September 8, local *campesinos* celebrate the **Fiesta de la Virgen de Guadalupe** with songs and poetry recitations. The following day, they dress in colorful costumes and parade around the main plaza carrying religious images and silver arches.

The **Fiesta de la Empanada**, which occurs several times a year at the Casa de la Libertad, draws chefs and bakers from around the country who compete for prizes with their original *salteña* and *empanada* recipes. The tourist office can provide specific dates. The festivities include folk music, dancing, costumes and artisans selling their handicrafts and weavings. Each September there's the **Festival International de la Cultura** (www.festivalsucre.org). On November 2 **Todos Santos** is celebrated with much fervor.

Sleeping

As Sucre has become more popular with well-heeled visitors, many budget accommodations are converting into more upmarket choices.

BUDGET

Sucre's best-value budget options are *casas de huéspedes* (guesthouses), which offer a distinctive, homey feel. Most places that charge in *bolivianos* rather than US currency are clustered near the market, and along Calles Ravelo and San Alberto.

Casa de Huéspedes San Marcos (☎ 646-2087; Arce 233; US$4, with bath US$5) Clean, quiet rooms plus kitchen and laundry access.

Casa de Huéspedes Colón 220 (☎ 645-5823; colon220@bolivia.com; Colón 220; d with bath & breakfast

US$5-16) A great little place with seven spotless rooms around a garden courtyard. English and German are spoken.

Hostal Charcas (☎ 645-3972; hostalcharcas@ yahoo.com; Ravelo 62; s/d US$5.35/8.50, with bath US$8.50/ 13.50) This long-time favorite continues to be one of Sucre's best-value accommodation options. Showers combine solar and electric heat, so hot water is available around the clock. Rooms are sparkling, breakfast is available, there's a pleasant rooftop area and the friendly staff can provide reliable tourist information.

Villa de la Plata (☎ 642-2577; isis208@yahoo.com; Arce 369; US$4-4.65) Tired of eating out? This *casa de huéspedes* provides long-term language school students and visiting local professionals with modern apartments with spacious living rooms and shared full kitchens. The breezy rooftop terrace is a brilliant place to stargaze. The owner seems to enjoy taking in stray travelers almost as much as she enjoys taking in stray cats.

Residencial Bolivia (☎ 645-4346; San Alberto 42; s/d with breakfast US$4/6.65) Breakfast is not memorable but the hostel is central, friendly and the spacious rooms are clean. It's an old building with a pleasant patio. Alcohol isn't allowed but it's still a Peace Corps favorite.

Hostal Veracruz (☎ 645-1560; Ravelo 158; US$2.65, s/d with bath US$5.35/9) The well-run Veracruz – a tour group favorite – is a renovated, good-value choice with a variety of rooms. Breakfast is available but at an extra cost.

HI Sucre Hostel (☎ 644-0471; www.hostellingboliv ia.org; Loayza 119; dm/d US$3-8/16-20; 🖳) Bolivia's flagship, full-service hostel – the country's swankiest – is clean and friendly and only 100m from the bus station (follow the signs). There's a shared kitchen and some private rooms even have Jacuzzis and cable TV. It's one of Bolivia's few purpose-built hostels and thus has most of the typical hostel amenities.

Alojamiento El Turista (☎ 645-3172; Ravelo 118; US$2) Tucked away behind a quick chicken joint, the friendly Turista is musty and mediocre, but it's good value for strict budgets. Request a room on the top floor – unless you feel the need to be close to the shared bathrooms (which are also open to the general public for a pittance).

Ten minutes from town on *micro* A are a few decent places directly opposite the bus terminal:

Austria Hostal (☎ 645-4202; US$3-6) Has a range of comfy rooms.

Residencial Gloria Sur (☎ 645-2847; US$3)

Alojamiento Central (☎ 645-3935; US$2.50)

Other reader recommendations include:

Hostal San Francisco (☎ 645-2117; hostalsf@cotes .net.bo; Arce 191; r per person with bath & breakfast US$6) A *tranquilo* option with an inviting patio.

Alojamiento San José (☎ 645-1475; Ravelo s/n; s/d US$3.25/5) A basic choice in an interesting old building.

MID-RANGE

Hostal de Su Merced (☎ 644-2706; www.boliviaweb .com/companies/sumerced; Azurduy 16; s/d/tr/ste US$30/ 45/60/60) In true Sucre style, this charming hotel is decorated with antiques and paintings, with rooms around an intimate, tiled courtyard. The hotel opened in 1997 to host a meeting of Andean presidents. Room No 7 is particularly nice and the view from the rooftop terrace is stunning.

Hostal Independencia (☎ 644-2256; jacosta@ mara.scr.entelnet.bo; Calvo 31; s/d/tr/ste US$20-27/30-36/ 40-45/48 with bath, breakfast & cable TV) Part of the crop of new spiffy mid-range places, this hotel features 19th-century architecture and a conference salon that emulates a colonial-era hall of government. The carpeted rooms are arranged around a lush garden courtyard, which adds to the colonial atmosphere.

Hostal Sucre (☎ 645-1411; hosucre@mara.scr .entelnet.bo; Bustillos 113; s/d with bath US$16/22) This pleasant hotel has a lovely antique dining room and a sunny, flower-filled courtyard, but rooms are old fashioned and a bit worn. The service is very attentive and breakfast is available for an extra couple of dollars.

Grand Hotel (☎ 645-2104/2461; grandhot@ mara.scr.entelnet.bo; Arce 61; s/d with bath, breakfast & TV US$13.50/16) A glowingly recommended hotel with comfortable rooms in an old but refurbished building.

Hostal Recoleta Sur (☎ 644-6603; hostalrecoleta@ hotmail.com; Ravelo 205; s/d/tr with bath US$17/25/30) More modern than its competition, this hotel offers the usual conveniences.

Hostal Libertad (☎ 645-3101; fax 646-0128; Arce 99; s/d/ste with bath & cable TV US$15/18/22) One block off the plaza, this modern hotel offers telephones, swanky pipe music and *frigobars*.

The spacious suite with huge wraparound windows and lots of light is perfect for families but suffers from traffic noise.

Hostal Los Pinos (☎ 645-4403; h_pinos@cotes .net.bo; Colón 502; s/d with bath, breakfast & cable TV US$13/17) For a quiet retreat, check out this homey place on the outer edge of town. It features spacious, sunny rooms, a beautiful courtyard and an overgrown garden.

Hotel Colonial (☎ 645-4709; northwest side of Plaza 25 de Mayo; s/d/tr/ste US$15/20/23/30) The carpeted suites and rooftop terrace overlook the plaza, and the interior fireplace keeps things toasty in the foyer. The service is good and the hotel caters mostly to a young Bolivian business clientele.

TOP END

Capital Plaza Hotel (☎ 642-2999; www.capitalplaza hotel.com; southeast side of Plaza 25 de Mayo; s/d/tr/ste with bath, breakfast & cable TV US$45/55/70/100; 🖳 🖭) Sucre's fanciest option is this elegant, four-star colonial hotel conveniently located on the principal square. The décor is French, the rooms are ample, the service is superb, breakfast is a buffet and the TVs are big-screen.

Hotel Real Audiencia (☎ /fax 646-0823; realaudi encia2000@hotmail.com; Potosí 142; s/d/tr/ste with bath, breakfast & cable TV US$40/50/60/80; 🖭) A modern, red-carpet, business-travel favorite. Bonuses include a sauna and Turkish baths, good views and good-value executive suites.

Eating

Sucre has a pleasant variety of quality restaurants and is a great place to spend time lolling around cafés while observing Bolivian university life.

CAFÉS

Good *salteñerías* include **Anita** (Siles at Arce) and **Lucy's** (Grau near Bolívar). Thanks to Sucre's status as Bolivia's chocolate capital, there are plenty of shops that cater to sweet tooths.

Joy Ride Café (Ortíz 14; 🕓 7:30am-late Mon-Fri, 9am-late Sat & Sun; mains US$2-5) Dutch-run bar, café and cultural space with live music and a book exchange. The tunes rock and the outback patio is a super hangout. There are plenty of imported beers and deli fixings that you're unlikely find elsewhere in South America. After-hours on weekends, expect lots of table dancing.

Café Mirador (Plaza la Recoleta; 🕓 9am-7pm Tue-Sun; mains US$1.50-3) The Museo de los Niños Tanga-Tanga's café (p220) overlooks a botanical garden that exhibits a range of foliage from around the country. The panoramic views are a sunset treat and worth the hike up the hill, and it's a sweet place to linger over juice, sandwiches, cocktails or the rich desserts.

Bibliocafé (Ortiz 50; 🕓 closed Mon; set lunch US$2-3, mains US$1-3.50) The dark but cozy atmosphere combined with 1980s and 1990s pop hits and stacks of *Geo* and *Der Spiegel* magazines make this place a hit with travelers. The pasta dishes – which include veggie options – are recommended, as are the sandwiches, Greek salads, and sweet and savory crêpes. It gets crowded, so show up early.

Café Tertulias (N side of Plaza 25 de Mayo; mains US$2-3) Writers, artists and journalists convene at this intimate hangout for chats over hearty food, principally pizza, salads and lasagna. Service can lag, but watching the people on the plaza is entertaining.

Café Hacheh (Sainz 233; 🕓 10am-1am; mains US$1-1) The café at this art gallery and cultural center is open primarily when school is in session. During the school year it often hosts live music and dancing. Edible specialties include sandwiches, coffee and fruit juice.

Kultur Café Berlin (Avaroa 340; 🕓 8am-midnight Mon-Sat; mains US$1-3) Affiliated with the ICBA, this café functions as a pub with strong coffee, draft beer, snacks and set lunches. Try the *papas rellenas* (spicy filled potatoes).

Café Capital (Arce at Arenales) This café is open early for *salteñas*, coffee, tea, juice and *licuados*.

Para Ti Chocolates (Arenales & Arce) Bolivian-made Breick bonbons are only the tip of the iceberg at this cacao-lover's dream shop.

QUICK EATS

For back-to-basics Bolivian, check the quick chicken-and-chips shops along Hernando Siles between Tarapaca and Junín.

Pastelería Amanecer (off Junín btwn Colón & Olañeta) Tucked away in a dead-end alley behind the police station, this petite, four-table non-profit bakery has delightful homemade goodies, breakfast, coffee and fresh juices. Proceeds benefit local children's projects.

RESTAURANTS

Café Monterosso (Bolívar 426; ☉ from 7pm; set dinner US$4) Intimate and candlelit with Carnaval masks on the walls, this place is romantic but casual. The owner is your waiter and he also makes the toothsome homemade pasta. The nightly set dinner deal attracts a loyal crowd.

La Taverna (Arce 835; mains US$1.50-4) Alliance Française's lively restaurant serves a mean ratatouille, as well as quiche Lorraine, coq au vin and other Continental favorites. Save room for the cheese plates and sinful desserts. There's a good wine selection and it can get crowded on weekends when there's live music and a small cover charge.

La Repizza (☎ 645-1506; Ortíz 78; set lunch US$1.50, mains US$2-4) Popular for its stone-baked pizzas, *milanesas*, *pacumutus* and pasta dishes which include vegetarian lasagna. The four-course *almuerzos* are a favorite with university students; it's a good place to meet them over cocktails and live music on Friday and Saturday nights.

La Vieja Bodega (Ortíiz near Grau; set lunch US$2, mains US$2-4) A warm pub with five-course *almuerzos*, fondue, salads and lasagna.

Restaurant La Plaza (southeast side of Plaza 25 de Mayo; mains US$2-4) The mostly meat-based meals are filling and the outdoor balconies are a great place for a beer on a lethargic Sunday afternoon.

Pizza Napolitana (southeast side of 25 de Mayo; set lunch US$3, pizza US$2-4) Enjoy US and British tunes over an (undercooked) pizza, pasta or ice-cream sundae at this popular student hangout. The meal deals are good value but drinks and coffee are a bit on the expensive side.

Arco Iris (Ortíz 42; mains US$2-5) Follow the rainbow to the Swiss pot of *roeschti* (hash browns), fondue and chocolate mousse. There's always veggie options and occasionally live music and dancing.

New Kactus (☎ 645-2788; España 176; mains US$2-4) Another pizza – as well as pasta, chicken and even ribs – spot. Kactus serves a wicked steak with baked potato and has a pool table, large-screen TV, bar, disco and other trendy amenities.

Pizza Cozzolisi (☎ 644-1720; SE side of Plaza 25 de Mayo; pizzas US$2-5) Bolivia's most reliable pizza chain also delivers.

Chifa New Hong Kong (☎ 644-1776; San Alberto 242; mains US$1-2.50) An expensive but good Chinese choice.

MSG lovers will appreciate the filling Chinese *almuerzos* at **Chifa Dragon Hong Kong III** (northeast side of Plaza 25 de Mayo; lunch US$1, mains US$1.25-2.50) and **Restaurant Shanghai 2** (Calvo btwn España & Bolívar; lunch US$1, mains US$1-$2.50), which both dish out Chinese and Bolivian favorites in a relatively clean environment.

Café Cultural Kaypichu (San Alberto 168; ☉ 7am-2pm & 5-9pm Tue-Sun; set lunch US$1.50, mains US$1.50-3) One of the country's best vegetarian options (best bathrooms too) is ultra-popular and run by a pair of upbeat Bolivians. For breakfast (available all day), they offer muesli, granola, yogurt and fresh fruit; lunch is a generous set *almuerzo* and dinners consists of á la carte options from pizza and pasta to soups and salads. They also host cultural events and sell a rotating assortment of fair-trade handicrafts from around the country.

El Germén (San Alberto 231; ☉ 8am-10pm Mon-Sat; set lunch US$1.50) The other candidate for Bolivia's best vegetarian kitchen serves up creative, well-spiced (is that real curry?) *almuerzos*, German-style gateaux and pastries in a bright and airy setting. Á la carte dinner highlights include pizza and veggie lasagna. There's also a German- and English-language book exchange.

SELF-CATERING

The **market** (☉ 7am-7:30pm Mon-Sat; Sun morning only) is home to some gastronomic highlights. Don't miss the fresh juices and fruit salads – they are among the best in the country. You'll have to search for the correct stalls, which are tucked in the northeast corner of the ground floor. Try *jugo de tumbo* (juice of unripe yellow passion fruit) or any combination of melon, guava, pomelo, strawberry, papaya, banana, orange, lime etc. The vendors and their blenders always come up with something indescribably delicious. Upstairs, you'll find good, filling, cheap meals in unusually sanitary conditions (for a market, anyway). For breakfast, tuck into a juicy *salteña* or *pastel* (pastry) and a glass of *api* for as little as US$0.25.

Super Abasto Sur (Bustillos at Colón) is the best-stocked central grocery store.

Drinking

Most of the bars and restaurants on or near the plaza have live music or *peñas* on weekends (cover charge around US$1) starting around 8pm. **Cavendash** (Dalence 170) is a favorite expat watering hole. For discos and karaoke, check Calle España just up from the plaza. The best places in town tend to move and change names frequently. Ask cabbies for a lift to the current hip places, which are usually out of the town center.

Entertainment

The **Centro Cultural los Masis** (☎ 645-3403; Bolívar 561; ☺ 10am-noon & 3:30-9pm Mon-Fri) hosts concerts and other cultural events, and has a small museum of local musical instruments. It also offers Quechua classes.

Southeast of the center, the **Teatro al Aire Libre** is a wonderful outdoor venue for musical and other performances. **Teatro Gran Mariscal de Ayacucho** (Plaza Pizarro), is an opulent old opera house. The tourist office and the Casa de la Cultura (p215) both distribute a monthly calendar of events. Keep an eye out for the municipal ballet and folkloric dance performances.

Shopping

The best place to learn about traditional local weavings is the ASUR Museo Textil-Etnografico (p217). Prices are steep by Bolivian standards, but the items are high quality and fair trade is maintained. Plan on US$100 to US$200 for a fine Jalq'a or Candelaria weaving. Alternatively, check out the little shop next door, which sells textiles and other traditional items for considerably less.

Inca Pallay (☎ 646-1936; incapallay@cotesnet.bo; Bolívar 682) This weaver's and artisan's cooperative has an impressive array of high-quality handmade crafts, not all from the Sucre area. The co-op also has another location in Tarabuco, which is only open on Sundays.

Ananay (☎ 644-0299; www.bolivianhandicrafts.com; Museo de los Niños Tanga-Tanga, Plaza la Recoleta) This boutique features export-quality crafts, home furnishings and adorable children's clothing. It's not cheap, but the designs are unique and the quality is high.

Doña Máxima (Junín 411, Centro Comercial Guadalupe No 8) After some bargaining, you'll find excellent deals on less decorative and more utilitarian Candelaria and Jalq'a weavings in this jam-packed cubbyhole.

Turismo Sucre (p222) organizes **Jatun Yampara** shopping tours (half/full day US$10/18) to textile- and ceramic-producing villages in the Tarabuco region.

Some of Bolivia's best *charango* makers are based around Sucre and several shops sell local pieces. Learning to play one is another matter, but some artisans may even throw in a lesson or two. Try the shops at Calle Junín 1190 and Destacamento 59.

Bolivia's best wines are available at the retail shop of **La Concepción** (☎ 644-2875; España at Camargo).

Getting There & Away

AIR

The domestic departure tax is US$1.35. **Aero-Sur** (☎ 645-4895; Arenales 31) and **LAB** (☎ 691-3181; Bustillos 121) have flights (some direct, some not) to most major cities. Note that when it's cloudy or raining Sucre's foggy mountain-girded airport resists the best efforts of the even most experienced pilot, so in inclement weather don't traipse out to the airport until confiming your flight with the airline. Detoured flights can turn a quick hop to Santa Cruz into a full-day aerial tour of the country. **TAM** (Airport ☎ 645-1310, Office ☎ 646-0944) flies on Friday to Cochabamba and Santa Cruz and on Sunday to La Paz.

BUS & SHARED TAXI

The full-service bus terminal (2km northeast of center) is not within easy walking distance of the center. It's accessed by *micro* A or 3 from along Calle España, but the *micros* are too crowded for lots of luggage. Unless you're headed for Potosí, it's wise to book long-distance buses a day in advance, in order to reserve a good seat. To save a trip to the bus station, book at the **Trans Real** office (Arce 95 at San Alberto).

Numerous daily buses run to Cocha-bamba (US$7 to US$10, 10 to 12 hours), which all depart at around 6pm or 7pm; several of these continue on to Santa Cruz (US$7 to US$10, 15 to 20 hours). Some buses follow the rough but scenic route via Samaipata rather than going through Cochabamba.

Lots of *flotas* have morning and evening departures for La Paz (US$7 to US$10, 14 to 16 hours) via Oruro (US$7.50, 12 hours). Numerous companies leave for Potosí (US$2.25, three hours) around 7am and at 5pm; some persevere to Tarija (US$9.50,

15 hours), Oruro and Villazón. You'll find daily connections to Uyuni (US$6, 10 to 12 hours), but they normally entail changing buses at Potosí.

Alternatively, you can take a shared taxi (US$4 per person with four people, 2½ hours), which is quicker, to Potosí. Most hotels can help arrange shared taxis. Try **Expreso Turismo Global** (☎ 642-5125) or **Auto Expreso Infinito del Sur** (☎ 642-2277).

Whenever the road is passable, Flota Chaqueño does the beautiful-but-brutal trip to Camiri (US$13.50, 18 hours), with connections to the Argentine border at Yacuiba.

TRAIN
Sucre's charming **train station** (☎ 644-0751) is no longer in use, though there has been talk of implementing a tourist-class rail service between Sucre and Potosí. Don't hold your breath.

Getting Around
TO/FROM THE AIRPORT
The airport, 9km northwest of town, is accessed by *micro* 1 or F (allow an hour to be safe) from Av Hernando Siles, by the *banderita blanca* taxi trufi from Av España or by taxi (negotiable US$2 to US$3.50).

BUS & MICRO
Lots of buses and *micros* (US$0.15) ply circuitous routes around the city's one-way streets, and all seem to congregate at or near the market between runs; they're usually crowded, but fortunately, Sucre is a town of short distances. The most useful routes are those that climb the steep Av Grau hill to the Recoleta, and *micro* A, which serves the main bus terminal.

RENTAL CAR
Imbex (☎ 646-1222; www.rentacarvillegas.entelnet.bo; Serrano 165) has 4WDs from US$29 a day.

TAXI
Taxis between any two points around the center, including the bus terminal, charge US$0.40 for up to three people, a bit more after midnight.

TARABUCO
elevation 3200m
This small, predominantly indigenous village, 65km southeast of Sucre via a good

paved road, enjoys a mild climate, just a bit cooler than Sucre's. Most *tarabuqueños* are involved in agriculture or textiles, and the textiles produced in the region are some of the most renowned in all of Bolivia. Tarabuco is best known for its Sunday market.

Sunday market
Although many visitors may miss the annual Phujllay celebrations in March (see below), you will want to catch Tarabuco's colorful, sprawling **Sunday market**, which features high-quality *artesanía*: pullovers, *charangos*, coca pouches, ponchos and weavings that feature geometric and zoomorphic designs.

However, much of the work for sale is not local, so don't expect many bargains. The colorful wares laid out in stalls around the plaza and on the side streets lend a festive and light-hearted atmosphere. Strolling, *charango*-playing *campesinos* model their local dress: the men wear distinctive *monteras* (also known as *morriones*), which are leather hats patterned after those worn by the *conquistadores*. You may also want to seek out the snake-oil vendors in the central market, who proffer the universal curative powers of leftover bits of snakes, dried starfish and Toucan beaks. This is one of the only places where you can still see and participate in *trueque* (barter) exchanges.

This scene draws independent, organized, Bolivian and foreign tourists. Even well-bargained prices tend to be high, and sales tactics are somewhat less than passive. Try and appreciate the skill and quality, even when it's being shoved up your nose! If it's all too overwhelming, you may want to visit other weaving villages in the area, such as Candelaria, southeast of Tarabuco, or Ravelo and Potolo, northwest of Sucre.

On market days the **Centro Artesanal Inca Pallay** (Murillo 25, near the market) sells an array of local weavings and serves local *comida* in the tourist-friendly restaurant.

Festivals & Events
On March 12, 1816, Tarabuco was the site of the Battle of Jumbati, in which the villagers defended themselves under the leadership of a woman, Doña Juana Azurduy de Padilla, and liberated the town from Spanish forces. In commemoration of the event the village stages **Phujllay** ('amusement' or 'play' in Quechua)

on the second or third weekend of March, when over 60 surrounding communities turn up in local costume. The celebration begins with a Quechua Mass and procession followed by the **Pukhara** ceremony, a Bolivian version of Thanksgiving. Folkloric dancers and musicians perform throughout the two-day weekend fiesta. It's one of Bolivia's largest festivals and is worth attending.

The smaller local celebration of **La Virgen de Rosario** takes place in October and features bullfights, Masses and parades.

Sleeping & Eating
During Phujllay accommodations fill up quickly, so you may want to hedge your bets and carry camping gear. The nicest digs are at **El Alojamiento** (on main plaza; US$2), which is run by a friendly woman. Half a block north of the plaza, **Alojamiento Florida** (☎ 691-2233; Potosí s/n; US$1.35), has shabby rooms and dirty communal facilities. The attached restaurant is a bit cleaner.

The plaza also has a couple of basic restaurants. Meals of *chorizo*, soup and *charque kan* are available from street stalls during market hours.

Getting There & Away
Sucre travel agencies offer bilingual guided tours to Tarabuco (about US$12 per person) on Sunday, but it's just as easy to take a charter bus (US$2.65 round-trip, 1½ hours each way), which leave from the center or pick up clients at their hotels around 7am. From Tarabuco, the buses return to Sucre anytime between 1pm and 3pm.

Alternatively, *micros* (US$0.75; 2½ hours) and *camiones* leave when full from Av de las Américas in Sucre on Sunday between 6:30am and 9:30am. Either walk from the center or take *micros* B or C. Transport returning to Sucre departs from the main plaza in Tarabuco, and leaves anytime between 11am and 3:30pm.

CORDILLERA DE LOS FRAILES
The imposing serrated ridge forming Sucre's backdrop creates a formidable barrier between the departments of Chuquisaca and Potosí.

Orientation
A recommended six-day circuit begins at Chataquila, on the ridge above Punilla, 25km northwest of Sucre. It begins with a side trip to Incamachay, then loops through Chaunaca, the Cráter de Maragua, the Termas de Talula and Quila Quila, taking in several Cordillera highlights before returning to Sucre from the south. Basic staples are available in Chaunaca. The Termas de Talula have now been damaged by flooding, but the semi-ghost town of Quila Quila remains charming. Note that no meals or formal accommodations are available anywhere in the Cordillera de los Frailes.

MAPS
There are numerous walking routes through the Cordillera de los Frailes, some of which are marked on the 1:50,000 topo sheets *Sucre*, sheet 6536-IV, and *Estancia Chaunaca*, sheet 6537-III.

Tours
Several Sucre travel agencies offer quick jaunts into the Cordillera – for example, a two-day circuit from Chataquila to Incamachay and Chaunaca. For an extended trip however, it's less expensive and more enjoyable to hire a private guide, who will allow you to customize your trip. Highly recommended is the Sucre-based guide **Lucho Loredo** (☎ 642-0752; turismo_lyd@hotmail.com; Comarapa 127, Barrio Petrolero, Sucre) who speaks Quechua and Spanish and is familiar with local customs, traditions and life in the *campo*. His family charges US$25 per person per day and can organize a range of customized itineraries, with meals and either camping or overnighting in homes or village schools.

Several Sucre travel agencies also arrange excursions – try **Sur Andes** (☎ /fax 645-2632; Ortíz 6) or **Eclipse Travel** (☎ /fax 644-3960; eclipse@mara.scr .entelnet.bo; Avaroa 310).

Getting There & Away
A couple of *camiones* leave Sucre for Potolo (US$1, three hours) via Punilla and Chataquila (US$0.65, two hours) daily between 10am and 11am from the Yuraj Yuraj *camión* terminal on the road to the airport. To connect with them, take *micro* 1 or *trufi* 1 from the corner of Hernando Siles and Loa. On weekends, *camiones* to Quila Quila and/or Talula (US$0.65, two hours) depart between 6am and 8am from Sucre's Barrio Aranjuez, returning the afternoon of the same day.

Hiking

The best way to see this region is on foot, but trekking on your own isn't recommended and a local guide will be indispensable when it comes to route-finding and communicating with the Quechua-speaking *campesinos*. A guide will also help to avoid misunderstandings, minimize your impact and help you get a better feeling for the local culture.

CHATAQUILA TO CHAUNACA

On the rocky ridge top at **Chataquila** is a lovely stone chapel dedicated to the Virgen de Chataquila, a Virgin-shaped stone that has been dressed in a gown and placed on the altar.

From Chataquila look around on the south side of the road for an obvious notch in the rock, which leads into a lovely pre-Hispanic route that descends steeply for 6km to the village of **Chaunaca** (39km from Sucre). Lots of good paved sections remain and it's easy to follow, but the route involves a couple of difficult scrambles over slides that have blocked the way.

Chaunaca is home to a school, a tiny church and the renovated colonial *hacienda* **Posada Samay Huasi** (☎ 645-2935; samay_huasi@latinmail.com). Very basic supplies are available in an uninspiring hovel along the main road. Guides may organize accommodations in the school, but otherwise try to camp away from the village to avoid disruption in this traditional area. The river banks downstream are ideal for picnics or camping.

INCAMACHAY

A worthwhile day trip from Chataquila leads to the two sets of ancient rock paintings collectively known as Incamachay. At the first major curve on the road west of Chataquila, a rugged track heads north along the ridge. For much of its length the route is flanked by rugged rock formations, but it's relatively easy going until you've almost reached the paintings, where you face a bit of a scramble. The first set, **Uracahuasi** lies well ensconced inside a rock cleft between two stone slabs. A more impressive panel, **Patatoloyo** is 15 minutes further along beneath a rock overhang. Note that these sites are virtually impossible to find without a guide.

From Incamachay, you can either return to Chataquila the way you came or continue downhill for a couple of hours until you strike the road at the **Tomo de Agua** aqueduct, where there's drinking water and a good campsite. From there take the road 6km to the Chataquila–Chaunaca road, where you can either ascend to Chataquila or descend to Chaunaca.

CHAUNACA TO THE CRÁTER DE MARAGUA

To experience some surreal scenery follow the road south from Chaunaca (not the one that continues toward Potolo) for 7km, passing brilliantly colored green-and-violet hillsides into the **Cráter de Maragua**. This unearthly natural formation, sometimes called the Umbligo de Chuquisaca (or Navel of Chuquisaca), features surreal settlements scattered across a red-and-violet crater floor, and bizarre slopes that culminate in the gracefully symmetrical pale green arches of the Serranías de Maragua. It's one of the most bizarre places in all Bolivia. From there you can either head back to Chaunaca or, if you have left early enough, continue to the Talula hot springs (see below).

CRÁTER DE MARAGUA TO TALULA

You can leave the **Cráter de Maragua** either toward the south through **Irupampa** and **Sisipunku** to Purunkilla, or west to Sapallu Khocha or Lajalaja. The latter route will take you over some challenging up-and-down terrain studded with brilliant mica deposits to **Hacienda Humaca**, past some isolated *huellas* (dinosaur tracks), and a lovely oasis between high peaks, with mud ruins, palm trees and the saline Río Khoya Mayu. From Hacienda Humaca, access to the **Termas de Talula**, 5km away, requires two fords of the Río Pilcomayo; it's best to cross in the morning when the water level is at its lowest.

Those who head directly south from Maragua can reach the Thermas de Talula by turning west at Purunkilla and sauntering 4km down the road. No river fords are required.

The Talula hot springs issue into three pools that have temperatures up to 45°C. Camping is possible anywhere in the vicinity, but unfortunately the bathhouse was severely damaged during floods and it may or may not reopen as a public spa.

CORDILLERA DE LOS FRAILES

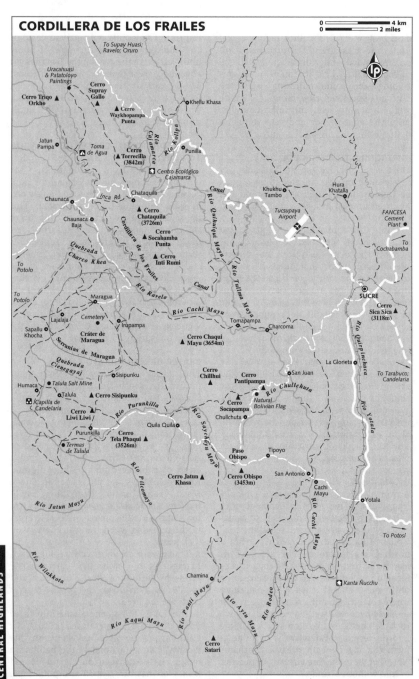

Either way, you should still be able to find some natural pools.

From Talula it's 500m to the constricted passage that conducts the Río Pilcomayo between the steep walls of the Punkurani gorge. When the river is low, you can cross over to the Potosí shore and see the many rock-painting sites above the opposite bank.

TALULA TO SUCRE

From **Talula** the route back to Sucre begins by following the road (which was constructed to serve fewer than a dozen vehicles per week!) back up to Purunkilla From there, it's 5km of well-kept farmland to **Quila Quila** (spelled Quilla Quilla on the topo sheet). This crumbling and bizarrely beautiful ghost village is now being revived by *sureños* exchanging city life for an agricultural lifestyle. There's little of interest here, but the enormous church does occupy an imposing position beneath the dramatic peak of **Cerro Tela Phaqui** (3526m). Soft drinks are sold at one home on the plaza, but no other supplies are available. The only vehicular traffic passes on weekends, when day-trippers travel between Sucre and Talula.

Continuing back toward Sucre, the road climbs through the barren but colorful landscape of red hills and maguey to the pass at the foot of **Cerro Obispo** (3453m). Here, you can turn off along the 12km track through **Tipoyo** and Hacienda Cachi Mayu to the colonial village of **Yotala**, about 16km south of Sucre on the main road. Alternatively, continue another 4km down the road past the well-watered flower-growing village of **Chullchuta**, over the shoulder of **Cerro Pantipampa**. About 2.5km further along, look across the *quebrada* at the bands of red, yellow and green in the hillside, which form a natural Bolivian flag.

From the crest the road drops steeply to **Hacienda San Juan** on the Río Cachi Mayu, where sand is extracted to make cement, then climbs to the plateau for the final – and rather tedious – 11km into Sucre.

POTOLO

The village of Potolo is the origin of some of Bolivia's finest Jalq'a tradition weavings, particularly the renowned red-and-black animal-patterned pieces sold throughout

the Andes and esteemed by experts worldwide. There's infrequent transport from Potolo to Chataquila.

SUPAY HUASI

Among the most interesting rock paintings in the Cordillera de los Frailes are those at Supay Huasi (House of the Devil). These unusual zoomorphic and anthropomorphic images in ochre, white and yellow include a white, long-tailed animal that could be a monkey, a humpbacked llama that bears a remarkable resemblance to a camel, a 12cm two-headed creature that may represent a pair of amorous canines; an ochre-colored 40cm man wearing a sunlike headdress, and several faded geometric figures and designs.

The paintings are a 2½ hour walk upstream from the point where the Río Mama Huasi crosses the Ravelo road, north of Punilla. However, they're almost impossible to find without a local guide.

POTOSÍ

pop 120,000 / elevation 4090m

> I am rich Potosí,
> The treasure of the world...
> And the envy of kings.

Potosí is renowned not only as the world's highest city but also for its silver. Its history and splendor as well as its tragedy and horror is inextricably tied to this precious metal. The legend from the city's first coat of arms (the above quote) wasn't far off the mark, but any city with a mountain of precious minerals in its backyard is certain to attract attention. The city was founded in 1545, following the discovery of ore in silver-rich Cerro Rico, and the Potosí veins quickly proved the world's most prolific – and lucrative.

Potosí blossomed, and toward the end of the 18th century it grew into the largest and wealthiest city in all of Latin America. Silver from Potosí underwrote the Spanish economy – and its monarchs' extravagance – for over two centuries. Even today, anything incredibly lucrative is said to *vale un Potosí* (be worth a Potosí). In fact, in the 1600s this mountain of wealth bestowed its name upon the city of San Luis Potosí in central Mexico, but those diggings, however productive, never did live up to that of its Bolivian namesake.

Visitors to modern Potosí will find remnants of a grand colonial city – ornate churches, monuments, and colonial architecture – in a most unlikely setting. This is truly a Bolivian highlight and is not to be missed.

History

No one is certain how much silver has been extracted from Cerro Rico (the 'rich hill' in Potosí's backdrop) over its four centuries of productivity, but a popular boast was that the Spanish could have constructed a silver bridge to Spain and still had silver left to carry across it. The Spanish monarchs, who personally received 20% of the take, were certainly worth more than a few *pesetas*.

Although the tale of Potosí's origins probably takes a few liberties with the facts, it's a good story. It begins in 1544 when a Peruvian Indian, Diego Huallpa, was tending his llamas. When he noticed that two of the beasts were missing, he set forth to search for them. By nightfall, however, he still hadn't found them and the cold grew fierce, so Diego stopped to build a fire at the foot of the mountain known in Quechua as 'Potojsi' (meaning 'thunder' or 'explosion' in Quechua, although it might also have stemmed from *potoj*, 'the springs'). The fire grew so hot that the very earth beneath it started to melt, and shiny liquid oozed from the ground.

Diego immediately realized he'd run across a commodity for which the Spanish conquerors had an insatiable appetite. Perhaps he also remembered the Inca legend associated with the mountain, which recounted that Inca Huayna Capac had been instructed by a booming voice not to dig in the hill of Potojsi, but to leave the metal alone, because it was intended for others.

At this juncture, accounts of the legend diverge. One version maintains that Diego Huallpa kept his discovery secret, lest he upset the mountain *apus* (spirits). Others relate that he informed a friend, Huanca, of the discovery, and together they formulated a plan to extract the silver themselves. According to the account, the vein proved extremely productive, but a dispute between the partners escalated into a quarrel about the division of profits and

Huanca, now weary of the whole mess, told the Spaniards about the mine.

Whatever the case, the Spanish eventually learned of the enormous wealth buried in the mountain of Potojsi and determined that it warranted immediate attention. On April 1 (according to some sources, April 10), 1545, the Villa Imperial de Carlos V was founded at the foot of Cerro Rico and large-scale excavation began. In the time it takes to say 'Get down there and dig', thousands of Indian slaves were pressed into service and the first of the silver was already headed for Spain.

The work was dangerous, however, and so many Indians died of accidents and silicosis pneumonia that the Spanish imported literally millions of African slaves to augment the labor force.

In order to increase productivity, in 1572 the Viceroy of Toledo instituted the Ley de la Mita, which required all Indian and black slaves over the age of 18 to work in shifts of 12 hours. They would remain underground without seeing the light of day for four months at a time, eating, sleeping and working in the mines. When they emerged from a 'shift', their eyes were covered to prevent damage in the bright sunlight.

Naturally these miners, who came to be known as *mitayos*, didn't last long. Heavy losses were also incurred among those who worked in the *ingenios* (smelting mills), as the silver-smelting process involved mercury. In all, it has been estimated that over the three centuries of colonial rule – 1545 to 1825 – as many as eight million Africans and Indians died from the appalling conditions.

Inside the mines, silver was smelted in small ovens known as *huayrachinas*, which were fueled with wood and the spiky grass *paja brava*. The silver was then transported by llama train to Arica (Chile), along the Camino de Plata, or to Callao (now Lima, Peru) on the Pacific coast. From there, it was carried by ship to Spain, providing spoils for English, Dutch and French freebooters along the way.

In 1672 a mint was established to coin the silver, reservoirs were constructed to provide water for the growing population, and exotic European consumer goods found their way up the llama trails from

TINKU – THE ART OF RITUAL MAYHEM

Native to the northern part of Potosí department, *tinku* fighting ranks as one of the few Bolivian traditions that has yet to be commercialized. This bizarre practice lies deeply rooted in indigenous tradition and is thus often misunderstood by outsiders, who can make little sense of the violent and often grisly spectacle.

Tinku may be best interpreted as a means for *campesinos* to forget the hardships of daily life. Festivities begin with singing and dancing, but participants eventually drink themselves into a stupor. As a result, celebrations may well erupt into drunken mayhem and sometimes violence, as alcoholically charged emotions are unleashed in hostile encounters. While some may claim that these brawls serve to release stress, frustration, anger and grudges, the sense of it all normally escapes any Western spectators.

A *tinku* usually lasts two or three days, when men and women in brightly colored traditional dress hike in from surrounding communities. The hats worn by the men strongly resemble those originally worn by the Spanish *conquistadores*, but are topped Robin-Hood-style with one long, fluorescent feather.

On the first evening, the communities parade through town to the accompaniment of *charangos* and *zampoñas*. Periodically, the revelers halt and form two concentric circles, with women on the inside and the men in the outer circle. The women begin singing a typically repetitious and cacophonous chant while the men run in a circle around them. Suddenly, everyone stops and launches into a powerful stomping dance. Each group is headed by at least one person – normally a man – who uses a whip to urge on any man whom he perceives isn't keeping up with the rhythm and the pace.

This routine may seem harmless enough, except that alcohol plays a significant and controlling role. All of the men and most of the women carry clear plastic bottles filled with *puro* (rubbing alcohol), which is the drink of choice if the intent is to quickly become totally plastered. By nightfall, each participating community retreats to a designated house to drink *chicha* until they pass out.

This excessive imbibing inevitably results in social disorder, and by the second day the drunk participants tend to grow increasingly aggressive. As they roam the streets, they encounter people from other communities with whom they may have some quarrel, either real or imagined. Common complaints include anything from land disputes to extramarital affairs to the theft of farm animals, and may well result in a challenge to fight.

The situation rapidly progresses past yelling and cursing to pushing and shoving, before it turns into a rather mystical – almost choreographed – warfare. Seemingly rhythmically, men strike each other's heads and upper bodies with extended arms (in fact, this has been immortalized in the *tinku* dance, which is frequently performed during Carnaval *entradas* – especially in highly traditional Oruro). To augment the hand-to-hand combat, the fighters may also throw rocks at their opponents, occasionally causing serious injury or death. Any fatalities however, are resignedly considered a blood offering to Pachamama in lieu of a llama sacrifice for the same purpose.

The best known and arguably most violent *tinku* takes place in Macha during the first couple of weeks of May, while the villages of Ocurí and Toracarí, among others, also host *tinkus*.

As you'd imagine, few foreigners aspire to witness this private and often violent tradition, and many people who have attended insist they'd never do it again. For the terminally curious, however, Koala Tours and Altiplano Tours in Potosí conduct culturally sensitive and patently less-than-comfortable – visits to several main *tinku* festivities. Note, however, that if you do go it will be at your own risk. Keep a safe distance from the participants and always remain on the side of the street to avoid being trapped in the crowd. When walking around the village, maintain a low profile, speak in soft tones and ignore any taunting cries of 'gringo'. Also, bear in mind that these traditional people most definitely do not want hordes of foreign tourists gawking at them and snapping photos; avoid photographing individuals without their express permission and do not dance or parade with the groups unless you receive a clear invitation to do so.

Most importantly, keep in mind that some violence can be expected during a *tinku*, especially on the final day.

Arica and Callao. Amid the mania, more than 80 churches were constructed, and Potosí's population grew to nearly 200,000, making it one of the largest cities in the world. One politician of the period put it succinctly: 'Potosí was raised in the pandemonium of greed at the foot of riches discovered by accident'.

As with most boom towns, Potosí's glory was not to last. During the early 19th-century independence struggles in Alto Perú, Potosí was naturally coveted by both sides. The city's many churches were looted, its wealth was removed to Europe or other parts of the Spanish realm and the population dropped to less than 10,000.

At the same time, Cerro Rico, the seemingly inexhaustible mountain of silver, began to play out, and by the time of Bolivian independence in 1825, the mines were already in decline. The mid-19th century drop in silver prices dealt a blow from which Potosí has never completely recovered.

In the present century only the demand for tin has rescued Potosí from obscurity and brought a slow but steady recovery. Zinc and lead have now taken over from tin as Bolivia's major metallic exports. Silver extraction continues only on a small scale, but reminders of the grand colonial city are still evident throughout the city.

The mining reforms of 1952 brought the Pailaviri mine under government control, and mining conditions improved immensely. Most of the Cerro Rico operations, however, are now in the control of miner-owned cooperatives. The government mine has closed, having been plagued by strikes, protests and general dissatisfaction, while the cooperatives continue operating under conditions that have changed shamefully little from the colonial period.

In 1987 Unesco named Potosí a World Heritage Site in recognition of its rich and tragic history and its wealth of colonial architecture.

Orientation

Everything is within easy walking distance, except the mines and the bus station. The lack of oxygen can be disorienting, so take it easy if you are a greenhorn arriving from the flatlands.

MAPS
Glossy city maps (US$0.65) are available at the tourist office, but most tour agencies include a useful city map on the reverse of their brochure. **Instituto Geográfico Militar** (IGM; Chayanta btwn 10 de Abril & Litoral) sells topo sheets of all areas of Potosí department.

Information
EMERGENCY
Tourist police (☎ 625-288)

INTERNET ACCESS
Tuko's (Junín & Bolívar, 3rd fl; ☺ 8am-11pm), Friendly and charges US$0.40 per hour for a fast connection.
Café Internet Candelaria (Ayacucho 5) Open daily.

LAUNDRY
Most hotels can organize laundry services for their guests. Failing that, try **Limpieza La Veloz** (Lanza at Matos), which charges US$1 per kilo.

MEDICAL SERVICES
If you need an English-speaking doctor or new spectacles, visit the **Clinica/Optica Esculapio** (☎ 622-3305; Antofagasta 666) or the **Hospital Daniel Bracamonte** (☎ 622-3900).

MONEY
ATMs are common in the center of town. Lots of businesses along Bolívar, Sucre and in the market change US dollars at reasonable rates. Cash advances are available at **Banco de Crédito** (Bolívar & Sucre) and **Banco Mercantil** (Paseo Blvd).

POST & TELEPHONE
The central **post office** (Lanza & Chuquisaca) has a good postcard shop run by friendly wonderboy Americo. Punto Entels are common around town and Internet phone calls are supposedly 'coming soon'.

TOURIST INFORMATION
Regional tourism office (☎ 622-5288; Ayacucho & Bustillos) Unhelpful.
Information kiosk (Plaza 6 de Agosto) Supposed to be staffed by local tour agencies; biased.

Sights & Activities
Such was the wealth of colonial Potosí that more than 80 churches were constructed here. It's worth visiting the roof of the Convento de San Francisco for a striking

panoramic view. See p240 for details about visiting the cooperative mines with a tour.

CASA REAL DE LA MONEDA

The **Royal Mint** (Ayacucho at Bustillos; admission US$2.65 for mandatory 2-3hr guided tour; ☻ 9am-12:30pm & 3-7pm Tue-Sat, 9am-12:30pm Sun) is Potosí's star attraction and one of South America's finest museums. Potosí's first mint was constructed on the present site of the Casa de Justicia in 1572 under orders from the Viceroy of Toledo. The knockout building, which has been painstakingly restored and occupies an entire block near the cathedral, was built between 1753 and 1773 to control the minting of colonial coins. These coins, which bore the mint mark 'P,' were known as *potosís*.

The building has walls that are more than a meter thick and it has not only functioned as a mint but also done spells as a prison, a fortress and, during the Chaco War, as the headquarters of the Bolivian army. As visitors are ushered into a courtyard from the entrance, they're greeted by the sight of a stone fountain and a mask of Bacchus, hung there in 1865 by Frenchman Eugenio Martin Moulon for reasons known only to him. In fact, this aberration looks more like an escapee from a children's fun fair, but it has become a town icon and, in fact, the Roman god of wine now figures prominently as the de facto patron saint of Potosí!

The museum houses a host of historical treasures. Among them are the first locomotive used in Bolivia and a beautiful salon brimming with religious paintings (lots of blood). In the basement are a couple of still-functional hand-powered minting devices that were in use until 1869, when the minting machines were imported from Philadelphia.

Whatever the outside temperature, wear thermal underwear and several layers of clothing, as the vast dungeon-like spaces in this building never feel the warmth of the sun! English- and French-language tours are occasionally available on request.

CATHEDRAL

Construction of Potosí's **cathedral** (Plaza 10 de Noviembre; half-hr tour US$0.75; ☻ 9:30-10am & 3-5:30pm Mon-Fri, 9:30-10am Sat) was initiated in 1564, officially founded in 1572 and finally completed around 1600. The original building lasted until the early 19th century, when it mostly collapsed. During the reconstruction (1808 to 1838) the original structure gained some neoclassical Greek and Spanish additions.

The interior décor represents some of the finest in Potosí. Note the bases of the interior columns, which still bear colonial-era tiles, the mid-17th century works of sculptor Gaspar de la Cueva titled *Señor de las Ánimas* and *Cristo de la Columna*, and the mausoleum, which holds the remains of colonial notables.

LOS INGENIOS DE LA RIBERA DE VERACRUZ

On the banks (*la ribera*) of the Río Huana Mayu, in the upper Potosí barrios of Cantumarca and San Antonio, are some fine ruined examples of the smelters. These were formerly used to extract silver from the ore hauled out of Cerro Rico. There were originally 82 *ingenios* along 15km of the stream. Some remaining ones date back to the 1570s and were in use until the mid-1800s.

Each *ingenio* consists of a floor penetrated by shallow wells (*buitrones*) where the ore was mixed with mercury and salt. The ore was then ground by millstones that were powered by water that was impounded in the 32 artificial Lagunas de Kari Kari (p244).

The renovated **San Marcos Smelter** (La Paz near Periodista; admission US$0.65; ☻ 11am-7:30pm Mon-Fri, 11am-3pm Sat) houses a fine restaurant (p243), museum and *artesanía* shop and has now become a solid Potosí attraction. Constructed in the 18th century, it belonged to the Condesa (Countess) de la Casa Real de la Moneda. Most of the original construction remains, but the highlight is the impressive and still-functional wooden water-wheel, which measures 5m in diameter; it once processed 120kg of silver per month and was later used in tin smelting. In the restaurant and museum all sorts of colonial mining equipment and paraphernalia are on display. Many tours to the cooperative mines stop here en route to Cerro Rico. There's also a Calcha weaving exhibit.

The **Ingenio Dolores**, on Calle Mejillones, actually still operates – or rather, the modern version does. Inside, however, remain the

POTOSÍ

0   300 m
0   0.2 mi

To Tranca (500m)

H Players

Litoral

10 de Abril

Former Train Station

Av Villazón

Calama

Av Carlos V

Santa Cruz

Av Cívica

Plaza Uyuni

78

C Llano

Plaza Vanguardia

7

To Hospital Daniel Bracamonte (1km); Bus Terminal & Camiones to Tarapaya (1km)

Av Sevilla

San Alberto

Av Antofagasta

América

45

Av del Maestro

74

Chayanta

Bustillos

Lucas Jaimes

La Paz

Quijarro

Sucre

5

Plaza Campero

Av Serrudo

43

49

50

17

M Omiste

77

26

47

F Cumiel

51

Plaza del Estudiante

36

Oruro

48

73

Caracas

Víctor Flores

22

61

37

64

Ingavi

To Tarapaya (25km)

Reg Chichas

Mini Market

Av Camacho

Héroes del Chaco

24

75

54

41

70

20

71

30

72

1

S Chacón

To Universitario Cinema (400m)

Bolívar

Bolívar

Plaza Vacuñas

Frías

Villavicencio

Juan de la Cruz Tapia

Plaza Arce

Oruro

68

Bustillos

18

10

66

S Matos

3

Paseo Blvd

13

67

To Iglesia San Marton (400m)

59

Junín

58

2

19

Hoyos

63

14

34

65

15

56

8

55

53

9

35

31

6

39

To Cerro Rico (3km); Lagunas de Kari Kari (8km)

29

C Santa Teresa

Ayacucho

4

16

Plaza 10 de Noviembre

32

11

52

Linares

38

Chuquisaca

Río Huana Mayu

C de Bolivia

Cobija

Arcos de Cobija

12

25

76

44

42

Lanza

62

57

60

40

Padilla

Tarija

69

23

27

Nogales

46

28

Millares

(underground river)

Cop Costrillo

Nicolás Ben

G de Rojas

E Cortés

33

Plaza Diego Huallpa

21

Mejillones

Fanola

Periodista

Av H Vásquez

Iglesia Copacabana

INFORMATION
Banco de Crédito (ATM)........................1 D4
Banco Mercantil..................................2 D5
Banco Nacional....................................3 D5
Café Internet Candelaria......................4 C5
Clinica/Optica Esculapio.......................5 A3
Information Kiosk.................................6 D5
Instituto Geográfico Militar..................7 D2
Limpieza La Veloz...............................8 C5
Regional Tourism Office.......................9 C5
Tuko's Café.......................................10 C4

SIGHTS & ACTIVITIES   (pp234–41)
Altiplano Tours.................................(see 4)
Andes Salt Expeditions.......................11 D5
Arcos de Cobija...................................12 B5
Balsa Turismo..................................(see 32)
Casa de las Tres Portadas...................13 D4
Casa Real de la Moneda......................14 C5
Cathedral...15 C5
El Cabildo...16 C5
Esquina de las Cuatro Portadas............17 D3
Hidalgo Tours.....................................18 C4
Iglesia de la Merced............................19 D5
Iglesia de San Agustín.........................20 C4
Iglesia de San Benito...........................21 A6
Iglesia de San Bernardo.......................22 B4
Iglesia de San Juan de Dios..................23 D5
Iglesia de San Lorenzo de Carangas......24 C4
Iglesia de Santo Domingo....................25 C5
Iglesia Jerusalén..................................26 B3
Ingenio Dolores...................................27 B6
Koala Tours.....................................(see 35)
Mercado Artesanal..........................(see 33)

Museo & Convento de San
  Francisco......................................28 D6
Museo & Convento de Santa
  Teresa..29 B5
Pasaje de Siete Vueltas.......................30 D4
Plaza 6 de Agosto...............................31 D5
Potosí Tours.......................................32 D5
San Marcos Smelter............................33 D6
Silver Tours..34 C5
South American Tours.........................35 C5
Sumaj Tours...................................(see 34)
Torre de la Compañía de Jesús........(see 9)
Victoria Tours.................................(see 42)

SLEEPING   (pp241–2)
Alojamiento San José..........................36 B4
Hospedaje La Paz................................37 B4
Hostal Carlos V...................................38 D5
Hostal Colonial...................................39 D5
Hostal Compañía de Jesús....................40 D5
Hostal Felimar....................................41 C4
Hostal María Victoria...........................42 C5
Hostal Santa María..............................43 C3
Hotel Central......................................44 C5
Hotel Cima Argentum..........................45 B2
Hotel El Turista...................................46 C6
Hotel Jerusalén...................................47 B3
Koala Den...48 D4
Residencial Copacabana.......................49 C3
Residencial Felcar...............................50 C3
Residencial Sumaj...............................51 B4

EATING   (pp242–3)
Cafe de la Plata..................................52 D5

Café Cultural Kaypichu........................53 D5
Café Imma Sumac................................54 C4
Café-Restaurant Potocchi.....................55 C5
Chaplin's..56 C5
Cherry's Salon de Té............................57 D5
Confitería Capricornio..........................58 D5
El Fogón...59 C5
El Mesón..60 D5
Kactus...61 B4
La Salteña...62 D5
Manzana Mágica.................................63 C5
Pizzarón...64 C4
Restaurant La Carreta..........................65 C5
Sumac Orcko.......................................66 C5

DRINKING   (p243)
La Bohemia Pub..................................67 D5
La Casona Pub....................................68 C5

ENTERTAINMENT   (pp243–4)
Imperial Cinema..................................69 D5
Nicko's Karaoke...................................70 C4
Rarcuso..71 D4

SHOPPING   (p244)
Arte Nativo...72 D4
Artesanía Andina.................................73 D4
Artesanías Palomita's...........................74 B3
Market...75 C4

TRANSPORT   (p244)
Aerosur..76 C5
Buses to Uyuni....................................77 A3
Micros to Sucre...................................78 D1

---

ruins of the colonial-era mill. It's open during business hours.

CALLE QUIJARRO & ESQUINA DE LAS CUATRO PORTADAS

North of the Iglesia de San Agustín, **Calle Quijarro** narrows as it winds between a wealth of colonial buildings, many with doorways graced by old family crests. It's thought that the bends in Calle Quijarro were an intentional attempt to inhibit the cold winds that would otherwise whistle through and chill everything in their path. This concept is carried to extremes on the **Pasaje de Siete Vueltas** – 'the passage of seven turns' – which is an extension of Calle Ingavi, east of Junín. During colonial times Calle Quijarro was the street of potters, but it's now known for its hat-makers. One shop worth visiting is that of **Don Antonio Villa Chavarría** (Quijarro 41). The intersection of Calles Quijarro and Modesto Omiste, further north, has been dubbed the **Esquina de las Cuatro Portadas** because of its four decorative colonial doorways.

MUSEO & CONVENTO DE SAN FRANCISCO

The **San Francisco Convent** (Tarija & Nogales; admission US$1.35, photo/video US$1.35/2.70; 9-11:30am & 2:30-5:30pm Mon-Fri, 9am-12:30pm Sat)

was founded in 1547 by Fray Gaspar de Valverde, making it the oldest monastery in Bolivia. Owing to its inadequate size, it was demolished in 1707 and recon-structed over the following 19 years. A gold-covered altar from this building is now housed in the Casa Real de la Moneda. The statue of Christ that graces the present altar features hair that is said to grow miraculously, and for some reason the stone cupolas have been painted to resemble brickwork.

The museum has examples of religious art, including various paintings from the Escuela Potosina Indígena (Indigenous Potosí School), such as *The Erection of the Cross* by Melchor Pérez de Holguín, various mid-19th century works by Juan de la Cruz Tapia, and 25 scenes from the life of St Francis of Assisi. Another notable painting is a portrait of Antonio López de Quiroga, a wealthy 17th-century philanthropist who donated generously to the Church.

The highlight of the obligatory tour (ask for an English-speaking guide) comes at the end, when you're ushered up the tower and onto the roof for a grand view of Potosí.

MUSEO & CONVENTO DE SANTA TERESA

The Carmelite **Santa Teresa Convent** (Ayacucho at Santa Teresa; admission & 1-hr guided tour US$1.75, photo permit US$1.35; ☾ 9am-noon & 3-5pm) was founded in 1685 by Mother Josepha de Jesús y María and a band of Carmelite nuns from the city of La Plata (now Sucre). The construction, which reflects heavy *mestizo* influence, was completed in 1692.

A visit to Santa Teresa may provide an unsettling vision into a hidden facet of the colonial Church. At the entrance you can still see the 17th-century wooden turnstile that sheltered the cloistered nuns from the outside world. Visitors to the convent may still hear them conducting prayers and songs from their self-imposed seclusion. The display of religious art is more interesting than most. It includes works of Bolivia's most renowned artist, Melchor Pérez de Holguín, as well as a collection of morbid disciplinary and penitential paraphernalia (fortunately no longer in use), a skeleton in the old dining room ('ashes to ashes, dust to dust') and – as one correspondent put it – 'evidence of lots of flagellation'.

Visitors can purchase *quesitos*, home-made marzipan sweets from the shop next door.

IGLESIA DE SAN BERNARDO

This immense former church and convent (Plaza del Estudiante) displays impressive Baroque architecture and an elaborate ornamented portal. The original structure dates back to 1590, but it was completely renovated in the late 1720s, and through the 19th century it was used as Potosí's parochial cemetery. It now houses an art restoration workshop for university students.

IGLESIA DE BELÉN & TEATRO OMISTE

The former Belén Church (☎ 622-2525; north side of Plaza 6 de Augosto; guided tour US$0.65) with its three-tiered Baroque façade, was constructed in 1735 as a church and later served as a hospital. It is now occupied by the **Café Museo Belén** (☾ 8am-noon & 3:30-10pm Mon-Sat) and **Omiste Theater**, which hosts folkloric music and theater a couple of nights a week. The optional tour ends at the rooftop *mirador* with the best views in town.

TORRE DE LA COMPAÑÍA DE JESÚS

The ornate and beautiful bell tower, on what remains of the former Jesuit church (☎ 622-7408; Ayacucho near Bustillos; mirador admission US$1.35;

☾ 8am-noon & 2-6pm Mon-Fri), was completed in 1707 after the collapse of the original church. Both the tower and the doorway are adorned with examples of Baroque *mestizo* ornamentation.

OTHER CHURCHES

Building began on the **Iglesia de San Benito** (Plaza Diego Huallpa) in 1711 and it's laid out in the form of a Latin cross and features Byzantine domes and a distinctive *mestizo* doorway. In fact, from a distance it resembles the traditional Christmas card rendition of the city of Bethlehem. It was completed in 16 years, which must have been a colonial construction record.

The rather ordinary-looking **Iglesia de San Martín** (☎ 622-3682; Hoyos near Almagro; ☾ 10am-noon & 3-6pm Mon-Fri, 3-6pm Sat) was built in the 1600s and is today run by the French Redemptionist Fathers. Inside is an art museum, with at least 30 paintings beneath the choir depicting the Virgin Mary and the 12 Apostles. The Virgin on the altarpiece wears clothing woven from silver threads. However, San Martín is outside the center and is often closed because of the risk of theft, so phone before traipsing out there. Try on weekdays after 3:30pm.

The ornate Baroque *mestizo* portal of **San Lorenzo de Carangas** (Héroes del Chaco at Bustillos; ☾ 10am-noon Mon-Sat) is probably one of the most photographed subjects in Bolivia. It was carved in stone by master Indian artisans in the 16th century, but the main structure wasn't completed until the bell towers were added in 1744. Inside are two Holguín paintings and handcrafted silverwork on the altar. The church was renovated in 1987.

Iglesia de San Agustín (Bolívar at Quijarro), with its elegant Renaissance doorway, is known for its eerie underground crypts and catacombs. To visit them, ask the security guard or join a spooky night-time visit with a tour agency.

The **Iglesia Jerusalén** (Camacho at Oruro; guided tours US$0.75; ☾ 4-8pm Mon-Fri, 8am-noon Sat), with its golden ornamentation and several paintings by Holguín, was constructed in the 17th century as a sanctuary in honor of the Virgen de Candelaria. It now houses a Museo Sacro of Viceroyalty-era art.

Other churches of note include **San Juan de Dios** (Chuquisaca at La Paz), which has stood since

THE JOB FROM HELL

In the cooperative mines on Cerro Rico, all work is done with primitive tools, and underground temperatures vary from below freezing – the altitude is over 4200m – to a stifling 45°C on the fourth and fifth levels. Miners, exposed to all sorts of noxious chemicals and gases, normally die of silicosis pneumonia within 10 to 15 years of entering the mines.

Contrary to popular rumor, women are admitted to many cooperative mines; only a few miners hang on to the tradition that women underground invite bad luck, and in many cases, the taboo applies only to miners' wives, whose presence in the mines would invite jealousy from Pachamama. At any rate, lots of Quechua women are consigned to picking through the tailings, gleaning small amounts of minerals that may have been missed.

Since cooperative mines are owned by the miners themselves, they must produce to make their meager living. All work is done by hand with explosives and tools they must purchase themselves, including the acetylene lamps used to detect pockets of deadly carbon monoxide gas.

Miners prepare for their workday by socializing and chewing coca for several hours, beginning work at about 10am. They work until lunch at 2pm, when they rest and chew more coca. For those who don't spend the night working, the day usually ends at 7pm. On the weekend, each miner sells his week's production to the buyer for as high a price as he can negotiate.

When miners first enter the mine, they offer propitiation at the shrine of the miners' god Tata Kaj'chu, whom they hope will afford them protection in the harsh underground world. Deeper in the mine, visitors will undoubtedly see a small, devilish figure occupying a small niche somewhere along the passageways. As most of the miners believe in a god in heaven, they deduce that there must also be a devil beneath the earth in a place where it's hot and uncomfortable. Since hell (according to the traditional description of the place) must not be far from the environment in which they work, they reason that the devil himself must own the minerals they're dynamiting and digging out of the earth. In order to appease this character, whom they call Tío (Uncle) or Supay – never Diablo – they set up a little ceramic figurine in a place of honor.

On Friday nights a cha'lla is offered to invoke his goodwill and protection. A little alcohol is poured on the ground before the statue, lighted cigarettes are placed in his mouth and coca leaves are laid out within easy reach. Then, as in most Bolivian celebrations, the miners smoke, chew coca and proceed to drink themselves unconscious. While this is all taken very seriously, it also provides a bit of diversion from an extremely difficult existence. It's interesting that offerings to Jesus Christ are only made at the point where the miners can first see the outside daylight.

In most cooperative operations there is a minimal medical plan in case of accident or silicosis (which is inevitable after seven to 10 years working underground) and a pension of about US$14.50 a month for those so incapacitated. Once a miner has lost 50% of his lung capacity to silicosis, he may retire, if he so wishes. In case of death, a miner's widow and children collect this pension.

the 1600s despite its adobe construction. Restored **La Merced** (Hoyos at Millares) is also lovely, with its carved pulpit and a beautiful 18th-century silver arch over the altarpiece. It was constructed between 1555 and 1687. The recently renovated **Santo Domingo** (Oruro at Cobija) contains an ornate portal, an unusual paneled ceiling and one of the eight original panels from the life of Santa Rosa de Lima, by Juan Díaz and Juan Francisco de la Puente. As well, there are other colonial paintings and sculptures located here. To gain admission to the church, visit on Sunday prior to the Mass.

HISTORIC BUILDINGS

Potosí's unique architecture merits a stroll around the narrow streets to take in the ornate doorways and façades, as well as the covered wooden balconies that overhang the streets and provide an almost Alpine sense of coziness to the city's bleak surroundings.

Architecturally worthy homes and monuments include **El Cabildo** (the old town hall) on Plaza 10 de Noviembre, the **Casa de las Tres Portadas** (Bolívar 1052) and the **Arcos de Cobija** (Arches of Cobija) on the street of the same name.

On Calle Junín, between Matos and Bolívar, is an especially lovely and elaborate *portón mestizo*, a *mestizo*-style doorway that's flanked by twisted columns. It once graced the home of the Marquez de Otavi, but now ushers patrons into the Banco Nacional.

VISITING THE COOPERATIVE MINES

A visit to the cooperative mines will almost surely be one of the most memorable experiences you'll have in Bolivia, providing an opportunity to witness working conditions that should have gone out with the Middle Ages. You may be left stunned and/or ill (see the boxed text, p239).

Quite a few young Potosí men offer guided tours through the mines, and each tour agency has its own pool of guides. Some guides are well known and well tested, but the adventurous may wish to try out new and enthusiastic guides.

Mine visits aren't easy, and the low ceilings and steep, muddy passageways are best visited in your worst clothes. Temperatures can reach 45°C, and the altitude can be extremely taxing. You'll be exposed to noxious chemicals and gases, including silica dust (the cause of silicosis), arsenic gas, acetylene vapors and other trapped mine gases, as well as asbestos deposits and the byproducts of acetylene combustion and the detonation of explosives. Anyone with doubts or medical problems should avoid these tours. The plus side is that you can speak with the friendly miners, who will share their insights and opinions about their difficult lot.

Mine tours begin with a visit to the market, where miners stock up on acetylene rocks, dynamite, cigarettes and other essentials. In the past, gifts weren't expected, but with the growing number of tourists through the mines, you'd be very unpopular if you didn't supply a handful of coca leaves and a few cigarettes – luxuries for which the miners' meager earnings are scarcely sufficient. Photography is permitted, but you'll need a flash.

Mine tours run in the morning or afternoon and last from three to five hours. The city permits agencies to charge up to US$10 per person, but lower rates are available during periods of low demand. This price includes a guide, transportation from town and equipment: jackets, helmets, boots and lamps (these days they're normally battery-powered rather than acetylene). Wear sturdy clothing and carry water and a handkerchief/headscarf to filter some of the noxious substances you'll encounter underground. Avoid companies willing take you on Saturday, Sunday or Monday when there is little activity in the mines. The last Friday of the month can be a particularly eventful day and is recommended for those who like to swill *puro*.

Tours

In addition to the cooperative mine tours described above, there are many guided tours offered and many agencies offering them. Other popular options include Tarapaya (US$7.50) and trekking and camping trips around the Lagunas de Kari Kari (US$20 to US$25 per day). Most agencies are professional, but it's still wise to seek recommendations from other travelers. Unless you're booking an upmarket tour or are short of time, Southwest Circuit tours are generally more inexpensively arranged in Uyuni (p166). Recommended agencies include:

Altiplano Tours (☎ /fax 622-5353; Ayacucho 19) Does all the standard tours plus *tinku* excursions.

Andes Salt Expeditions (☎ /fax622-5175; www.andes -salt-uyuni.com.bo; Padilla at Linares) Raúl Braulio Mamani organizes tours through several cooperative mines and guarantees at least one dynamite detonation.

Balsa Turismo (☎ /fax 622-6270; Padilla at Linares) Does upmarket trips around the Southwest Circuit in addition to the standard tours.

Hidalgo Tours (☎ 622-5186; fax 061-227077; www.salardeuyuni.netuy; Bolívar at Junín) Owns several upscale hotels around the salar, making it one of the best upmarket options for the Southwest Circuit.

Koala Tours (☎ 622-4708; wgarnica@hotmail.com; Ayacucho 5) In addition to the standard mine tours, which are very good, they offer culturally sensitive three-day excursions to local *fiestas* that feature *tinku* fighting.

Potosí Tours (☎ 622-5786; Padilla at Linares) Offers all the standards.

Silver Tours (☎ /fax 622-3600; www.silvertours.8m .com; Edificio Cámara de Minería, Quijarro 12) All the standard tours around Potosí and adventure tours to the *salares*.

South American Tours(☎ /fax 622-8919; sud_ american@hotmail.com; Ayacucho 11) Visits the mine San Miguel la Poderosa and also does the standard tours.

Sumaj Tours (☎ 622-4633; hoteljer@cedro.pts.entelnet
.bo; Oruro 143) This friendly agency mainy organizes mine
tours.

Victoria Tours (at Hostal María Victoria; ☎ /fax 622-
2132; Chuquisaca 148) Budget agency running mine tours,
as well as city tours, Tarapaya, Lagunas de Kari Kari and
hot springs trips.

Festivals & Events

Held during the third weekend in March at
Plaza Ingenio San Marcos, the **Feria Artesenal
& Comida Tipica Andina** features craft exhibitions
from around Potosí department plus all the
typical music, food and dance. The national
holiday **Día del Trabajador** (Labor Day, May 1)
is celebrated most enthusiastically in Potosí –
watch out for dynamite in the plaza. The
International Festival of Culture happens in late
October or early November.

FIESTA DEL ESPÍRITU

Potosí's most unusual event takes place
on the last three Saturdays of June and the
first Saturday of August. It's dedicated to
the honor of Pachamama, the earth mother,
whom the miners regard as the mother of
all Bolivians.

Campesinos bring their finest llamas to
the base of Cerro Rico to sell to the miners
for sacrifice. The entire ritual is conducted
according to a meticulous schedule. At
10am, one miner from each mine purchases
a llama and their families gather for the
celebrations. At 11am, everyone moves to
the entrances of their respective mines.
The miners chew coca and drink alcohol
from 11am to 11:45am. Then, at precisely
11:45am, they prepare the llama for
Pachamama by tying its feet and offering
it coca and alcohol. At high noon, the
llama meets its maker. As its throat is slit,
the miners petition Pachamama for luck,
protection and an abundance of minerals.
The llama's blood is caught in glasses and
splashed around the mouth of the mine in
order to ensure Pachamama's attention,
cooperation and blessing.

For the following three hours, the men
chew coca and drink while the women
prepare a llama *parrillada*. The meat is
served traditionally with potatoes baked
along with *habas* (fava beans) and oca in a
small adobe oven. When the oven reaches
the optimum temperature, it is smashed in
on the food, which is baked beneath the hot

shards. The stomach, feet and head of the
llama are buried in a three-meter hole as
a further offering to Pachamama, and then
the music and dancing begin. In the evening,
truckloads of semi-conscious celebrants are
escorted home in transportation provided
by the honored miner who secured the
llama for his respective mine.

FIESTA DE SAN BARTOLOMÉ (CHU'TILLOS)

This rollicking celebration takes place on
the final weekend of August or the first
weekend of September and is marked by
processions, student exhibitions, traditional
costumes and folk dancing from all over
the continent. In recent years it has even
extended overseas and featured musical
groups and dance troupes from as far
away as China and the USA. Given all
the practicing during the week leading
up to the festival, you'd be forgiven for
assuming it actually started a week early.
Booking accommodations for this period
is essential.

EXALTACIÓN DE LA SANTA VERA CRUZ

This festival, which falls on September
14, honors Santo Cristo de la Vera Cruz.
Activities occur around the church of San
Lorenzo and the railway station. Silver
cutlery features prominently, as do parades,
dueling brass bands, dancing, costumed
children and, of course, lots of alcohol.

Sleeping

Usually only the top-end hotels have heating,
and there may be blanket shortages in the
cheapies, so you'll want a sleeping bag.
Unless your hotel has water tanks or goes
through an arduous daily water-collection
ritual, water is available only in the morning.
Some bottom-end places charge an extra
US$0.50 for hot showers.

BUDGET

Koala Den (☎ 622-6467; ktours_potosi@hotmail.com;
Junín 56; dm US$2.65) Heating, 24/7 gas showers,
a shared kitchen, a good book exchange
and a bar make the new Koala the current
traveler's favorite. There are 20 beds spread
out in several dorms around a central
common room and TV lounge.

Residencial Felcar (☎ 622-4966; Serrudo 345;
US$2.65) Clean, simple rooms, reliable hot
showers and a sunny, flower-filled patio

make the Felcar good value. Full breakfast is available for US$0.75. New rooms with private baths were in progress at last look.

Residencial Copacabana (☎ 622-2712; Serrudo 319; US$2.65) The large and less-personal Copacabana works for a night or two. Hot water pumps from 6am to 6pm and there's a decent attached restaurant.

Residencial Sumaj (☎ 622-3336; Gumiel 12) Long-time budget favorite for its shared kitchen, laundry service and TV lounge. It's a fringe location, however, and the downstairs rooms are small and dark.

Hostal Carlos V (☎ 622-5121; Linares 42; US$3.25) Another budget favorite is this cozy colonial building with a covered patio. The 'hot' showers available from 7am to noon barely rate as tepid.

Hotel Central (☎ 622-2207; Bustillos & Cobija; US$3, with bath US$4.65) In a quiet old part of town, the adequate Central has a traditional *potosino* overhanging balcony in the interior courtyard. The aging management gives guests piles of blankets to make up for chilly rooms.

Hotel El Turista (☎ 622-2492; Lanza 19; s/d/tr with bath US$8/12/16) Drafty but pleasant rooms with sporadic electric showers and superb views from the top floor. The new owners plan to install gas heating and color TVs.

Hostal Santa María (☎ 622-3255; Serrudo 244; s/d with bath & TV US$7.50/12) Comfortable carpeted rooms have private, piping-hot showers and phones, and the on-site eatery is pleasant.

Hostal María Victoria (☎ 622-2144; Chuquisaca 148; dm/d US$2/5.50, d with bath US$8) This agreeable but rather overpriced hostal occupies an old home at the end of a quiet passageway. The rooms surround a classic courtyard that is being impinged upon by an extension. There's also a bright terrace. Breakfast costs US$1 and the tour agency sells bus tickets to Sucre.

The best of the bottom of the barrel is represented by **Alojamiento San José** (☎ 622-2632; Oruro 173; US$3.25), which features llama wool mattresses and is favored by locals in town for the market. Nearby, the less desirable **Hospedaje La Paz** (☎ 22632; Oruro 262; US$2) is cheap but dank.

MID-RANGE & TOP END
Hostal Colonial (☎ 622-4809; www.redboliviana.com /hostalcolonial; Hoyos 8; s/d with bath & cable TV US$33/ 43) In a well-kept colonial building near the main plaza, this warm, centrally heated retreat has spacious rooms with *frigobars*; a few even have bathtubs. The English-speaking staff is very helpful and breakfast is available.

Hostal Compañía de Jesús (☎ 622-3173; Chuquisaca 445; s/d US$6/10, with bath, breakfast & TV US$7/12) For sparkling clean rooms, firm mattresses, lots of blankets and a friendly atmosphere, stay in this old Carmelite monastery. It's a bit cloistered and the rooms with wood floors can be cold. There are a couple of triple rooms and room No 18 is especially nice.

Hotel Jerusalén (☎ 622-4633; hoteljer@cedro.pts .entelnet.bo; Oruro 143; s/d in summer US$10/18.50, in winter with bath & breakfast US$19.50/26) Recommended and welcoming, this HI-affiliate has friendly staff, nice balconies, quality gas showers, rooms with TV and a mellow atmosphere, but it's a bit expensive for what you get. Rates vary seasonally and include a buffet breakfast.

Hostal Felimar (☎ /fax 622-4357; Junín 14; US$4.65, s/d with bath & breakfast US$9/14.65) This pleasant and centrally located, solar-powered hostal has some very nice upstairs rooms with balconies affording views over the colonial street below. The top floor suite is US$20.

Hotel Cima Argentum (☎ 622-9538; www.hca -potosi.com; Villazón 239; s/d/tr/q with bath & breakfast US$33/46/60/68) This new deluxe, tour-group oriented hotel has modern family suites with marble bathrooms, heating, telephone, and room service from the international restaurant.

Eating
Few folks trek all the way here for the cuisine. That said, stylish places are popping up and it's a good place to sample traditional dishes.

QUICK EATS
Café de la Plata (east side of Plaza 10 de Noviembre; mains US$1.50-3) Artsy, cozy and chic in a restored sort of way, this Argentine-run hangout steams rich espressos and is a fine place to read over a beer or glass of international wine. It's also a good place to find out about cultural happenings around town while munching on pasta and sandwiches.

Cherry's Salon de Té (Padilla 8; mains US$1-2) Open all afternoon, this café makes a nice but very slow pit stop while you're out exploring the town. The apple strudel, chocolate cake and lemon meringue pie are superb, but the coffee is mediocre and the pastries can be stale.

Confitería Capricornio (Padilla at Hoyos; ☺ 7am-10pm; mains US$1-2) Packed with students in the evening, this quick-bite option serves soup, fast food, pizza, spaghetti, coffee and juices.

Café Internet Candelaria (Ayacucho 5; ☺ from 7:30am; everything under US$2) Adjacent to a popular Internet café, Candelaria is well known for its full breakfasts and coffee specialties in the morning and pizza, burgers and healthy lunch specials (with veggie options) later on.

Stalls in the market comedor serve inexpensive breakfasts of bread, pastries and coffee. Downstairs there are some excellent juice stands. For great *salteñas*, check out **La Salteña** (Padilla 6) or **Café Imma Sumac** (Bustillos 987). In the morning, street vendors sell meatless *salteñas potosinas* near Iglesia de San Lorenzo. Meat *empanadas* are sold around the market until early afternoon, and in the evening, street vendors sell cornmeal *humitas*.

RESTAURANTS

El Fogón (☎ 622-4969; Oruro & Frías; ☺ 11am-midnight; mains US$2.50-5) In a modernized but drafty colonial space, this bright and spacious (if a bit stark) upscale restaurant serves contemporary Bolivian gourmet meals as well as quality *platos típicos*. It has an impressive wine list, toasty fireplace and a full bar. Come for a meal or just a drink – it's a social place.

San Marcos (☎ 623-0260; La Paz at Betanzos; ☺ 8am-midnight; lunch US$2.50, mains US$2-4) Inside the beautifully restored Ingenio San Marcos (p235) is this comfortable and creative restaurant, which serves a range of well-prepared soups, salads and main courses: *ceviche*, shellfish and fish, beef, chicken and llama. Reservations are recommended, especially if you have a group or come for Sunday brunch.

El Mesón (☎ 622-3087; Tarija & Linares; mains with wine US$5) This romantic, if a tad dungeon-like, restaurant with cloth napkins was long considered Potosí's finest. The service and the food (steak, pasta, salads) are excellent, though a bit old-fashioned.

Restaurant La Carreta (Lanza btwn Matos & Ayacucho; mains US$2) The best spot near the

cathedral for pizzas, burgers and *almuerzos*, including vegetarian alternatives.

Sumac Orcko (Quijarro 46; set meals US$1.35, mains US$1.50-3) Serves filling, four-course *almuerzos* of salad, soup, a meat dish and dessert, plus à la carte dinners including divine *trucha al limón* (lemon trout) and *picante de perdíz* (spicy partridge).

Kactus (Camacho near Antofagasta; set meals under US$1) If there's any place in town where locals run a tab, it's this family-run hole-in-the-wall. Lunch is big, tasty and cheap and everything else is straightforward fare.

Pizzarón (Oruro 257; ☺ from 7pm; pizzas US$1.50-3) Signless but no secret, this is the place to go if you're hankering for pizza in the evening.

Café-Restaurant Potocchi (☎ 622-2759; Millares 13; lunch US$1.50) A pleasant and inexpensive place serving a range of meals. It also hosts a *peña* (US$1.50 cover) several nights a week.

Chaplin's (Matos near Quijarro; meals US$1.50-2.50) Friendly and comfortable, this place serves mostly Bolivian fare with a few international and Mexican dishes.

Café Cultural Kaypichu (☎ 622-6129; Millares 24; ☺ 7:30am-2pm, 5-9pm Tue-Sun; mains US$2) As in Sucre, starting the day here with a healthy vegetarian breakfast is a real treat. The generous set lunches are a good deal and the à la carte pasta and pizza dinners are worthwhile too. Call ahead to see what's on for evening entertainment.

Manzana Mágica (Bustillos & Ayacucho; ☺ 8am-10pm Mon-Sat; meals US$2) A cramped, strictly vegetarian refuge known for its breakfast – muesli, juice, eggs and brown bread. Lunch is ultra-healthy and à la carte dinners are assertively spiced and portions are big.

Drinking

The atmospheric **La Casona Pub** (☎ 622-2954; Frías 41; ☺ 10am-12:30pm & 6pm-midnight Mon-Sat), is tucked away in the historic 1775 home of the royal envoy sent to administer the Casa Real de la Moneda. It's a memorable watering hole with greasy pub grub. On Friday it stages live music performances. **La Bohemia Pub** (☎ 622-4348; Matos at La Paz; ☺ from 7pm) serves cocktails and light pub meals.

Entertainment

Tuesday through Friday nights, **Café-Restaurant Potocchi** (above) hosts traditional folk music *peñas* (US$1.50). For karaoke and disco dancing, try the locally popular **Rarcuso** (Junín near Bolívar) or **Nicko's Karaoke** (Bolívar at Junín) around the corner.

Potosí has two cinemas, the **Imperial** (☎ 622-6133; Padilla 31) and the **Universitario** (Bolívar 893), which both screen relatively recent releases.

Shopping

Favored Potosí souvenirs include silver and tin articles available in stands near the market entrance on Calle Oruro; many of them were produced in the village of Caiza, 80km south of Potosí, which now has its own co-op shop featuring naturally dyed wool items. Here, small dangly earrings, hoop earrings, spoons and platters cost between US$1 and US$5.

A recommended shop is **Arte Nativo** (☎ 622-3544; Sucre 30), which sells indigenous handiwork and thereby improves the economic condition of rural women. Another possibility is **Artesanía Andina** (Sucre 92). The **Mercado Artesanal** (Omiste at Sucre), or the *artesanía* shop in the **San Marcos Smelter** (p235) cater specifically to tourists. The smaller shops along Sucre north of Bolívar are even cheaper. **Artesanías Palomita's** (Museo Etno-Indumentario; ☎ 622-3258; Serrudo 148-152; ☯ 9am-noon & 2-6pm Mon-Fri, 9am-noon Sat) is half shop, half museum and features costumes and weavings from each of the 16 provinces of Potosí department.

Getting There & Away

Potosí boasts the world's highest commercial airport, Aeropuerto Capitán Rojas. In the early 1990s the runway was extended to 4000m to accommodate larger planes. **Aerosur** (☎ 622-8988; Cobija 25) had flights for a while, but their five putative weekly connections with La Paz were invariably canceled for one reason or another. In any case, it's not that inconvenient to fly into Sucre and travel to Potosí by bus.

All road routes into Potosí are quite scenic, and arriving by day will always present a dramatic introduction to the city. The **bus terminal** (☎ 624-3361) is about half an hour on foot downhill (1km) from the center, and *micros* and minibuses (US$0.15) run every minute or two.

Numerous *flotas* offer a daily overnight service to La Paz (US$5 to US$7, 11 hours)

via Oruro (US$4, eight hours) departing around 7pm or 8pm; you can also opt for a bus *cama* (US$12, 10 hours).

Buses leave for Tupiza (US$3.35, seven hours) and Villazón (US$5.50, 10 to 12 hours) daily in the morning and evening. Buses to Tarija (US$7, 14 hours) run at least three times daily, and there are numerous night-time services to Cochabamba (US$7 to US$9; 12 to 15 hours). Several *flotas* also have daily services to Santa Cruz (US$8; 16 to 20 hours), but it's a long, arduous trip; it's better to take a break in Sucre or Cochabamba.

Quite a few *flotas* leave for Sucre (US$2, 3½ hours) between 7am and 5pm. Alternatively if you have four people, you can take a shared taxi to Sucre (US$4 per person, 2½ hours). Most hotels can help you organize a group or you can phone **Expreso Turismo Global** (☎ 624-5171) or **Auto Expreso Infinito del Sur** (☎ 624-5040). Alternatively just head for the bus terminal where taxis wait until they are full. If you prefer to take the least expensive route, *micros* (US$1.35, five hours) leave from the *tranca* 500m north of Plaza Uyuni all day when full.

Buses to Uyuni (US$2 to US$3.50, six to seven hours) depart between 9:30am and noon from just below the railway line, higher up on Av Antofagasta. The rugged route is quite spectacular.

Camiones to Uyuni leave from roughly the same place as the bus, but unless you're a real glutton for punishment, you're better off on the bus.

Getting Around

Micros and minibuses (US$0.15) shuttle between the center and the Cerro Rico mines, as well as the bus terminal. Taxis charge US$0.40 per person around the center and to the bus terminal. The main stands are on the northern side of Plaza 10 de Noviembre.

AROUND POTOSÍ
Lagunas de Kari Kari

The artificial lakes of Kari Kari were constructed in the late 16th and early 17th centuries by 20,000 Indian slaves to provide water for the city and for hydropower to run the city's 82 *ingenios*. In 1626 the retaining wall of Laguna San Ildefonso broke and caused an enormous flood that destroyed operations along La

Ribera de los Ingenios and killed 2000 people. Of the 32 original lakes, only 25 remain and all have been abandoned – except by waterfowl, which appreciate the incongruous surface water in this otherwise stark region.

LAGUNAS DE KARI KARI HIKE

The easiest way to visit Lagunas de Kari Kari is with a Potosí tour agency (p240). If you prefer to strike out on your own, carry food, water and warm clothing. In a long day, you can have a good look around the lagunas and the fringes of the Cordillera de Kari Kari, but it may also be rewarding to camp overnight in the mountains.

Access is fairly easy. Take a *micro* heading toward Cerro Rico (Pailaviri or Calvario) and get off at the Tupiza turnoff. Follow that road until the pavement ends at a *tranca*, then head southeast along a stream. Any of the numerous uphill tracks will lead onto an open plain, where you should bear left and climb past a llama pasture and onto a ridge where you'll have a superb view of the **Lagunas San Sebastián**. At this point, you're about 4km southeast of central Potosí. Continue along this ridge until you cross a track, which will lead you through a hamlet and along the Río Masoni into the mountains.

Alternatively, cross the Masoni valley and scramble up the ridge on the other side and climb to the summit of **Cerro Masoni** for an excellent view of **Lagunas San Ildefonso** and **San Pablo**. Descending along the same ridge will lead you back to Potosí.

Another option is to descend to Laguna San Ildefonso, then follow the track around its northern shore and continue up the valley or strike off eastward into the hills. The higher you go, the more spectacular the views become. The area is riddled with open mine entrances, mining detritus and remains of mining equipment.

Those prepared for an overnight stay can travel even further into the mountains, since there are no difficult summits in the area. As long as you can catch sight of Cerro Rico, the route back to Potosí will be obvious. Remember, however – as if you could forget – that the altitude hereabouts ranges from 4400m to 5000m. The Cordillera de Kari Kari is included on the IGM topo sheet *Potosí (East) – sheet 6435*.

Hacienda Cayara

For a peaceful retreat or some comfortable hill walking, visit Hacienda Cayara, which lies 25km down the valley northwest of Potosí. Set amid lovely hills at 3550m, this beautiful working farm produces vegetables and milk for the city. It dates back to colonial times, when it was owned by the Viceroy of Toledo. In the name of King Felipe II, its title was later handed to Don Juan de Tendones and was then transferred to the Marquez de Otavi, whose coat of arms the ranch still bears.

In 1901 it was purchased by the English Aitken family, who still own it. The family converted it into a hostel in 1992. 'Cayara' is the Aymará name for the *Puya raimondii* plant, which flowers after 100 years then decomposes.

The hostel is like a museum: an opulent colonial mansion furnished with original paintings and period furniture. Guests have the use of the fireplace and extensive library, which includes works dating from the 17th century.

For bookings, go to the office 10m up the street from Entel in Potosí, in the back of the glass-fronted shop selling cakes and cheese. Alternatively, phone Señora Luisa Serrano (☎ /fax 622-6380; cayara@cotepnet.com.bo; Cochabamba 532 in Potosí; r per person US$25, day use US$5, meals US$7).

Transportation can be arranged in Potosí at the time of booking the hostel, but it's cheaper to go by taxi, especially if you're in a group; have the driver take the left fork to La Palca instead of heading through the canyon toward Tarapaya. Otherwise, *micros* (US$0.50) that pass the turnoff depart from Mercado Quichimi daily around noon.

Betanzos

Set in a landscape of rugged, rocky mountains, the traditional town of Betanzos is about an hour from Potosí along the Sucre road. On Sunday, when the **market** is in full swing, *campesinos* wearing local dress bring their weavings, ceramics and crops from the countryside to sell. The surrounding hills are full of **ancient rock paintings**; the beautiful sites of Lajas-Mayu and Inca Cueva are only 5km from Betanzos.

On April 4 and 5, Betanzos celebrates the **Fiesta de la Papa** (Potato Festival), which features up to 200 varieties of tubers.

AROUND POTOSÍ

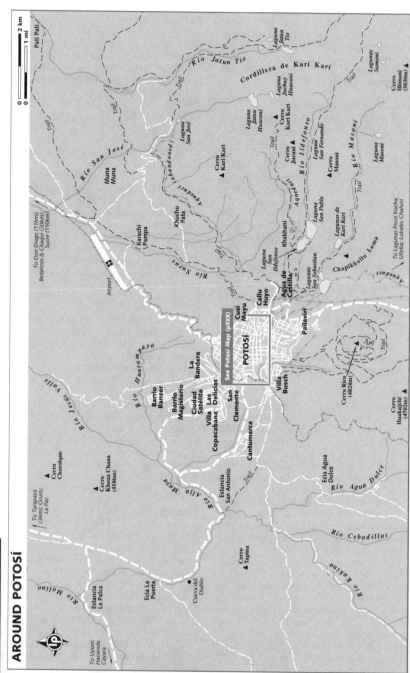

Although it isn't well known, it does attract major Andean dance and musical groups from all over Bolivia.

If you want to crash in town, the best option is the **Residencial Bolívar** (US$2), but it's pretty grubby and lacks water.

Micros and *camiones* leave for Betanzos from Plaza Uyuni, north of the town centre, in Potosí early in the morning, with extra departures on Sunday. All Sucre buses also pass Betanzos, but make sure they drop you in the village, which is 1km off the main road.

Tarapaya

Belief in the curative powers of Tarapaya (3600m), the most frequently visited **hot-springs** area around Potosí, dates back to Inca times. It even served as the holiday destination for Inca Huayna Capac, who would come all the way from Cuzco (now in Peru) to bathe.

The most interesting sight is the 30°C **Ojo del Inca**, a perfectly round, green lake in a low volcanic crater, 100m in diameter. Along the river below the crater are several *balnearios* (resorts) with medicinal thermal pools utilizing water from the lake.

Locals claim that in the morning it's safe to bathe in the Ojo del Inca, but that *remolinos* (whirlpools) may develop early in the afternoon and cause drowning. There have indeed been bizarre disappearances here, and it would be wise to err on the side of caution and avoid swimming at any time.

To reach Ojo del Inca, cross the bridge 400m before the Balneario de Tarapaya, turn left and walk about 200m. Just past the waterfall on the right, a washed-out road leads uphill about 400m to the lake.

The **Balneario Paraíso** has a hostel for overnight guests and there's also lodging at **Balneario de Tarapaya**. Self-contained backpackers will find a number of level and secluded campsites near the river, but all water should be purified.

Camiones leave for Tarapaya (US$0.40, half hour) from Plaza Chuquimia near the bus terminal in Potosí roughly every half hour from 7am to 7pm. Taxis are US$6 for up to four people. The last *micro* back to Potosí leaves Tarapaya around 6pm.

Ask the driver to let you off at the bridge where the gravel road turns off. The Balneario de Tarapaya is 400m from the bridge along the paved road. Balneario Paraíso is over the bridge and 400m down the road to the right.

Chaqui

Another major **hot spring** bubbles away 3km uphill from the village of Chaqui, 45km by road east of Potosí. The countryside around nearby Puna and Belen is particularly interesting, but transportation may be a problem. On Sunday, *potosinos* come with loads of sugar, flour, rice and bread to exchange in the markets for potatoes, cheese and local farm products. The climate is considerably more agreeable than in Potosí, and superior-quality **handicrafts**, are sold in the small villages.

If you wish to stay, **Hotel Termas de Chaqui** (☎ 622-2158; Chuquisaca 587 in Potosí; US$10) has room rates that include the use of the hot pools, but backpackers may feel less than welcome. Nonguests may use the pools and sauna (US$1.35 per person). Chaqui village also has a couple of basic *alojamientos*, but they're 3km downhill from the resort. There are a couple of cheaper non-hotel soaking options too.

To get to Chaqui, hop on a *micro* or *camión* from Plaza Uyuni in Potosí (US$0.40, two hours); the first one leaves at around 8am. Alternatively, arrange transportation through Hotel Termas de Chaqui; inquire at its office in Potosí. Getting there is one thing, but returning to Potosí can be more difficult, as some drivers won't leave until there's sufficient interest (or until you're prepared to hire an entire vehicle).

Don Diego

The **hot springs** at Don Diego are along the Sucre road and can be reached by *micro* or *camión* from Plaza Uyuni, or on a Sucre bus. The rustic resort has a **hostel** (US$2), including use of the baths.

CENTRAL HIGHLANDS

South Central Bolivia & The Chaco

CONTENTS

With a land drier and more desolate than areas further north, the inhabitants of the isolated Tarija department have historically identified more with Argentina than Bolivia. In fact the department bills itself as the Andalucia of Bolivia, in reference to its dry, eroded badlands, neatly groomed vineyards and orchards, and white-stucco and red-tile architecture, all of which are reminiscent of the Iberian Peninsula. Chapacos – as Tarijeños prefer to refer to themselves – speak a lilting dialect of European Spanish, and even the river flowing past the departmental capital is called the Guadalquivir.

In the far eastern regions of Tarija and Chuquisaca departments, the highlands roll down into the petroleum-rich scrublands and red earth of the Gran Chaco. Villamontes, a small stop on the Santa Cruz–Yacuiba railway line, is very proud of its status as Bolivia's hottest spot.

Down in the country's southernmost tip, lush sugarcane-producing valleys and oil-bearing veins fuel the prosperous town of Bermejo, on the Argentine border.

TOP FIVE

- Sample vintages from Bolivia's best – and the world's highest – vineyards outside **Tarija** (p254)
- Spot rare wildlife and hike the well-preserved Inca Trail in the **Reserva Biológica Cordillera de Sama** (p259)
- Track endangered Chaco wildlife in the **Parque Nacional Aguaragüe** (p265), and the **Corvalán** (p266) and **Tariquía** (p262) **Reserves**
- Tackle the rugged journey between Bolivia and Paraguay on the rough-and-ready **Trans-Chaco Road** (p264)
- See dogs with flowery collars and hear some bizarre musical instruments at Tarija's **Fiesta de San Roque** (p255)

HISTORY

Before the Chaco War (1932–1935), most of Paraguay northeast of the Paraguay and Pilcomayo Rivers – encompassing about 240,680 sq km – and the 168,765-sq km chunk of Argentina north of the Río Bermejo lay within Bolivian territory. The dispute between Bolivia and Paraguay that led to the Chaco War had its roots in Paraguay's formal 1842 declaration of independence, which omitted official demarcation of Paraguay's boundary with Bolivia.

In 1878 the Hayes Arbitration designated the Río Pilcomayo as the boundary between Paraguay and Argentina, which was duly accepted. The empty land to the north however, became a matter of conflict between Paraguay and Bolivia. Subsequent attempts at arbitration failed and Bolivia began pressing for a settlement.

After losing the War of the Pacific in 1884, Bolivia needed the Chaco as an outlet to the Atlantic via the Río Paraguay more than ever. Hoping that physical possession would be interpreted as official

sovereignty, the Bolivian army set up a fort at Piquirenda on the Pilcomayo.

Arbitration attempts failed because Bolivia refused to relinquish rights to Fuerte Vanguardia, its only port on the Río Paraguay. Paraguay was unwilling to concede and, in 1928, the Paraguayan military seized the fort. Although the situation heated up, both sides maintained a conciliatory attitude, hoping that a military solution would not be necessary.

While negotiations were under way in Washington (the USA never could stay out of a good conflict), unauthorized action on the part of the Bolivian military erupted into full-scale warfare. While casualties on both sides were heavy, the highland Bolivians, unaccustomed to the subtropical terrain, fared miserably. No decisive victory was reached, but the 1938 peace negotiations awarded most of the disputed territory to Paraguay. Bolivia retained only the town of Villamontes, where, in 1934, it saw its most successful campaign of the war.

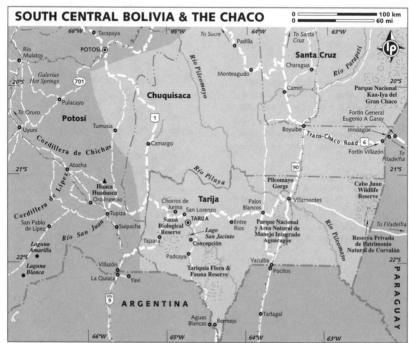

SOUTH CENTRAL BOLIVIA & THE CHACO

CLIMATE

This is the area of Bolivia where you feel the country's proximity to the equator and its distance from the sea. Tarija's Mediterranean climate quickly disappears as soon as you head downhill and Villamontes proudly claims the title of the country's hottest spot. As in most of Bolivia, the dry season lasts from April to November.

NATIONAL PARKS & RESERVES

Remote, wild and off the beaten track, South Central Bolivia's parks and reserves are for hardcore adventure seekers. Infrastructure is less than basic, but a visit to any one of the reserves will make a lasting impression. Those covered in this chapter include Sama Biological Reserve (p259), Reserva Nacional de Flora y Fauna Tariquía (p262), Parque Nacional y Area Nacional de Manejo Integrado Aguaragüe (p265), Reserva Privada de Patrimonio Natural de Corvalán (p266) and Cabo Juan Wildlife Reserve.

GETTING THERE & AROUND

Most people visit Bolivia's far south on the way to or from somewhere else. Overland connections from Argentina and Paraguay and other regions within the country involve long bus rides. The Trans-Chaco Road (see the boxed text, p264) from Paraguay has improved in recent years but is still an arduous journey. Tarija has the biggest airport in the area but scheduled flights to places like La Paz are less than daily.

Public transport runs frequently between towns, but you'll need a 4WD to get almost anywhere else. Few roads are paved so prepare yourself for hauls that take longer than they should.

SOUTH CENTRAL BOLIVIA

In spite of Tarija's grand illusions of spiritual kinship with Andalucia, urban Bolivians regard South Central Bolivia as a half-civilized backwater. 'Chapaco' all too often forms the standard butt of tasteless jokes told in La Paz. In rebuttal the regionalistic southerners note that in 1810, the year that followed Chuquisaca department's 'first cry

of independence in the Americas', part of Tarija department declared independence from Spain and operated briefly under a sovereign government with its capital at Tarija.

TARIJA

pop 132,000 / elevation 1850m

Tarija's valley climate resembles the eternal spring of Cochabamba, although winter nights may be slightly cooler. The region's distinctly Mediterranean flavor is evident in its climate, architecture and vegetation. Its inhabitants are proud to be accused of considering themselves more Spanish or Argentine than Bolivian; many are descended from Argentine *gauchos*. Stately date palms line the main plaza and the wildly eroded surrounding landscape includes badlands reminiscent of the Spanish *meseta*. As many immigrants have discovered, Tarija makes a nice stopover on the way to or from Argentina.

History

Tarija was founded on July 4, 1574, as La Villa de San Bernardo de Tarixa, by Don Luis de Fuentes y Vargas under the orders of Viceroy Don Francisco de Toledo. In 1810 the region declared independence from Spanish rule. Although the breakaways weren't taken seriously by the Spanish, the situation did erupt into armed warfare on April 15, 1817. At the Batalla de la Tablada, the Chapacos won a major victory over the Spanish forces. In the early nineteenth century, Tarija actively supported Bolivia's struggle for independence. Although Argentina was keen to annex the agriculturally favorable area, Tarija opted to join the Bolivian Republic when it was established in 1825.

Orientation

Street numbers are preceded by an O (*oeste*/west) for those addresses west of Calle Colón and an E (*este*/east) for those east of Colón; addresses north of Av Victor Paz Estenssoro (Av Las Américas) take an N.

Information

Between 1pm and 4pm Tarija becomes a virtual ghost town. Conduct all your business in the morning or you'll have to wait until after the siesta.

EMERGENCY
Hospital San Juan de Dios (☎ 664-5555; Santa Cruz s/n)
Police (☎ 664-2222; Campero & 15 de Abril)

IMMIGRATION
Migración (☎ 664-3450; Bolívar at Ballivián) Get entry/exit stamps or to extend your stay.

INTERNET ACCESS
Internet Bunker (Saracho 456; ☾ until 1pm Sat & Sun) Non-smoking; US$0.50 per hour.

LAUNDRY
Lavandería La Esmerelda (☎ 664-2043; La Madrid 0-157) Does quick machine wash-and-dry service for US$0.80 per kilo.

MONEY
ATMs are numerous around the plaza. **Casas de cambio** (Bolívar btwn Sucre & Campos) change US dollars and Argentine pesos. Banco Bisa and Banco Nacional, both on Sucre, will change up to US$1000 of travelers checks for US$6 commission.

POST & TELEPHONE
The main **post office** (Sucre & Lema) and **Entel** (Lema & Campos) are conveniently located.

TOURIST INFORMATION
Departmental tourist office (☎ 663-1000; south-west cnr of Plaza Luis de Fuentes y Vargas; ☾ 8:30am-noon & 3-6pm Mon-Fri) Distributes basic town maps (US$1) and is reasonably helpful with queries regarding sites both within the city and out of town.
Municipal tourist office (☎ 663-8081; Bolívar & Sucre) More friendly than helpful and is shut more often than open.

Sights
A stroll around the center to see what remains of the colonial atmosphere is worth an afternoon.

MUSEO DE ARQUEOLOGÍA Y PALEONTOLOGÍA
The free university-run **Archaeology & Paleontology Museum** (Lema & Trigo; ☾ 9am-noon & 3-6pm) provides a convenient overview of the prehistoric creatures and the early peoples that once inhabited the Tarija area.

Downstairs you'll see the well-preserved remains of several animals: *megatherium*, a giant ground sloth; *glyptodon*, a prehistoric armadillo; *lestodon*, which resembled a

giant-clawed aardvark; *scelidotherium*, a small ground sloth; *smilodon*, the saber-toothed tiger; and *toxodon*, a large and dozy-looking creature with buck teeth.

Items of note are the nearly complete *glyptodon* carapace, and the tail and a superb hand of a *megatherium*. Displays are accompanied by artistic representations of how the animals appeared in the flesh. The archaeological section displays ancient tools, weapons, copper items, textiles and pottery from all over southern Bolivia.

The rooms upstairs focus on history, geology and anthropology, containing displays of old household implements, weapons, an old piano and various prehistoric hunting tools, including a formidable-looking cudgel known as a *rompecabezas* (head-breaker). One inter-esting item is an old bit of presidential stationery bearing the letterhead 'Mariano Melgarejo, President of the Republic of Bolivia, Major General of the Army, etc, etc, etc'. That is topped, however, by a hideously bizarre representation of the Antichrist made from nuts, seeds, grass, wool, hair, shells, flowers, wood and lichen.

CASA DORADA (CASA DE CULTURA)
The **Gilded House** (☎ 664-4606; Ingavi 0-370; ☾ 8am-noon & 2:30-6:30pm Mon-Fri) dates back to 1930, when it was one of the several properties of the wealthy Tarija landowner Moisés Navajas (often described as Bolivia's Teddy Roosevelt) and his wife, Esperanza Morales. The building could be described as imposing but, amusingly, the exterior has been sloppily splashed with gold and silver paint, the roof is topped with a row of liberating angels and the interior reflects equally questionable taste.

The ground floor is painted a scintillating shade of purple and the frescoes could have been the work of precocious preschoolers. There's also a winning collection of lamps: rose lamps, peacock lamps, morning glory lamps and, of course, crystal chandeliers that sprout light bulbs. Perhaps the most worthwhile relic is the *funola*, an early type of player piano that produced music by forcing air through a strip of perforated paper. The recently restored building now belongs to the university and houses the Casa de Cultura. Brief guided tours are sometimes offered for a small donation.

TARIJA

To Hotel Los Parrales (3km);
Tomatitas (5km);
Coimata Falls (12km);
Villazón (12km);
San Lorenzo (15km);
Potosí (366km)

Zoo

Loma de San Juan

Río Guadalquivir

Stadium

Plaza Unión

Parque Bolívar

Mercado Central

Plaza Luis de Fuentes y Vargas

Plaza Sucre

Cathedral

Plaza Heroes de la Tablada

To Parque Heroes de la Tablada

Río Guadalquivir

Puente Bolívar

To Airport (3km); Campos de
Solana; Casa Real & Kohlberg (17km);
Centro Nacional Vitivinícola (20km);
La Concepción (25km);
Bermejo (209km) Yacuíba (351km);
Centro Nacional Vitivinícola (20km)

To Aranjuez (2km)

INFORMATION		(pp252-5)
Argentine Consulate	1	B1
Banco Bisa (ATM)	2	C2
Banco Mercantil (ATM)	3	C2
Banco Nacional	4	C2
Casas de Cambio	5	C2
Departmental Tourist Office	6	C2
Entel	7	C2
Honorary German Consul	8	B3
Hospital San Juan de Dios	9	E1
Immigration	10	B1
Internet Bunker	11	B2
Lavandería La Esmeralda	12	C2
Municipal Tourist Office	13	C2
Prometa	14	D3

SIGHTS & ACTIVITIES		(pp252-5)
Basílica de San Francisco	15	C2
Campos de Solana	(see 17)	
Casa Dorada (Casa de Cultura)	16	C2
Casa Real (Office)	17	D3
Castillo de Moisés Navajas (Castillo de Beatriz)	18	E2
Iglesia de San Juan	(see 59)	
Iglesia de San Roque	19	C1
Kohlberg (Office)	20	D3
La Concepción/Rujero	21	E3
Mirador Loma de San Juan	22	B1
Museo de Arqueología y Paleontología	23	C2
Museo Franciscano Frey Francisco Miguel Mari	(see 15)	
Vinos Aranjuez (Office)	24	D3
Viva Tours	25	D3
Viva Tours	26	E4
VTB Tours	27	B2

SLEEPING		(pp256-7)
Alojamiento El Hogar	28	E4
Alojamiento Ocho Hermanos	29	C2
Gran Hotel Tarija	30	C2
Hostal Bolívar	31	D2
Hostal La Costañera	32	B3
Hostal Libertador	33	B1
Hostal Miraflores	34	C1
Hostería España	35	C1
Residencial El Rosario	36	B2
Residencial Zeballos	37	C1
Victoria Plaza Hotel	38	C2

EATING		(p257)
Bagdad Café	39	D3
Cafe Campero	40	C2
Cafe Mokka	41	D2
Chifa New Hong Kong	42	C3
Chingo's	43	C3
Churrasquería El Rodeo	44	E2
Club Social Tarija	45	C2
El Tropero	46	C3
Heladería Napoli	47	C2
Mr Pizza	(see 41)	
Snack Vicky	48	C2
Supermercado Tarija	49	D3
Taverna Gattopardo	50	C2

DRINKING		(p257)
Auto Mania Sports Bar	51	C2
Karaoke Discoteca Amor	52	C2
Karaoke Tom-Thonn	53	D3

ENTERTAINMENT		(pp257-8)
Asociación Tarijeña de Ajedrez	(see 56)	
Cafe Teatro Caretas	54	C3
Cine Gran Rex	55	C2
Coliseo Deportivo	56	C2

TRANSPORT		(p258)
AeroSur	57	C2
Barron's Rent-a-Car	58	D2
Bus Stop for San Lorenzo	59	B1
Bus Terminal	60	E4
LAB Office	61	C3
Micro Stop for San Jacinto	62	C2
Micros to Terminal, Airport & Tomatitas	63	C1
TAM	64	C2

800 m
0.5 mi

CHURCHES

Architecturally, Tarija's most unusual church is the 1887 **Iglesia de San Roque**, which crowns the hill at the end of General Bernardo Trigo. This imposing landmark is visible from all over town, and its balcony once served as a lookout post.

The **cathedral** (Campero & La Madrid) contains the remains of prominent Chapacos, including Tarija's founder, Don Luis de Fuentes y Vargas. It was constructed in 1611 and expanded and embellished in 1925. By Bolivian standards, the interior is fairly ordinary.

The **Basílica de San Francisco** (Campos at La Madrid) was founded in 1606 and is now a national monument. The 16th-century convent library and archives, which may conjure up images from *The Name of the Rose*, may be used only by researchers with permission from the Franciscan order. Inside the basilica, the free **Museo Franciscano Frey Francisco Miguel Mari** (☺ 8am-6pm Mon-Fri) displays ecumenical painting, sculpture and artifacts.

The **Iglesia de San Juan** at the top of Bolívar, was constructed in 1632. Here the Spanish signed their surrender to the liberation army after the Batalla de la Tablada. The garden affords a sweeping view over Tarija and its dramatic backdrop of brown mountains.

WINERIES (BODEGAS & VINEYARDS)

The Tarija region is known for its wines, most of which are palatable and a few of which produce a spontaneous reaction of the facial muscles. The first grapevines were brought by 17th-century missionaries who recognized the region's climate and soils as similar to those they'd known in wine-growing regions of Iberia. The region now produces well over two million liters annually, and the wines improve all the time.

To visit the wineries and sample their products, inquire at their town offices. The best is **La Concepción/Rujero** (☎ 664-5040; concepbv@ceibo.entelnet.bo; O'Connor N-642), which exports and promotes its vintages as the 'world's highest wines'; the most modern is **Campos de Solana/Casa Real** (☎ 664-8481; www.csolana.com; 15 de Abril E-259); the oldest is **Kohlberg** (☎ 663-6366; 15 de Abril E-275); and the least-palatable is **Vinos Aranjuez** (☎ 664-5651; 15 de Abril E-241). The offices sell bottles at factory prices (US$1.50 to US$10). Besides bottled poetry, the bodegas all produce *singani*, a distilled grape spirit of varying quality.

Only the **Aranjuez cellars** (☎ 664-2552; Los Sauces 1976), a short jaunt southwest across the river, are within walking distance of town. Kohlberg and Casa Real are in Santa Ana, 17km southeast of Tarija via an indirect route that passes the Campos de Solana bodega. La Concepción, worth the extra effort for enophiles, is 25km south on the same road as the **Centro Nacional Vitivinicola** (Cenavit; ☎ 665-1054). Cenavit performs laboratory quality-control of all alcohol entering and exiting Bolivia, provides technical support to local vintners and produces its own experimental wines.

Travelers without transportation may approach the in-town offices politely and see if they may be able to organize lifts. Alternatively, both Viva Tours and VTB Tours (below) offer recommended half-day and day-long wine-tasting tours for US$15 to US$25 per person.

In town the best places to sample local vintages are the wine bar at **Taverna Gattopardo** (p257) and the **Viva Tours** (☎ /fax 663-8325; 15 de Abril & Delgadillo) branch near the bus terminal.

MIRADOR LOMA DE SAN JUAN

This park area above the tree-covered slopes of San Juan hill provides a grand city view and is a favorite with students. Climb uphill to the end of Calle Bolívar, then turn right behind the hill and follow the footpath up the slope that faces away from the city.

CASTILLO DE MOISÉS NAVAJAS

The exterior of this oddly prominent and deteriorating private mansion (aka Castillo de Beatriz; Bolívar E-644) is worth a look for its garish extravagance. It's currently inhabited but is occasionally open for informal tours.

Tours

For wine tours and adventurous eco-trips to Tarija's hinterlands – including four nearby national reserves – it's tough to beat **Viva Tours** (☎ /fax 663-8325; vivatour@cosett.com.bo; 15 de Abril & Delgadillo) and its branch office (☎ 666-1169; La Paz 252), which charges around US$15 per person or US$25 per person for half- or full-day tours. **VTB Tours** (☎ 664-3372;

MUSIC & DANCE, CHAPACO-STYLE

Not only is Tarija Bolivia's land of wine, it's also rich in music and song, as shown by its musical and dance traditions, which are unique in the country.

The traditional dance *La Rueda* is featured at all Tarijeño festivities, as are the *chunchos*. These men have vowed to the Virgin Mary to perform their gyrating Bolivian version of British morris dancing every year for 10 to 50 years. Their colorful costumes are assembled from half-length silk shirts, scarves, veils and stockings, clown shoes, gaudy silk hearts decorated with shells, and polychrome feather top-hats adorned with assorted bangles. The lively, rhythmic music is accompanied by the clicks of their small metal castanets.

Woodwind instruments unique to the Tarija area are the *erke*, the *caña* and the *camacheña*. The *erke*, also known as the *phututu*, is made from a cow's horn and is played exclusively between New Year's Day and Carnaval. From San Roque to the end of the year, the *camacheña*, a type of flute, is featured. The *caña*, a 3m-long cane pole with a cow's horn on the end, is similar in appearance and tone to an alphorn. It's played throughout the year in Tarija. The stringed *violín chapaco*, a variation on the European violin, originated in Tarija and is the favored instrument between Easter and San Roque. Among percussion instruments, Tarija loves the *caja*, a tambourine-like drum played with one hand. Instruments popular elsewhere in Bolivia, such as *charangos*, guitars and flutes, also feature prominently in Tarijeño merrymaking.

---

vtb@olivo.entelnet.bo; Ingavi 0-784) also runs trips to most sites of interest around the city and the region.

Festivals & Events

Tarija is one of Bolivia's most festive towns, especially around Carnaval.

MARCH

If you're in town during the last week of March, check out the **Fiesta de Leche y Queso** (Festival of Milk & Cheese) outside of town in Rosillas (p259).

Tarija's **Carnaval** is one of the most animated in Bolivia and is well worth attending. To launch the festivities, two Thursdays before Carnaval Tarija celebrates the **Fiesta de Compadres**, and then, the following Thursday the unique **Fiesta de Comadres**. The latter, which is Tarija's largest pre-Carnaval festival, was probably inspired by the wives of Spanish colonial authorities and soldiers, who saw to it that strict social customs and morals were followed in this sophisticated community. This festival, which originated in Pola de Siero, Asturias, Spain, was eventually adopted by the indigenous population and is now celebrated by the entire community with music, dancing and special basket tableaux constructed of bread known as *bollus preñaus*, flowers, fruits, tubers, small cakes and other gifts, which are passed between female friends and relatives.

Throughout the Carnaval season, the festivities are dedicated to good fun and the streets fill with joyful dancing, original Chapaco music and colorfully costumed country folk who come to town for the event. There's a **Grand Ball** in the main plaza after the celebration and the entire town turns out for dancing and performances by folkloric groups, bands and orchestras. Gringos beware: water balloons figure prominently in the festivities.

On the Sunday after Carnaval, the *barrio* near the cemetery enacts a bizarre 'funeral' in which the devil is burned and buried in preparation for Lent. Paid mourners lend the ritual a morose air – but they're actually lamenting that they must remain free of vice for the 40 days until Easter!

APRIL

In keeping with its gaucho heritage, Tarija stages an annual rodeo in Parque Héroes de la Tablada, beginning on the departmental holiday. **Rodeo Chapaco** (April 15–21) includes all the standard cowboy events. Take *micro* C from the center.

AUGUST

Tarija's well-known **Fiesta de San Roque** (August 16) features canines parading through the street in festive dress (San Roque is the patron saint of dogs). The main celebration however, doesn't begin until the first Sunday of September and then continues for eight days; it features traditional musical performances and a *chuncho* procession. During the procession, participants wearing costumes highlighted with bright feathers, ribbons, glittering sequins and other small, festive objects masquerade as members of a Chaco tribe that has been recently converted to Christianity.

OCTOBER

The annual **Fiesta de las Flores** (2nd Sunday in October) is a religious celebration dedicated to the Virgen de Rosario. It begins with a procession of the faithful, which sets off from the **Iglesia de San Juan**. Along the route, spectators shower participants with flower petals. The highlight of the day is a colorful fair and bazaar in which the faithful spend lavishly for the benefit of the Church.

Ask around about the artesanal in October and about the **Serrano Ham & Cheese Festival**.

Sleeping

BUDGET

Alojamiento Ocho Hermanos (☎ 664-2111; Sucre N-782; s/d US$5/8) A favorite, centrally located budget choice, with a sun-filled courtyard surrounded by tidy rooms with shared bath. Bonuses include a terrace and cheap laundry service. It was closed for repairs but scheduled to re-open in 2004.

Residencial Zeballos (☎ 664-2068; Sucre N-966; US$3.35, with bath & breakfast US$6.35) Bright, comfortable rooms and a million potted plants make this friendly joint a good choice. The relaxing courtyard, cable TV and laundry service add to the value.

Hostería España (☎ 664-1790; Corrado O-546; US$3.35, with bath US$5.35) This welcoming *hostería* with helpful staff makes a smart all-round choice. The hot showers and a pleasant flowery patio keep it popular with long-term university student residents.

Residencial El Rosario (☎ 664-3942; Ingavi 777; US$3.35, with bath US$5.35) This favorite haunt of volunteer workers doesn't have the warmest atmosphere, but it's comfortable and good value. Advantages include the

reliable gas-heated showers, the laundry sinks and the common cable-TV room. Breakfast is available for US$1.

Hostal Bolívar (☎ 664-2741; Bolívar N-256; s US$5.50-9.50, d US$10-16) The warm and quiet courtyard is inviting and all of the hot showers work. Only the cheapest rooms lack TV.

Hostal Miraflores (☎ 664-3355; Sucre N-920; US$3.25, with bath US$6.35) In a restored colonial-style building near the market, Miraflores is far from perfect. Some rooms occupy a dark warren at the back and the cheapest rooms are windowless, but the rooms upstairs are just fine.

Alojamiento El Hogar (☎ 6643964; Paz Estenssoro at La Paz; US$2) Opposite the bus terminal, this dirt-cheap crash pad offers basic accommodations in a friendly, family-run atmosphere.

MID-RANGE

Hostal La Costañera (☎ 664-2851; Paz Estenssoro & Saracho; s US$15-20, d with bath & cable TV US$30; free 🖳) This pleasantly posh hostel is popular with business people and NGO workers for its amenities: phone, *frigobar*, heaters (upon request) and parking. Good-value rooms include a full buffet breakfast and lower rates may be negotiated for longer stays or in the low season. A good vegetarian buffet *almuerzo* (US$1.75) is served daily except Sunday.

Victoria Plaza Hotel (☎ 664-2600; hot_vi@ entelnet.bo; La Madrid at Sucre; s US$25-40, d with cable TV US$35-50) This four-star, business traveler's choice on the main plaza has modernized rooms with phones and *frigobars*. A stylish café-bar, La Bella Epoca, is downstairs.

Gran Hotel Tarija (☎ 664-2893; fax 664-4777; Sucre N-770; s/d with breakfast & cable TV US$15/29; 🐶) The carpeted rooms are a tad old but spacious and comfortable at this convenient choice only a block from the plaza.

Hostal Libertador (☎ 664-4231; Bolívar O-649; s/d US$8/12) A passable lower-mid-range choice, this central and welcoming place has rooms with phones and cable TV. Breakfast runs an additional US$0.75.

TOP END

Hotel Los Parrales (☎ 664-8444; www.losparrales hotel.com; Urbanización Carmen de Aranjuez; s/d with full breakfast US$95/115; 🐶) In a relaxed setting 3.5km from the center, Tarija's only five-star option has a spa and all the other trappings of a business-class resort, plus a lovely open-air dining area overlooking the countryside. Transfers from the center cost US$10 for up to three people. Taxis are US$1. Significant discounts (up to 45%) are available for stays of more than one night during the low season.

Eating

At the northeast corner of the **Mercado Central** (Sucre & Domingo Paz), street vendors sell snacks and pastries unavailable in other parts of Bolivia, including delicious crêpe-like *panqueques*. Breakfast is served out the back, other cheap meals are upstairs and fresh juices are in the produce section. Don't miss the huge bakery and sweets section off Bolívar.

QUICK EATS

Cafe Mokka (north side of Plaza Sucre; meals US$1-2) A stylish newcomer with sidewalk seating that's open all day for strong espresso, breakfast, cocktails and good light grub.

Cafe Campero (Campero near Bolívar) The range of breads, cakes and pastries, including French-style baguettes, chocolate cake, *cuñapes* (cassava and cheese rolls), is what makes this place a gem.

Heladería Napoli (Campero N-630) Serves simply divine scoops of ice cream until 8pm.

Snack Vicky (La Madrid at Trigo; mains & meals US$1-1.50) A local favorite for a quick bite, also serves steaks, sandwiches and *almuerzos*.

Bagdad Café (east side of Plaza Sucre; ⏰ 9am-midnight Mon-Fri, 9am-2am Sat & Sun; snacks & mains under US$2) A popular youth hangout, has a full bar and light dinner menu.

RESTAURANTS

Taverna Gattopardo (☎ 663-0656; north side of main plaza; mains US$2-5, wine tasting US$6-10) Tarija's most popular hangout is this welcoming European-run tavern. It's decorated with Chaco War antiques and is a pleasure at any time of the day: for espresso or cappuccino in the morning; well-prepared salads, soups and pasta, burgers, *ceviche* or pizzas at midday; chicken fillets and fish to fondue bourguignonne in the evening; and rich desserts at night. There's a cozy, stone-lined alcove at the back, a social bar and a new wine-tasting area where you can sample a flight of the region's best vintages

between bites of local Serrano ham. When the weather's good, quaff a beer outside and admire the (lack of) urgency of life on the plaza.

Chingo's (☎ 663-2222; west side of Plaza Sucre; ⏰ 11am-midnight; snacks US$1-2, meals US$3-4) Specializing in hefty Argentine beef *parrillada* with all the standard trimmings – rice, salad and potatoes – Chingo's also serves burgers, pizza, chicken and chips and other fried things. Delivery is available for a nominal fee.

Churrasquería El Rodeo (Oruro E-749; meals US$4) With Argentina so close, it's not surprising that big slabs of red meat are popular. This sparkling choice also has a salad bar.

El Tropero (Lema O-226; meals US$4) This rustic spot is another good choice for hungry carnivores. Steak is all that's for dinner with only a salad bar to complement it.

Chifa New Hong Kong (☎ 663-7076; Sucre N-235; lunch US$2.25, mains US$2.50-4) The best Chinese choice, with cheap cocktails, huge lunches and an extensive menu featuring all the usual suspects.

Mr Pizza (☎ 665-0505; north side of Plaza Sucre; pies US$2-3.50) Next door to Cafe Mokka, this no-nonsense parlor delivers until midnight.

Club Social Tarija (☎ 664-2108; 15 de Abril E-271; ⏰ lunch only Mon-Fri; lunch US$1) Serves inexpensive, old-fashioned *almuerzos* to a loyal crowd of monthly meal-plan subscribers.

SELF-CATERING

Supermercado Tarija (15 de Abril at Delgadillo) Tarija's best supermarket is well-stocked with imported foodstuffs and a good wine selection.

Entertainment

Plaza Sucre is Tarija's youth hangout. **Cafe Teatro Caretas** (Suipacha & Carpio) is a bohemian, all-ages cultural center. It presents live music, theater, chess lessons and art exhibitions. There is something happening most nights and the cover is minimal. Drinks and snacks are served and late-night burger stands wait outside.

To watch big games, head to Tarija's only fully fledged sports bar, **Auto Mania** (Sucre & Carpio).

Earplug alert: karaoke runs rampant around Plaza Sucre. For tone-deafness try **Karaoke Tom-Thonn** (15 de Abril & Méndez) or the hip **Karaoke Discoteca Amor** (Sucre at La Madrid).

Keep an eye out for flyers advertising *peñas*, usually held at restaurants on weekends. **Cine Gran Rex** (La Madrid btwn Campos & Colón) screens double-feature first-run flicks for a couple of bucks.

Entertaining basketball, *futsal* and volleyball games are played at the **Coliseo Deportivo** on Campero. After 6pm, chess heads can pick up a game next door at the **Asociación Tarijeña de Ajedrez**, where you can play for free if you respect club rules: no smoking and quiet, please.

Getting There & Away
AIR
The Oriel Lea Plaza Airport is 3km east of town off Av Victor Paz Estenssoro. **LAB** (☎ 664-2195; Trigo N-329) has regular services to Cochabamba and a couple of flights a week to Santa Cruz. **TAM** (☎ 664-2734; La Madrid 0-470) has Saturday flights to Santa Cruz (US$55) and Sunday flights to La Paz (US$75) via Sucre (US$40). **AeroSur** (☎ 663-0893; Ingavi at Sucre) flies three times a week to La Paz and Santa Cruz.

BUS & CAMIÓN
The **bus terminal** (☎ 663-6508) is at the east end of town, a 20-minute walk from the center along Av Victor Paz Estenssoro. Several *flotas* run buses to Potosí (US$6.50, 12 to 15 hours), with connections to Uyuni (US$8, 20 hours), Oruro (US$9, 20 hours), Cochabamba (US$12, 26 hours) and Sucre (US$9, 18 hours); most leave daily in the afternoon.

Buses to Tupiza (US$4 to US$5, nine to 10 hours) and Villazón (US$4 to US$5, 10 hours) depart daily in the evening. Buses leave every morning to Yacuiba (US$4, 12 hours); this is a lovely journey. Daily buses for La Paz (US$15, 24 hours) leave at 7:30am. There are also daily services to Camiri (US$8, 14 hours), with connections to Santa Cruz (US$11, 24 hours) and numerous buses head daily for Bermejo (US$3.50, six hours).

You can also travel directly to most Argentine cities daily, including Buenos Aires (US$50, 32 hours). There is a daily service to Santiago, Chile (US$65, 34 hours), via Mendoza, Argentina, as well. International services to Asunción (Paraguay), Iquique (Chile) and Montevideo (Uruguay) are also regular.

To go to Yacuiba or Villamontes, the best place to wait for a *camión* is at the *tranca* east of town. Although it's an uncomfortable ride, you'll pass through some fabulous scenery, especially the stretch between Entre Ríos and Palos Blancos, and through the Pilcomayo Gorge. Use the north *tranca* for Villazón and Potosí and the southeast *tranca* for Yacuiba and Bermejo.

Getting Around
TO/FROM THE AIRPORT
Taxis from the airport to the center cost around US$1, but if you walk 100m past the airport gate (visible from outside the terminal), you'll pay as little as US$0.40 per person. Otherwise, cross the main road and take a passing *micro* A or *trufi* (US$0.20), which passes by the Mercado Central.

BUS
City *micros* and *trufis* cost US$0.20 per ride; routes are clearly marked on the front windows of the vehicles.

CAR
Barron's Rent-a-Car (☎ 663-6853; Ingavi E-339)

TAXI
Although you can walk just about anywhere in Tarija (including the airport), taxis cost US$0.50/0.75 per person for day/night trips around the center, including the bus terminal. For a radio taxi, ring **4 de Julio** (☎ 664-6555/7676).

AROUND TARIJA
San Jacinto Reservoir
This 1700-hectare reservoir, 7km southwest of town, provides landlocked Tarija with watery recreation. There's a tourist complex with little *cabañas* serving *dorado* (a delicious local fish), a canoe rental place and nice walks along the shore and surrounding ridges. It's popular with chapacos on Sunday afternoons. *Micro* H and the *trufi* Línea San Jacinto (US$0.20, 10 minutes) leave every 20 minutes from the **Palacio de la Justicia** (Ingavi & Campos) in Tarija.

San Lorenzo
San Lorenzo, 15km north of Tarija along the Tupiza road, is a quaint colonial village with cobbled streets, carved balconies, a 1709 church and a flowery plaza. It's best

known however, as the home of one José Eustaquio 'Moto' Méndez, the hero of the Batalla de la Tablada, whose home now houses the free **Museo Moto Méndez** (9am-12:30pm & 3-5pm Mon-Sat, 10am-noon Sun). Displays consist mainly of his personal belongings, which he bequeathed to the people of Tarija. As in so many such museums, they've been left exactly as they were when he died. The popular **Fiesta de San Lorenzo** takes place on August 10 and features Chapaco musical instruments and dancing.

After seeing the museum, head 2km north to the **Capilla de Lajas**, a delicate chapel of exquisite proportions and fine colonial architecture. It was once the Méndez family chapel and remains in private hands. Just to the north is the former home of Jaime Paz Zamora, with an adjacent billboard paying homage to the ex-president.

Micros and *trufis* (US$0.35, half-hour) leave from **Plaza Guemes** (Iglesia de San Juan) in Tarija approximately every 20 minutes during the day.

El Valle de la Concepción

The Concepción Valley, or simply 'El Valle', is the heart of Bolivian wine and *singani* production. The town itself still bears many picturesque colonial elements and the plaza sports some lovely endemic flowering ceibo trees. To visit the valley's wineries, contact **Viva Tours** (p254) or the winery offices in Tarija (p254). The **Fiesta de la Uva** (Grape Festival) is held here for three days in March, corresponding with the grape harvest.

El Valle lies off the route toward Bermejo; take the right fork at the *tranca* east of Tarija. *Trufi* Línea V leaves for Concepción from Tarija's Plaza Sucre (US$0.40, half-hour) approximately every half-hour during the day.

Padcaya

About all that remains of Padcaya's touted colonial heritage are a couple of buildings on the plaza and one other edifice (now a truck repair shop) with a plaster colonial façade peeling to its adobe innards. While the town does enjoy a nice setting, nestled in a hollow with lots of eucalyptus trees, what makes Padcaya worthwhile is the trip itself – 50km of lovely mountainous desert with green river valleys.

For an interesting walk from Padcaya, continue south along the road toward Chaguaya (not toward Bermejo – turn right at the *tranca*) for 3km to a hamlet known as **Cabildo**. Tanning seems to be an important cottage industry here, done the old-fashioned way with pits of vile-looking liquids and hides strung on lines.

At Cabildo turn right on a llama track, then walk 5km further until you reach a **cave** with petroglyphs. This is a popular field trip for Tarija students. You'll probably need help to find the paintings, but don't ask a child to guide you: locals believe the devil inhabits this enchanting spot and they don't allow their own children to go near it.

If you're up for something totally off the beaten track, check out the annual **Fiesta de Leche y Queso** (Festival of Milk & Cheese) in Rosillas (population 1000), west of Padcaya. It takes place during the last week of March and admirably celebrates the contributions of local cows.

Micro P leaves for Padcaya (US$1, half-hour) hourly from Plaza Sucre, at the intersection of Colón and 15 de Abril.

Chaguaya

In Chaguaya, 51km south of Tarija near Padcaya, you'll find the pilgrimage shrine Santuario de la Virgen de Chaguaya. The **Fiesta de la Virgen de Chaguaya** begins on August 15; celebrations follow on the subsequent Sunday. Alcohol is forbidden at this time. Pilgrims from all over Bolivia arrive during the following month, some on foot (including the annual 12-hour, 45km procession from Tarija). *Micros* (US$0.75) from Tarija to Chaguaya leave from the main bus terminal at 4pm daily.

Reserva Biológica Cordillera de Sama (Sama Biological Reserve)

This reserve protects representative samples of both the Altiplano and the inter-Andean valley ecosystems. In the highland portion of the reserve (11,000 feet above sea level) one can visit the Tajzara lakes, which serve as a stop for over 30 species of migrating aquatic birds, including three of the world's six flamingo species and the rare horned coot and giant coot. Temperatures in the highlands stay quite chilly year-round but are slightly more comfortable in the drier

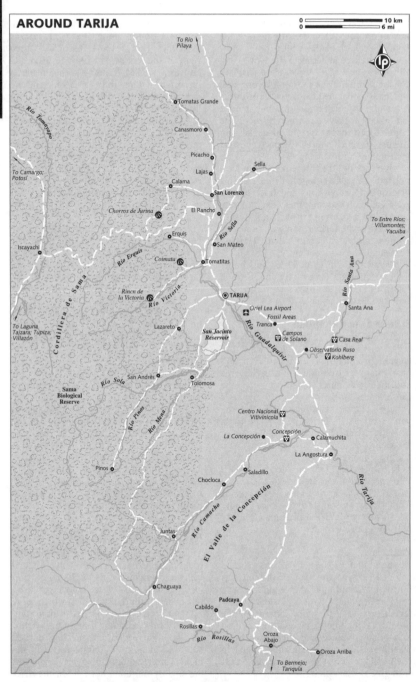

AROUND TARIJA

| 0 | 10 km |
| 0 | 6 mi |

To Río Pilaya

Río Tomayapo

Tomatas Grande

Canasmoro

To Camargo;
Potosí

Picacho

Sella

Lajas

Calama

San Lorenzo

Chorros de Jurina

El Rancho

Río Sella

Erquis

Río Erquis

San Mateo

Coimata

Tomatitas

To Entre Ríos;
Villamontes;
Yacuiba

Iscayachi

Río Santa Ana

Rincn de
la Victoria

Río Victoria

TARIJA

Oriel Lea Airport
Fossil Areas

Santa Ana

Cordillera de Sama

To Laguna
Tajzara; Tupiza;
Villazón

Lazareto

San Jacinto
Reservoir

Tranca

Campos
de Solano

Río Guadalquivir

Casa Real

Observatorio Ruso
Kohlberg

Sama
Biological
Reserve

Río Sola

San Andrés

Río Pinos

Río Mena

Tolomosa

Centro Nacional
Vitivinicola

La Concepción

Concepción

Calamuchita

La Angostura

Pinos

Río Tarija

Chocloca

Saladillo

Río Camacho

El Valle de la Concepción

Juntas

Chaguaya

Padcaya

Cabildo

Rosillas

Río Rosillas

Oroza
Abajo

Oroza Arriba

To Bermejo;
Tariquía

winter months (May to August). The best time to visit the lower elevations is in the summer, when it's warm enough to swim.

The reserve is jointly administered by Sernap and **Protection of the Environment of Tarija** (Prometa; ☎ 663-3873; www.prometabolivia.org; Carpio E-659), which may implement an admission fee in 2004.

TAJZARA SECTION

The area known as Tajzara lies high on the cold and windy *puna* of western Tarija department. Here, several shallow flamingo-filled lagoons appear like jewels in the harsh Altiplano, vegetated only by *thola* (a small desert bush) and spiky *paja brava*. Tarija's New Agers consider Tajzara to be a natural power site and indeed, it could easily be mistaken for an estranged corner of Tibet. Highland people believe the lakes are haunted by spirit voices that call out at night, and that to be out after dark would invite disaster. The night air does produce some eerie voice-like cries, but unimaginative people have ascribed the phenomenon to winds rushing through the *thola*.

Along the eastern shores of the lagoons, the wind has heaped up large *arenales* (sand dunes). An interesting climb takes you to the symmetrical peak of **Muyuloma**, which rises about 1000m above the plain. The summit affords views across the lagoons and beyond to the endless expanses of the southern Altiplano. The return climb takes the better part of a day.

Near the **Tajzara visitors' center**, Prometa is building an **albergue** (under/over 25 years old US$10/ 13) with hot showers, communal kitchen and an observatory where bird-watchers will be able to spot the 45 resident species including the three flamingo species. Hikers can spend a very enjoyable six to eight hours on the wonderful **Inca Trail** as it descends 2000m to the valley below. With luck, hikers may see vicuñas, condors, the rare Andean deer or mysterious petroglyphs of unknown origin. Arrive the night before you intend to hike and bring all your food from elsewhere.

INTER-ANDEAN VALLEYS

During the summertime, there are several places in the valley to go swimming in the rivers, including Tomatitas, Coimata and Chorros de Jurina.

Tomatitas, with its natural swimming holes, its three lovely rivers (the Sella, Guadalquivir and Erquis) and its happy little eateries, is popular with day-trippers from Tarija. The best swimming is immediately below the footbridge, where there's also a park with a campground and barbecue sites. From here you can walk or hitch the 5km to **Coimata**. From Tarija, turn left off the main San Lorenzo road. After less than 1km, you'll pass a cemetery on the left, which is full of flowers and brightly colored crosses. Just beyond it, bear right toward Coimata. Once there, turn left at the soccer field and continue to the end of the road. Here you'll find a small cascade of water and a **swimming hole** that makes a great escape, as lots of Tarijeño families can attest. There's also a choice of small restaurants serving *misquinchitos* and *doraditos* (fried local fish with white corn), as well as *cangrejitos* (small freshwater crabs). From this point, you can follow a walking track 40 minutes upstream to the base of the two-tiered **Coimata Falls**, which has a total drop of about 60m.

Another swimming hole and waterfall are found at **Rincón de la Victoria**, 6.5km southwest of Tomatitas in a green plantation-like setting. Instead of bearing right beyond the colorful cemetery, as you would for Coimata, follow the route to the left. From the fork, it's 5km to Rincón de la Victoria.

The twin 40m waterfalls at **Chorros de Jurina** also make an agreeable destination for a day trip from Tarija. Set in a beautiful but unusual landscape, one waterfall cascades over white stone while the other pours over black stone. In late winter, however, they may diminish to a mere trickle or even be dry.

The route from Tarija to Jurina passes through some impressive rural landscapes. From near the flowery plaza in San Lorenzo, follow the Jurina road, which turns off beside the **Casa de Moto Méndez**. After 6km, you'll pass a school on the left side. Turn left 200m beyond the school and follow that road another 2.5km to the waterfalls. From the end of the road, it's a five-minute walk to the base of either waterfall. The one on the left is reached by following the river upstream; for the other, follow the track that leads from behind a small house.

GETTING THERE & AWAY

From Tarija, **Viva Tours** (☎ /fax 663-8325; 15 de Abril & Delgadillo) organizes overnight trips to several areas of Sama. However, it is possible to reach Tajzara by local transport, but often only at night. From Tarija take a bus toward Villazón and ask the driver to point out the Tajzara visitors' center, a 20-minute walk from the road. Otherwise, you can get off at **Pasajes**, 7km from the visitors' center. Or contact **Prometa** (☎ 663-3873) about other transport options.

Micros A and B to Tomatitas leave frequently from the western end of Av Domingo Paz in Tarija, and on weekends occasional *trufis* go all the way to Coimata. A taxi from Tomatitas to Coimata costs US$2 with up to four people; all the way from Tarija to Coimata costs US$4. *Trufis* San Lorenzo leave for Jurina from near the Iglesia de San Juan in Tarija around 8:30am, 2:45pm and 5pm. Get off near the school and then walk the rest of the way. Hitching is only feasible on weekends.

TARIQUÍA FLORA & FAUNA RESERVE

Created in 1989 the lovely and little-known 247,000-hectare **Reserva Nacional de Flora y Fauna Tariquía** protects a large portion of the dense cloud-forest ecosystem on the eastern slopes of Tarija department's mountains. Ranging in altitude from 400m to 1500m, the reserve features such rare animals as the spectacled bear, jaguar, tapir, collared peccary and Andean fox, as well as hundreds of bird species. Visitors to the reserve's southern sector are charged US$10 if they wish to fish.

The only way to see this largely wild reserve is on foot, but hiking can be challenging and is most comfortably done with a guide and pack animal. The best time to visit Tariquía is during the dry winter months (May–September), since river crossings become treacherous during the rainy season. In winter the climate is generally mild and sometimes even quite warm, especially at the lower altitudes.

Prometa (☎ 663-3873; www.prometabolivia.org; Carpio E-659) operates seven camps in Tariquía, including a simple **albergue** (US$15-20) with cooking and free camping facilities, and the **Tariquía Community Center** in the heart of the reserve. From the road it's a two-day hike to the center and requires camping

gear, but allow six days to fully explore the area on foot.

Transportation may be organized through Prometa, which does day trips and sometimes sponsors guided hikes. Alternatively, you can go with Viva Tours in Tarija.

BERMEJO

pop 1500 / elevation 415m

Bolivia's southernmost town is a hot, muggy and dusty community on the banks of the Río Bermejo, at the southwest end of the country's oil-bearing geological formation. Most of its residents earn their living from the YPFB petroleum plant or from the refinery that processes locally grown sugarcane. The international bridge, 5km upriver from the town, provides a highway link with **Aguas Blancas**, Argentina. Note that Bolivia is always one hour behind Argentine time.

Thanks to its border location, Bermejo has plenty of *casas de cambio* that change cash. Check email at **Café Internet Cotabe** (Arce at Ameller). Both the Bolivian and Argentine border posts are open the same hours: 7am to 4pm *mas o menos* in Bolivia and a more reliable 8am to 5pm in Argentina. *Chalanas* (ferries) over the river (US$0.15) leave every few minutes. Be sure to pick up an exit stamp before crossing.

There's a surprising choice of accommodations in Bermejo. **Hotel Paris** (☎ /fax 696-4562; Tarija at La Paz) is pretty nice, as is **Hotel San Diego** (☎ 696-1333; Cochabamba 118). The clean **La Casona del Turista** (☎ 696-3342; carello@cotabe.com; Barranqueras 147; r per person with bath US$5) has rooms with hot water. There are no accommodations in Aguas Blancas.

On the plaza, **Don Javier** serves standard Bolivian favorites for equally standard prices. Nothing outstanding – just *lomo*, chicken, soup and rice. There is, however, a good *heladería* on the plaza.

The bus terminal is eight blocks southeast of the main plaza. Hourly buses connect Bermejo and Tarija (US$6, six hours). From Aguas Blancas, Argentine buses to Orán (US$1.50, one hour) depart hourly from the terminal opposite the immigration office. From Orán, you can connect to Salta, Jujuy, Tucumán, Tartagal (the connection to Pocitos and Yacuiba) and Asunción (Paraguay).

THE CHACO

Parceled into vast *estancias*, this immense flat expanse of thorn scrub takes in most of southeastern Bolivia and western Paraguay and spills into neighboring Argentina. The human population of this expansive region is limited to a handful of widely dispersed ranchers, isolated indigenous groups, resourceful Mennonite colonists and troops at police and military posts.

The flat Chaco may lack undulating scenery, but it is South America's second most diverse ecosystem (after the Amazon Basin). Butterflies and birds are abundant and it's one of the continent's dwindling strongholds of larger mammals such as the tapir, jaguar and peccary or *javeli*. The thorny scrub that characterizes the Chaco's unusual flora is enlivened by brilliant flowering bushes and trees, including the yellow *carnaval* bush; the yellow-and-white *huevo*; the pink or white thorny bottle tree, locally known as the *toboroche* or *palo borracho* (drunken branch); and the red-flowering *quebracho* ('break-axe' tree). Beautiful *quebracho* wood, which is too heavy to float, is one of the Chaco's main exports. There are also numerous cactus species.

YACUIBA
elevation 625m

As a typical frontier town, Yacuiba has many shoddy commercial goods for sale and many shoppers scrambling to buy stuff nobody really wants or needs. The town and the surrounding area are of little interest, but bad karma could leave you stranded here overnight. Tiny **Pocitos**, 5km south, is the easternmost Bolivia–Argentina border crossing.

Yacuiba straddles the transition zone between the Chaco and the Argentine Pampa and is the terminus for both the railway from Santa Cruz and the YPFB oil pipeline from Camiri. The railway line was constructed with Argentine capital according to the terms of a 1941 treaty in which Bolivia agreed to export surplus petroleum to Argentina in exchange for a 580km rail approach from Buenos Aires. Although construction began immediately, it wasn't completed until the 1960s.

Information

Yacuiba's main north–south street is flanked by several *casas de cambio*, which only deal in cash. Calculate the amount you're to receive before leaving the window and beware of counterfeit US bills. Pickpocketing and petty theft have been reported, especially in crowded shopping areas. There's no consulate here for either Bolivia or Argentina.

Sleeping & Eating

The number of hotels, bars and restaurants in Yacuiba is disproportionate to its size. The best value is **Hotel Valentín** (☎ 682-2645; San Martín 1153; s/d US$4/7, d with bath US$14), opposite the railway station, with an attached bar/restaurant. The next-best alternative is the older **Hotel Monumental** (☎ 682-2088; Comercio 1270; s/d with bath US$9/14), where you'll pay considerably less in the older annex. The **Hotel Paris** (☎ 682-2182; Comercio at Campero; US$15/20; ❊) has private baths and air-con. Passable budget options include **Residencial Aguaragüe** (s/d US$2.50/3), **Alojamiento Ferrocarril** (US$2) and **Residencial San Martín** (US$2).

For a taste of Argentina north of the border – most notably huge racks of meat – try any of the several *parrilladas*. Decent breakfasts and typical Bolivian meals are served at Swin. There are also numerous snack stands peppered around the shopping district.

Getting There & Around

TAM (☎ 682-3853) flies to Santa Cruz on Saturday afternoons and to La Paz on Sunday mornings, via Tarija and Sucre.

There are morning and evening buses to Tarija (US$4, 12 hours) and numerous *flotas* leave every evening for Santa Cruz (US$9, 15 hours) via Villamontes and Camiri. You can purchase Veloz del Norte Argentine bus tickets in Yacuiba at TVO Expreso Café.

Shared taxis (US$0.75 per person) shuttle between Yacuiba and Argentine immigration at Pocitos. After crossing the border on foot, you can connect with onward Argentine bus services to Tartagal and Embarcación every couple of hours, where you can make connections to Salta, Jujuy, Orán and Buenos Aires.

Yacuiba's **railway station** (☎ 682-2308) ticket window opens in the morning on the day of departure; line up early. Reasonably quick and comfortable *Ferrobus* service to Santa Cruz (3rd/2nd/1st class US$5/6.50/13.50, nine hours) leaves on Wednesday and Sunday at 8pm.

Localiza Rent-a-Car (☎ 682-5600; Comercio at Juan XXIII) rents ordinary cars as well as 4WD vehicles.

VILLAMONTES
elevation 380m

Bolivia's main Chaco outpost prides itself on being the hottest place in the country. The mercury often rises above 40°C as the hot, dry winds coat everything with a thick layer of red dust. Like the rest of the Chaco, Villamontes is famous for

---

THE TRANS-CHACO ROAD

One of South America's great journeys stretches across the vast Gran Chaco between Filadelfia in Paraguay and Villamontes in Bolivia. Now that several bus lines have taken up the Santa Cruz–Asunción challenge, the route has lost some of its romanticism, but most of the old uncertainties remain, and you can be assured that it's still an exciting haul through raw, wild and thorny country. Between Filadelfia and La Patria on the Paraguayan side, the road is good gravel, but from there it's little more than deep, parallel sand ruts. You can choose between buses, *camiones* and private 4WD vehicles – however you go, expect lots of jolts, bounces and repeated immigration, customs, police and military checkpoints. During the wet season, however, the rough, sandy stretches become impassable quicksand and slimy mud. As one traveller describes the experience:

> However you look at it, this trip is still an adventure through one of South America's wildest regions. Two friends and I traveled the Chaco Road in the bed of a *camión* carrying a load of uncured cowhide, which oozed rancid fat and saturated the 40°C heat with an aromatic bovine perfume. On one 5km stretch immediately south of Fortín General Eugenio A Garay, the crew and passengers spent 12 hours digging sand, cutting trees and laying branches to make the road passable. At the end of the day, the always jolly Bolivian crew rewarded the exhausted passengers – the three of us, a German backpacker and a Colombian Hare Krishna devotee – with a delicious meal around a cowboy-style campfire.

> The bugs were as bad as rumored, but the big surprise is the butterfly population. When they're in season, the poor mosquitoes and flies don't stand a chance because there is simply no room for them in the air. At least the butterflies only sit on your toes and lick your sweat!

> In the bus, they wouldn't open the toilet for fear of cholera, so when nature called, passengers headed into the bush with warnings from the drivers about pumas, jaguars and lurking vipers. At the Bolivian border post, our bus stopped to give the guards a few supplies – not a bribe but rather an act of mercy. Then it began to drizzle – drizzle, mind you, not gush down – and the road quickly turned to mud. Now I understood why we were carrying tree trunks in the aisle of the bus. Off we got – not the women, children or bus owners (who were monitoring the expedition) – and stuck the trunks under the wheels. The bus heaved, jerked, spun and got lodged in a ditch. Three hours later we had pushed the bus onto slightly drier ground and were off again.

The Trans-Chaco Road may be as adventurous as the above traveler describes, but it's also fraught with bureaucracy. In Bolivia the best bet for picking up exit stamps is in Tarija or Santa Cruz, or from the military post at Boyuibe (along the railway south of the village) and from the immigration/police post on the highway 1km further out. At the Bolivian border post at Picada Sucre, your passport will be checked and you may receive another exit stamp. The Paraguayan border post is at Fortín Infante Rívarola, a few kilometers further along. Between there and Mariscal Estigarribia there are a couple more checkpoints, one at a remote police post and another at La Patria.

Coming from Paraguay, you must obtain your entry stamp within 72 hours of entering the country.

DEANNA SWANEY

Dinosaur tracks, **Sapallu Khocha** (p229)

WOODS WHEATCROFT

Volcán Licancabur (p177)

Mercado Lanza (p54), La Paz

KRZYSZTOF DYDYNSKI

Ancient rock paintings, **Incamachay** (p229)

Village church, **Chaunaca** (p229)

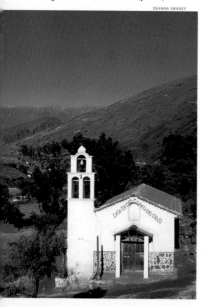

Chewing **coca leaves** (p110)

its wildlife, particularly small buzzing varieties like flies and mosquitoes. In the market look for baskets and furniture made from natural Chaco materials by the indigenous Guaraní people. If you are nearby don't miss the annual August **fishing festival** on the Río Pilcomayo or the **cattle fair** held at the end of August or beginning of September.

History

During Inca times Guaraní tribes immigrated here from present-day Paraguay and their descendants now make up most of the town's indigenous population. Villamontes remained a lonely outpost until it emerged as a strategic Chaco War stronghold. The Paraguayans considered Villamontes their key to undisputed victory over the Bolivian resistance. In the 1934 Battle of Villamontes, the Bolivian army enjoyed its most significant victory. The momentum gained in that battle allowed them to recapture portions of the eastern Chaco and some Santa Cruz department oil fields.

Cañón del Pilcomayo

In the beautiful Pilcomayo Canyon at **El Chorro Grande** waterfall, fish are prevented from swimming further upstream. Abundant *surubí*, *sábalo* and *dorado* are easily caught, making the area a favorite with anglers from all over the country. The prized *dorado* is particularly interesting because it has an odd hinge at the front of its jawbone that allows the mouth to open wide horizontally. There are great views from the restaurants seven to 10km west of town where you can sample local fish dishes.

To reach the gorge, take any Tarija-bound transport, or taxi to the *tranca* and hitch or walk from there (as usual, weekends are the best time to hitchhike). Where the road forks, bear right and continue another 2km to the mouth of the gorge.

Sleeping & Eating

The nicest central hostel is **Gran Hotel Avenida** (☎ 684-2297; s/d with bath & breakfast US$12/15; 🟩), which has rooms with cable TV. Opposite the railway station, the appealing **Hotel El Rancho** (☎ 684-2049; r per person with bath US$8) has bungalows with TV. Cheaper rooms

are available in the older section, and it also has a pleasant restaurant. Two blocks east of the plaza near the railway line, **Residencial Raldes** (☎ 684-2086; US$3.50) isn't that clean but the grounds are flowery. There are a couple good *parilladas* and *churrasquerías*, plus a *chifa* near the plaza.

Getting There & Away

Buses run several times daily to Yacuiba, Tarija and Santa Cruz. The Trans-Chaco Road (see the boxed text, p264) heads out southeast along the Río Pilcomayo. *Camiones* line up near the northern end of the market. By train, Villamontes is two hours north of Yacuiba and 10 hours south of Santa Cruz. Taxis (US$0.40 per person) frequent the railway station, 2km north of town. Inquire at **TAM** (☎ 684-2135) to see if they have resumed Saturday flights to Yacuiba, Santa Cruz and Tarija.

PARQUE NACIONAL Y AREA NATURAL DE MANEJO INTEGRADO AGUARAGÜE

The long and narrow 108,000-hectare Aguaragüe National Park takes in much of the **Serranía de Aguaragüe**, which divides the vast Gran Chaco and the highlands of Tarija department. The region is also well known as having Bolivia's hottest climate, with summer temperatures as high as 46°C.

Although it currently lacks visitor facilities, the **Cañón del Pilcomayo** is readily accessible from Villamontes (p264). The Guaraní name of the park means 'lair of the jaguar,' and the range protects not only this rare cat, but also the fox, tapir, anteater, lynx, assorted parrots, numerous plant species and 70% of the region's potable water sources. **Viva Tours** (☎ /fax 663-8325; 15 de Abril & Delgadillo) conducts guided hikes and visits.

BOYUIBE

Sitting on the fringes of the Chaco along the Santa Cruz–Yacuiba railway line, diminutive Boyuibe serves mainly as a transit point. Roads head north to Camiri and Sucre, south to Argentina and east into Paraguay. The new Trans-Chaco Road (see the boxed text, p264), however, now ends at Villamontes.

Boyuibe's two crash pads, **Hotel Rosedal** and **Hotel Guadalquivir** (both around US$3), are both on the main street. For meals the best bet is Pensión Boyuibe, also on the main street.

A motley assortment of *movilidades* to Camiri (US$1.25, one hour), Villamontes and Yacuiba wait in front of the Tránsito office on the main drag. All Yacuiba- and Santa Cruz–bound trains stop here.

RESERVA PRIVADA DE PATRIMONIO NATURAL DE CORVALÁN

This private 4500-acre reserve on the Paraguayan border was established in 1996 to protect an ideal slice of the arid Gran Chaco. In addition to the jaguar, puma, tapir, giant anteater and armadillo, it's also home to the *ñandu* (rhea), iguana, alligator and all the classic Chaco vegetation. The only access route is the poor road from Villamontes, which takes at least four hours with a good vehicle. Accommodations are limited to a simple park rangers' camp, and visitors should be self-sufficient in food, water and other supplies. Currently the only commercial access is with **Viva Tours** (☎ /fax 663-8325; 15 de Abril & Delgadillo).

CAMIRI

pop 35,000 / elevation 825m

Situated at the Chaco's western edge with a favorable climate, Camiri grew phenomenally in the 1990s due to rapid growth of the national oil company, YPFB (known affectionately as 'Yacimientos'). It's a center for the production of petroleum and natural gas, and bills itself as the Capital Petrolífero de Bolivia (Oil Capital of Bolivia). The city is also poised to become the southern staging point for the developing Che Trail (p293).

In 1955 two pipelines were constructed to carry natural gas and petroleum to Yacuiba on the Argentine frontier. The following year a US$1.5-million natural gas re-injection plant was built atop Cerro Sararenda to recover liquid petroleum gas by injecting natural gas into oil-bearing formations. Another plant to process this liquid petroleum gas was built and began functioning in 1968, and a refrigeration and dehydration plant to recover liquid petroleum was put into operation nearby at Taquiparenda in 1983. Decreased production closed it however, after only three years of operation. Camiri has since experienced ups and downs in the industry, but it remains one of Bolivia's fossil fuel production centers.

Information

Visitors arriving from Paraguay must register with **immigration** (Av 1 de Mayo s/n), downhill from Calle Tarija. **Librería Ramirez** changes cash and travelers checks. **Hotel Ortuño** changes US dollars at decent rates and will sometimes change travelers checks. **Entel** and Internet places are near the plaza. The friendly **post office** (Av Santa Cruz) is a relic from the days when people had a lot more time to do than they do now.

Sights & Activities

Camiri may not be well endowed with attractions, but it's damn proud of its **YPFB plant**. There's no formal tour, but if you turn up at 8am and appear to be interested in oil, you may get a look around. Even if you're not into oil, don't miss the **Petrolero (Oil Worker) monument** in the middle of Av Petrolero.

There are also a couple of nice **walks**. One will take you up to the statue of **St Francis of Assisi** on the hill behind the market for a super view over town. Another pleasant walk is down Av Mariscal Sucre to the **Río Parapeti**. On the bank, turn south and walk several hundred meters downstream, where you'll find a clean sandy beach and a good, deep swimming hole.

Sleeping & Eating

The friendly **Hotel JR** (☎ 952-2200; Sánchez 247; s/d with bath US$12/20; 🅿) is a favorite of visiting oil barons. Rooms all have phone, heat and cable TV. Peripherals include a good restaurant, a bright sitting area and good views. A block from the plaza, the spiffy **Residencial Premier** (☎ 952-2204; Busch 60; with fan US$4, with bath US$6.50; 🅿) has clean rooms with cable TV and hot showers. Request one of the light and airy upstairs rooms that open onto a leafy patio. Next door, **Gran Hotel Londres** is grubby but noteworthy for Che Guevara aficionados as the place where a sheaf of the revolutionary's papers was found. Another squeaky-clean choice is the friendly **Residencial Las Mellizas** (☎ 952-2614; Manchego 300; r per person with bath US$4).

By Bolivian standards, Camiri's choice of restaurants is limited. In the morning, street vendors near the **market** (Bolívar & Comercio) sell hot drinks, bread and delicious *licuados*. Inside you'll find basic meals. **La Estancia** (Comercio at Busch) does *almuerzos* for

US$1.35 and evening à la carte meals. On the plaza, Chifa Hong Kong is a decent lunch option but seems to be closed most evenings. For some greasy lubrication, try El Palacio del Pollo, near the plaza, and El Pollo Ejecutivo, opposite the LAB office, which both serve chicken and fries. Visiting business people frequent **Gambrinus Grill** (Santa Cruz 149), which has an international menu.

Getting There & Away

There's no central bus terminal, but most buses leave from the corner of Bolívar and Cochabamba. After 7pm, numerous *flotas* have nightly services to Santa Cruz (US$8, seven to eight hours); buses coming from Yacuiba via Villamontes normally pass in the middle of the night. When the road is passable, *Flota* El Chaqueño leaves for Sucre (US$15, 24 hours) several times a week in the morning. The road to Boyuibe (US$1.25, one hour) passes through some beautiful hilly Chaco scrub; *micros* leave from Bolívar, four blocks uphill from the main market. *Camiones* to Santa Cruz and Sucre leave when full from Calle Comercio near the market.

Santa Cruz & Eastern Lowlands

CONTENTS

Traveling through the Bolivian Oriente is like taking a walk through time. From bustling Santa Cruz you can visit pre-Inca ruins and the relatively undisturbed Parque Nacional Amboró, home to several species of endangered wildlife.

Santa Cruz' longstanding reputation as a drug-trafficking mecca is now being eclipsed by an agriculture boom. Large corporate sugarcane, rice, cotton and soybean plantations now dominate the lowlands east of the city, which only a decade ago were covered with thick tropical forest. This economic and agricultural potential has attracted not only optimistic settlers from the highlands, but also folks from many other walks of life. The region boasts rice-growing Japanese colonies as well as settlements of Italians, Palestinians, Indian Sikhs and thousands of German–Canadian Mennonites fleeing conflicts in Belize and Mexico. Once upon a time, the region was a haven for escaped Nazis but it now attracts more Brazilian opportunists, foreign oil workers, agribusiness tycoons, drug traffickers, scientific researchers, missionaries and environmental activists.

The 1986 film *The Mission*, which was set in the South American Jesuit missions, awakened an interest in Jesuit work in the continent's interior regions. Perhaps the height of mission architecture is represented in the unique and well-preserved churches in the lowlands north and east of Santa Cruz that form the Jesuit Mission circuit.

Culturally and economically, the Oriente looks toward Brazil rather than La Paz, and the 'Death Train' between Santa Cruz and Quijarro on the Brazilian border is its lifeline; over this dilapidating link flows a stream of largely contraband commerce and undocumented imports.

SANTA CRUZ & EASTERN LOWLANDS

TOP FIVE

- Hike and search for the blue-horned curassow in **Parque Nacional Amboró** (p283)
- Wander through **San José de Chiquitos** (p300) and its restored Jesuit mission complex
- Explore cosmopolitan **Santa Cruz** (p270) and its hedonistic range of clubs, resorts and eateries
- Acclimatize in the laid-back village of **Samaipata** (p288) and explore the mysterious pre-Inca ruins of El Fuerte
- Follow in the footsteps of **El Ché** (p293) from Vallegrande to Pucará and La Higuera

Parque Nacional Amboró ★
Santa Cruz ★
San José de Chiquitos & Jesuit Mission Circuit ★
★ Samaipata
★ Ché Guevara Trail

- TELEPHONE CODE: 03
- ELEVATION: 0 – 1300M

HISTORY

Santa Cruz de la Sierra was founded in 1561 by Ñuflo de Chavez, a Spaniard who hailed from what is now Paraguay. The town originated 220km east of its current location. However, around the end of the 16th century, it proved too vulnerable to attack from local tribes and was moved to its present position 50km east of the Cordillera Oriental foothills.

The city was founded to supply the rest of the colony with products such as rice, cotton, sugar and fruit. Its prosperity lasted until the late 1800s, when transportation routes opened up between La Paz and the Peruvian coast and made imported goods cheaper than those hauled from Santa Cruz over mule trails.

During the period leading up to Bolivia's independence in 1825, the eastern regions of the Spanish colonies were largely ignored. Possession of the hostile lowlands and the hazy boundaries between Alto Peru, the Viceroyalty of La Plata and Portuguese territory was of little concern. Although agriculture was thriving around Santa Cruz, the Spanish remained intent upon extracting every scrap of mineral wealth that could be squeezed from the rich and more hospitable highlands.

In 1954 a highway linking Santa Cruz with other major centers was completed, and the city sprang back from the economic lull imposed by its remoteness. The completion of the railway line to Brazil in the mid-1950s opened trade routes to the east. Tropical agriculture prospered and the city began a flurry of growth that has continued to the present day.

For more on the pre-independence history of the Oriente, see History in the Eastern Lowlands section of this chapter, p295.

CLIMATE

The Oriente's overall climate is tropical, but because it occupies the transition zone between the Amazon rainforest, the highlands and the dry Chaco plains, Santa Cruz enjoys more sun and less stifling temperatures than the humid Amazon Basin further north and west. Winter rainfalls mean little more than 10-minute downpours, but a single summer deluge can last for days. Santa Cruz also experiences heavy winds that rarely subside and, at times during winter, chilly winds *(surazos)* blow in from Patagonia and the Argentine pampas. Outside of Santa Cruz, the Lowlands experience hot sunny days and an occasional afternoon shower to cool things off and settle the dust.

NATIONAL PARKS

Parque Nacional Amboró (p283) is an unquestionable highlight of the region. The remote Parque Nacional Kaa-Iya del Gran Chaco (p303) is Latin America's largest park. It includes the vast Bañados del Izozog wetlands and will be another highlight when access is improved.

GETTING THERE & AWAY

Many flights from Europe and neighboring countries come direct to Santa Cruz and are worth considering if you're arriving from sea level and don't want to spend days acclimatizing in La Paz. Direct flights depart daily for Buenos Aires, Miami, São Paulo and Rio de Janeiro.

Trains trundle south to Argentina and east to the Brazilian Pantanal. With long-distance buses running along paved roads to the west and south and frequent domestic flights, Santa Cruz is the country's most connected city.

SANTA CRUZ

Since 1950 Santa Cruz has mushroomed from a backwater cattle-producing town to its present position as Bolivia's most populous city – it surpassed La Paz in 2003 – and a trade and transport hub. With well over one million inhabitants, it's a metropolis on the fringe of a diminishing wilderness, displaying an incongruous amount of affluence not normally associated with Bolivia.

Despite its phenomenal growth rate, Santa Cruz retains traces of its dusty past, evident in its wide streets, frontier architecture and a rapidly fading small-town atmosphere. Few foreign visitors fail to notice that the streets shaded with colonnade-supported awnings recall the days of the North American Wild West, which leaves Santa Cruz looking like a bizarre cross between Miami and Tombstone!

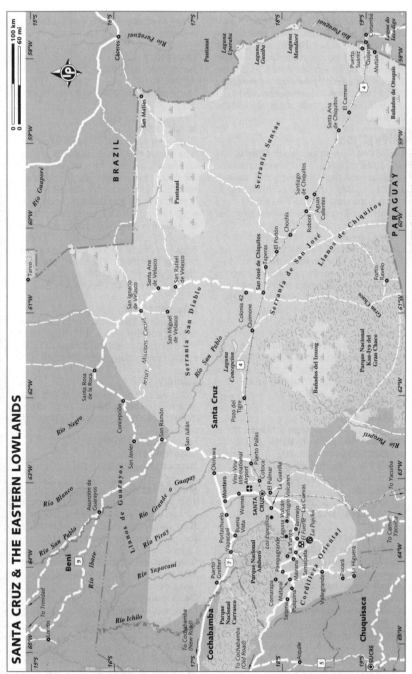

SANTA CRUZ & THE EASTERN LOWLANDS

As the country's richest city, this is where the action is, and while some people love it, others find it too North American for their tastes. If you're young and Bolivian, or a businessperson interested in cutting deals, you're likely to be numbered among the former. However, travelers in search of the 'real' Bolivia usually don't linger here too long.

ORIENTATION

Roughly oval in shape, Santa Cruz is laid out in *anillos* (rings), which form concentric circles around the city center, and *radiales*, or the 'spokes' that connect the rings. Radial 1, the road to Viru-Viru airport, runs roughly north–south; the *radiales* progress clockwise up to Radial 27.

Most commercial enterprises, hotels and restaurants lie within the *primer* (1st) *anillo*, which is centered on the Plaza 24 de Septiembre. The railway station is within the 3rd *anillo* but is still only a half-hour walk from the center. The 2nd to 7th *anillos* are mainly residential and industrial.

Maps

The best city map, *Multiplano Santa Cruz City Guide*, covers the 1st to 4th *anillos* and is available free from larger hotels or for a couple dollars from the tourist office.

INFORMATION
Bookshops

Near the plaza, **Los Amigos del Libro** (☎ 332-7937; Ingavi 114) and **Lewy Libros** (☎ 332-7937; lewylibros@cotas.com.bo; Junín 229) both stock Lonely Planet guidebooks and have limited selections of foreign-language books for sale or trade.

International periodicals are sold at street kiosks around the plaza.

Cultural Centers

Casa de la Cultura Raúl Otero Reiche (west side of Plaza 24 de Septiembre) Hosts free music and modern art exhibitions plus theater performances.
Centro Boliviano-Americano (CBA; ☎ 342-2299; Cochabamba 66) Has an English-language library.
Centro Cultural Franco Alemán (Velarde 200; ☙ 9am-noon & 3-8pm Mon-Fri) Houses the **Alliance Française** (☎ 333-3392) and **Goethe Institut** (☎ 332-9906; icbasc@sccbs-bo.com) and offers courses in French, German, Spanish and Portuguese. Facilities include a multimedia, trilingual Medioteca, the outdoor Kulture

Café and an art exhibition gallery; it also sponsors lectures and screens foreign films.

Emergency

Private ambulance (Foianini; ☎ 336-2211, mobile ☎ 716-27647)
Tourist police (☎ 322-5016; north side of Plaza 24 de Septiembre)

Immigration

Migración (☎ 333-2136; ☙ 8:30am-4:30pm Mon-Fri) is north of the center, opposite the zoo's entrance. Visa extensions are available and overland travelers arriving from Paraguay must pick up a free entry stamp here. There is an office at the **train station** (supposedly ☙ 10am-noon & 1:30-7pm), which is more convenient but the station is plagued by phony officials and thus should be a last-ditch resort. The most reliable office is at the airport. For those braving the Death Train, exit stamps are reportedly only available at the Brazilian frontier – ask around before departing.

Internet access

The arcade at España and Junín has a couple of good Internet places, the best of which is hyper-fast, air-conditioned **Meganet** (US$0.50 an hour), open daily until midnight.

Laundry

Central, efficient wash-and-dry places offering same-day service (with drop-off before noon) for around US$1 per kilo include:
España Lavandería (España 160)
Lavandería La Paz (La Paz 42)
Nameless Lavandería (Bolívar 490) Ring the bell.

Medical Services

The best pharmacy is the efficient and inexpensive **Farmacia América** (Libertad 333). Next door is the **Policonsultorio Central**, with the recommended **Dr Ana María López**, who trained in the USA and speaks English.
Clínica Japonesa (☎ 346-2031) On the 3rd *anillo*, east side, recommended for inexpensive and professional medical treatment.
Clínica Foianini (☎ 336-2211; Irala 468) Hospital used by embassies, but travelers have reported unnecessary tests and longer stays than necessary.

Money

The easiest place to change cash or travelers checks (2% to 3% commission) is **Casa de Cambio**

Alemán (east side of Plaza 24 de Septiembre). Cash advances are available at most major banks and Enlace ATMs, which are found at most major intersections. Street moneychangers flaunt their fat wads along Av Cañoto between Calles Ayacucho and Junín as well as occasionally around the main plaza. **Magri Turismo** (☎ 334-5663; Warnes & Potosí) is the American Express agent but doesn't cash travelers checks.

Telephone

Public telephone boxes here – shaped like anything from toucan birds to *surubí* fish – scream 'photo op'. The main **Entel office** (Warnes 82) is between La Paz and Chuquisaca. Cheap international Internet calls are offered by several telecom shops along Bolívar. The **Punto Entel** (Junín 284) near the plaza has land lines.

Tourist Information

Main tourist office (☎ 336-9595; west side of Plaza 24 de Septiembre) Ground floor, Casa de la Cultura.

Departamental de Turismo (☎ 336-8901; north side of Plaza 24 de Septiembre) Inside the Palacio Prefectural.

Fundación Amigos de la Naturaleza (FAN; ☎ 355-6800; www.fan-bo.org; Km7.5, Carretera a Samaipata) Contact for Amboró and Noel Kempff Mercado National Parks information; west of town (*micro* 44) off the old Cochabamba road.

DANGERS & ANNOYANCES

Beware of bogus immigration officials, particularly at the bimodal bus/train station – carefully check the credentials of anyone who demands to see your passport or other ID. If you're suspicious, insist that they accompany you to the police station, where things can be legitimately be sorted out. Readers have reported several violent robberies in broad daylight during the week at Río Piray; it's best only to venture out there on weekends when there's safety in numbers.

SIGHTS & ACTIVITIES
Plaza 24 de Septiembre

If you find yourself stuck here for a day, Santa Cruz' tropical main plaza is an attractive place to relax by day or night. As a telling sign of the times, the plaza's longtime resident jaywalking sloths were recently relocated to the zoo in an effort to protect them from electrocution and increasing traffic hazards in the city center.

Basílica Menor de San Lorenzo & Museo de la Catedral

Although the original cathedral on Plaza 24 de Septiembre was founded in 1605, the present structure dates from 1845 and wasn't consecrated until 1915. Inside, the decorative woodwork on the ceiling and silver plating around the altar are worth a look.

The cathedral's air-conditioned **Museo de Arte Sagrado** (admission US$0.65; ⊗ 8:30am-noon & 2:30-6pm Tue & Thu) has a collection of religious icons and artifacts but very little typical religious art. Most interesting are the many gold and silver relics from the Jesuit Guarayos missions. There's also a collection of religious vestments and medallions, as well as one of the world's smallest books, a thumbnail-sized volume containing the Lord's Prayer in several languages.

Museo de la Historia Natural

The **Natural History Museum** (☎ 336-6574; Irala 565; admission by donation; ⊗ 9am-noon & 3-6pm) gives you the lowdown on the flora, fauna and geology of eastern Bolivia. Exhibits include pickled frogs and the usual stuffed animals, fish and birds, as well as information on seeds, wood, fruit, gardening and other lowland pursuits. The bug collections include specimens large enough to keep many people out of rainforests forever.

Parque El Arenal & Museo Etno-Folklórico

Locals relax around the lagoon at Parque El Arenal, but it's best not to dawdle here at night. On an island in the lagoon, a bas-relief mural by renowned Bolivian artist Lorgio Vaca depicts historic and modern-day aspects of Santa Cruz. On a peninsula, the **Ethno-Folkloric Museum** (admission US$0.75; ⊗ 9:30am-noon & 2:30-5:30pm Mon-Fri) has a small collection of traditional art and artifacts from several *camba* (lowland) cultures.

Jardín Zoológico

Santa Cruz' **zoo** (☎ 342-9939; admission adults/kids US$0.65/0.40; ⊗ 9am-7pm) was once one of the few on the continent that was worth the time, but indications are that it has been going downhill in recent years. Its collection is limited to South American birds, mammals and reptiles, and all appear to be humanely treated (although the llamas

SANTA CRUZ & EASTERN LOWLANDS

SANTA CRUZ

INFORMATION

Argentine Consulate.................	**1** D3
ATM..	(see 46)
Banco de Bolivia (ATM)..............	**2** D4
Banco de Santa Cruz (ATM)........	**3** D3
Brazilian Consulate....................	**4** C1
Casa de Cambio Alemán.............	**5** D3
Casa de la Cultura Raúl Otero	
Reiche...................................	(see 16)
Centro Boliviano Americano.......	**6** E3
Clínica Foianini.........................	**7** C5
Departamental de Turismo.......	(see 19)
Entel Office..............................	**8** D4
España Lavandería.....................	**9** C3
Farmacia América......................	**10** D3
Honorary German Consul...........	**11** E4
Internet Arcade.......................	(see 17)
Lavandería La Paz......................	**12** D3
Lewy Libros..............................	**13** D3
Los Amigos del Libro.................	**14** D4
Magri Turismo..........................	**15** E4
Main Tourist Office...................	**16** D3
Meganet...................................	**17** C3
Nameless Lavandería.................	**18** E3
Palacio Prefectural....................	**19** D3
Policonsultorio........................	(see 10)
Punto Entel..............................	**20** C3
Tourist Police...........................	(see 19)

SIGHTS & ACTIVITIES   (pp273–5)

Alliance Française.....................	(see 22)
Balas..	**21** D3
Centro Cultural Franco Alemán..	**22** D6
Forest Tour..............................	**23** D2
Fremen Tours...........................	**24** D3
Gama Tours..............................	**25** E3
Goethe Institut........................	(see 22)
Mau-Mauin auditorium.............	**26** C2
Museo de Arte Sagrado.............	**27** D3
Museo de la Historia Natural.....	**28** D5
Museo Etno-Folklórico..............	**29** D2
Rosario Tours...........................	**30** D3
Totaitu Tours............................	**31** D4
Tuyuyú.....................................	**32** D4

SLEEPING   (pp276–7)

Alojamiento Santa Bárbara........	**33** C3
Hotel Amazonas........................	**34** C3
Hotel Bibosi.............................	**35** C3
Hotel Copacabana.....................	**36** C3
Hotel Excelsior.........................	**37** D3
Hotel Globetrotter....................	**38** C3
Hotel Italia...............................	**39** D4
Hotel Las Américas...................	**40** C3
Hotel Lido................................	**41** C2
Residencial Ballivián.................	**42** D3
Residencial Bolívar...................	**43** D3

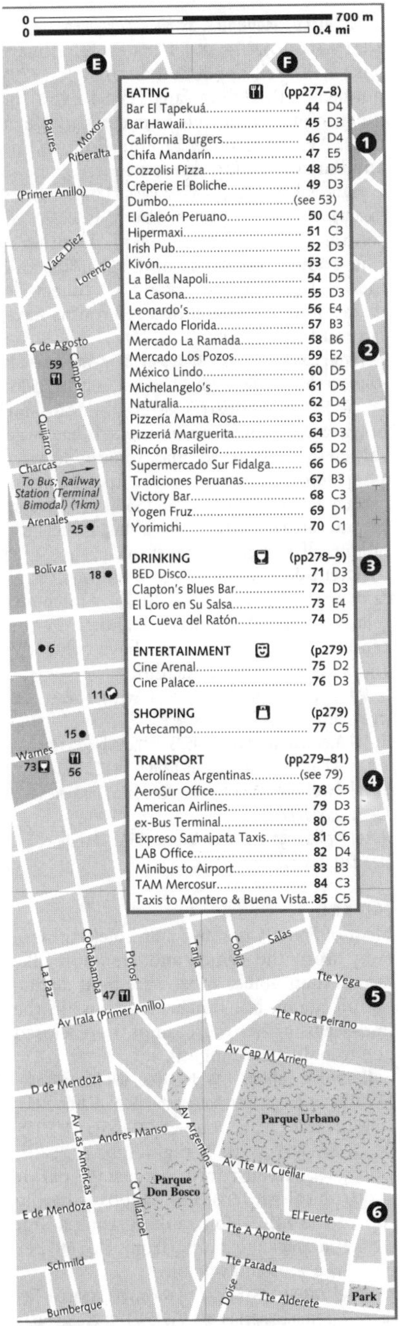
0 700 m
0 0.4 mi
E
F
EATING (pp277–8)
Bar El Tapekuá 44 D4
Bar Hawaii 45 D3
California Burgers 46 D4
Chifa Mandarín 47 E5
Cozzolisi Pizza 48 D5
Crêperie El Boliche 49 D3
Dumbo (see 53)
El Galeón Peruano 50 C4
Hipermaxi 51 C3
Irish Pub 52 D3
Kivón 53 C3
La Bella Napoli 54 D5
La Casona 55 D3
Leonardo's 56 E4
Mercado Florida 57 B3
Mercado La Ramada 58 B6
Mercado Los Pozos 59 E2
México Lindo 60 D5
Michelangelo's 61 D5
Naturalia 62 D4
Pizzería Mama Rosa 63 D5
Pizzeriá Marguerita 64 D3
Rincón Brasileiro 65 D2
Supermercado Sur Fidalga 66 D6
Tradiciones Peruanas 67 B3
Victory Bar 68 C3
Yogen Fruz 69 D1
Yorimichi 70 C1
DRINKING (pp278–9)
BED Disco 71 D3
Clapton's Blues Bar 72 D3
El Loro en Su Salsa 73 E4
La Cueva del Ratón 74 D5
ENTERTAINMENT (p279)
Cine Arenal 75 D2
Cine Palace 76 D3
SHOPPING (p279)
Artecampo 77 C5
TRANSPORT (pp279–81)
Aerolíneas Argentinas (see 79)
AeroSur Office 78 C5
American Airlines 79 D3
ex-Bus Terminal 80 C5
Expreso Samaipata Taxis 81 C6
LAB Office 82 D4
Minibus to Airport 83 B3
TAM Mercosur 84 C3
Taxis to Montero & Buena Vista 85 C5
Baures
Moxos
Riberalta
(Primer Anillo)
Vaca Diez
Lorenzo
6 de Agosto
Campero
Quijarro
Charcas
To Bus; Railway Station (Terminal Bimodal) (1km)
Arenales
Bolívar
Warnes
Cochabamba
Potosí
Tarija
Cobija
Salas
La Paz
Tte Vega
Av Irala (Primer Anillo)
Tte Roca Peirano
Av Cap M Arrien
D de Mendoza
Parque Urbano
Av Las Américas
Andres Manso
Av Argentina
Av Tte M Cuéllar
Parque Don Bosco
G Villarroel
E de Mendoza
El Fuerte
Tte A Aponte
Schmild
Tte Parada
Doise
Tte Alderete
Bumberque
Park

are a bit overdressed for the climate). It features endangered and exotic species such as tapirs, pumas, jaguars and spectacled bears. Sloths, which are too slow and lazy to escape successfully, are not confined to cages and hang about in the trees.

Take *micro* No 58 or 55 from Vallegrande, No 76 from Calle Santa Bárbara or anything marked 'Zoológico'. Taxis for up to four people cost around US$1.35.

Other Activities

For a real splash, dive into **Aqualand** (☎ 385-2500; www.aqualand.com.bo; admission half-day US$5-8, day US$7.50-10; 10am-5:30pm Fri-Sun), a water park near the airport. For something more sedate, try the **mini-golf** course across the street from Hotel Los Tabijos (p276).

Tours

Numerous companies offer organized tours. A highly recommended agency is **Forest Tour** (☎ 337-2042; www.forestbolivia.com; Cuéllar 22), which specializes in nature and adventure tours and custom trips to the Pantanal, the Volcanes region and Amboró and Noel Kempff Mercado National Parks.

Rosario Tours (☎ 336-9977; aventura@cotas.com.bo; Arenales 193) offers tours to sights including the Pantanal, Jesuit missions, Parque Nacional Amboró and Samaipata.

Uimpex Travel (☎ 333-6001; Moreno 226) is a long-established agency that runs tours to the Bolivian Pantanal, Jesuit missions and imaginative city sights.

Other recommended agencies include:

Balas (☎ 333-3933; www.turismobalas.com; Beni 218)
Fremen Tours (☎ 333-8535; www.andes-amazonia.com; Beni & Bolívar)
Gama Tours (☎ 334-0921; gamatur@roble.scz.entelnet.bo; Arenales 566)
Totaitu Tours(☎ 333-3672; totaitu@em.daitec-bo.com; Warnes 105)
Tuyuyú (☎ /fax 336-4003; Chuquisaca 232)

FESTIVALS & EVENTS

If you're in Santa Cruz during **Carnaval**, you can either head for the paintball-plagued streets and join in the melee or pick up a few supplies and hole up somewhere until the chaos clears. Alternatively, check out the **Mau-Mauin**, the auditorium on the corner of Ibáñez and 21 de Mayo. It attracts over 10,000 people with its dancing, music shows and coronation of the carnival queen.

Every year in mid- to late September, Santa Cruz hosts an enormous two-week **ExpoCruz** (www.fexpocruz.com.bo) fair where you can buy anything from a toothbrush or clothing to a new house, a combine harvester or a 20-ton truck. It's worthwhile even if you're not shopping, especially at night when it takes on a carnival atmosphere as local families stroll, browse, listen to music, eat, drink and be merry.

SLEEPING
Budget

In a pinch, there are several cheap indistinguishable places to crash across from the bimodal terminal. Otherwise, there are few stellar in-town budget options.

Alojamiento Santa Bárbara (☎ 332-1817; alojsta barbara@yahoo.com; Santa Bárbara 151; US$2.65) Appealing for its friendly staff and simple rooms arranged around a sunny courtyard, the Santa Bárbara is popular with young Bolivians and travelers alike. There's no sign and the beds are funky, but it's cheap and convenient.

Residencial Bolívar (☎ 334-2500; Sucre 131; s/d with breakfast US$6/11) A longtime backpackers' favorite, the clean and bright Bolívar has an inviting courtyard, hammocks, good hot showers and a charming toucan (who has the run of the place).

Residencial Ballivián (☎ 332-1960; residencial ballivian@yahoo.es; Ballivián near Chuquisaca; US$4) A fine alternative if the Bolívar is full, the Ballivián has a lovely courtyard and decent rooms, but it's been going downhill as of late. If you believe the rumors, Ché Guevara once stayed here. According to one reader, 'It's like staying at your grandmother's house'.

Mid-Range

Santa Cruz has a growing number of mid-range hotels, all with private baths and reasonable prices, which cater mainly to business travelers.

Hotel Globetrotter (☎ 337-2754; Sara 49; s/d US$22/25) More like a large modern home than a hotel, you'll feel like you're in the suburbs in the middle of the city. Rooms are big, comfortable and updated. The well-traveled management appropriately speaks a smorgasbord of languages: Swedish, German, French, English and Danish.

Hotel Copacabana (☎ 336-2770; Junín 217; s/d with breakfast US$20/24; 🏊) The new HI affiliate has small, well-appointed disco-style 1970s doubles with ceiling fans (US$4 extra for quiet, remote-controlled air-con) and firm beds. Avoid the noisy ground-floor rooms and bargain during slow periods.

Hotel Bibosi (☎ 334-8548; Junín 218; bibosi@scbbs -bo.com; s/d with breakfast & cable TV US$13/20) A central choice with a cheery proprietor. The rooms are clean and spacious and there's a great rooftop view but otherwise it's nothing to brag about. All rooms have fans and telephones.

Hotel Las Américas (☎ 336-8778; www.lasamericas -hotel.com.bo; 21 de Mayo at Seoane; s/d US$55/65; 🏊 🖥) This industrial-strength, four-star hotel caters to business travelers. It has large carpeted, air-con rooms, superb service, a top-floor restaurant and a free business center. The best deal is its US$30 per person promo rate (including a breakfast buffet) for holders of AeroSur ticket stubs.

Hotel Lido (☎ 336-3555; www.lido-hotel.com; 21 de Mayo 527; s/d/tr US$55/65/80; 🏊 🖥) A nice but relatively simple upmarket choice in the center. Comfortable rooms have color TV and access to laundry facilities.

Also close to the action with the usual in-room conveniences are:

Hotel Amazonas (☎ 333-4583; leanch@bibosi.scz .entelnet.bo; Junín 214; s/d with bath & TV US$10/14)

Hotel Excelsior (☎ 334-0664; fax 332-5924; Moreno 70; s/d US$12/22)

Hotel Italia (☎ 332-3119; Moreno 167; s/d with breakfast US$14/22)

Top End

Most of Santa Cruz' five-star hotels are well away from the center and are more like resorts than hotels. Most were built during the oil boom, but things went bust in the mid-1990s when the casinos were closed due to political wrangling.

Hotel Los Tajibos (☎ 342-1000, toll-free ☎ 800-10-2210; www.lostajiboshotel.com; San Martín 455, Barrio Equipetrol; s/d/ste with breakfast US$155/175/185; 🏊 🏊 🖥 🍸) With a nightclub, a health club, racquetball courts, a massage parlor and tropical gardens, Los Tajibos is hardly run-of-the-mill. Nonsmoking rooms and weekend package rates (from US$60 per person) are often available.

Hotel Yotaú (☎ 336-7799; www.yotau.com.bo; San Martín 7, Barrio Equipetrol; s/d US$159/179; 🏊 🖥 🍸)

This beautiful tropical-style high-rise has fitness facilities and a sauna, as well as executive and family rooms for up to six people, which cost US$300. Lunches and dinners are US$7 each.

EATING
When it comes to culinary matters, cosmopolitan Santa Cruz won't disappoint; it has a staggering number of fine restau-rants. The better places, however, can be quite expensive and most are found outside the center, primarily in Barrio Equipetrol.

Restaurants
La Casona Bistro (☎ 337-8495; Arenales 222; ☒ closed Sun; mains US$5-7) Hurray! A German-run splash of California gourmet in the heart of Bolivia. The salad has *arugula* and the chicken is basted in a balsamic vinaigrette. There are also quality cheeses and cold cuts available at the deli next door.

Crêperie El Boliche (☎ 333-9053; Arenales 135; ☒ 7:30pm-1am; dinner US$5-10) A fine place to splurge: choose from salads, crêpes, cakes, cocktails and ice-cream confections, all served up in an elegant setting. You might ask yourself 'Am I really in Bolivia?' A good diversity of vegetarian options only adds to the charm.

La Bella Napoli (☎ 332-5402; Independencia 635; pizzas & mains US$4-6) In a rustic barn six blocks south of the plaza, this place serves fine pizza and pasta dishes – including ravioli, cannelloni and lasagna – on chunky hardwood tables, some outside. It's a short taxi (or dark walk) back to the center at night.

Michelangelo's (☎ 334-8403; Chuquisaca 502; mains US$5-10) Housed in a classy home, complete with fireplaces and marble floors, this is a good choice for a romantic evening or a little Italian self-indulgence.

Leonardo's (☎ 333-8282; Warnes 366; mains US$5-10) Continuing with the Italian Renaissance art theme, you can enjoy another cozy candlelit dinner of pasta or shellfish in this beautiful old converted mansion.

Pizzería Marguerita (☎ 37-0285; north side of the plaza) Long known for its high-quality pizza, pasta and salads, this well-located place is good for a casual meal.

Yorimichi (☎ 334-7717; Busch 548; meals US$10) Santa Cruz' Japanese immigrants fill a wide-open Bolivian culinary niche. This unforgettable choice for sushi, sashimi, tempura and other specialties gets plenty of votes for the Oriente's best Asian food.

Pizzería Mama Rosa (Velasco near Irala; ☒ noon-midnight; mains US$2-4) Ambitious Mama Rosa aims to do it all – pizzas, chicken dishes, Mexican burgers, hot dogs, fast food and big *almuerzos* – but some of the creative meat concoctions miss their mark.

México Lindo (☎ 332-3056; Independencia 561; mains US$3-6) For superlative south-of-the-border fare, crowds flock here for the *muy rico* tacos, fajitas and *enchiladas de mole*, plus ice-cold Coronas and margaritas to ease the heartburn.

Texas Rodeo Grill (☎ 352-7214; 26 de Febrero s/n, Barrio Urbarí; mains US$4-8) For those who prefer more Tex with their Mex, this grill serves nachos slathered with cheese and salsa, *quesadillas*, chili and other favorites of expat oil workers.

Texas Burger (☎ 342-2138; San Martín 918, Barrio Equipetrol; mains US$3-6) Relaxed and more low-key than the Rodeo Grill, this joint is great for grabbing a burger while watching live American football. The food is genuine (the owner worked in Texas for years), the prices are fine and the fries are among the best in town.

Rincón Brasileiro (☎ 333-1237; Libertad 358; buffet US$2-3 per kg) Brazilian places are the rage in Santa Cruz these days, mainly because the food is filling, fresh and typically sold by the kilo. This is one of the best in town with top-notch steak and *feijoada* (pork and beans stew) on weekends.

Tradiciones Peruanas (Cañoto & Florida; mains US$2.50-5) A good bet for flown-in Peruvian specialties of the sea like *ceviche* and shellfish.

Chifa Mandarín (☎ 334-8388; Potosí 793; mains US$2-5) Decent Chinese food done pagoda-style. Phone ahead for pick-up or send a cab for delivery.

Casa Típica de Camba (☎ 342-7864; Mendoza 539; www.casadelcamba.com; mains US$3-8) You're likely to end up at this lively, sprawling landmark if you ask Bolivian friends where to find the 'most typical' *crucena/camba* experience. National and Argentine meat comes sizzling off the grill while live crooners belt out traditional tunes to the accompaniment of a Casio keyboard – *buen provecho*.

CAFÉS
Irish Pub (☎ 333-8118; east side of Plaza 24 de Septiembre; ☒ 9am-midnight) A hit with travelers.

You'll find not only your favorite dishes from home, but also local specialties for breakfast, lunch and dinner. The service and music are outstanding, and you can easily pass an afternoon here nursing a beer or three while watching life on the plaza below.

Victory Bar (Junin & 21 de Mayo, Galería Casco Viejo; lunch US$4, lager US$1.50) For a great lunch in the sun or just a large afternoon beer, head for the palm-shaded terrace of this popular bar where you can also enjoy salads, sandwiches, burgers, pasta and Bolivian dishes. They do Western breakfasts in the morning too.

Bar El Tapekuá (☎ 334-5905; La Paz & Ballivián; ☽ from 6pm Wed-Sat; cover US$1) This casual yet upscale Swiss–Bolivian-owned hangout serves pub grub and there's live music (US$1 cover) most nights.

Mr Café (Rivero 260) A favorite local hangout for sandwiches, juices, cakes, light meals and ice cream to complement its rich espresso drinks.

Quick Eats

As Bolivia's most modern, hustle-and-bustle town, Santa Cruz also boasts more fast-food outlets than you can shake a happy meal at. It's difficult to walk more than a few blocks without scraping your head against the awning of a sidewalk hamburger stand and there's an endless supply of roast chicken, fries and fried plantain along Av Cañoto (also known as Pollo Alley).

El Galeón Peruano (Ingavi at Colón; lunch US$2, mains US$3) Always busy thanks to its delicious lunches and reasonable prices.

Kivón (☎ 333-1333; Ayacucho 267 & 239) When it comes to over-the-top ice-cream places, Santa Cruz outdoes itself. The American-style food is a bit bland and expensive, but when you're young and in Santa Cruz, this is the place to be and be seen.

Dumbo (☎ 336-7077; Ayacucho 247) Almost as extravagant as its neighbor, Dumbo serves gourmet frozen yogurt in the usual flavors plus maracuya, papaya, guayaba, almond, tangerine and so on.

Bar Hawaii (Sucre at Beni; meals US$3) An expansive cross between an ice-cream joint and a fast-food eatery. It's popular for sundaes, cakes, light meals and good coffee.

California Burgers (☎ 333-4054; Independencia 481; tacos US$1, doughnuts US$0.35) Serves coffee, burgers, tacos, burritos and sticky doughnuts.

Yogen Fruz (☎ 337-7221; Rivero at Cañada Strongest; US$1-2) The franchised frozen yogurt is a big hit with weight-watching Mormon missionaries.

Cozzolisi Pizza (Independencia & La Riva) A cheap, reliable outpost of the national chain.

Self-Catering

For simple, cheap eats, try Mercado La Ramada or the mall-like Mercado Los Pozos with food stalls on the top floor. The latter is especially good for unusual tropical fruits. It's hard to tear yourself away after only one glass of *licuado de papaya* or *guineo con leche* (US$0.35) – puréed papaya or banana with milk, whipped in a blender and served cold. Mercado Florida is wall-to-wall blender stalls serving exquisite juices and fruit salads for US$0.50.

For a good variety of (relatively expensive) fixings to prepare meals yourself, try mini-mart **Hipermaxi** (21 de May & Florida). **Supermercado Sur Fidalga** (east side of Plaza Héroes del Chaco) is the best stocked, cheapest self-catering option. The **Naturalia** (Independencia 452) organic grocery store has a wide selection of locally produced, healthy goodies.

DRINKING

The hottest nightspots are along Av Gral San Martín, between the 2nd and 3rd rings in Barrio Equipetrol, a US$1 to US$2 taxi from the center. Cover charges run US$2 to US$10 and drinks are expensive; most places start selling drinks between 6pm and 9pm but don't warm up until 11pm, then continue until 3am or 4am. Hotspots change frequently so it's best to dress to impress and cruise the strip (*piranhar*, literally 'to go piranha fishing') and see what catches your fancy. In the center, try BED. On Av San Martín in Barrio Equipetrol ask around for Mad, Varadero or Number One.

North of the plaza between the 1st and 2nd *anillos*, Av Monseñor Rivero is chockablock with see-and-be-seen cafés and trendy late-night restaurants with sidewalk seating. Near the university, Av Busch is lined with places catering to more serious, mostly male drinkers.

Popular late-night travelers' hangouts near the plaza include the Victory Bar (above) and the Irish Pub (p277). Another pleasant hideaway with live music is Bar El Tapekuá (p278).

La Cueva del Ratón (☎ 332-6163; La Riva 173), a barnlike bar with big-screen music videos, is also relatively central and offers live music most weekends.

Clapton's Blues Bar (Murillo at Arenales; ☺ Sat & Sun; cover US$2) is friendly and can be great fun.

ENTERTAINMENT

Traditional *peñas* are scarce in modern Santa Cruz. However, an excellent choice is **El Rincón Salteño** (☎ 353-6335; 26 de Enero at Charagua; ☺ from 10pm Fri, Sat & Sun), in the 2nd *anillo*. Nowhere else in Santa Cruz will you hear such a variety of musical styles, from Argentine guitarists to Cuban village drummers and local singers and dancers in local costume.

The city also has a number of cinemas, and the films are generally better and more recent than elsewhere in Bolivia. First-run flicks are shown nightly at **Cine Palace** (west side of plaza; admission US$2.25). Older releases play at **Cine Arenal** (Beni 555; admission US$2), which faces Parque Arenal. For movie schedules and other venues, see the daily newspapers *El Mundo* and *El Deber*.

Santa Cruz has a disproportionate number of discos and karaoke bars, which reflects the young city's liberal and cosmopolitan character.

The most central disco (inside the 1st *anillo*) is the tropically themed **El Loro en Su Salsa** (Warnes at Cochabamba; ☺ 8pm-late).

SHOPPING

There are *artesanía* shops scattered around town at which you can buy attractive Western-style clothing made of llama and alpaca wool.

Woodcarvings made from the tropical hardwoods *morado* and the more expensive *guayacán* (from US$20 for a nice piece) are unique to the Santa Cruz area. Relief carvings on *tari* nuts are also interesting and make nice portable souvenirs. Locals also make beautiful macramé *llicas* (root-fiber bags). Santa Cruz leatherwork is expert, but most items are unfortunately adorned with kitsch slogans and designs.

The best place to find fine *artesanía* is **Artecampo** (☎ 334-1843; Salvatierra 407), which provides an outlet for the work of 1000

rural *cruceña* women and their families. The truly inspired and innovative pieces include leatherwork, hammocks, weavings, handmade paper greeting cards and lovely natural-material lampshades. You may also find some examples for sale at the Casa de la Cultura (p272).

Mercado Los Pozos is good for inexpensive basketry, but if you're after genuine indigenous articles, wait until you get to the Altiplano.

GETTING THERE & AWAY
Air

Viru-Viru international airport (VVI; ☎ 181), 15km north of the center, handles domestic and international flights. Both **AeroSur** (☎ 336-4446; Irala at Colón) and **LAB** (☎ 334-4896; Chuquisaca 126) have daily services to Cochabamba, La Paz and Sucre, as well as several other Bolivian cities.

American Airlines (☎ 334-1314; Beni 167) flies direct daily to Miami; **Aerolíneas Argentinas** (☎ 333-9776; Junín 22) flies several times a week to Buenos Aires; **Varig** (☎ 334-1114; Edificio Nago, Barba 39) flies daily to Rio de Janeiro and São Paulo; and **TAM Mercosur** (☎ 337-1999; 21 de Mayo at Florida) flies to Asunción Monday to Saturday, with connections to Miami, Buenos Aires and several Brazilian cities.

TAM (☎ 353-2639) flies direct to La Paz (US$67) on Monday morning and roundabout a couple more times a week from the military's El Trompillo airport, just south of the center. It also runs popular direct flights to Puerto Suárez (US$65) a couple of times a week.

Bus, Micro & Shared taxi

The new, full-service **bimodal terminal** (☎ 348-8382; US$0.40 terminal fee), the combo long-distance bus and train station, is 1.5km east of the center, just before the 3rd *anillo* at the end of Av Brasil.

There are plenty of daily services morning and evening to Cochabamba (US$4–6, 10 to 12 hours), where there are plenty of connections to La Paz, Oruro, Sucre, Potosí and Tarija. Cosmos has a daily direct service to La Paz (US$6 to US$12, 16 to 25 hours).

Several companies offer daily evening services to Sucre (US$4 to US$13.50, 16 to 25 hours), with connections for Potosí. Most services to Camiri (US$8, seven to eight hours) and Yacuiba (US$9, 15 hours) depart in the mid-afternoon. Buses to Vallegrande (US$5, six hours) leave in the morning and afternoon.

To the Jesuit missions and all of Chiquitanía, Misiones del Oriente buses leave in the morning and afternoon. Buses run to San Ramón (US$2.50, 2¾ hours), Asunción de Guarayos (US$3.50, five hours), San Javier (US$3.50, three hours), Concepción (US$4, six hours), San Ignacio de Velasco (US$8, nine hours), San Miguel de Velasco (US$10, 10 hours) and San Rafael de Velasco (US$11, 11 hours). Several other companies do the same routes but may be less comfortable.

To Trinidad (US$4 to US$10, at least 12 hours) and beyond, a number of buses leave every evening. Although the road is theoretically open year-round, at least to Trinidad, the trip gets rough in the rainy season and is frequently canceled for weeks on end.

Several companies also offer international services. Daily services connect Santa Cruz with Buenos Aires (US$60, 42 hours). In the dry season, you can attempt the Chaco Road (see the boxed text, p264) to and from Asunción, Paraguay (around US$50, 30 hours minimum).

Smaller *micros* and *trufis* to Viru-Viru airport, Montero (with connections to Buena Vista and Villa Tunari), Samaipata and other communities in Santa Cruz department leave regularly from outside the bus terminal. To Buena Vista, they wait along Izozog (Isoso). To Samaipata (US$3, three hours), *trufis* leave on the opposite side of Av Cañoto, about two blocks from the old bus terminal. Alternatively, ring **Expreso Samaipata Taxis** (☎ 333-5067; Ortíz 1147), which charges US$13.50 for up to four passengers.

Train

The *Expreso del Oriente* (the infamous Death Train) runs to Quijarro, on the Brazilian border, daily except Sunday around 3pm (2nd/1st/Pullman class US$7/15.50/20). It takes at least 21 hours and in the wet season may not run at all. The train chugs through soy plantations, forest, scrub and oddly shaped mountains to the steamy, sticky Pantanal region on the Brazilian frontier. Bring plenty of food and water and mosquito repellent for long stops in swampy areas. About halfway, the train stops in San José de Chiquitos (p300) on the mission circuit, a good place to layover before continuing to Brazil.

Trains arrive the following day in Quijarro (p304), from where taxis shuttle passengers to the Brazilian border town of Corumbá, 2km away. Don't pay more than US$2 per person for the taxi – rip-offs are common. You can change dollars or *bolivianos* into *reais* (R$; pronounced HAY-ice) on the Bolivian side, but rates are poor. Note that there's no Brazilian consulate in Quijarro, so if you need a visa, get it in Santa Cruz. Bolivian officials may demand a bribe for an exit stamp at Quijarro. From Corumbá there are good bus connections into southern Brazil, but no passenger trains.

Train tickets can be scarce and carriages are often so jammed with people and contraband that there's nowhere to sit. Ticket windows (supposedly) open at 8am, and you can only buy your ticket on the day of departure, when lines reach communist proportions. A funkier alternative is to stake out a place in the *bodegas* (boxcars) of a mixed train and purchase a 2nd-class ticket on board (for 20% over the ticket window price). The upmarket option is to buy a 1st-class ticket through a Santa Cruz travel agent – try **Bracha** (☎ 346-7795), which may still have an office in the train station. You must pay a US$1.35/4 national/international departure tax after purchasing your ticket.

Rail service to Yacuiba, on the Argentine border, is a reasonably quick and comfortable *Ferrobus* (US$5/6.50/13.50, nine hours), which supposedly departs at 5pm on Monday, Wednesday and Friday, returning on Wednesday and Sunday at 8pm.

GETTING AROUND
To/From the airport

Handy minibuses leave Viru-Viru for the center (US$0.60, 30 minutes) when flights arrive. Minibuses to the airport leave every 20 minutes starting at 5:30am from the Av Cañoto at stops along the 1st *anillo*. Taxis for up to four people cost US$5 to US$6.

To/From the bus & train stations

The bimodal bus/train station is beyond easy walking distance, but you can get to the center in about 10 minutes on *micro* No 12 or 20.

Bus

Santa Cruz' handy system of city *micros* (US$0.20) connect the transport terminals and all the *anillos* with the center. *Micros* Nos 17 and 18 circulate around the 1st *anillo*. To reach Av San Martín in Barrio Equipetrol, take *micro* No 23 from anywhere on Vallegrande.

Car

American Rent-a-Car (☎ 334-1235; Justiniano 28 at Uruguay)

Barron's Rent-a-Car (☎ 3420-160; www.rentacar bolivia.com; Alemania 50 at Tajibo; also at Viru-Viru airport)

International Rent-a-Car (☎ 334-4425; Uruguay at Antelo)

Localiza Rent-a-Car (☎ 343-3939; Banzer Km 3.5, Carretera al Norte; ☎ 385-2190; Viru-Viru airport)

Taxi

Generally, taxis are more expensive here than the rest of Bolivia, and overcharging is common. The official rate is US$1 to anywhere in the 1st *anillo* for one person, plus US$0.25 for each additional person and about US$0.25 for each additional *anillo*. If you have lots of luggage, however, drivers may try to extract up to 50% more.

AROUND SANTA CRUZ

BUENA VISTA

This pleasant little town two hours (100km) northwest of Santa Cruz is an ideal staging point for trips into Parque Nacional Amboró's forested lowland section. New accommodations and restaurants spring up often here, and the region is becoming a Gringo Trail fixture.

Information

The municipal government is planning to open its own tourist office on the plaza. For information on Parque Nacional Amboró, visit the **Sernap office** (☎ 932-2054), two blocks southwest of the plaza, where you can pick up an entry permit and inquire about current park regulations and accommodation options.

There's no bank or ATM here, so bring cash from elsewhere. Dial-up Internet connections (US$2 an hour) are available after 7pm during the week and all day on

weekends at a couple of places around the plaza.

English-speaking **Amboró Tours** (☎ 932-2093, Santa Cruz ☎ 358-5383; www.vektron.net/amborotours; off northeast cnr of plaza) runs adventurous trips to the northern section of the park, starting at US$45 per person per day for two people, including transport, guide and food. They offer 15% discounts for walk-in bookings in Buena Vista.

Sights & Activities

IGLESIA DE LOS SANTOS DESPOSORIOS

Buena Vista's Jesuit mission was founded in 1694 as the fifth mission in the Viceroyalty of Perú. The need for a church was recognized, and 29 years later, after a search for a high-standing location with sufficient water and potential cropland, the first building was finally constructed.

By the mid-1700s, 700 Chiraguano people had been converted to Christianity. The Swiss Jesuit missionary and architect Padre Martin Schmid recognized the need for a new church and, in 1767, the current structure was completed. When the Jesuits were expelled from Bolivia later that year, the administration of the church passed to the Bishop of Santa Cruz. Although the building is deteriorating, its lovely classic form merits a look.

CURICHI MARSH

This beautiful marshy wetland, a 30-minute walk south of the main plaza, is a municipal reserve (admission US$1.35 or US$4 with guide). It provides Buena Vista's water supply and serves as a habitat and breeding site for both migratory and native birds. There is an elevated boardwalk and two viewing towers. It's best to visit at dawn or dusk. You can set up a guided visit with any of the tour companies around the plaza.

RÍO SURUTÚ, SANTA BÁRBARA & EL CAIRO
Surutú River is a popular excursion for locals. There's a pleasant sandy beach ideal for picnics, swimming and camping during the dry season. From Buena Vista it's an easy 3km walk to the river bend nearest town. The opposite bank is the boundary of Parque Nacional Amboró.

A good longer option is the six-hour **circuit walk** through the community of **Santa Bárbara**, through partially forested tropical plantation country. From Buena Vista, follow the unpaved road to Santa Bárbara and ask for the track that leads to an idyllic river beach on the Río Ucurutú. After a picnic and a dip, you can return to Buena Vista via the Huaytú road.

An even better swimming hole is at **El Cairo**, which is an hour's walk from town. To get there, pass Los Franceses and follow the unpaved road as it curves to the right. About 2km from town, take the left fork and cross over a bridge. After passing El Cairo, on your right, keep going until you reach the river.

Festivals & Events
The local fiesta, **Día de los Santos Desposorios** (November 26), features bullfights, food stalls and general merrymaking. Culinary festivals include the **Chocolate Festival**, last Sunday in January; the **Coffee Festival**, third Sunday in April; and the **Rice Festival** in early May after the harvest.

Sleeping
One good-value option is the German- and Bolivian-run **Cabañas Quimorí** (☎ 932-2081, Santa Cruz ☎ 342-7747; hamel@cotas.com.bo; with breakfast US$10), just off the road toward Santa Bárbara. The simple individual cabins are spread over a large area with a great view over Amboró. They charge a bit more on weekends.

Residencial Nadia (☎ 932-2049; Sevilla 186; with bath US$4) Nadia has firm beds and the owner

is a good source of park information. All rooms have fans. The main drawback is the blaring disco across the street – try for a room in back.

Hotel Sumuqué (☎ 932- 2080; Steinbach s/n; cabin US$20) The cabins here are comfortable but lack views and the rates do not include breakfast.

Hotel Flora & Fauna (Double F; ☎ 710-43706; amboroadventures@hotmail.com; 4km south of plaza off Huaytú road; US$50 all-inclusive) British ornithologist and entomologist Robin Clarke runs this modern, utilitarian collection of cabins that sit atop a breezy, bird-rich ridge overlooking Amboró, surrounded by 200 acres of primary forest. Pluses include wildlife-viewing platforms, an extensive book exchange and guided walks (for guests only) from US$10. Access is by car/motorbike taxi (US$2.65/1.35) from Buena Vista.

Amboró Eco-Resort (☎ 932-2048, Santa Cruz ☎ 342-2372; www.amboro.com; s/d/ste US$80/90/140; ✗ ☀) Surrounded by its own tropical forest complete with walking paths and fenced-in forest animals. Amenities include a swim-up bar in the pool, a sauna, a disco and several sporting options. They also run the Mataracú Tent Camp, a relatively luxurious new complex on the edge of Amboró National Park (p283).

Ask around about Hotel Amboró, which was being refurbished by the owners of the Irish Pub and has great views of Amboró. A couple of the cheaper places allow camping on their grounds.

Eating
Los Franceses (1 block southwest of plaza; meals US$2.50-4.50) and its *tres* jovial owner from Bourguignon are a highlight of a visit to Buena Vista. The menu includes pan-fried steak, Provençal chicken, pork in white wine sauce, and *surubí* in a tomato and garlic sauce. All dishes come with bread, salad, french fries and rice, and vegetarian options are available on request.

Another excellent choice is **La Tranquera Kaffee Pub** (northwest side of plaza; mains US$3-4), which serves beef and chicken as well as wild game – agouti, peccary and armadillo; in the interest of wildlife, you might want to avoid these and opt instead for the exotic rainforest juices (US$3 for a jug). Main dishes are accompanied by salads and a major starch blitz: chips, yucca, plantains and rice.

In a kiosk in the middle of the plaza, the Irish Pub is open all day for coffee, muffins, juice, wine and cocktails. There are several other cheap family-run places on the plaza and along the highway serving burgers and specials.

Shopping

The **Jipijapa shop** (one block northwest of the plaza), sells lampshades, handbags, boxes and panama hats made from *jipijapa*, the fronds of the *cyclanthaceae* fan palm tree. Up the street, the recommended **Artecampo** shop also sells *jipijapa* products, plus other local creations.

Getting There & Away

From Santa Cruz, shared taxis (US$2.75 per person) leave for Yapacaní from behind the old long-distance bus terminal. Make it clear that you want to get off at Buena Vista. You can also take a slow *micro* to Montero and change to one that continues to Buena Vista. In Buena Vista, the bus stop is near the pharmacy.

To return to Santa Cruz, either take the *micro* to Montero or wait for a shared taxi coming from Yapacaní, which will cruise around the plaza in search of passengers with its horn blaring.

Getting Around

Car- and moto-taxis (US$0.20) wait at one corner of the plaza; there's also another taxi stand along the road to Santa Bárbara for Cabañas Quimorí and Hotel Flora & Fauna.

PARQUE NACIONAL & ÁREA DE USO MÚLTIPLE AMBORÓ

This 430,000-hectare park lies in a unique geographical position at the confluence of three distinct ecosystems: the Amazon Basin, the northern Chaco and the Andes.

The park was originally created in 1973 as the Reserva de Vida Silvestre Germán Busch, with an area of 180,000 hectares. In 1984, thanks to the efforts of British ornithologist Robin Clarke and Bolivian biologist Noel Kempff Mercado, it was given national-park status and in 1990 was expanded to 630,000 hectares. In late 1995, however, amid controversy

surrounding *campesino* colonization inside park boundaries, it was pared down to its current size (see the boxed text, p285).

The park's range of habitats means that both highland and lowland species are found here. All species native to Amazonia, except those of the Beni savannas, are represented, including the elusive spectacled bear. Jaguars, capybaras, river otters, agoutis, tapirs, deer, peccaries and various monkeys still exist in relatively large numbers, and more than 700 species of birds have been identified. The unfortunately tasty *mutún* or razor-billed curassow, is still native to the area, and even rare quetzals have been spotted. The park is also one of the only remaining habitats of the rare and endangered blue-horned curassow, also known as the unicorn bird.

To see most of these wild creatures, however, you will have to spend several days getting deep into the park.

Buena Vista Section

Access to the eastern part of the reserve requires crossing over the Río Surutú, either in a vehicle or on foot. Depending on the rainfall and weather, the river may be anywhere from knee- to waist-deep. For details on huts and campsites throughout the park, contact the Sernap office in Buena Vista (p281). For a list of companies running guided excursions into this section of the park, see Tours in Santa Cruz, p275.

RÍO MACUÑUCU

The Río Macuñucu route is the most popular into the Área de Uso Múltiple Amboró and begins at **Las Cruces**, 35km southeast of Buena Vista. It's a US$4 taxi ride from Buena Vista. From there it's 7km to the Río Surutú, which you must drive or wade across. Just beyond the opposite bank you'll reach **Villa Amboró**. Be aware that villagers may illegally try to charge an entrance fee to any tourist who passes their community en route to Macuñucu, regardless of whether you intend to stay there or not. The only body authorized to charge a fee is the park administration, which plans to begin charging a fee in 2004.

Here you'll pick up a track that continues several kilometers through the trees and homesteads and past a few cattle gates to the

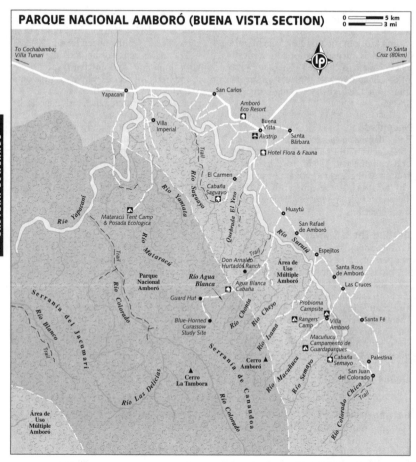

PARQUE NACIONAL AMBORÓ (BUENA VISTA SECTION)

banks of the **Río Macuñucu**. The track continues upriver through thick forest for about two hours, then disappears into the river course. Continue upstream another hour or so, hopping over river stones past beautiful red rocks, cliffs and overhangs. Beyond a particularly narrow canyon, which confines hikers to the river, you'll reach a large rock overhang accommodating up to 10 campers. If you have a tent, the sandy river beaches also make pleasant campsites.

At this point, the upriver walk becomes increasingly difficult and entails negotiating some large and slippery river boulders and scrambling past obstructing landslides. After several hours of heavy slogging upstream from the cave you reach a nice

waterfall and another potential campsite. The daring can continue the treacherous boulder-hopping to more overhangs further upstream. The terrain becomes more rugged, so a guide is recommended for overnight or extended trips above the waterfall.

RÍO ISAMA & CERRO AMBORÓ

The Río Isama route turns off at the village of **Espejitos**, 28km southeast of Buena Vista, and provides access to the base of 1300m Cerro Amboró, the bulbous peak for which the park is named. It's possible to climb to the summit, but it is a difficult trek and a guide is essential.

THE STRUGGLE FOR AMBORÓ

The location of Parque Nacional Amboró is a mixed blessing; although it's conveniently accessible to visitors, it also lies practically within spitting distance of Santa Cruz, Bolivia's second-largest city, and squarely between the old and new Cochabamba–Santa Cruz highways. At a time when even the remote parks of the Amazon Basin are coming under threat, this puts Amboró in an especially vulnerable position.

The first human settlers in the area were Chiriguano and Yuracare Indians, who occupied the lowlands, while Altiplano peoples, such as the Aymará, probably settled parts of the highland areas. Although agriculture was introduced after the arrival of the Spanish in the late 16th century, the remote Amboró region remained untouched until the late 20th century, when unemployed opportunity-seekers began migrating from the highlands in search of land.

When Parque Nacional Amboró was created in 1973, its charter included a clause forbidding settlement and resource exploitation. Unfortunately for naturalists and conservationists, hunters, loggers and *campesino* settlers continue to pour in – many of them displaced from the Chapare region by the US Drug Enforcement Agency – and the northeastern area is already settled, cultivated and hunted out. For poor farmers, cultivation practices have changed little since the 1500s, and slash-and-burn is still the prevailing method of agriculture.

Although NGOs have attempted to train committed *guardaparques* and educate people about the value of wilderness, more land is lost every year and the park's future is far from certain. In 1995 conflicts between colonists and authorities heated up, and as a result the park was informally redefined to include only land that lay 400m beyond the most remote cultivated field, effectively shrinking the protected area by about 200,000 hectares.

In July of the same year, *campesinos* pressing for official recognition of their rights to occupy the land prevented tourists and researchers from entering the park. The following October, with regional elections coming up, the government abandoned the struggle and issued an official decree reducing the park by over 200,000 hectares. The decommissioned area was then redesignated as the Área de Uso Múltiple Amboró, which effectively opened it up for settlement. The affected portion includes a band across the southern area from Comarapa to Samaipata, all of the eastern bit up to the headwaters of the Surutú tributaries, and parts of the far north.

UPPER SAGUAYO

The objective of this route is the study site on the upper Río Saguayo, where researchers rediscovered the rare blue-horned curassow, once thought to be extinct. It's very rough-going in places, so prospective hikers need a guide and a good machete. Without a 4WD to take you to the end of the motorable track, the return trip requires about five days.

The hike begins at the mouth of the **Río Chonta**. To get there, take a taxi or *micro* from Buena Vista to Huaytú. Here, turn right (southwest) and walk 5km to the Río Surutú. In the dry season, you can ford the river by vehicle or on foot. From the opposite bank it's 12km along the 4WD track to the end of the motorable track at Don Arnaldo Hurtado's ranch.

From the ranch, keep going a short distance along the track to the **Agua Blanca Cabaña**, watching along the way for herons, toucans, parrots, kingfishers and other colorful birds. If the route to the study site proves impassable, this makes a pleasant base for a couple of days exploring.

Beyond the *cabaña*, the track crosses the boundary between the Área de Uso Múltiple and the Parque Nacional Amboró, and descends through thick forest to the Río Saguayo. On the bluff above the opposite bank is an abandoned **guard hut** and a viable campsite.

If you do get as far as the guard hut, look for a trail heading upstream. If the way has been cleared, you can also explore side streams and observe an amazing variety of birdlife including tanagers, *orpendolas* (blackbirds), honeycreepers, humming-birds, warblers and herons. After about five hours, you'll reach the **abandoned hut** that served as the research base and study site for the blue-horned curassow, but you'll need a great deal of luck to see one. This is also an ideal habitat for the colorful military macaw.

The downhill return to the road is the same way you came; on foot, this takes about two days from the research camp and one long day from the Agua Blanca Cabaña.

MATARACÚ

From near Yapacaní, on the main Cochabamba road, a 4WD track heads south across the Río Yapacaní into the northern reaches of the Área de Uso Múltiple Amboró and, after a rough 18km, rolls up to Amboró Eco Resort's new **Mataracú Tent Camp** (p282) and community-run **Posada Ecologica** (☎ 716-74582; dm/d US$4/5.35), which offers all-you-can-eat meals (breakfast/lunch US$1/$2) and can be booked through any agency in Buena Vista. This is the only Sernap *cabaña* accessible by motor vehicle. Except in the driest part of the year, however, crossing the Río Yapacaní may be a problem.

Samaipata Area

Samaipata sits just outside the southern boundary of the Área de Uso Múltiple Amboró and is the best access point for the Andean section of the former park. There's no real infrastructure, and public facilities and walking tracks are still largely in the planning stages or privately maintained by local guides.

The best guides to the region are available in Samaipata. The road uphill from Samaipata ends at a small cabin, and from there it's a four-hour walk to a camping spot near the boundary between the primary forest, giant ferns and Andean cloudforest. From this point, you can continue an hour further into the park.

If you can't find a guide, a recommended **two-day walk** is the 23km traverse between Samaipata and Mairana via the hamlet of La Yunga. Most of the route is depicted on the IGM 1:50,000 topo sheet *Mairana – 6839-IV*. Samaipata appears at the northern edge of *Samaipata – 6839-III*.

For details, see Tours in Samaipata, p288.

Mairana Area

From Mairana, it's 7km uphill along a walking track, or taxi, to **La Yunga** where there's a community-run guest hut and FAN office. It's in a particularly lush region of the Área de Uso Múltiple Amboró, surrounded by tree ferns and other cloudforest vegetation. From La Yunga, a 16km forest traverse connects with the main road near Samaipata.

To enter the park here, visit the guard post at the south end of the soccer field in La Yunga. Access to Mairana is by *micro* or *camión* from Santa Cruz or Samaipata.

Comarapa Area

You may be able to find local Spanish-speaking guides in Comarapa. Northwest of Comarapa, 4km toward Cochabamba, is a little-used entrance to the Área de Uso Múltiple Amboró. After the road crosses a pass between a hill and a ridge with a telephone tower, look for the minor road turning off to the northeast (right) at the settlement of **Khara Huasi**. This road leads uphill to verdant stands of cloudforest, which blanket the peaks.

Other worthwhile visits in this area include the 36-sided **Pukhara de Tuquipaya**, a set of pre-Inca ruins on the summit of **Cerro Comanwara**, 1.5km outside of Comarapa; and the colonial village of **Pulquina Arriba**, several kilometers east of Comarapa.

Sleeping

Note that the following *cabañas* may or may not be available to the public depending on regulations in the forthcoming park-use plan.

That said, inside the park you'll find five wilderness *cabañas* that used to rent for US$2 per person per day. For bookings and information, contact **Sernap** (☎ Buena Vista 932-2054). The *cabañas* are very basic, so you'll need your own sleeping bag. The most popular and accessible *cabaña* is the one on the Río Macuñucu. Others can be found on the lower Río Semayo, above the Río Mataracú, on the Río Agua Blanca and on the lower Río Saguayo.

The **Macuñucu Campamento de Guardaparques**, 4km upstream, has a sleeping loft and rudimentary cooking facilities. The main camp activity is sitting beside the river and waiting for wildlife to wander past. Jaguar and puma tracks are frequently seen along the riverbank, but large cats are rarely observed.

At Villa Amboró, near the mouth of the Macuñucu, the NGO **Probioma** (☎ 343-1332; www.probioma.org.bo; Córdoba 7 Este No 29, Barrio Equipetrol, Santa Cruz) helped establish a community-run campsite with clean showers, toilets and several hiking trails, including a two-hour route to a lovely 50m waterfall and a four-hour return hike to a marvelous viewpoint over Cerro Amboró. Local Spanish-speaking guides can provide information on the flora and fauna, and the community can organize meals and arrange horse transportation for visitors who might not want to walk. A two-day stay, including guides, horses, camping gear and meals costs around US$30 per person. With your own food and camping equipment, you'll pay half price.

Getting There & Away

Every morning a *micro* heads south from Buena Vista through Huaytú, San Rafael de Amboró, Espejitos, Santa Rosa de Amboró, Santa Fé and Las Cruces. This boundary provides access to several rough routes and tracks that lead southwest into the interior, following tributaries of the Río Surutú. Note that all access to the park along this road will require a crossing of the Río Surutú. In Buena Vista you can hire a 4WD vehicle to reach Macuñucu Camp.

SANTA CRUZ TO SAMAIPATA

Thirty kilometers west of Santa Cruz on the road to Samaipata, 1km north up a valley in the village of El Torno, **Tapekuá Le Mayen** (☎ 382-2925; Warnes 999; ⏱ Sat & Sun 11:30am-6pm; mains US$4-8) serves gourmet Swiss–French fare in a lovely rural setting and has four charming, rustic *cabañas* (one night US$50-70, additional nights each US$4-5), which are superb value for extended stays.

Los Espejillos

The name of this popular retreat, which means 'the little mirrors', is derived from the surrounding smooth black rock, polished by a small mountain river. The site, which features cascades and refreshing swimming holes, is across the Río Piray 18km north of the highway.

About 400m beyond the free public site is the mediocre **Hotel Espejillos** (☎ 333-0091; d weekdays/weekends US$40/50, camping US$5/6), which has a clean private stretch of the river for bathing, an unremarkable restaurant and a bar that's good for a beer in the sun.

Catch any *micro* or *trufi* going toward Santiago del Torno, Limoncito, La Angostura or Samaipata, and get off just beyond

the village of San José. From here, Los Espejillos is a long walk or hitch north along the 4WD track (which isn't passable by vehicle at all during the rainy season). Weekends are the most crowded and chaotic but are also the best for finding taxis or catching lifts from the turnoff.

Bermejo & Volcanes Region

Bermejo, 85km southwest of Santa Cruz on the Samaipata road, is marked by a hulking slab of red rock known as **Cueva de los Monos**, which is flaking and chipping into nascent natural arches.

The intriguing crater lake **Laguna Volcán** is 6km up the hill north of Bermejo. Once a popular stopover for migrating ducks, in the late 1980s a *cruceño* developer cleared all the vegetation with the idea to build condos here. His time-share scheme fell flat and the foliage and wildlife are returning, so it makes for a pleasant walk from the highway. A lovely **walking track** climbs from the lake to the crater rim; it begins at the point directly across the lake from the end of the road. Coming from Santa Cruz, take a *micro* or *trufi* toward Samaipata and get off 1km beyond Bermejo.

More amazing is the bizarre nearby region known as **Los Volcanes**, which is north of the main road and features an otherworldly landscape of tropical sugarloaf hills. In the dry season, **Refugio Volcanes** (☎ 337-2042; forest@mail.zuper.net; www.forestbolivia.com; all-inclusive, plus transport US$65) offers sensitively developed *cabañas* with hot showers, meals, transport from the main road and guided hikes through the impossible landscapes. This wonderfully wild slice of paradise is 4km off the main road (two hours on foot or 45 minutes from the end of the easily motorable section of the side road into the complex). In addition to more than 10km of **hiking trails** through the tropical forests, you'll find paradisiacal waterholes where you can cool off; fascinating flora, including several unusual species of wild orchids; and also some of the Bolivia's most interesting bird-watching. The juice here is definitely worth the squeeze.

Las Cuevas

Las Cuevas (admission US$1) is 100km south-west of Santa Cruz and 20km east of Samaipata. If you walk upstream on a clear path away from the road, you'll reach two lovely waterfalls that spill into eminently swimmable lagoons bordered by sandy beaches. Camping is also possible here for a small fee.

SAMAIPATA

This sleepy village (elevation 1650m) in the foothills of the Cordillera Oriental is a popular weekend destination for *cruceños* and a pleasant place to hole up for a couple of days. The Quechua name, meaning 'rest in the highlands', could hardly be more appropriate. This quiet village has also attracted a growing cadre of foreign settlers and both highland and lowland Bolivians, and a cosmopolitan society is developing. If you're coming from the lowlands, it's also a good place to begin altitude acclimatization by degrees.

The region's main attraction is the pre-Inca ceremonial site of El Fuerte (p291). It's also the jumping-off point for Parque Nacional Amboró (p283) and forays to the site of Ché Guevara's last stand outside Vallegrande (p293).

Information

Reliable tourist information is available at **Café Bar Amboró** (☎ 944-6293; Bolívar s/n) and at the restaurant **La Chakana** (☎ 944-6146; www.geocities.com/chakanabol; west side of Plaza). **Sernap** has a new office 1km outside of town on the road to Santa Cruz. The **FAN** office (Sucre & Murillo) can arrange trips to the community of La Yunga at the edge of the park. See www.samaipata.info for an illustrated overview of the town and its surroundings.

Several telecom places near the plaza are working on getting the Internet (US$2 per hour) going; try **Snack Dany** (west side of plaza) or Roadrunners (below). There are a couple of Punto Entels for phone calls but there are no banks or ATMs. It's best to bring cash with you even though some upmarket places will accept, and might even cash, travelers checks. The post office only delivers mail; they can't accept outgoing post (and if they did, it would probably never be seen again).

Museo Arqueológico

Samaipata's small **archaeological museum** (admission US$0.65; 🕑 8:30am-12:30pm & 2:30-6:30pm) makes an interesting visit, but offers little

explanation of El Fuerte (p291). It does have a few Tiahuanaco artifacts and some local pottery. Admission to the ruins (student/adult US$1.65/2.35) covers the cost of the museum.

Tours

Several agencies organize trips to nearby attractions (US$10 to US$50 per person per day). Longer guided overnight trips on foot and horseback start around US$75 per person per day.

In addition to Amboró adventure tours, the recommended **Boliviajes** (☎ /fax 944-6082; at Finca La Víspera; www.lavispera.org) offers several exciting hiking, horseback and 4WD trips into wonderfully remote places south of Samaipata.

Biologist **Michael Blendinger** (☎ 944-6186; www.discoveringbolivia.com; Bolívar s/n, opposite the museum) is best for orchid, birding and full moon tours in English and German.

AmboróTours (☎ 944-6293; erickamboro@yahoo.com; Bolívar s/n) does park trips and bike rentals. Visit Olaf and Frank at German- and English-speaking **Roadrunners** (☎ 944-6153/93; dustyroad99@hotmail.com) for self-guided hikes with GPS and guided hikes to Amboró's waterfalls and cloudforests and to El Fuerte.

Spanish-speaking Samaipata native **Don Gilberto** (☎ 944-6050; Sucre 2) lived inside what is now the national park for many years and runs tours to his own simple encampment inside the park.

Sleeping
BUDGET

Paola Hotel (☎ 944-6903; northwest cnr of plaza; US$2, with bath & breakfast US$3.35) A new family-run place with spotless rooms and good beds plus shared kitchen, laundry sinks, cheap meals, a sunny mirador reading room and terrace overlooking the plaza. There's a basic restaurant and no alcohol allowed in rooms.

Palacio del Ajedrez (☎ 944-6196; paulin-chess@ cotas.com.bo; Bolívar s/n; US$5, s/d with bath US$8/13) Next to the archeological museum, the quiet, modern rooms at the Chess Club have quality beds. It's a quiet place to stay for the night or to pick up a game with Bolivian junior champions at the attached café.

Mi Casa Hostería (US$3.35, with bath US$4.65) Behind the church, the recently restored Mi Casa shines with a lush garden and rustic, clean rooms with a view.

Residencial Don Jorge (☎ 944-6086; Bolívar 20; US$3.35, with bath US$4) The courtyard is pleasant but beware of mosquitoes in the rooms at this friendly pad. Reasonably priced meals are available for guests upon request.

Achira Resort (☎ 352-2288; bolivia.resort@scbbs -bo.com; at Km 112; camping US$3.50, cabañas US$5; ⬛) Bolivia's leap into European-style camping begins 8km east of Samaipata. This family-style complex has *cabañas*, campsites, baths, showers and washing sinks, as well as a social hall with a restaurant and a games room.

More basic camping is available at the secluded **Mama Pasquala's** (camping US$3.50, cabins US$5), set in a beautiful valley near some great swimming holes. It's 500m upstream from the river crossing en route to El Fuerte.

Other basic choices include:
Residencial Chelo (☎ 944-6014; Sucre s/n; US$2-4) Just off the plaza.
Residencial Kim (☎ 944-6161; US$2.65, with bath US$3.35) A quiet, sunny place a half-block north of the plaza.

Hostal Saldías (☎ 944-6023; Bolívar s/n; US$1.35, with bath US$1.65) The funkiest acceptable cheapie.

MID-RANGE
Finca La Víspera (☎ /fax 944-6082; www.lavispera.org; US$12, walk-ins US$7, camping with/without your own tent US$4/5) A gregarious Dutch couple run this relaxing organic farm and retreat. Margarita sells all sorts of herbal remedies for whatever ails you and her piano-tuning partner Peter rents horses (US$7 an hour or US$25 a day) and organizes adventurous trips throughout the region. The well-built rooms with communal kitchens and four self-contained guesthouses (for two to 12 people) are warm and clean and enjoy commanding views across the valley. Camping includes hot showers and kitchen facilities. Bring a flashlight, as there's no street lighting between the village and the guesthouse, an easy 15-minute walk southwest of the plaza.

Campeche Cabañas (☎ 944-6046, Santa Cruz ☎ 333-6607; www.campechebolivia.com; cabañas weekdays US$20-25, weekends US$30-35) This HI affiliate has cozy, fully equipped cabins with

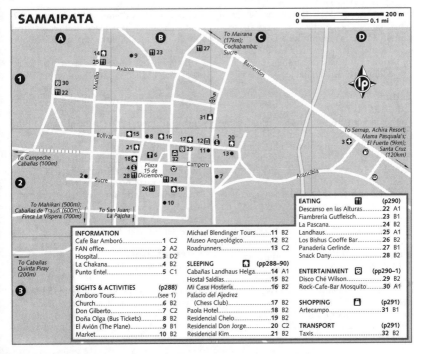

SAMAIPATA

INFORMATION	
Cafe Bar Amboró.....................**1** C2	
FAN office.................................**2** A2	
Hospital....................................**3** D2	
La Chakana.............................**4** B2	
Punto Entel.............................**5** C1	
SIGHTS & ACTIVITIES (p288)	
Amboró Tours.....................(see 1)	
Church......................................**6** B2	
Don Gilberto...........................**7** C2	
Doña Olga (Bus Tickets)........**8** B2	
El Avión (The Plane)................**9** B1	
Market....................................**10** B2	

Michael Blendinger Tours.......**11** B2	
Museo Arqueológico..............**12** B2	
Roadrunners..........................**13** C2	
SLEEPING (pp288-90)	
Cabañas Landhaus Helga......**14** A1	
Hostal Saldías........................**15** B2	
Mi Casa Hostería...................**16** B2	
Palacio del Ajedrez	
(Chess Club)........................**17** B2	
Paola Hotel............................**18** B2	
Residencial Chelo..................**19** B2	
Residencial Don Jorge...........**20** C2	
Residencial Kim.....................**21** B2	

EATING (p290)	
Descanso en las Alturas.........**22** A1	
Fiambrería Gutfleisch.............**23** B1	
La Pascana.............................**24** B2	
Landhaus...............................**25** A1	
Los Bishus Cooffe Bar...........**26** B2	
Panadería Gerlinde................**27** B1	
Snack Dany............................**28** B2	
ENTERTAINMENT (pp290-1)	
Disco Ché Wilson...................**29** B2	
Rock-Cafe-Bar Mosquito.......**30** A1	
SHOPPING (p291)	
Artecampo.............................**31** B1	
TRANSPORT (p291)	
Taxis......................................**32** B2	

Scale: 0 — 200 m / 0 — 0.1 mi

To Mairana (17km); Cochabamba; Sucre

To Sernap, Achira Resort; Mama Pasquala's; El Fuerte (9km); Santa Cruz (120km)

To Campeche Cabañas (100m)

To Mahikari (500m); Cabañas de Traudi (600m); Finca La Víspera (700m)

To San Juan; La Pajcha

To Cabañas Quinta Piray (200m)

Plaza 15 de Diciembre

fireplaces and kitchens just five minutes uphill from the plaza. With luxuriant gardens and spectacular views, it's a good deal. Prices depend on number of people, length of stay and type of accommodation.

Cabañas de Traudi (☎ 944-6094; www.traudi.com; US$5, s/d with bath US$10/15, cabañas US$30-70; 🏊) Across from La Víspera, this amenable Austrian-run spread has ample manicured grounds and horses for rent. It's set up as a family- oriented recreation center with ping-pong, tennis and equipment for other activities. The swimming pool is open to nonguests for US$2 per person.

Cabañas Landhaus Helga (☎ 944-6033; www .samaipata-landhaus.com; Murillo; s/d US$5/8, with bath US$10/16, cabañas US$30-70; 🏊) More upmarket, these tasteful *cabañas*, behind the Landhaus restaurant near the landmark airplane, El Avión have their own cooking and bathroom facilities. They accommodate up to seven people in three bedrooms, making it ideal for families. Breakfast costs an additional US$1 to US$2 and Finnish saunas are available with two hours' notice (US$20 for up to five people).

Cabañas Quinta Piray (☎ /fax 944-6136; www .samaipata.com; s/d US$10/15, cabañas US$20-65) This big, gated complex of modern self-contained cabins resembles a US suburban development. Rates depend on the number of rooms and beds and simpler 'backpack-ers' rooms are also available.

Eating
QUICK EATS
Panadería Gerlinde (☎ 944-6175; 🕐 8am-10pm, also at the market Sat & Sun) For baked goods, cheese, yogurt, muesli, organic produce, meats and healthy snacks and herbal remedies, don't miss this very popular German-run bakery.

Café Bar Amboró (☎ 944-6220; Bolívar s/n) Coffee, snacks, ice-cream and Internet (US$2 an hour).

Snack Dany (☎ 944-6063; west side of plaza) Offers much the same as Bar Amboró, with phone calls and Internet 'coming soon'.

La Pascana (southeast cnr of plaza) The local favorite for cheap, filling *almuerzos*.

Fiambrería Gutfleisch (🕐 7am-6pm Mon-Fri, at market 8am-4pm Sat & Sun) Sells some of Bolivia's best cheese, salami and cold cuts at their factory during the week and at the market on weekends.

Along the road to La Víspera, the Japanese religious sect **Mahikari** (🕐 2-6pm Tue-Sun) sells organic vegetables fertilized with divine light. Followers also offer spiritual sustenance for a pittance: for under US$1 you can be blessed with the 'energy' of the Mahikari Luz Divina – go on, don't be shy.

RESTAURANTS
La Chakana (☎ 944-6207; chakanabol@yahoo.com; west side of plaza; mains US$1.25-2.50) Samaipata's best and friendliest eatery is the Dutch- and Hungarian-run 'Southern Cross', where Erik and Krisztina Velde serve up breakfast, sandwiches, vegetarian meals, excellent pizza, homemade sweets, cocktails and European specialties. All that plus a welcome dose of hospitality and good conversation, a book exchange and foreign reading material make this a favorite travelers' haunt.

Garden Café (at Finca La Víspera; ☎ /fax 944-6082; www.lavispera.org; meals US$1.50-3) La Víspera's sunny, al fresco café features amazing breakfasts and lunches using fresh organic ingredients, and special dietary needs are catered to on request.

Descanso en las Alturas (☎ 944-6072; mains US$2-4) A welcoming little place that serves great breakfasts, meat, pasta, pizza and home-baked goodies.

Landhaus (☎ 944-6257; 🕐 dinner only Thu-Sun; mains US$2-4) If you are hankering for a European gourmet-style meal, this is the place. The food here is superb by anyone's standards and they have veggie options and a salad bar. It's near the airplane at the northern end of town.

Campeche (☎ 944-6046; 🕐 dinner weekends only; mains US$3-5) The elegant cuisine – salads, European-style meals and vegetarian fare – is accompanied by an excellent view.

Los Bishus Cooffe Bar (south side of plaza; lunch US$1.35) This small café has a full bar and serves a range of coffee drinks and a good-value set Bolivian lunch.

Entertainment
A slice of Santa Cruz teenage nightlife is transported to Samaipata each weekend and revived at the popular **Disco Ché Wilson**. Anyone over 21 will probably prefer the Saturday disco at the **Landhaus** (above), which cranks up as the restaurant winds down, normally around 10pm.

Rock-Café-Bar Mosquito (☎ 944-6232; behind Descanso en las Alturas; ☉ 7pm-late Tue-Sat) is the most happening watering hole in town, with full bar and a hell-bent-for-leather theme. Also look for the new incarnation of **Café Hamburg** (Bolívar s/n), which was planning to move down the street and change its name at time of writing.

Shopping
Saturday and Sunday are market days. You'll find locally produced ceramics at the Landhaus. Opposite the museum, Artecampo sells the work of women from around Santa Cruz department. Vendors show up on the plaza on weekends with homemade wine and artesanal food stuffs.

Getting There & Around
Four-passenger Expreso Samaipata Taxis (US$3.50 per person, 2½ hours) leave Santa Cruz when full from the corner of Chávez Ortíz and Solis de Olguin, two blocks south of the old bus terminal, and from outside the bimodal terminal. Alternatively, a *micro* (US$2, three hours) departs from Av Grigotá in the 3rd *anillo* at 4pm daily.

From Samaipata, **shared taxis** (☎ 944-6133/ 6016) depart for Santa Cruz from the gas station on the highway. *Micros* leave from the plaza daily around 4:30am and between noon and 5pm on Sunday.

From Samaipata to Santa Cruz, you can buy bus tickets at Snack Dany or from Doña Olga's shop, a block north of the plaza. You'll find public taxis at the gas station and *micros* around the main plaza between 5am and 7am and Sunday from noon to 5pm. Alternatively, wait by the highway for *trufis* returning in the afternoon. Finding a lift west to Mairana, Comarapa, Siberia, Vallegrande or Cochabamba is a bit trickier, but if you wait along the main highway, something will eventually come along. For a **private taxi** ring (☎ 944-6050).

AROUND SAMAIPATA
El Fuerte
Inscribed in 1998 as a Unesco World Heritage site, Samaipata's main attraction (admission adults/kids US$2.65/$1.35 plus US$0.25 local tax; ☉ 9am-5pm) is the remains of a pre-Inca ceremonial site. It occupies a hilltop about 10km from the village and affords a commanding view across the rugged transition zone between the Andes and low-lying areas further east. There's a new observation tower to allow visitors to view the ruins from above. Allow at least two hours to fully explore the complex.

Early conquerors assumed the site had been used for defense, hence its Spanish name, 'the fort'. In 1832 French naturalist Alcides d'Orbigny proclaimed that the pools and parallel canals had been used for washing gold. In 1936 German anthropologist Leo Pucher described it as an ancient temple to the serpent and the jaguar.

Recently the place has gained a New Age following, and in one of his fits of extraterrestrial fancy Erich von Daniken visited El Fuerte and proclaimed that it was a takeoff and landing ramp for ancient spacecraft. (One can hardly blame him; take a look into the valley below and you'll see a large flying saucer that has landed – and remains – at the Achira Resort complex.)

In fact, no one knows the exact purpose of El Fuerte. The site has been radiocarbon-dated at approximately 1500 BC. There are no standing buildings, but the remains of 500 dwellings have been discovered in the immediate vicinity and ongoing excavation reveals more every day. The main site, which is almost certainly of religious significance, is a 100m-long stone slab with a variety of sculpted features: seats, tables, a conference circle, troughs, tanks, conduits and *hornecinos* (niches), which are believed to have held idols. Zoomorphic designs on the slab include a raised relief of a puma and numerous serpents, which probably represented fertility. Most intriguing are the odd parallel grooves that appear to shoot off into the sky and inspired von Daniken's UFO launch-ramp hypothesis.

About 300m down an obscure track behind the main ruin is **El Hueco**, a sinister hole in the ground that appears all the more menacing by the concealing vegetation and sloping ground around it. It's almost certainly natural, but three theories have emerged about how it might have been used: that it served as a water-storage cistern; that it functioned as an escape-proof prison; and that it was part of a subterranean communication system between the main ruin and its immediate surroundings. El Hueco has been partially explored, but the project was abandoned when excavators heard mysterious sounds emanating from the walls. Openings of suspected side passages are now shut tight. On weekends snacks and refreshments are served from trailers outside the entrance.

GETTING THERE & AWAY

Hitching from Samaipata is easiest on weekends – especially Sunday – but the 20km round-trip walk also makes a fine day-long trip. Or, better yet, taxi up and walk back down. Follow the main highway back toward Santa Cruz for 3.5km and turn right at the sign pointing uphill. From here it's a scenic 5km to the summit. Watch for condors, and in the morning and afternoon for the flocks of commuting parakeets that chatter overhead.

Taxis for the round-trip, including a one-hour stop (negotiate for more time) at the ruins, charge US$7.50 for up to four people from Samaipata.

La Pajcha

A series of three beautiful waterfalls on a turbid mountain river, La Pajcha has a sandy beach for swimming and some inviting campsites. It's 42km (one to two hours by car) south of Samaipata, toward San Juan, then 7km on foot off the main road. The site is privately owned and visitors are charged a small fee to visit and swim here. You'll occasionally find transportation from Samaipata but, unless you have guaranteed transport back, take camping gear and plenty of food, or join a tour from Samaipata (p288).

Pampagrande

An especially nice spot is Pampagrande, which is surrounded by a desertlike landscape of cactus and thorny scrubland. There are no hotels, but the Dominican friar **Hermano Andres** (☎ 911-3155, Samaipata ☎ 944-6011) operates a basic bunkhouse with cooking facilities. He also guides informal and highly worthwhile **tours** into the surrounding hills and imparts his extensive knowledge of the local flora and fauna (especially birds and snakes). The only charge for these tours is a donation to the

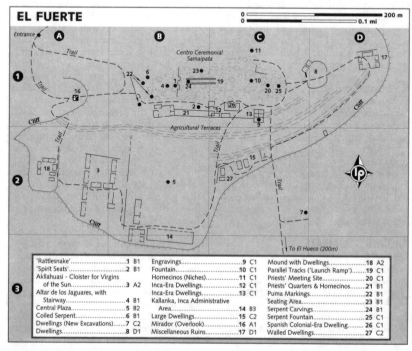

EL FUERTE

'Rattlesnake'..............................1 B1	Engravings..............................9 C1	Mound with Dwellings.................18 A2
'Spirit Seats'.............................2 B1	Fountain..................................10 C1	Parallel Tracks ('Launch Ramp')......19 C1
Akllahuasi - Cloister for Virgins	Hornecinos (Niches)..................11 C1	Priests' Meeting Site....................20 C1
of the Sun...............................3 A2	Inca-Era Dwellings.....................12 C1	Priests' Quarters & Hornecinos......21 B1
Altar de los Jaguares, with	Inca-Era Dwellings.....................13 C1	Puma Markings..........................22 B1
Stairway..................................4 B1	Kallanka, Inca Administrative	Seating Area..............................23 B1
Central Plaza.............................5 B2	Area......................................14 B3	Serpent Carvings........................24 B1
Coiled Serpent...........................6 B1	Large Dwellings........................15 C2	Serpent Fountain........................25 C1
Dwellings (New Excavations)......7 C2	Mirador (Overlook).....................16 A1	Spanish Colonial-Era Dwelling...26 C1
Dwellings...................................8 D1	Miscellaneous Ruins...................17 D1	Walled Dwellings........................27 C2

church so, if you've enjoyed yourself, please don't skimp. For meals there's only the small eatery near the market, three blocks north of the plaza.

Micros to Pampagrande leave from Santa Cruz late in the afternoon; they leave for the return journey at 7am daily.

VALLEGRANDE
Set in the Andean foothills at 2100m, Vallegrande enjoys a lovely temperate climate. Like most rural towns in Bolivia, life starts up around 4:30am, when the *micros* start arriving from the campo, delivering people to the markets.

After Ché Guevara was executed in La Higuera, south of Vallegrande, his body was brought to the now-dilapidated hospital laundry here, where graffiti lends its homage to this controversial figure. The revolutionary's body was clandestinely buried beneath the airstrip and stayed there until 1997, when the responsible official admitted to the cover-up (see the boxed text, p294). Most visitors to the town are passing through on a Ché pilgrimage, but Vallegrande is also a nice spot to relax and walk in the hills.

Vallegrande is the northern end of the developing 815km **Ché Trail** community-based tourism project, with Camiri (p266) anchoring the southern end. The route will trace Ché's final movements on foot, mule, bicycle and boat with basic, rustic accommodation at encampments and with local families. For an update on the project's development, contact America Tours in La Paz (p60).

Information
Vallegrande's **alcaldía** (☎ 942-2149) is keen to promote tourism and is happy to answer questions. For cultural or historical information, see the Casa de la Cultura, which has a small archeological museum and a Ché Guevara room with a video in Spanish. For information on local rock paintings, fossils and archeological sites, seek out Don Lalo Carrasco, president of the Grupo Yungauri; try first at Librería Acuarela.

Festivals & Events
The daily market begins in the plaza about 5am and a bigger **weekly fería** is held every Sunday. Nearly every week, there's some sort of small festival at the sports ground featuring traditional music and dancing. Around February 23 the town marks its anniversary with various sporting and cultural events. Since the bodies of Ché and several of his comrades were recovered from the airport in 1997, the town has celebrated an annual **Ché Guevara festival** in October, featuring folk art and cultural activities.

Sleeping & Eating
Vallegrande has a growing number of hostelries, so you're unlikely to be without a bed. **Hotel Sede Ganaderos** (☎ 942-2176; Bolívar 115; with bath & breakfast US$4) is the best place in town to look for the latest tourist information. **Alojamiento Teresita** (☎ 924-2151; Escalante/Mendoza 107), **Hotel Copacabana** (☎ 942-2014; Escalante/Mendoza 100) and **Residencial Vallegrande** all charge around US$3.50 per person.

Among the eating choices are the chicken joint La Casita, near the cathedral; La Chujlla, near the post office, which charges US$1.25 for an *almuerzo*; and **El Mirador** (El Pichacu near La Cruz), where you'll find trout, pork, steak and other carnivorous goodies for a couple of bucks. The cheap **Los Chinos** *pensión*, near the police station, serves set *almuerzos* and *cenas*.

Getting There & Away
From the terminal in Santa Cruz, buses leave for Vallegrande (US$5, six hours) from around 9am to 2pm. There may also be a later bus, but don't count on it. From Samaipata, an unreliable Vallegrande bus leaves around 2pm. If you're hitching, get off at Mataral, 55km north of Vallegrande, and wait there (and pray) for something headed south. From Cochabamba (US$4, 11 hours), buses leave several times weekly in the morning. Buses return to Cochabamba from near the market several times a week.

PUCARÁ & LA HIGUERA
To reach La Higuera, the site of Ché Guevara's final struggle and execution, you must first go to Vallegrande then catch a taxi or *camión* to Pucará. Camiones leave around 8am from a couple of blocks uphill from the market. For a taxi, ask around on Pedro Montano, near the school.

CHÉ GUEVARA – THE MOST COMPLETE MAN

Ernesto 'Ché' Guevara de la Serna was born on June 14, 1928, in Rosario, Argentina, to wealthy middle-class parents. He qualified as a doctor at the University of Buenos Aires, but his conscience was awakened at an early age. Idealistically, he decided that personal sacrifice and violent revolution were the only ways to create an equal society. Rejecting his comfortable life, he set off to travel penniless around Latin America.

His travels took him to Guatemala, where in 1954 he held a minor position in Jacobo Arbenz' communist government. It was around this time that he earned his nickname, Ché (buddy), after the Argentine habit of punctuating sentences with that word. After the CIA-aided overthrow of Arbenz the following year, Ché fled to Mexico, where he and his first wife, Peruvian socialist Hilda Gadea, met Fidel Castro. Guevara decided his calling was to bring about a worldwide socialist revolution, first by overthrowing the administration of Fulgencio Batista in Cuba, which was accomplished on January 2, 1959, after much bloodshed on both sides.

Through the late 1950s Guevara worked as a doctor, military commander and adviser in Castro's revolutionary forces. In 1959 Castro appointed him president of the Banco Nacional de la Cuba. In 1961 he became the Minister of Industry and was responsible for land redistribution and industrial nationalization. He persuaded Castro to ally Cuba with other communist nations.

What happened next is rather mysterious. In 1965 the ever-zealous Guevara decided to take his Marxist message to Africa. Before he left, Castro required him to sign a letter of resignation. While Guevara was in the Congo, Castro made public Guevara's resignation, making it clear that his African activities were not sanctioned by the Cuban government.

When he returned to Cuba in 1965, feeling betrayed by Castro's bureaucratization of the Marxist ideal, Ché turned back to Latin America. The following year, with a motley band of guerrillas, he set up a base at the farm Ñancahuazú, 250km southwest of Santa Cruz. Marching through the hinterlands of western Santa Cruz department, he attempted to convince the *campesinos* that they were oppressed, and to inspire them to social rebellion. Rather than being supported, however, he was met only with suspicion, and not even the local communist party would take up his cause.

On the plaza in Pucará, a grizzled *campesino* runs the local bar/*tienda*, and his daughter serves meals in a basic *comedor*. They're both very kind, and if you buy the man a couple of beers, he'll probably share a few Ché tales or suggest people who rent horses to go to La Higuera. They also have a room to rent on the roof at the back of the house, with marvelous views over the mountains and the upper Río Grande.

From Pucará, the 15km trip to La Higuera requires seven or eight hours on foot, five hours on horseback or a fortuitous hitch or taxi ride. Along the route, signposts point out Ché-related sites of historic interest.

Approaching La Higuera, you'll see the long *barranca* where Ché was captured. Apart from that, there's little to recall the incident but the schoolroom – now the local clinic – where Ché was kept before being executed. It's the yellow building just off the plaza, with a solar panel on the roof.

La Higuera has few amenities, but there is a small bar/shop where you can buy a beer and chat with locals about the historical events – and also about the devoted aficionados who turn up every October for the anniversary of the shootout. La Higuera has no formal accommodations, so you may wind up camping. Unless you're invited to do otherwise, select a secluded spot outside the village.

EASTERN LOWLANDS

The vast, sparsely populated lowlands of the Bolivian Oriente take in all of crescent-shaped southeastern Bolivia. The region is bounded on the west by the foothills of the Cordillera Oriental, on the north by Llanos de Guarayos and on the south and east by the international boundaries of Paraguay and Brazil.

The rejection took its toll. On October 8, 1967, when he was captured near La Higuera by the CIA-trained troops of Bolivian military dictator René Barrientos Ortuño, Guevara wasn't the T-shirt icon of his sympathizers, but a pathetically emaciated figure, suffering at the age of 39 from chronic asthma, arthritis and malnutrition. He was taken to a schoolroom in La Higuera and, just after noon the next day, was executed by the Bolivian army.

Ché's body was flown to Vallegrande, where it was displayed until the following day in the hospital laundry room. Local women noted an uncanny resemblance to the Catholic Christ and took locks of his hair as mementos. His hands, which were cut off to prevent fingerprint identification, were smuggled to Cuba by a Bolivian journalist and remain there in an undisclosed location.

The same night, he was buried with his comrades in an unmarked grave to deny him a place of public homage. In 1995 General Vargas, one of the soldiers who carried out the burial, revealed that the grave was beneath Vallegrande's airstrip. The Bolivian and Cuban governments called for exhumation, which resulted in the July 13, 1997, return of Ché's body to Cuba. He was officially reburied in Santa Clara de Cuba on October 17, 1997.

Ché's final speech, relayed from the Bolivian forests via the Tri-Continental Conference in Havana in April 1967, became a rallying cry around the world: 'Wherever death may surprise us, let it be welcome, provided that this, our battle cry, may have reached some receptive ear and another hand be extended to wield our weapons and other men be ready to intone the funeral dirge with the staccato singing of machine guns and new battle cries of war and victory. *Venceremos* (We shall overcome).'

According to philosopher Jean-Paul Sartre, Ché Guevara was 'the most complete man of our age'. Ché's international appeal, however, rests in his greatest quotation, which transcends any political ideology and taps into universal spirituality: 'I'm not a liberator – they do not exist. Only the people can achieve their own liberation'.

For more on Ché's extraordinary life – straight from the horse's mouth – look for *Bolivian Diary*, which was written during the final months of his life, or his myth-shattering book *The Motorcycle Diaries* (translated by Ann Wright), which presents a less politically correct side of this enduring legend. A recent attempt to follow his South American escapades by motorbike is chronicled in *Chasing Ché*, by Patrick Symmes.

The land is generally flat, broken by long, low ridges and odd monolithic mountains. Much of the territory lies soaking under vast marshes such as the Bañados del Izozog (part of the Parque Nacional Kaa-Iya del Gran Chaco) and the magnificent Pantanal on the Brazilian frontier. Mostly, however, it serves as a transition zone between the hostile, thorny Chaco scrubland in the south and the low, jungle-like forests and savannas of the Amazon Basin to the north.

HISTORY

In the days when eastern Bolivia was still unsurveyed and largely unorganized territory, the Jesuits established an autonomous religious state in Paraguay. From there they spread outwards founding missions and venturing into wilderness previously unexplored by other Europeans. The northern reaches of this territory were inhabited by indigenous tribes – including the Chiquitanos, Chiriguanos, Moxos and Guaraníes – whose descendants inhabit the area to the present day.

Each mission became an experiment in communal living for the original indigenous inhabitants, who had survived by their wits in a nomadic environment from time immemorial. The Jesuits established what they considered an ideal community hierarchy. Each population unit, known as a *reducción*, was headed by two or three Jesuit priests. A self-directed military unit was attached to each of these *reducciones*, and for a time the Jesuit armies were the strongest and best trained on the continent. This makeshift military force shielded the area from both the Portuguese in Brazil and the Spanish to the west, creating what was in effect an autonomous theocracy.

Politically, the *reducciones* were under the nominal control of the *audiencia* of

Chacras, and ecclesiastically under the bishop of Santa Cruz, although the relative isolation of the settlements meant that the Jesuits controlled things. Internally the settlements were jointly administered by a few priests and a council of eight natives representing specific tribes (a rare example of Colonial-era power sharing) who met daily to monitor community progress. A less altruistic motive for the Indians' cooperation was that those who elected to live in the missions (residence was voluntary, not enforced) could escape the harsh *encomienda* system or, worse still, outright slavery that awaited them elsewhere.

The mission settlements reached their apex under the indefatigable Swiss priest Father Martin Schmidt, who not only built the missions at San Javier, Concepción and San Rafael de Velasco, but also designed many of the altars, created the musical instruments, acted as the chief composer for the *reducciones*, and published a Spanish–Chiquitano dictionary. Schmidt was among those later expelled from the region and died in Europe in 1772.

Ironically, the Jesuits' growing strength proved their eventual undoing. By the mid-1700s political strife in Europe had escalated into a power struggle between the Church and the governments of France, Spain and Portugal. When the Spanish in South America fully realized the extent of Jesuit influence and got wind of all the wealth being produced in the wilderness, they decided the Jesuits had usurped too much power from the State. Portuguese slave traders were encroaching westward as Spanish imperial troops marched eastward to fortify the vague eastern border of Alto Perú. Caught in the military–political crossfire, the lucrative missions proved easy pickings for the Spanish. In 1767, swept up in a whirlwind of political babble and religious dogma, the missions were disbanded, and King Carlos III signed the Order of Expulsion, which evicted the Jesuits from the continent.

In the wake of the Jesuit departure, the carefully managed balance between the Europeans and local peoples shifted dramatically. The Spanish overlords, after realizing that their newly acquired lands were sources of neither unlimited mineral wealth nor slave labor for the Potosí mines, essentially abandoned the settlements, allowing them to decline. Without the Jesuits' adeptness at integrating the two cultures, the Indians soon left, and the towns became little more than agricultural backwaters, their amazing churches standing as mute testimony to the incredible experiment that ended so abruptly.

JESUIT MISSIONS CIRCUIT

The Oriente's vast expanses may at first glance appear to offer little to the traveler. But in fact some of the country's richest cultural and historic accomplishments are found within the seven-town region known as Las Misiones Jesuíticas. To travel through the entire circuit takes five or six days, but for those with an interest in architecture or history, it's one of Bolivia's most rewarding excursions.

Hidden in obscurity for more than two centuries, the area was raised to international prominence by the 1986 film *The Mission*, which gave impetus to the growing interest in the unique synthesis of Jesuit and native Chiquitano Indian culture in the South American interior. Five years later, Unesco declared the region a World Heritage site. Thanks largely to 25 years of painstaking restoration work directed by the late architect Hans Roth, all but one of the region's magnificent, centuries-old mission churches have been restored to their original splendor.

The circuit can be traversed either clockwise or counterclockwise: that is, going by bus from Santa Cruz around the circuit to San José de Chiquitos (p300), or by train to San José de Chiquitos and then between the missions by bus or by hitching.

Tours

See Tours under Santa Cruz (p275) for a list of agencies that organize trips through the Jesuit Missions circuit.

San Ramón

Although dusty San Ramón lacks a mission-era church, it's a significant cross-road between Santa Cruz, Trinidad, the missions and Brazil. It may be the site of a gold mine, but anything taken out of the ground is quickly transported somewhere else. **Hotel Manguarí** (☎ 965-6011; US$5), two blocks from the plaza on the Trinidad road,

A curassow

TOM BOYDEN

DEANNA SWANEY

Jesuit mission church, **San José de Chiquitos** (p301)

El Fuerte (p291), Samaipata

DEANNA SWANEY

House on Río Beni, **Rurrenabaque** (p314)

Baby capybaras

Parque Nacional Madidi (p320)

DEANNA SWANEY

has basic facilities. For meals, wander the few meters to the recommended **Boliche de Arturo**. Buses to Trinidad pass between 10pm and midnight, as do those headed east to San Ignacio de Velasco. The first bus leaves for Santa Cruz at 7am, but *camiones* also run relatively frequently.

San Javier
Founded in 1691, this pleasant little settlement is the mission circuit's oldest town and is becoming a favorite holiday destination for wealthy *cruceño* families. Martin Schmidt arrived in 1730 and founded the region's first music school and workshop to produce violins, harps and harpsichords. He also designed the present church, which was constructed between 1749 and 1752. It sits on a forested ridge with a commanding view over the surrounding low hills. Restoration work was completed in 1992 and the newly restored building appears pleasantly old.

San Javier is quite proud of its **cheese factory**, which you can visit. In addition, there are some inviting **hot springs** (US$6.50 via moto-taxi) 14km northwest of town. A further 6km along is a natural pool and waterfall, **Los Tumbos de Suruquizo**.

SLEEPING & EATING
The four-star **Cabañas Totaitu** (☎ 963-5063; 4/6/8 people US$75/96/110 weekends, US$20 less weekdays; 🏊), easily the mission circuit's nicest accommodations, occupies a dairy farm 4km northwest of town. Amenities include a pool, golf and tennis. There are some lovely walks as well as horses and mountain bikes for rent to explore the area. Camping may also be available – call ahead to check.

In town itself, you can choose between **Ame-Tauna** (US$5.50) on the plaza, which means 'welcome friend' in Guaraní and has comfortably cool rooms with shared

---

THE JESUITS & THE TRANSFORMATION OF LOWLAND CULTURE

Upon the arrival of the Jesuit missionaries, the native Chiquitano Indians, traditionally nomadic hunters and gatherers, were instructed in animal husbandry and European agricultural techniques and successfully integrated into a predominantly agricultural economy. The reverse also held true: the native inhabitants, with more than a millennium of nomadic existence behind them, showed the Europeans how to adapt to the demanding tropical environment. Unlike some of their contemporaries, the Jesuits were wise enough to heed the Indians' suggestions, and as a result the missions grew. Over the years a trade network was established between these communities and the Aymará and Quechua villages in the Altiplano. Beeswax, cotton, honey and indigenous textiles were exchanged for imported goods and raw silver mined in the highlands.

The Indians also were exposed to and inculcated with Christianity. Although subtle at first, the cumulative effect was that the new religion eventually obliterated any trace of their original tenets. To this day almost nothing is known of the beliefs and practices of these tribes prior to the arrival of the Jesuits.

In addition to economic and religious ventures, the Jesuits promoted cultural and educational expansion, cautiously avoiding the all too typical 'all or nothing' approach. The Jesuits sought to incorporate the best of both cultures, and to an astonishing extent succeeded. With Jesuit training, the Indians became accomplished artisans and produced outstanding work in cloth, silver and wood, even handcrafting the renowned harps and violins that still play a prominent role in traditional Paraguayan music. They also became formidable artists: at the height of this revolutionary cultural transition, the inhabitants of the missions were performing concerts, dances and plays that rivaled the best of Europe – in the Bolivian wilderness. Each mission had its own complete orchestra, furnished with handcrafted instruments, in many cases qualitatively superior to their European counterparts. These communities even performed sophisticated Italian Renaissance madrigals and Baroque masques and operas.

For those interested in learning more about this fascinating culture, two books, both in Spanish, are highly recommended: *Misiones Jesuíticas*, by Jaime Cisneros, and the preeminent *Las Misiones Jesuíticas de Chiquitos*, edited by Pedro Querejazu.

facilities, and the simple **Alojamiento San Javier** (☎ 963-5038; US$4). Offering the most amenities plus a good restaurant is the more upscale **Gran Hotel El Reposo del Guerrero** (Warrior's Rest; ☎ 963-5022, 332-7830 in Santa Cruz; with bath & breakfast US$10), a couple of blocks from the plaza.

Restaurants include **El Turista**, frequented by mission-bound tour groups, as well as the more down-to-earth **La Pascana**, **El Snack** and the highly regarded **El Ganadero**.

GETTING THERE & AWAY
All Santa Cruz–San Ignacio de Velasco buses pass through San Javier, 68km west of Concepción (US$1.35, 1½ hours) and 229km from Santa Cruz (US$3.50, five hours).

Concepción
Sleepy Concepción is 182km west of San Ignacio de Velasco in an agricultural and cattle-ranching area. The dusty village's main appeal is its friendliness and tranquility. Possibly because it's the nerve center for all the mission restoration projects, the extensively restored **church** (founded in 1709) appears to have fallen prey to kitsch tendencies, with much gaudy plastic and Disney-like décor.

For architectural aficionados, the **restoration workshops** (☉ 10:30am-3:30pm) behind the mission, where many of the fine replicas and restored artworks are crafted, merit a visit. The new **Museo Misional** (south side of plaza; ☉ 8:30am-noon, 2:30-6:30pm Tue-Sat, 10am-12:30pm Sun) in the old Cabildo building is also worth a look.

SLEEPING & EATING
The most upscale lodging is at the charming, three-star **Gran Hotel Concepción** (☎ 964-3031; west side of plaza; s/d with bath US$25/40; ☒), which features a pool, a quiet patio with an exotic garden, and intricately carved wooden pillars. A block west of the plaza, the recommended **Hotel Sede Ganaderos** (☎ 964-3055; with bath US$4.65) is also good value, with shaded hammocks in the courtyard. The best budget hostelry is **Residencial 6 de Agosto** (US$4).

Recommended restaurants include **El Buen Gusto** (south side of plaza) and **Club Social Ñuflo de Chavez** (west side of plaza), which has bargain set meals, live music on Friday nights and bats in the rafters.

GETTING THERE & AWAY
All Santa Cruz–San Ignacio de Velasco buses (US$5, seven hours) pass through Concepción, stopping on the main road 1km from the plaza (only buses destined for Concepción actually enter the center). From Trinidad, take a Santa Cruz bus and get off at San Ramón, where you can pick up a bus to Concepción and points east. *Micros* leave for San Javier (US$1.35, 1½ hours) and Santa Cruz (US$4, six hours) daily at 7:30am, 2pm and 6pm. Otherwise, wait near the gas station and flag down whatever may be passing (usually a *camión*).

San Ignacio de Velasco
The first mission church at San Ignacio de Velasco, which was founded in 1748, was once the largest and perhaps the most elaborate of all the missions. Unfortunately the original structure was demolished in the 1950s and replaced by a modern abomination. Realizing they'd made a hash of it the first time, the architects razed the replacement and designed a reasonable facsimile of the original structure. This new version is now nearly completed, and has incorporated the altar and wooden pillars from the original 18th-century church.

The town still has a large indigenous population and remains the 'capital' and commercial center of the Jesuit missions. Along with San Javier, it is also falling prey to Brazilian-influenced agribusiness, commercialization and development. Just a few years ago, visitors could expect to see mules and *burros* wandering about, but now the scene is set by modern commercial pursuits and foreign hunters in search of rare bird species. On Sundays, however, you can still see chicken fights near the airport.

SIGHTS & ACTIVITIES
The several large **wooden crosses** that have been erected at intersections just off the plaza create an appealing effect. Also check out the wooden pillars in front of the **Casa Miguel Areijer** on the plaza; one pillar is beautifully carved with the image of a group of Bolivian musicians. The owner intended to carve all the posts, but the city preferred the plain colonial style, and the municipal fate of the carved pillar remains in doubt. Attached to the **Casa de la Cultura** is

a small **museum**, which is noteworthy for its collection of musty, centuries-old musical instruments.

Only 700m from the church is the imposing **Laguna Guapomó**, where you can swim or rent a boat and putter around.

FESTIVALS & EVENTS

There's a big party celebrating the **election of Miss Litoral** during the last weekend in March. San Ignacio fetes its patron saint every July 31. Every summer, the Chiquitania hosts the **International Baroque & Renaissance Music Festival**, which runs for several weeks and centers on San Ignacio de Velasco.

SLEEPING

Because San Ignacio de Velasco is the commercial heart of the mission district, there's a good choice of accommodations. The nicest place in town is the **Apart-Hotel San Ignacio** (☎ 962-2157; 24 de Septiembre & Cochabamba; d with bath & breakfast US$16). The helpful proprietor at **Casa Suiza** (with meals US$8.50), seven blocks west of the plaza, speaks German and Spanish, has a wonderful library and can organize horseback riding, fishing trips and visits to surrounding *haciendas*.

Also recommended are **Hotel Palace** (☎ 962-2063; west side of plaza; US$6) and **Plaza Hotel** (☎ 962-2035; east side of plaza; US$3, with bath US$6).

Other basic and inexpensive possibilities include:

Alojamiento Guapomó (☎ 962-2094; 24 de Septiembre & Sucre)

Hotel Oriental (☎ 962-2150; 24 de Septiembre at Cochabamba)

Hotel 31 de Julio (west side of plaza)

Hotel Misión (east side of plaza)

EATING

On the plaza are **Restaurant Acuario** (west side of plaza), which specializes in Greek barbecue; **Pizzería Pauline** (south side of plaza); and **Snack Marcelito** (south side of plaza). Parrillada Las Palmares serves up beef dishes and Hamburguesas Chachi, two-and-a-half blocks south of the plaza, also does a range of snacks. You'll also find decent meals at the market, one block west and three blocks south of the plaza. Note that on Sunday everything is locked up tight except Snack

Marcelito, which on the Sabbath dispenses only sinful ice cream.

GETTING THERE & AWAY

Bus travelers will want to cover their luggage to prevent it from arriving in a thick coating of red dust. Several Santa Cruz-based flotas serve San Ignacio de Velasco (US$4 to US$5, 11 hours) via San Javier, Concepción and Santa Rosa de la Roca. Some buses continue from San Ignacio to San Miguel (US$1, one hour). Most buses and *micros* leave San Javier from near the market.

Coming from Trinidad, take a Santa Cruz bus and get off at San Ramón (usually in the middle of the night); there you can hitch or wait for an eastbound bus to San Ignacio.

In the dry season, several Santa Cruz bus companies operate services between the mission towns. A couple of Brazilian companies leave San Ignacio daily from early to mid-morning for San Matías, on the Brazilian border, where you'll find connections to the Brazilian towns of Cáceres and Cuiabá. The Flota Trans-Bolivia *micro* departs daily to San Miguel (US$1, half hour), San Rafael (US$1, one hour) and Santa Ana around 8am.

TAM and LAB used to run flights from Santa Cruz and TransBrasil used to offer flights to Cáceres, Brazil, but for now all flights have been suspended.

San Miguel de Velasco

Lost in the scrub 38km south of San Ignacio, San Miguel seems to be permanently on siesta. Its church was founded in 1721 and is, according to the late Hans Roth, the most accurately restored of all the Bolivian Jesuit missions. Its spiral pillars, carved wooden altar with a flying San Miguel, extravagant golden pulpit, religious artwork, toylike bell tower and elaborately painted façade are simply superb.

Although not designed by Martin Schmidt, the church does reflect his influence and is generally considered the most beautiful of Bolivia's Jesuit missions. During the restoration (1978–1984), Hans Roth and his colleagues set up workshops and trained local artisans, probably much as the Jesuits did two centuries earlier. The restoration artisans remained and now work in cooperatives making furniture and carvings, such as small, carved-cedar chests painted in pastels.

The best time to photograph the church is in the morning light. The nightly mass at 7pm will also provide a pleasant local perspective.

SLEEPING & EATING

On the plaza is the basic but acceptable **Alojamiento Pascana** (US$2.50). The attached restaurant serves cold drinks and simple meals. Just off the plaza, Alojamiento Pardo charges the same but you may have to chase up the owner to get a room. If you'd prefer to camp, speak with the nuns at the church, who can direct you to a suitable site.

GETTING THERE & AWAY

A *micro* leaves daily at 8:30am for San Ignacio de Velasco and returns, then leaves at about 10am for San Rafael. Next it travels back through San Miguel at around noon before returning to San Ignacio. It's also easy to get to San Ignacio with the *camionetas* that buzz around town honking for passengers in the early morning and after lunch.

Santa Ana de Velasco

The mission at this tiny Chiquitano village, 24km north of San Rafael de Velasco, was established in 1755. The church, with its earthen floor and palm-frond roof, is more rustic than the others and recalls the first churches constructed by the Jesuit missionaries upon their arrival. In fact the building itself is post-Jesuit, but the interior contains exquisite religious carvings and paintings.

Given its age, the original structure is in remarkable condition. Sadly, its ongoing 'renovation' is more utilitarian than preservationist and is limited to 'band-aid' repairs made as bits of the building collapse. So far, the work has been done by unskilled labor using cheap modern materials and shoddy techniques, but thanks to well-conceived plans by Roth and others, the church will eventually be professionally restored to its original state.

You shouldn't have problems finding transportation from either San Ignacio or San Rafael. Most days, *micros* run between San Ignacio and San Rafael via Santa Ana.

Because most traffic now uses this route, hitching is also a possibility.

San Rafael de Velasco

San Rafael de Velasco, 132km north of San José de Chiquitos, was founded in 1696. Its church was constructed between 1740 and 1748 – the first of the mission churches to be completed in Bolivia. In the 1970s and 1980s, the building was restored by the same Swiss architects responsible for the restoration of the churches in Concepción and San José de Chiquitos.

The interior is particularly beautiful, and the original paintings and woodwork remain intact. The pulpit is covered with a layer of lustrous mica, the ceiling is made of reeds and the spiral pillars were carved from *cuchi* (ironwood) logs. It's the only mission church to retain the original style, with cane sheathing. Of perhaps the most interest are the lovely music-theme paintings in praise of God along the entrance wall, which include depictions of a harp, flute, bassoon, horn and maracas.

At the corner of the main road and the street running south from the church is Alojamiento San Rafael (no sign). There's also Alojamiento La Pascana, on the plaza. Both are very basic and charge around US$3 per person.

The best place to wait for rides south to San José de Chiquitos (five to six hours) or north to Santa Ana, San Miguel or San Ignacio is on the main road in front of Alojamiento San Rafael. In the morning, buses run in both directions. To reach Santa Ana, use the right fork north of town.

San José de Chiquitos

One of the most accessible Jesuit missions, San José (population 13,000) was named for the original Chiquitano Indian inhabitants of the area. Just 4km to the west was the original location of Santa Cruz de la Sierra, but the city moved to its present site soon after its founding in 1561. The Jesuits arrived sometime in the mid-1740s, and construction of the magnificent mission church that today dominates the town was begun around 1750.

San José de Chiquitos surprises its few visitors with the atmosphere and beauty of an Old West frontier town, complete with dusty streets straight out of *High Noon* and footpaths shaded by pillar-supported roofs. Flanked on the south by a low escarpment and on the north by flat, soggy forest, San José is developing into a cattle ranching center and oil exploration is an ongoing concern. There's also a lively trade in undocumented goods from Brazil, made all the more prevalent by the completion of the gas pipeline between Santa Cruz and Brazil.

INFORMATION

The bank on the plaza may change cash US dollars if it has sufficient *bolivianos* on hand. Most businesses will accept cash dollars for purchases and a few will change small amounts for non-customers. Check around the plaza for telecom and Internet services.

JESUIT MISSION CHURCH

Even if you've had your fill of ho-hum monuments to New World colonialism, San José's unique, beautiful stone Jesuit mission church won't fail to impress. Although the main altar is nearly identical to those in other nearby missions and vague similarities to churches in Poland and Belgium have been noted, there is no conclusive evidence about the source of its unusual exterior design.

The Jesuits could not find a ready source of limestone for making cement mortar, so they built with wood and mud plaster. The church compound consists of four principal buildings arranged around the courtyard and occupying an entire city block. The bell tower was finished in 1748, the *funerario* (death chapel) is dated 1752 and the *parroquio* (living area) was completed in 1754. It is believed, however, that only the façades were completed before the Jesuits were expelled in 1767. All construction work was done by the Chiquitano Indians under Jesuit direction. The doors, some of the altar and one magnificent bench seat were hand-carved in wood by expert Chiquitano artisans.

Massive renovations and restorations have been underway for over a decade and are still incomplete, and the altar is currently a series of bare, empty niches. Nevertheless, what has been accomplished to date is amazing; the restored altar and front pews are especially noteworthy.

Phone the **church rectory** (☎ 972-2156) for up-to-date information on what's open, closed or under renovation. Chances are the person answering will speak not only Spanish but German, French, English or Portuguese.

PLAZA 26 DE FEBRERO

The *toboroche* trees on the town's huge plaza were once occupied by a family of sloths, but a flowering of the trees several years ago sent them off to search for leafier pickings. The trees now shelter noisy green parrots, and during the rainy season the ground beneath hops with thousands of frogs and large toads. Note also the bust of Ñuflo de Chavez, founder of Santa Cruz, and the rather odd and erotic fountain off to one side of the plaza; it's a safe bet you won't see anything like it in highland Bolivia.

SANTA CRUZ LA VIEJA WALK

Just south of town, the road passes beneath an **archway** supported by bikini-clad ferro-concrete nymphs welcoming you to the old Santa Cruz highway (the route to the original Santa Cruz de la Sierra). These beauties were obviously designed by the same person responsible for the Chiquitano maiden and the plaza fountain. About 1km further along, through dusty ranchland, you'll pass an abandoned schoolhouse from bygone days. After 3km or so, the road enters more jungle-like vegetation, which supports throngs of squawking green parrots.

Along this road, 4km south of town, is the **Parque Histórico Santa Cruz la Vieja** (admission US$1.75), on the site of the original Santa Cruz de la Sierra, but there's little to see other than an abandoned guard house. Over the road is a small park where locals go to cool off in a murky green swimming pool, but the walk itself is more appealing than the water. In the forest nearby is a **waterfall**, the source of San José's drinking water; it's a cool spot sheltered from the tropical heat, but swarms of biting insects may limit you to a fleeting visit. Carry insect repellent and wear good shoes and pants to protect your feet and legs from ferocious ants.

If you continue another 2km to 3km up the switchbacks onto the escarpment, you'll have a far-ranging view of San José and the surrounding plains. Further along are some nice eroded landscapes and a series of lovely waterfalls known as the **Cascadas del Suruquizo**.

SLEEPING

Despite its lackadaisical staff, the best place to stay is **Hotel Raquelita** (☎ 972-2037; west side of plaza; US$4.25, with bath US$6), which has a laundry service, fans and sparkling clean facilities. The rate schedule is rather complicated, depending on the time of your visit, the number of people in your party and whether or not they size you up as a tourist.

Opposite the railway station, **Alojamiento San Silvestre** (☎ 972-2041; with bath & breakfast US$4) has double rooms with private baths. Guests may use the pool table, but beware of the stereo system that swallowed South America.

A block north of the plaza is the more basic **Hotel Denisse** (☎ 972-2230; Ñuflo de Chavez s/n; US$3.65).

If you prefer to camp, ask the priest at the mission church whether you can pitch a tent in the courtyard.

EATING

There's a good, clean snack bar in Hotel Raquelita where you'll find breakfast, lunches and delicious homemade ice cream. Next door, Sombrero é Sao serves chicken and beef dishes with rice, fries and salad. It's a great spot to sit outside and down a couple of cold brews. Another decent spot for an evening meal is the cheaper Casa é Paila, around the corner, but it's closed more often than it's open.

On the Virrey Mendoza side of the plaza, Pollo Pio-Pio dishes out chicken and fries but is notorious for overcharging foreigners. A better choice is Pollo Barbaroja a few meters further along. Brazilian influences are evident at the Enca Restaurant, north of the railway line.

Watch for the army of lads who emerge from plaza doorways selling *salteñas* in the morning and cheese bread in the afternoon from heaped trays, often tellingly recycled from lard tins. There are also some informal restaurant stalls near the railway station and along the road toward San Ignacio, north of the railway line, which serve snacks and inexpensive lunch and dinner specials.

On Mondays the Mennonites come into town from the colonies and sell homemade cheese, butter, bread and produce.

GETTING THERE & AWAY

There are no bus or *micro* services between San José de Chiquitos and Santa Cruz, although various government agencies have promised 'tourist-class' bus services. At present, you must first reach San Ignacio and pick up transport from there. On Monday, Wednesday and Friday morning, *micros* leave from San Ignacio for San José (via San Rafael and San Miguel); they return on Tuesday, Thursday and Saturday afternoons.

If you prefer to take your chances with a *camión*, wait at the *tranca* beyond the railway line 300m north of town. In the dry season, *camiones* go to San Ignacio at least a couple times daily. Plan on about US$4 per person as far as San Ignacio.

The easiest way to travel between San José de Chiquitos and Santa Cruz or Quijarro, both roughly eight hours away, is via train. Many trains arrive and depart at night, which is a shame because the countryside here – especially to the east of San José – is the most scenic stretch of the Red Oriental.

The eastbound *Expreso del Oriente* (the Death Train) passes daily except Sunday at 9:30pm to Quijarro and the westbound train to Santa Cruz passes daily except Sunday at 2am. The *tren mixto* leaves Santa Cruz on Monday and Friday at 7:15pm and arrives in San José de Chiquitos at around 5am; it leaves less than an hour later and arrives in Quijarro at around 3pm the next day. The ironically named *tren rápido* passes (very slowly) on Tuesday and Sunday at 9:50pm eastbound and Monday and Thursday at 9:45pm westbound; note however, that the days of this service may be numbered.

Freight trains run at any time; in theory you can simply hop into the passenger *bodega* and pay the 2nd-class fare to either Santa Cruz or Quijarro, although polite inquiries beforehand are appreciated. The ticket window opens whenever the ticket seller rolls up and feels ready to work, which may be anytime between 6am and 3pm. Buying train tickets is a slow process, and you need to show a passport for each person traveling (to forestall ticket scalping). Intermediate stations such as San José de Chiquitos receive only a few ticket allotments, and they are sold only on the day of departure (or, in the case of departures in the wee hours, on the previous day).

FAR EASTERN BOLIVIA

Between Roboré and San José de Chiquitos the railway line passes through a bizarre and beautiful wilderness region of hills and monoliths. Further east, along the Brazilian border, much of the landscape lies soaking beneath the wildlife-rich swamplands of the Pantanal, while the southern area of the region is dominated by the equally soggy Bañados del Izozog. This latter wetland area has recently been incorporated in the Parque Nacional Kaa-Iya del Gran Chaco (below), which is Latin America's largest national park.

Roboré

The town of Roboré, about four hours along the railway east of San José de Chiquitos, began in 1916 as a military outpost, and the military presence remains a bit overwhelming. You can probably imagine what happens when a lot of bored soldiers posted in the middle of nowhere encounter tourists in a town that rarely sees outsiders. The situation seems to have improved over the past few years, but it's still best to keep a low profile.

SIGHTS & ACTIVITIES

The cool and clean **Río Roboré**, which flows through town, offers some pleasant and refreshing swimming. You may want to move several hundred meters upstream from the bridge to avoid the curious eyes of local crowds. A pleasant day-trip will take you to **El Balneario**, a mountain stream with a waterfall and natural swimming hole. It's a two-hour walk each way from town, and you'll need a local guide to find it. There's another closer swimming hole that is accessible by taxi for US$1.50 round-trip.

Culturally, the Jesuit mission at **Santiago de Chiquitos**, 20km from Roboré, is more interesting than San José de Chiquitos. It's set in the hills, and the cooler climate provides a welcome break from the tropical heat of the lowlands. The round-trip taxi fare from Roboré is US$10 for up to four

people. *Camiones* and military vehicles occasionally do the run from the east end of town for US$1 per person one way.

The 40°C thermal baths at **Aguas Calientes**, 31km east of Roboré, are popular with Bolivian visitors who believe in their curative powers. The Santa Cruz–Quijarro train stops in Aguas Calientes, and *camiones* (US$1 per person) leave from the eastern end of Roboré. Taxis charge US$12 for up to four passengers. There are no accommodations, so the baths are best visited on a day trip.

Chochís, two stops along the railway toward San José de Chiquitos, has a lovely church.

Finally, if you're keen to see the best of the landscape between Roboré and San José de Chiquitos, the most convenient station is **El Portón**, which lies immediately west of the spectacular and oft-photographed rock pillar of the same name. There are no tourist facilities, so carry food and camping gear.

SLEEPING & EATING

Roboré's best accommodation option is **Hotel Pacheco** (☎ 974-2074; 6 de Agosto s/n; d US$5, with bath US$7). The alternative is **Residencial San Martín** (☎ 974-2192; Av Ejército Nacional). For meals, apart from the hotels, you can check out Pollo de Oro near the railway station. In the evening, it livens up appreciably when the alcohol-assisted celebrants provide a bit of a diversion to accompany the inevitable wait for the *tren atrasado* (late train).

GETTING THERE & AWAY

By train, Roboré is about four hours west of Quijarro and the same distance (time-wise) east of San José de Chiquitos. **TAM** (☎ 974-2035) flies from Santa Cruz to San Matías on Friday mornings, returning via Roboré.

Parque Nacional Kaa-Iya del Gran Chaco

In the late 1990s the Guaraní people, in conjunction with the Bolivian Ministerio de Desarrollo, the World Bank, the Swiss government, the Wildlife Conservation Society and the Armonía Foundation, succeeded in having their ecological treasure protected in a two-million-hectare reserve, which is now Latin America's largest national park. The huge and enigmatic **Bañados del Izozog** wetland, in the heart of this vast wilderness, lies buried in a wild and relatively inaccessible expanse of territory between San José de Chiquitos and the Paraguayan border.

Of the total area, 800,000 hectares belong to the Guaraní people and 300,000 hectares to the neighboring Ayoreos. Currently, the only access into this fabulous region is by 4WD or on foot from El Tinto, on the railway line west of San José de Chiquitos, but organized tours from Santa Cruz may begin someday. This is a true wilderness and there are no facilities or services in the area. If you enjoy places that recall the Brazilian Pantanal and have a way to get into the area, a visit is emphatically recommended.

PUERTO SUÁREZ

If it could only get its act together, Puerto Suárez, set in a watery wilderness with some of the densest wildlife populations on the continent, could be a legitimately profitable and attractive tourist center. Although it's improving, this hot, steamy backwater remains infamous as the place where São Paulo car thieves dump their spoils and the majority of the community is in some way involved in illicit dealings.

Hotel Bamby (☎ 976-2015; 6 de Agosto s/n; d US$8) offers the best value. Alternatively, try the less expensive **Hotel Sucre** (☎ 976-2069; Bolívar 63), **Frontera Verde** (☎ 976-2468, fax 976-2469), or **Residencial Puerto Suárez** (☎ 976-2750; Bolívar 105), among numerous others.

TAM (☎ 976-2205) runs popular Tuesday and Saturday morning flights from Santa Cruz to Puerto Suárez (US$59), returning the same afternoon. These flights actually land in Corumbá, but passengers intending to cross into Brazil must first return to Bolivia to exit the country before checking into Brazil at the Polícia Federal in Corumbá.

Puerto Suárez is also on the railway line, 15km west of Quijarro.

QUIJARRO

Quijarro, a muddy collection of shacks at the eastern terminus of the Death Train, sits on slightly higher and drier ground than Puerto Suárez and serves as the border crossing between Bolivia and Corumbá (Brazil). Visitors heading east will be treated to a wonderful preview

of Corumbá; from muddy Quijarro, it appears on a hill in the distance, a dream city of sparkling white towers rising above the vast green expanses of the Pantanal. In Mutún, just south of Quijarro, what may be the richest deposits of iron manganese on the continent are currently being 'developed'.

Bolivian Pantanal

Hotel Santa Cruz in Quijarro organizes boat tours through the wetlands of the Bolivian Pantanal and provides an alternative to the well-visited Brazilian side. A comfortable three-day excursion, including transportation, food and accommodations (on the boat) costs around US$100 per person.

Sleeping & Eating

The friendly **Hotel Bilbosi** (☎ 978-2113; s/d with bath US$10/16; ❄), two blocks from the railway station, has clean, air-con rooms. The three-star **Hotel Oasis** (☎ 978-2159) offers pleasant rooms for the same rates. More basic accommodations are available for around US$2 per person at several *alojamientos* on the left as you exit the railway station; a recommended cheap one is the spartan **Hotel Carmen**.

The five-star **El Pantanal Hotel Resort** (☎ 978-2020, Santa Cruz ☎ 355-9583; www.elpantanalhotel.com; ❄ ❢) is in the beautiful Arroyo Concepción, 12km from Puerto Suárez and 7km from Corumbá, Brazil. With over 600 hectares of grounds, it sits atop a bluff overlooking the Río Paraguai and the Cidade Branca of Corumbá. All of its 75 rooms have private baths, a TV, phones and air-conditioning, and guests have access to the swimming pool, jacuzzi, game rooms, tennis and volleyball courts, child care, indoor tropical gardens (the point of this is lost on many...) and several restaurants, including an Argentine *churrasquería*. Standard two-day, three-night packages, with meals and airport transfers, cost around US$100 per person. The current program may attract Bolivian interest, but foreigners would probably expect more emphasis on the Pantanal and wildlife-viewing.

Lots of good inexpensive restaurants are lined up along the street perpendicular to the railway station entrance.

Getting There & Away
TRAIN
By rail the trip between Quijarro and Santa Cruz takes anywhere from 16 to 23 hours, depending on which train you take. The *Expreso del Oriente* leaves Quijarro in the afternoon daily except Sunday (2nd/1st/Pullman class US$7/15.50/20) but departure times depend entirely on when the train arrives from Santa Cruz. The slow, cumbersome and slightly cheaper *tren mixto* chugs out on Wednesday and Saturday. You'll pay the same to ride in a *bodega* on a freight train. The ticket office opens around 7am and only sells tickets on the day of departure; depending on the lines, you may be better off buying tickets for a few dollars more from an agency on the Bolivian side of the frontier.

TO BRAZIL
When the train pulls into Quijarro, a line of taxis waits to take new arrivals to the border. The border post is just 2km from the station, so if you can't bargain the drivers down to something reasonable – say US$0.65 per person – it's a pretty easy walk to the border. Travelers report being charged up to US$10 for Bolivian exit stamps, but this is entirely unofficial; politely explain that you understand there is no official charge for the stamp, and appear prepared to wait until they get real.

Over the bridge, you pass through Brazilian customs. From there, city buses will take you into Corumbá. Brazilian entry stamps are given at the Polícia Federal, at the *rodoviária* (Portuguese for 'bus terminal,' pronounced haw-doo-*vyahr*-ya); it's open until 5pm.

Technically, travelers arriving in Brazil from Bolivia need a yellow fever vaccination

certificate. Officials don't always ask for one, but when they do, the rule is inflexibly enforced. In a pinch, a clinic in Corumbá provides the vaccine. You can change US dollars in cash or travelers checks at the Banco do Brasil, two blocks from Praça Independência.

To reach the Bolivian border from Corumbá, catch a bus from Praça Independência, opposite the cathedral. If you're entering Bolivia, you can change Brazilian *reais* and US dollars at the frontier.

SAN MATÍAS
The border town of San Matías is the main Bolivian access point into the northern Brazilian Pantanal. Travelers between Cáceres and Bolivia must pick up Brazilian entry or exit stamps from the Polícia Federal office at Rua Antônio João 160 in Cáceres. On the Bolivian side, you'll have to hunt up the immigration officer; otherwise, pick up your entry or exit stamp in Santa Cruz.

For accommodations you're limited to the basic, stifling rooms at **Hotel San José** (US$3). The best restaurant, which serves a very limited menu, is **BB's** (it stands for Bolivia/Brazil – cute).

TAM (☎ 968-2256) may offer an occasional unscheduled flight between Santa Cruz and San Matías. In the dry season, a Trans-Bolivia bus leaves from Cáceres (Brazil) to Santa Cruz (US$25, 30 hours), via San Matías (US$5, four hours) between 5am and 6am daily.

Coming from Brazil, get your exit stamp the night before; in San Matías, the bus will stop and wait while you visit immigration (US$0.75 by taxi from the bus terminal). It's possible to change dollars or *reais* to *bolivianos* at the Trans-Bolivia bus office.

Amazon Basin

Although it lies more than 1000km upstream from the great river, Bolivia's portion of the Amazon Basin better preserves the classic image many travelers associate with the mother of all rivers than the real thing itself. While Brazilian rainforests continue to suffer heavy depredation, the archetypal Amazon forests of northern Bolivia remain relatively intact. Although facing similar threats, they still offer a glimpse of the deep and mysterious Eden (they've also been called the Green Hell) that beckons from the glossy pages of travel brochures and adventure magazines.

Despite all the attention focused on the drug issue and the environment, northern Bolivia is not all cocaine and rainforest. Cattle ranching continues on a large scale, especially in the savannas around Trinidad. All the region's main thoroughfares are Amazon tributaries that elsewhere would be considered great rivers in their own right. Along these jungle waterways, riverboats, barges and bathtubs are the predominant modes of transportation. Villages are still thin on the ground, and some remote tribes have had only minimal contact with modern civilization. All that is changing however, with the recent spate of road construction, leading to an influx of highland settlers and a subsequent upsurge in logging and slash-and-burn agriculture.

The Beni, Pando and surrounding Amazon Basin areas have weathered continuous human immigration and boom-bust cycles. Only a few of the original forest-dwelling tribes remain, and even fewer have been able to maintain their traditional subsistence hunting-and-gathering lifestyles.

TOP FIVE

- Go gaga over wildlife on a jungle or pampas trip from **Rurrenabaque** (p314)

- Hop on a slow boat down the **Río Mamoré** (p338) between Trinidad and Guayaramerín

- Immerse yourself in the richness of the jungle at Chalalán Ecolodge, deep inside **Parque Nacional Madidi** (p320)

- Explore the transition between savanna and rainforest and observe wildlife at **Reserva Biosférica del Beni** (p322)

- Float by the impressive waterfalls and hike through the fabulous landscapes of **Noel Kempff Mercado National Park** (p330)

- TELEPHONE CODE: 03 (EXCEPT WHERE NOTED) - ELEVATION: 0–200M

HISTORY

Indigenous peoples occupying the western Bolivian Amazon were conquered early on by the Inca. Then came the Spanish, who wandered all over the Americas chasing rumors of a mystical city of unimaginable wealth, which they called El Dorado (The Gilded One).

One such tale was of Paititi, an unfathomably opulent land east of the Andean Cordillera near the source of the Río Paraguai. It was said to be governed by a particularly affluent king named El Gran Moxo. Though the would-be looters scoured the region for traces of the coveted booty, they found nothing but a few muddy jungle villages and hostile tribes. There was neither a single street paved with gold nor a single royal treasury. In the mid-17th century the Spanish turned elsewhere in their quest for El Dorado.

The Spanish may have found nothing in the Moxos region that interested them, but the Jesuits did, seeing an area that was rich in souls that were ripe for the plucking. The first significant European penetration of these lowlands was staged by these hardy missionaries, whose first mission was founded at Loreto, in the Moxos region, in 1675.

The Jesuits set up a society similar to the one they would establish in the Llanos de Chiquitos and Llanos de Guarayos during the following century. While they imposed Christianity and European ways, they also recognized the indigenous people's natural expertise in woodcarving, which eventually produced the brilliant carvings now characteristic of the missions. They imported herds of cattle and horses to some remote outposts, and, thanks to the prolific natural vegetation, the animals fared well. The descendants of these herds still thrive throughout most of the department.

From the locals the Jesuits learned about tropical agricultural methods. They, in turn, introduced unfamiliar crops, and the Beni today produces bananas, coffee, tobacco, cotton, cacao, peanuts and a host of other warm-weather crops.

After the expulsion of the Jesuits in 1767, the Franciscan and Dominican missionaries, as well as the opportunistic settlers who followed, brought slavery and disease. Otherwise, the vast, steamy forests and plains of northern Bolivia saw little activity for decades.

CLIMATE

The seasons are less pronounced here than in other parts of Bolivia, and temperatures are uniformly hot year-round. Most of the rain falls during the summer in unrelenting downpours and, during wet times, the streets fill with mud and the air fills with the sound of croaking frogs. Although winter is drier than summer, it also sees a good measure of precipitation. Even in the hot, humid forest regions of the north, frosts are not unheard of during a *surazo*, a cold wind blowing from Patagonia and the Argentine pampas.

NATIONAL PARKS & RESERVES

Blessed with some of the richest wildlife habitats on earth, the Bolivian Amazon is home to some of the country's best-known national parks and reserves. For bird watchers, monkey lovers and jaguar seekers, this region is heaven. From the jungles and wild rivers of Parque Nacional Madidi (p320) to the less-frequented, wildlife-rich Reserva Biosférica del Beni (p322) and the virtually unexplored 'lost world' of Parque Nacional Noel Kempff Mercado (p330), the Amazon Basin has it all. Conservation International is attempting to raise awareness of the need for protection of the headwaters of several major Amazon tributaries with their ambitious new Vilcabamba–Amboró Conservation Corridor initiative.

GETTING THERE & AROUND

Rurrenabaque is by far the Amazon's most visited settlement. Although it's worth the treacherous bus ride from La Paz, flying is highly recommended. It's no coincidence that buses heading back to La Paz from Rurre are less crowded – many people decide to wing it (or take a faster Jeep) after surviving the initial bus ride.

Transportes Aéreos Militares (TAM) and Amazonas fly daily between La Paz and Rurrenabaque. Their low-flying planes afford great glimpses of Lake Titicaca after takeoff before squeezing past Chacaltaya and soaring over the Yungas. You can see the landscape change from desolate, rugged highlands to lush, forested lowlands. And

THE AMAZON BASIN

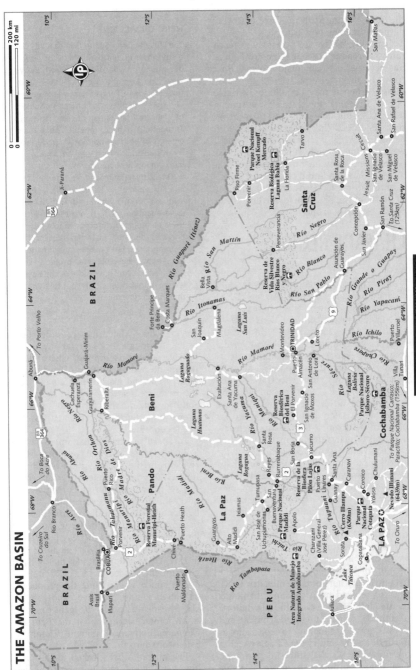

the grass landing strip in Rurre is worthy of more than one post-trip tale.

Generally, 4WDs are necessary to reach most off-road spots, but there are regular bus services between major towns. Boat travel is big here, especially in the rainy season, when it may be your only viable option. Riverboat travel isn't for everyone: it's relaxing but slow going and there are no real schedules. While riverside scenery can be mesmerizing, it changes little, so you'll want to bring a couple of books along. Passenger comfort is the last thing cargo-boat builders have in mind, but Bolivian accommodation standards are still superior to those on the Brazilian 'cattle boats' that ply the Amazon proper.

CHAPARE REGION

☎ 04

'The Chapare' is synonymous with both coca and Drug Enforcement Agency (DEA) attempts to eradicate it, which have resulted in ongoing, messy confrontations between *cocaleros* (coca growers), the DEA and the Bolivian government. The Bolivian media frequently expose cases of human-rights abuse and disregard for property. Although it isn't inherently unsafe to travel in the Chapare, road blockades are common and independent adventurers should inquire locally about safety before straying too far off the Cochabamba–Santa Cruz highway. The spectacular route from Cochabamba to Villa Tunari (now *asfaltado* except for a geologically unstable 20km stretch that's been approved for paving) passes between peaks and mountain lakes before dropping steeply into deep, steaming valleys and leveling out into remnants of tropical forest.

HISTORY

Less than a century after the rubber boom went bust in the early 1900s, another member of the infamous Suárez family came to control another booming industry. Coca, the leaf revered by Altiplano inhabitants for its ability to stave off the discomforts of altitude, thirst, hunger, discontent and stress, grows primarily in the Yungas north of La Paz and in the Chapare region of northern Cochabamba department. The Yungas produce the more palatable

HERO OR VILLAIN?

The life of Roberto Suárez Gómez reads like a spy novel in which the hero (or villain, depending on your point of view) always stays one step ahead of the CIA – or, in this case, the US Drug Enforcement Agency. The great-nephew of Nicolás Suárez, he amassed a narcotrafficking fortune. Throughout Bolivia, people perpetuate legends of philanthropic deeds performed by this enigmatic man who became a folk hero among his compatriots.

One story has him landing unannounced in a Piper aircraft at Reyes airport, walking into a poor neighborhood and flinging large quantities of cash into the air. From there he reportedly proceeded to a nearby bar and declared an open tab for the evening. Other tales speak of his donations to schools, development projects and health clinics. And now and again he's been known to make significant contributions to the federal government.

leaves, while the Chapare crop tastes bitter. Although locals prefer the former for everyday consumption, Chapare coca has an international market. Dried, soaked in kerosene and mashed into a pasty pulp, the leaves are treated with hydrochloric and sulfuric acid until they form a foul-smelling brown base. Further treatment with ether creates cocaine.

It's been estimated that up to half of Bolivia's gross national product is derived from the cocaine industry. By the mid-1980s, US yuppiedom was snorting so much Bolivian coke that the US government decided something had to be done about it. Realizing that it would be unpopular to bomb the users among its own population, the USA pointed an accusing finger at Bolivia and threatened drastic DEA action should the Bolivian government not cooperate with military action aimed at curtailing the production of Bolivia's most lucrative export. When US President Ronald Reagan proposed some joint cleaning up of the Beni and Chapare, Bolivian President Victor Paz Estenssoro agreed.

The operation was leaked to the press, however, giving remote processing labs sufficient warning to clear out before the bombs arrived. Only minor damage was done, and the US government found itself in a rather embarrassing situation. In 1987 the Bolivian army raided the ranch of the elusive Roberto Suárez Gómez by helicopter, but failed to make any arrests. In Suárez' absence, the Bolivian government sentenced him to 12 years in prison, and in 1988 Bolivian soldiers finally managed to arrest the cocaine king while he slept.

VILLA TUNARI
pop 2000 / elevation 300m
Villa Tunari is a major truck stop and a tropical resort for cold-weary highlanders. Away from the highway, it's a quiet spot to relax, hike and swim in cool rivers.

Information
There's no ATM here yet, but the Prodem bank and some hotels may change cash – bring some bills with you just to be safe. There are several telecom places along the highway but nobody is offering public Internet service to date.

Sights & Activities
In addition to Hotel El Puente's Los Pozos (p312), there are several free *pozos* (swimming holes) in town along the Río San Mateo. The potential fishing, kayaking and white-water rafting is unlimited in the surrounding rivers.

A good independent hike will take you to the friendly village of **Majo Pampa**. Follow the route toward Hotel El Puente and turn right onto the walking track about 150m before the hotel. After crossing the Valería Stream, it's 8km to the village.

PARQUE MACHÍA (INTI WARA YASSI)
This 36-hectare wildlife refuge (☎ 413-6572; www.intiwarayassi.org; admission US$0.75, photo/video permit US$2/$3.35; camping US$2) rescues injured wild animals, abandoned tropical pets, former zoo inhabitants, old circus animals and other abused critters, and provides volunteers with a sense of satisfaction in exchange for their sweat. It's also a relaxing place to camp and wander through the forest, taking in the sights, sounds and tranquility. The alternative name, Inti Wara Yassi, means 'sun', 'moon', 'stars' in Quechua, Aymará and Guaraní, respectively.

> **DEMOCRACY IN ACTION?**
> Speak Spanish and want to see Bolivian democracy in action? Check out the live soap opera that takes place most weeknights when the open-air court is in session across the street from Alojamiento Pilunchi in the Poder Judicial sentencing tribunal.

The best times to see animals are at noon and 5pm during feeding. Tours for prospective volunteers are conducted daily at 10am. Volunteers must stay for a minimum of 15 days and can choose between rustic camping and the hostel, both of which cost US$70 for the first two weeks, including showers and cooking facilities.

The reserve's founders may be opening a larger refuge off the highway halfway between Santa Cruz and Trinidad in 2004.

ORCHIDEARIO VILLA TUNARI
Lovingly tended by German botanists, Villa Tunari's **orchid nursery** (☎ 413-4153; www.orchidarium.org) is a beautiful garden that's home to over 70 species of tropical orchids. There's also a small museum, El Bosque restaurant and a couple of *cabañas* for rent. It's just north of the highway, 2km west of town near the *tranca*.

Tours
Villa Tunari is a main focus for Cochabamba-based **Fremen Tours** (☎ 425-9392; www.andes-amazonia.com; Tumusla N-245, Cochabamba), which arranges all-inclusive tours, accommodations, river trips and other activities at out-of-the-way sites. It also offers live-aboard riverboat cruises around Trinidad and adventure tours in Parque Nacional Isiboro-Sécure (when it's safe to do so).

Festivals & Events
The town festival of its patron saint, **San Antonio**, consumes the entire first week of June. During the first week of August, unique Amazonian fish dishes are served up at the **Feria Regional del Pescado**.

Sleeping
BUDGET
Hotel Villa Tunari (☎ 413-6544; US$3, d with bath US$8.50) Villa Tunari's newest budget option is above a corner store opposite

AMAZON BASIN

Alojamiento Pilunchi. The owner is friendly and keen on providing great-value, clean accommodations.

Camping is possible at Parque Machía and also at the sporting ground, north of the center. Other *alojamientos* may allow emergency camping when they are full.

Other classic cheapies (which are often overrun by feral Parque Machía volunteers) include:

Hotel Las Vegas (Arce S-325; US$2) Friendly but run-down. Serves decent meals.

Alojamiento San Mateo (US$2, camping US$1) Just beyond Hotel Las Vegas.

Alojamiento Pilunchi (US$1.75) Super simple with open-roofed rooms with mosquito nets.

La Querencia (☎ 413-4189; Beni 700; US$2.50) Tranquil riverfront place serving basic meals.

MID-RANGE & TOP END

Hotel El Puente (Cochabamba ☎ 425-9392; s/d/tr/q US$19/27/38/45; 🐾) Operated by Fremen Tours, this delightful hideout in a remnant island of rainforest 4km outside Villa Tunari sits near the Ríos San Mateo and Espíritu Santo confluence. The highlight is a walk around **Los Pozos**, 14 idyllic natural swimming holes (US$2 for nonguests) deep in the forest, where you're guaranteed to see blue morpho butterflies. To get here, catch a *micro* heading east from Villa Tunari; get off at the first turnoff after the second bridge, turn right and walk for 2km. Taxis from the center charge around US$3 for up to four people.

Hotel Victoria Resort (☎ 413-4176, Cochabamba ☎ 445-1239; off highway 1.5km west of town; US$35) Popular with families from Cochabamba, this self-contained family-oriented resort and time-share condo complex is the fanciest place in town.

Los Tucanes (☎ 413-4108; with breakfast US$30; 🍴 🐾) The five-star *cabañas* at this country clubesque resort are among Villa Tunari's most luxurious options.

Las Araras (☎ 413-4116; s/d with breakfast US$18/ 28) This modern hotel in a tropical garden setting is just over the first bridge east of the highway. It offers good mid-week package discounts.

Hotel/Restaurant Las Palmas (☎ 413-4163, Cochabamba ☎ 427-7762; s/d/tr US$30/40/45; 🍴 🐾) The air-con rooms aren't the best deal in town, but cheaper rooms with fans and the family *cabañas* are a good option for big

groups. The open-air restaurant (mains US$1.50 to US$4) serves well-prepared locally caught fish and great fresh tropical juices.

The friendly **Residencial San Martín** (☎ 413-4115; s/d US$15/25; 🐾) also has a pool.

Eating & Drinking

A rank of food stalls along the highway sells all manner of inexpensive tropical fare. The *comedores* in the new sparkling market are also worth a look. Otherwise, the restaurants mentioned in the Sleeping section above are your best bets.

Entertainment

Nightlife revolves around Restaurant Karaoke Jazmin del Tropico, the steamy place to sweat and be seen on the dance floor after hours.

Getting There & Away

The bus and *micro* offices are sandwiched amid the line of food stalls along the main highway. From Cochabamba (US$2, four to five hours), *micros* leave in the morning from the corner of 9 de Abril and Oquendo; some continue on to Puerto Villarroel (US$1, two hours). From Villa Tunari to Santa Cruz, several services operate in the early afternoon, but most Santa Cruz traffic departs in the evening. To Cochabamba, *micros* leave at 8:30am.

PARQUE NACIONAL CARRASCO

Created in 1988, this 622,600-hectare park takes in some of Bolivia's most readily accessible cloudforest. It skirts a large portion of the road between Cochabamba and Villa Tunari, and also includes a large lowland area of the Chapare region. Most rainforest mammal species are present, as is an array of birds, reptiles, amphibians, fish and insects.

The easiest way to visit is with Fremen Tours (p311). Tour programs include the **Cavernas del Repechón** (Caves of the Night Birds), where you'll see the rare nocturnal *guáchero* (oilbird) and six bat species. Access is from the village of **Paractito**, 8km west of Villa Tunari. This half-day excursion includes a short slog through the rainforest and a zippy crossing of the **Río San Mateo** in a cable-car contraption.

Another emerging option is the Conservation International-backed **Camino en las Nubes** (Walk in the Clouds) project, a three-day

AMAZON BASIN

trek through the park's cloudforests, descending with local guides from 4000m to 300m along the old Cochabamba–Chapare road. For details, contact **Conservation International** (CI; ☎ 717-3527; Hans Gretel 10, Villa Tunari) or Fremen Tours (p311).

PUERTO VILLARROEL

This muddy tropical settlement, one of northern Bolivia's major river ports, is two hours northeast of Villa Tunari. Although it's little more than a collection of tumbledown wooden hovels, a military installation, a YPFB petroleum plant and a loosely defined port area, it's a vital transportation terminal and gateway to the Amazon lowlands. For a quick look at the rainforests, it makes an easy two-day round-trip from Cochabamba. Bring lots of insect repellent and wear strong old shoes with lots of tread. Even in the dry season, the muddy streets will submerge your ankles and devour your footwear.

The best sleeping option is the 10-room **Amazonas Eco-Hotel** (☎ 424-2431; tombol@ hotmail.com; s/d US$3/6, with bath US$7/12), which also serves meals. None of Puerto Villarroel's other hotels will win any awards. **Hotel Amazonas** (US$2) is probably the best choice. The alternative, **Hotel Sucre** (US$2), suffers from an excess of noise, thanks to the attached bar and disco. Fortunately, those who've arranged river transportation will normally be permitted to sleep on the boat.

Half a dozen restaurant shacks opposite the port captain's office serve up fish and chicken dishes. For good *empanadas*, snacks, hot drinks and fresh juices, try the market on the main street.

Micros from Cochabamba to Puerto Villarroel (marked 'Chapare,' US$2, seven hours) leave from the corner of Av 9 de Abril and Oquendo, near Laguna Alalay. The first one sets off around 6:30am, and subsequent buses depart when full. The first *micro* back to Cochabamba leaves around 7am from the bus stop on the main street. *Camiones* leave from the same place at any hour of the day, especially when there are boats in port. Note that transportation between Cochabamba and Santa Cruz doesn't stop at Puerto Villarroel.

Two types of boats run between Puerto Villarroel and Trinidad. The small family-run cargo boats that putter up and down the Ríos Ichilo and Mamoré normally only travel by day and reach Trinidad in around six days. Larger commercial crafts travel day and night and do the run in three or four days.

In Puerto Villarroel the **Capitanía del Puerto** and other related portside offices can provide sketchy departure information on cargo transporters. Unless military exercises or labor strikes shut down cargo services, you shouldn't have more than a three- or four-day wait.

The average fare to Trinidad on either type of boat is US$15 to US$20, including food (but it's still wise to carry emergency rations), a bit less without meals. The quality of food varies from boat to boat, but overall the shipboard diet consists of fish, dried meat, *masaco* and fruit; avoid endangered turtle eggs if they're offered. Few boats along the Ichilo have cabins. Most passengers sleep in hammocks (sold in Cochabamba markets) slung out in the main lounge.

PARQUE NACIONAL ISIBORO-SÉCURE

Created in 1965, this 1.2-million-hectare park occupies a large triangle between the Ríos Isiboro and Sécure and the Serranías Sejerruma, Mosetenes and Yanakaka. It takes in mountains, rainforest and savanna and, in its more remote sections, is home to profuse wildlife. However, an obscure 1905 resolution opening the region to settlers has resulted in much of it being overrun by squatters with no way to halt the influx. As a result, the natural environment and the once-prevalent Indian population, which consisted of Yuracarés, Chimanes, Sirionós and Trinitarios, have been compromised.

As if that's not enough, the park also lies along drug-running routes, so independent visitors must exercise extreme caution. Thanks to DEA activity, locals may regard any foreigner as an anti-*cocalero* and hence fair game for abuse. Independent travelers would be wise to carry letters of introduction from the coca growers' association. There's also a dispute over whether Isiboro-Sécure belongs to Cochabamba department or whether it lies in the Beni. The suspected presence of oil makes the issue all the more relevant.

Owing to seasonal flooding, the park is inaccessible between November and March.

AMAZON BASIN

For more information, contact **Sernap** (☎ 448-6452/53) in Cochabamba.

Currently, the only truly safe way to visit the park is with Fremen Tours (p311). Their worthwhile seven-day boat trip from Trinidad to Laguna Bolivia, the park's best-known destination, includes stops at riverside settlements, rainforest walks, horseback riding, wildlife viewing and a canoe trip on the Río Ichoa.

WESTERN BOLIVIAN AMAZON

The wildlife-rich bit of the Bolivian Amazon closest to La Paz is an ideal introduction to the country's northern rainforests. The lovely town of Rurrenabaque is now a primary Gringo Trail hangout: pampas, jungle and ethno-ecotourism options are innumerable and Parque Nacional Madidi is one of South America's finest wilderness gems.

For background reading, pick up *Phoenix: Exploration Fawcett* (2001), by early explorer Colonel Percy Harrison Fawcett, or *Back from Tuichi* (1993; also published as *Heart of the Amazon*, 1999), about the 1981 rescue of Israeli Yossi Ghinsberg, whose expedition was lost in the rainforest and rescued by locals.

RURRENABAQUE
pop 15,000

This bustling little frontier town on the Río Beni is Bolivia's most appealing lowland settlement. Its changing moods can be magical: the sunsets are superb and at night dense fog rolls down the river and creates beautiful effects, especially during the full moon. The area's original people, the Tacana, were one of the few lowland tribes that resisted Christianity. They are responsible for the name Beni, which means 'wind', as well as the curious name of 'Rurre', which is derived from 'Arroyo Inambaque', the Hispanicized version of the Tacana name 'Suse-Inambaque', the 'Ravine of Ducks'.

Information
BOOKSHOPS
For reading material, try **Café Motacú** (Santa Cruz near Comercio s/n; ☒ 8:30am-noon & 6:30-9:30pm Mon-Sat), where there's a book exchange (US$4 a book or US$0.65 on loan). Otherwise, check the popular hotels.

IMMIGRATION
Extend your stay by visiting **Migracíon** (☎ 892-2241; ☒ 8:30am-4:30pm Mon-Fri) on the plaza's northeast corner.

INTERNET ACCESS
Access (via temperamental satellite) is best when the sun is shining but can be painfully slow at times. Try **Camila's** (Santa Cruz at Avaroa; US$2 per hr) or American-run **Librería Sembrador** (Bolívar at Arce; US$1.60 per hr; ☒ 9am-10pm).

LAUNDRY
Recommended **Laundry Service Rurrenabaque** and neighboring **Number One** promise same-day machine-wash-and-dry service (US$1.35 per kilo).

MONEY
There's no bank (the closest one is in Reyes), but cash dollars can be changed at Cactri, next to Bala Tours. Some tour agencies change travelers checks (4 to 5% commission), as will Red Expreso Oriental, which can also handle overseas money orders. Tours can usually be paid for with credit cards and *simpatico* bars, agencies and hotels may be willing to facilitate cash advances.

TELEPHONE
Punto Entel (☎ 892-8510; Comercio & Santa Cruz; ☒ 7am-10pm) is a better place to make calls than the main Entel office.

TOURIST INFORMATION
Sernap's main **Parque Nacional Madidi's office** (☎ 892-2540), where independent visitors must register and pay the US$5.35 entrance fee, is across the river in San Buenaventura. Inquire at **Conservation International** (CI; ☎ 892-2015/2495; www.conservation.org.bo; south side of Plaza 2 de Febrero) about new community ecotourism developments in the region.

Keep an eye out for the new municipal tourist office opening a couple of doors down from the Amazonas office, which plans to maintain a complaint registry and publish a qualitative ranking of Rurre's tour agencies, compiled from visitor evaluations.

AMAZON BASIN

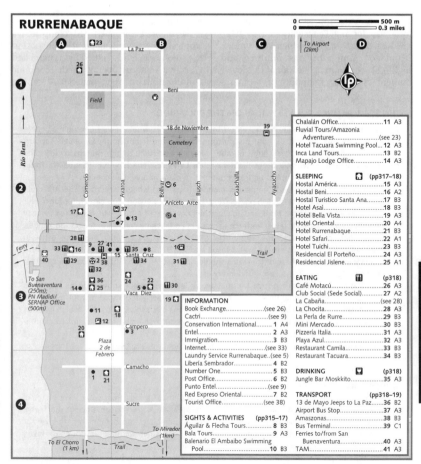

RURRENABAQUE

Chalalán Office	11 A3
Fluvial Tours/Amazonia	
Adventures	(see 23)
Hotel Tacuara Swimming Pool	12 A3
Inca Land Tours	13 B2
Mapajo Lodge Office	14 A3

SLEEPING (pp317–18)
Hostal América	15 A3
Hostal Beni	16 A2
Hostal Turístico Santa Ana	17 B3
Hotel Asaì	18 B3
Hotel Bella Vista	19 A3
Hotel Oriental	20 A4
Hotel Rurrenabaque	21 B3
Hotel Safari	22 A1
Hotel Tuichi	23 B3
Residencial El Porteño	24 A3
Residencial Jislene	25 A1

EATING (p318)
Café Motacú	26 A3
Club Social (Sede Social)	27 A2
La Cabaña	(see 28)
La Chocita	28 A3
La Perla de Rurre	29 B3
Mini Mercado	30 B3
Pizzería Italia	31 B3
Playa Azul	32 A3
Restaurant Camila	33 A1
Restaurant Tacuara	34 B3

INFORMATION
Book Exchange	(see 26)
Cactri	(see 9)
Conservation International	1 A4
Entel	2 A3
Immigration	3 B3
Internet	(see 33)
Laundry Service Rurrenabaque	(see 5)
Librería Sembrador	4 B2
Number One	5 B3
Post Office	6 B2
Punto Entel	(see 9)
Red Expreso Oriental	7 B2
Tourist Office	(see 38)

SIGHTS & ACTIVITIES (pp315–17)
Águilar & Flecha Tours	8 B3
Bala Tours	9 A3
Balenario El Ambaibo Swimming	
Pool	10 B3

DRINKING (p318)
| Jungle Bar Mokkkito | 35 A3 |

TRANSPORT (pp318–19)
13 de Mayo Jeeps to La Paz	36 B2
Airport Bus Stop	37 B3
Amazonas	38 B3
Bus Terminal	39 C1
Ferries to/from San	
Buenaventura	40 A3
TAM	41 A3

AMAZON BASIN

Sights & Activities

Most of Rurrenabaque's appeal is the surrounding natural beauty. It's easy to pass a day or three here while waiting to join a tour. Behind town is a low but steep **mirador** that affords a view across the seemingly endless Beni lowlands; it's reached by climbing up the track at the southern end of Bolívar.

Another nice excursion is **El Chorro**, an idyllic waterfall and pool 1km upstream. A track leads from the wet-sand beach to this favorite swimming hole, which is accessible only by boat. On a rock roughly opposite El Chorro is an ancient **serpentine engraving**, which was intended as a warning to travelers: whenever the water reached serpent level, the Beni was considered unnavigable.

When you can't stand the heat, cool off at **Balenario El Ambaibo** (US$2) or, in the high season, at **Hotel Tucuara's pool**, on the north side of the plaza.

Tours

Jungle and pampas tours (see the boxed text, p316) are Rurre's bread and butter, but a number of emerging community-based ethno-ecotourism projects also merit mention.

The community-run **Mapajo Lodge** (☎ 892-2317; www.mapajo.com) is one outstanding alternative. It offers all-inclusive overnight visits to the Mosetén-Chimán community of Asuncíon. It's three hours upriver from Rurre inside the Reserva de la Biosfera Pilón-Lajas (p319).

Inquire at the tourist office about day-long **Day for the Community** tours (US$25; www.rurrenabaquebolivia.com), which visit unique Altiplano immigrant communities and highlight alternative sustainable development projects, including a women's *artesanía* co-op, a sustainable agroforestry experiment, a carpentry workshop and a tropical fruit processing plant. Transport to the colonies recently settled by Aymará and Quechua refugees fleeing harsh economic conditions is in open trucks and can be

AMAZON BASIN

JUNGLE & PAMPAS TOURS: WALKS ON THE WILD SIDE

Tourism around Rurrenabaque has taken off to an extent that would have been unimaginable a decade ago. The main draws are the surrounding rainforest and pampas, which support Amazonian wildlife in relatively large numbers. Recent additions to the options include the culturally sustainable **Reserva de la Biosfera Pilón Lajas** and the fabulous **Parque Nacional Madidi**, which is home to a mind-boggling number of plant and wildlife species.

Numerous agencies run both jungle and pampas tours, and while no two agencies offer the same trips, most include hiking, fishing, relaxing and wildlife viewing. You can either form your own group or let the agencies hook you up with their next tour. The trips, which aren't as touristy as they may sound, normally last from three to six days and include canoe transportation, guides, food and plenty of hammock time. The official rates for both tours (which are likely to rise in 2004) are set at US$25 per day in the rainy season and US$30 during the drier period after June 1. Any agency undercutting these official rates should be regarded with a bit of caution – consider where they might cut corners before forking over less.

Note that to get the most out of these tours, at least a minimal knowledge of Spanish is requisite. Even more essential however, is a strong insect repellent; without it, your misery will know no bounds, especially when you're faced with the insidious *marigui* sandfly, which inhabits the riverbanks. Please also advise your guides not to disturb animals – that is, not to capture caimans, anacondas or capybaras for photo opps.

Finally, avoid leaving valuables in storage with tour agencies, as there have been reports of items disappearing.

Jungle Tours

The Bolivian rainforest is full of more interesting and unusual things than you'd ever imagine. Local guides, most of whom have grown up in the area, are knowledgeable about the fauna, flora and forest lore; they can explain animals' habits and habitats and demonstrate the uses of some of the thousands of plant species, including the forest's natural remedies for colds, fever, cuts, insect bites (which come in handy!) and other ailments.

Most trips begin by canoe upstream along the Río Beni as it winds between high, steep hills. Then you ascend the Río Tuichi, camping and taking shore and jungle walks along the way, with plenty of swimming opportunities and hammock time. Accommodation is either in agencies' private camps or on the river sand beneath a tarpaulin tent and a mosquito net.

Rain, mud and badass insects make the wet season (especially January to March) particularly unpleasant for jungle tours, but some agencies have jungle camps set up for good wildlife watching at this time.

Note that only Sernap-authorized operators are allowed to enter Parque Nacional Madidi and that foreigners must be accompanied by a local guide. Authorized agencies are planning to open an information office in San Buenaventura in 2004.

Pampas Tours

It's often easier to see wildlife in the wetland savannas northeast of town, but the sun is more oppressive, and the bugs can be worse, especially in the rainy season. Bring binoculars, a good flashlight, extra batteries and plenty of strong anti-bug juice. Highlights include swimming with pink river dolphins, piranha fishing, horseback riding, feeding bananas to monkeys, hunting for anacondas and nighttime canoe trips to search for caimans.

a bit dusty and rough, but it's reportedly worth the hassle.

The community-based **San Miguel** project is Conservation International's latest foray into ethno-ecotourism, with plans for seven self-contained *cabañas*, community visits and interpretive trails tracing traditional Tacana hunting routes. It's scheduled to be up and running by mid-2004 – inquire at CI's office on the plaza in Rurre.

Jungle and pampas tours are excellent value and most people are very happy with them, but the guide's treatment of the wildlife depends on your group's demands. A lack of drinking water and biting insects are the main complaints. All guides should be licensed – ask to see *la autorización*. Keep in mind that most guides speak Spanish and no agency has a sterling record. It's worth seeking out a local guide who can provide insights on the fauna, flora, indigenous people and forest lore. Most agencies in Rurre have offices on Avaroa.

If the new municipal tourist office's agency ranking system is implemented without bias, it should prove a useful tool for travelers, but nothing substitutes for talking to recent trip returnees.

The following agencies consistently receive the more positive reports:

Águilar & Flecha Tours (☎ 892-2476/2478; Avaroa & Santa Cruz)

Bala Tours (☎ 892-2527; www.mirurrenabaque.com; Santa Cruz at Comercio) Has its own jungle camp and comfortable pampas lodge on Río Yacumo.

Fluvial Tours/Amazonia Adventures (☎ 892-2372; www.megalink.com/rurrenabaque; at Hotel Tuichi) Rurre's longest-running agency.

Inca Land Tours (La Paz ☎ 231-3589; www.incaland tours.com; Arce & Avaroa) Private pampas lodge on Río Yacumo but some complaints as well.

Sleeping
BUDGET

Hostal Turístico Santa Ana (☎ 892-2399; Avaroa btwn Diez & Campero; US$3.35, with bath US$5.35) Rurre's best budget value is this clean, cheery place with a couple of leafy courtyards, a shady *palapa*, and hammocks and tables for enjoying the sun. Laundry facilities are also available.

Residencal El Porteño (☎ 892-2558; Comercio at Diez; US$3.35, with bath US$4.65) This sprawling place is run by a motherly *dueña* and features a prolific *carambola* (starfruit) tree that provides

delicious free juice for guests. As elsewhere, the garden hammocks encourage lazing.

Hotel Asaí (☎ 892-2439; Diez at Busch; s/d with bath US$6.65/10) It's newer than most places and all rooms have good fans, firm beds, private baths and electric showers. The shaded courtyard has several hammocks under a *palapa*.

Hotel Tuichi (☎ /fax 892-2372; Avaroa s/n; US$2-3, with bath US$4-5.50) The backpacker scene is most evident here. Laundry service, cooking facilities and hammocks in a pleasant garden lure travelers. It's a good place to form tour groups with Fluvial Tours, but patrons of other agencies get a less enthusiastic reception.

Hotel Bella Vista (☎ 892-2328; Comercio at Campero; US$2, with bath US$3.35) This recently refurbished, Korean-run place faces the plaza and has riverfront access out back and simple but clean rooms (but no matrimonial beds).

Residencal Jislene (☎ 892-2526/2552; Comercio near Beni; US$2, with bath US$3.35) This basic, reader-recommended, riverfront spot is an Israeli favorite with shared kitchen facilities. It makes up for what it lacks in creature comforts with family-run hospitality. The rooms with private baths are new and all rooms have fans and mosquito nets. Good meals are available on request.

Hostal América (☎ 892-2413; Santa Cruz near Comercio; US$2.65) The only worthwhile rooms at this basic pad are on the top floor, which affords superb views.

MID-RANGE

Hotel Rurrenabaque (☎ 892-2481, La Paz ☎ 279-5917; Diez at Bolívar; s/d US$4.65/9, with bath & breakfast US$8/13.35) Far from the maddening late-night disco crowd, the welcoming Rurre has basic but clean rooms with fan, and hammocks on a breezy balcony.

Hotel Oriental (☎ 892-2401; south side Plaza 2 de Febrero; US$3-4, s/d with bath US$9.25/13.35) An excellent, friendly choice, within earshot of the nightly frog chorus on the plaza. In the stifling afternoon hours, you can read or snooze in the garden hammocks until the heat subsides. Breakfast and drinks available.

Hostal Beni (☎ 892-2408; fax 892-2273; Comercio; s/d US$4/6.65, d with bath & TV US$9.35; ⊠) Centrally located and popular with tour groups. All rooms have fans and TV. Air-conditioned doubles are US$20.

Hotel Safari (☎ /fax 892-2210; Comercio Final; s/d/q with bath & breakfast US$20/30/45; 🖭) Rurre's only true upmarket option is this riverfront spread well beyond the noisy center of town. It's a quiet, Korean-run place with simple but comfortable rooms with fans. Amenities catering to tour groups include a restaurant and karaoke bar.

Eating

Rurre's eating options are numerous and varied, from good market meals and quick chicken to fresh river fish and applaudable attempts at international fare. Freshly brewed Yungas coffee is widely available. For groceries, try the *tiendas* along Comercio or the **Mini Mercado** (Santa Cruz at Busch), where you'll find a selection of canned rations, snacks and alcohol.

Several fish restaurants line the riverfront: basic **La Chocita**, candlelit **La Cabaña** and **Playa Azul** grill or fry up the catch of the day. In addition to the Beni standard, *masaco* (mashed yucca or plantain), try the excellent *pescado hecho en taquara*, fish baked in a special local pan, or *pescado en dunucuabi*, fish wrapped in a rainforest leaf and baked over a wood fire.

Café Motacú (Santa Cruz near Comercio s/n; ☽ 8:30am-noon & 6:30-9:30pm Mon-Sat; mains US$1-3) The perfect place to sit beneath the streetside awning and watch Rurre's comings and goings over breakfast, coffee or snacks – including homemade sweets and veggie burgers. It's especially useful for those awaiting the latest flight news from TAM, next door.

Restaurant Camila (Santa Cruz at Avaroa; mains US$1-4; 🖭) This friendly travelers' hangout serves muesli breakfasts, juices, salads, pasta, burgers, vegetarian lasagna, *burritos* and chicken dishes, plus unbeatable milkshakes.

Restaurant Tacuara (Santa Cruz at Avaroa; mains US$1-3) Open-air eatery with shaded sidewalk seating and an ambitious breakfast through dinner menu. It's friendly and popular, especially for its lasagna.

La Perla de Rurre (Bolívar at Diez; mains US$2-3) Often cited as Rurre's best restaurant, La Perla specializes in fresh fish and chicken dishes, but also prepares red meat well. Service is superlative.

Club Social (Comercio near Santa Cruz; lunch US$1.25, dinner US$2-4) Atmospheric, open-air riverfront setting with full bar with meat, chicken and à la carte international dishes for dinner. It's a pleasant place to enjoy a cocktail.

Pizzería Italia (Comercio near Santa Cruz; pizza US$2-4) Pizza, pasta and other savory Italian choices, as well as wine and vegetarian options. Shares the *palapa* with the Moskkito Bar. The pizza is good and they deliver next door.

Drinking & Entertainment

Rurre doesn't see a lot of action, but there are a couple of bars and discos. The **Jungle Bar Moskkito** (☎ 892-0267; Comercio s/n; moskkito@terra.com; ☽ happy hour 7-9pm; drinks US$2-3) is the undisputed travelers' favorite. Diversions include darts, pool tables and an extensive menu of CDs played by request. It's Peruvian-run, English is spoken and there's a positive vibe, super-lindo service and wide selection of tropical cocktails. It's a good spot to form tour groups.

A pleasant place for a quiet drink after dinner is the **Club Social**, where the river slides by as the beer slides down. It's hard to miss the thumping, locals-only discos and karaoke bars full of off-duty soldiers on weekends – especially if they are near your hotel. Gringos may feel less than welcome, except perhaps at the **Hotel Safari's** black-lighted karaoke bar. The billiards halls along Comercio are mellower, more gringo-friendly options.

Shopping

The cheap clothing stalls near the market are a good place to pick up hammocks (*hamacas*; US$5/10 single/double) and finely woven cotton and synthetic mosquito nets (*mosquiteros*; from US$5). Café Motacú has the best selection of local handicrafts.

Getting There & Away

Apparently not realizing that tourists are the town's bread and butter, Rurre charges foreigners a rather unfriendly 'tourist tax' of US$1 at the airport. That's in addition to the bus terminal tax and the US$0.80 airport tax.

AIR

Rurre's humble airport is a grassy landing strip a few kilometers north of town. The number of flights to Rurre is increasing all the time, but tickets still sell out fast in the high season. Even when the windows are hopelessly scratched, these glorious flights afford superb views of 6000m peaks as they climb over the Cordillera Real, then pass over the Yungas, where the land dramatically drops away and opens onto the forested expanses of the Amazon Basin. Have your tour agency purchase your return ticket in advance. If you're stuck, try using the Reyes airport, an hour northeast by bus or shared taxi.

In theory, **TAM** (☎ 892-2398) flies between La Paz and Rurre (US$50, one hour) daily except Tuesday. In reality, flights are often canceled or diverted to Reyes in the rainy season. Note that TAM tickets are standby; reserving a seat does not guarantee a place on the return flight, so be sure to confirm your return booking at the in-town office as soon as you arrive.

Amaszonas (☎ 892-2472; Santa Cruz near Avaroa) attempts two daily La Paz (US$50) round-trips, but isn't much more reliable. It also flies daily to Trinidad (US$50) and Santa Cruz (US$79).

SAVE runs charter flights from La Paz (US$65) during the high season; book through Inca Land Tours in La Paz (p317).

BOAT
Thanks to the Guayaramerín road, there's little cargo transport down the Río Beni to Riberalta. There's no traffic at all during periods of low water. If you do find something, plan on at least four or five days at around US$7 per day, including meals, for the 1000km trip. Going upstream to Guanay, the journey takes as many as 10 days. Except at times of low water, motorized canoe transportation upriver (US$15, 12 hours) may be occasionally available; ask around at the port or larger tour agencies.

BUS & JEEP
The bus terminal is a good 20-minute walk northeast of the center. Minibuses and shared taxis to Reyes (US$1.35, half an hour) leave when full from the corner of Santa Cruz and Comercio. When the roads are passable, **Totai** and **Yungueña** (☎ 892-2112) run daily buses between Rurrenabaque and La Paz (US$6.50, 18 hours), via Yolosa (US$6, 15 hours), 7km from Coroico. There

are also Thursday and Saturday dry-season runs to Trinidad (US$17/22 normal/*cama*, 17 hours) via Yucumo, San Borja and San Ignacio de Moxos. Dry-season services sometimes reach Riberalta (US$18, 17 to 40 hours) and Guayaramerín (US$22, 18 hours to three days). 13 de Mayo Jeeps to La Paz (US$20 to US$25, 12 hours) leave in the morning whenever there is enough demand (minimum five or six, maximum eight passengers).

Getting Around
Stifling TAM and Amaszonas *micros* (US$0.65, 10 minutes) shuttle between the airport and in-town airline offices; the quicker and breezier moto-taxis (US$0.65) require that you carry all your luggage on your back. Moto-taxis around town cost US$0.35 per ride. Taxi ferries to San Buenaventura (US$0.15) set sail frequently from the riverbank.

SAN BUENAVENTURA
Since residents mostly conduct their business across the river in Rurre, nothing much happens in sleepy San Buena – and that's how they seem to like it. The only access is via the ferry across the Río Beni from Rurre.

If you're looking for fine Beni leather goods, visit the well-known shop of leather artisan Manuel Pinto, but avoid purchasing anything made from wild rainforest species. The on-again, off-again **Centro Cultural Tacana** (☎ 892-2394; west side of plaza; admission US$0.50; 🏵 closed Fri & Sat) has a handicrafts shop and celebrates the Tacana people's unique cosmovision. Sernap's **Parque Nacional Madidi headquarters** (☎ 892-2540) and a new tourist information office staffed by agencies authorized to conduct tours in the park provide visitor information.

The best lodging choice is **Residencial Madidi** (US$1.35), near the Sernap office. The only other reliable option is the basic **Alojamiento Florida** (US$2).

RESERVA DE LA BIOSFERA PILÓN LAJAS
The **Mapajo Ecoturismo Indígena** project, an experiment in community-based tourism, functions in the Reserva de la Biosfera Pilón Lajas. The project takes in six traditional communities of Tacana, Chimane and

Mosetén peoples, upstream from Rurrenabaque. Because lumbering was stopped in 1998, the ecosystem is relatively intact and the wildlife is quickly returning to the region. All-inclusive overnight visits to the community of Asuncíon, three hours upriver from Rurre just below the confluence of the Ríos Beni and Tuichi on the Rió Quiquibey, include bow-and-arrow fishing, rainforest hiking and unchoreographed visits to the community. The cost is around US$50 per person, per day. The individual *cabañas* are comfy, the hosts are simpatico and the food is great and plentiful. Guides speak Spanish. The project's profits finance community health and education projects. To arrange a visit, contact their office in Rurrenabaque (☎ 892-2317; Comercio near Santa Cruz).

PARQUE NACIONAL MADIDI

The Río Madidi watershed is one of South America's most intact ecosystems. Most of it is protected by the 1.8-million-hectare Parque Nacional Madidi, which takes in a range of wildlife habitats, from the steaming lowland rainforests to 5500m Andean peaks. This wild, little-trodden utopia is home to a mind-boggling variety of Amazonian wildlife, including 44% of all New World mammal species, 38% of tropical amphibian species, more than 10% of all bird species known to science and more protected species than any park in the world.

The populated portions of the park along the Río Tuichi have been accorded a special Unesco designation permitting indigenous inhabitants to utilize traditional forest resources, but the park has also been considered for oil exploration and as a site for a major hydroelectric scheme (see *National Geographic*, March 2000). In addition, illicit logging has affected several areas around the park perimeter and there's been talk of a new road between Apolo and Ixiamas that would effectively bisect the park.

The US$5.35 admission fee is payable via tour agencies or at the Sernap office in San Buenaventura. An excellent publication for visitors is *A Field Guide to Chalalán*, sold at the project's office in Rurre.

San José de Uchupiamonas

This lovely traditional village operates **Chalalán**, the Bolivian Amazonia's most successful community-based ecotourism project. The village alone merits a visit, and both jungle walks and boat trips are available with local guides. San José celebrates its patron saint with a weeklong **fiesta** around May 1.

While day-long tours to the village can be arranged at Chalalán itself, there are a couple of more adventurous approaches. First, it's possible to hire a guide in **Apolo** (where you can stay overnight at the monastery) and hike for four days down to the village, following the historic route taken by Colonel Percy Harrison Fawcett. To reach Rurre from here, you'll have to chase up a canoe for the six-hour downstream trip.

Alternatively, take a ferry from Rurre to San Buenaventura, where *vagonetas* depart daily from around 8am for **Ixiamas**. Get off at the village of **Tumupasa** (US$2, 1½ hours), which has an *alojamiento* half a block from the plaza. From here, it's a relatively easy 30km, eight-hour hike along a rough dry-season road to San José de Uchupiamonas; throw in rocks or slap the water with a stick before crossing the numerous river fords to disperse the stingrays.

Sleeping & Eating

At the idyllic oxbow lake, Laguna Chalalán, is the park's only formal visitor accommodation, Chalalán Ecolodge. This simple but comfortable lodge, surrounded by relatively untouched rainforest, provides the opportunity to amble through the jungle and appreciate the incredible richness of life. Although the flora and fauna are lovely, it's sounds more than sights that provide the magic here: the incredible dawn bird chorus, the evening frog symphony, the collective whine of zillions of insects, the roar of bucketing tropical rainstorms and, in the early morning, the thunderlike chorus of every howler monkey within a 100km radius.

Most of the park is effectively inaccessible, which is why it remains such a treasure. For a high-season stay in a simple but comfortable lodge made of natural materials, you'll pay US$280 per person (all-inclusive) for two nights and three days in groups of two to five, or US$225 for groups of six or more. What the rooms lack in privacy (was that a howler monkey or your neighbor snoring?) they make up for in creature comforts. Rates include transfers to and from the airport, one night in Rurre, three good meals per day, a well-trained English-speaking guide from the community for wildlife- and bird-watching hikes, canoe trips on the beautiful black waters of the lake, nighttime excursions in search of spiders, surreptitious snakes and colorful tree frogs, plus local taxes and a community levy. Profits benefit potable water and community health and education projects.

For reservations, visit the **Chalalán office** (☎ 892-2419; www.chalalan.com; Comercio at Campero) in Rurre or contact America Tours in La Paz (p47).

REYES & SANTA ROSA

In the area of Reyes and Santa Rosa, you'll find lovely lagoons with myriad birds, alligators and other local wildlife. Reyes is less than an hour east of Rurre. Santa Rosa, with its attractive **Laguna Rogagua**, is two rough hours further along. Both places are popular pampas tours destinations (p316).

Reyes' best place to stay, **Alojamiento Santa Tereza** (24 de Septiembre at Fernandez; US$2), has a beautiful garden. In Santa Rosa, recommended places include **Hotel Oriental** (US$2-3) and the more basic **Residencial Los Tamarindos** (US$2). For meals, try Bilbosi or Restaurante Triángulo.

If you can't get a **TAM** (☎ 825-2168/2083) flight to Rurre, it's easy enough to land in Reyes instead; collective transport to Rurre (US$1.35, 30 minutes) leaves the airport after flights arrive. *Micros* between Santa Rosa and Rurre (US$4.50, four hours) normally leave in the morning.

YUCUMO

The main thing to know about this frontier El Dorado populated by development-crazed settlers is how to escape as quickly as possible. It's at the intersection of the La Paz–Guayaramerín road and the Trinidad turnoff. The Rurre–Yucumo road passes through a devastated environment of cattle ranches and logged-out forest. If biding your time here, a decent hike leads along the road south of town; after the bridge, turn left and follow the walking track to a scarlet macaw colony.

If stuck here overnight, try **Hotel Tropical** (US$6, with bath US$8) or **Hotel Palmeras** (US$2).

All transport between Rurre and La Paz or Trinidad passes through Yucumo. Once in Yucumo, connect with a *camioneta*, which will take you through the savanna to San Borja (US$1.75, one hour), which has onward connections for Reserva Biosferíca del Beni, San Ignacio de Moxos and Trinidad.

SAN BORJA

Many visitors sense unsettling vibes in this hamlet with a penchant for illicit dealings. However, it's only dangerous to those involved in drug smuggling. There's not much to keep one occupied here. The town's prosperity is revealed in the palatial homes that rise on the block behind the church. A long day's walk along the relatively little-traveled road west of town will take you through a wetlands area frequented by numerous species of tropical birds. At night, life literally revolves around the plaza, where everything with wheels zips around in typical lowland fashion.

Sleeping & Eating

At the top of the sleep heap is the clean and friendly **Hotel San Borja** (US$3.35, with bath US$5), facing the plaza, where the only drawback is the 6am gospel wakeup call courtesy of the nearby Catholic church. Other good choices are **Hotel Manara** (US$6) and **Hostal Jatata** (US$9). Meals are available at both and the latter has a beautiful patio enhanced by hammocks.

Lomo and *pollo* are king at the simple eateries near the plaza on the way to the airport.

Getting There & Away

In the dry season buses pull out several times daily from the bus terminal (3km south of the plaza; US$0.40 moto-taxi) for the Reserva Biosférica del Beni (US$1.50. 1½ hours), San Ignacio de Moxos (US$3, five hours), Trinidad (US$6.75, eight to 12 hours) and Santa Cruz (US$15, 20 to 24 hours). There are daily services to Rurrenabaque (US$5, five to eight hours) and masochists can travel several times weekly to La Paz (US$20, 23 to 27 hours). The best spot to wait for infrequent *camiones* is at the gas station at the south end of town.

If you're Trinidad-bound, note that the Mamoré balsa crossings close at 6pm, and you need five to six hours to reach them from San Borja. There are no accommodations on either side of the crossing. Between San Borja and San Ignacio de Moxos, watch for birds and wildlife. You may also spot capybaras and pink river dolphins at small river crossings.

Amazonas (☎ 895-3185; Bolívar 157) has daily round-trip flights between La Paz, San Borja and Trinidad. **TAM** (☎ 895-3609) sometimes makes a surprise landing, but doesn't have any regularly scheduled flights.

RESERVA BIOSFÉRICA DEL BENI

Created by Conservation International in 1982 as a loosely protected natural area, the 334,200-hectare Beni Biosphere Reserve was recognized by Unesco in 1986 as a 'Man & the Biosphere Reserve'. The following year it received official recognition through a pioneering debt swap agreement with the Bolivian government.

The abutting **Reserva Forestal Chimane**, a 1.15-million-hectare buffer zone and indigenous reserve, has also been set aside for sustainable subsistence use by the 1200 Chimane people living there. The combined areas are home to at least 500 tropical bird species as well as more than 100 mammal species, including monkeys, jaguars, deer, two species of peccary, river otters, foxes, anteaters and bats.

In 1990 the Chimane reserve was threatened when the government opened it up to logging interests. In response, 700 Chimanes and representatives of other tribes staged a march from Trinidad to La Paz to protest what would amount to the wholesale destruction of their land. Logging concessions were rezoned but not altogether revoked and colonization pressures continue to escalate.

Owing to increasing human pressures, the degraded western 20% of the reserve has been lopped off and sacrificed to settlement and exploitation in hopes that the remaining pristine areas can be more vigilantly protected.

Information

The reserve is administered by the **Bolivian Academy of Sciences** (La Paz ☎ 235-2071). Admission to the **reserve** (☎ 895-3385) is US$5 per person. Horse rentals are available for US$7 per eight-hour day. Information is available by shortwave radio on 5850-USB

at 9:30am and noon and on 8550-USB at 3:30 and 6pm.

When to Visit

The best months to visit the reserve are June and July, when there's little rain and the days are clear; bring warm clothing to protect against the occasional *surazo*. During the rainy season, days are hot, rainy, muggy and miserable with mosquitoes, so bring plenty of repellent. In August and September the atmosphere becomes somber thanks to El Chaqueo smoke (see the boxed text, p34).

The reserve headquarters, **El Porvenir**, is in the savannas quite a distance from the true rainforest, so walks around the station will be of limited interest. The best way to observe its wildlife is to hire a guide for a hike through the savannas and the primary- and secondary-growth rainforests.

From El Porvenir, several tours are offered: a four-hour canoe trip to see the black caimans in **Laguna Normandia** (US$8 per person) at 4pm daily; a four-hour savanna hike to several monkey-infested rainforest islands (US$11); and a full-day **Las Torres tour** (US$20, including food) on horseback to three wildlife-viewing towers where you can observe both savanna and rainforest ecosystems and fish piranha for dinner. When flocks of white-eyed parrots pass through the reserve, you can take the **Loro tour** (US$10) on foot or horseback to see the colorful spectacle – or you can check them out in the palms at El Porvenir, where they provide a raucous 6am wakeup call.

Perhaps the most interesting option is the four-day **Tur Monitoreo** (US$80/90 without/with food), during which visitors accompany park rangers on their wildlife-monitoring rounds into the reserve's farthest reaches to search for monkeys, macaws and pink river dolphins.

Laguna Normandia

This savanna lake, an hours' walk from El Porvenir, is the reserve's most popular destination. It's crawling with rare black caimans – 400 at last count – which are descendants of specimens originally destined to become shoes and handbags. When the caiman breeder's leather business failed, the animals were left to fend for themselves, and the vast majority perished from neglect, crowding and hunger. The survivors were confiscated by Bolivian authorities and airlifted to safety. Fortunately, the caimans have little interest in humans, so it's generally safe to observe them at close range while rowboating around with a guide. If you're feeling skiddish, there's an 11m **viewing tower**.

Rainforest Tours
Beyond Laguna Normandia, you'll need to take a tour. From the lake, it's a four-hour walk to the margin of the secondary-growth rainforest. A further four hours' walk through secondary forest takes you to the primary forest. Along the way, a 6m viewing tower provides a vista over an island of rainforest, and a 4m tower along the Río Curiraba provides views over the forest and savanna in the remotest parts of the reserve.

Totaizal & Reserva Forestal Chimane
A stone's throw from the road, 40 minutes' walk from El Porvenir, is **Totaizal**. This friendly and well-organized village of 140 people lies hidden in the forest of the Chimane reserve. The Chimane, traditionally a nomadic forest tribe, are currently being driven from their ancestral lands by lumber companies and highland settlers. Skilled hunters, they also catch fish with natural poisons and are particularly adept at avoiding the stickier drawbacks of wild honey collection. People living in the settlement of **Cero Ocho**, a four-hour walk from Totaizal, trudge into the village to sell bananas, while others provide guiding services for visitors.

Sleeping & Eating
Accommodation at **El Porvenir** is in airy bunk-bed rooms (including three simple meals cooked up by the affable Doña Rosa) that cost US$12 per person. Amenities include a library, a researchers' workshop, an interpretive center and a small cultural and biological museum. There's plenty of potable water but you'll want to bring snacks and refreshments as there's nothing available for miles around. Unless this book becomes a best-seller, it's quite likely you'll have this peaceful place all to yourself.

Getting There & Away
Don't blink or you'll miss El Porvenir, which is 200m off the highway, 90 minutes east of San Borja, and is accessible via any *movilidad* between Trinidad and San Borja or Rurrenabaque. On the way out, Trinidad-bound buses pass by between 9:30am and 10:30am. Buses heading for San Borja pass by anytime between 4pm and 7pm. Otherwise, there's surprisingly little traffic. You might be able to arrange a lift with reserve personnel at the office in San Borja, but don't bet the *estancia* on it.

SAN IGNACIO DE MOXOS
This Moxos Indian village, 89km west of Trinidad, was founded as San Ignacio de Loyola by the Jesuits in 1689. In 1760 the village suffered pestilence and had to be shifted to its present location on higher and healthier ground. Although the Jesuits were expelled from South America in 1767, Jesuit priests are now returning not only to work among the Moxos but also to strike an understanding among the Moxos, the dispossessed Chimane people and the newly arriving settlers and loggers.

Despite all the outside factions in the Beni, San Ignacio de Moxos remains a friendly and tranquil agricultural village with an ambience quite distinct from any other in Bolivia. The people speak an indigenous dialect known locally as Ignaciano, and their lifestyles, traditions and foods are unique in the country.

Sights & Activities
In the **main plaza** is a **monument** to Chirípieru, El Machetero Ignaciano, with his crown of feathers and formidable-looking hatchet. The relatively recent **church** on the plaza is filled with local art and Ignaciano religious murals.

At the **museum** in the **Casa Belén**, near the northwest corner of the plaza, you'll see elements of both the Ignaciano and Moxos cultures, including the *bajones*, or immense flutes introduced by the Jesuits.

North of town at the large **Laguna Isirere**, you can go fishing and swimming, or just observe the profuse bird life. It's accessible on a 30-minute walk or by hitching from town.

The greater area also boasts a number of obscure – and hard-to-reach – sights of interest: the **Lomas de Museruna**, several

AMAZON BASIN

archaeological ruins, and the ruins of the missions San José and San Luis Gonzaga.

Festivals & Events
Annually, July 31 is the first day of the huge **Fiesta del Santo Patrono de Moxos**, in honor of the sacred protector of the Moxos. As in most Bolivian parties, the celebration includes games, music, dancing and drinking. The festivities culminate at 2pm on the final day of the fiesta, when wildly clad dancers led by El Machetero himself proceed from the church, accompanied by fiddles and woodwind instruments.

Sleeping & Eating
Prices double during the fiesta. The outstanding **Residencial Don Joaquín** (US$2.50, with bath US$4.50), at the corner of the plaza near the church, has a nice patio. Also on the plaza, the cheery **Plaza Hotel** (US$2, with bath US$4.50) has spacious doubles with fans. A block off the plaza, the friendly **Residencial 31 de Julio** (US$2) maintains clean and basic accommodations. On the plaza to the right of the church, **Residencial 22 de Abril** (US$2) occasionally has hot water and is known for its good breakfasts. Another similarly priced place is Residencial Tamarindo, on the main street. During the fiesta, visitors can camp at established sites just outside town.

The recommended eating establishment here is the wonderfully friendly Restaurant Don Chanta, on the plaza; don't miss the Ignaciano specialties: *chicha de camote* (sweet potato chicha) and the interesting *sopa de joco* (beet and pumpkin soup). Another good choice is Restaurant Cherlis, a block east of the southeast corner of the plaza.

Getting There & Away
From Trinidad, *micros* and *camionetas* (US$2, three hours) leave for San Ignacio when full from the terminals on Calle La Paz, and *camiones* leave in the morning from the east end of La Paz, near the river. There's good forest scenery all along the way, but prepare for delays at the Río Mamoré balsa crossing between Puerto Barador and Puerto Ganadero. From March to October, it's two to three hours from Trinidad to San Ignacio, including the balsa crossing, but this route is impassable during the summer rainy season.

Note that the balsa shuts down at 6pm (it may stay open later at times of heavy traffic) and there are no accommodations on either side, so check the timing before setting out.

EASTERN BOLIVIAN AMAZON

The migration of the Suárez family from Santa Cruz to Trinidad in the late 19th century marked the beginning of serious economic exploitation of this region. While the senior Suárez was occupied with cattle ranching, young Nicolás Suárez set off to explore the inhospitable wilderness of Bolivia's northern hinterlands. He developed a substantial business dealing in quinine, derived from the bark of the *cinchona* tree.

When the rubber boom descended upon Amazonian Brazil, it was a simple matter for Suárez to arrange a system for transporting rubber around the Mamoré rapids into Brazil, and then down the Río Madeira to the Amazon and the Atlantic. Before the turn of the century, the Suárez family owned six million hectares of lowland real estate. However, a good proportion of these holdings lay in the remote Acre territory, which Bolivia lost to Brazil in 1903. Although a large percentage of the Suárez fortune was lost and Bolivia's rubber boom ground to a halt, the family was by no means devastated (see History in the Chapare Region, p310, for the rest of the story).

Trinidad is the Bolivian Amazon's population center but is still very much a frontier settlement. It's also an access point for dozens of smaller communities, wild rivers and remote jungle reserves. The region's treasure, however, is the spectacular Parque Nacional Noel Kempff Mercado, which sees an average of 600 visitors a year and has only recently become known to adventurers, bird watchers and wildlife enthusiasts.

TRINIDAD
pop 80,000 / elevation 235m
The Beni's tropical capital and nerve center of the Bolivian Amazon looks somewhat like Santa Cruz did 30 years ago. Although not Bolivia's most prepossessing city – the open

sewers are a nauseating health hazard – 'Trini' is still growing rapidly. Only 14 degrees south of the equator, Trinidad has a humid tropical climate. Its main attraction is as a stopover between Santa Cruz and Rurrenabaque or as a place to organize a Mamoré river trip.

History
The city of La Santísima Trinidad (the Most Holy Trinity) was founded in 1686 by Padre Cipriano Barace as the second Jesuit mission in the flatlands of the southern Beni. It was originally constructed on the banks of the Río Mamoré 14km from its present location, but floods and pestilence along the riverbanks necessitated relocation. In 1769 it was moved to the Arroyo de San Juan, which now divides the city in two.

Information
Trinidad's helpful municipal **tourist office** (☎ 462-1722; Santa Cruz at La Paz) is inside the Prefectura. Several Enlace ATMs near the main plaza accept international cards. Moneychangers gather on Av 6 de Agosto between Suárez and Av 18 de Noviembre. You can change travelers checks at Banco Mercantil.

For telephone calls, see **Entel** (Cipriano Barace 23-A). Fast Internet access is available on the west side of the plaza at **Siscotri**, **Kayak-Red Internet Café** (Bolívar at Cochabamba) and at several other places, all charging US$0.35 to US$0.65 per hour. **Lavandería Pro-Vida** (☎ 462-0626; Sattori at Suárez) charges US$0.80 per dozen stinky items. The provincial **immigration** office (upstairs on Busch) may grant length-of-stay extensions.

Dangers & Annoyances
Although mud is the biggest problem for pedestrians, the open sewers will make anyone retch – except perhaps the 3m boa constrictors sometimes seen swimming in them! Take special care at night. Note also – especially if you're staying near the plaza – that a sort of town reveille sounds at about 6:15am.

Sights & Activities
For a nostalgically retro visit to American Graffiti with a tropical twist, spend an evening snacking on popcorn and ice cream on the main plaza, where you can watch hundreds of motorbikes orbiting with more urgency than would seem necessary in the tropics – and with up to four people perched on each bike. Until just a few years ago, it was all refereed by a police officer who sat in a big wooden chair and conjured up red, yellow and green traffic lights by touching an electric wire against one of three nails. Alas, technology has prevailed and this stalwart public servant has now been replaced by automatic traffic lights. As another sign that Trinidad is going the same way as Santa Cruz, the lethargic sloths that used to hangout in the plaza's trees have vanished without a trace. Locals don't seem to know what became of them, but rumor is that they were relocated after a couple of gnarly traffic accidents.

Festivals & Events
The mid-June town **founding fiesta** features a big loud drunken *choupe* at the Plaza de la Tradición, climbing of greased poles for prizes and a *hocheadas de toros* (teasing of bulls).

Tours
Several agencies run tours into the city's hinterlands. **Turismo Moxos** (☎ 462-1141; turmoxos@sauce.ben.entelnet.bo; 6 de Agosto 114) organizes three-day cruises on the Río Ibare, visits to Sirionó villages, four-day canoe safaris into the jungle and one-day horseback trips into remote areas. **Paraíso Travel** (☎ /fax 462-0692; paraiso@sauce.ben.entelnet.bo; 6 de Agosto 138) does four-day bird-watching safaris, jungle camping trips, day cruises on the Rio Mamoré and excursions to Laguna Suárez.

Fremen Tours (☎ /fax 462-1834; www.andes-amazonia.com; Barace 332) specializes in all-inclusive river cruises on their posh hotel-boat *Flotel Reina de Enin*; cabins include private baths and there's an excellent dining room and bar. They also own the houseboat *Ebrio*, with four berths and hammock space, which does the run down into Parque Nacional Isiboro-Sécure (p313).

Sleeping
BUDGET
Hostal Palmas (☎ 462-6979; La Paz 365; s/d US$3.25/5.35, with bath US$10/15.50; 🖳) Nice rooms with TV and air-con upgrades available.

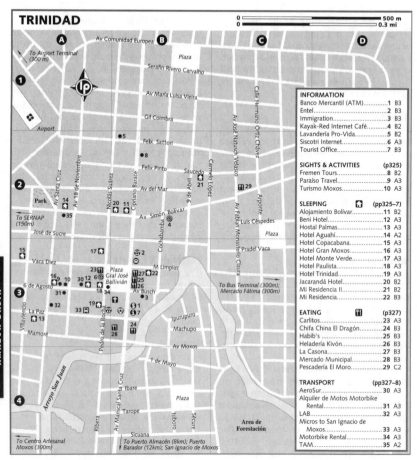

TRINIDAD

Hotel Monte Verde (☎ 462-2750, fax 462-2044; 6 de Agosto 76; s/d with bath US$10/13.50; 🖳) Central; rooms with cable TV and phones.

Hotel Copacabana (☎ 462-2811; Villavicencio 627; US$4, with bath US$9) A friendly, good value place with basic rooms with fans.

Beni Hotel (☎ 462-2788; benihotel@latinmail.com; 6 de Agosto 68; s/d with bath US$9/13.50) Has decent rooms with fans but avoid the ground floor, where the high water table often causes plumbing odors.

Other passable options include:

Alojamiento Bolívar (☎ 462-1726; Bolívar 235; US$2.65), which lacks singles, and the welcoming but tattered **Hotel Paulista** (☎ 462-0018; 6 de Agosto & Suárez; US$2.65, s/d with bath US$8/13.50).

MID-RANGE

Jacarandá Hotel (☎ 462-1659; Bolívar 229; s/d with bath, breakfast & cable TV US$35/50; 🖳 🖳) A solid modern, three-star choice with good firm beds plus air-con, phones and *frigobar*; children under 12 stay free of charge.

Hotel Trinidad (☎ /fax 462-1380; Pedro de la Rocha 80; s/d with bath, breakfast & cable TV US$35/45; 🖳) The pleasant carpeted rooms here aren't cheap but they come with more than just the basics.

Mi Residencia (☎ 462-1529; fax 4622464; Limpias 76; s/d/tr with bath & breakfast US$30/40/60) A very friendly, excellent-value mid-range choice in the center. Its out-of-the-way annex, **Mi Residencia II** (☎ 462-1543; fax 462-2464; Saucedo 555; s/d US$45/60) has larger rooms with similar amenities and is on a quiet street within walking distance of the plaza.

TOP END

Hotel Aguahí (☎ 462-5569; aguahi@sauce.ben .entelnet.bo; Bolívar at Santa Cruz; s/d with bath & breakfast US$50/60; ❄ ▢ ☎) This comfortable and convenient hotel is in a quiet barrio just a few blocks from the center. Amenities include air-conditioning, TVs and a nice swimming pool.

Hotel Gran Moxos (☎ 462-2462; moxostdd@sauce .ben.entelnet.bo; 6 de Agosto 146; s/d with bath, breakfast & cable TV US$50/65; ❄ ☎) The conference center and convenient location make this four-star place the business travelers' choice. Rates include use of the gym, pool and sauna (which is fairly redundant in this climate). Credit cards accepted.

Eating

Since Trinidad is the heart of cattle country, it's the place to indulge in beef, and all of the major hotel dining rooms feature it on the menu. A popular and inexpensive place to enjoy *parrillada* is **Carlitos** (northwest side of plaza) inside the Social Club, which sizzles up some of the best steaks you'll ever taste.

Light meals, full breakfasts, ice cream, cakes, sweets, pastries, sandwiches, coffee and juice are served at **Heladería Kivón** (on the plaza), a family hangout. It's open when everything else is closed, including mornings and Saturday afternoons. Sit upstairs for good views of the cruising scene. Next door there's Habib's, an unassuming little kebab stall. **La Casona** (east side of plaza) is a welcoming place with sidewalk tables, good pizza and inexpensive *almuerzos*.

A friendly choice is the long-standing **Chifa China El Dragón** (opposite the Mercado Municipal), which does Beijing/Bolivian fare. Feeling fishy? Drop anchor at **Pescadería El Moro** (Bolívar at Velasco), which is just a short hike from the center. After dark, you may want to catch a taxi. For something less formal, head out to Puerto Barador (p328) on weekends, where *palapa* restaurants serve up the catch of the day.

If budget is a major concern, head for the Mercado Municipal. For a pittance, you can pick up tropical fruits or sample the local specialty, *arroz con queso* (rice with cheese), as well as *pacumutu* (shish kebabs), yucca, plantains and salad. The main plaza is home to plenty of popcorn, ice cream and *refresco* vendors.

Entertainment & Shopping

Apart from the bars in the main hotels and restaurants, your entertainment options are limited to motorbike cruising, the lovely frog choruses that resonate through the evening and the several discos along Av Santa Cruz. Keep an eye out for a new watering hole called the Drunken Boat, which is slated to open somewhere near the plaza in a retired riverboat.

Local Beni crafts, including weavings, woodwork and ceramics, are sold at the **Centro Artesanal Moxos** (☎ 462-2751; Bopi s/n).

Getting There & Away

AIR

The airport is a feasible half-hour walk northwest of the center. In addition to the US$1.35 Aasana tax, departing air travelers must pay US$0.40 to support senior citizens and finance public works. Note that the inter-Beni flights are frequently suspended for long periods.

Subject to seasonal fluctuations, **LAB** (☎ 462-1277; La Paz 322) and **AeroSur** (☎ 462-3402/5443; 6 de Agosto s/n) both fly several times a week to Cochabamba, La Paz, Santa Cruz, Riberalta and Guayaramerín. **Amazonas** (☎ 462-2426/7575; 18 de Noviembre 267) shuttles daily between La Paz, San Borja, Riberalta and Guayaramerín.

TAM (☎ 462-2363; Bolívar at Santa Cruz) has a couple of flights a week to Cobija (US$65), Cochabamba (US$38), Guayaramerín (US$57), La Paz (US$55) and Riberalta (US$57).

BOAT

Trinidad isn't actually on the bank of a navigable river; Puerto Almacén is on the Ibare, 8km southwest of town, and Puerto Barador is on the Río Mamoré, 13km in the same direction. Trucks charge around US$1 to Puerto Almacén and US$2 to Puerto Barador.

If you're looking for river transportation north along the Mamoré to Guayaramerín, or south along the Mamoré and Ichilo to Puerto Villarroel, inquire at the **Distrito Naval** (☎ 462-3000). If nothing turns up, head for Puerto Barador and check departure schedules with the Capitanía del Puerto or inquire around the riverboats themselves.

DOWN THE LAZY RIVER

River trips from Trinidad will carry you to the heart of Bolivia's greatest wilderness area, where you'll experience the mystique and solitude for which the Amazonian rainforests are renowned. For optimum enjoyment, go during the dry season, which lasts roughly from May or June to October.

Although the scenery along the northern rivers changes little, the diversity of plant and animal species along the shore picks up any slack in the pace of the journey. The longer your trip, the deeper you'll gaze into the forest darkness and the more closely you'll scan the riverbanks for signs of movement. Free of the pressures and demands of active travel, you'll have time to relax and savor the passing scene.

In general, the riverboat food is pretty good, but meals consist mainly of *masaco*, *charque*, rice, noodles, thin soup and bananas in every conceivable form. After a couple of days you'll probably start dreaming of pizza, so bring along some treats to supplement the daily fare. It's also wise to carry your own water or some form of water purification.

Be sure to discuss sleeping arrangements with the captain before setting out. Passengers must usually bring their own hammocks (available in Trinidad), but you may be allowed to sleep on deck or on the roof of the boat. You'll also need a sleeping bag or a blanket, especially in the winter, when jungle nights can be surprisingly chilly. If you're fortunate enough to be on a boat that travels through the night, a mosquito net isn't necessary, but on one that ties up at night passengers without a mosquito net will find the experience ranges from utterly miserable to unbearable.

The Guayaramerín run takes up to a week (larger boats do it in three to four days) and should cost no more than US$25, including food. To Puerto Villarroel, smaller boats take four to six days and cost US$13.50 to US$20, normally including meals.

BUS & CAMIÓN

The rambling bus terminal is a 10-minute walk east of the center. Road conditions permitting, several *flotas* depart nightly between 6pm and 9pm for Santa Cruz (normal/*cama* US$2.50/5.50, eight to 10 hours). Several companies serve Rurrenabaque (US$7, 12 hours) daily via San Borja. Flota Copacabana beelines direct to La Paz (US$24 bus *cama*, 30 hours) daily at 5:30am. There are also daily dry-season departures to Riberalta, Guayaramerín and Cobija. *Micros* and *camionetas* run to San Ignacio de Moxos (US$2.50, three hours) when full from opposite the Municipality. Some continue to San Borja (US$6, eight hours).

Getting Around
TO/FROM THE AIRPORT
Taxis to and from the airport charge around US$1 per person (beware of overcharging), but if you don't have much luggage, moto-taxis charge US$0.65 – you'll be surprised

how much luggage they can accommodate with a bit of creativity.

MOTORCYCLE

Moto-taxi drivers are normally happy to take the day off and rent out their vehicles, but you'll need a regular driving license from home. Plan on US$1.35 per hour or around US$10 for a 24-hour day. Idle moto-taxi drivers hang out around the southwest corner of the plaza. Alternatively, you can rent motorbikes at Alquiler de Motos for US$1.35 per hour, US$8 from 8am to 6pm, or US$12 for 24 hours.

TAXI

Moto-taxis around town cost US$0.25 (B$2), while car taxis charge US$0.40 (B$3). A taxi to the bus terminal costs US$0.80. For rides to outlying areas, phone **Radio Taxi Progreso Beniano** (☎ 462-2759). It's important to know the distances involved and to bargain well for a good rate, which should be no more than US$4 per hour for up to four people. Be sure to include any waiting time you'll need to visit the sights.

AROUND TRINIDAD
Puertos Almacén & Barador
Puerto Almacén is best known for its lineup of rickety fish restaurants, which provide

excellent lunch options. Otherwise, this pointless little place is the proud home of a massive concrete bridge, and vehicles no longer have to be shunted across on *balsas*.

You may prefer to continue 5km further to Puerto Barador, where you can observe pink river dolphins in small Mamoré tributaries or sample fresh fish at one of several pleasant portside restaurants. One of the best is **El Pantano**, which serves excellent *surubí* for US$2. It's very popular with locals, especially on Sunday.

Taxis from Trinidad to either port cost about US$8 each way and moto-taxis charge US$3 round-trip. *Camiones* and *camionetas* leave frequently from Av Santa Cruz, one and a half blocks south of Pompeya bridge in Trinidad. All transportation to San Ignacio de Moxos also passes both Puerto Almacén (US$0.75) and Puerto Barador (US$1). For information on boat travel from Puerto Barador, see Getting There & Away in Trinidad, p328.

Santuario Chuchini

In the Llanos de Moxos, between San Ignacio de Moxos and Loreto, the heavily forested landscape is crossed with more than 100km of canals and causeways and dotted with hundreds of *lomas* (artificial mounds), embankments and more fanciful prehistoric earthworks depicting people and animals. One anthropomorphic figure measures over 2km from head to toe – a rainforest variation on Peru's famed Nazca Lines. The original purpose of the earthworks was probably to permit cultivation in a seasonally flooded area, but inside the mounds were buried figurines, pottery, ceramic stamps, human remains and even tools made from stone imported into the region.

According to archaeologists, the prehistoric structures of the Beni were constructed by the Paititi tribe 5500 years ago and provide evidence of much larger pre-Columbian populations than were previously suspected. It's likely that this ancient Beni civilization was the source of popular Spanish legends of the rainforest El Dorado known as Gran Paititi.

The Santuario Chuchini (Jaguar's Lair), 14km northwest of Trinidad, is one of the few easily accessible Paititi sites. This wildlife sanctuary sits on an eight-hectare artificial *loma*, which is only one of many dotted throughout the surrounding forest. From the camp, you can take short walks in the rainforest to lagoons with profuse bird life, caimans and other larger animals.

The camp has shady, covered picnic sites, trees, children's swings and a variety of native plants, birds and animals. There's also an archaeological museum displaying articles excavated from the *loma*, including bizarre statues with distinctly Mongol queues and slanted eyes as well as a piece that appears to be a female figure wearing a bikini (it's actually thought to be an identification of and homage to specific body areas rather than an article of clothing).

Chuchini may be a lovely place, but it's overpriced for what's offered. For a day visit, including admission, a three-hour cruise and a meal, the price is US$50, and to stay overnight it's US$100. Package tours booked in Trinidad may work out a bit cheaper. Further information is available from **Lorena** or **Efrém Hinojoso** (☎ 462-1968/1811) or travel agencies in Trinidad.

Hitching is best on Sunday, though you may have to walk the last 5km from Loma Suárez. It's also a good destination for those who've rented motorbikes. Boat transport may be possible in the wet season.

SLEEPING & EATING

Bungalows, with meals included, cost US$55 per person. If you're not staying, exotic dishes are available in the restaurant; the food is great but again, it's pricey. If you just want a snack, try the tasty *chipilos* (fried green plantain chips).

Magdalena

In the heart of vast, low-lying forest and pampa beside the Río Itonamas, 220km northeast of Trinidad, is this little settlement. It was founded by the Jesuits in 1720 and was the northernmost of the Bolivian missions. Today, the atmosphere surpasses *tranquilo*, and most of the local vehicles are horse- or ox-drawn carts. The area is rich in birds and other wildlife and has yet to be discovered by tourism. Magdalena's biggest festival, **Santa María de Magdalena**, takes place on July 22.

AMAZON BASIN

About 7km upstream is the inviting **Laguna Baíqui**, which is excellent for swimming, picnics and fishing, and is accessible by boat from town (US$1 per person, 30 minutes). Another pleasant excursion will take you to **Bella Vista**, which is considered one of the Beni's most charming villages – and one of its finest fishing venues – at the junction of the Ríos San Martín and Blanco. In the dry season, minibuses do the two-hour trip, passing en route through the rustic village of **Orobayaya**.

SLEEPING & EATING

The best accommodations are at the lovely Swiss-run **Hotel Internacional** (☎ 886-2210; www.hwz-inc.com; s/d/ste with bath & breakfast US$33/45/50; 🏊), which has become an Amazonian standard, with a fine restaurant/bar and two pools to help you cope with the tropical heat. The friendly management is happy to help guests in organizing excursions through the sur-rounding region.

Budget choices include **Hotel Ganadero** (US$6, with bath US$8), near the plaza and **Hotel San Carlos** (US$6.50, with bath US$10).

GETTING THERE & AWAY

TAM lands here once a week, usually on Wednesday, and the Oasis del Aire air taxi service (US$35 to US$40 one way) shuttles daily between Trinidad and Magdalena. The poor dry-season-only road from Trinidad is served by hardy *camiones* and an occasional bus, but realistically it should only be tackled in a 4WD.

RESERVA DE VIDA SILVESTRE RÍOS BLANCO Y NEGRO

This 1.4-million-hectare reserve, created in 1990, occupies the heart of Bolivia's largest wilderness area and contains vast tracts of undisturbed rainforest with myriad species of plants and animals. These include giant anteaters, peccaries, tapirs, jaguars, bush dogs, marmosets, river otters, capuchin monkeys, caimans, squirrel monkeys, deer and capybaras. The diverse bird life includes curassows, six varieties of macaw and over 300 other bird species.

The area's only settlement, the privately owned *estancia* of **Perseverancia**, is 350km north of Santa Cruz. It started as a rubber production center in the 1920s and continued until the last *seringueros* (rubber tappers) left in 1972. When the airstrip was completed, professional hunters went after river otters and large cats. By 1986 the *estancia* had again been abandoned, and it remained so until tourism – albeit scanty – began to be promoted in 1989.

In the mid-1990s Moira logging concerns began encroaching on the eastern portion of the reserve and USAID recommended that loggers clear a section of the forest rather than cut selective trees. They apparently considered it preferable to endure a total loss over a small area than partial loss of a large area.

Tours

The best way to visit Ríos Blanco y Negro is with Santa Cruz-based **Last Frontiers** (☎ 357-3429; lastfrontiers@yahoo.co.uk). Adventurous, year-round camping tours along wild rivers start at US$30 per person per day, including boat transport, a guide and meals. Rosario Tours (p275) also offers occasional excursions to the park.

Getting There & Away

The privately owned *estancia* of Perseverancia is most easily accessible by a 1½-hour charter flight from El Trompillo airport in Santa Cruz. There's a 100km 4WD track between Asunción de Guarayos and Perseverancia that's passable year-round – with considerable perseverance.

PARQUE NACIONAL NOEL KEMPFF MERCADO

The remote Noel Kempff Mercado National Park is an Amazonian highlight. It lies in the northernmost reaches of Santa Cruz department, between the Serranía de Huanchaca (aka Meseta de Caparú) and the banks of the Ríos Verde and Guaporé (Río Iténez on Bolivian maps). Not only is it one of South America's most spectacular parks, but it also takes in a range of dwindling habitats, lending it world-class ecological significance. The park encompasses 1.5 million hectares of the most dramatic scenery in northern Bolivia including rivers, rainforests, waterfalls, plateaus and rugged 500m escarpments. As well, the park is home to a broad spectrum of Amazonian flora and fauna (see the boxed text, p334).

History

Originally known as Parque Nacional Huanchaca, the fabulous park was created in 1979 to protect the wildlife of the Serranía de Huanchaca. Many of the people living around the fringes of the park are descended from rubber tappers who arrived during the 1940s. When synthetic rubber was developed, their jobs disappeared and they turned to hunting, agriculture, logging and the illegal pet trade.

Tragically, on September 5, 1986, distinguished Bolivian biologist Noel Kempff Mercado, who had originally lobbied for the creation of the park, was murdered by renegades at a remote park airstrip east of the Río Paucerna, along with pilot Juan Cochamanidis and guide Franklin Parada. In 1988 the park's name was officially changed to Noel Kempff Mercado in honor of its de facto founder. In 1995 two Brazilians and a Colombian were convicted of the murders. In 2000 the park was inscribed by Unesco as a World Heritage site.

When to Go

There's no wrong season to visit the park. The wet season is great for river travel, especially if you want to boat up to the two big waterfalls. The wettest months are from December to March. The dry season is obviously better for vehicles, but in the late winter months smoke from forest burning can obliterate the scenery, especially from mid-August to October. March to June is pleasant and not overly hot or rainy, and from October to December the spring blooms add another fabulous dimension.

Information

The park is co-administered by **Sernap** (p34) and **Fundación Amigos de la Naturaleza** (p273). Every prospective visitor to the park must first visit a park information office in either Santa Cruz, Concepción or on San Ignacio de Velasco's main plaza, in order to ensure that park personnel will be available to accompany them on their visit. Visit www.noelkempff.com for an excellent overview of what makes the park so special and for details about the park's ongoing, award-winning Climate Action carbon sequestration program.

The park administration and the **Noel Kempff Mercado Natural History Museum** (p273)

in Santa Cruz organize low-budget transportation and facilities for visitors interested in backpacking, wilderness canoeing and mountain biking, in hopes of demonstrating to local people that conservation pays. Local Spanish-speaking Chiquitano guides are mandatory and charge US$10 to US$15 per day for groups of up to four. They are very familiar with the area's natural history and they'll help carry gear, set up camp and keep visitors out of danger.

Dangers & Annoyances

A major concern will be *bichos* (insects). During rainy periods, the mosquitoes are fierce and voracious and tiny *garapatilla* ticks can be especially annoying. In the wet season, be especially wary of blood-sucking sandflies, which carry leishmaniasis. These flies are a real pest at some campsites, particularly in the high forest around the Huanchaca I laboratory ruins.

Between September and December there's a phenomenal bee hatch-out, when the bees seek out human campsites for salt. At such times it's not unusual to have as many as 10,000 bees hanging around a single site so, if you're allergic, avoid the park during these months. The best way to avoid attracting such numbers is to change campsites daily.

Leafcutter ants can also be problematic and, although their six-inch-wide forest highways, choked with trains of leaf-bearing workers, can be fascinating to watch, they also seem to thrive on the rip-stop nylon used in tents. In fact, they can destroy a tent in less than an hour – even while you're sleeping in it. Don't set up camp anywhere near an ant trail. If that isn't enough, termites have a taste for backpacks that have been left lying on the ground.

Fire is also a concern. The main natural fire season in the park is from July to November and, since the savanna doesn't burn every year, the amount of dead vegetation is substantial. Never cook or even camp in grassland habitat, no matter how flat and inviting, and never leave a cooking fire unattended, even in the forest.

The park's surface water, which can be scarce between August and November, is delicious and safe to drink, but it's still wise to purify it.

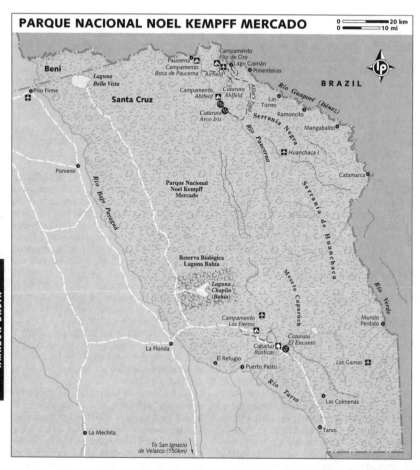

La Florida

Essentially the only access point to the park's interior, La Florida is the headquarters for budget travelers. The community rents bicycles, dugout canoes, tents and backpacks (US$5 to US$10 each per day) and has a couple of low-budget hostels and basic eateries.

By canoe, you can visit the black-water oxbow lakes and backwater channels of the **Río Bajo Paraguá**. Camping is restricted to designated sites. Wildlife is abundant around the river: you're likely to see river otters, howler monkeys, black caimans and dozens of bird species.

There are three ways to enter the park from La Florida. You can hike 40km (two days) through the forest along the old logging road, rent a mountain bike or hire a 4WD taxi (US$50; April to December only). Alternatively, you can hitch a ride with the park rangers to Campamento Los Fierros, but this is likely to change as soon as the local taxi service takes hold. If you decide to hike, allow two days and carry plenty of water.

Campamento Los Fierros

This is an excellent staging point for jaunts around the southern end of the park, lying in the high Amazonian forest, 2km from the ecological habitat known as 'seasonally inundated termite savanna' (that is, plains dotted with termite mounds). Nearby excursions include bicycle trips to **Laguna**

Chaplin and **Catarata El Encanto** and steep hikes up onto the wild **Huanchaca Plateau**.

There's excellent bird-watching along the forested roads near Los Fierros, and a nearby creek for cooling off or watching fish-eating bats at night. An early-morning visit to the termite savanna will frequently yield glimpses of rare wildlife: maned Andean wolves, crab-eating foxes and even the odd jaguar.

CATARATA EL ENCANTO

The spectacular 150m **waterfall** that spills off the Serranía de Huanchaca is the main objective of most visitors to Los Fierros. It makes for an enchanting three-day hike from Los Fierros. With a mountain bike, it's a long and tiring day-trip; with a vehicle, it can be done in a day, with lots of time for stops along the way.

The excursion begins along the 4WD track that heads east from Los Fierros. Along the way you'll pass through high Amazonian forest, seasonally inundated termite savanna and the threatened *cerrado* (gallery forest) savanna.

Once you've crossed the savanna area, continue until you reach a fork in the road; take the left fork. This abandoned logging road passes through some attractive forest, and you're almost guaranteed to observe – or at least hear – spider monkeys.

Eventually you'll reach a brook with potable water. Here the logging road ends and you follow a trail running alongside the stream to the foot of the waterfall. **Camping** is allowed along the stream below the trailhead, but not along the trails to the waterfall. In the evening ask your guide to take you to **natural salt licks** *(salitrals)* which attract tapirs, peccaries and other large mammals.

SERRANÍA DE HUANCHACA (LA SUBIDA DE LAS PELADAS)

This excursion begins the same as the trip to Catarata El Encanto but, while crossing the seasonally inundated termite savanna, you'll see a small track that turns left (northeast) off the road and leads through the *cerrado* and forest to the foot of the escarpment. From here it's a steep 500m climb up a footpath that crosses three bald hills known as **Las Peladas**. On the way you'll pass through dry forest on the lower slopes, and *cerrado* and bamboo groves on the

upper slopes. Once at the top you're ushered onto a spectacular grassy plain dotted with unusual rock outcrops that lend it the name **Campo Rupestre** (Rocky Landscape). There are also plenty of islands of gallery forest with some excellent campsites.

From the escarpment on a clear day you can see the Amazon forests, termite savannas, Laguna Chaplin and the gallery forests of the Río Bajo Paraguá. It's also a good vantage point to watch hawks and vultures riding the thermals and flocks of blue and yellow macaws migrating between their nesting sites in the highland palm groves and their feeding grounds in the forests below.

On the plateau you can hike for two or three days north to a spectacular unnamed **waterfall** or south to the escarpment overlooking the Catarata El Encanto. Along the way watch for the endangered *gama* (white-tailed deer), which has its last stronghold here. You'll also pass numerous **crystalline ponds** that make for refreshing swimming holes; at least one species of fish here is found nowhere else on earth and, although it may nip at your legs, it's not dangerous.

Those with adequate financial resources can fly into one of two remote airstrips at the abandoned drug-processing laboratories **Huanchaca I** (now used as an overnight camp on FAN's extension tour) and **Las Gamas**, a beautiful place at the southern end of the escarpment. The former lies on the northern end of the plateau amid *cerrado* savanna dotted with islands of Amazonian forest. From there it's a short day hike to the upper reaches of the **Río Paucerna**, which is a fast-running blackwater river. Strong swimmers will be OK, but drag yourself out before you reach the **Arco Irís waterfall**!

Flor de Oro

FAN runs a comfortable lodge at the airstrip for its package visitors. Around the camp you'll find examples of periodically inundated termite savanna, degraded *cerrado*, oxbow lakes and riverine flooded forests, all of which afford superb bird-watching opportunities. More than 300 bird species have been recorded here, and sightings of pink river dolphins are almost guaranteed. It's a 30-minute motorboat

AMAZON BASIN

ride or four-hour hike upstream to **Lago Caimán**, a superb spot for bird-watching and seeing caimans. The lagoon is the trailhead for **Allie's Trail** which climbs up through dry forest to the **Mirador de los Monos** for great scenery along the edges of the escarpment.

Two spectacular **waterfalls** tumble down the **Río Paucerna** above the Campamento Boca de Paucerna ranger station. From December to late June, the boat trip from Flor de Oro to the rustic **Campamento Ahlfeld** takes about five hours each way, depending on water levels. From the *campamento* it's an easy 30-minute walk to the spectacular 35m **Catarata Ahlfeld** and its lovely **swimming hole**. The more adventurous can hike four hours beyond to the fabulous **Catarata Arco Iris**.

Tours

FAN (Santa Cruz ☎ 355-6800; www.fan-bo.org) offers a variety of package tours to the park, including both wet- and dry-season options, as well as other tours that run year-round. All include guides, accommodation, food and local transportation (but not transport to/from Santa Cruz). In the rainy season a five-/seven-day package at Flor de Oro costs around US$700/1100 per person with two people and US$525/875 with four people. In the dry season a seven-day excursion to both Los Fierros and Flor de Oro costs around US$1100/800 with two/four people. A 10-day bird-watching expedition costs around US$2000/1500. Special four-day, three-night discount trips (from US$465 per person) run several times a year during

---

WILDLIFE OF NOEL KEMPFF MERCADO NATIONAL PARK

Noel Kempff Mercado National Park is both spectacularly scenic and ecologically extraordinary because of the diversity of its habitat. It protects five distinct ecosystems – broadleaf evergreen forest, dry forest, inundated forest, dry savanna and inundated savanna – each of which is composed of numerous distinct biological communities.

Recent studies put the number of mammal species at 130, birds at 630, reptiles at 75, frogs at 63 and fish at 260. In addition, it's estimated that the park supports over 4000 plant species, including dozens of orchids and some of the last remnants of *cerrado* vegetation in South America. This is one of the most biologically rich parks in the world, surpassed only by parks in the Andean foothills (such as Manu in Peru or Madidi in Bolivia), which have the advantage owing to their 3000m altitudinal ranges.

Patient and observant visitors are likely to see a rich variety of wildlife. If you're very lucky, you may even see a jaguar. Note, however, that full-time researchers only see them perhaps twice in a year. More predictably observed is the maned wolf, found mainly around Los Fierros. It's the most endangered species in the park – not to mention the most glamorous. Go out onto the termite savanna in the early morning and the odds are that you'll see one when they come to the road culverts to drink. You can sometimes hear them barking at night. The best time is June and July. Also relatively easy to see are pampas deer. These are most readily observed on the track up onto the plateau from Los Fierros, or around Las Gamas.

In the rivers you'll see alligators, caimans, pink river dolphins and perhaps even a rare river otter. Also around are peccaries, tapirs and spider monkeys, which are frequently spotted around Lago Caimán and Catarata El Encanto, and along the plateau track from Los Fierros. Less common are howler monkeys, giant anteaters, bush dogs, short-eared dogs and giant armadillos, all of which are considered endangered or threatened species.

And don't forget your binoculars – Noel Kempff Mercado has more bird species than all of North America! Especially interesting are the very rare grassland species that are largely restricted to Brazil but are becoming threatened there by conversion of their *cerrado* habitat to cattle ranches and soybean farms. Species that will get birders' juices flowing include the rusty-necked piculet, Zimmer's tody tyrant, collared crescent-chest, ocellated crake, rufous-winged antshrike, rufous-sided pygmy tyrant, campo miner, yellow-billed blue finch, black and tawny seed-eater, and a host of others. For the beginner, there is easy bird-watching at Flor de Oro along the river. The guans and curassows are especially tame, as there hasn't been much hunting pressure during the past decade.

Timothy J Killeen, Bolivia

Bolivian holiday weekends – contact FAN for the current schedule.

Sleeping & Eating

In the park's southwest sector, 10km directly west of the escarpment, **Campamento Los Fierros** provides dorm beds (US$20) and private *cabañas* (US$60). Camping in your own tent is free. In addition, there is running water, showers, meals and kitchen facilities. There are also rustic *cabañas* just below Catarata El Encanto.

At the more plush **Campamento Flor de Oro** in the park's northwest sector, you'll pay US$65 per person per day, including delicious typical Brazilian and Bolivian meals.

The simple **Campamento Ahlfeld**, a 45-minute walk downstream from the waterfall of the same name, is accessible by boat from Flor de Oro during periods of high water – normally from December to June.

Getting There & Away

AIR

The easiest – and most expensive – way into the park is via one of FAN's private Cessna aerotaxis. Round-trip charter flights for up to five passengers from Santa Cruz cost US$1200 to Los Fierros (two hours) and US$1300 to Flor de Oro (2¾ hours) and are the major costs of package tours.

BOAT

From the pleasant little Bolivian village of Piso Firme (which has several humble *alojamientos* and restaurants as well as a small shop selling staples), there's infrequent barge service upriver to Pimenteiras, Brazil (12 hours). From there it's a 30-minute boat ride upstream to Flor de Oro. Otherwise you'll have to swim or negotiate a hired motorboat (up to US$200 one way). There's also a fair amount of Brazilian cargo transport along the Ríos Mamoré and Guaporé between Guajará-Mirim and Costa Marques, in the Brazilian state of Rondônia. If coming from Brazil, there's no immigration officer in the park, so afterwards you'll have to return to Brazil or make a beeline for immigration in Santa Cruz.

BUS & CAMIÓN

Without your own transport, reaching the park independently overland will require a great deal of effort, patience and a good measure of your own steam.

When the roads are driest (normally from June to November), **Trans-Bolivia** (☎ 336-3866; Arana 332) buses depart Santa Cruz every Thursday at 7pm, passing Concepción, San Ignacio de Velasco and La Mechita en route to Piso Firme (US$15, 18 hours). For La Florida, get off at La Mechita, a wide spot in the road 55km west. This is a popular route so book well in advance

If you're traveling this route, it's wise to speak with Susy at the FAN office in San Ignacio and see if she can arrange to have a 4WD taxi meet you in La Mechita. Alternatively, you can try to hitch a ride with the park rangers or a passing logging truck. There are also plans to provide bicycle rental in La Mechita.

At other times take an overnight bus from Santa Cruz to San Ignacio de Velasco (US$6.75, 10 to 12 hours) – most companies leave between 6pm and 8pm. Once there visit the FAN office and speak with Susy about your plans to visit the park; she'll generally be able to help you find a 4WD taxi service. Similar arrangements can be made in Concepción, where the taxi stand is just off the plaza. Costs are negotiable, but drivers tend to charge by the kilometer (and it's 250km to the park!); you can minimize costs by sharing transportation with four or five travelers.

Alternatively, take the Santa Cruz–San Ignacio de Velasco bus to Santa Rosa de la Roca (US$6.50, nine hours), or take a *micro* there from San Ignacio. After you've secured a good supply of food and drink, find the restaurant El Carretero, five minutes' walk from Santa Rosa de la Roca along the road toward San Ignacio, and look for a *camión* headed north toward La Mechita. If you're unsuccessful – which will be rare – you can always stay overnight in Santa Rosa at Alojamiento Bárbara (US$3 per person) or Alojamiento La Chocita (US$4 per person).

At La Mechita you'll find a couple of *alojamientos* but, with luck, your *camión* may be passing the La Florida turnoff, 20km away, where it's possible to camp. From the turnoff you'll probably have to walk the remaining 35km to La Florida. After 34km from the turnoff, turn right and continue the last kilometer into the village.

AMAZON BASIN

Here it's possible to camp. On the next day, register at the park rangers' office and embark on the 40km hike to Los Fierros.

CAR & MOTORCYCLE
The easiest way to reach the park is via 4WD (US$75 to US$100 per day) from Santa Cruz. From Santa Cruz it takes at least 14 hours to reach Los Fierros, so most people take two days for the trip, spending the night in Concepción en route.

TO BRAZIL
A more radical alternative is the Brazilian connection to Flor de Oro. After picking up a visa in Santa Cruz, take a bus to San Matías (on the Brazilian border) and then on to Cáceres, four hours into Brazil. From there catch another bus to Vilhena (with a federal police post for entrance stamps) in the southern part of Rondônia state. From there daily buses leave for the village of Pimenteiras, 25 minutes by boat downstream from Flor de Oro. Alternatively, from San Ignacio de Velasco (exit stamps sporadically available), you can catch a direct Trans Joao bus into Brazil via San Vincente to La Cerda (R$35, 10 hours) and change buses for Vilhena (R$22, 4½ hours). If stuck overnight Vilhena has a couple of recommendable hostelries near the *rodoviária* (bus terminal): **Santa Rosa** (r per person with bath & breakfast R$20-35) and the more basic **Victoria** (R$15).

THE NORTHERN FRONTIER

While the once-untouched rainforests of Bolivia's little-regulated northern frontier are rapidly being tamed by fire, chainsaws and grazing cattle, the region's wild spirit continues to attract dreamers, developers and renegades from around the country. Visitors are rare and facilities are scarce but, for adventurous travelers who do make the effort to reach the far north, memorable experiences are guaranteed.

GUAYARAMERÍN
pop 14,000 / elevation 130m
Guayaramerín, on the Río Mamoré opposite the Brazilian town of Guajará-Mirim,

is a rail town where the railway never arrived. The line that would have connected the Río Beni town of Riberalta and the Brazilian city of Porto Velho was completed only as far as Guajará-Mirim and never reached Bolivian territory.

Historically, the area was a center of rubber production; in fact, Nicolás Suárez had his rubber-exporting headquarters at Cachuela Esperanza, 40km northwest of Guayaramerín. From there he transported cargo overland past the Mamoré rapids to the Río Madeira and shipped it downstream to the Amazon, the Atlantic and on to markets in Europe and North America (see the boxed text, p339).

A typically friendly Amazon town, Guayaramerín serves as a river port and a back door between Bolivia and Brazil. It's now the northern terminus for river transportation along the Río Mamoré, thanks to the same rapids that plagued the rubber boomers and rendered the river unnavigable just a few kilometers to the north.

Of late, Guayaramerín has sprung to life with a thriving commercial trade. Although it retains its frontier atmosphere, the town is growing rapidly – a constant stream of motorcycles buzz around the streets, and the shops overflow with black market Asian goods.

Information
The tourist office (of sorts) at the port rarely has any literature but the staff are happy to answer questions. A block east of the plaza, the relatively efficient **Brazilian consulate** (☎ /fax 855-3766; Beni & 24 de Septiembre; ⊙ 9am-1pm & 3-5pm Mon-Fri) issues visas in two days. Exchange US dollars at the Banco Mercantil, Hotel San Carlos or the *casas de cambio* around the plaza. For travelers checks, try Bank Bidesa. Moneychangers hanging around the port area deal in US dollars, Brazilian *reais* and *bolivianos*.

Tours
Amazonas Tours (☎ /fax 855-4000; Román 680) conducts five-hour city tours of Guayaramerín and Guajará-Mirim, as well as La Ruta de la Goma (The Rubber Trail) to Cachuela Esperanza. You can also arrange one-day cruises on the Río Yata or fishing trips to Rosario del Yata, and four-day tours that include hiking and fishing at the

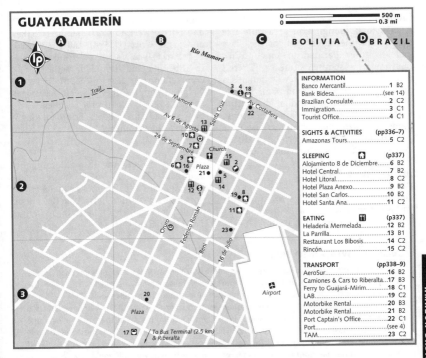

GUAYARAMERÍN

Lago Santa Cruz and a cruise along the Río Guaporé to Brazil's Forte Principe da Beira. Camping equipment is available for rent if you are planning a multi-day trip.

Sleeping

The most mellow budget place is **Hotel Litoral** (☎ 855-2016; with bath US$3), with clean rooms and refreshingly tepid showers. In the courtyard there's a snack bar and a TV set eternally playing Brazilian soap operas to a full house.

Opposite Litoral is the quiet and shady **Hotel Santa Ana** (☎ 855-3900; 25 de Mayo 611; US$2.65, with bath US$3.50) with similar amenities. **Hotel Plaza Anexo** (☎ 855-2086; with bath US$3.25) has clean rooms and a pleasant ambience.

Down the block, the friendly, well-kept **Hotel Central** (☎ 855-3911; s/d US$2.50/3.50) has rooms with shared baths. Even cheaper is **Alojamiento 8 de Diciembre** (US$2).

If you can't cope with the heat, head for **Hotel San Carlos** (☎ 855-3555; s/d with bath & breakfast US$15/25; ⚌ ⚎), which has a restaurant, redundant sauna, hydromassage, billiards room and 24-hour hot water.

Eating

The home cooking at Rincón's, located on the plaza, satisfies Brazilian expats. Try an enormous *prato feito* (*almuerzo*, Brazilian style); *baião de dois com carne de sol*; Brazil's national dish, *feijoada carioca*; or pizza, fish, chicken and beef dishes. It charges in reais, which makes it a bit more expensive than the Bolivian-run restaurants in town.

Churrasquería Patujú (6 de Agosto s/n) serves up tasty, good-value steak-oriented meals.

At La Parilla, which is just as beefy, *almuerzos* cost US$1.35 and evening meals go for around US$3.

The quieter out-of-town steak house Churrasquería Sujal, most readily accessible by motorbike taxi, has set *almuerzos* for under US$1 and à la carte dinners for around US$3.

Back on the plaza, Heladería Mermelada is renowned for its mountainous fruit and ice-cream creations, while Snack Paulita is a good spot for juices, burgers, beer and snacks. Most of Guayara's lager louts pass their days at Restaurant Los Bibosis.

AMAZON BASIN

Shopping

Thanks to its designation as a duty-free zone (authorities couldn't fight the illicit trade, so they decided to sanction it), Guayara is a shopper's mecca. There's nothing of exceptional interest, but it's a good place to pick up brand name knock-off shoes and clothes, Indian drawstring skirts and fake brand-name electronic goods. For *artesanía*, visit Caritas, near the airfield, which sells locally produced wooden carvings for reasonable prices.

Getting There & Away

AIR

The airport is on the edge of town. **TAM** (☎ 855-3924) flies twice a week from La Paz (US$88) to Riberalta (US$20) and Guaya-ramerín, twice a week to Trinidad (US$57) and once a week to Cochabamba (US$85) and Santa Cruz (US$94). **LAB** (☎ 855-3540; 25 de Mayo 652) lands several times a week in Riberalta and Trinidad, with La Paz connections. **AeroSur** (☎ 855-3731) serves Cobija a couple times a week. **Amaszonas** (☎/fax 855-3731; Mamoré 100) shuttles daily between La Paz, San Borja, Trinidad, Riberalta and Guayaramerín.

BOAT

Cargo boats up the Río Mamoré to Trinidad (around US$25 with food) leave almost daily. The noticeboard at the port captain's office lists departures. For details, see Getting There & Away in Trinidad, p328.

OVER THE RIVER & INTO BRAZIL

The happy words on the railway water tower in the Brazilian town of Guajará-Mirim (pronounced gwa-zha-*ra* mee-*reeng*), over the Río Mamoré from Guayaramerín, read *Seja Bem Vindo* (Be Welcome!) and travelers can pop across on a day visit without restrictions.

Between early morning and 6:30pm, frequent motorboat ferries cross the river between the two ports; they cost US$0.75 from Bolivia and US$1.50 from Brazil. After hours there are only express motorboats (US$4 to US$5 per boat). Once you're across the river, the Portuguese words *onde fica* (pronounced *awn*-jee *fee*-ca), meaning 'where is,' will go a long way, and *gracias* is replaced by *obrigado* (bree-*gah*-doo) if you're a man or *obrigada* (bree-*gah*-dah) if you're a woman.

While you're here, check out the free **Museu Histórico Municipal de Guajará-Mirim** (🕑 8am-noon & 2:30-6:30pm Mon-Fri, 9am-noon & 3-7pm Sat & Sun), in the old Madeira-Mamoré railway station, which focuses on regional history and contains the remains of some of Rondônia's fiercely threatened wildlife. Note the tree full of moth-eaten dead animals, the brilliant butterfly collection, the hair-raising assortment of enormous bugs, the huge anaconda that stretches the length of the main salon, the *sucurí* (the snake of your nightmares), an eye-opening history of Brazilian currency inflation and the lovable turtle that inhabits one aquarium. The collection of historical photographs includes an especially intriguing portrayal of an Indian attack taken in the 1960s. Also check out the classic steam locomotives in the square outside – especially the smart-looking *Hidelgardo Nunes*.

To travel further into Brazil or to enter Bolivia, you'll have to complete border formalities. The Bolivian **immigration office** (🕑 8am-8pm) is at the port in Guayaramerín. On the Brazilian side you pass through customs at the port in Guajará-Mirim and have your passport stamped at the port. They may also ask you to visit the Polícia Federal, on Av Presidente Dutra, five blocks from the port. Leaving Brazil you may also need to pick up a stamp at the Bolivian consulate in Guajará-Mirim.

Although officials don't always check, technically everyone needs a yellow-fever vaccination certificate to enter Brazil. If you don't have one, head for the convenient and relatively sanitary clinic at the port on the Brazilian side. For more information see Lonely Planet's *Brazil* guide.

For onward travel, at least eight daily buses connect Guajará-Mirim and Porto Velho (US$10, 5½ hours) along an excellent road, commonly known as the Trans-Coca highway. In addition, Brazilian government boats ply the Ríos Mamoré and Guaporé from Guajará-Mirim to the military post at Forte Príncipe da Beira in two to three days. They then continue to nearby Costa Marques, where food and accommodations are available. Inquire about schedules at the Capitânia dos Portos.

AMAZON BASIN

BUS, CAMIÓN & TAXI

The bus terminal is on the west end of town, beyond the market. With the exception of Riberalta, the only bus services to and from Guayaramerín operate during the dry season – roughly June to October. Buses run to Riberalta (US$2.75, three hours) several times daily. Foolhardy Flota Yungueña *flotas* depart daily in the morning for Rurrenabaque (US$18, 14 to 36 hours) and La Paz (US$21.50, 30 to 60 hours) via Santa Rosa and Reyes. There are four brave buses weekly to Cobija (US$14, 16 hours) and Trinidad (US$25, 22 hours). Beware that if enough tickets aren't sold, any of these runs may be summarily canceled.

Shared taxis to Riberalta (US$4.25, two hours) leave from the terminal when they have four passengers. *Camiones* to Riberalta leave from opposite the 8 de Diciembre bus terminal. *Camiones* charge the same as buses but make the trip in less time. To Cobija, YPFB gasoline trucks and a Volvo freight carrier depart occasionally from the same place as the *camiones* to Riberalta.

Getting Around

Guayaramerín is small enough to walk just about anywhere. Motorbike taxis and auto rickshaws charge US$0.40 to anywhere in town. To explore the area, you can hire motorbikes from the plaza (US$1.35 per hour) or negotiate all-day rentals – figure US$15 for 24 hours.

RIBERALTA

pop 60,000 / elevation 115m

The major town in Bolivia's northern frontier region sits on the banks of the Río Beni near its confluence with the Río Madre de Dios. Riberalta was once a thriving center of rubber production, but declined with increased Asian competition and the development of synthetics. Since the opening of the road link to La Paz and Guayaramerín, Riberalta's importance as a port has also ebbed. The town has fallen back on its current mainstay industry: the cultivation, production and export of Brazil nuts.

Information

As a service to travelers, Brother Casimiri at the vicarage changes US dollars cash and

MEMORIES OF MAD MARÍA

In 1907 the US company of May, Jeckyll & Randolph began work on a 364km railway to link Riberalta with the village of Santo Antônio on the Río Madeira. The original idea was to compensate Bolivia for the loss of the Acre territory (annexed by Brazil in 1903) by providing a transportation outlet to the Atlantic that was otherwise blocked by the Mamoré rapids 25km north of Guayaramerín. German, Jamaican and Cuban workers, and even Panama Canal hands, were brought in to work on the project. When the track was finished in 1912, more than 6000 workers had perished from malaria, yellow fever, gunfights and accidents, and the railway came to be known as A Via do Diabo (The Devil's Line).

The towns of Guajará-Mirim and Porto Velho owe their existence to the project, but since the railroad never arrived at Riberalta and the world market price of rubber plummeted while it was still under construction, the line became a white elephant before the first train even chugged along it. Today the road between Porto Velho and Guajará-Mirim uses the railway bridges, but the line itself is used only occasionally as a tourist novelty from the Porto Velho end.

Márcio Souza chronicles the brutal story in *Mad María* (1985), out-of-print but mandatory reading for anyone interested in how humanity briefly conquered this small parcel of the Green Hell.

travelers checks. Although there are lots of *compro dólares* signs in shops around town, they change only cash, and at a relatively poor rate. The post office and Entel are near the main plaza.

Keep in mind that the town's municipal water supply is contaminated; the heat and open sewers create a rather pungent atmosphere. Stick to bottled or thoroughly purified water.

Sights & Activities

Riberalta is a pleasant enough town, but it doesn't cater to visitors. In the paralyzing heat of the day, strenuous activity is suspended and locals search out the nearest hammock. If you're feeling motivated, don't miss the novel **monument** to Riberalta's

RIBERALTA

0 — 200 m
0 — 0.1 mi

Río Beni

Flood Plain

To Old rubber plantation
& carpentry workshop (1.5km)

INFORMATION
Entel....................................1 A1

SIGHTS & ACTIVITIES (pp339–41)
Mario Vargas Brazil Nut Factory..2 C3
Moghul Palace........................3 B1
Motorbike Monument..............4 B2
Parque Mirador La Costañera.....5 A1
Vicarage................................6 A1

SLEEPING (p341)
Hostal Tahuamanu...................7 B1
Hotel Amazonas......................8 A2
Hotel Colonial.........................9 B1
Hotel Villa Bahía....................10 B1

Residencial Julita....................11 B2
Residencial Katita...................12 A2
Residencial Las Palmeras.........13 B2
Residencial Los Reyes.............14 A3

EATING (p341)
Cabaña de Tío Tom................15 B1
Churrasquería El Pahuichi........16 A2
Club Social Boliviano-Japonés...17 A2
Club Social............................18 B1
Heladería Cola.......................19 A1
Heladería Vienesa...................20 A1

TRANSPORT (pp341–2)
AeroSur................................21 A2
Camiones a Tumi-Chúcua........22 C3
Capitanía del Puerto...............23 B1
LAB.....................................24 A2
Motorcycle Hire.....................25 A2
Puerto Beni-Mamore...........(see 23)
TAM....................................26 B3

favorite invention – the motorbike – on Av Nicolás Suárez.

For some minor amusement, stroll past the bizarre **Moghul palace**; although the prevailing theme is clearly Rajasthani, the architecture schizophrenically integrates Roman columns and arches, a couple of lounging lions and some raised-relief palm trees, as well as an odd grassy knoll that sprouts from the roof.

Parque Mirador La Costañera, on Riberalta's river bluff, overlooks a broad, sweeping curve of the Río Beni and affords the standard Amazonian view over water and rainforest. Planted in cement 20m above the river here sits the steamer *Tahuamanu*, which could readily pass for the African Queen. Inaugurated in 1899, it served in the Acre War (1900–1904) and the Chaco War (1932–1935), and was the first and last steamer used in the Bolivian Amazon.

Alternatively, you can rent a **motorbike** and explore the surrounding jungle tracks or take a **swim** in the river; ask locals where it's safe. At **Puerto Beni-Mamoré**, within

walking distance of the center, you can watch the hand-carving and construction of small boats and dugouts by skilled artisans. Two kilometers east of the plaza along Ejército Nacional, you can visit an **old rubber plantation**, watch coffee beans being roasted and visit a **carpentry workshop**. Riberalta carpenters specialize in high-quality rocking chairs and furniture made from tropical hardwoods.

The **Mario Vargas Brazil nut factory**, one of many in Riberalta, is happy to conduct tours. Here thousands of women enjoy a smashing career cracking Brazil nuts. Once extracted, the nuts are dried for 24 hours prior to shipment to prevent their going rancid, and the shells are hauled off to massive dumps to be turned into road-building material. The region exports millions of kilos of the nuts annually. Perhaps even more significant is the fact that this renewable resource protects rainforests that might otherwise fall to logging operations. So go out and buy more Brazil nuts!

Tumi-Chúcua once served as the Summer Institute of Linguistics of the Wycliffe

Bible Society and as the headquarters for translation of the Bible into local indigenous languages. When the work was finished, most of the Indians left and the site and school were turned over to the Bolivian government. With a pleasant lake, gardens and a picnic site, it's now Riberalta's get-away-from-it-all spot, 25km from town on the road toward Santa Rosa. Lifts are easiest to come by on weekends, particularly with the *camionetas* that leave from the Plaza del Periodista, southeast of the center.

Sleeping

The best value place is the spotless **Residencial Los Reyes** (☎ 852-8018; US$3, with bath US$4), near the airport, where the shady courtyard provides a respite from the afternoon heat, and iced water and hot coffee are always available.

The atmosphere is tropical at **Hotel Amazonas** (☎ 852-2339; with bath US$7), a favorite with local business travelers. A carpeted three-bed suite with TV is US$25. The scene is enhanced by the presence of two little *jochis*, whose happiness undoubtedly comes from the fact that they aren't on the menu.

The quirky **Hotel Colonial** (☎ 852-8212; US$4, with hot shower & breakfast US$6) isn't the best, but it's well meaning. Breakfast (which includes toast, eggs and coffee) is also available for nonguests for US$1.35.

The quiet, pink, B&B-style **Residencial Las Palmeras** (☎ 852-8353; s/d US$12/17), 15 minutes' walk from the center, has clean rooms with private baths and serves breakfast.

Residencial Julita (US$2) may be a bit scruffy, but the owner is friendly. The new **Residencial Katita** (☎ 852-8386; US$2) is a friendly and welcoming place with a public restaurant.

The most upmarket choice is **Hostal Tahuamanu** (☎ 852-8006; s/d US$9/14, with bath & breakfast US$15/20; ✷), a block off the plaza toward the river. Air-con is available for a few bucks extra. Not quite as classy but still nice and similarly priced is the laid-back **Hotel Villa Bahía** (s/d with breakfast & bath US$17/20; ✷).

Eating

The most interesting eateries are around the plaza. The reliable Cabaña de Tío Tom serves good coffee, ice cream, juices, shakes and sandwiches, as well as fish and Beni beef. What's more, the sidewalk seating provides a front-row view of the nightly Kawasaki derby. It also does breakfast, but doesn't get going until at least 8:30am.

Early risers should try the Hotel Colonial, or the market, which opens around 7am and is the best place to cobble together a classic breakfast of *api*, juice and *empanadas*. The plaza also has two *heladerías*, Vienesa and Cola.

Also on the plaza, Club Social serves inexpensive set lunches, superb filtered coffee, drinks and fine desserts. This isn't to be confused with Club Social Boliviano-Japonés, near the market, which doesn't serve anything Asian, but does dish up Bolivian and Amazonian standbys. Nearby, Churrasquería El Pahuichi has al fresco seating and an endless supply of Beni beef.

For an unforgettable Riberalta specialty, sample its famous Brazil nuts (*almendras*) which are roasted in sugar and cinnamon and sold by children around the bus terminals and the airport for US$0.15 per packet. Another local specialty, which can't be recommended (for sentimental and ecological reasons), is *carne de jochi*. The *jochi* (agouti), is a lively long-legged rodent that scurries around rainforests and is, in fact, the only wild creature with jaws strong enough to penetrate the shell of the Brazil nut.

Getting There & Away
AIR

The airport is a 15-minute stroll south of the main plaza. Departing flights are subject to an airport tax of US$1 and US$0.60 municipal tax. In the rainy season, however, flights are often canceled and you may be stuck awhile.

AeroSur (☎ 852-2798) and **LAB** (☎ 852-2239; Martinez 77) fly several times weekly to Trinidad, with connections to La Paz, Santa Cruz and Cochabamba. LAB also flies a couple of times a week to and from Cobija and Guayaramerín. **TAM** (☎ 852-2646) flies from La Paz to Riberalta (US$88) Tuesday and Thursday, returning to La Paz on Wednesday and Saturday. TAM's 20-minute, five-times-a-week Riberalta–Guayara flight (US$20) is surely one of Bolivia's cheapest thrills. **Amaszonas** (☎ 852-3933; Chuquisaca at Sucre) shuttles daily between La Paz, San Borja, Trinidad, Riberalta and Guayaramerín.

BOAT

The Río Beni passes through countless twisting kilometers of virgin rainforest and provides Bolivia's longest single-river trip. Unfortunately, boats upriver to Rurrenabaque are now rare and, in any case, they normally only run when the road becomes impassable (October to May). For information on departures, check the notice board at the Capitanía del Puerto at the northern end of Calle Guachalla. Budget US$20 to US$30 (including meals and hammock space) for the five- to eight-day trip. Lucky Peru-bound travelers may also find cargo boats to the frontier at Puerto Heath, which has onward boats to Puerto Maldonado.

BUS & CAMIÓN

During the soggy rainy season (November to at least March), the mucky Riberalta–Guayaramerín road opens sporadically but, at such times, the La Paz road is closed. The bus terminal is 3km east of the center, along the Guayaramerín road.

In the dry season, several *flotas* do daily runs to and from Guayaramerín (US$2.75, three hours). Alternatively, try hitching or waiting for a *camión* along Av Héroes del Chaco. This typically dusty trip passes through diminishing rainforest. All *flotas* between Guayaramerín and Cobija (US$12, 12 hours), Rurrenabaque (US$18, 17 to 40 hours) and La Paz (US$28, 35 to 60 hours) stop at Riberalta. Several *flotas* also go to Trinidad (US$20 to US$25, 17 hours) daily.

Getting Around

Motorbike taxis (US$0.40) will take you anywhere but *colectivos* (US$0.40) are scarce. With a driver's license from home, you can rent motorbikes (US$15 per 24 hours) from *taxistas* at the corner of Nicolás Suárez and Gabriel René Moreno.

RIBERALTA TO COBIJA

Not so long ago, the route between Riberalta and Cobija was negotiated only by hardy 4WD vehicles and high-clearance *camiones*. Nowadays, it's a high-speed gravel track that connects the once-isolated Pando department with the rest of the country. In the few years it has been open, the road has attracted unprecedented development.

Virgin rainforest is being cleared at a rate of knots and scarcely a scrap remains untouched.

At **Peña Amarilla**, two hours outside Riberalta, the route crosses the **Río Beni** by *balsa* raft. On the western bank, a friendly woman sells *empanadas* and other snacks.

The most interesting crossing on the trip, however, traverses the **Río Madre de Dios**. From the eastern port, the 45-minute crossing begins with a 500m cruise along a backwater tributary onto the great river itself. Along the way listen for the intriguing jungle chorus that characterizes this part of the country.

The last major *balsa* crossing is over the **Río Orthon**, at **Puerto Rico**. From Puerto Rico to Cobija, development is rampant. The scene is one of charred giants, a forest of stumps and smoldering bush; often the sun appears like an egg yolk through the dense smoke.

COBIJA

pop 15,000 / elevation 140m

The hot and sticky capital of the Pando, Bolivia's youngest department, sits on a sharp bend of the Río Acre. Cobija means 'blanket' and, not surprisingly, the climate creates the sensation of being smothered beneath a whopping duvet. With 1770mm of precipitation annually, it's Bolivia's wettest and most humid spot.

Cobija was founded in 1906 under the name 'Bahía', and in the 1940s it boomed as a rubber-producing center. When that industry declined, so did Cobija's fortunes, and the town was reduced to little more than a forgotten village. The original intent was to include Vaca Diez province, with Riberalta as the Pando capital (and Cobija left out in the cold, so to speak). However, when Riberalta opted to stay with Beni department, Cobija happily took over the role of departmental capital.

Cobija's most recent town plan shows lots of streets that have now been overgrown by jungle. In fact it once seemed that the town might someday be entirely swallowed up but, thanks to the road from Riberalta, a Japanese-funded hospital, a high-tech Brazil-nut processing plant and a pork-barrel international airport, its fortunes may be turning around. The big question is, why?

Information

The soporific Pando tourist office on the plaza operates...sporadically. The **Brazilian consulate** (☎ 842-2110; ⏱ 8:30am-12:30pm Mon-Fri) is on the corner of Beni and Fernández Molina. **Bolivian immigration** (⏱ 9am-5pm Mon-Fri) is in the Prefectural building on the main plaza.

Casas de Cambio Horacio and Horacio II change *reais*, *bolivianos* and US dollars at official rates, and will occasionally change travelers checks, for an arm and a leg. The post office is on the plaza and Entel is a block away, toward the river.

Sights

Cobija rambles over a series of hills, giving it a certain desultory charm. Of interest in the center are the remaining **tropical wooden buildings** and the lovely avenues of royal palms around the plaza. The **church** has a series of naive paintings from the life of Christ.

In Cobija's hinterlands, you can visit rubber and **Brazil nut plantations**, and there are also several lakes and places to observe rainforest wildlife, but transportation is difficult. The very adventurous can hire a motorized dugout and head upriver from nearby **Porvenir** to visit remote villages around the Peruvian border. It's recommended to take a guide with experience in navigating the overgrown waterways.

The Pando's biggest annual bash, the **Fería de Muestras** (August 18 to 27), features local artisans and is held at the extreme western end of town, near the Río Acre.

Sleeping & Eating

Residencial Frontera (☎ 842-2740; 9 de Febrero s/n; US$4, s/d with bath US$8/10) is clean but a bit overpriced. Request a room with a window onto the patio. Just off the plaza, the nicer **Hostería Sucre** (☎ 842-2797; Cornejo & Suárez; s/d with bath US$9/13) includes breakfast. **Residencial Cocodrilo** (☎ 842-2215; Molina s/n; s/d US$2.50, with bath US$7.50) has clean but far from opulent quarters.

In the early morning, the market sells chicken *empanadas*, fresh fruit and vegetables and lots of canned Brazilian products. Unfortunately, nothing stays fresh very long in this sticky climate, and most people won't touch the meat. For a tropical treat, head for the juice bar on the plaza.

Cobija's nicest eatery is **Esquina de la Abuela** (Molina s/n; mains US$2-4), which sports outdoor tables and fresh, well-cooked chicken and meat dishes. For a real pig-out, finish off across the street with an ice-cream sundae at Heladería El Tucano.

On the same street, five minutes' walk from the center, is Churrasquería La Cabaína del Momo, where you can chow on cheap *churrasco* on an elevated balcony. Curichi del Coco, which is better known as a disco, also serves beef and other traditional meals.

For lunch and dinner Pescadería Danielita specializes in freshwater fish, but obnoxious drunks may cause some discomfort. Another good choice is Restaurant Baixinho (Portuguese for 'shorty'), run by an affable chap who's at least 2m tall.

Getting There & Away

AIR

For some bizarre reason, Cobija has two airports. Despite the fact that the white elephant Aeropuerto Internacional Anibal Arab (CIJ) can accommodate 747s, most flights use the domestic airport just outside the town. Flights are sporadic at best, and although three airlines advertise services, it's largely a matter of luck to connect with something. You'll generally have the best luck flying with TAM or heading to Riberalta.

TAM (☎ 842-2267) flies directly to and from La Paz (US$85) on Wednesday and Friday morning. The **LAB** office (☎ 842-2170; Molina 139) is near the Policía Nacional. **AeroSur** (☎ 842-3132; Molina 41) is a block away.

BUS & CAMIÓN

In the dry season, buses to Riberalta (US$12, 12 hours) and Guayaramerín (US$16, 14 hours) leave at 6am daily. There you can connect with services to Rurrenabaque, Trinidad and La Paz. Three times daily Flota Cobija heads 30km south to Porvenir (US$0.80, one hour). In the dry season, *camiones* travel 'direct' to La Paz (around US$30 after bargaining). In the wet, *camiones* may still get through, but plan on at least three hot, wet days.

TO BRAZIL

Entry/exit stamps are available at immigration in Cobija and from Brasiléia's

Polícia Federal. A yellow-fever vaccination certificate is required to enter Brazil, but there's no vaccination clinic in Brasiléia, so you'll have to chase up a private physician.

It's a long, hot slog across the bridge to Brasiléia. With some negotiation, taxis will take you to the Polícia Federal in Brasiléia, wait while you clear immigration, then to the center or to the *rodoviária* (bus terminal). Alternatively, take the rowboat ferry (US$0.40) across the Río Acre. At the Brazilian landing, you're greeted by a topiary turkey, from where it's a 1km hike to the *rodoviária* and another 1.5km to the **Polícia Federal** (⊗ 8am-noon & 2-5pm). Dress neatly (no shorts!) or you may be refused entry. Check official rates before changing money in Brasiléia. None of Brasiléia's banks accept travelers checks.

From Brasiléia's *rodoviária*, several daily buses leave for Rio Branco (US$14, six hours), where there are many buses and onward flights.

Getting Around

Motorbike and automobile taxis charge a set US$0.40 to anywhere in town, including the domestic airport. Taxis charge US$0.85 to Brasiléia and US$2.50 to the international airport.

Directory

CONTENTS

PRACTICALITIES

- Use the metric system for weights and measures – except when buying produce at street markets, where everything is sold in *libras* (1 pound = 0.45kg).

- s/n (*sin numero*; without number) is commonly used in addresses in Bolivia where building numbers do not exist.

- Buy or watch videos on the VHS system.

- Most electricity currents are 220V AC, at 50Hz. Most plugs and sockets are the two-pin round-prong variety.

- Most locals take their *mate* with *La Razón*, the nation's biggest daily newspaper. In Sucre seek out *El Correo del Sur*, or *El Deber* in Santa Cruz.

- In La Paz, tune into non-commercial 96.5FM for folk tunes or 100.5FM for a catchy English-Spanish language pop mix. In Cochabamba Radio Latina 97.3FM spins a lively blend of Andean folk, salsa and rock. For a 24/7 stream of Andean artists, browse Bolivia Web Radio (www.boliviaweb.com/radio).

- Switch on the TV to watch the government-run Canal 7 or the private ATB TV network. Cable (with BBC, CNN, and ESPN) and international stations is available in most upmarket hotels.

ACCOMMODATIONS

Bolivian accommodations are among South America's cheapest, though price and value are hardly uniform. Prices in this chapter reflect standard, mid-season rates – prices can be up to 20% more in the high season (late June to early September) and can double during fiestas. Room availability is usually only a problem during fiestas (especially Carnaval in Oruro) and at popular weekend getaways.

The Bolivian hotel-rating system divides accommodations into *posadas, alojamientos, residenciales, casas de huéspedes, hostales* and *hoteles*. This subjective zero- to five-star rating system reflects the price scale and, to some extent, the quality.

The listings in the accommodation sections of this book are budget followed by mid-range followed by top-end options. Budget typically means less than US$7 per person per night with shared a bathroom. Mid-range facilities are usually around US$7 to US$20 per person (most often with private bath and breakfast), while the top-end tag is applied to places charging more than US$25 per person. Of course, in bigger cities like La Paz and Santa Cruz, mid-range can mean paying more than US$50 per double and top-end places fetch upwards of US$100 per night.

Hotels

Bolivia has plenty of pleasant mid-range places and five-star luxury resorts in and around larger cities and vacation destinations. Standard hotel amenities include breakfast, private bathrooms with 24/7 hot showers (gas- or electric-heated), phones and color TV, usually with some sort of cable. Luxury accommodations are a great bargain where they exist, but they don't exist outside of the major cities and weekend resort areas.

HI Hostels

Hostelling International (HI; www.hostellingbolivia .org) has recently affiliated with a nascent network of 14 existing accommodations. Unlike other 'hostelling' networks, members range from two-star hotels to camping places, but few offer traditional amenities like dorm beds or shared kitchens. HI membership cards may be for sale at the flagship hostel in Sucre (p223) or at Valmar Tours in La Paz (p49) but aren't always necessary to secure the standard 10% discount.

Posadas, Alojamientos, Residenciales & Casas de Huéspedes

Quality varies little at the bottom of the range, except at the worst *posadas* (US$1 to US$2 per person) where the shared facilities can be smelly, showers are scarce and hot water is unknown. Most *alojamientos* (US$2 to US$5 per person) have communal bathing facilities with electric showers. Most travelers end up at *residenciales*, which charge US$5 to US$20 for a double with private bath, about 30% less without. *Casas de huéspedes* (guesthouses) are appearing in cities and often offer a more mid-range, B&B-like atmosphere.

Camping

Bolivia offers excellent camping, especially along trekking routes and in remote mountain areas. Gear (of varying quality) is easily rented in La Paz and popular trekking base camps like Sorata. There are few organized campsites, but you can pitch a tent almost anywhere outside population centers. Remember, however, that highland nights are often freezing. Theft from campers is reported in some areas – inquire locally about security.

ACTIVITIES
Adrenaline-Charged Activities

Mountaineering is the most developed adventure sport in Bolivia. Other radical possibilities are just beginning to be explored. Emerging extreme-sports possibilities include paragliding (*parapente*; the national 2003 reunion was held in Copacabana), rock climbing (*escalada deportiva*; La Paz, Oruro and Cochabamba are the main bases) and skiing (p79).

Key thrill-seeking contacts are the Oruro-based **Club de Montañismo Halcones** (www.geocities.com/msivila) and the **Club Andino Boliviano** (http://geocities.com/Yosemite/Trails/7553/cab1 .html) in La Paz.

Bird-Watching & Wildlife-Watching

Fauna and flora fanatics are spoilt for choice in Bolivia. There are many world-class wildlife-watching destinations in Bolivia that are the primary objectives of many travelers' visits. The diversity of intact habitats throughout the country account for the huge number of surviving species.

Parque Nacional Madidi (p320), for example, harbors 1200 species, the world's most dense concentration of avifauna species. It is home to wildlife endemic to all Bolivian ecosystems, from tropical rainforest and tropical savanna to cloudforest and alpine tundra.

Count yourself lucky if you see any elusive species, such as *vicuña*, *huemules* (Andean deer), maned wolves, condors, jaguars, pumas, tapir, giant anteaters or the spectacled bear. If you don't see a llama or alpaca, well, you simply haven't been to Bolivia.

There are believed to be at least 19 endemic bird species. Other bird hotspots include the highlands around La Paz and Cochabamba, Parque Nacionales Amboró (p283), Noel Kempff Mercado (p330) and the Reserva Biosférica del Beni (p322).

Contact **Asociación Armonía** (www.birdbolivia .com), the Bolivian partner of BirdLife International, for further birding information.

Hiking & Trekking

Hiking and trekking are arguably the most rewarding Andean activities. Bolivia rivals

Nepal in trekking potential, but has only recently been discovered by enthusiasts. The most popular hikes and treks in Bolivia begin near La Paz, traverse the Cordillera Real along ancient Inca routes and end in the Yungas. Many other areas of the country are also suitable.

See the Cordilleras & Yungas chapter (p108) for more information and Lonely Planet's *Trekking in the Central Andes* for more detail. Maps are discussed below.

Serious incidents and robberies continue to be reported, so be sure to inquire locally about the safety of trails before heading out.

Mountaineering & Climbing

Climbing in Bolivia, in common with the country itself, is an exercise in extremes. In the dry southern winter (May to September) temperatures may fluctuate as much as 40°C in a single day, but the weather is better than can be expected when compared to other mountain ranges in the world, except in winter when conditions can be as uncomfortable as any other range. Another plus point is ease of access; although public transport may not always be available, roads pass within easy striking distance of many fine peaks.

Trekkers will find that the 160km-long Cordillera Real northeast of La Paz offers the easiest access and most spectacular climbing in the country. Six of its peaks rise above 6000m and there are many more gems in the 5000m range. Because of the altitude, glaciers and ice or steep snow, few of the peaks are 'walk-ups', but most are well within the capability of the average climber, and many can be done by beginners with a competent guide.

The dangers of Bolivian climbing are due to the altitude and the difficulties in mounting any sort of rescue, as well as the small but potentially serious avalanche danger. For information on dealing with altitude problems, it's wise carry the practical and easily transportable *Mountain Sickness*, by Peter Hackett, whenever you ascend to high altitude. See Health chapter for information regarding altitude sickness (p374).

Those who've spent some time in the highlands will have a head start on acclimatization, but newly arrived climbers should spend a week in La Paz or on the Altiplano, including some hiking (staying as high as possible), before attempting their climb. Once you're acclimatized to the Altiplano's relatively thin air, remember there are still 2500m of even thinner air lurking above, so climb smart. Drink plenty of fluids, sleep as low as possible, and descend at any sign of serious altitude sickness before a headache, troubled breathing or lethargy turn into life-threatening pulmonary or cerebral edema (see the Health chapter, p374).

Climbers should be aware that should they get in trouble the few helicopters Bolivia possesses generally cannot fly above 5000m. Emergency help is more likely on the frequently climbed routes up Huayna Potosí and Illimani, but transport difficulties and the lack of phones mean any rescuers not already on the mountain will take many hours to arrive. Mountaineering insurance is essential to cover the high costs of rescue and to ensure medical evacuation out of the country in the event of a serious accident.

MAPS

Historically, maps of Bolivian climbing areas have been or poor quality and difficult to obtain. Even now, elevations of peaks are murky, with reported altitudes varying as much as 600m – it's seems that the rumor that Ancohuma is taller than Aconcagua won't die.

Liam O'Brien's 1:135,000-scale *Cordillera Real* shows mountains, roads and pre-Hispanic routes. Roughly two-thirds of Bolivia is covered by 1:50,000 topo sheets produced by the Instituto Geográfico Militar (IGM). Notable exceptions include the areas north of Sorata, the Cordillera Apolobamba and Parque Nacional Noel Kempff Mercado. Walter Guzmán Córdova has produced 1:50,000 color maps of *Choro-Takesi-Yunga Cruz*, *Muru-rata-Illimani*, *Huayna Potosí-Condoriri* and *Sajama*.

The Deutscher Alpenverein (German Alpine Club) produces the excellent and accurate 1:50,000 maps *Alpenvereinskarte Cordillera Real Nord (Illampu)*, which includes the Sorata area, and *Alpenvereinskarte Cordillera Real Süd (Illimani)*, which centers on Illimani.

See Maps, p353, later in this chapter, for map sources.

GUIDEBOOKS

The best mountaineering guide is *Bolivia – a Climbing Guide* by Yossi Brain; the late author worked as a climbing guide in La Paz and also served as secretary of the Club Andino Boliviano. *Los Andes de Bolivia* by Alain Mesili, was recently reprinted in Spanish and an English translation is forthcoming.

AGENCIES & GUIDES

Many La Paz travel agencies offer to organize climbing and trekking trips in the Cordillera Real and other areas (p357). Some, however, are not all they claim to be. Guides have gotten lost, even on Huayna Potosí, and others have strung 10 or more climbers on the same rope. These sorts of things aren't uncommon, so it's worth sticking to reputable specialist climbing agencies.

Specialist agencies in La Paz can do as much or as little as you want – from just organizing transport to a full service with guide, cook, mules, porters and so forth, providing a full itinerary. Trekking guides generally charge US$25 per day, plus their food. Mountain guides cost US$50 per day and also must be fed. In addition you need your food, technical equipment and clothing and – often the most expensive part of any trip – transport to and from the base camp or the start of the trek. Some people do resort to public transport or hitching on *camiones*, but this requires more time and logistics.

In addition to the agencies, mountain guide information is available from the Club Andino Boliviano (p346) which is mainly a ski organization but also has a number of top climbers as members.

Mountain Biking

Bolivia is blessed with some of the most dramatic mountain-biking terrain in the world, seven months every year of near-perfect weather and relatively easy access to mountain ranges, magnificent lakes, pre-Hispanic ruins and trails, and a myriad of ecozones. Mountain biking is relatively new to the country; generally speaking many areas have yet to be explored properly by bike.

Travelers with their own bikes need to consider several factors. During the December to February wet season, some roads become mired in muck, and heavy rain can greatly reduce visibility, creating dangerous conditions (even in the dry season, conditions on some roads could be considered hazardous). Also worth noting are Bolivia's lack of spare parts and shortage of experienced mechanics. While some bike shops in larger cities do have competent mechanics, most lack experience with complicated systems, such as hydraulic and disk brakes, and newer suspension systems. In short, independent cyclists will have to carry all essential spares from outside and know how to make their own repairs.

While mountain bikes aren't suited to all parts of Bolivia, most highland areas and some lowland regions present great potential. Hard-core, experienced, fit and acclimatized riders can choose from a wide range of possibilities; either work out a route on a map and take a gamble on it, or find a guide and tackle some really adventurous rides.

The Bolivian highlands are full of long and thrilling descents, as well as challenging touring possibilities, such as the Apolo road, which descends from the Cordillera Apolobamba to Apolo. In addition, one of the world's longest downhill rides will take you from Sajama National Park down to the Chilean coast at Arica, a total descent of more then 5000m. In the dry season you can even tackle the mostly level roads of the vast Amazonian lowlands.

Some rides from La Paz can be done by riders of any experience level. The best known is the thrilling 3600m descent down 'The World's Most Dangerous Road' from La Cumbre to Coroico (p55). Other popular routes from the highlands into the Yungas include the descent into the lush Zongo Valley and the twisting route from near Lake Titicaca to Sorata. Alternatively, you can opt for a descent from the 5300m summit of Chacaltaya, which winds up in central La Paz! For descriptions of these routes, see the boxed text, p138, in the Cordilleras & Yungas chapter.

Whitewater Rafting & Kayaking

One of Bolivia's greatest secrets is the number of white-water rivers that drain the eastern slopes of the Andes between the Cordillera Apolobamba and the Chapare. Here, thousands of rivers and streams provide thrilling descents for avid rafters and kayakers. While access will normally require long drives and/or treks – and considerable expense – several fine rivers are relatively accessible.

Organizing rafting and kayaking trips could prove difficult for individual travelers, but most La Paz tour agencies can organize day trips on the Río Coroico and Río Huarinilla. Other options include the Río Unduavi, Río Tuichi and numerous wild Chapare rivers.

For major adventure trips – which will require a great deal of planning and expense – a good operator to use is Explore Bolivia. Within Bolivia, their trips can be organized through America Tours (p357), in La Paz.

BUSINESS HOURS

Few businesses open before 9am, though markets stir as early as 6am. Cities virtually shut down between noon and 2pm, except markets and restaurants serving lunch-hour crowds. Most businesses remain open until 8pm or 9pm. If you have urgent business to attend to, don't wait until the weekend as most offices will be closed.

CHILDREN

Few foreigners visit Bolivia with children, but those who do are usually treated with great kindness. Children with fair hair are especially likely to receive local attention.

Civilian airlines allow children under 12 to fly at half fare, but on long-distance buses, those who occupy a seat will normally have to pay the full fare. Most hotels have family rooms with three or four beds. Restaurants rarely advertise children's portions, but will often offer a child-sized serving at a lower price, or will allow two kids to share an adult meal.

Safety seats, diaper-changing facilities and child-care services are only available in the finest hotels. Breast feeding in public is widespread. But formula is available in modern supermarkets in big cities, as are disposable diapers.

There are fantastic children's museums in Sucre and La Paz, and a water park in Santa Cruz, but most Bolivians spend Sunday afternoons picnicking with the family in parks and zoos or strolling the trafficless Prados of La Paz and Cochabamba. For more information, advice and anecdotes, see Lonely Planet's *Travel with Children*.

CLIMATE CHARTS

The following climate charts provide an indication of temperature and rainfall around the country. See also the When to Go section (p9).

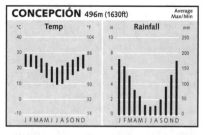

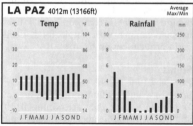

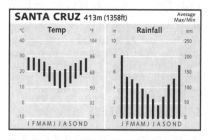

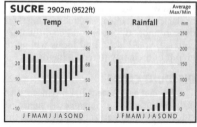

CUSTOMS

When entering Bolivia you can bring most articles duty-free provided that you can convince customs that they are for personal use. There's also a loosely-enforced duty-free allowance of 200 cigarettes and one liter of alcohol per person.

DANGERS & ANNOYANCES

Bolivia is a comparatively mellow travel destination, but certain dangerous and/or annoying instances may arise. First there's a strong tradition of social protest – demonstrations are a weekly occurrence. These are usually peaceful, but police occasionally deploy force and tear gas to disperse crowds. The Bolivian workforce is heavily unionized, and work stoppages by bus drivers, teachers and others can affect travelers. Roadblocks (bloqueos) and strikes by transportation workers often lead to long delays. The rainy season means flooding, landslides and road washouts, causing delays. Getting stuck overnight behind a slide is common: you'll be a happier camper with ample food, drink and warm clothes on hand.

Scams

Psst, hey, my friend: One popular scam involves a shill spilling something on you and while you or they are wiping it off, another lifts your wallet or slashes your pack. The ruse often starts with a fat luggi or phlegm ball being spat on your shoulder; the perpetrator may be an innocent granny or young girl. After dark outside dodgy bus stations, beware of hopping into shared cabs with strangers – several violent assaults have been reported in the past few years, usually targeting solo female travelers.

DISABLED TRAVELERS

The sad fact is that Bolivia's infrastructure is ill-equipped for disabled travelers. You will, however, see locals overcoming myriad obstacles and challenges while making their daily rounds. If you encounter difficulties yourself, you'll likely find locals willing to go out of their way to lend a hand.

DISCOUNT CARDS

The **International Student Travel Confederation** (ISTC; www.istc.org) is a network of specialist student travel organizations. It's also the body behind the International Student Identity Card (ISIC), which gives carriers discounts on a few services in Bolivia. La Paz-based Valmar Tours (p49) is the local representative.

Most Bolivian airlines offer 5% student discounts, but they may not be available to foreigners. AeroSur has more generous discounts for passengers over 65, and Amaszonas may give steep discounts (up to 90%) for seniors and children when space is available.

EMBASSIES & CONSULATES

The Minister of Exterior Relations's website (www.rree.gov.bo) has a full listing of Bolivian diplomatic missions overseas (click on 'Representaciones diplomáticas y consulares'), as well as a complete listing of foreign diplomatic representation in Bolivia (click on 'Guía Diplomática').

Bolivian Embassies & Consulates

Australia Sydney Honorary Consul (☎ 02-9247-4235; 305/4 Bridge St, NSW 2000)
Canada Ottawa (☎ 613-236-5730; fax 613-236-8237; 130 Albert St, Suite 416, Ontario K1P 5G4)
France Paris (☎ 01-42 24 93 44; fax 01-45 25 86 23; embolivia.paris@wanadoo.fr; 12 Ave du President Kennedy, F-75016)
Germany Berlin (☎ 030 2639 150; fax 030 2639 1515; www.bolivia.de; Wichmannstr. 6, PLZ-10787)
UK London (☎ 020-7235 4248/2257; fax 020-7235 1286; www.embassyofbolivia.co.uk; 106 Eaton Square, SW1W 9AD)
USA Embassy (☎ 202-483-4410; 202-328-3712; www .bolivia-usa.org; 3014 Massachusetts Ave NW, Washington, DC 20008); Consulate General (☎ 202-232-4828, 202-232-4827; bolivianconsulatewdc@starpower.net; 2120 L St NW, Suite 335, Washington, DC 20037)

Embassies & Consulates in Bolivia

Argentina La Paz (☎ 02-241-7737; embarbol@caoba .entelnet.co; Aspiazu 497); Cochabamba (☎ 04-422-9347; fax 04-425-5859; Blanco 0-929); Villazón (Saavedra 311); Santa Cruz (☎ 03-334-7133; Junín 22, above Banco de la Nación Argentina facing Plaza 24 de Septiembre); Tarija (☎ 04-664-2273; Ballivian N-699)
Australia La Paz (☎ 02-244-0459; Arce 2081, Edificio Montevideo)
Brazil La Paz (☎ 02-244-0202; fax 02-244-0043; embajad brasil@acelerate.com; Arce at Gutierrez, Edificio Multicentro); Cochabamba (☎ 04-425-5860; fax 04-411-7084; Edificio Los Tiempos II, 9th floor); Guayaramerín (☎ /fax 03-855-3766; Beni & 24 de Septiembre); Santa Cruz (☎ 03-334-4400; Busch 330); Sucre (☎ 04-645-2661; Arenales 212)

YOUR OWN EMBASSY

It's important to realize what your own embassy can and can't do for you. Generally speaking your embassy won't be much help in emergencies if the trouble you're in is remotely your own fault. Remember that while in Bolivia you are bound by Bolivian laws. Your embassy will not be sympathetic if you end up in jail after committing a crime locally, even if such actions are legal in your own country.

In genuine emergencies you might get some assistance, but only if other channels have been exhausted. For example if you need to get home urgently, a free ticket home is exceedingly unlikely – the embassy would expect you to have insurance. If you have all your money and documents stolen, embassy staff might assist with getting a new passport, but a loan for onward travel is out of the question.

Canada La Paz (☎ 02-241-5021; lapaz@dfait-maeci.gc.ca; Sanjinés 2678, Edificio Barcelona, 2nd fl)
Chile La Paz (☎ 02-278-3018; Siles 5843, Obrajes); Santa Cruz (☎ 03-343-4272; Calle 5 Oeste 224, Barrio Equipetrol)
Colombia La Paz (☎ 02-278-6841; emcol@acelerate.com; Calle 9 No 7835, Calacoto)
Ecuador La Paz (☎ 02-233-1588; fax 02-2319739; mecuabol@entelnet.bo;16 de Julio s/n, Edificio Herrmann, 14th floor); Sucre (☎ 04-648-0205; Beni s/n)
France La Paz (☎ 02-278-6114; www.ambafrance-bo.org; Siles 5390 at Calle 8, Obrajes); Santa Cruz (☎ 03-343-3434; 3rd Anillo between Alemana & Mutualista); Sucre (☎ 04-645-3018; Bustillos 206)
Germany La Paz (☎ 02-244-0066, 02-244-1133/66; www.embajada-alemana-bolivia.org; Arce 2395); Cochabamba (☎ 04-425-4024; fax 04-425-4023; Edificio La Promontora, 6th floor); Santa Cruz Honorary (☎ 03-336-7585; dconsscz@cotas.com.bo; Nuflo de Chavez 437); Sucre (☎ 04-645-1369; Rosendo Villa 54); Tarija Honorary (☎ 04-664-2062; methfess@olivio.tja.entelnet.bo; Campero 321)
Italy La Paz (☎ 03-243-4955/29; ambitlap@ceibo.entelnet.bo; 6 de Agosto 2575, Sopocachi); Santa Cruz (☎ 03-353-1796; El Trompillo, Edificio Honnen, 1st floor); Sucre (☎ 04-645-4172; Santa Cruz s/n)
Netherlands La Paz (☎ 02-244-4040; nllapos@caoba.entelnet.bo; 6 de Agosto 2455, Edificio Hilda, 7th floor); Santa Cruz (☎ 03-358-1866; Aguilera 300, 3rd Anillo)
Paraguay La Paz (☎ 02-243-3176; embapar@acelerate.com; 6 de Agosto at Pinilla, Edificio Illimani); Cochabamba (☎ /fax 04-425-0183; Edificio El Solar, 16 de Julio 211)
Peru La Paz (☎ 02-244-1250; embbol@caoba.entelnet.bo; Guachalla 300, Sopocachi); Cochabamba (☎ 04-424-6210; Pando 1143, Recoleta); Santa Cruz (☎ 03-336-8979; Edificio Oriente, 2nd floor); Sucre (☎ 04-645-5592; Avaroa 462)
Spain Santa Cruz (☎ 03-332-8921; Santiesteban 237)
UK La Paz (☎ 02-243-3424; www.embassyofbolivia.co.uk; Arce 2732)
USA La Paz (☎ 02-243-3812; http://lapaz.usembassy.gov; Arce 2780); Cochabamba (☎ 04-425-6714;

fax 04-425-7714; Torres Sofer, Oquendo E-654, Rm 601); Santa Cruz (☎ 03-333-0725; Gu\:emes Este 6B, Barrio Equipetrol) Moving to a new bunker in 2004.

FESTIVALS & EVENTS

Bolivian *fiestas* are invariably of religious or political origin, and typically include lots of music, drinking, eating, dancing, processions, ritual and general unrestrained behavior. Water balloons (gringos are sought-after targets!) and fireworks (all too often at eye-level) figure prominently. On major holidays banks, offices and other services are closed, and public transport is often bursting at the seams; book ahead if possible.

Every first Friday of the month is celebrated in big cities and traditional communities with a *cha'lla*, the burning of *mesa blanca* (literally 'white table') offerings and incense while sitting outside homes and businesses with friends and family in huge clouds of smoke.

The following is a snapshot of nationwide festivals and events that are not confined to one city or town. See the destination chapters for city- and town-specific festivals or events that are held around Bolivia during the year; dates are subject to change.

January
Día de los Reyes 'Kings' Day' (Epiphany) is celebrated on January 6 as the day the three wise kings visited the baby Jesus after his birth. The largest celebrations are in Reyes (Beni); Sucre; Tarija; and rural villages in Oruro, Cochabamba and Potosí departments.

February/March
Fiesta de La Virgen de Candelaria This week-long festival is held during the first week of February in Aiquile (Cochabamba); Samaipata (Santa Cruz); Angostura (Tarija)

and Cha'llapampa (Oruro). The biggest celebration, however, is at Copacabana in La Paz department.

Carnaval Celebrations are held nationwide the week before Lent. Celebrations start with enthusiastic processions and booming brass bands, but – with the addition of alcohol –a crescendo into madness. In most parts of the world, Lent grinds to a halt with the dawning of Ash Wednesday. In Bolivia, hair-of-the-dog celebrations may continue for several days later than the Catholic Church would consider appropriate.

March/April
Semana Santa One of the most impressive of the nationwide Holy Week activities is the Good Friday fiesta in Copacabana, when hundreds of pilgrims arrive on foot from La Paz.

May
Fiesta de la Cruz The Festival of the Cross (May 3) commemorates the cross on which Christ was crucified (or the Southern Cross, in pagan circles). Despite the somber theme, the celebrations are quite upbeat. The greatest revelry takes place in Tarija, with two weeks of music, parades, and alcohol consumption. The fiesta is also big in Vallegrande (Santa Cruz), Cochabamba and Copacabana (both in La Paz).

Día de la Madre Mother's Day celebrations (May 27) are held nationwide. In Cochabamba the festivities are known as Heroínas de la Coronilla in honor of the women and children who defended their cities and homes in the battle of 1812.

June
San Juan Bautista Held nationwide (June 24) but the largest bash takes place in Santa Cruz.

August
Independence Day Fiesta Held August 6 this highly-charged anniversary provides inspiration for excessive raging nationwide. The largest celebration is held at Copacabana.

October
Vírgen del Rosario This celebration is held on different days during the first week of the month and in different locations, including Warnes (Santa Cruz); Tarata, Morochata and Quillacollo (Cochabamba); Tarabuco (Chuquisaca); Viacha (La Paz) and Potosí.

November
Día de Todos los Santos All Saints' Day (November 1 and 2) sees cemetery visits, much mouring and celebration, and colorful decoration of graves nationwide.

December
Christmas Celebrated throughout Bolivia on December 25. Some of the most unique festivities take place in San Ignacio de Moxos (Beni) and Sucre.

FOOD
Bolivian food generally is palatable, filling and ho-hum. For the larger cities the eating recommendations provided in this book are often broken down by style of eatery. It's definitely an acquired taste, but the best-value meals are found at midday in and around markets (often under US$1) and at nicer restaurants, where four courses run US$2 to US$5. A meal at one of the best cosmopolitan restaurants with internationally-trained chefs costs around US$25 a head with wine. See the Food and Drink chapter (p36) for more specific information.

Formal tipping is haphazard except in nicer restaurants – the most formal places will add 10% to your bill. Elsewhere, locals leave coins amounting to a maximum of 10% of the total in recognition of good service.

GAY & LESBIAN TRAVELERS
Homosexuality exists and is legal in Bolivia (though the constitution does prohibit same-sex marriages). The government merely defines homosexuality as 'a problem'.

Gay bars and venues are limited to the larger cities, but due to bashings and police raids, they come and go with some regularity. As for hotels, sharing a room is no problem as long as you don't request a double bed; discretion is still in order.

Gay rights lobby groups are active in La Paz (MGLP Libertad), Cochabamba (Dignidad) and most visibly in progressive Santa Cruz. In June 2003 Santa Cruz' La Comunidad Gay, Lésbica, Bisexual y Travestí (GLBT) replaced their fourth annual Marcha de Colores on Día del Orgullo Gay (Gay Pride Day, June 26) with a health fair called Ciudadanía Sexual in an effort to gain wider public acceptance. In La Paz watch for flyers advertising drag performances by La Familia Galan, the capital's most fabulous group of cross-dressing queens.

HOLIDAYS
Public Holidays
Public holidays vary from province to province. The following is a list of the main national and provincial public holidays;

for precise dates (which vary from year to year), check locally.

New Year's Day January 1
Carnaval February/March
Semana Santa Easter Week: March/April
Labor Day May 1
Corpus Christi May
Independence Days August 5–7
Columbus Day October 12
Día de los Muertos All Souls' Day; November 2
Christmas December 25

Departmental Holidays

Not about to be outdone by their neighbors, each department has its own holiday.

February 22 Oruro
April 1 Potosí
April 15 Tarija
May 25 Chuquisaca
July 16 La Paz
September 14 Cochabamba
September 24 Pando & Santa Cruz
November 18 Beni

INSURANCE

A good travel-insurance policy to cover theft, loss and medical mishaps is important. Nothing is guaranteed to ruin your holiday plans quicker than an accident or having that brand new digital video camera stolen.

There is a wide variety of policies available: shop around and scrutinize the fine print. Some policies specifically exclude 'dangerous activities', which can include skiing, motorcycling, mountain biking, even trekking. Check that the policy covers ambulances and emergency airlift evacuations. You may prefer a policy which pays doctors or hospitals directly, rather than you having to pay on the spot and claim later. If you have to claim later, make sure you keep all documentation.

Also see Health Insurance (p368). For information on insurance matters relating to motoring around, see Car & Motorcycle (p365) in the Transport chapter.

INTERNET ACCESS

Nearly every corner of Bolivia has a cybercafé. Rates run from US$0.25 to US$3 per hour. In smaller towns check the local Entel office for access.

Most travelers make constant use of Internet cafes and free web-based email such as Yahoo! (www.yahoo.com) or Hotmail

---

> **NEVER TOO OLD...**
>
> For the record:
>
> - The legal age for voting in Bolivia is 18.
> - You can drive when you're 18.
> - Hetrosexual sex is legal when you turn 18, or 15 if you're married.
> - Homosexual sex is legal but same-sex marriages are prohibited by the constitution.
> - The legal drinking age is 21, but that doesn't seem to deter anyone.

(www.hotmail.com). Lonely Planet's ekno global communication service (www.ekno .lonelyplanet.com) offers an online travel vault, where you can securely store all your important documents.

For a list of useful Bolivia-savvy websites, see Internet Resources (p10).

LEGAL MATTERS

Bolivia may be the land of cocaine, but rumors that a cheap and abundant supply is readily available to the general public are unfounded. Refined cocaine is highly illegal in Bolivia – the standard sentence for possession of cocaine in Bolivia is eight years – so it's clearly best left alone.

The big guys get away with processing and exporting because they're able to bribe their way around the regulations. Backpackers and coca farmers become statistics to wave at foreign governments as proof, if you will, that Bolivia is doing something about the drug problem. Although foreign travelers are rarely searched, it's still unwise to carry drugs of any kind, as the consequences are just too costly.

If the worst happens – you're caught with drugs and arrested – the safest bet is to pay off the arresting officer(s) before more officials learn about your plight and want to be cut in on the deal. It's best not to call the payoff a bribe per se. Ask something like: '¿Cómo podemos arreglar este asunto?' ('How can we put this matter right?'). They'll understand what you mean.

If the officer refuses, then you're on your own, as foreign embassies are normally powerless, and in most cases they simply don't want to know.

MAPS

Maps are available in La Paz, Cochabamba and Santa Cruz through Los Amigos del Libro. Government 1:50,000 topographical and specialty sheets are available from the Instituto Geográfico Militar (IGM), with two offices in La Paz (p45) and in other most major cities.

For detailed trekking maps, the colorful contour maps produced by Walter Guzmán Cordova are hard to beat, though they are based on the IGM maps and contain many of the same errors. In La Paz try the trekking agents and tourist shops along Sagárnaga, or watch for ambulatory vendors prowling the Prado; you'll often find them lurking around the entrance to the Gravity Assisted and America Tours office.

The superb *New Map of the Cordillera Real,* published by O'Brien Cartographics, is available at various gringo hangouts. O'Brien also publishes the *Travel Map of Bolivia,* which is one of the best country maps. Freddy Ortiz' widely available, inexpensive *Journey Routes* map series covers the major touristic regions and includes a good *Bolivia Highlights* country map. The **South American Explorers** (www.samexplo.org) distribute the O'Brien sheets, plus maps of major cities.

International sources for hard-to-find maps include the US-based **Maplink** (www.maplink.com) and **Omnimap** (www.omnimap.com) and the UK-based **Stanfords** (www.stanfords.co.uk). In Germany, try **Deutscher Alpenverein** (www.alpenverein.de), which publishes its own series of climbing maps.

MONEY

ATMs

Just about every sizable town has a *cajero automatico* (ATM) – look for the 'Enlace' sign. They dispense *bolivianos* in 50 and 100 notes (sometimes dollars as well) on Visa, Plus and Cirrus cards, but many Europeans have reported trouble using their cards.

Change

Finding change for bills larger than B$10 is a national pastime as change for larger notes is scarce outside big cities. When exchanging money or making big purchases, request the *cambio* (change) in small denominations. If you can stand the queues, most banks will break large bills.

Credit Cards & Cash Advances

Brand-name plastic, such as Visa, Master-Card and (less often) American Express, may be used in larger cities at better hotels, restaurants and tour agencies. Cash advances of up to US$1000 per day are available on Visa (and less often MasterCard), with no commission, from most Banco Nacional de Bolivia, Banco Mercantil and Banco de Santa Cruz braches. Travel agencies in towns without ATMs will often provide cash advances for clients for 3% to 5% commission.

Currency

Bolivia's unit of currency is the *boliviano* (B$), which is divided into 100 *centavos*. *Bolivianos* come in 10, 20, 50, 100 and 200 denomination notes, with coins worth 10, 20 and 50 *centavos*. Often called *pesos* (the currency was changed from *pesos* to *bolivianos* in 1987), *bolivianos* are extremely difficult to unload outside the country.

Exchanging Money

As a rule, visitors fare best with US dollars. Currency may be exchanged at *casas de cambio* (exchange houses) and at some banks in larger cities. You can often change money in travel agencies and jewelry stores. *Cambistas* (street moneychangers) operate in most cities but only change cash dollars, paying roughly the same as *casas de cambio*. They're convenient after hours, but guard against rip-offs. The rate for cash doesn't vary much from place to place, and there is no black-market rate. Currencies of neighboring countries may be exchanged in border areas and at *casas de cambio* in La Paz. Beware of mangled notes; unless both halves of a repaired banknote bear identical serial numbers, the note is worthless.

International Transfers

The fastest way to have money transferred from abroad is with Western Union. It has offices in all major cities, but charges hefty fees. Your bank can also wire money to a cooperating Bolivian bank for a smaller fee; it may take a couple business days.

Travelers Checks

The rate for travelers checks (1% to 3% commission) is best in La Paz, where it nearly equals the rate for cash; in other large cities it's 3% to 5% lower, and in smaller towns it's sometimes impossible to change checks at all. American Express is the most widely accepted brand, though with persistence you should be able to change other major brands.

PHOTOGRAPHY & VIDEO

Bolivian landscapes swallow film, so don't be caught without a healthy supply. Keep in mind, however, that the combination of high-altitude ultraviolet rays and light reflected off snow or water will conspire to fool both your eye and your light meter.

A polarizing filter is essential when photographing the Altiplano, and will help to reveal the dramatic effects of the exaggerated UV element at high altitude. In the lowlands, conditions include dim light, humidity, haze and leafy interference. For optimum photos, you need either fast film or a tripod for long exposures.

La Paz is generally the best place to pick up film and for repairs; for suggested shops, see p71. As always, avoid exposing your equipment to sand and water.

Photographing People

While some Bolivians are willing photo subjects, others – especially traditional women – may be superstitious about your camera, suspicious of your motives or simply interested in whatever economic advantage they can gain from your desire to photograph them. Whatever the case, be sensitive to the wishes of locals, however photogenic. Ask permission to photograph if a candid shot can't be made; if permission is denied, you should neither insist or snap a picture anyway.

POST

Even the smallest towns have post offices – some are signposted 'Ecobol,' (Empresa Correos de Bolivia). From major towns, the post is generally reliable, but when posting anything important, pay the additional US$0.20 to have it certified.

Postal Rates

Airmail postcards (postales) or letters weighing up to 20g cost US$0.65 to the USA, US$1.10 to Europe and US$1.25 to the rest of the world. For items up to 40g, it's actually a bit cheaper to send things in two separate 20g envelopes. Relatively reliable express-mail service is available for rates similar to those charged by private international couriers.

Parcels

To mail an international parcel in La Paz, take it to the customs desk and have it inspected before sealing it and going to the parcels desk. Parcels to Bolivian destinations should be taken to the desk marked encomiendas. A large notice board in the main hall lists airport departure times for mail to various destinations. A 2kg parcel will cost about US$50 to the USA or US$80 by air; to airmail it to Australia costs US$150. Posting by sea is s-l-o-w but considerably cheaper.

In cities without in-house customs agents, you may have to trek across town to the customs office (aduana). A parcel's chances of arriving at its destination are inversely proportional to its declared value, and to the number of 'inspections' to which it is subjected.

Sending & Receiving Mail

Reliable free poste restante (lista de correos) is available in larger cities. Mail should be addressed to you c/o Poste Restante, Correo Central, La Paz (or whatever city), Bolivia; using only a first initial and capitalizing your entire last name will help avoid confusion. Mail is often sorted into foreign and Bolivian stacks, so those with Latin surnames should check the local stack.

SHOPPING

Each town or region has its own specialty. For traditional musical instruments, head for Tarija or Calle Sagárnaga in La Paz. For weavings, head for the Cordillera Apolobamba or the environs of Sucre. Ceramics are a specialty around Cocha-bamba and lowland arts in tropical woods are sold in Santa Cruz, Trinidad and the Amazon Basin.

Although prices for artesanía (handicrafts) are generally lower at the point of original production, in La Paz and Copacabana you'll find a range of work from all over the country. All sorts of clothing are available in wool, llama and alpaca (which is the finest). Some pieces are hand-dyed and woven or knitted while others are mass-produced by machine.

SOLO TRAVELERS

Bolivia is still very much a man's country, and for a woman traveling solo, this can prove frustrating. Things are changing – Bolivia has had a woman president, Lidia Gueiller Tejada (1979–1980), and from 1993 to 1995 Mónica Medina de Palenque served as mayor of La Paz. Even so, the machismo mind-set remains, and the mere fact that you appear to be unmarried and far from your home and family may cause you to appear suspiciously disreputable.

Because many South American men have become acquainted with foreign women through such reliable media as girlie magazines and North American films and TV, the concept of *gringa fácil* (loose foreign woman) has developed. As Bolivia has cultural roots in southern Europe, it has been subjected to over four centuries of machismo, and many men consider foreign women – especially those traveling alone – to be fair and willing game. Fortunately, the recent increase in tourism to Bolivia has meant that locals are becoming more accustomed to seeing Western travelers, including unaccompanied women. This has significantly reduced the incidence of sexual harassment, but in some places you may still face unwanted attention.

For your part, bear in mind that modesty is expected of women in much of Spanish-speaking Latin America. Short sleeves are more or less acceptable, but hemlines shouldn't be above knee level and trousers should be loose-fitting. The dress code tends to be more liberal the lower you go in altitude, but the men are more aggressive. The best advice is to watch the standards of well-dressed Bolivian women in any particular area and follow their example.

A 100% effective alternative is to find a male traveling companion, but then you may have to contend with being ignored while Bolivians direct their comments to your companion – even if you speak Spanish and he doesn't! If you prefer to travel alone, it's wise to avoid such male domains as bars, sports matches, mines and construction sites. It's all right to catch a lift on a *camión* (truck), especially if there are lots of other people waiting; otherwise, women shouldn't hitchhike alone.

TELEPHONE

The frequency of phone number changes has become something of a shared nationwide joke; most numbers have changed at least a couple of times since the last edition of this book. Recently they seem to have stablized, now that all numbers are seven digits. See www.sittel.gov.bo/mennpn.htm for an thorough explanation (in Spanish) of the new numeration plan which took effect in late 2001.

The Empresa Nacional de Telecomunicaciones (Entel) has telephone offices in nearly every town, usually open 7am to 11:30pm daily. Local calls cost just a few B$s from these offices. Punto Entels are small privately-run outposts offering similar services. Alternatively, street kiosks are often equipped with telephones that charge B$1 for brief local calls. In some tiny villages you'll find pay telephone boxes, but card phones are much more common. While cards come in both magnetic and computer chip varieties, phones only take one or the other. Both card types come in denominations of B$10, 20, 50 and 100.

Area Codes & Long-Distance Calls

Two-digit area codes change by province: 02 for La Paz, Oruro and Potosí; 03 for Santa Cruz, Beni and Pando; and 04 for Cochabamba, Sucre and Tarija. You must add the initial code if you're calling outside your province. If calling from abroad, drop the 0 from the code. If ringing a local mobile phone, dial the 8-digit number; if the mobile is from another city, you must first dial 0 then a two-digit carrier code (10 through 17). In this book, when the given phone number is in another city or town (eg some rural hotels have La Paz reservation numbers), the telephone code is provided along with the number.

International Calls

Bolivia's country code is ☎ 591. The international direct-dialing access code is 00. Calls from Entel offices are getting cheaper all the time to the USA (60¢ per minute), more expensive to Europe (US$1 per minute) and still more to Asia, Australia and Oceania (US$1.50 per minute). Reduced rates take effect nights and weekends.

Some Entel offices accept reverse-charge (collect) calls; others will give you the office's number and let you be called back. For reverse-charge calls from a private line, ring an international operator: for the USA (AT&T toll-free ☎ 800-10-1111; MCI ☎ 800-10-2222), Canada (Teleglobe ☎ 800-10-0101) or UK (BT ☎ 800-10-0044) – beware that these calls can be bank-breakers.

INTERNET CALLS

Much cheaper Net2Phone Internet call centers, charging as little as US$0.15 a minute to the USA and less than US$1 a minute to anywhere in the world, are springing up in major cities but in many cases connections are shaky at best.

TIME

Bolivian time is four hours behind Greenwich Mean Time (GMT). When it's noon in La Paz, it's 4pm in London, 11am in New York, 8am in San Francisco, 4am the following day in Auckland and 2am the following day in Sydney.

TOILETS

First and foremost, learn to live with the fact that facilities are nonexistent in most buses. Smelly, poorly-maintained *baños publicos* abound and charge around US$0.15 (B$1). Carry toilet paper with you wherever you go at all times! Don't put anything in the toilet that didn't come out of you, unless you want to see it again – use the wastebaskets provided for toilet paper. In an emergency, you can always follow the locals' lead and drop your drawers whenever and wherever you feel the need. Some of the most popular spots seems to be below 'No Orinar' signs threatening *multas* (fines) equal to the average Bolivian monthly wage. Whatever you do, wash your hands when you are finished and think about using the facilities at your hotel before heading out.

TOURIST INFORMATION

Although Bolivia's appeal should not be underestimated, much of its attraction lies in the fact that it has been largely ignored by large-scale tourism. While this is changing, the Bolivian tourist industry is still in its formative stages, and government tourist offices still concentrate more on statistics and bureaucratic spending than on promotion of the country's attractions. In fact, most real development and promotion have been courtesy of the private sector.

As a result, domestic tourist offices run by the **Secretaría Nacional de Turismo** (Senatur; www.desarrollo.gov.bo/turismo/Bolivia-Travel) and municipal tourism bodies range from helpful to worthless. Most can provide street plans and answer specific questions about local transport and attractions. The most worthwhile are those in Cochabamba, La Paz and Oruro, while those in other major cities seem to be considerably less useful. There are no tourist offices abroad.

In this book, tourist offices are marked on city maps where applicable. As with many Bolivian operations, posted opening hours are often superseded by the personal whims of their employees.

TOURS

Arrange organized tours in La Paz or the town closest to the attraction you wish to visit. Tours are a convenient way to visit a site when you're short on time or motivation; they are frequently the easiest way to visit remote areas. They're also relatively cheap, but the cost will depend on the number of people in your group. Popular organized tour destinations include Tiahuanaco, the Chacaltaya ski slopes and excursions to remote attractions such as the Cordillera Apolobamba.

There are scores of outfits offering trekking, mountain-climbing and rainforest-adventure packages. For climbing in the Cordilleras, operators offer customized expeditions. They can arrange anything from just a guide and transport right up to equipment, porters and even a cook. Some also rent trekking equipment. Recommended agencies include:

America Tours (Map pp52-3; ☎ 02-237-4204; www.america-ecotours.com; 16 de Julio 1490, Edificio Avenida, No 9, La Paz) Warmly recommended English-speaking agency that organizes trips to anywhere in the country. Specializes in new routes and community-based ecotourism in such places as Parque Nacional Madidi, Parque Nacional Sajama, Rurrenabaque and the Salar de Uyuni.

Andean Summits (☎ 02-242-2106; www.andeansummits.com; Aranzaes 2974, Sopocachi, La Paz) Mountaineering & trekking all over Bolivia, plus adventure tours and archaeology trips.

Colibri (☎ 02-237-8098; www.colibri-adventures.com; Sagárnaga 309, La Paz) Offers comprehensive trekking, mountaineering, mountain biking, jungle trips and 4WD tours; rents gear. French and English spoken.

Diana Tours (Map pp52-3; ☎ 02-235-1158; hotsadt@ ceibo.entelnet.bo; Sagárnaga 328, Hotel Sagárnaga, La Paz) Good-value La Paz city tours, plus day trips to Tiahuanaco, Valle de la Luna, Chacaltaya and the Yungas; cheap tours to Copacabana and Puno.

Fremen Tours (☎ 02-240-7995; www.andes -amazonia.com; Santa Cruz & Socabaya, Galeria Handal, No 13, La Paz) Upmarket agency with offices in Cochabamba, Santa Cruz and Trinidad. Specializes in soft adventure trips in the Amazon and Chapare.

Gravity Assisted Mountain Biking (Map pp52-3; ☎ 02-231-3849; gravity@unete.com; www.gravity bolivia.com; 16 de Julio 1490, Edificio Avenida, No 10, La Paz) Downhill mania on two wheels, from the 'World's Most Dangerous Road' to stylin' singletrack. Ask about Customized Hell Missions and exploratory adventures. Reserve a few days in advance online to avoid missing the experience of a lifetime.

Huayna Potosí Tours (☎ /fax 02-274-0045; berrios@ mail.megalink.com; Sagárnaga 398, La Paz) Runs Refugio Huayna Potosí, which serves as expedition base camp; organizes good-value treks and climbs in the Cordillera Real, Cordillera Apolobamba and elsewhere; English and French spoken.

Inca Land Tours (☎ 02-231-3589; www.incalandtours .com; Sagárnaga 213, No 10, La Paz) Established Peruvian budget operation running tours out of Rurrenabaque and Coroico; it arranges its own charter flights to Rurre and will book tickets in advance with TAM – at a premium.

Neblina Forest (☎ /fax 03-347-1166; www.neblina forest.com; Paraguá 2560, Santa Cruz) Specializes in bird-watching and natural-history tours throughout Bolivia, especially to Noel Kempff Mercado, Amboro and Madidi National Parks, along with the Beni region and the Pantanal.

Pachamama Tours (Map pp52-3; ☎ 02-211-3179; www .magicbolivia.com; Sargárnaga 189, Galería Doryan, No 35, La Paz) Full-service travel agency specializing in soft adventures, 'mystical' and multisport trips and ecotourism, all with bilingual native guides. Branch offices in Santa Cruz and Trinidad offer trips to lesser-known Amazonia and Beni destinations.

Tawa Tours (☎ 02-232-5796; tawa@ceibo.entelnet.bo; Sagárnaga 161, La Paz) French-speaking agency with wide selection of adventure options: mountaineering, jungle trips, trekking, horseback riding and mountain biking.

Turisbus (☎ 245-1341; www.travelperubolivia.com; Hotel Rosario, Illampu 702, La Paz) Upmarket agency specializing in Lake Titicaca tours.

VISAS

Passports must be valid for one year beyond the date of entry. Entry or exit stamps are free, and attempts at charging should be met with polite refusal; ask for a receipt if the issue is pressed. Personal documents – passports, visas or photocopies of these items – must be carried at all times, especially in lowland regions.

Bolivian visa requirements can be arbitrarily changed and interpreted. Each Bolivian consulate and border crossing may have its own entry requirements, procedures and idiosyncrasies.

Citizens of most South American and Western European countries can get a tourist card on entry for stays up to 90 days. Citizens of the USA, Canada, Australia, New Zealand, Japan, South Africa, Israel and many other countries are usually granted 30 days. If you want to stay longer, ask at the point of entry for 90 days and officials will likely oblige. Otherwise, you have to extend your tourist card (easily accomplished at the immigration office in any major city – some nationalities pay for extensions) or apply for a visa. Visas are issued by Bolivian consular representatives, including those in neighboring South American countries. Costs vary according to the consulate and the nationality of the applicant – up to US$50 for a one-year multiple-entry visa.

Overstayers can be fined US$2 per day and may face ribbons of red tape at the border or airport when leaving the country. See the Ministerio de Relaciones Exteriores y Culto website (www.rree.gov.bo) for a complete list (in Spanish) of overseas representatives and current regulations.

In addition to a valid passport and visa, citizens of many Communist, African, Middle Eastern and Asian countries require 'official permission' by cable from the Bolivian Ministry of Foreign Affairs before a visa will be issued.

Vaccination Certificates

Anyone coming from a yellow-fever infected area needs a vaccination certificate to enter Bolivia. Many neighboring countries, including Brazil, also require anyone entering from Bolivia to have proof of a yellow-fever vaccination. If necessary, a jab can often be administered at the border.

WOMEN TRAVELERS

Women's rights in Bolivia are nearing modern standards. That said, avoid testing the system alone in a bar in a miniskirt. Conservative dress and confidence without arrogance are a must for *gringas*. Men are generally more forward and flirtatious in the lowlands than in the Altiplano. See Solo Travelers, p356, for more information.

WORK & VOLUNTEERING

There are hundreds of voluntary and nongovernmental organizations working in Bolivia, but travelers looking for paid work on the spot shouldn't hold their breath. Qualified English teachers angling for work can try the professionally run Centro Boliviano-Americano (p46) in La Paz; there are also offices in other cities.

New, unqualified teachers must forfeit two months' salary in return for their training. Better paying are private school positions teaching math, science or social studies. Accredited teachers can expect to earn up to US$500 per month for a full-time position.

Other popular options include:

Parque Machía (p311; www.intiwarayassi.org; Parque Machía, Villa Tunari, Chapare) Volunteer-run wild animal refuge; minimum commitment is 15 days and no previous experience working with animals is required.

Volunteer Bolivia (p195; www.volunteerbolivia.org; Ecuador 342, Cochabamba) Arranges short- and long-term volunteer work, study and homestay programs throughout Bolivia.

Transport

GETTING THERE & AWAY

AIR

Only a few airlines offer direct flights to Bolivia, thus fares are as high as the altitude; there are direct services to most major South American cities, with flights to/from Chile and Peru being the cheapest. Santa Cruz is an increasingly popular entry point from western European hubs. Due to altitude-related costs, flying into La Paz is more expensive than into Santa Cruz. High season for most fares is from early June to early September, and mid-December to mid-January.

THINGS CHANGE...

The information in this chapter is particularly vulnerable to change. Check directly with the airline or a travel agent to make sure you understand how a fare (and ticket you may buy) works and be aware of the security requirements for international travel. Shop carefully. Details given in this chapter should be regarded as pointers and are not a substitute for your own careful, up-to-date research.

INTERNATIONAL DEPARTURE TAX

The international departure tax, payable in cash only at the airport, is US$25, no matter how long you've been in Bolivia. There's also a 15% tax on international airfares purchased in Bolivia.

Airports & Airlines

Bolivia's principal international airports are La Paz' **El Alto** (LPB; ☎ 02-281-0240), infrequently referred to as the John F Kennedy Memorial, and Santa Cruz' **Viru-Viru International** (VVI; ☎ 181).

Airlines with international flights and offices in La Paz include:

AeroSur (☎ 02-243-0430, 02-231-3233; www.aerosur .com; airline code 5L; hub Santa Cruz, Bolivia)

Aerolíneas Argentinas (☎ 02-235-1711/1624; www.aerolineas.com.ar; airline code AR; hub Buenos Aires, Argentina)

American Airlines (☎ 02-235-5384; www.aa.com; airline code AA; hub Dallas, TX and Chicago, IL)

Grupo Taca (☎ 02-231-3132; www.taca.com; airline code TA; hubs Lima, Peru, San Jose, Costa Rica, San Salvador, El Salvador)

LanChile/LanPeru (☎ 02-235-8377; www.lanchile.com, www.lanperu.com; airline code LA; hub Santiago, Chile)

Lloyd Aéreo Boliviano (LAB; ☎ 02-237-1020/24, 800-10-4321 or 800-10-3001; www.labairlines.com; airline code LB; hub La Paz)

TAM Mercosur(☎ 02-244-3442; www.tam.com.py; airline code PZ; hub Asunción, Paraguay)

Varig (☎ 02-231-4040; www.varig.com.br; airline code RG; hub São Paolo, Brazil)

Tickets

World aviation has never been so competitive, making air travel better value than ever. Research your options carefully to get yourself the best deal. Online ticket sales work well if you are doing a simple one-way or return trip on specified dates. However, whiz-bang online fare generators are no substitute for a knowledgeable travel agent.

If you're time-rich and money-poor, try an air-ticket auction site such as **Priceline .com** (www.priceline.com) or **SkyAuction.com** (www.sky auction.com), where you bid on your own fare.

The restrictions are not crippling, but read the fine print.

Some of the better international online ticketing sites include:

Expedia (www.expedia.msn.com) Microsoft's USA travel site has links to sites for Canada, the UK and Germany.

Flight Centre International (www.flightcentre.com) Respected operator for direct flights with sites for Australia, New Zealand, the UK, USA and Canada.

Flights.com (www.eltexpress.com) A truly international site for flight-only tickets; cheap fares and an easy-to-search database.

STA (www.sta.com) The leader in world student travel but you don't necessarily have to be a student.

Travel.com.au (www.travel.com.au) A good Australian site – you can look up fares and flights into and out of the country.

Travelocity (www.travelocity.com) This US site allows you to search fares (in US$) from/to practically anywhere.

INTERCONTINENTAL (RTW) TICKETS

Round-the-world (RTW) tickets can be real bargains if you are coming to South America from the other side of the world. They are generally put together by the airline alliances, and give you a limited period (usually a year) in which to circumnavigate the globe.

An alternative type of RTW ticket is one put together by a travel agent. These tickets are more expensive than airline RTW fares, but you chose your itinerary. Travel agents, by combining tickets from two low-cost airlines, can also offer multiple destination fares which are cheaper than a RTW ticket, and allow for two stops on the way to and from South America.

Some online ticket sites for intercontinental tickets include:

Airbrokers (www.airbrokers.com) A US company specialising in cheap RTW tickets.

Oneworld (www.oneworld.com) Airline alliance that offers a cheaper version of its RTW ticket.

Roundtheworld.com (www.roundtheworldflights.com) An excellent site that allows you to build your own trip from the UK.

Star Alliance (www.staralliance.com) Another airline alliance that offers a cheaper version of its RTW ticket.

From Australia & New Zealand

Travel between Australasia and South America ain't cheap, so it makes sense to think in terms of a RTW ticket, or a round-trip ticket to Europe with a stopover in the USA, Rio de Janeiro, Buenos Aires or Santiago. Round-trip fares from Sydney to La Paz via Auckland and Santiago start around A$2200/2600 in low/high season. Fares via the USA are considerably more expensive, starting around A$2600 return in the low season. RTW ticket including La Paz start around A$2420/2780 low/high.

For discount fares check **STA Travel** (☎ 1300-733 035; www.statravel.com.au) or **Flight Centre International** (☎ 1300-133 133; www.flightcentre.com.au). For online bookings, try www.travel.com.au or www.travel.co.nz. **Destination Holidays** (☎ 03-9725 4655, 800-337 050 outside Melbourne; www.south-america.com.au) specializes in Latin American travel. Also check the advertisements in Saturday editions of newspapers, such as Melbourne's *Age* or the *Sydney Morning Herald*.

The most direct routes on Qantas and its partners are from Sydney to Santiago or Buenos Aires. The other South American route is with Qantas or Air New Zealand from Sydney to Papeete (Tahiti), connecting with a LanChile flight via Easter Island to Santiago, with a free onward flight to either Rio or Buenos Aires.

The best RTW options are probably those with Aerolíneas Argentinas combined with other airlines, including Air New Zealand, British Airways, Iberia, Singapore Airlines, Thai or KLM. A 'Visit South America' fare, good for three months, allows you two stops in South America plus one in the US, then returns to Auckland. The Qantas version of an RTW ticket is its 'OneWorld Explorer' fare, which allows you to visit up to six continents with three stopovers in each one.

From Continental Europe

The best places in Europe for cheap airfares are student travel agencies (you don't have to be a student to use them). If airfares are expensive where you live, try contacting a London agent, who may be able to issue a ticket by mail. The cheapest flights from Europe are typically charters, usually with fixed outward and return flight dates.

Some fares include a stopover in the USA. Note that passengers through New York (JFK) or Miami must pass through US immigration procedures, even if they won't be visiting the USA. That means you'll either need a US visa or be eligible for the Visa Waiver Program, which is open to Australians, New Zealanders and most Western Europeans, unless they're traveling on a non-accredited airline (which includes most Latin American airlines).

From Europe, you can search for cheap airfares at **DiscountAirfares.com** (www.etn.nl).

There are bucket shops by the dozen in Western European capitals. Many travel agents in Europe have ties with STA Travel, where you'll find cheap tickets that may be altered once without charge. Other discount outlets in major transport hubs include:

Alternativ Tours Berlin (☎ 030-881 2089; www.alternativ-tours.de)

CTS Rome (☎ 199/840-501150; www.cts.it)

Kilroy Travel Amsterdam (☎ 20 524 5100; www.kilroy travel.com)

NBBS Reizen Amsterdam (☎ 0900-10 20 300; www.nbbs.nl)

SSR/STA Zürich (☎ 297 11 11; www.statravel.ch)

USIT Dublin (☎ 0818 20020; www.usitworld.com)

Voyages Wasteel Paris (☎ 825-887-070; www.wasteels.fr)

From South America

LAB connects La Paz to Rio de Janiero, Buenos Aires, Lima, Cusco, Santiago, Arica and Iquique several times a week if not daily. Aerolíneas Argentinas flies daily between Santa Cruz and Buenos Aires. Varig flies daily between La Paz and Rio de Janiero via Santa Cruz. LanPeru shuttles frequently between Lima and La Paz.

LanChile connects La Paz with Arica, Iquique and Santiago. Passengers departing Chile are subject to a departure tax of US$20, and Australians, Canadians and US citizens landing in Santiago must pay an 'entry tax' of US$100 per person.

Paraguayan TAM Mercosur connects Asuncíon with La Paz and Santa Cruz.

LanPeru flies daily to Cusco (often via Lima) and LAB flies there three times weekly. Peru levies an air-ticket tax of 21% for Peruvian residents and 7% for non-resident tourists.

From the UK

Discount air travel is big business in London. Advertisements for many agencies appear in the travel pages of the weekend broadsheet newspapers, in *Time Out*, the *Evening Standard* and in the free magazine *TNT*. It's considerably cheaper to fly to one of the other South American cities than direct to La Paz. From London most of the cheaper flights are via a couple of USA cities, usually Washington and Miami. Expect to pay around US$900 for a return to Rio de Janeiro, or US$1300 for a return to La Paz in the low season. RTW's from London that take in South America (Santiago and Rio de Janeiro) start from US$2650.

London-based South American specialists include **Journey Latin America** (JLA; ☎ 020-8747 8315; www.journeylatinamerica.co.uk); **South American Experience** (☎ 020-7976 5511; www.southamerican experience.co.uk); and **Austral Tours** (☎ 020-7233 5384; www.latinamerica.co.uk).

Recommended travel agencies include:

Bridge the World (☎ 0870 444 7474; www.b-t-w.co.uk)

Flightbookers (☎ 0870 010 7000; www.ebookers.com)

Flight Centre (☎ 0870 890 8099; flightcentre.co.uk)

North-South Travel (☎ 01245 608 291; www.north southtravel.co.uk) Donates profits to projects in the developing world.

Quest Travel (☎ 0870 442 3542; www.questtravel.com)

STA Travel (☎ 0870 160 0599; www.statravel.co.uk) Well-established student-focused budget agency serving travelers aged 26 and under.

Trailfinders (Long-haul line ☎ 020-7938 3939; www.trailfinders.co.uk) Good general agency with offices throughout the UK.

Travel Bag (☎ 0870 890 1456; www.travelbag.co.uk)

From the USA & Canada

Inexpensive tickets from North American gateways (Miami is cheapest) usually have restrictions. Often there's a two-week advance-purchase requirement, and usually you must stay at least one week and no more than three months (prices often double for longer periods). For an idea of what's available, peruse the Sunday travel sections of major newspapers and free alternative weeklies.

Look for agencies specializing in South America, such as **eXito** (☎ 800-655-4053; www.exitotravel.com), which has an expert staff and is superb for anyone traveling with special interests. Also recommended is the **Educational Travel Center** (☎ 800-747-5551; www.edtrav.com).

The following are recommended Internet-only consolidators:

Airtech (☎ 212-219-7000; www.airtech.com)

Airtreks (☎ 877-247-8735; www.airtreks.com)

Cheap Tickets (☎ 888-922-8849; www.cheaptickets.com)

Most flights from Canada involve connecting via a US gateway like Miami or Los Angeles. Canada's national student travel agency is **Travel Cuts** (☎ 866-246-9762 in Canada & USA; www.travelcuts.com). It offers great deals for students and those under 26 there are good fares for the general public as well. It has offices in several US cities. Owned by Travel Cuts, **The Adventure Travel Company** (☎ 1-888-238-2887 in Canada, ☎ 415-247-1800 in USA; www.atcadventure.com) deals with the general public as much as it does with students, and offers some excellent prices.

LAND
Border Crossings
If your documents are in order and you are willing to answer a few questions about the aim of your visit, entry into Bolivia should be a breeze. If crossing at a smaller border post, you may be asked to pay an 'exit fee'. Unless otherwise noted in the text, these fees are strictly unofficial.

ARGENTINA
There are two major overland crossings: at Yacuiba/Pocitos and between Villazón and La Quiaca. The crossing between Bermejo and Aguas Blancas is minor. Argentine officials are vigilant about drugs and no one entering from Bolivia escapes suspicion. Expect thorough customs searches both at the frontier and 20km down the road, inside Argentina.

BRAZIL
Corumbá, opposite the Bolivian border town of Quijarro, is the busiest port of entry, and has both train and bus connections from São Paulo, Rio de Janeiro, Cuiabá and southern Brazil.

From Brasiléia in Acre you can cross into Cobija, Bolivia, where you'll find a dry-season road and unreliable year-round flights to Riberalta and on to La Paz. A more popular crossing is by ferry from Guajará-Mirim, across the Río Mamoré in Brazil, into Guayaramerín. From there, you can fly to Trinidad, Santa Cruz or La Paz, or travel the long and dusty bus routes to Riberalta and on to Cobija, Rurrenabaque or La Paz.

CHILE
Note that meat and produce cannot be carried from Bolivia into Chile and will be confiscated at the border. Owing to the high altitudes, warm clothing is essential for any land crossing between Bolivia and Chile.

The most popular route is from La Paz to Arica via Tambo Quemado and Lauca National Park. The San Pedro Atacama to Salar de Uyuni crossing is gaining popularity. Going to or coming from Antofagasta is more complicated, but do-able.

PARAGUAY
The three-day overland Trans-Chaco route (p264) between Villamontes, Bolivia and Asunción, Paraguay now has a daily bus service, but it still ain't a breeze.

The easiest route between Paraguay and Bolivia is to cross from Pedro Juan Caballero (Paraguay) to Ponta Porã (Brazil), and then travel by bus or train to Corumbá (Brazil) and Quijarro (Bolivia).

PERU
Puno is Peru's main access point for Bolivia. The quicker but less interesting route is via the frontier at Desaguadero, where there are frequent *micros* to La Paz. The more scenic route is via Copacabana and the Estrecho de Tiquina (Straits of Tiquina). It's also possible to use the obscure border crossing near Puerto Acosta, north of Lake Titicaca.

Car & Motorcycle
Details on how to enter South America in your own vehicle are beyond the scope of this book. Suffice it to say that you can enter Bolivia by road from any of the neighboring countries. The routes from Brazil and Chile are poor, and the one from Paraguay should be considered only with a 4WD. The routes from Argentina and Peru pose no significant problems.

Foreigners entering Bolivia from another country need a circulation card *(hoja de ruta)*, available from the Servicio Nacional de Tránsito at the frontier. This document must be presented and stamped at all police posts – variously known as *trancas*, *tránsitos* or *controles* – which are spaced along highways and just outside major cities. *Peajes* (tolls) are often charged at these checkpoints and vehicles may be searched for contraband.

For details about driving in Bolivia, see Getting Around (p365).

TRANSPORT

RIVER
Brazil & Paraguay
Ferries facilitate short hops across borders in the Amazon Basin at far flung locales such as Cobija, Guayaramerín and from Parque Nacional Noel Kempff Mercado to Pimienteras in Brazil.

River transport between Asunción, Paraguay and Bolivia (via Corumbá, Brazil) is likely to involve a series of adventurous short journeys and informal arrangements with individual boat captains. From Asunción, there's a regular river service to Concepción (Paraguay). Beyond Concepción is where the informal arrangements begin. You'll probably wind up doing it in two stages: Concepción to Bahía Negra (northern Paraguay), then Bahía Negra to Corumbá.

Peru
An adventurous riverboat route is possible through the rainforest from Puerto Heath in Bolivia to Puerto Maldonado in Peru.

GETTING AROUND

AIR
Air travel in Bolivia is inexpensive and it's the quickest and most reliable means of reaching out-of-the-way places. It's also the only means of transport that isn't washed out during the wet season. Although weather-related disruptions definitely occur, planes eventually get through even during summer flooding in northern Bolivia.

Bolivian Airlines
Bolivia's national carrier LAB, private carrier AeroSur and upstart Amaszonas (www.amaszonas.com) connect the country's major cities and remote corners. They all charge similar fares and allow 15kg of luggage, excluding 3kg of carry-on luggage. With LAB you must reconfirm your reservations 72 hours before the flight or your reservations may be canceled.

The military airline, Transportes Aéreos Militares (TAM), operates cheaper domestic flights in smaller planes that fly closer to the landscape. As military operations go, TAM is remarkably reliable, but schedules can change without notice and reservations can only be made in the town of departure. They are strict with the 15kg baggage limit; each additional kilo costs around US$0.50, depending on the length of the flight.

Air Passes
LAB offers a 45-day Visite Bolivia (VIBOL) air pass, which must be purchased abroad and allows a circuit through four different major Bolivian cities. If you're flying into Bolivia with LAB, it costs US$150; those traveling on other airlines pay US$225 (US$145 for kids). The LAB pass, on sale only within Bolivia, also costs US$225. AeroSur offers a similarly priced pass.

Domestic Departure Taxes
AASANA, the government agency responsible for airports and air traffic, charges a US$1–$2 domestic departure tax, which is payable at their desk after check-in. Some airports also levy a municipal tax of up to US$1.

BICYCLE
For cyclists who can cope with the challenges of cold winds, poor road conditions, high altitude and steep terrain, Bolivia is a paradise. Traffic isn't a serious problem, but intimidating buses and *camiones* may leave cyclists lost in clouds of dust or embedded in mud. Finding supplies may prove difficult, so cyclists in remote areas must carry ample food and water. Given these challenges, many prefer to leave the work to a tour company. Mountain-biking hubs and hotspots include La Paz, Sorata and the Yungas.

Bolivia has its fair share of inexpensive bikes – mostly supermarket beaters from China. Quality new wheels are few and far between. Your best bet for purchasing a used, touring-worthy stead is through agencies in La Paz. Try Gravity Assisted Mountain Biking (p358) for spare parts and help with repairs.

See Mountain Biking (p348) for details.

BOAT
Ferry
Bolivia's only public ferry service operates between San Pedro and San Pablo, across the Straits of Tiquina on Lake Titicaca. To visit any of Lake Titicaca's Bolivian islands, you can travel by launch or rowboat. To

the Huyñaymarka islands in the lake's southernmost extension, boats and tours are available in Huatajata. To visit Isla del Sol, you can take a tour, hire a launch or catch a scheduled service in Copacabana, or look for a lift in Yampupata. Cruises by motorboat or hydrofoil are provided by a couple of well-established tour companies.

River Boat

The most relaxing way to get around the Amazon is by river. There's no scheduled passenger service, so travelers almost invariably wind up on some sort of cargo vessel. The most popular routes are from Puerto Villarroel to Trinidad and Trinidad to Guayaramerín. There are also much less frequented routes from Rurrenabaque or Puerto Heath to Riberalta.

BUS

Buses and their various iterations are the most popular form of Bolivian transport. It's relatively safe and cheap, if a bit uncomfortable or nerve-wracking at times. Long-distance bus lines in Bolivia are called *flotas*, large buses are known as *buses* (*boo-sehs*) and small ones are called *micros* (*mee-*cros). If looking for a bus terminal, ask for *la terminal terrestre* or *la terminal de buses*.

Thankfully, the Bolivian road network is improving as more kilometers are paved. Modern coaches use the best roads, while older vehicles ply minor secondary routes.

It's safer and the views are better during the day. Drunken driving is illegal, but bus drivers have been known to sip the hard stuff on long nighttime hauls. Except on the most popular runs, most companies' buses inexplicably depart at roughly the same time, regardless of the number of competitors.

Between any two cities, you should have no trouble finding at least one daily bus. On the most popular routes you can choose between dozens of daily departures.

Classes & Costs

The only choices you'll have to make are on major, long-haul routes, where the better companies offer *coche cama* (sleeper) service for around double the *común* or normal going rate. The VCR on the newest buses will be in better shape than the

reclining seats, heaters *may* function and toilets (yes, toilets) *may* work. Whether you will actually be able to sleep is another matter.

Reservations

To be safe, reserve bus tickets at least several hours in advance. For the lowest fare, purchase immediately after the driver starts the engine. Many buses depart in the afternoon or evening, to arrive at their destination in the wee hours of the morning. Often you can crash on these buses until sunrise. On most major routes there are also daytime departures.

CAR & MOTORCYCLE

The advantages of a private vehicle include schedule flexibility, access to remote areas and the chance to seize photo opps. However, only a few Bolivian roads are paved and others are in varying stages of decay, so high-speed travel is impossible (unless, of course, you're a Bolivian bus driver), The typically narrow and winding mountain roads often meander along contours and rocky riverbeds.

The undaunted should prepare their expeditions carefully. Bear in mind that spare parts are a rare commodity outside cities. A high-clearance 4WD vehicle is essential for off-road travel. You'll need a set of tools, spare tires, a puncture repair kit, extra gas and fluids, and as many spare parts as possible. For emergencies, carry camping equipment and plenty of rations.

Low-grade (85-octane) gasoline and diesel fuel are available at *surtidores de gasolina* (gas dispensers) – also known as *bombas de gasolina* (gas pumps) – in all cities and major towns. Gas costs around US$0.50 per liter.

Motorcycle

In lowland areas, where temperatures are hot and roads are scarce, motorbikes are popular for zipping around the plazas, as well as exploring areas not served by public transportation. They can be rented for around US$12 to US$15 per 24 hours from moto-taxi stands. Gringo-run agencies offering motorcycle tours through the rugged highland are popping up like mushrooms in the larger cities.

TRANSPORT

Bear in mind that many travel insurance policies will not cover you for injuries arising from motorbike accidents, so check your policy carefully.

Drivers

Many people just want transport to trailheads or base camps rather than a tour. Examples of one-way transport prices from La Paz with a private driver *(chofer)*, regardless of the number of passengers (6 to 8 maximum), include the following: Refugio Huayna Potosí – US$50; Estancia Una (for Illimani climb) – US$120 to US$140; Curva, for the Cordillera Apolobamba trek – US$250 to US$350; Chuñavi or Lambate, for the Yunga Cruz trek – US$150; Sajama – US$300; and Rurrenabaque – US$300. Private Salar de Uyuni and Southwest Circuit tours cost from US$150 per day.

Several La Paz drivers are recommended for their value. Bolivian Climbing Federation secretary **Carlos Aguilar** (☎ 715-25897) speaks some English and provides safe, informative and inexpensive jeep trips. He also works as a climbing guide and is especially popular with mountaineers. **Oscar L Vera Coca** (☎ 223-0453; 715-61283) also speaks some English. Another recommendation is **Romero Ancasi** (☎ 283-1363; 719-21318), who offers experienced driving in well-maintained Toyota Landcruisers.

Another option is **Minibuses Yungueña** (☎ 221-3513), which contracts drivers and 2WD minibuses.

Driving License

Most Bolivian car-rental agencies will accept your home driver's license, but if you're doing a lot of driving, it's wise to back it up with an International Driver's License. Bolivia doesn't require special motorcycle licenses, but neighboring countries do. For motorcycle and moped rentals, all that is normally required is a passport.

Rental

Few travelers in Bolivia rent self-driven vehicles. Only the most reputable agencies service vehicles regularly, and insurance bought from rental agencies may cover only accidental damage; breakdowns may be considered the renter's problem.

You must be over 21 or 25 years, have a driver's license from your home country, have a major credit card or cash deposit (typically around US$1000) and, usually, accident insurance. You'll be charged a daily rate and a per-kilometer rate (some agencies allow a set number of free kilometers). They'll also want you to leave your passport as a deposit.

Costs vary widely but the average daily rate for a small VW or Toyota starts at US$25, plus an additional US$0.30 to US$0.35 per kilometer. For the least expensive 4WD, companies charge US$40 per day plus US$0.40 to US$0.45 per kilometer. Weekly rates (with up to 1600km free) start around US$250 for a compact and US$450 in a 4WD pickup.

For listings of better-known agencies, see the Getting Around section in the major cities.

Road Rules

Traffic regulations aren't that different than those in North America or Europe. Speed limits are infrequently posted, but in most cases the state of the road will prevent you from exceeding them anyway.

Bolivians keep to the right. When two cars approach an uncontrolled intersection from different directions, the driver who honks first has right of way if intending to pass straight through. Turning vehicles, of course, must wait until the way is clear before doing so. When two vehicles meet on a narrow mountain road, the downhill vehicle must reverse until there's room for the other to pass.

HITCHING

Thanks to relatively easy access to *camiones* and a profusion of buses, hitching isn't really popular in Bolivia. It's not unknown and drivers of *movilidades* – *coches* (cars), *camionetas* (pickup trucks), NGO vehicles, gas trucks and other vehicles – are usually happy to pick up passengers when they have room. Always ask the price, if any, before climbing aboard; if they do charge, it should amount to about half the bus fare for the equivalent distance.

Please note that hitchhiking is never entirely safe in any country. If you decide to hitch, you should understand that you are taking a small but potentially serious risk. Travel in pairs and let someone know where you're planning to go.

LOCAL TRANSPORT
Micros, Minibuses & Trufis

Micros – half-size buses – are used in larger cities and serve as Bolivia's least expensive form of public transport. They follow set routes, and the route numbers or letters are usually marked on a placard behind the windshield. This is often backed by a description of the route, including the streets that are followed to reach the end of the line. They can be hailed anywhere along their routes. When you want to disembark, move toward the front and tell the driver or assistant where you want them to stop.

Colectivos (minibuses) and *trufis* (which may be either cars or minibuses) are prevalent in both La Paz and Cochabamba, and follow set routes that are numbered and described on placards. They are always cheaper than taxis and they're nearly as convenient. As with *micros*, you can board or alight anywhere along their route.

Taxis

Urban taxis are relatively inexpensive. Few are equipped with meters, but in most cities and towns there are standard per-person fares for short hauls. In some places taxis are collective and behave more like *trufis*, charging a set rate per person. However, if you have three or four people all headed for the same place, you may be able to negotiate a reduced rate for the entire group.

Radio taxis, on the other hand, always charge a set rate for up to four people; if you squeeze in five people, the fare increases by a small margin. When using taxis, try to have enough change to cover the fare; drivers often like to plead a lack of change in the hope that you'll give them the benefit of the difference. As a general rule, taxi drivers aren't tipped, but if an individual goes beyond the call of duty, a tip of a couple B$s wouldn't be amiss.

TRAIN

Since privatization in the mid-1990s, passenger rail services have been cut back. The western network operated by the **Empresa Ferroviaria Andina** (FCA; www.fca.com.bo) runs from Oruro to Villazón (on the Argentine border); a branch line runs southwest from Uyuni to Avaroa, (on the Chilean border).

In the east, there's a line from Santa Cruz to the Brazilian frontier at Quijarro, where you cross to the Pantanal. An infrequently used service goes south from Santa Cruz to Yacuiba on the Argentine border.

Reservations

Even in major towns along the routes, tickets can be reserved only on the day of departure. At smaller stations tickets may not be available until the train has arrived. Larger intermediate stations are allotted only a few seat reservations, and tickets go on sale quite literally whenever employees decide to open up. The best infomation is usually available from the *jefe de la estación* (stationmaster).

When buying tickets, make sure you have a passport for each person for whom you're buying a ticket. This is a remnant from the days when ticket scalping was profitable.

Health

CONTENTS

BEFORE YOU GO

Prevention is the key to staying healthy while abroad. Travelers who receive the recommended vaccines and follow common-sense precautions usually come away with nothing more than a little diarrhea.

Since most vaccines don't produce immunity until at least two weeks after they're given, visit a physician four to eight weeks before departure. Ask your doctor for an International Certificate of Vaccination (otherwise known as the yellow booklet), which will list all the vaccinations you've received. This is mandatory for countries that require proof of yellow fever vaccination on entry, but it's a good idea to carry it wherever you travel.

INSURANCE

If your health insurance does not cover you for medical expenses abroad, consider supplemental insurance. (Check the subwwway section of the Lonely Planet website at www.lonelyplanet.com/subwwway for more information.) Find out in advance if your insurance plan will make payments directly to providers or reimburse you later for overseas health expenditures.

MEDICAL CHECKLIST

- Antibiotics
- Antidiarrheal drugs (eg loperamide)
- Acetaminophen (Tylenol) or aspirin
- Anti-inflammatory drugs (eg ibuprofen)
- Antihistamines (for hay fever and allergic reactions)
- Antibacterial ointment (eg Bactroban) for cuts and abrasions
- Steroid cream or cortisone (for poison ivy and other allergic rashes)
- Bandages, gauze, gauze rolls
- Adhesive or paper tape
- Scissors, safety pins, tweezers
- Thermometer
- Pocket knife
- DEET-containing insect repellent for the skin
- Permethrin-containing insect spray for clothing, tents and bed nets
- Sun block
- Oral rehydration salts
- Iodine tablets (for water purification)
- Syringes and sterile needles
- Acetazolamide (Diamox) for altitude sickness

Bring medications in their original containers, clearly labeled. A signed, dated letter from your physician describing all medical conditions and medications, including generic names is also a good idea. If carrying syringes or needles, be sure to have a physician's letter documenting their medical necessity.

ONLINE RESOURCES

There is a wealth of travel health advice on the Internet. For further information, the Lonely Planet website at www.lonelyplanet.com is a good place to start. The World Health Organization publishes a superb book, called *International Travel and Health*, which is revised annually and is available online at no cost at www.who.int/ith/. Another website of general interest is MD Travel Health at www.mdtravelhealth.com, which provides complete travel health recommendations for every country, updated daily, also at no cost.

RECOMMENDED VACCINATIONS

The only required vaccine is yellow fever, and that's only if you're arriving in Bolivia from a yellow-fever-infected country in Africa or the Americas. However, a number of vaccines are recommended:

Vaccine	Recommended for	Dosage	Side effects
Hepatitis A	All travelers	One dose before trip; booster 6–12 months later	Soreness at injection site; headaches; body aches
Typhoid	All travelers	Four capsules by mouth, one taken every other day	Abdominal pain; nausea; rash
Yellow fever	Travelers to Beni, Cochabamba, Santa Cruz, La Paz, possibly other areas	One dose lasts 10 years	Headaches; body aches; severe reactions are rare
Hepatitis B	Long-term travelers in close contact with the local population	Three doses over 6-month period	Soreness at injection site; low-grade fever
Rabies	Travelers who may have contact with animals and may not have access to medical care	Three doses over 3–4 week period	Soreness at injection site; headaches; body aches.
Tetanus-diphtheria	All travelers who haven't had booster within 10 years	One dose lasts 10 years	Soreness at injection site
Measles	Travelers born after 1956 who've had only one measles vaccination	One dose	Fever; rash; joint pains; allergic reactions
Chickenpox	Travelers who've never had chickenpox	Two doses one month apart	Fever; mild case of chickenpox

It's usually a good idea to consult your government's travel health website before departure, if one is available:

United States – www.cdc.gov/travel/
Canada – www.hc-sc.gc.ca/pphb-dgspsp/tmp-pmv/pub_e.html
United Kingdom – www.doh.gov.uk/traveladvice/index.htm
Australia – www.dfat.gov.au/travel/

FURTHER READING

For further information see *Healthy Travel Central & South America*, also from Lonely Planet. If you're traveling with children, Lonely Planet's *Travel with Children* may be useful. The *ABC of Healthy Travel*, by E. Walker et al, is another valuable resource.

IN TRANSIT

DEEP VEIN THROMBOSIS

Blood clots may form in the legs (deep vein thrombosis) during plane flights, chiefly because of prolonged immobility. The longer the flight, the greater the risk. Though most blood clots are reabsorbed uneventfully, some may break off and travel through the blood vessels to the lungs, where they could cause life-threatening complications.

The chief symptom of deep vein thrombosis is swelling or pain of the foot, ankle or calf, usually but not always on just one side. When a blood clot travels to the lungs, it may cause chest pain and difficulty breathing. Travelers with any of these symptoms should immediately seek medical attention.

To prevent the development of deep vein thrombosis on long flights you should walk about the cabin, perform isometric compressions of the leg muscles (ie contract the leg muscles while sitting), drink plenty of fluids, and avoid alcohol and tobacco.

JET LAG & MOTION SICKNESS

Jet lag is common when crossing more than five time zones resulting in insomnia, fatigue, malaise or nausea. To avoid jet lag try drinking plenty of fluids (non-alcoholic) and eating light meals. On arrival get exposure to natural sunlight and readjust your schedule (for meals, sleep, etc) as soon as possible.

Antihistamines such as dimenhydrinate (Dramamine) and meclizine (Antivert, Bonine) are usually the first choice for treating motion sickness. Their main side-effect is drowsiness. An herbal alternative is ginger, which works like a charm for some people.

IN BOLIVIA

AVAILABILITY & COST OF HEALTH CARE

Good medical care is available in the larger cities, but may be difficult to find in rural areas. Many doctors and hospitals expect payment in cash, regardless of whether you have travel health insurance. For a medical emergency in La Paz, call **SAMI ambulance** (☎ 279-9911) or go directly to the **Clinica del Sur emergency room** (☎ 278-4001/02/03; Hernando Siles Ave, cnr Calle 7, Obrajes). In Cochabamba, call the **Medicar Emergency Ambulance Service** (☎ 453-3222) or go to the emergency room of **Centro Medico Boliviano Beluga** (☎ 422-9407, 425-0928, 423-1403; Antezana St between Venezuela and Paccieri N-0455). In Santa Cruz, go to the emergency room of **Clinica Angel Foianini** (☎ 336-2211, 336-6001/02/03/04; Av Irala 468). A taxi may get you faster to the emergency room than an ambulance.

For the names of physicians, dentists, hospitals and laboratories for routine medical problems, the US Embassy provides an online directory of medical resources at http://bolivia.usembassy.gov/english/con sular/medicalresources.htm.

If you develop a life-threatening medical problem, you'll probably want to be evacuated to a country with state-of-the-art medical care. Since this may cost tens of thousands of dollars, be sure you have insurance to cover this before you depart. You can find a list of medical evacuation and travel insurance companies on the US State Department website at www.travel.state .gov/medical.html.

Bolivian pharmacies offer most of the medications available in other countries.

In general it's safer to buy pharmaceuticals made by international manufacturers rather than local companies. Make sure you use a pharmacy staffed by a pharmacist, not just a clerk. For a list of pharmacies, see the US Embassy website above.

INFECTIOUS DISEASES
Malaria

Malaria occurs in every South American country except Chile, Uruguay and the Falkland Islands. It's transmitted by mosquito bites, usually between dusk and dawn. The main symptom is high spiking fevers, which may be accompanied by chills, sweats, headache, body aches, weakness, vomiting or diarrhea. Severe cases may involve the central nervous system and lead to seizures, confusion, coma and death.

Taking malaria pills is strongly recommended for areas below 2500 m (8202 ft) in the departments of Beni, Chuquisaca, Cochabamba, La Paz, Pando, Santa Cruz and Tarija. The risk is highest in the departments of Beni, Pando, Santa Cruz and Tarija, and in the provinces of Lacareja, Rurenabaque, and North and South Yungas in La Paz Department. Falciparum malaria, which is the most dangerous kind, occurs in Beni and Pando.

There is a choice of three malaria pills, all of which work about equally well. Mefloquine (Lariam) is taken once weekly in a dosage of 250 mg, starting one to two weeks before arrival, and continuing through the trip and for four weeks after return. The problem is that a certain percentage of people (the number is controversial) develop neuropsychiatric side effects, which may range from mild to severe. Atovaquone/proguanil (Malarone) is a newly approved combination pill taken once daily with food, starting two days before arrival and continuing through the trip and for seven days after departure. Side effects are typically mild. Doxycycline is a third alternative, but may cause an exaggerated sunburn reaction.

In general Malarone seems to cause fewer side effects than mefloquine and is becoming more popular. The chief disadvantage is that it has to be taken daily. For longer trips it's probably worth trying mefloquine; for shorter trips, Malarone will be the drug of choice for most people.

Protecting yourself against mosquito bites is just as important as taking malaria pills (see the recommendations below), since none of the pills are 100% effective.

If you may not have access to medical care while traveling, you should bring along additional pills for emergency self-treatment, which you should take if you can't reach a doctor and you develop symptoms that suggest malaria, such as high spiking fevers. One option is to take four tablets of Malarone once daily for three days. However Malarone should not be used for treatment if you're already taking it for prevention. An alternative is to take 650mg quinine three times daily, and 100mg doxycycline twice daily for one week. If you start self-medication, see a doctor at the earliest possible opportunity.

If you develop a fever after returning home, see a physician, as malaria symptoms may not occur for months.

Yellow Fever

Yellow fever is a life-threatening viral infection transmitted by mosquitoes in forested areas. The illness begins with flu-like symptoms, which may include fever, chills, headache, muscle aches, backache, loss of appetite, nausea and vomiting. These symptoms usually subside in a few days, but one person in six enters a second, toxic phase characterized by recurrent fever, vomiting, listlessness, jaundice, kidney failure and hemorrhage, leading to death in up to half of the cases. There is no treatment except for supportive care.

Yellow-fever vaccine is strongly recommended for all those visiting areas where yellow fever occurs, which at time of publication included the departments of Beni, Cochabamba, Santa Cruz and La Paz. For the latest information on which areas in Bolivia are reporting yellow fever, go to the 'Blue Sheet' on the CDC website at www.cdc.gov/travel/blusheet.htm.

Proof of vaccination is *required* from all travelers arriving from a yellow-fever-infected country in Africa or the Americas.

Yellow-fever vaccine is given only in approved yellow-fever vaccination centers, which provide validated International Certificates of Vaccination ('yellow booklets'). The vaccine should be given at least 10 days before any potential exposure to yellow fever, and remains effective for approximately 10 years. Reactions to the vaccine are generally mild, and may include headaches, muscle aches, low-grade fevers or discomfort at the injection site. Severe, life-threatening reactions have been described but are extremely rare. In general the risk of becoming ill from the vaccine is far less than the risk of becoming ill from yellow fever, and you're strongly encouraged to get the vaccine.

Taking measures to protect yourself from mosquito bites, as described on p374, is an essential part of preventing yellow fever.

Dengue Fever

Dengue fever is a viral infection found throughout South America. Dengue is transmitted by Aedes mosquitoes, which bite preferentially during the daytime and are usually found close to human habitations, often indoors. They breed primarily in artificial water containers, such as jars, barrels, cans, cisterns, metal drums, plastic containers and discarded tires. As a result, dengue is especially common in densely populated, urban environments.

Dengue usually causes flu-like symptoms, including fever, muscle aches, joint pains, headaches, nausea and vomiting, often followed by a rash. The body aches may be quite uncomfortable, but most cases resolve uneventfully in a few days. Severe cases usually occur in children under age 15 who are experiencing their second dengue infection.

There is no treatment for dengue fever except to take analgesics such as acetaminophen/paracetamol (Tylenol) and drink plenty of fluids. Severe cases may require hospitalization for intravenous fluids and supportive care. There is no vaccine. The cornerstone of prevention is insect protection measures, see page 374.

Hepatitis A

Hepatitis A is the second most common travel-related infection (after travelers' diarrhea). It's a viral infection of the liver that is usually acquired by ingestion of contaminated water, food or ice, though it may also be acquired by direct contact with infected persons. The illness occurs throughout the world, but the incidence

HEALTH

is higher in developing nations. Symptoms may include fever, malaise, jaundice, nausea, vomiting and abdominal pain. Most cases resolve without complications, though hepatitis A occasionally causes severe liver damage. There is no treatment.

The vaccine for hepatitis A is extremely safe and highly effective. If you get a booster six to twelve months later, it lasts for at least 10 years. You really should get it before you go to Bolivia or any other developing nation. Because the safety of hepatitis A vaccine has not been established for pregnant women or children under age two, they should instead be given a gammaglobulin injection.

Hepatitis B
Like hepatitis A, hepatitis B is a liver infection that occurs worldwide but is more common in developing nations. Unlike hepatitis A, the disease is usually acquired by sexual contact or by exposure to infected blood, generally through blood transfusions or contaminated needles. The vaccine is recommended only for long-term travelers (on the road more than six months) who expect to live in rural areas or have close physical contact with the local population. Additionally, the vaccine is recommended for anyone who anticipates sexual contact with the local inhabitants or a possible need for medical, dental or other treatments while abroad, especially if a need for transfusions or injections is expected.

Hepatitis B vaccine is safe and highly effective. However, a total of three injections are necessary to establish full immunity. Several countries added hepatitis B vaccine to the list of routine childhood immunizations in the 1980s, so many young adults are already protected.

Typhoid Fever
Typhoid fever is caused by ingestion of food or water contaminated by a species of *Salmonella* known as *Salmonella typhi*. Fever occurs in virtually all cases. Other symptoms may include headache, malaise, muscle aches, dizziness, loss of appetite, nausea and abdominal pain. Either diarrhea or constipation may occur. Possible complications include intestinal perforation, intestinal bleeding, confusion, delirium or (rarely) coma.

Unless you expect to take all your meals in major hotels and restaurants, typhoid vaccine is a good idea. It's usually given orally, but is also available as an injection. Neither vaccine is approved for use in children under age two.

The drug of choice for typhoid fever is usually a quinolone antibiotic such as ciprofloxacin (Cipro) or levofloxacin (Levaquin), which many travelers carry for treatment of travelers' diarrhea. However, if you self-treat for typhoid fever, you may also need to self-treat for malaria, since the symptoms of the two diseases may be indistinguishable.

Plague
Small outbreaks of the plague sometimes occur in Bolivia, most recently in the town of San Pedro (department of La Paz) in the mid-1990s. The plague is usually transmitted to humans by the bite of rodent fleas, typically when rodents die off. Symptoms include fever, chills, muscle aches and malaise, associated with the development of an acutely swollen, excruciatingly painful lymph node, known as a bubo, most often in the groin. Most travelers are at extremely low risk for this disease. However, if you might have contact with rodents or their fleas, you should bring along a bottle of doxycycline, to be taken prophylactically during periods of exposure. Those less than eight years old or allergic to doxycycline should take trimethoprim-sulfamethoxazole instead. In addition you should avoid areas containing rodent burrows or nests, never handle sick or dead animals, and follow the guidelines on p374 for protecting yourself from insect bites.

Rabies
Rabies is a viral infection of the brain and spinal cord that is almost always fatal. The rabies virus is carried in the saliva of infected animals and is typically transmitted through an animal bite, though contamination of any break in the skin with infected saliva may result in rabies. Rabies occurs in all South American countries. In Bolivia most cases are related to dog bites. Risk is greatest in the southeastern part of the country.

Rabies vaccine is safe, but a full series requires three injections and is quite expensive. Those at high risk for rabies, such as animal handlers and spelunkers (cave explorers), should certainly get the vaccine. In addition, those at lower risk for animal bites should consider asking for the vaccine if they might be traveling to remote areas and might not have access to appropriate medical care if needed. The treatment for a possibly rabid bite consists of rabies vaccine with rabies-immune globulin. It's effective, but must be given promptly. Most travelers don't need rabies vaccine.

All animal bites and scratches must be promptly and thoroughly cleansed with large amounts of soap and water, and local health authorities contacted to determine whether or not further treatment is necessary (see Animal Bites, p375).

Cholera

Cholera is an intestinal infection acquired through ingestion of contaminated food or water. The main symptom is profuse, watery diarrhea, which may be so severe that it causes life-threatening dehydration. The key treatment is drinking oral rehydration solution. Antibiotics are also given, usually tetracycline or doxycycline, though quinolone antibiotics such as ciprofloxacin and levofloxacin are also effective.

Cholera sometimes occurs in Bolivia, but it's rare among travelers. Cholera vaccine is no longer required, and is in fact no longer available in some countries, including the United States, because the old vaccine was relatively ineffective and caused side effects. There are new vaccines that are safer and more effective, but they're not available in many countries and are only recommended for those at particularly high risk.

Chagas' Disease

Chagas' disease is a parasitic infection that is transmitted by triatomine insects (reduviid bugs), which inhabit crevices in the walls and roofs of substandard housing in South and Central America. In Bolivia most cases occur in temperate areas, especially the Altiplano. The triatomine insect lays its feces on human skin as it bites, usually at night. A person becomes infected when he or she unknowingly rubs the feces into the bite wound or any other open sore. Chagas' disease is extremely rare in travelers. However, if you sleep in a poorly constructed house, especially one made of mud, adobe or thatch, you should be sure to protect yourself with a bed net and a good insecticide.

Leishmaniasis

Leishmaniasis occurs in the mountains and jungles of all South American countries except for Chile, Uruguay and the Falkland Islands. The infection is transmitted by sandflies, which are about onethird the size of mosquitoes. In Bolivia, risk is greatest in the forested foothill regions east of the Andean Cordillera. Most cases are limited to the skin, causing slowlygrowing ulcers over exposed parts of the body. The more severe type of leishmaniasis, which disseminates to the bone marrow, liver and spleen, occurs only in the Yungas. Leishmaniasis may be particularly severe in those with HIV. There is no vaccine. To protect yourself from sandflies, follow the same precautions as for mosquitoes (p374) below, except that netting must be finer-mesh (at least 18 holes to the linear inch).

Bartonellosis

Bartonellosis (Oroya fever) is carried by sandflies in the arid river valleys on the western slopes of the Andes in Peru, Bolivia, Colombia and Ecuador between altitudes of 800m and 3000m. The chief symptoms are fever and severe muscle and joint pains according to several sources. Complications may include marked anemia, enlargement of the liver and spleen, and sometimes death. The drug of choice is chloramphenicol, though doxycycline is also effective.

Bolivian hemorrhagic fever

Bolivian hemorrhagic fever has been reported from the Beni Department in the northeastern part of the country. The causative organism, known as Machupo virus, is thought to be acquired by exposure to rodents.

Typhus

Typhus may be transmitted by lice in mountainous areas near La Paz.

HIV/AIDS

HIV/AIDS has been reported from all South American countries. Be sure to use condoms for all sexual encounters.

TRAVELERS' DIARRHEA

To prevent diarrhea, avoid tap water unless it has been boiled, filtered or chemically disinfected (iodine tablets); only eat fresh fruits or vegetables if peeled or cooked; be wary of dairy products that might contain unpasteurized milk; and be highly selective when eating food from street vendors.

If you develop diarrhea, be sure to drink plenty of fluids, preferably an oral rehydration solution containing lots of salt and sugar. A few loose stools don't require treatment but, if you start having more than four or five stools a day, you should start taking an antibiotic (usually a quinolone drug) and an antidiarrheal agent (such as loperamide). If diarrhea is bloody, or persists for more than 72 hours or is accompanied by fever, shaking chills or severe abdominal pain, you should seek medical attention.

ENVIRONMENTAL HAZARDS
Altitude sickness

Altitude sickness may develop in those who ascend rapidly to altitudes greater than 2500m (8100 feet). In Bolivia this includes La Paz (altitude 4000m). Being physically fit offers no protection. Those who have experienced altitude sickness in the past are prone to future episodes. The risk increases with faster ascents, higher altitudes and greater exertion. Symptoms may include headaches, nausea, vomiting, dizziness, malaise, insomnia and loss of appetite. Severe cases may be complicated by fluid in the lungs (high-altitude pulmonary edema) or swelling of the brain (high-altitude cerebral edema).

To protect yourself against altitude sickness, take 125mg or 250mg acetazolamide (Diamox) twice or three times daily, starting 24 hours before ascent and continuing for 48 hours after arrival at altitude. Possible side effects include increased urinary volume, numbness, tingling, nausea, drowsiness, myopia and temporary impotence. Acetazolamide should not be given to pregnant women or anyone with a history of sulfa allergy. For those who cannot tolerate acetazolamide, the next best option is 4mg dexamethasone taken four times daily. Unlike acetazolamide, dexamethasone must be tapered gradually on arrival at altitude, since there is a risk that altitude sickness will occur as the dosage is reduced. Dexamethasone is a steroid, so it should not be given to diabetics or anyone for whom steroids are contraindicated. A natural alternative is gingko, which some people find quite helpful.

When traveling to high altitudes, it's also important to avoid overexertion, eat light meals and abstain from alcohol.

If your symptoms are more than mild or don't resolve promptly, see a doctor. Altitude sickness should be taken seriously; it can be life-threatening when severe.

Insect Bites & Stings

To prevent mosquito bites, wear long sleeves, long pants, hats and shoes (rather than sandals). Bring along a good insect repellent, preferably one containing DEET, which should be applied to exposed skin and clothing, but not to eyes, mouth, cuts, wounds or irritated skin. Products containing lower concentrations of DEET are as effective, but for shorter periods of time. In general, adults and children over 12 should use preparations containing 25% to 35% DEET, which usually lasts about six hours. Children between two and 12 years of age should use preparations containing no more than 10% DEET, applied sparingly, which will usually last about three hours. Neurologic toxicity has been reported from DEET, especially in children, but appears to be extremely uncommon and generally related to overuse. DEET-containing compounds should not be used on children under age two.

Insect repellents containing certain botanical products, including oil of eucalyptus and soybean oil, are effective but last only 1½ to two hours. DEET-containing repellents are preferable for areas where there is a high risk of malaria or yellow fever. Products based on citronella are not effective.

For additional protection you can apply permethrin to clothing, shoes, tents and bed nets. Permethrin treatments are safe and remain effective for at least two weeks, even when items are laundered. Permethrin should not be applied directly to skin.

Don't sleep with the window open unless there is a screen. If sleeping outdoors or in an accommodation that allows entry of mosquitoes, use a bed net, preferably treated with permethrin, with edges tucked in under the mattress. The mesh size should be less than 1.5mm. If the sleeping area is not otherwise protected, use a mosquito coil, which will fill the room with insecticide through the night. Repellent-impregnated wristbands are not effective.

Animal Bites

Do not attempt to pet, handle or feed any animal, with the exception of domestic animals known to be free of any infectious disease. Most animal injuries are directly related to a person's attempt to touch or feed an animal.

Any bite or scratch by a mammal, including bats, should be promptly and thoroughly cleansed with large amounts of soap and water, followed by application of an antiseptic such as iodine or alcohol. The local health authorities should be contacted immediately for possible post-exposure rabies treatment, whether or not you've been immunized against rabies. It may also be advisable to start an antibiotic, since wounds caused by animal bites and scratches frequently become infected. One of the newer quinolones, such as levo-floxacin (Levaquin), which many travelers carry in case of diarrhea, would be an appropriate choice.

Snake Bites

Snakes and leeches are a hazard in some areas of South America. In Bolivia there are two species of poisonous snakes: pit vipers (rattlesnakes) and coral snakes. These are found chiefly in the sugar and banana plantations, and in the dry, hilly regions. In the event of a venomous snake bite, place the victim at rest, keep the bitten area immobilized and move the victim immediately to the nearest medical facility. Avoid tourniquets – they are no longer recommended.

Water

Tap water in Bolivia is not safe to drink. Vigorous boiling for one minute is the most effective means of water purification. At altitudes greater than 2000m (6500 feet), boil for three minutes.

Another option is to disinfect water with iodine pills. Instructions are usually enclosed and should be carefully followed.

Or you can add 2% tincture of iodine to one quart or liter of water (five drops to clear water, 10 drops to cloudy water) and let stand for 30 minutes. If the water is cold, longer times may be required. The taste of iodinated water may be improved by adding vitamin C (ascorbic acid). Iodinated water should not be consumed for more than a few weeks. Pregnant women, those with a history of thyroid disease and those allergic to iodine should not drink iodinated water.

A number of water filters are on the market. Those with smaller pores (reverse osmosis filters) provide the broadest protection, but they are relatively large and are readily plugged by debris. Those with somewhat larger pores (microstrainer filters) are ineffective against viruses, although they remove other organisms. Manufacturers' instructions must be carefully followed.

Sun

To protect yourself from excessive sun exposure, you should stay out of the midday sun, wear sunglasses and a wide-brimmed sun hat, and apply sunscreen with SPF 15 or higher, with both UVA and UVB protection. Sunscreen should be generously applied to all exposed parts of the body approximately 30 minutes before sun exposure and should be reapplied after swimming or vigorous activity. Travelers should also drink plenty of fluids and avoid strenuous exercise when the temperature is high.

TRAVELING WITH CHILDREN

Since there's little information concerning the medical consequences of taking children to high altitudes, it's probably safer not to do so. Also, children under nine months should not be brought to areas where yellow fever occurs, since the vaccine is not safe in this age group.

When traveling with young children, be particularly careful about what you allow them to eat and drink, because diarrhea can be especially dangerous in this age group and also because the vaccines for hepatitis A and typhoid fever are not approved for use in children under age two.

The two main malaria medications, Lariam and Malarone, may be given to children, but insect repellents must be applied in lower concentrations.

FOLK MEDICINE

Problem	Treatment
Altitude sickness	Gingko
	Coca leaf tea
Jet lag	Melatonin
Motion sickness	Ginger
Mosquito-bite prevention	Oil of eucalyptus
	Coconut oil

WOMEN'S HEALTH

There are English-speaking obstetricians in Bolivia, listed on the US Embassy website at http://bolivia.usembassy.gov/english/consular/medicalresources.htm. However medical facilities will probably not be comparable to those in your home country. It's safer to avoid travel to Bolivia late in pregnancy, so that you don't have to deliver there.

If pregnant, you should avoid travel to high altitudes. The lower oxygen levels that occur at high altitudes can slow fetal growth, especially after the 32nd week. Also it's safer not to visit areas where yellow fever occurs, since the vaccine is not safe during pregnancy.

If you need to take malaria pills, mefloquine (Lariam) is the safest during pregnancy.

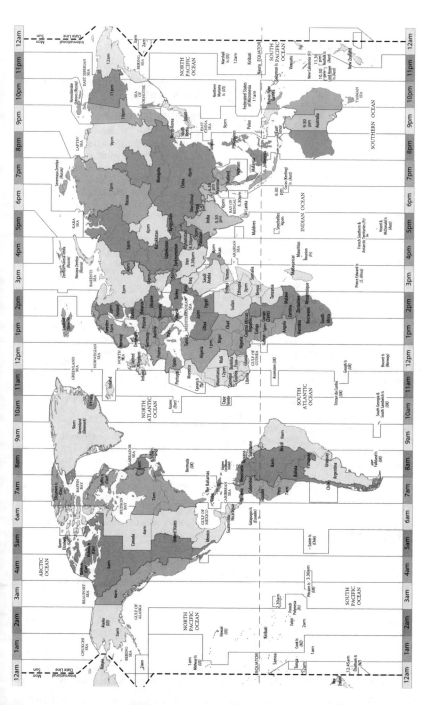

Language

The official language of Bolivia is Latin American Spanish, but only 60 to 70% of the people speak it, and then often only as a second language. The remainder speak Quechua (the language of the Inca conquerors) or Aymara (the pre-Inca language of the Altiplano). In addition, a host of other minor indigenous tongues are used in limited areas throughout the country. English in Bolivia won't get you very far, but fortunately it's not difficult to learn the basics of Spanish. After a short course or self-teaching program, you mightn't be able to carry on philosophical or political discussions, but you'll have the tools you need for basic communication.

SPANISH

Spanish courses in Bolivia are available in La Paz (p58), Cochabamba (p198) and Sucre (p222) for those who want to learn the language in greater depth while in the country.

For a more comprehensive guide to the Spanish of Bolivia than we can offer here, pick up a copy of Lonely Planet's *Latin American Spanish phrasebook*. Another useful resource is the compact *University of Chicago Spanish-English, English-Spanish Dictionary*. For words and phrases for use when ordering at a restaurant, see Eat Your Words on p39.

PRONUNCIATION

Spanish spelling is phonetically consistent, meaning that there's a clear and consistent relationship between what you see in writing and how it's pronounced. In addition, most Spanish sounds have English equivalents, so English speakers should not have much trouble being understood if the rules listed below are adhered to.

Vowels

a	as in 'father'
e	as in 'met'
i	as in 'marine'
o	as in 'or' (without the 'r' sound)
u	as in 'rule'; the 'u' is not pronounced after **q** and in the letter combinations **gue** and **gui**, unless it's marked with a diaeresis (eg *argüir*), in which case it's pronounced as English 'w'
y	at the end of a word or when it stands alone, it's pronounced as the Spanish **i** (eg *ley*); between vowels within a word it's as the 'y' in 'yonder'

Consonants

As a rule, Spanish consonants resemble their English counterparts, with the exceptions listed below.

While the consonants **ch**, **ll** and **ñ** are generally considered distinct letters, **ch** and **ll** are now often listed alphabetically under **c** and **l** respectively. The letter **ñ** is still treated as a separate letter and comes after **n** in dictionaries.

b	similar to English 'b,' but softer; referred to as 'b larga'
c	as in 'celery' before **e** and **i**; otherwise as English 'k'
ch	as in 'church'
d	as in 'dog,' but between vowels and after **l** or **n**, the sound is closer to the 'th' in 'this'
g	as the 'ch' in the Scottish *loch* before **e** and **i** ('kh' in our guides to pronunciation); elsewhere, as in 'go'

LANGUAGE

h	invariably silent. If your name begins with this letter, listen carefully if you're waiting for public officials to call you.	
j	as the 'ch' in the Scottish *loch* (written as 'kh' in our guides to pronunciation)	
ll	as the 'y' in 'yellow'	
ñ	as the 'ni' in 'onion'	
r	a slap of the tongue against the palate (like the 'd' in 'ladder'); at the beginning of a word or after **l**, **n** or **s**, it's strongly rolled, though some Bolivians pronounce it as the 's' in 'pleasure'	
rr	very strongly rolled	
v	similar to English 'b', but softer; referred to as 'b corta'	
x	as in 'taxi' except for a very few words, when it's pronounced as **j**	
z	as the 's' in 'sun'	

Word Stress

In general, words ending in vowels or the letters **n** or **s** have stress on the next-to-last syllable, while those with other endings have stress on the last syllable. Thus *vaca* (cow) and *caballos* (horses) both carry stress on the next-to-last syllable, while *ciudad* (city) and *infeliz* (unhappy) are both stressed on the last syllable.

Written accents will almost always appear in words that don't follow the rules above, eg *sótano* (basement), *América* and *porción* (portion). When counting syllables, be sure to remember that diphthongs (vowel combinations, such as the 'ue' in *puede*) constitute only one. When a word with a written accent appears in capital letters, the accent is often not written, but is still pronounced.

GENDER & PLURALS

In Spanish, nouns are either masculine or feminine, and there are rules to help determine gender (there are of course some exceptions). Feminine nouns generally end with **-a** or with the groups **-ción**, **-sión** or **-dad**. Other endings typically signify a masculine noun. Endings for adjectives also change to agree with the gender of the noun they modify (masculine/feminine -**o**/-**a**). Where both masculine and feminine forms are included in this language guide, they are separated by a slash, with the masculine form first, eg *perdido/a*.

If a noun or adjective ends in a vowel, the plural is formed by adding **s** to the end. If it ends in a consonant, the plural is formed by adding **es** to the end.

ACCOMMODATION

I'm looking for ...	*Estoy buscando ...*	e·*stoy* boos·*kan*·do ...
Where is ...?	*¿Dónde hay ...?*	*don*·de ai ...
a hotel	*un hotel*	oon o·*tel*
a boarding house	*una pensión/ residencial/ un hospedaje*	*oo*·na pen·*syon*/ re·see·den·*syal*/ oon os·pe·*da*·khe
a youth hostel	*un albergue juvenil*	oon al·*ber*·ge khoo·ve·*neel*
I'd like a room.	*Quisiera una habitación ...*	kee·*sye*·ra oo·na a·bee·ta·*syon* ...
double	*doble*	*do*·ble
single	*individual*	een·dee·vee·*dwal*
twin	*con dos camas*	kon dos *ka*·mas
How much is it per ...?	*¿Cuánto cuesta por ...?*	*kwan*·to *kwes*·ta por ...
night	*noche*	*no*·che
person	*persona*	per·*so*·na
week	*semana*	se·*ma*·na

MAKING A RESERVATION
(for phone or written requests)

To ...	*A ...*
From ...	*De ...*
Date	*Fecha*
I'd like to book ...	*Quisiera reservar ...* (see the list under 'Accommodations' for bed/ room options)
in the name of ...	*en nombre de ...*
for the nights of ...	*para las noches del ...*
credit card ...	*tarjeta de crédito ...*
number	*número*
expiry date	*fecha de vencimiento*
Please confirm ...	*Puede confirmar ...*
availability	*la disponibilidad*
price	*el precio*

Does it include breakfast?
¿Incluye el desayuno?   een·*kloo*·ye el de·sa·*yoo*·no
May I see the room?
¿Puedo ver la habitación?   pwe·do ver la a·bee·ta·*syon*
I don't like it.
No me gusta.   no me *goos*·ta

LANGUAGE

It's fine. I'll take it.
OK. La alquilo.   o·kay la al·kee·lo
I'm leaving now.
Me voy ahora.   me voy a·o·ra

full board	pensión	pen·syon
	completa	kom·ple·ta
private/shared	baño privado/	ba·nyo pree·va·do/
bathroom	compartido	kom·par·tee·do
too expensive	demasiado caro	de·ma·sya·do ka·ro
cheaper	más económico	mas e·ko·no·mee·ko
discount	descuento	des·kwen·to

CONVERSATION & ESSENTIALS

In their public behavior, South Americans are very conscious of civilities, sometimes to the point of ceremoniousness. Never approach a stranger for information without extending a greeting and use only the polite form of address, especially with the police and public officials. Young people may be less likely to expect this, but it's best to stick to the polite form unless you're quite sure you won't offend by using the informal mode. The polite form is used in all cases in this guide; where options are given, the form is indicated by the abbreviations 'pol' and 'inf.'

Hello.	Hola.	o·la
Good morning.	Buenos días.	bwe·nos dee·as
Good afternoon.	Buenas tardes.	bwe·nas tar·des
Good evening/	Buenas noches.	bwe·nas no·ches
night.		
Goodbye.	Adiós.	a·dyos
Bye/See you soon.	Hasta luego.	as·ta lwe·go
Yes.	Sí.	see
No.	No.	no
Please.	Por favor.	por fa·vor
Thank you.	Gracias.	gra·syas
Many thanks.	Muchas gracias.	moo·chas gra·syas
You're welcome.	De nada.	de na·da
Pardon me.	Perdón.	per·don
Excuse me.	Permiso.	per·mee·so
(used when asking permission)		
Forgive me.	Disculpe.	dees·kool·pe
(used when apologizing)		
How are things?	¿Qué tal?	ke tal

What's your name?
¿Cómo se llama?   ko·mo se ya·ma (pol)
¿Cómo te llamas?   ko·mo te ya·mas (inf)
My name is ...
Me llamo ...   me ya·mo ...

It's a pleasure to meet you.
Mucho gusto.   moo·cho goos·to
The pleasure is mine.
El gusto es mío.   el goos·to es mee·o
Where are you from?
¿De dónde es/eres?   de don·de es/e·res (pol/inf)
I'm from ...
Soy de ...   soy de ...
Where are you staying?
¿Dónde está alojado?   don·de es·ta a·lo·kha·do (pol)
¿Dónde estás alojado?   don·de es·tas a·lo·kha·do (inf)
May I take a photo?
¿Puedo sacar una foto?   pwe·do sa·kar oo·na fo·to

DIRECTIONS

How do I get to ...?
¿Cómo puedo llegar a ...?   ko·mo pwe·do lye·gar a ...
Is it far?
¿Está lejos?   es·ta le·khos
Go straight ahead.
Siga/Vaya derecho.   see·ga/va·ya de·re·cho
Turn left.
Voltée a la izquierda.   vol·te·e a la ees·kyer·da
Turn right.
Voltée a la derecha.   vol·te·e a la de·re·cha
I'm lost.
Estoy perdido/a.   es·toy per·dee·do/a
Can you show me (on the map)?
¿Me lo podría indicar   me lo po·dree·a een·dee·kar
(en el mapa)?   (en el ma·pa)

north	norte	nor·te
south	sur	soor
east	este/oriente	es·te/o·ryen·te
west	oeste/occidente	o·es·te/ok·see·den·te

SIGNS

Entrada	Entrance
Salida	Exit
Información	Information
Abierto	Open
Cerrado	Closed
Prohibido	Prohibited
Comisaria	Police Station
Servicios/Baños	Toilets
Hombres/Varones	Men
Mujeres/Damas	Women

---

here	aquí	a·kee
there	allí	a·yee
avenue	avenida	a·ve·nee·da
block	cuadra	kwa·dra
street	calle/paseo	ka·lye/pa·se·o

mountain
   montaña/cerro/nevado mon·*ta*·nya/*se*·ro/ne·*va*·do
mountain pass
   paso/pasaje/abra/ *pa*·so/pa·*sa*·khe/*a*·bra/
   portachuel por·ta·*chwel*

EMERGENCIES

Help!	*¡Socorro!*	so·*ko*·ro
Fire!	*¡Incendio!*	een·*sen*·dyo
I've been robbed.	*Me robaron.*	me ro·*ba*·ron
Go away!	*¡Déjeme!*	*de*·khe·me
Get lost!	*¡Váyase!*	*va*·ya·se

Call ...!	*¡Llame a ...!*	*ya*·me a
the police	*la policía*	la po·lee·*see*·a
a doctor	*un médico*	oon *me*·dee·ko
an ambulance	*una ambulancia*	oo·na am·boo·*lan*·sya

It's an emergency.
   Es una emergencia. es oo·na e·mer·*khen*·sya
Could you help me, please?
   ¿Me puede ayudar, me *pwe*·de a·yoo·*dar*
   por favor? por fa·*vor*
I'm lost.
   Estoy perdido/a. es·toy per·*dee*·do/a
Where are the toilets?
   ¿Dónde están los baños? don·de es·*tan* los *ba*·nyos

HEALTH
I'm sick.
   Estoy enfermo/a. es·toy en·*fer*·mo/a
I need a doctor.
   Necesito un médico. ne·se·*see*·to oon *me*·dee·ko
Where's the hospital?
   ¿Dónde está el hospital? don·de es·*ta* el os·pee·*tal*
I'm pregnant.
   Estoy embarazada. es·toy em·ba·ra·*sa*·da
I've been vaccinated.
   Estoy vacunado/a. es·toy va·koo·*na*·do/a

I'm allergic to ...	*Soy alérgico/a a ...*	soy a·*ler*·khee·ko/a a ...
antibiotics	*los antibióticos*	los an·tee·*byo*·tee·kos
penicillin	*la penicilina*	la pe·nee·see·*lee*·na
nuts	*las fruta secas*	las *froo*·tas *se*·kas

I'm ...	*Soy ...*	soy ...
asthmatic	*asmático/a*	as·*ma*·tee·ko/a
diabetic	*diabético/a*	dya·*be*·tee·ko/a
epileptic	*epiléptico/a*	e·pee·*lep*·tee·ko/a

I have ...	*Tengo ...*	*ten*·go ...
altitude sickness	*soroche*	so·*ro*·che
diarrhea	*diarrea*	dya·*re*·a
nausea	*náusea*	*now*·se·a
a headache	*un dolor de cabeza*	oon do·*lor* de ka·*be*·sa
a cough	*tos*	tos

LANGUAGE DIFFICULTIES
Do you speak (English)?
   ¿Habla/Hablas (inglés)? *a*·bla/*a*·blas (een·*gles*) (pol/inf)
Does anyone here speak English?
   ¿Hay alguien que hable ai al·*gyen* ke *a*·ble
   inglés? een·*gles*
I (don't) understand.
   Yo (no) entiendo. yo (no) en·*tyen*·do
How do you say ...?
   ¿Cómo se dice ...? *ko*·mo se *dee*·se ...
What does ...mean?
   ¿Qué quiere decir ...? ke *kye*·re de·*seer* ...

Could you please ...?	*¿Puede ..., por favor?*	*pwe*·de ... por fa·*vor*
repeat that	*repetirlo*	re·pe·*teer*·lo
speak more slowly	*hablar más despacio*	a·*blar* mas des·*pa*·syo
write it down	*escribirlo*	es·kree·*beer*·lo

NUMBERS

1	*uno*	*oo*·no
2	*dos*	dos
3	*tres*	tres
4	*cuatro*	*kwa*·tro
5	*cinco*	*seen*·ko
6	*seis*	says
7	*siete*	*sye*·te
8	*ocho*	*o*·cho
9	*nueve*	*nwe*·ve
10	*diez*	dyes
11	*once*	*on*·se
12	*doce*	*do*·se
13	*trece*	*tre*·se
14	*catorce*	ka·*tor*·se
15	*quince*	*keen*·se
16	*dieciséis*	dye·see·*says*
17	*diecisiete*	dye·see·*sye*·te
18	*dieciocho*	dye·see·*o*·cho
19	*diecinueve*	dye·see·*nwe*·ve
20	*veinte*	*vayn*·te
21	*veintiuno*	vayn·tee·*oo*·no
30	*treinta*	*trayn*·ta
31	*treinta y uno*	*trayn*·ta ee *oo*·no
40	*cuarenta*	kwa·*ren*·ta
50	*cincuenta*	seen·*kwen*·ta

60	sesenta	se·sen·ta
70	setenta	se·ten·ta
80	ochenta	o·chen·ta
90	noventa	no·ven·ta
100	cien	syen
101	ciento uno	syen·to oo·no
200	doscientos	do·syen·tos
1000	mil	meel
5000	cinco mil	seen·ko meel
10,000	diez mil	dyes meel
50,000	cincuenta mil	seen·kwen·ta meel
100,000	cien mil	syen meel
1,000,000	un millón	oon mee·yon

SHOPPING & SERVICES

I'd like to buy ...
Quisiera comprar ... kee·sye·ra kom·prar ...
I'm just looking.
Sólo estoy mirando. so·lo es·toy mee·ran·do
May I look at it?
¿Puedo mirar(lo/la)? pwe·do mee·rar·(lo/la)
How much is it?
¿Cuánto cuesta? kwan·to kwes·ta
That's too expensive for me.
Es demasiado caro es de·ma·sya·do ka·ro
para mí. pa·ra mee
Could you lower the price?
¿Podría bajar un poco po·dree·a ba·khar oon po·ko
el precio? el pre·syo
I don't like it.
No me gusta. no me goos·ta
I'll take it.
Lo llevo. lo ye·vo

Do you accept ...?	*¿Aceptan ...?*	a·sep·tan ...
American dollars	*dólares americanos*	do·la·res a·me·ree·ka·nos
credit cards	*tarjetas de crédito*	tar·khe·tas de kre·dee·to
travelers checks	*cheques de viajero*	che·kes de vya·khe·ro

less	*menos*	me·nos
more	*más*	mas
large	*grande*	gran·de
small	*pequeño/a*	pe·ke·nyo/a

I'm looking for (the) ...	*Estoy buscando ...*	es·toy boos·kan·do
ATM	*el cajero automático*	el ka·khe·ro ow·to·ma·tee·ko
bank	*el banco*	el ban·ko
bookstore	*la librería*	la lee·bre·ree·a
embassy	*la embajada*	la em·ba·kha·da

exchange house	*la casa de cambio*	la ka·sa de kam·byo
general store	*la tienda*	la tyen·da
laundry	*la lavandería*	la la·van·de·ree·a
market	*el mercado*	el mer·ka·do
pharmacy/ chemist	*la farmacia/ la botica*	la far·ma·sya/ la bo·tee·ka
post office	*el correo*	el ko·re·o
supermarket	*el supermercado*	el soo·per·mer·ka·do
tourist office	*la oficina de turismo*	la o·fee·see·na de too·rees·mo

What time does it open/close?
¿A qué hora abre/cierra? a ke o·ra a·bre/sye·ra
I want to change some money/travelers checks.
Quiero cambiar dinero/ kye·ro kam·byar dee·ne·ro/
cheques de viajero. che·kes de vya·khe·ro
What is the exchange rate?
¿Cuál es el tipo de kwal es el tee·po de
cambio? kam·byo
I want to call ...
Quiero llamar a ... kye·ro lya·mar a ...

airmail	*correo aéreo*	ko·re·o a·e·re·o
black market	*mercado (negro/ paralelo)*	mer·ka·do ne·gro/ pa·ra·le·lo
letter	*carta*	kar·ta
registered mail	*certificado*	ser·tee·fee·ka·do
stamps	*estampillas*	es·tam·pee·lyas

TIME & DATES

What time is it?	*¿Qué hora es?*	ke o·ra es
It's one o'clock.	*Es la una.*	es la oo·na
It's seven o'clock.	*Son las siete.*	son las sye·te
midnight	*medianoche*	me·dya·no·che
noon	*mediodía*	me·dyo·dee·a
half past two	*dos y media*	dos ee me·dya

now	*ahora*	a·o·ra
today	*hoy*	oy
tonight	*esta noche*	es·ta no·che
tomorrow	*mañana*	ma·nya·na
yesterday	*ayer*	a·yer

Monday	*lunes*	loo·nes
Tuesday	*martes*	mar·tes
Wednesday	*miércoles*	myer·ko·les
Thursday	*jueves*	khwe·ves
Friday	*viernes*	vyer·nes
Saturday	*sábado*	sa·ba·do
Sunday	*domingo*	do·meen·go

| **January** | *enero* | e·ne·ro |
| **February** | *febrero* | fe·bre·ro |

March	marzo	mar·so
April	abril	a·breel
May	mayo	ma·yo
June	junio	khoo·nyo
July	julio	khoo·lyo
August	agosto	a·gos·to
September	septiembre	sep·tyem·bre
October	octubre	ok·too·bre
November	noviembre	no·vyem·bre
December	diciembre	dee·syem·bre

TRANSPORT
Public Transport

What time does	¿A qué hora ...	a ke o·ra ...
... leave/arrive?	sale/llega?	sa·le/ye·ga
the bus	autobus	ow·to·boos
the plane	el avión	el a·vyon
the ship	el barco/buque	el bar·ko/boo·ke
the train	el tren	el tren

airport	el aeropuerto	el a·e·ro·pwer·to
train station	la estación de ferrocarril	la es·ta·syon de fe·ro·ka·reel
bus station	la estación de autobuses	la es·ta·syon de ow·to·boo·ses
bus stop	la parada de autobuses	la pa·ra·da de ow·to·boo·ses
luggage check room	guardería/ equipaje	gwar·de·ree·a/ e·kee·pa·khe
ticket office	la boletería	la bo·le·te·ree·a

I'd like a ticket to ...
Quiero un boleto a ... kye·ro oon bo·le·to a ...
What's the fare to ...?
¿Cuánto cuesta hasta ...? kwan·to kwes·ta a·sta ...

student's	de estudiante	de es·too·dyan·te
1st class	primera clase	pree·me·ra kla·se
2nd class	segunda clase	se·goon·da kla·se
single/one-way	ida	ee·da
return/round trip	ida y vuelta	ee·da ee vwel·ta
taxi	taxi	tak·see

Private Transport

I'd like to hire a ...	Quisiera alquilar ...	kee·sye·ra al·kee·lar ...
4WD	un todo terreno	oon to·do te·re·no
car	un auto	oon ow·to
motorbike	una moto	oo·na mo·to
bicycle	una bicicleta	oo·na bee·see·kle·ta

pickup (truck)	camioneta	ka·myo·ne·ta
truck	camión	ka·myon
hitchhike	hacer dedo	a·ser de·do

Is this the road to (...)?
¿Se va a (...) por esta carretera? se va a (...) por es·ta ka·re·te·ra
Where's a petrol station?
¿Dónde hay una gasolinera/un grifo? don·de ai oo·na ga·so·lee·ne·ra/oon gree·fo
Please fill it up.
Lleno, por favor. ye·no por fa·vor
I'd like (20) liters.
Quiero (veinte) litros. kye·ro (vayn·te) lee·tros

diesel	diesel	dee·sel
leaded (regular)	gasolina con plomo	ga·so·lee·na kon plo·mo
petrol (gas)	gasolina	ga·so·lee·na
unleaded	gasolina sin plomo	ga·so·lee·na seen plo·mo

ROAD SIGNS

Acceso	Entrance
Aparcamiento	Parking
Ceda el Paso	Give way
Despacio	Slow
Dirección Única	One-way
Mantenga Su Derecha	Keep to the Right
No Adelantar/ No Rebase	No Passing
Peaje	Toll
Peligro	Danger
Prohibido Aparcar/ No Estacionar	No Parking
Prohibido el Paso	No Entry
Pare/Stop	Stop
Salida de Autopista	Exit Freeway

(How long) Can I park here?
¿(Por cuánto tiempo) Puedo aparcar aquí? (por kwan·to tyem·po) pwe·do a·par·kar a·kee
Where do I pay?
¿Dónde se paga? don·de se pa·ga
I need a mechanic.
Necesito un mecánico. ne·se·see·to oon me·ka·nee·ko
The car has broken down (in ...).
El carro se ha averiado (en ...). el ka·ro se a a·ve·rya·do (en ...)
The motorbike won't start.
No arranca la moto. no a·ran·ka la mo·to
I have a flat tyre.
Tengo un pinchazo. ten·go oon peen·cha·so
I've run out of petrol.
Me quedé sin gasolina. me ke·de seen ga·so·lee·na
I've had an accident.
Tuve un accidente. too·ve oon ak·see·den·te

TRAVEL WITH CHILDREN

I need ...	Necesito ...	ne·se·*see*·to ...
Do you have ...?	¿Hay ...?	ai ...
a car baby seat	un asiento de seguridad para bebés	oon a·*syen*·to de se·goo·ree·*da* pa·ra be·*bes*
a child-minding service	un servicio de cui dado de niños	oon ser·*vee*·syo de kwee·*da*·do de nee·nyos
a children's menu	una carta infantil	oona *kar*·ta een·*fan*·*teel*
a creche	una guardería	oo·na gwar·de·*ree*·a
(disposable) diapers/nappies	pañoles (de usar y tirar)	pa·*nyo*·les de oo·*sar* ee tee·*rar*
an (English-speaking) babysitter	una niñera (de habla inglesa)	oo·na nee·*nye*·ra (de a·bla een·*gle*·sa)
formula (milk)	leche en polvo	*le*·che en *pol*·vo
a highchair	una trona	oo·na *tro*·na
a potty	una pelela	oo·na pe·*le*·la
a stroller	un cochecito	oon ko·che·*see*·to

Do you mind if I breast-feed here?

¿Le molesta que dé de pecho aquí?	le mo·*les*·ta ke de de pe·cho a·*kee*

Are children allowed?

¿Se admiten niños?	se ad·*mee*·ten nee·nyos

AYMARA & QUECHUA

Here's a brief list of Quechua and Aymara words and phrases. The grammar and pronunciation of these languages are quite difficult for native English speakers, but those who are interested in learning them will find language courses (p378) in La Paz, Cochabamba and Sucre.

Dictionaries and phrasebooks are available through Los Amigos del Libro and larger bookstores in La Paz, but to use them you'll first need a sound knowledge of Spanish.

Lonely Planet's *Quechua phrasebook* provides useful phrases and vocabulary in the Cuzco (Peru) dialect, but it will also be of use in the Bolivian highlands.

The following list of words and phrases (with Aymara listed first, Quechua second) is obviously minimal, but it should be useful in the areas where these languages are spoken. Pronounce them as you would a Spanish word. An apostrophe represents a glottal stop, which is the 'non-sound' that occurs in the middle of 'uh-oh.'

Hi!
  Laphi!   Raphi!
Hello.
  Kamisaraki.   Napaykullayki.
Please.
  Mirá.   Allichu.
Thank you.
  Yuspagara.   Yusulipayki.
It's a pleasure.
  Take chuima'hampi.   Tucuy sokoywan.
Yes/No.
  Jisa/Janiwa.   Ari/Mana.
How do you say ...?
  Cun sañasauca'ha ...?   Imainata nincha chaita ...?
It is called ...
  Ucan sutipa'h ...   Chaipa'g sutin'ha ...
Please repeat that.
  Uastata sita.   Ua'manta niway.
Where is ...?
  Kaukasa ...?   Maypi ...?
How much?
  K'gauka?   Maik'ata'g?

Also available from Lonely Planet:
Latin American Spanish and *Quechua phrasebooks*

distant	haya	caru	**1**	maya	u'
downhill	aynacha	uray	**2**	paya	iskai
father	auqui	tayta	**3**	quimsa	quinsa
food	manka	mikíuy	**4**	pusi	tahua
mother	taica	mama	**5**	pesca	phiska
lodging	korpa	pascana	**6**	zo'hta	so'gta
near	maka	kailla	**7**	pakalko	khanchis
river	jawira	mayu	**8**	quimsakalko	pusa'g
snowy peak	kollu	riti-orko	**9**	yatunca	iskon
trail	tapu	chakiñan	**10**	tunca	chunca
very near	hakítaqui	kaillitalla	**100**	pataca	pacha'g
water	uma	yacu	**1000**	waranka	huaranca

Glossary

For a glossary of food and drink items, see the Food &
Drink chapter on p40.

A

abra – opening; refers to a mountain pass, usually flanked
by steep high walls

achachilas – Aymará mountain spirits, believed to be
ancestors who look after their *ayllus* and provide bounty
from the earth

aguayo – colorful woven square used to carry things on
one's back, also called a *manta*

alcaldía – municipal/town hall

Altiplano – High Plain; the largest expanse of level
(and, in places, arable) land in the Andes. It extends from
Bolivia into southern Peru, northwestern Argentina and
northern Chile.

Alto Perú – the Spanish colonial name for the area now
called Bolivia

anillos – literally 'rings'; the name used for main orbital
roads around some Bolivian cities

apacheta – mound of stones on a mountain peak or pass.
Travelers carry a stone from the valley to place on top of
the heap as an offering to the *apus*. The word may also be
used locally to refer to the pass itself.

apu – mountain spirit who provides protection for
travelers and water for crops, often associated with a
particular *nevado*

arenales – sand dunes

artesanía – locally handcrafted items, or a shop selling
them

ayllus – loosely translates as 'tribe'; native groups
inhabiting a particular area

Aymará or Kolla – indigenous Indian people of Bolivia.
'Aymará' also refers to the language of these people. Also
appears as 'Aymara.'

azulejos – decorative tiles, so-named because most early
Iberian *azulejos* were blue and white

B

bajones – immense flutes introduced by the Jesuits
to the lowland Indian communities. They are still featured
in festivities at San Ignacio de Moxos.

balsa – raft; in the Bolivian Amazon, *balsas* are used to
ferry cars across rivers that lack bridges.

barranca – cliff; often refers to a canyon wall

barranquilleros – wildcat gold miners of the Yungas
and Alto Beni regions

barrio – district or neighborhood

bodega – boxcar, carried on some trains, in which
2nd-class passengers can travel; or a wine cellar

bofedales – swampy alluvial grasslands in the *puna*
and Altiplano regions, where Aymará people pasture their
llamas and alpacas

boletería – ticket window

bolivianos – Bolivian people; also the Bolivian unit
of currency

bombas de gasolina – gasoline pumps

bus cama – literally 'bed bus'; a bus service with
fully reclining seats that is used on some international
services, as well as a few longer domestic runs. It's often
substantially more expensive than normal services.

C

cabaña – cabin

cama matrimonial – double bed

camarín – niche in which a religious image is displayed

camba – a Bolivian from the Eastern Lowlands; some
highlanders use this term for anyone from the Beni, Pando
or Santa Cruz departments (oddly enough, the same term
applies to lowlanders in eastern Tibet!)

cambista – street moneychanger

camino – road, path, way

camión – flatbed truck; a popular form of local
transportation

camioneta – pickup truck, used as local transportation
in the Amazon Basin

campesinos – peasants or common folk, normally
of indigenous heritage

cancha – open space in an urban area, often used for
market activities; soccer field

casilla – post-office box

cerrado – sparsely forested scrub savanna, an
endangered habitat that may be seen in Parque Nacional
Noel Kempff Mercado

cerro – hill; this term is often used to refer to mountains,
which is a laughably classic case of understatement given
their altitudes!

chacra – cornfield

cha'lla – offering or toast to an indigenous deity

chapacos – residents of Tarija; used proudly by *tarijeños*
and in misguided jest by other Bolivians

chaqueo – annual burning of Amazonian rain forest to
clear agricultural and grazing land; there's a mistaken
belief that the smoke from chaqueo forms clouds and
ensures good rains.

charango – a traditional Bolivian ukulele-type
instrument

cholo/a – Quechua or Aymará person who lives in the
city but continues to wear traditional dress

chompa – sweater, jumper

chullo – traditional pointed woolen hat, usually with earflaps

chullpa – funerary tower, normally from the Aymará culture

colectivo – minibus or collective taxi

Colla – alternative spelling for *Kolla*

Comibol – Corporación Minera Boliviana (Bolivian Mining Corporation), now defunct

contrabandista – smuggler

cordillera – mountain range

D

DEA – Drug Enforcement Agency, the US drug-offensive body sent to Bolivia to enforce coca-crop substitution programs and to apprehend drug magnates

denuncia – affidavit

derecho – a right; a privilege provided in exchange for a levy or tax

dueño/a – proprietor

E

edificio – building

EFA – Empresa Ferroviaria Andina; the new private railway company, also known as FVA, or 'Ferroviarias Andinas'

ejecutivo – executive

Ekeko – household god of abundance; the name means 'dwarf' in Aymará

Entel – Empresa Nacional de Telecomunicaciones (Bolivian national communications commission)

Entelito – 'Little Entel', a small outlet providing Entel services; aka Punto Entel

esquina – street corner, often abbreviated esq

estancia – extensive ranch, often a grazing establishment

F

feria – fair, market

ferretería – hardware shop

ferrobus – bus on rail treads

flota – long-distance bus company

FVA – see EFA

G

garapatillas – tiny ticks that are the bane of the northern plateaus and savanna grasslands

guardaparque – national park ranger

H

hechicería – traditional Aymará witchcraft

hoja de ruta – circulation card

hornecinos – niches commonly found in Andean ruins, presumably used for the placement of idols and/or offerings

huemul – Andean deer

I

iglesia – church

Inca – dominant indigenous civilization of the Central Andes at the time of the Spanish conquest; refers both to the people and to their leader

ingenio – mill; in Potosí, it refers to silver smelting plants along the Ribera, where metal was extracted from low-grade ore by crushing it with a mill wheel in a solution of salt and mercury

J

jardín – garden

javeli – peccary

jefe de la estación – stationmaster

jipijapa – the fronds of the cyclanthaceae fan palm (*Carludovica palmata*)

jochi – agouti, an agile, long-legged rodent of the Amazon basin. It's the only native animal that can eat the Brazil nut.

K

Kallahuayas – itinerant traditional healers and fortunetellers of the remote Cordillera Apolobamba. Also spelled 'Kallawaya'.

koa – sweet-smelling incense bush (*Senecio mathewsii*), which grows on Isla del Sol and other parts of the Altiplano and is used as an incense in Aymará ritual; also refers to a similar-smelling domestic plant *Mentha pulegium*, which was introduced by the Spanish

Kolla – the name used by the Aymará to refer to themselves. Also spelt Colla.

Kollasuyo – Inca name for Bolivia, the 'land of the Kolla,' or Aymará people. The Spanish knew the area as Alto Perú, 'upper Peru.'

L

LAB – Lloyd Aéreo Boliviano, the Bolivian national airline

La Diablada – Dance of the Devils, a renowned Bolivian carnival held in Oruro

lago – lake

laguna – lagoon; shallow lake

legía – alkaloid usually made of potato and quinoa ash that is used to draw the drug from coca leaves when chewed

liquichiris – harmful spirits who suck out a person's vitality, causing death for no apparent reason

llanos – plains

llapa – bargaining practice in which a customer agrees to a final price provided that the vendor augments or supplements the item being sold

llareta – combustible salt-tolerant moss (*Azorella compacta*) growing on the salares of the southern Altiplano that oozes a turpentine-like jelly used by locals as stove fuel; also spelled *yareta*

M

Manco Capac – the first Inca emperor

mariguí – a small and very irritating biting fly of the Amazon lowlands. The bite initially creates a small blood blister and then itches for the next two weeks, sometimes leaving scars.

menonitas – Mennonites of the Eastern Lowlands, Paraguay, northern Argentina and southwestern Brazil

mercado – market

mestizo – person of Spanish-American and indigenous parentage or descent; architectural style incorporating natural-theme designs

micro – small bus or minibus

minifundio – a small plot of land

mirador – lookout

mobilidad – any sort of motor vehicle

moto-taxi – motorbike taxi, a standard means of public transportation in the Eastern Lowlands and Amazon Basin

mudéjar – Spanish name for architecture displaying Moorish influences

N

ñandu – rhea, a large, flightless bird also known as the South American ostrich

nevado – snowcapped mountain peak

P

Pachamama – the Aymará and Quechua goddess or 'earth mother'

pahuichi – straw-thatched home with reed walls, a common dwelling in Beni department

paja brava – spiky grass of the high Altiplano

peajes – tolls sometimes charged at a tranca or toll station

peña – folk-music program

piso – floor

pongaje – nonfeudal system of peonage inflicted on the Bolivian peasantry; abolished after the April Revolution of 1952

pullman – 'reclining' 1st-class rail or bus seat; it may or may not actually recline

puna – high open grasslands of the Altiplano

Q

quebrada – ravine or wash, usually dry

Quechua – highland (Altiplano) indigenous language of Ecuador, Peru and Bolivia; language of the former Inca empire

quena – simple reed flute

queñua – dwarf shaggy-barked tree (*Polylepis tarapana*) that grows at higher altitudes than any other tree in the world; it can survive at elevations of over 5000m.

quinoa – highly nutritious grain similar to sorghum, used to make flour and thicken stews; grown at high elevations

quirquincho – armadillo carapace used in the making of *charangos*; nickname for residents of Oruro

R

radiales – 'radials', the streets forming the 'spokes' of a city laid out in *anillos*, or rings. The best Bolivian example is Santa Cruz.

reais – pronounced 'hey-ice'; Brazilian unit of currency (R$). Singular is *real* pronounced 'hey-ow'.

refugio – mountain hut

río – river

roca – rock

S

salar – salt pan or salt desert

saya – Afro-Bolivian dance that recalls the days of slavery in Potosí. It's featured at festivities.

Senatur – Secretaria Nacional de Turismo (Bolivian national tourism authority)

seringueros – rubber tappers in the Amazon region

soroche – altitude sickness, invariably suffered by newly arrived visitors to highland Bolivia

surazo – cold wind blowing into lowland Bolivia from Patagonia and Argentine pampa

surtidores de gasolina – gas dispensers/stations

T

Tahuatinsuyo – the Inca name for their entire empire

tambo – wayside inn, market and meeting place selling staple domestic items; the New World counter-part of the caravanserai

tarijeños – residents of Tarija

taxista – taxi driver

termas – hot springs

terminal terrestre – long-distance bus terminal

thola – small desert bush

tienda – small shop, usually family-run

tinku – traditional festival that features ritual fighting, taking place mainly in northern Potosí department. Any blood shed during these fights is considered an offering to Pachamama.

totora – type of reed, used as a building material around Lake Titicaca

tranca – highway police post, usually found at city limits

tranquilo – 'tranquil', the word most often used by locals to describe Bolivia's relatively safe and gentle demeanor. It's also used as an encouragement to slow down to the local pace of life.

tren expreso – reasonably fast train that has 1st- and 2nd-class carriages and a dining car

tren mixto – very slow goods train. Any passengers normally travel in *bodegas*.

trufi – collective taxi or minibus that follows a set route

V

vicuña – a small camelid of the high puna or Altiplano, a wild relative of the llama and alpaca
viscacha – small long-tailed rabbit-like rodent (*Lagidium viscaccia*) related to the chinchilla; inhabits rocky outcrops on the high Altiplano

W

Wara Wara – slow train on the Red Occidental that stops at most stations

Y

yagé – a hallucinogenic drug used by certain tribes of the upper Amazon
yareta – see *llareta*
yatiri – traditional Aymará healer/priest or witch doctor

Z

zampoña – pan flute made of hollow reeds of varying lengths, lashed together side by side. It's featured in most traditional music performances.

Behind the Scenes

THIS BOOK

This 5th edition of *Bolivia* was written by Andrew Dean Nystrom and Morgan Konn. Andrew acted as Coordinating Author, and he and Morgan traveled and worked together on all sections of the book except the Health chapter, which was written by Dr David Golberg. Deanna Swaney wrote each of the previous editions of the book.

THANKS from the Authors

Morgan Konn & Andrew Dean Nystrom Without a supporting cast of thousands, our seven-month *recorrido* would have been impossible. Many thanks to Peace Corps Volunteers Brad Kenedy, Coach Marty Williams, Mimi Kil, Josh Canfield and Max in Oruro; Fabiola, Beatriz, Eddie and the entire Tupiza Tours crew; Chris Sarge and the Toñito family in Uyuni; Martha Cáceres, Alistair and Karen at Gravity, Jazmin and Miguel Caballero, Coco Cardenas, Eduardo Zeballos, Vania Rivero, Elizabeth J Vera Loza and the entire Hotel Rosario staff in La Paz; Rusty Young; Miguel Piaggio; Mariel Rivera de Morales; Peter and Wendy McFarren; Drs Fernando Patino and Elbert Orellana; Sandro, Pedro and the San Joséanos at Chalalán; Lizette and the Chimane and Mosetén comunarios at Mapajo; Don Alcides at Bala Tours; Stephan and Petra in Sorata; Louis Demers; Javier Sarabia; Sergio Ballivian; Oscar and Jorge Schmidt; Sigrid Frönius in Coroico; Peter, Margarita, Sandra and the chess champs in Samaipata; Don Ricardo in Yumani; Mauricio at La Cupula; Marcelo Arze at Conservation International in Villa Tunari; Oscar and Mariam de Abajo in Tarija;

Walter Guzmán and Norah Ferrel Urquidi in Santa Cruz; Veronica Vargas Ríos; Romulo Trujillo in Rurre; Juan Mamani and Pedro Blanco in Potosí; Francisco Ishu and Saira Duque at FAN; Bernhard and Justina Maierhofer; LP *Chile* author Carolyn Hubbard; and Capitán Pibe de Los Lagos. A sincere *mil gracias* to all the pilots and bus, flota, macro and micro drivers who spared our lives.

At LP, big thanks to Andreas Schueller and Graham Neale (in your absence we've grown fonder), Leonie Mugavin, Anneka Imkamp, Alison Lyall, Alex Hershey, Wendy Smith and Maria Donohoe.

Thanks also to Deanna Swaney, author of the book's previous editions, and the many other contributors along the way.

Finally, without the unconditional love and support of our parents Joe, Dolores, John and Barbra, the journey would have ever been possible.

CREDITS

This title was commissioned and developed in Lonely Planet's Oakland office by Wendy Smith. Overseeing production were Bridget Blair (Project Manager) and Kyla Gillzan (Editorial House Style Coordinator). Cartography for this guide was developed by Alison Lyall and Graham Neale. Cartography was coordinated by Andrew Smith and Herman So, with assistance from Marion Byass, Karen Fry, Anneka Imkamp, Louise Klep, Valentina Kremenchutskaya, Kim McDonald, Jolyon Philcox, Sarah Sloane, Natasha Velleley and Celia Wood. Editing was coordinated by EdInk. Thanks to the editors and proofreaders

---

THE LONELY PLANET STORY

The story begins with a classic travel adventure: Tony and Maureen Wheeler's 1972 journey across Europe and Asia to Australia. There was no useful information about the overland trail then, so Tony and Maureen published the first Lonely Planet guidebook to meet a growing need.

From a kitchen table, Lonely Planet has grown to become the largest independent travel publisher in the world, with offices in Melbourne (Australia), Oakland (USA), London (UK) and Paris (France).

Today Lonely Planet guidebooks cover the globe. There is an ever-growing list of books and information in a variety of media. Some things haven't changed. The main aim is still to make it possible for adventurous travellers to get out there – to explore and better understand the world.

At Lonely Planet we believe travellers can make a positive contribution to the countries they visit – if they respect their host communities and spend their money wisely.

who helped EdInk including Miriam Cannell, Kate Church, Alexandra Payne and Felicity Shay, and to Max McMaster for creating the index. Early editorial assistance was provided by Barbara Delissen and Craig Kilburn, and Quentin Frayne compiled the Language chapter. The cover was designed by Simon Bracken and the cover artwork prepared by Daniel New. Thanks to PAGE people, Jenni Quinn and Peter Dyson, who laid the book out and made everything fit on the page.

Series Publishing Manager Virginia Maxwell oversaw the redevelopment of the country guides series with help from Regional Publishing Manager Maria Donohoe, who also steered the development of this title. The series was designed by James Hardy, with series mapping development by Paul Piaia. The series development team included Shahara Ahmed, Susie Ashworth, Gerilyn Attebery, Jenny Blake, Anna Bolger, Verity Campbell, Erin Corrigan, Nadine Fogale, Dave McClymont, Leonie Mugavin, Rachel Peart, Lynne Preston and Howard Ralley.

ACKNOWLEDGMENTS

Many thanks to the following for the use of their content:

Mountain High Maps® © 1993 Digital Wisdom, Inc.

THANKS FROM LONELY PLANET

Many thanks to the travellers who used the last edition and wrote to us with helpful hints, useful advice and interesting anecdotes:

A Olivier Abon, Mark Addinall, Yoav Adomi, Sushil Aerthott, Peggy Aerts, Tineke Aertsen, Anwar Ali, Jason Allard, Maricruz Almanza, Klaus Altman, Emma Andrews, Jochen R Andritzky, Sergio Antezana, Diana Armstrong, Hilmir Asgeirsson, Karen Askew, John Atkins, Anne Auchatraire, Julie Aucoin, Nicole Avallone, Daniel Axelsson **B** Dirk Bachmann, Fay Baildon, Jorge Baldivieso, Julian Barbar, Ines Barbieri, Horst Bardorf, Arnold Barkhordarian, Richard Barragan, Kathy Barragan, Florence Barrere, Colin Barton, Alfredo Bauman, Chuck Bauman, Ralf Behrens, Mike Beishuizen, Sam Bell, Diana Benedetto, Petter Bengtsson, Arne Beniest, Didrik Berntsen, Cecile Bertout, Antoine Beurskens, Filippo Bianco, Sally Birchenough, Eliza Bird, Camila Bjorkbom, Carolina Blanco, Soren Boel, Salome Bolliger, Marleen Bos, Robert Bowker, Ben Brabazon, Mikael Bredberg, Micaela Bredberg, Nynke Brett, Martin Brewerton, Ian and Sally Britton, Eric Brouwer, Eric M Brown, Andrew Bunbury, Agi & Shanf Burra, Annette Busch, Melissa Butler, Marie Button, Nic Bye **C** Alberto Cabana, Philippe Cambres, David Cameron, John Campbell, Richard Campero, Tamara Campero, Claudia Canales, Mike & Amy Capelle, Stephen Carlman, Rulan Carr, Michael Carrigan, Sofie &

Roel Castelein, Sharon Cawood, Sirman Celayir, Jane Chambers, Carolynn Chaput, Matthias Chardon, Dominique Chauvet, Matthew Chell, Martin Chlodnicki, Na Choo, Jacky Chrisp, Uwe Christener, Becky Christiansen, Nicolas Claire, Helene Clappaz, Lucy Claridge, Pia Claudius, Helen Cole, Andrew Condell, Norbert Conti, Grace Cook, Heather N Cook, Alisha Cooper, Toyan Copeland, Arnaud Corin, Theresa Costigan, Susan Crawford, Matthew Creeden, Katja Cronauer, Daniel E Cronk, Hugh Cropp, Oliver T Cunningham, Tamara Cuppens, Ralf Czepluch **D** Ivar Dalén, Adam Danek, Jonathan Davies, Michael Davies, Keith Davis, Nicki Davis, Robert de Graaf, Michel de Groot, Jan-Willem de Jong, Sjoerd de Wit, Catherine Dean, Maria del Soto, Kate Delaney, Fernando Delgado, Rach Demp, Sanne Derks, Nathalie Desseux, Jeffrey Dhont, Conny Dietrich, Jane Dillon, Markus Doebele, Serge Dolcemascolo, Scott Doolittle, Tomas Dostal, Sarah Dotson, Arthur Dover, Laura Cecilia Driau, Jan Dudeck, Jean Marc Dugauquier, Ilse Duijvestein, Linda Duits, Jennifer Duncan, Anne Dupont, Abby Dupuy **E** Yasmin Ebrahim, Oliver Eck, Todd Edgar, Roger Paul Edmonds, Michelle Edwards, Jolanda Eelderink, Johan Ellborg, Maren Erchinger, Gilat Eshed, Lucy Esplin-Jones, Ingrid Estrella, Heike Eujen, Karl Evans **F** Kristen Faith, Jonathan Falby, Ed Fec, Jordan Feld, Berta Fernandez Rodriguez, Gyan Fernando, Andreas Fertin, Christian Feustle, Andrew Firth, J Patrick Fischer, John Fogg, Pernille & Kennet Foh, Mara Folz, Lisa Fowler, R Steve Fox, Steve Fox, Bernard Francou, Bryan & Sonja Fraser, Anna Freeman, Tamar Friedlander, Thomas Friedli, Caroline Frostick, Dave & Lina Fuller, George Fullerlove, B Sue Futrell, Erik Futtrup **G** Susanne Galla, Kathleen Gallichan, Marcel Gareau, Venyamin Gendrikovich, Axarlis Georgios, Christine Gesseney, Sean Gibson, Ian Gilmore, Malcolm Gladdish, Martin Gluckman, Nick Golding, Petra Golja, Harry Goovaarts, Silvia Gordini, Anthony J Gorski, Wendy Govaers, Andy Graham, Candi Greaves, Steven Greenall, Josh Griff, Karin & Martin Grubes, Gschwind, Chris Gudgin, Paulina Guerrero, Alf Amund Gulsvik, Kristina Gutschow **H** Robert Hance, Roly Hancock, Gemma Handy, Jenny Harding, Cristina Harnischmacher, Edwina Hart, Imke & Markus Hartig-Jansen, Philip Harvey, Michael Haschka, Jeff Haslam, Jenny Hawkins, Rodrigo Heidorn, Dagmar Heinen, Imogen Heldt, David Higgs, Jeroen Hilak, Deborah Hill, Julie Hinckley, Jason Hingley, Raul Hinojosa, Maximilian Hirn, Len Hobbs, Britta Hoffman, Martine Hofstede, Roos Hollenberg, Anne Hollier, Richard Holmes, Brian Horkan, David Horkan, Sheila Horkan, Miriam Horne, Chris Horsfall, David Hoskins, Melanie Howlett, Lee Huntington, Jon Huss, Eva Huthoefer, Shelley Hutson **I** Trebor Iksrazal, Patricia Inarrea, Adrienne Inglis, Laurent Iseli, Olivier Issaverdens, Pico Iyer **J** Bastiaan Jaarsma, Ellen Jacobs, Karin Jacobsson, Stephanie Jamison, Johana Janson, Susanne Janssen, Lauren Jarvis, Alden Jencks, Eric Jensen, Carina Johnson, Richard Johnson, Ard Jonker, Veronika Jonker, Isabelle & YC Jost, Howard Judd, Nina Junghans, Cleve Justis **K** Claudia Kalin, Melissa Kallas, Bernd Kaltenhaeuser, Nadia Kamal, Darl Kamm, Kenneth Kartchner, Georgina Kearney, Patrick LW Kearney, Ute Keck, Christophe Keckeis, Tom Keith-Roach, Ben Kelly, Charlotte Kelly, Lucille Kemp, Brad Kenedy, Kevin Kichinka, Bob Klingenberg, Karin Klitgaard, Beate Klugmann, Hans

Klugmann, Joreg Knapke, Chris Knutson, Stefan Koetter, Rok Kofol, Kirstin Koller, Jenifer Kooiman, Frans Koopman, Dorothea Koschmieder, Johanna Koskinen, Angela Kotsopoulos, Andrew Koutsaplis, Oliver Krause, Ulrich Kreuth, Uwe Krieger, Ulrik Kristiansen, Olga Kroes, Johan Kruseman, Agnieszka Kula, Oskar Kullingsjo **L** Ann Lager, Christel Lammertink, Jasmin Lappalainen, Pierre Larose, Tony Larsen, Ib Laursen, Justin Lawson, Sandra Leathwick, Sung Yun Lee, Toby Leeming, Zoe Leighton, Helen Leivers, Richard Leon, Charles Lew, Robert Lewis, Hilary Lewison, Kerstin Lichtenberg, David Lifschitz, David Limacher, Christian Linder, Manuel Lins, Jen Little, Anneli Lofgren, Frederic Lopez, Anna Lovejoy, Katie Luxton, Toby Lynns **M** Campbell Macdonald, Jane L Macdonald, Ian Mace, Gordon Machin, Mary Machin, Cedric Maizieres, Anne Margrethe, Mary Markotic, Sunny Maroo, Dominique Marsh, Carolyn Marshall, John Martin, Russel Martin, Vique Martin, Ruben Martinez, David Matthews, Bartholdi Matthias, Bruno Maul, Steve McElhinney, Norm McIver Jr, Roy McKenzie, R James McLeod, Brian McNicholas, Mark McNulty, Robert Medaris, Guus Meeuwsen, Marieke Meijer, Fabian Mentink, Asha Metharam-Jones, Susan Mew, Rudolph Meyer, Lloyd Michaels, Birte Mikkelsen, Lucas Mile, Lynda Miller, Ashild Mjanger, Paul Moir, Antony Montoya, Ian Moody, Lorn Moran, Itzik Morthehay, Thierry Moschetti, Patricia Mulkeen, Camilo Muñoz, David Muntslag, Angus Murray, Marcus Murray, Gustavo Musto, Jens Myhre **N** Ingrid Naden, David Naderi, Ishay Nadler, Goyo Nagai, Sean Nagle, Moran Nahum, Kiran Nandra, Roger Nash, Craig Nelson, Catherine Newman, Pete Newman, May Ng, Greg Nielsen, Neil Nordstrom, Christo Norman, Katharina Nothelfer, Mary Nowakowski **O** Rainer Oberguggenberger, Izaskun Obieta, Jane O'Brien, Olivia O'Callaghan, Colm O'Cuinann, Mark O'Day, Mark O'Flaherty, Georg Ohler, Deirdre O'Kelly, Michelle Okouneff, Sissel Helen Ommedal, Justin Ooi, Rijk Oosterhoff, Connie Orias, Yoshitomo Osawa, Aidan O'Shaughnessy, Erik Oskamp, Birke Otto **P** Melanie Pardo, Helen Paterson, Fernando Patino, Stuart Pattullo, Thies-Peter Paukner, Johan Pauvert, Kevin Pegram, Jose Luis Pena, Alan Perry, Andrew Perry, Kris M Piorowski, Cesar Piotto, Robert Matthew Poccia, Judith Polak, Helen Poole, Boris Popov, Carine Porret, Lonnie Porro, Steve Porter, Danielle Powley, Selma Pozzo, Chris Preager, Yvonne Press, Karl Pruckner **Q** Natascha Quadt **R** Eynay Rafalin, Marek Rajnic, Nicole Rankin, Thomas Rau, Sophie Raworth, Sally Reader, Gal Regev, Ine Reijnen, Franziska Reinhard, Kay Renius, Marco Antonio Reyes, Cory Reynolds, Harmony Reynolds, Kathy Rice, Adam Richardson, Graham Robertson, Becki Robinson, Andrew Roddick, Stephan Roess, Elaine Rogers, Andrea Rogge, Andrea Rostek, Thomas Roth, Catherine Rourke, Karen Rowland, Andrew Ruben, Debra Ruben, Dan Ruff, Jan Ruis, Patrice Rutten **S** Claude Sabatier, Rania Salameh, Monica & Noel Salazar Espinosa, Carl Salk, Peter Sanders, Sten Rune Sannerholt, Christopher Santander, Nathaniel Scharer, Lena Schiess, Vicki Schilling, Ingrid Schlepers, Matthias Caton Schlesiger, Judith Schmid, Robin Schmidt, Matthias Schmutz, Joerg Schneider, Matt Schoenfelder, Herdis Helga Schopka, Peer Schouten, Ingo Schultz, Michael Schwartz, Andrew Sciascia, Stephan Segers, Katja Seifert, Sharon Selby, Saeed Shah, Danielle Sharkan, Michael & Lisa Sharpe, Lydia Shaw, Michael Shaw, Nicola Shaw, Fred Sheckells, Mercedes Shelby, Rossie Shelty, Bill Shemie, Yinon Shiryan, Jonathan Sibtain, Veronika Siebenkotten, Dan & Kirsten Simpson, Madeleine Sinclair, Leena Sisodia, Jeffrey Slater, Rowan Slattery, Kristoffer Sletten, Jeroen Slikker, John Smith, Jon Even Soerlie, Ernie Soh, Martin Sohngen, Tracy Sparkes, Frans Spijkers, Bronwyn Spiteri, Ann & Frank Spowart Taylor, Frank & Ann Spowarttaylor, Elena Springer, Mary Ann Springer, Mark Stables, John Staelens, Rob Stainsby, Andrea Stallkamp, Pierre Stangherlin, Martin Staniforth, Lisa Starr, Urs Steiger, Juerg Steiner, Sibylle Steiner, Gunhild Stenersen, Colin Steward, Milada Stipetic, Fess Stone, Debbie Stowe, Hannes Stradmann, Adrian Stuerm, Judy & Ariana Svenson, Deborah Sweeney, Meredith Sweeney, Catriona Syme, Eileen Synnott, Andrew Szefler, Micole Sztanski **T** Ritu Tariyal, Lee Tatham, Shawn Teague, Ruben A Terrazas, Manuel Teunissen, Sabine Thielicke, Fiona Thiessen, Sophie Thomas, Isobel Thompson, Mark Thompson, Martin Thompson, Tim Thompson, Martijn Tillema, Sally Tillett, Edward Timpson, Julia Timpson, Luiz Toledo, Carole Tomaszewicz, Mike Tompson, Brian Torvik, Gilles Tournois, Ivo Troost, Vangelio Trova, Bob Truett, Ed Tyson **U** Silvia Ugarte, Ute Ulsch, Monique Unger **V** Marcelo Vallejos, Erik van Roovert, Henk van Caan, Marcel van de Pol, Annette van der Donk, Kris van der Starren, Daphne van der Velden, John van der Woude, Natalie van Eckendonk, Bart-Jan van Hees, Luc van Hensberg, Andre van Leeuwen, Elles van Loo, Chris van Lottum, Tessa van Schijndel, Andrea Veller, Eddy Veraghtert, Mariska Verplanke, Bert Viel, Arlinde Vletter, Cees Vletter, Rick Vogel, Ludwig Vogler, Kristina

SEND US YOUR FEEDBACK

We love to hear from travelers – your comments keep us on our toes and help make our books better. Our well-traveled team reads every word on what you loved or loathed about this book. Although we cannot reply individually to postal submissions, we always guarantee that your feedback goes straight to the appropriate authors, in time for the next edition. Each person who sends us information is thanked in the next edition – and the most useful submissions are rewarded with a free book.

To send us your updates – and find out about LP events, newsletters and travel news – visit our award-winning website: **www.lonelyplanet.com**.

Note: We may edit, reproduce and incorporate your comments in Lonely Planet products such as guidebooks, websites and digital products, so let us know if you don't want your comments reproduced or your name acknowledged. For a copy of our privacy policy visit www.lonelyplanet.com/privacy.

von Stosch, Jaron Vreman **W** Thomas Wagner, Henri Wahl, Jonathan Waldie, Matt Walker, Richard C Walker, Charmian Walker-Smith, Claire Wallder, Julie Wang, Therese Wanzenried, Michael Ward, Ruth Wembridge, Linda White, Sonia I White, Nina Wilbrink, Dianne Wild, Harold Willaby, Byron Williams, Wendy Wilson, Mikael Winblad, Richard Winchester, Sue Windmill, James Wix, Natasha Wolmarans, Alice L Wood, Helen Wood, Rachel Wrench, Bernie Wright, Samantha L Wronski, Melanie Wynter **Y** Tetsuhiko Yagami, Andrew Yale, Simone Yamashita, Mong Yang Loh, Jeff Young **Z** Sher Zaman, Elles Zandhuis, Ryette Zandt, Lital Zelinger, Tymoteusz Zera, Ralph Zimmermann, Denise Zumpe, Magda Zupancic

Index

INDEX

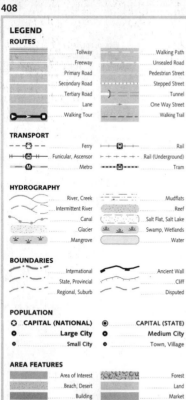

LEGEND

ROUTES

Tollway	Walking Path
Freeway	Unsealed Road
Primary Road	Pedestrian Street
Secondary Road	Stepped Street
Tertiary Road	Tunnel
Lane	One Way Street
Walking Tour	Walking Trail

TRANSPORT

Ferry	Rail
Funicular, Ascensor	Rail (Underground)
Metro	Tram

HYDROGRAPHY

River, Creek	Mudflats
Intermittent River	Reef
Canal	Salt Flat, Salt Lake
Glacier	Swamp, Wetlands
Mangrove	Water

BOUNDARIES

International	Ancient Wall
State, Provincial	Cliff
Regional, Suburb	Disputed

POPULATION

○ CAPITAL (NATIONAL)	◉ CAPITAL (STATE)
● Large City	● Medium City
● Small City	● Town, Village

AREA FEATURES

Area of Interest	Forest
Beach, Desert	Land
Building	Market
Campus	Park
Cemetery, Christian	Sports
Cemetery, Other	Urban

SYMBOLS

SIGHTS/ACTIVITIES
- Beach
- Buddhist
- Canoeing, Kayaking
- Castle, Fortress
- Christian
- Diving, Snorkeling
- Drinking
- Hindu
- Islamic
- Jewish
- Monument, Palace
- Museum, Gallery
- Picnic Area
- Point of Interest
- Ruin
- Skiing
- Snorkeling
- Surfing, Surf Beach
- Taoist
- Winery, Vineyard
- Zoo, Bird Sanctuary

INFORMATION
- Bank, ATM
- Embassy/Consulate
- Hospital, Medical
- Information
- Internet Facilities
- Parking Area
- Petrol Station
- Police Station
- Post Office, GPO
- Telephone
- Toilets

SLEEPING
- Sleeping
- Camping

EATING
- Eating

DRINKING
- Drinking
- Café

ENTERTAINMENT
- Entertainment

SHOPPING
- Shopping

TRANSPORT
- Airport, Airfield
- Border Crossing
- Bus Station, Stop
- Cycling, Bicycle Path
- General Transport
- Taxi Rank
- Trail Head

GEOGRAPHIC
- Hazard
- Lighthouse
- Lookout
- Mountain, Volcano
- National Park
- Oasis
- Pass
- River Flow
- Shelter, Hut
- Spot Height
- Waterfall

NOTE: Not all symbols displayed above appear in this guide.

LONELY PLANET OFFICES

Australia
Head Office
Locked Bag 1, Footscray, Victoria 3011
☎ 03 8379 8000, fax 03 8379 8111
talk2us@lonelyplanet.com.au

USA
150 Linden St, Oakland, CA 94607
☎ 510 893 8555, toll free 800 275 8555
fax 510 893 8572, info@lonelyplanet.com

UK
72–82 Rosebery Ave,
Clerkenwell, London EC1R 4RW
☎ 020 7841 9000, fax 020 7841 9001
go@lonelyplanet.co.uk

France
1 rue du Dahomey, 75011 Paris
☎ 01 55 25 33 00, fax 01 55 25 33 01
bip@lonelyplanet.fr, www.lonelyplanet.fr

Published by Lonely Planet Publications Pty Ltd
ABN 36 005 607 983

© Lonely Planet 2004

© photographers as indicated 2004

Cover photographs: Young child on its mother's back, La Paz, Anthony Cassidy/Getty Images (front); Alpacas by Laguna Verde, Southern Altiplano, Andrew Peters/Lonely Planet Images (back). Many of the images in this guide are available for licensing from Lonely Planet Images: www.lonelyplanetimages.com.

Printed by SNP SPrint (M) Sdn Bhd, Malaysia